The Ivory Throne

Praise for the Book

'The wealth of information crammed into this book is bewildering. If *Mastermind* did a special episode on Travancore, all you would have to read to max it is *The Ivory Throne*.'

—Mint

'This 700-page whopper of a book ... swirls through Kerala's history like a dervish possessed by the intention of telling a magnificent story, and telling it marvellously well.'

—The New Indian Express

'A detailed work of history ... The achievement of the book matches its ambition ... You will not regret the many hours you commit.'

—Business Standard

'A brilliant debut ... *The Ivory Throne* is an exceptional work; the achievement falls into perspective when you realize that Pillai is just 25 years old.'

—DNA

'A particularly fascinating account ... *The Ivory Throne* is also a sociological study – perhaps the first of its kind.'

—The Tribune

'A riveting read ... Even a cursory glance makes one forget that it is a debut work by a writer in his mid-twenties ... an awesome achievement.'

—The Hindustan Times

'A gripping historical account.'

—The Telegraph

'A clear-headed history ... Well-researched and well-written, *The Ivory Throne* adds a new point of view to the study of Kerala.'

—Outlook

'Vast and learned ... Pillai has given us a wonderful book.'

—Asian Review of Books

Celebrating
30 Years of Publishing
in India

Éléphants du Radja de Travancor (Elephants of the Rajah of Travancore) (1848), lithograph by L.H. de Rudder based on a drawing by Prince Aleksandr Mikhailovich Saltuikov.

The Ivory Throne

Chronicles of the House of Travancore

MANU S. PILLAI

HarperCollins *Publishers* India

First published in India by
HarperCollins *Publishers* India 2015

HarperCollins Publishers India, Cyber City, Building 10-A, Gurugram,
Haryana-122002, India
www.harpercollins.co.in

2 4 6 8 10 9 7 5 3 1

This edition published in hardback by HarperCollins *Publishers* India 2023

P-ISBN: 978-93-5629-655-8
E-ISBN: 978-93-5177-643-7

Typeset in 11/14 Garamond Premier Pro
By Saanvi Graphics Noida

Printed and bound at
MicroPrints India, New Delhi

MIX
Paper
FSC FSC® C218906

This product is made of FSC®-certified and other controlled material.

HarperCollins Publishers, Macken House, 39/40 Mayor Street
Upper, Dublin 1, D01 C9W8, Ireland

For Indrani

Contents

Introduction: The Story of Kerala

In July 1497 when Vasco da Gama set sail for India, King Manuel of Portugal assorted a distinctly expendable crew of convicts and criminals to go with him. After all, the prospects of this voyage succeeding were rather slender considering that no European had ever advanced beyond Africa's Cape of Good Hope before, let alone *reached* the fabled spice gardens of India. Da Gama's mirthless quest was essentially to navigate uncharted, perilous waters, and so it seemed wiser to invest in men whose chances in life were not especially more inspiring than in death. Driven by formidable ambition and undaunted spirit, it took da Gama ten whole months, full of dangerous adventures and gripping episodes, to finally hit India's shores. It was the dawn of a great new epoch in human history and this pioneer knew he was standing at the very brink of greatness. Prudence and experience, however, dictated that in an unknown land it was probably wiser not to enter all at once. So one of his motley crew was selected to swim ashore and sense the mood of the 'natives' there before the captain could make his triumphant, choreographed entrance. And thus, ironically, the first modern European to sail all the way from the West and to set foot on Indian soil was a petty criminal from the gutters of Lisbon.[1]

For centuries Europe had been barred direct access to the prosperous East, first politically when international trade fell into Arab hands in the third century after Christ, and then when the emergence of Islam erected a religious obstacle in the seventh. Fruitless wars and bloodshed followed, but not since the heyday of the Greeks and Romans had the West enjoyed steady contact with India. Spices and other oriental produce regularly reached the hungry capitals of Europe, but so much was the distance, cultural and geographic, that Asia became a sumptuous cocktail of myth and legend in Western imagination. It was generally accepted with the most solemn conviction, for instance, that the biblical Garden of Eden was located in the East and that there thrived all sorts of absurdly exotic creatures like unicorns, men with dogs' heads, and supernatural races called 'The Apple Smellers'. Palaces of gold sparkled in the bright sun, while precious gems were believed to casually float about India's serene rivers. Spotting phoenixes, talking serpents, and other fascinating creatures was a mundane, everyday affair here, according to even the most serious authorities on the subject. But perhaps the most inviting of all these splendid tales was that lost somewhere in India was an ancient nation of Christians ruled by a sovereign whose name, it was confidently proclaimed, was Prester John.[2]

It was long believed that there lived in Asia a *prestre* (priest) called John who, through an eternal fountain of youth, had become the immortal emperor of many mystical lands. Some accounts said he was a descendant of one of the three Magi who visited the infant Jesus, while a more inventive version placed him as foster-father to the terrible Genghis Khan. Either way, Prester John was rumoured to possess infinite riches, including a fabulous mirror that reflected the entire world, and a tremendous emerald table to entertain thirty thousand select guests. Great sensation erupted across Europe in AD 1165, in fact, when a mysterious letter purportedly from the Prester himself appeared suddenly in Rome. In this he elaborately gloated about commanding the loyalties of 'horned men, one-eyed men, men with eyes back and front, centaurs, fauns, satyrs, pygmies, giants, cyclops' and so on. After vacillating for twelve years, Pope Alexander III finally couriered a reply, but neither the messenger nor this letter was ever seen again.[3] Luckily for Europe, the travels of Marco Polo in the thirteenth century and of Niccolo di Conti in the fifteenth painted a rather more rational picture of Asia on the whole, but they were still convinced of the presence of lost Christians there, egged on by religious fervour and the commercial incentives of breaching the monopolised spice trade.

If da Gama and his men, weighed down by centuries of collective European curiosity and imagination, anticipated the legendary Prester as they stepped on to the shores of Kerala in India, they were somewhat disappointed. For when envoys of the local king arrived, they came bearing summons from Manavikrama, a Hindu Rajah famed across the trading world as the Zamorin of Calicut.[4] This prince was the proud lord of one of the greatest ports in the world and a cornerstone of international trade; even goods from the Far East were shipped to Calicut first before the Arabs transported them out to Persia and Europe. Until the Ming emperors elected to isolate themselves from the world, huge Chinese junks used to visit Calicut regularly; between 1405 and 1430 alone, for instance, the famed Admiral Zheng called here no less than seven times with up to 250 ships manned by 28,000 soldiers.[5] In fact, even after the final departure of the Chinese, there remained for some time in Calicut a half-Malayali, half-Chinese and Malay community called Chinna Kribala, with one of its star sailors called Chinali.[6] The city itself was an archetype of commercial prosperity and medieval prominence; it hosted merchants and goods from every worthy trading nation in its lively bazaars, its people were thriving and rich, and its ruler potent enough to preserve his sovereignty from more powerful forces on the Indian peninsula.

Da Gama and his men received one courtesy audience from the Zamorin and they were greatly impressed by the assured opulence of his court. But when they requested an *official* business discussion, they were informed of the local custom of furnishing presents to the ruler first. Da Gama confidently produced 'twelve pieces of striped cloth, four scarlet hoods, six hats, four strings of coral, a case of six wash-hand basins, a case of sugar, two casks of oil, and two of honey' for submission, only to be jeered into shame. For Manavikrama's men burst out laughing, pointing out that even the poorest Arab merchants knew that nothing less than pure gold was admissible at court. Da Gama tried to make up for the embarrassment by projecting himself as an *ambassador* and not a mere merchant, but the Zamorin's aides were not convinced. They bluntly told him that if the King of Portugal could afford only third-rate trinkets as presents, the mighty Zamorin had no interest whatever in initiating any diplomatic dealings on a basis of equality with him.[7] Manavikrama, it was obvious, could not care less about an obscure King Manuel in an even more obscure kingdom called Portugal, and with a pompous flourish of royal hauteur, he brushed aside da Gama's lofty ambassadorial claims.

The Zamorin was not unreasonable, however. He clarified that the Portuguese were welcome to trade like ordinary merchants in the bazaar if they so desired, even if no special treatment was forthcoming. Da Gama, though livid at his less-than-charming reception, had no option but to comply, having come all the way and being too hopelessly outnumbered to make a military statement to the contrary. And so his men set up shop in Calicut, under the watchful eyes of the Arabs, peddling goods they had brought from Europe; goods, they quickly realised, nobody really wanted here in the East. The hostility of the Arabs did not help either; for they, recognising a threat to their commercial preponderance, initiated a policy of slander, painting him and his men as loathsome, untrustworthy pirates. When complaints about this were made to the

Zamorin, they were met with yawning disdain, not least because the Portuguese had precious little to contribute to business or to the royal coffers. The first European trade mission, thus, was a resounding flop as far as the Indians were concerned, and when da Gama's fleet departed Calicut three months later, they left behind a distinctly unflattering impression on the locals.[8]

In Europe, however, the expedition was received as a great success, as it had finally broken the thousand-year Arab monopoly, and also because the few goods da Gama had successfully bartered in Calicut fetched sixty times their price in Western markets. In March 1500, therefore, King Manuel assembled a second armada to go to India. This time they were better prepared and more confident, led by the redoubtable Pedro Alvarez Cabral. It also helped that by the time they arrived in Calicut, the forbidding Manavikrama had died and a younger, more amenable prince was parked on the throne. The Portuguese got off to a more promising start, as a result. But their enthusiasm waned when they realised that demand for European goods continued to be feeble at best. In the spice auctions too, wealthy Arabs consistently outbid them and Cabral's ships were not filling up as expected. As the weeks passed he began to grow impatient and belligerent. The policy of defamation unleashed by the Arabs incensed him, and he suspected they were colluding with local suppliers to prevent the sale of spices to the Portuguese. At one point, then, Cabral sacked an Arab vessel, provoking retaliation from Muslim merchants who burned down his warehouse and killed between fifty and seventy Portuguese men. Cabral took to the safety of the sea and looted every ship he could find and, in what was meant as a lesson to the Zamorin, bombarded Calicut from afar for an entire day, killing nearly 600 people.

Cabral had realised by now that there was no way he could trade in this city so long as the Arabs held sway. He decided, in what was a calculated move, therefore, to sail south into an alternative harbour and try his luck there. During his months in Kerala, he had learnt a fair deal about regional politics and identified a very useful chink in the Zamorin's armour. And this was the port of Cochin in the south, held by a Rajah called Unni Goda Varma. This prince was a dynastic descendant of the Chera kings of yore and possessed a pedigree and caste superior to that of the haughty Zamorin. Yet he had been enslaved by Calicut: he had to pay tribute; all his pepper had to be submitted to his overlord; he was not allowed to mint currency; and perhaps most humiliatingly, the scion of the Cheras was prohibited from tiling the roof of his own palace, forced to thatch it instead, like the hut of a common peasant.[9] Cochin resented this debasing treatment imposed by the Zamorin and so, when Cabral's ships appeared by his shores, the Rajah received them with open arms, magnanimously granting several trade privileges and much pepper. He hoped, as Cabral knew and exploited, that with the aid of the Portuguese, he would finally be able to throw off Calicut's yoke and regain his independence and dignity.

It was a fateful juncture in the history of Kerala. Essentially, at this moment, Cabral had declared war between Portugal and Calicut, and Unni Goda Varma had rebelled against his feudal master after generations of servitude. The Zamorin, when he heard of these proceedings, was furious. He resolved not only to cut down the arrogant foreigners, whose only advantage was a superiority of arms and better navigational skill, but also to punish his audacious tributary. An enormous army started southwards while a massive fleet of eighty ships sailed out of Calicut to confront the Portuguese. Unni Goda Varma, incidentally, was prepared for a showdown and began to gear up for war. Cabral, however, knew that for all his bravado and grandstanding, the Portuguese were no match for the Zamorin and would only be utterly routed if they engaged in a full-fledged military conflict. To the great chagrin and disappointment of his new ally, then, Cabral had the lights of all his ships put out and in the dead of the night slunk out of the harbour and sailed off to Portugal, leaving a trembling and perfectly betrayed Unni Goda Varma to the mercies of an incandescent Zamorin.

For quite some time the Portuguese repeated this exercise of harassing Calicut from a distance, sailing out to Cochin to load their ships, and then fleeing the moment the Zamorin's forces arrived to face them. In 1502, for instance, da Gama himself returned and irrevocably upped the ante by not only looting Arab ships in the vicinity of Calicut, but also sinking a vessel full of pilgrims returning from Mecca, including women and children. He instigated the Kolathiri Rajah of Cannanore, another resentful foe of the Zamorin,[10] to open hostilities and then demanded that every one of the 5,000 families of Arabs in Calicut be expelled and the Portuguese be awarded an absolute monopoly over the spice trade. In another merciless episode, da Gama captured and sacked twenty-four ships headed for Calicut, and then set them as well as the 800 crew inside on fire. To add insult to the injury, an exalted envoy was tortured and returned with dogs' ears sewn on his head, with a note suggesting that perhaps the Zamorin should 'have a curry made' of the burning human flesh.[11] As usual, the moment 50,000 soldiers marched into Cochin, the Portuguese set sail, abandoning Unni Goda Varma once again to his own feeble defences.[12] The Rajah, as it happened, had to flee with his life and seek refuge inside a temple sanctuary this time.

For many years after this, the Zamorin was engaged in an uneasy tango with the Portuguese, on land and at sea. Trade, in the meantime, suffered as the latter initiated a policy of blatant terrorism in the Indian Ocean, with the Arabs unable to hold their own against these aggressions. In 1508, then, the Zamorin in alliance with the Sultan of Egypt and the Ottoman Turks inflicted defeat on the Portuguese, only to have the favour returned in 1510 when the latter invaded Calicut itself and set the royal palace on fire. When such multinational partnerships failed, some decades later the Zamorin forged an alliance with the Adil Shah of Bijapur and the Nizam Shah of Ahmednagar, and together they battled the Portuguese in 1571. The Zamorin, as his part of the joint offensive, seized their fort at Chaliyam and 'demolished it entirely, leaving not one stone upon another', according to a contemporary account.[13] But, as usual, the enemy was quick to recover, and this costly sequence of sanguinary war and desultory peace cascaded into the seventeenth century as well.

It was only after the arrival of other Europeans in India that the Zamorin was finally able to expel the Portuguese from Kerala. In 1663, in alliance with the Dutch, he mounted his strongest campaign ever and together they conquered Cochin. But if anyone expected an era of peace to follow, it was rendered only a daydream. For the Dutch smoothly slid into the political vacuum left by the retreat of the Portuguese and, to the abiding resentment of Calicut, assumed the mantle of protecting the Rajah of Cochin. They even went out proactively to interfere in regional affairs, instigating a rebellion here or settling a succession dispute there, and otherwise undermined the Zamorin's power. This, in fact, was a deliberate strategy on their part, for they wanted the Kerala princes and chieftains to remain forever embroiled in petty warfare, which produced ample opportunities for the sale of the by now prized European weapons in return for pepper and other spices, not to speak of widening Dutch influence on the coast.[14] This would only be possible so long as there was no dominant authority in Kerala and so one by one they signed independent treaties with even the smallest princelings and chieftains, all at the expense of an increasingly exhausted Zamorin.[15]

By the end of the seventeenth century, Calicut's pre-eminence in Kerala lay in complete shambles and the Zamorin's influence was at its lowest ebb. As the traveller Jacobus Visscher noted, his splendour had been 'considerably diminished' by war and it was 'quite a fiction' to claim he was the leader of all Kerala now.[16] The Kolathiri Rajah in Cannanore, who ruled over the northern extremity of the coast, was now completely independent; in central Kerala the Rajah of Cochin remained safe under Dutch assurances; and further south, whatever distant standing the Zamorin commanded came to naught.[17] These territories were further divided under smaller chieftains, and the whole region turned into one messy political scramble, with the Dutch having the last laugh as they walked away with heaps of pepper and money. In earlier days spices produced in the region were by and large channelled to Calicut, and the harbours of the minor Rajahs were only really ports of call for those headed to the Zamorin's famed capital. Now, however, each of them attempted autonomously to woo anyone who would heed their call to patronise their respective cities, actively instigated by the Dutch. Commerce began to become irregular and less profitable while petty squabbles grew aplenty all across the land.

At the turn of the eighteenth century, Kerala's last great age before the advent of the colonial era was inching towards a traumatic conclusion. Calicut's glory, built through a dynamic partnership between its cultivated Hindu princes and spirited Muslim merchants, characterised by an equally sophisticated internationalism, was reduced to a wistful memory. Beleaguered by incessant war and refractory allies, the diminished Zamorins were no longer lords of one of the world's great free cities; they were fighting now for their very political survival. They were rendered ordinary, like the other parvenu forces thrashing about on the coast. In the face of determined hostility from European powers that demanded unfair privileges and discriminatory concessions, striking at the very roots of the free trade that had brought prosperity to Kerala, the Zamorins floundered and fell. They did, however, fight valiantly for many long years, and as late as 1607, after a century of battling the Portuguese, the traveller Pyrard de Laval was still able to write:

> There is no place in all India where contentment is more universal than at Calicut, both on account of the fertility and beauty of the country and of the intercourse with the men of all religions who live there in free exercise of their own religion. It is the busiest and most full of all traffic and commerce in the whole of India; it has merchants from all parts of the world, and of all nations and religions, by reason of the liberty and security accorded to them there.[18]

But despite their best efforts, Manavikrama's heirs were destined to fail. The eighteenth century revealed a Kerala that was only a shadow of its former greatness, a civilisation devastated by internal tumult and external assault. It would never regain its former stature in the world, and another brutal century would pass before even a semblance of peace was restored in the region. And this was achieved not through the wise endeavours of its quarrelling princes, but by the superior forces of powers foreign to the land. Marching in by land and from sea, they would brush aside the wreckage of the past and painfully initiate Kerala into the modern age, defining the land as we see it today.

Nestled between the mighty mountains of the Western Ghats and the sparkling waters of the Arabian Sea, exposure to the wider world is an ancient feature of Kerala's heritage. Since biblical times men came in search of this land, enriching it with wealth, fame and culture. The Babylonians and Assyrians traded here in the centuries before Christ, and the edicts of the celebrated Emperor Asoka name the Keralaputras as an independent country in south India in his day, corresponding with 'the *Celobotras* of Pliny, the *Keprobotras* of Periplus, [and] the *Kerobotras* of Ptolemy'.[19] In the early years of the Common Era this narrow seaboard was a renowned cosmopolitan centre, where men of every country and race were welcomed with open arms. After the destruction of their second Temple in AD 70, Jews escaping persecution in Jerusalem sought refuge in Kerala where they lived in prosperity until the Portuguese arrived 1,500 years later to harass them afresh. Islam too found a home here, not by means of the sword but through the peaceful embassies of commerce. Indeed, such was the level of free multiculturalism at one time that the Zamorin even decreed that every fisherman in his realm should bring up one son as a Muslim so as to become a merchant and sail in the Eastern seas.[20] Kerala flourished as an exceptional realm of liberty, peace and plenty, reputed as a haven for one and all.

It is no wonder, then, that the Portuguese were drawn to Kerala. But what set them apart from other merchants was that they came in search not only of spices but also of Christians. The aim, dramatically enough, was to reunite with lost Christians in the East and retake Jerusalem after an ultimate confrontation with Islam. This religious zeal was a legacy of the violent Crusades that had tormented Europe for generations, and there was a rather fundamentalist spark motivating this higher purpose of the explorers.[21] And indeed when they reached Calicut, they were thrilled not so much by the magnificent commerce they witnessed there, but by the happy intelligence that resident on this sliver of the Indian coast was an ancient community of indigenous Christians. The old tales that had exhilarated Europe for centuries were finally confirmed and it was with great eagerness that the early Portuguese went out to meet their Indian brethren. But if they expected the Christians of Kerala to revel in joy at being united with them and pledge unconditional loyalty, they were somewhat disappointed. For the Malayali Christians responded with polite bewilderment and courtly indifference, rendering the Portuguese disheartened first and then positively enraged.[22]

Keen as the Portuguese were to impart their religious wisdom and light in the East, Christianity had in fact arrived in Kerala as early as AD 52, when St Thomas the Apostle ('Doubting Thomas') is believed to have set foot on the shores of Cranganore near Cochin. He traversed the region, winning over substantial sections of people with the intellectual and religious merits of his faith. He established seven churches in Kerala, and over time a proud Christian community evolved in the region. Like the Arabs, they were masters of business and emerged as a premier entrepreneurial class, even establishing partnerships with the immigrant Jews. They maintained intimate links with Hindu society as well, developing a fascinating syncretism of culture in Kerala. Their churches, for instance, were modelled on Hindu temples and da Gama himself worshipped in a shrine to Bhagavathi (the goddess), mistaking it for a chapel to the Madonna. St Thomas is even supposed to have had an intellectual *debate* on religion with the goddess at the Cranganore Temple. According to legend, the discussion got rather heated and a weary Bhagavathi decided to decamp and go back to rest in her shrine. 'St Thomas,' as Francis Day records, 'not to be out done, rapidly gave chase, and just as Bhagavathi got inside the door post, prevented its closing.' And there they stood, for a long time, with the goddess barring St Thomas entry, and he refusing to let her shut him out, until the door turned to stone. As the scholar Susan Bayly states, both Bhagavathi and St Thomas are seen in this story as equally divine figures and in the end, even though the Apostle (representing Christianity) did not gain access into the *entire* shrine (symbolising the Hindu populace), he secured a 'significant foothold' in the region.[23]

Naturally, then, the Christians of Kerala developed a unique personality of their own, quite unlike the version of their faith practised in faraway Europe. Identities were plastic and even Brahmins, who belonged to the highest Hindu echelons, often converted to St Thomas's religion, seasoning its indigenous flavour. Many Christians served alongside Hindu soldiers in regional militias and at the end of the sixteenth century, for example, the Rajah of Cochin is said to have employed thousands of Christians in his service. In daily life too, Hindus and Christians interacted freely and the former treated them with great honour and respect. One traveller recorded that 'there is no distinction either in their habits, or in their hair, or in anything else, betwixt the Christians of this diocese and the heathen' Hindus, and as late as the closing years of the sixteenth century there was tolerance of intermarriage between the communities.[24] In the Krishna Temple in Ambalapuzha an image of St Thomas used to be carried in procession alongside those of Hindu divinities on festive occasions. Across the coast there were temples where only oil 'purified' by the touch of a Malayali

Christian could be used to light lamps and holy fires. There was a fascinating intermingling of faith and culture throughout Kerala, and Christians were integral constituents of this rich social fabric, arguably more cosmopolitan and certainly less fanatic than in contemporary Europe.[25]

It was hence that neither the Portuguese nor their pontifical enterprise to unite Christians into one integrated bloc against Islam (and Arab competition) evoked any great enthusiasm in Kerala. After all, these Malayalis had been Christian long before Christianity had reached even the outskirts of Europe. They were heirs to a tradition more ancient than the Roman Catholicism of the Portuguese and had never, for instance, even heard of the Pope; when the Portuguese presumed to claim that the Kerala churches 'belonged' to the Pope, quick came the retort, 'Who is the Pope?'[26] The Malayali Christians, as it turned out to the great mortification of the Portuguese, adhered not to the Vatican but to the Nestorian Church in modern-day Iraq. Their liturgical language, similarly, was not Latin but Syriac, by virtue of which they were known as Syrian Christians. In other words, the celebrated Father of Roman Catholicism held little consequence for them, and besides the common tag of being all 'Christians' they could not be more unlike the Portuguese. Thus, the local Christians whom the Europeans 'rediscovered' observed a branch of the faith that Roman Catholicism neither approved of nor upheld.

As was almost habitual with them at the time, when the Portuguese could not find what they sought in the local Christians, they abandoned all fraternal pretensions and went on to diligently persecute the latter. Over the following centuries many were compelled to accept the Catholic faith and denounce the East Syrian rites of their ancestors. The Portuguese also set out to purge Hindu elements from their rites, and ruthlessly applied themselves to rid local Christianity of what they derided as 'Pagan' influences. They may have reconciled to not finding the fabled Prester John and his legendary treasures, but the zealous Portuguese could never come to terms with a flock of 'corrupted', non-Catholic Christians. Eventually, a sizeable Catholic following also grew in the region under the Portuguese banner, along with a minor Luso-Indian population. In the years ahead, as more and more European missions reached Kerala, many new brands of the faith found welcome in the land, establishing other churches with their own distinctive features along the coast.

But if the nature of Christianity in Kerala seemed outlandish, what positively befuddled the Europeans were the peculiarities of Hindu society here. While they did not encounter men with dogs' heads or the so-called 'Apple Smellers', they were most astonished by the principal class of 'Pagans' in Kerala. The Nairs, as these serpent worshippers were known, were a martial group, and the most exalted of them was none other than the Zamorin himself. And *their* customs appeared even more bizarre than those of the Christians. Describing the Nairs, the diarist Duarte Barbosa paints a picturesque, typically exoticised summary of their general way of life:

> In these kingdoms ... there is another sect of people called Nairs, who are the gentry, and have no other duty than to carry on war, and they continually carry their arms with them, which are swords, bows, arrows, bucklers, and lances. They all live with the kings, and some of them with other lords, relations of the king, and lords of the country, and with the salaried governors ... And no one can be a Nair if he is not of good lineage. They are very smart men, and much taken up with their nobility. They do not associate with any peasant, and neither eat nor drink except in the houses of other Nairs. These people accompany their lords day and night ... These Nairs, besides being all of noble descent, have to be armed as knights by the hand of the King or lord with whom they live, and until they have been so equipped they cannot bear arms or call themselves Nairs ... In general when these Nairs are seven years of age they are immediately sent to school to learn all manner of feats of agility and gymnastics for the use of their weapons ... These Nairs when they enlist to live with the king, bind themselves and promise to die for him; and they do likewise with any other lord from whom they receive pay. This law is observed by some and not by others; but their obligation constrains them to die at the hands of anyone who should kill the king or their lord; and some of them so observe it so that if in any battle their lord should be killed, they go and put themselves in the midst of the enemies who killed him, even should those be numerous, and he alone by himself dies there; but before falling he does what he can against them; and after that one is dead, another goes to take his place, and then another, so that sometimes ten or twelve Nairs die for their lord.[27]

Indeed to the first Europeans, Kerala seemed to marinate in blood as Nairs, serving their numerous lords and princes, lived in a state of perpetual warfare and violent enmity; as Galleti would dryly remark, 'War was in fact the natural state' here.[28] Perhaps the most emblematic of their ingrained will to kill (or to get killed) was the custom of blood feuds known as *kudipaka*. If a Nair died at the hands of an enemy, the slain warrior's family vowed not to rest until they had exterminated the killer's clan, avenging their dead kin. Families in such epic vendettas often prepared doggedly for years before assaulting each other on a chosen date in a great duel or full-fledged battle, witnessed by massive baying crowds.[29] Bloodthirsty loyalty of this nature extended to feudal overlords also. In 1502, for example, when the Zamorin's soldiers killed three princes of Cochin, 200 Nairs serving as the latter's bodyguard set out to avenge their dead masters' honour. Their mission was to claim the lives of an equal number of princes from the house of the Zamorin, and it is said to have taken five years before the soldiers of Calicut put the last of these warriors to death, just outside the capital city. Until then, these *chavers*, as they were called, persevered on, advancing further and further into the Zamorin's country, acting as a deadly squad of killing machines, cutting down every enemy Nair they encountered.[30] 'Their chief delight,' Francis Buchanan would write about the Nairs, 'is in parading up and down fully armed. Each man has a firelock, and at least one sword; but all those who wish to be thought as men of extraordinary courage carry two sabres.'[31]

If the reckless bravery of the Nairs (sometimes induced by opium[32]) impressed the Portuguese, what provoked great sensation and even a degree of romanticism were their exotic marriage customs. Indeed, parallels to their way of cohabitation were difficult to find even in other parts of India, leave alone Europe. The Nairs, it so happened, were what we would today define as extremely liberal, and their women had enough personal freedom to scandalise foreign observers. While everywhere else in the familiar world it was ordinary for men to keep numerous wives, here custom granted that privilege to women as well. As Barbosa exaggerated, 'the more lovers a woman has, greater is her honour'. And ladies, high and low, vied to collect beaus and husbands with great avidity. Even princesses and queens were not excluded from this inviting polyandrous tradition; to quote Barbosa once again, 'these [princesses] do not marry, nor have fixed husbands, and are very free and at liberty in doing what they please with themselves'.[33] Wave after wave of Europeans was enchanted (and occasionally horrified) by these exotic customs, inspiring James Lawrence, years later, to pen a twelve-volume novel called *The Empire of the Nairs: An Utopian Romance.* Since this was translated into both French and German, it was presumably received with great interest and is now considered an early feminist work arguing for parity between the genders.[34]

Women, in general, enjoyed individual personalities and often ran vast estates and even kingdoms on their own. They were normally educated at least to a basic level and very often grew adept in the art of warfare also. One local Rajah in Kerala, for instance, maintained a palace guard of 300 female archers when the Portuguese first met him, much to their astonishment.[35] Country bards sang of gallant heroines putting dreadful villains to death with their superior swordsmanship and prowess. In the Muslim royal family of Arakkal, women had equal rights of succession with male members of the house, ruling in their own right. Females of royal blood moved about freely in society, unencumbered by purdah and that severe seclusion that was their fate in other parts of India. They commanded tremendous respect, besides actively participating in affairs that were the strict preserve of men in less-inclusive societies. When the Italian, Pietro Della Valle, visited the court of the Zamorin in 1623, for instance, he observed many ladies in attendance there and two princesses even came up and studied him with a casual, self-assured confidence, as the following description confirms:

> Suddenly two girls, about twelve years of age, entered the court. They wore no covering of any kind except a blue cloth about their loins; but their arms, ears, and necks were covered with ornaments of gold and precious stones. Their complexion was swarthy but clear enough; their shape was well proportioned and comely; and their aspect was handsome and well favoured ... These two girls were in fact *Infantas* of the kingdom of Calicut. Upon their entrance all the courtiers paid them great reverence; and Della Valle and his companions rose from their seats, and saluted them ... The girls talked together respecting the strangers; and one of them approached Della Valle and touched the sleeve of his coat with her hand, and expressed wonder at his attire. Indeed they were as surprised at the dress of the strangers, as the strangers were at the strange appearance of the girls .... There were higher cloisters round the court filled with women, who had come to behold the strangers. The Queen ... stood apart in the most prominent place, with no more clothing than her daughters, but abundantly adorned with jewels.[36]

Thus, in Kerala women enjoyed a position of singular importance, not least due to its matrilineal system of inheritance, about which more will be said later.[37] Even their highly abbreviated sense of dress seemed outrageously uninhibited to the more conservative and culturally judgemental Europeans, for it was unusual for women to cover themselves above the waist. It was as if they all lived in a state of perpetual dishabille but the fact was that being bare-bosomed was considered perfectly respectable. Outsiders did feel this was somehow immoral but as F. Fawcett would opine, 'Dress is, of course, a conventional affair, and it will be a matter of regret should false ideas of shame supplant those of natural dignity such as one sees expressed in the carriage and bearing of the well-bred Nair lady.'[38] In fact, in one instance in the seventeenth century when a local woman appeared before a princess covered in Western style, she was actually *punished* for doing this. Her breasts were mutilated by royal order, since covering them were 'a mark of disrespect to the established manners of the country'. The princess too, of course, was unabashedly bare-breasted.[39]

By the eighteenth century, however, all this was beginning to change. In 1766, Kerala was unexpectedly drenched in war and blood as the dreaded armies of Hyder Ali of Mysore rained death on the Zamorin and his hapless aristocracy. The Muslim king pillaged and plundered, unleashing such formidable chaos that the Zamorin was compelled to send even his own women and children south as broken refugees. As the marauders gained on his ancestral seat in Calicut, Manavikrama's heir, by his own hand, set fire to the palace where his ancestors once sat in state and lorded over the riches of their trade. And while the last of the great Zamorins of Calicut perished, thus, in inglorious flames, his feudatories and generals fled en masse, abandoning Kerala to the fiery ambitions of its invaders.[40] With their exodus, the old ways of life in the region were devastated. Into the 1790s the English East India Company took over the province, and the ancient clans, once active participants in that enthralling theatre of commerce and power, were reduced to mere landlords with hollow, wistful titles. There was now no leader in the northern half of the coast, and all looked south where alone one prince succeeded in withstanding these convulsions of time, carrying his dynasty and house into modernity. As the Zamorins of Calicut faded into oblivion, it was time for the Maharajahs of Travancore to emerge from the shadows.

In 1752, shortly before the last Zamorin was toppled in Calicut, a hitherto forgotten dynasty made a thunderous reappearance upon the political landscape of Kerala. They had a pedigree that matched the Zamorin's, and at one time it was to their port of Quilon that the world came in avid search of spices and trade. Their Jewish and Christian merchants had dominated commerce for long years until the Arabs combined with Calicut and transformed the rules of the game, leaving Quilon a shadow of its former greatness. In the centuries that followed, the royal family there became so divided and diminished into feuding households, that they were practically nobodies in the larger scheme of things, their land a political backwater. In the sixteenth and seventeenth centuries when the Zamorin was forging grand alliances with Turkey and

Egypt, deploying colossal armies in his wars against the Portuguese, here in the south its princes were fighting petty clannish battles with minor militias supplied by petty warlords.[41] While Manavikrama sneered at presents Vasco da Gama offered him, the humble ruler in Quilon not only lapped up similar trinkets but also submitted gifts in return to honour the Portuguese.[42] The wide disparity in prestige between the Zamorin and these southern princes could not be overstated.

In the early eighteenth century, however, this house, known as Kupaka, was to experience such a wonderful resurgence that all Kerala sat up and took notice. They had carved up the south into small principalities among their various offshoots, with the extreme south in the hands of the Rajah of Travancore. He ruled over a tiny patch of land between Cape Comorin and Trivandrum, hovering at the periphery of Kerala's dynamics, with a voice so feeble that it was universally neglected. Travancore cut a miserable figure before the remainder of Kerala's princes; in fact if any of the Kupakas possessed at least a semblance of power, it was the branch in Quilon. Like Cochin, the prince of Travancore was perpetually vassal to one force or another. In the sixteenth century the emperors of Vijayanagar seem to have levied tribute from him, and by the seventeenth it was the Nayaks of Madurai who periodically plundered his lands. The Nawab of Arcot, a representative of the mighty Mughal emperor, followed, adding ignominy to the prince's unglamorous circumstances by treating him merely as a zamindar (landlord) at his court.[43] It was with some surprise, then, that Kerala awoke with a jolt when this house of perennial tributaries produced a valiant prince determined to rewrite history and drive a fear of mortal existence through the heart of the coastal polity, saving his lands from that destructive wave of invasive war that would engulf all else very shortly.

It was a prince of Travancore by the now-hallowed name of Martanda Varma who achieved this dramatic revitalisation of the Kupaka dynasty, resurrecting their former pride and standing. Born in 1706, he was, in the words of a contemporary, a 'man of great pride, courage, and talents, capable of undertaking grand enterprises'.[44] These were desperately desired qualities at the time, for by now his house had hit rock bottom. Respect for royal authority was at a complete discount and it was Nair chieftains who decided all affairs at court. Atop every hillock and across every river ruled a Nair lord, enjoying hereditary sway over his estates and engaged in fickle battles with assorted neighbours.[45] But for all their ceaseless infighting, the Nairs were wholly united in the preservation of their mutual interests by keeping the Rajah permanently emasculated. Temples too, controlled by influential Brahmin grandees, existed in *imperium in imperio*, as states within a state, and together these factions jealously guarded their privileges from any encroachment by the monarch. As one of Martanda Varma's powerless predecessors lamented bitterly, 'the nobles only desire that the kings sit on the throne like mute statues and do only what the nobles wish them to do!'[46]

Martanda Varma, however, was determined to put an end to this, and enthusiastic about employing all varieties of violence and intimidation to achieve his goals. Even before he succeeded to the throne, he was thoroughly despised by the most powerful clique in Travancore. Known as the Ettuveetil Pillamar (Lords of the Eight Houses), these Nairs had for long harassed the royal family and tamed the king into spectacular impotence. They whimsically played one branch of the Kupaka clan against the other, keeping its princes forever at war while reaping all the rewards of the attendant lawlessness. The Rajahs were unable to retaliate, as custom precluded fealty to any one king alone, and the Nairs were free to make or break their promiscuous allegiances as they pleased. Their impunity was also due to the fact that tradition denied Rajahs the power to divest any noble family of its ancestral rights. Martanda Varma, however, had scant respect for such usages. He earned the wrath of the Pillamar in the 1720s by scheming to rein them in with the aid of superior mercenary forces from outside Kerala, demonstrating early on that he was thirsting for a fight. For years, then, legend has it, these nobles hounded and chased him from one place to the next, reducing him into an illustrious fugitive in constant fear of physical liquidation. Meanwhile, he could only bide his time patiently and vow ultimate revenge on his adversaries when his day came.

That day came in 1729. Upon his accession, Martanda Varma, as a confirmed enemy of the aristocracy, sent a chilling message across Kerala, showing himself capable of not only breaching age-old mandates of tradition, but also of exercising ruthless force to satisfy his ambitions. He set an eerie example, for instance, by slaughtering his own cousins in cold blood when they refused to fall in line with him.[47] While this was essentially a family affair, it spelled out to one and all that Martanda Varma hadn't any scruples about breaking rules or committing sin. He had a cold, calculating zeal that sent a shiver down the back of the feudal class. The Pillamar were promptly on their guard, for they had supported these murdered cousins, and it was patent they would be next to confront Martanda Varma's vendetta. Soon enough, when evidence fell into the Rajah's hands of a conspiracy at court, he had the Pillamar arrested summarily and presented proof of their perfidy. In what was unprecedented, instead of chastising the nobles by demoting their powers but otherwise leaving them unharmed, Martanda Varma ordered their immediate execution.[48] Their properties were attached and their women and children sold into slavery, with not a hint of mercy or sympathy. And thus perished forty-two noble houses of the realm, obliterating internal opposition from the Rajah's path and ringing the death knell of feudalism in the region.[49]

Over the next two decades, Martanda Varma unleashed a formidable military campaign in south Kerala. He first went to war against his uncle who ruled Quilon. Having annexed his territories and acquired the old port, he moved to conquer other branches of the Kupaka dynasty. He suffered a number of defeats and reversals and at one point nearly lost everything when rival relations united to destroy him. But then, he recruited a contingent of Tamil mercenaries, and with their aid regained the upper hand, using stratagems of war traditionally never observed in Kerala.[50] In 1746, the last of his fierce opponents gave up resistance and fled, paving the way for Martanda Varma to claim unchallenged sovereignty over the now-united Kupaka kingdom. By 1749, he began to muscle into domains of other dynasties as well, beyond the frontiers of the old Kupaka country, reducing them to ashes.[51] One clever pretext after another was always tailored to justify these aggressions, and with his growing military clout, few were able to stall his advances. There was no clemency and by 1752 the armies of Travancore were hammering at the trembling gates of Cochin, having taken by force all the lands south, destroying also, in the process, the final vestiges of Dutch influence in Kerala.[52]

While Martanda Varma was building strong armies and emerging as the new fountain of power along the coast, the proud Zamorin had turned into a forlorn relic of the past. All that was needed to shatter his derelict jigsaw state was a fateful confrontation with the arriviste warrior from the south. In 1762, Travancore's soldiers, under the united command of a central authority, routed the paralysed jumble of feudal lords and spiritless retainers deployed by the Zamorin, decisively crushing any remaining prestige that ancient dynasty could claim in Kerala. The balance of power firmly tilted south, and it was up to Martanda Varma's house to guide the future destinies of the land in a changing world. In 1766, when Hyder Ali dispossessed the Zamorin and other northern chieftains forever, it was only Travancore that could withstand his threat, holding its own in the south until the Lion of Mysore, Tipu Sultan, marched in and waged a bloody war in 1789. But he too failed, ultimately, to take Travancore. A terrible heavenly downpour reinforced the bravery of the Nairs (aided by the English East India Company) to destroy the invaders. Martanda Varma's legacy was destined to survive for many more years.[53]

Travancore's unchallenged pre-eminence in Kerala was short-lived, however, as the political winds were blowing in a new, unprecedented direction, mortgaging its destiny to the newest foreign entrants in the subcontinent. The sceptre of colonialism commenced its rise in India, and this foreign power was shortly to dispose of even such tremendous powers as the Mughal emperor and the Marathas, claiming a right of conquest over the entire subcontinent for the first time in history. Martanda Varma apparently recognised this turn of the tide well beforehand. The Zamorins had taken a hostile position against the Portuguese and the Dutch in the name of dynastic gallantry. And they had lost. Discerning a lesson in political pragmatism, Martanda Varma chose, therefore, not to stand in the way of the ascent of the British and sacrifice the conquests of his lifetime at the altar of princely vanity. He satisfied himself instead with the role of a secondary partner to India's new rulers. On his deathbed in 1758 he issued seven injunctions for political survival to his heirs, the most crucial of which was that 'the friendship existing between the English East India Company and Travancore should be maintained at any risk, and that full confidence should always be placed in the support and aid of that honourable association'.[54] His successors followed this fiat to the letter, making up with grumbling obedience to their foreign overlords what they often lacked in personality and vigour.

Their *people*, of course, were rather less well disposed to this colonial marriage of expediency between a monarchy of recent vintage and an empire of foreign origins. As in the rest of the world, the dawn of the nineteenth century witnessed a Kerala at the very cusp of modernity, set to unleash many waves of change and turmoil upon its restless society. The old ways were discarded in favour of new. Victorian morality and views on life were superimposed awkwardly on the 'heathen' practices of yore. In the hasty name of 'progress', many of those remarkable distinctions that had once set Kerala apart from the rest of India, and indeed the rest of the world, were relinquished. Material prosperity of the classes and, to a lesser extent, the masses, grew. Modern forces were painfully birthing a new people, inching towards a common nationality alongside the remainder of India that was to fulfil its 'tryst with destiny' only in 1947. In the interim, rebellions, first violent and armed, then cultural and socio-economic, were provoked, and that strategic relationship advocated by a dying Martanda Varma was more than once challenged. The aspirations of the people were given expression in communal rivalries among themselves first before they integrated against the princely government ruling over them, in effect as a glorified, worshipped, and romanticised local arm of the empire; as a client regime of the

British. The fact, it was ultimately realised, was that the fortunes of Kerala's last prominent princely line were inextricably intertwined in an umbilical bond with the fate of the imperial enterprise in India. So long as the sun did not set on the British Empire, Travancore would endure.

This book is a chronicle of those fascinating times, from the era of Martanda Varma, the masterful warrior king, down to India's liberation from colonial rule two centuries after his passing. It is the story of those intervening years when the region became a smouldering cauldron of social, political and cultural contestations, which would leave in their wake a new land so different from its incredible ancestor in the era of the Zamorins and the Portuguese. It is the story also of a monarchy that was constantly reconciling its dynastic prerogatives with the demands of its colonial masters, or trying hard to harmonise social forces that slowly drained power from its hands. Martanda Varma's heirs were enlightened despots, offering their people many material rewards of modernity and standards of living superior to elsewhere in India (with enduring results in present-day Kerala). But these very gifts of noblesse oblige mutated into tools with which the masses would clamour for power and the right to determine their own course devoid of inherited dynastic paternalism. While the Maharajahs began to get comfortable on their thrones and convinced themselves of their own benevolent despotism, the people rose to challenge that entire world and chart a future guided by their collective aspirations alone.

The story of this tremendous transformation is told through the life and times of perhaps one of the most distinguished rulers of Travancore in the modern period. During the 1920s the stormy fortunes of the five million subjects of the state were entrusted into the misleadingly gentle hands of a *female* monarch, destined to go down in history as the penultimate ruler of Travancore and the last queen of the Kupaka dynasty and its Ivory Throne. She presided over the state during a most critical period, serving her people with considerable ability even as she watched her dynasty suffer inevitable strategic attacks outside while crumbling with dissent within. She occupied a riveting world of court intrigues and illicit conspiracies, hatched not only by scheming politicians beyond the walls of her palace but also by ambitious members of her family in an all-engulfing contest for power. With remarkable stoicism, however, she navigated her troubles—personal, political and dynastic—winning the reverence and love of her people through far-sighted policy and good government. Reigning with much aplomb and majesty on the eve of the dissolution of India's gilded world of Rajahs and Maharajahs, she earned the unstinting admiration of both the colonial empire that had shaped the country's past and of nationalists like Gandhi who were moulding its future. And when the final moment of reckoning came in 1947 and Travancore faded before a greater idea of India, she renounced her illustrious (and frequently violent) heritage and effaced herself from the land of her ancestors, as a romantic emblem of a Kerala that once was. Years later this last heiress of Martanda Varma's line would die faraway from the kingdom she once ruled, concluding with a tragic dignity a story that had begun generations before.

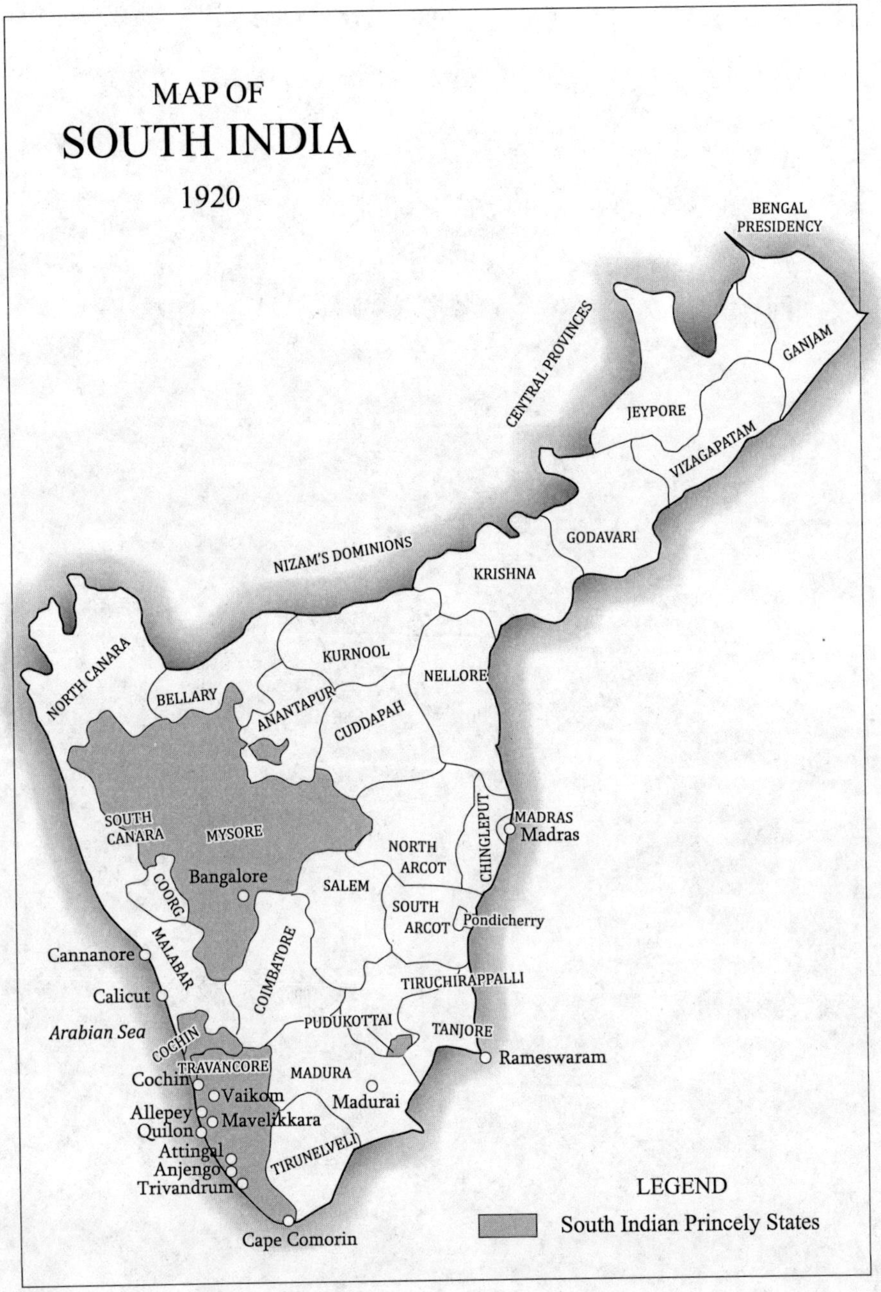
MAP OF
SOUTH INDIA
1920
BENGAL PRESIDENCY
CENTRAL PROVINCES
GANJAM
JEYPORE
VIZAGAPATAM
GODAVARI
NIZAM'S DOMINIONS
KRISHNA
NORTH CANARA
KURNOOL
NELLORE
BELLARY
ANANTAPUR
CUDDAPAH
SOUTH CANARA
MYSORE
MADRAS
Madras
NORTH ARCOT
CHINGLEPUT
COORG
Bangalore
SALEM
SOUTH ARCOT
Pondicherry
MALABAR
Cannanore
COIMBATORE
TIRUCHIRAPPALLI
Calicut
PUDUKOTTAI
TANJORE
Arabian Sea
COCHIN
Rameswaram
TRAVANCORE
MADURA
Cochin
Vaikom
Madurai
Allepey
Mavelikkara
Quilon
Attingal
TIRUNELVELI
Anjengo
Trivandrum
Cape Comorin
LEGEND
South Indian Princely States

THE HOUSE OF TRAVANCORE

The Kolathiri Princess
Chathayam Tirunal Mahaprabha
'of violent, profligate, and sordid character'

Mahaprabha

Arya — Chamunda

Mahaprabha

Uma
(*Adopted 1788*)

Gowri Lakshmi Bayi
(*r. 1810-1814*)

Parvathi
(*Adopted 1788*)

Gowri Parvathi Bayi
(*r. 1814-1829*)

Bhageerathi — The Pretender of 1810

- Rani Rukmini Bayi
  - Maharajah Ayilyam Tirunal (*r. 1860-1880*)
  - Maharajah Visakham Tirunal (*r. 1880-1885*)
  - Rani Lakshmi Bayi
    - Maharajah Mulam Tirunal (*r. 1885-1924*)
- Rajah Swathi Tirunal (*r. 1829-1846*)
- Rajah Uthram Tirunal (*r. 1846-1860*)

- Mahaprabha (*Kochupanki, wife of Raja Ravi Varma*)
  - Bhageerathi (*Kochukunji*) — Maharani Sethu Parvathi Bayi (*Adopted 1900*)
    - Maharajah Chithira Tirunal (*The Last Maharajah*) (*r. 1931-1949*)
  - Mahaprabha
    - Maharani Sethu Lakshmi Bayi (*Adopted 1900*) (*r. 1924-1931*)
- Rani Lakshmi Bayi (*The Barren Queen*) (*Adopted 1857*)
- Rani Parvathi Bayi (*Adopted 1857*) (*The mother of Prince Chathayam Tirunal and Prince Asvathi Tirunal*)

Note to the Reader

The names in this book follow a certain pattern. For male rulers of the House of Travancore I have used their star-names (*tirunals*) to avoid confusion. For instance, between 1829 and 1924 all the Maharajahs of Travancore, with one exception, had the personal name, Rama Varma. They are therefore distinguished by their star-names as Swathi Tirunal, Ayilyam Tirunal, Visakham Tirunal, and Mulam Tirunal.

For women, I have retained their personal names in most instances, but wherever confusion is likely to arise, I have relied on nicknames, while full names are given in the endnotes. Thus, for instance, where three women—grandmother, daughter and granddaughter—are all named Mahaprabha, I have retained the proper name for one of them while the others are referred to by their nicknames.

Some titles and names in this book have also been standardised throughout the main text. For instance, the word 'Maharajah' alone has variously been spelt in different sources as 'Maharaja', 'Maha Raja', 'Maha Rajah' and so on. So too surnames like 'Iyer' have been spelt sometimes as 'Aiyar' or 'Aiyer'. Original versions may be found in the endnotes and the bibliography, but throughout the principal text, I have chosen the ordinarily used version and employed that alone for consistency.

The images in this book, unless specifically mentioned, are either from open resources (such as the paintings by Raja Ravi Varma) or from private collections and the albums of members of the Travancore family.

ORIGINS

The matriarch of Mavelikkara

1
A Painter Prince

In 1862 when Ravi Varma was presented at court to the Maharajah of Travancore, little did he presume he was destined to emerge as one of the great luminaries of his generation. He had arrived in Trivandrum, the principality's capital, as a physically unprepossessing, swarthy stripling, whose facility and sophistication, however, belied his age. At fourteen, he had, in the manner of the Malayali aristocracy of the day, had an education in Sanskrit and Malayalam, with an honourable appreciation of music, drama and, rather unusually, painting. His family were country aristocrats lording over a few thousand acres of freehold at the grace and favour of the Maharajah, who was closely connected to them by marriage. It was, in fact, the principal occupation of the men of Ravi Varma's clan to marry princesses of Travancore and to spend the remainder of their days in splendid luxury. But that was if they were fortunate, for the number of princesses unengaged at any time did not always match the hordes of eligible young noblemen in waiting, and more aristocrats were left disappointed than exalted to a life of courtly recreations.

Used as he was to a country setting of fields, temples and rustics, for the young boy Trivandrum was a majestic change. Its architecture, a charming blend of the Kerala and European styles, was vastly different from that of his traditional home in Kilimanoor. There were leafy avenues and well-kept boulevards where the Maharajah went out for his drives, surrounded by public buildings, libraries, schools and all the other accessories of a nascent modern state. There were Englishmen and women, novelties he had never before seen, while at court munificent patronage was extended to some of the best musicians, artists and scholars in southern India. The Maharajah, having taken a liking to the boy from Kilimanoor, gave him leave to stay in the capital under a special sponsorship to study art. Accordingly, the uncle, who had chaperoned him to Trivandrum, installed Ravi Varma at their family's townhouse and departed, leaving the teenager a responsible master of his own destiny.[1]

In the palace, young Ravi Varma 'wandered the halls and corridors, studied the artists paint, observed their paintings, saw colourful processions, and pored over albums of European art, which the Maharajah collected'.[2] The royal library and manuscript collection were at his welcome disposal and he read and absorbed with an enthusiastic voracity. He had seen tales from Hindu mythology depicted on the walls of temples and in the murals at his family home, but what he really wanted to do was to bring them to life himself in paint; and specifically in oil paint. At the time, the chief durbar artist was Ramaswami Naidu of Madurai who alone knew how to mix and paint in oil, a technique he jealously guarded from rivals at court. Ravi Varma was no exception and consequently found himself kept at a watchful distance. 'Despondent,' one account goes, 'he marked his time, with none to initiate him into the mysteries of perspective and chiaroscuro, of compositions and complementary colours' with 'all the encouragement he received being the occasional advice of the Maharajah that perseverance is the best guru'.[3]

The young painter seems to have taken this royal counsel, probably given out of impatience than with pregnant meaning, to heart. For by the time he died in 1906 he would become one of colonial India's great artists, a celebrity whose life the press followed keenly, and whose paintings collectors vied to obtain. With typical panache and style, he would divide his seasons between Bombay, Delhi, Calcutta, Agra and other urban centres of the British Raj, entertained by one fawning patron after another. He was paid not only in money but also with more prestigious gifts of jewels, gold, robes of honour and even elephants. His social circle included Congress leaders like Dadabhai Naoroji and Gopal Krishna Gokhale; the crème de la crème of Bengali intelligentsia such as Surendranath Banerjea and the Tagore family; pro-imperialist statesmen like Sir Sheshiah Shastri and Sir T. Madhava Rao; alongside an impressive assortment of opulent Maharajahs and zamindars. Everywhere he always found 'opened for him the gates to the rich and powerful', although, ultimately, 'it was his personal charisma that enabled him to hold on to this milieu'. For he was also by this time 'a likeable socialite, equal in status to most of his clientele, with a gift for being able to flatter with his art even the least attractive features of his customers'.[4]

Indeed, Ravi Varma's success came not only because of his innate talent and hard work, but also because he had the advantage of high birth and social cultivation (not to speak of canny networking skills) that made him seem an exotic catch to many of his adoring patrons. He spoke several languages in varying degrees of proficiency, such as English, Tamil, Hindustani, Gujarati, Marathi, and even some German. His close links with the royal house of Travancore distinguished him from the legions of nameless artists and painters in India. To his credit, Ravi Varma did not rest idle with the rewards of his fame. He succeeded in taking his art into the homes of millions of Indians through a popular lithograph press, despite grave financial losses, and gave dignity to the profession of painting. Unlike Indian artists before him, whose identities are largely lost to posterity, he signed his name on his work with pride and confidence, imbuing the entire craft with those qualities. That is also why, when he died in 1906, people from many walks of life mourned him with creditable sincerity. He was not exceptionally wealthy ('Had brother taken care to save the money he had earned by painting, he would have been one of the richest men,' a sibling regretted),[5] but left behind, in the admiring estimate of a contemporary, a name and legacy on 'fame's lofty pinnacle'.[6]

Yet this path to glory and greatness was not easy for Ravi Varma, and in his marriage to art much else had to be sacrificed. For a few years after his arrival in 1862 at the durbar, he was engaged mainly in self-study as the other artists, with all their internecine rivalries, refused to guide or assist him in any way. 'What really sustained him during these years,' one biographer writes, 'was his will to break through and excel, and an abiding faith in divine grace.'[7] Tenacity was definitely a pronounced feature in the boy, but Ravi Varma did have a few other tricks up his sleeve than entrusting the matter entirely to divine offices. When the proud Ramaswami Naidu refused to initiate him into oil painting, he succeeded, most likely by underhand inducements, to persuade Arumugham Pillai, one of Naidu's apprentices, to give him secret lessons by the darkness of dusk. With all the watchful distrust among court painters, it was no mean accomplishment for the young boy to orchestrate a clandestine arrangement with none other than the trusted pupil of the biggest notable in Trivandrum's clannish art circles. An ingenious wit and a perfectly comfortable approach towards manipulation in the attainment of his own artistic ambitions were also, then, unabridged features of Ravi Varma's fascinating personality.

In 1868, however, a new chapter began in his life when a sensational character arrived at court in the form of Theodore Jensen. He was a Danish painter of no great ability but whose flawless white skin opened him many princely doors in the East. 'It was not,' says E.M.J. Venniyur, 'uncommon with European portrait painters of those days, who were probably none too successful at home, to come to India and extol in gold and velvet ... the Maharajahs wreathed in oriental splendour.' The Maharajahs, for their part, were equally enthusiastic to entertain Europeans, 'for these were times when the elite of the country cultivated British tastes most assiduously'.[8] Jensen got down to business and Ravi Varma promptly sought the honour of becoming his student, no doubt eager to learn from a bona fide 'master'. The Dane, predictably enough, was no less unwelcoming than Naidu and the others, aware, as he was, that he too came only with the dubious distinction of oil painting with a white hand. At the Maharajah's insistence, though, Ravi Varma was reluctantly granted permission to watch Jensen at work. And as it happened, the boy, now aged twenty, decided he would one day give these haughty artists, Indian and foreign, a run for their money.

By 1870, Ravi Varma was able to acquit himself in oil painting with much promise and intuitive flair. But a new set of problems arrived as friends and relations realised he intended to make a living out of art. The Varmas in Kerala were an aristocracy steeped in meticulous ceremony and endless ritual that built around them an aura they much enjoyed. They were once a ruling class and even in the late nineteenth century controlled vast swathes of land, keeping memories of bygone times alive through their traditions and antiquated way of life. There was, in 1870, no precedent of any of them having worked at all, leave alone working as a painter, which was seen more as a profession of lowborn artisans. In the face of opposition, however, the Maharajah came to Ravi Varma's rescue. Declaring that art was divine, he gave the painter his blessings and wholehearted encouragement. Reinvigorated by royal support (and the attendant silencing of the conservative faction), Ravi Varma went on a forty-one-day pilgrimage to Mookambika and propitiated the goddess Sarasvati. On his way back, in what was seen as a good omen, he received his first paid commission from a judge in Malabar, the northern portion of Kerala, once the domain of the Zamorin and now under direct British administration. He was hereafter officially a professional painter.[9]

Back in Trivandrum the talented Ravi Varma now commanded the complete attention and support not only of the Maharajah but also of his singularly attractive consort, Kalyani Pillai. This was a woman of tremendous personality, and a mind of her own, that often upset more orthodox sections at court. Born in 1839 as a subject of the neighbouring Rajah of Cochin, she was the only daughter of a former minister there, and a consummate mistress of all the cultural refinements of her class. She arrived in Trivandrum quite unexpectedly sometime in the 1850s, with scandal in hot pursuit. For local gossip has it that she had eloped, in a rather unladylike fashion, with a famous actor called Easwara Pillai, a member of the palace drama troupe.[10] At some point the Maharajah became acquainted with her and fell in love, so that in 1862 she dissolved her marriage to Easwara Pillai and became the ruler's consort.[11] Slowly a coterie of young intellectuals, artists, musicians, and others began to revolve around her, a fine poet and composer of Sanskrit plays herself, and her obliging husband. She went on to learn English, even interacting with Christian missionaries and reading the Bible, with an urbane irreverence that at once attracted and infuriated less liberal souls outside her ring. Ravi Varma, now a member of the elite inner circle of the Maharajah and his enigmatic consort, became so close to her that some even hint at a romantic liaison.[12] In any case, after his return to Trivandrum in 1870 he executed a portrait of the royal couple, which was close to such remarkable perfection that he was instantly elevated as a favourite. The Bangle of Honour (called *Veera Srinkhala*) was awarded him, no mean distinction for a painter, and for the next decade the Maharajah and Kalyani Pillai unstintingly championed Ravi Varma and his art, giving him the wings he needed to flourish.

Naidu, of course, did not appreciate his own fall from royal favour and the introduction of Ravi Varma, with all his personal rapport with the monarch, into that coveted spot. In 1873, both sent their paintings to the Fine Arts Exhibition sponsored by Lord Hobart, the Governor of Madras. Ravi Varma not only won the Gold Medal, but his *Nair Lady at the Toilet* was 'much admired' and is said to have become 'the talk of the town'.[13] In the same year he sent the painting to an international exhibition in Vienna, winning another medal that brought him coverage in all major newspapers of the day. In 1874 and 1875 he won Gold again in Madras, and his work was offered as an official present to the visiting Prince of Wales, a serious honour at the time for so young a 'native' artist. By 1876, the Governor of Madras was *collecting* his work, and his *Sakuntala's Love Letter* was sought by Sir Monier Monier-Williams as frontispiece for his famous translation of the Sanskrit *Abhijnana Sakuntalam*. Soon after this, in what a bitter Naidu only viewed as another testament to Ravi Varma's audacity and arrogance, the star artist declared that he would no longer compete for prizes and would only *exhibit* his work at public platforms. By now he was a popular member of Madras society, and an established painter with very pleased royal patrons in Trivandrum. Nothing could, it seemed, halt the meteoric ascent of Ravi Varma into the towering heights of history.

In 1880, however, all this began to unravel and Ravi Varma was to shortly be cast adrift. The reigning Maharajah, Ayilyam Tirunal, died unexpectedly after a brief ailment only to be succeeded by his staid, colourless brother, Visakham Tirunal, who was more a botanist than a connoisseur of the arts. For years there had been no love lost between these siblings, and one of the first acts of the new ruler was to dismantle the palace establishment, comprising his late brother's favourites, replacing them with his own loyalists. Naidu, interestingly, was one of the *new* Maharajah's partisans, and Ravi Varma realised his position was now untenable. In 1881 there was a public falling out between him and the Maharajah during a state visit by the Governor of Madras. Lord Buckingham considered Ravi Varma a friend and asked to see him during his meeting with the ruler at the palace. Visakham Tirunal had the artist summoned but was livid when he saw the Governor receiving him with a warmth and familiarity that he had not shown him. When Buckingham invited Ravi Varma to *join* them, the meeting turned awkward, for according to the dictates of court etiquette, the artist could not sit down in the presence of the Maharajah. The entire discussion had to be conducted with all three men standing, and the protocol-obsessed Visakham Tirunal became more and more incensed with every passing moment. He was furious that a subject of his should be seen as an equal and that he should have the temerity to publicly act friendly with a visiting dignitary, demeaning the Maharajah who could but swallow his pride. The story goes that the very next day Ravi Varma left Trivandrum, never to return during the reign of the hateful Visakham Tirunal. This may well be apocryphal but there was certainly a quarrel followed by the artist's unceremonious departure from court in 1881.[14]

But the ever-resourceful Ravi Varma only turned calamity into opportunity as usual. Determined to continue his work with or without royal backing, he now left for Bombay. Making full use of the many contacts he had made in Madras over the years he found new vistas of patronage and help. The Maharajahs of Baroda and Mysore gave him important commissions and soon he was able to build up a formidable reputation across India that brought him only more acclaim, while old Naidu and the wrathful Maharajah continued to fret and fume in Trivandrum. His stipend from the durbar was cut off and attempts were made by Visakham Tirunal to have him ostracised from his caste. Again Ravi Varma, who knew he was in a different league now, managed to foil this through his influential friends.[15] By 1904 the Viceroy of India, on behalf of the King of England, awarded him the Kaiser-i-Hind, a distinction that his first patron Ayilyam Tirunal had once received, truly elevating the artist to equality with his royal sponsors, no matter how much the latter resented this. He was now known popularly as Raja Ravi Varma and, to add to his prestige, in 1903 he also succeeded as head of the Kilimanoor family, making him a leading figure of the Malayali aristocracy. By his fifties, thus, Ravi Varma, the country boy who had come to Trivandrum with oil paint on his adolescent mind, was firmly at the pinnacle of worldly success, while those who stood against him faded into history or respectable oblivion.

While Ravi Varma earned himself a place among the great personalities of India, in Trivandrum, Ayilyam Tirunal's glamorous widow was fated for a joyless eclipse from public imagination. With the death of her husband, the bewitchingly beautiful and talented Kalyani Pillai was disengaged, in keeping with tradition, from all society, and prohibited further unorthodox cultural pursuits.[16] A 'liberal provision' was granted from the state treasury for her 'maintenance in comfort and dignity',[17] but she was for all real purposes restricted in her residence as was conventional with royal widows in Travancore. Occasionally her irresistible appetite for life saw her mildly breaching the rule, as witnessed, for instance, during Queen Victoria's golden jubilee celebrations in Trivandrum in 1887, when she sent felicitations to be read out at a public durbar. But for the most part she had mellowed, and disappeared prematurely into the twilight of her life, which came to an end at two o'clock on 18 January 1909, nearly thirty years after her beloved Maharajah had died.[18]

Kalyani Pillai, for all her inner magnetism and strength of personality, always knew her life was destined to conclude in this manner. For under the matrilineal law of succession prevalent in Kerala, even though she was married to the ruler, she was not his queen. On the contrary, she was merely his *consort*, whose status was by no means set in stone. She lived at the Maharajah's favour, and could easily be discarded if he tired of her or preferred a new candidate as his partner. Indeed, Ayilyam Tirunal, while highly regarded for his perspicacity and for laying the foundations of modern government in Travancore, was personally 'notorious as a moral wreck', with 'a flood of local stories prevalent about his perversions'.[19] It was to Kalyani Pillai's credit that she not only retained the official position of consort for herself, but also succeeded in adopting children with the Maharajah when she could have none of her own. But this pre-eminence was still enjoyable only during his lifetime, and after his death she had to invariably reconcile to uncomplaining anonymity, making way for Visakham Tirunal's preferred spouse. Even her official title as the wife of a Maharajah of Travancore was not Rani but *Ammachi*, which as a 1912 feature in London's *The Lady* pointed out, merely meant, 'The mother of his children'. Nobody could have stated the fact more succinctly:

> Whenever a stranger goes to Travancore, one of the largest and most picturesque native States, situated in south-western India, they always tell him not to address her as 'Your Highness'. They think this word is too dignified to apply to her. No doubt she is the Ruler's spouse; but that does not make her the Maharani or even the Rani. She is only Ammachi, just the mother of His Highness' children, and they believe that word is good enough to express her relationship to the man who is autocrat of more than 2,950,000 people, inhabiting [over] seven thousand square miles of territory, yielding an annual revenue of about £700,000.[20]

The author of this piece captured the simple essence of matrilineal society in Kerala. For here, a family did not take after the patriarchal model of man, wife and their children. Instead, it consisted, to put it simplistically, of man, *sister*, and *her* children. The crown passed not from father to son but from maternal uncle to nephew, and the Rani was never the Maharajah's wife, but his sister or niece or great-niece. Ayilyam Tirunal, for instance, did not inherit his title or throne from his father, who was only a glorified nobleman, but from his mother, the Rani, and her brother, the previous Maharajah. His heirs too were, first, his younger brother, and then the son of their sister. And thus the crown passed in this somewhat topsy-turvy fashion down the ages. The Maharajahs' own children were merely nobles with the consolation of certain exclusive titles and estates, fated as they were for oblivion after the lifetimes of their exalted fathers. 'I have seen standing unnoticed in a shop,' Henry Bruce wrote with surprise during his travels in Kerala, 'the son of [a] highly distinguished late Maharajah.'[21] And he was not exaggerating. For 'The Ammachi [like her children],' confirms Samuel Mateer, was 'not a member of the royal household, and is in nowise associated with the royal court. She has neither official nor social position at court, and cannot even be seen in public with the ruler whose wife she is.'[22] 'Her sole interests in life,' *The Lady* concludes, '[were] to anticipate the wishes of her royal husband and amuse herself.'[23] In this Kalyani Pillai was a greater success than most Ammachis, whose very names were forgotten the moment their illustrious spouses left this world.

In a similar manner, the sister-Ranis also selected nobles of superior caste as their partners, and these gentlemen, chosen invariably from Ravi Varma's clan, were equally disposable at will. Fancy titles were granted them but never any real power or royal status, and they were expected mainly to serve their wives by fathering the next generation of the dynasty. Indeed, as late as the 1920s, the Ranis' husbands were 'entitled only to a monthly allowance from the durbar of Rs 200 per mensem with meals from the palace and the use of a brougham and pair of horses'.[24] Even into the 1940s, at grand banquets, while the Ranis and their children would be served four varieties of dessert, the consorts were entitled to only two, while ordinary guests had to satisfy themselves with a single option.[25] Custom discouraged them from living with the Ranis, and they had to await royal summons whenever their wives wished to entertain them. Indeed, they were disallowed even from travelling in the same carriage as the Ranis, and if due to any reason they had to, it was essential that they sat opposite and not next to their wives.[26] In public they had to bow to them and refer to them always as 'Your Highness'. They were certainly fathers of Maharajahs, but in the matrilineal system it did not matter who your father was, as much as who your mother and uncle were. To those more accustomed to the patriarchal tradition, all this seemed rather outlandish and perhaps even unnatural. But as the writer in *The Lady* wistfully remarks, these sons and husbands were 'used to this sort of procedure from long centuries of customary practice' and would say with 'smiles playing upon their lips' that they were meant to be private citizens, even if they were born or married to royalty.[27]

The Travancore dynasty, however, was not really known for its fecundity and historically there was always a lack of girls born of blood royal. The family produced males in healthy abundance, but usually with fewer sisters to continue the line. Since the fourteenth century, in such instances it was customary to adopt girls from another old family in Kerala and install them as Ranis in Travancore, with their issue taking the dynasty into the next generation. These adoptions were always made from the house of the Kolathiri Rajah of Cannanore. Once a proud prince in Malabar (though nowhere as grand as the Zamorin), this was a Rajah who used to lord over a thriving port and, like all petty potentates worth their salt, flaunted a fanciful pedigree from ancient dynasties and mythical kings not to speak of the sun, moon and other heavenly entities. In other words, the Kolathiri line was equal in stature to Travancore's, and their females were eminently qualified to replace the latter's Ranis. In fact, Ayilyam Tirunal and Visakham Tirunal themselves were descendants of one such royal adoptee who was brought in from Cannanore and installed as Rani in 1788. By this time, however, the Kolathiri Rajah's circumstances were rather appalling, and his family had swollen into several unwieldy, quarrelling branches. Its members, in the words of Canter Visscher, 'both male and female, [were] so numerous that they [lived] in great poverty for the most part'.[28] To add to their agonies, soon after 1788 they were forced into exile and had to abandon their ancestral lands altogether, when the fearsome armies of Tipu Sultan of Mysore routed their feeble defences and overran all of Malabar. Eventually the English East India Company annexed the region and most constituents of the no-longer-royal Kolathiri dynasty accepted the invitation of the Maharajah of Travancore, their affluent and still afloat relative, to settle in his state, where estates, pensions and the offer of a better life were placed at their grateful disposal. They were accommodated in various parts of the principality, with one division of these immigrants establishing themselves in the town of Mavelikkara, a hub of the pepper trade in bygone times.[29]

Among the Mavelikkara stock was a young princess by the name of Arya. She was considered especially important among all the exiles on account of the fact that it was *her* older sister who had been adopted in 1788 as the Rani of Travancore. In the decades that followed, Arya's offspring became comfortably ensconced as aristocrats in Mavelikkara, when in 1857 the Kolathiris, despite their loss of princely status, were again called upon to supply two Ranis to the Maharajah of Travancore. That year, it so happened, the sole female member in the royal family, the only sister of Ayilyam Tirunal and Visakham Tirunal, died giving birth to a boy. This infant was expected to succeed his uncles one day as Maharajah, but without any sisters of his own, the line would terminate with him. It was to avoid this eventuality that Arya's heirs, as close cousins of the royal house, were asked to provide two girls to be installed as Senior Rani and Junior Rani respectively. They were to be entrusted with the lofty task of furnishing successors for their adoptive baby brother, and it was thus that two children, great-granddaughters of Princess Arya, were separated from their mother and siblings in Mavelikkara and escorted to Trivandrum. Their ties with the Kolathiri dynasty were ritually severed and they were duly consecrated as Ranis of Travancore, with the elaborate names of Bharani Tirunal Lakshmi Bayi Tampuran and Bharani Tirunal Parvathi Bayi Tampuran.

Neither of the sisters was destined to lead particularly happy lives, however. This was partly on account of the onerous dynastic task they were encumbered with, as also because of the intrigues that inevitably plagued royal courts. The Junior Rani was widowed while in her teens, and selected a second husband in order to do her duty to the royal family. She produced five children but all three that survived were boys. They, of course, joined the ranks of future Maharajahs of Travancore but in turn had no sisters to give them royal heirs. In 1893, then, the Junior Rani herself died of cancer and any hopes of her producing female children were permanently dashed.[30] Lakshmi Bayi, the Senior Rani, on the other hand, did not have any children at all, even though she emerged as a remarkable lady of considerable ability and personal accomplishments. Like Kalyani Pillai, she commanded excellent cultural attainments, especially when it came to music, and played the veena with expert facility. Her beauty is believed to have been quite exquisite; as Pierre Loti, the French novelist wrote, with forgivable Western hyperbole: 'her face does not seem to belong to our times, and it is only in old Indian miniatures that I have had a glimpse of such princesses.'[31] Following in Kalyani Pillai's footsteps, Lakshmi Bayi also obtained a sound English education, and her letters to her consort, with such unorthodox romantic salutations as 'My darling husband', 'My most beloved husband', etc., are delightful works of prose that bespeak impressive literary potential.[32] She also possessed considerable self-confidence that enabled her to call a spade a spade, and stand up even to dominating Maharajahs like Ayilyam Tirunal. At one time, when the latter wanted to dismiss her husband and select her a fresh consort, she stuck by her marriage, winning the appreciation of Queen Victoria for her 'womanly' loyalty and virtue, of which much was made in those days.[33] In the 1880s, on a visit to Madras, large crowds of people came out to catch a glimpse of the Rani, who was something of a celebrity, perceived by many, to quote Loti again, as 'a charming personification of India'.[34]

By the 1890s, however, Lakshmi Bayi's singular preoccupation was posterity. Having no children of her own, and with the Junior Rani leaving behind only sons, it was evident to everybody at court that yet again the royal family would have to bring in girls through adoption. 'Many thoughts in connection with this trouble my mind perpetually,' the Rani wrote to a niece. 'Oh God! I do not have the strength to think on this! The fortunate ones are those who can live happily without such thoughts.'[35] As the eldest member of the dynasty it was up to her to set the wheels in motion and ask her adoptive brother, by now the Maharajah of Travancore, to adopt girls to succeed her as Ranis and to provide their lineage male and female heirs for the future. Lakshmi Bayi only hoped 'to be spared long enough to bring up two girls as to inherit my estate and its appurtenances', concerned as she also was that, like the Junior Rani, she too might die leaving the precarious issue of succession unsettled.[36] To resolve this, however, she did not have to look very far, turning instinctively to her relations in Mavelikkara to select suitable girls there. And the children she had in mind came not merely with the conventional Kolathiri bloodline that was mandatory for adoption, but also with a more fashionable distinction that rendered them immensely attractive as candidates. For they were grandchildren of none other than the most prominent subject of the state and that pioneering artist, Raja Ravi Varma.

The greatest casualty of Ravi Varma's successes in the world of art was his family life. In 1866 he married a child bride aged about eleven, called Mahaprabha. Lovingly known by her vernacular pet name of Kochupanki, she was a member of the Kolathiri family with more than one intimate connection at the royal court. Her uncle was an influential grandee in Trivandrum,[37] but in what was certainly more salient, Kochupanki was the youngest sister of the Senior and Junior Ranis of Travancore. Ravi Varma, in other words, was married to the sister Lakshmi Bayi and Parvathi Bayi left behind in Mavelikkara when they were adopted in 1857.[38] The match was probably arranged by the Senior Rani herself, and proved most propitious for the young artist at the time. For Kochupanki brought him even closer to the royal house and her sisters went out for their way to help him navigate court politics, not to speak of frequently assisting him with presents of expensive art supplies. At the time of his marriage with Kochupanki, however, he was not so famous as an artist as much as another member of the court who happened to like to paint, and his intentions to take this up as a profession were unclear. The marriage, then, was just another alliance between two leading families of the principality. But, as fate would have it, the relationship was doomed to be unhappy from the beginning. For Ravi Varma was devoted to his art, with a vision that transcended the cloistered environs of feudal Kerala, looking out at the world beyond and all that it offered to a man of his creative temperaments. What Kochupanki, whose sex and circumstances precluded her from a broader world view, desired on the other hand, was her own notion of a regular marriage and domestic fulfilment.

At the time of their wedding she was still a child and did not make too many demands of her husband, happy to let him pursue his studies and spend all his time in Trivandrum. Even when she matured, Kochupanki is said to have been exceedingly understanding in the beginning, even if she did not comprehend why her aristocrat husband had to work so much at all or why, of all things in the world, he wished to be a painter. But with time the gaps of intellect and ambition between them, not to speak of their entirely divergent views on life, began to impose a strain on the marriage. Ravi Varma's absences from Mavelikkara grew, and resentment and depression crept into Kochupanki's life. Reports of his activities in Bombay and other great cities, that she could only vaguely and incoherently have known about, reached Mavelikkara. Exaggerated by gossipmongers and delivered to jealous relatives, Kochupanki found herself facing a frustrating combination of embarrassment and anxiety about a husband whose personality she failed to fathom and whose intellectual spirit she could never match. In the words of a descendant, 'She was utterly incompatible with her husband, and his highly developed aesthetic sense and urges found no sympathy in her. She was exactly the opposite: a down-to-earth, plain, unimaginative woman while he took his sense of creativity to the heights of worship. She was often enraged at his using models for his paintings, and had no taste for beautiful things. The play of light upon skin or leaf would send her husband into ecstasies. But Kochupanki could not have cared less.'[39] Ravi Varma too made few efforts to alleviate his wife's stress, or sympathise with her unhappy situation, distracted and immersed in the artistic (and possibly equally material) opportunities the more cosmopolitan world outside Kerala presented him. Husband and wife seemed to occupy entirely different milieus to all who beheld them.

By the 1880s the marriage of the celebrated artist and his orthodox wife lay in a predictable shambles. Kochupanki, miserable and lonely, lost interest in living life for the sake of it and became, in the words of her nephew, 'addicted to drink'.[40] Her temper became uncontrollable; once when her husband brought home 'a huge crystal chandelier of Murano workmanship, Kochupanki, angry at his protracted absence, threw it out of the door and the priceless artefact shattered to pieces'.[41] It is also believed that both of them may have been tempted to pursue other relationships, given their prolonged separations,[42] but Kochupanki had to grapple with an especially difficult psychological strain. She now had the unenviable reputation of being the neglected wife of a flamboyant Ravi Varma whose successes rendered him an object of envy and sarcasm among less gifted but stingingly vocal members of their class. This was in addition to her general feeling of inadequacy that came from having to live all her life in the shadows of her exalted royal sisters in Trivandrum. Alcoholism fused with relentless depression into a deadly cocktail and in 1891, while her husband sojourned in Bombay, Kochupanki died an inglorious and premature death. She was only thirty-six, leaving behind sorrowful memories of a life unfulfilled. Ravi Varma is said to have felt a sense of remorse when he heard the news, but this did not prompt him to hasten to Kerala. Instead, he continued with his commitments elsewhere, and by the time he returned home many months later, Kochupanki's remains had already been turned to ashes and dissolved into sacred waters by her sons, where finally, one presumes, she found the peace that had always eluded her.

For all its tribulations, however, the marriage of Ravi Varma and Kochupanki was not without offspring, and five children were born to this unlikely couple. Two of these were boys named Kerala Varma and Rama Varma respectively. The former inherited his mother's addiction to alcohol and 'belying much early promise, turned a profligate'.[43] Like her, he too did not survive his thirty-sixth birthday and is believed to have died in 1912 in an accident in the Himalayas where he was wandering for unknown reasons.[44] The other boy followed in the creative footsteps of his father and studied painting at the Sir J.J. School of Art in Bombay, going on to live a constructive life, even if he never achieved any comparable fame or celebrity as an artist. Of the three daughters, the eldest born in 1872 was named, like her mother, Mahaprabha, and was followed by Bhageerathi in 1878 and Uma in 1882.[45] Mahaprabha was the beauty of the family. Fair-skinned, with very attractive features, rendered all the more appealing by an aristocratic demeanour, she was, according to a descendant, 'an artist's dream'.[46] Her father recognised this and featured her in one of his most famous paintings, *There Comes Papa* (1893), and proceeded to depict many of his goddesses and celestial beauties in her image. The youngest girl, Uma, was also pretty but Bhageerathi, known within family circles as Kochukunji, presented a stark contrast to her sisters. Photographs reveal a much less appealing countenance, not helped by a conspicuous squint, and it is very likely she did not win any particular appreciation for her looks as a young girl.

In the late 1880s, before her mother's death, Mahaprabha married a nephew of her father's from the Kilimanoor family. Known as Kuttan Tampuran, he was an erudite scholar and one of the first members of the aristocracy to obtain a college education in Madras. He was also the author of a comprehensive and scholarly translation of the Sanskrit dictionary into Malayalam and English, and was to spend much of his life in similar intellectual pursuits.[47] Sometime later, Kochukunji, the second sister, married a gentleman called Bhagavan Tampuran,[48] and if Mahaprabha was the beauty among the sisters, he was the more handsome of their husbands. Tall, with a very strong, masculine appearance, he also possessed in great abundance something Malayalis were obsessed with: hair! For both men and women a wealth of hair was considered a major attraction and Bhagavan Tampuran was blessed with long, lustrous locks that are said to have reached down well below his waist. This he would tie up on the side of his head in an enormous (and then stylish) bun called *kudumi*, provoking much envy in less endowed men around him.[49] Uma, the youngest, was also married in due course, although it was through the first two daughters that Ravi Varma's name would gain an added sheen of princely class in the decades to come.

With the passing of Kochupanki, and with Ravi Varma travelling endlessly across India with his art, Lakshmi Bayi assumed the responsibility of looking after his motherless children. She was not involved in the humdrum decisions about their lives but had tremendous influence over bigger matters, including their weddings. The Rani after all did have a vested interest in this, for her intention was for her nieces to give her baby girls she could adopt into the royal family as future Ranis and mothers of prospective Maharajahs of Travancore. With this in mind, she embarked upon a long pilgrimage in 1894 to the Tamil temple town of Rameswaram, accompanied by Mahaprabha and Kochukunji. The royal party journeyed hundreds of miles through the heat and dust of the peninsula, all the way to the eastern coast of India.

Rameswaram is considered one of India's holiest cities, and legend places its origins in a deeply spiritual act by Rama, the mythological hero of the Ramayana. The story goes that after vanquishing the evil King of Lanka, Rama bathed in the sapphire seawaters at Rameswaram to wash away the bloody sins of war. He also consecrated a temple to Mahadeva here and for thousands of years pilgrims travelled to this town to undertake the ritual bath called Sethu Snanam and to worship Rama's deity. Lakshmi Bayi too arrived here with the same intentions, and undertook that ceremonial dip in the sea, to wash away the accumulated sins of her ancestors, and propitiated Mahadeva for the baby girls she so ardently desired. And of course the locals were fascinated. For the custom among other pilgrims was to ask the gods for baby boys, but here was a devout queen who had travelled an enormous distance with the sole purpose of seeking a boon of little girls.

By the time the royal party departed Rameswaram, a great aura of magic and divine mystery had been built around them. It was said that the Rani, with her piety and absolute devotion, had succeeded in pleasing the deity. So much so that one day while she stood before the sanctum sanctorum of the temple, she had a divine vision of Mahadeva himself. He appeared before Lakshmi Bayi, the story goes, in all that majesty typical to gods while making such appearances in the mortal world, and proceeded to personally promise her the gift of female heirs in her line.[50] Another version states that the deity featured in a dream the Rani had, for the same purpose of guaranteeing baby girls to her family.[51] Either way, a fittingly dramatic and certainly apocryphal tale was woven around the whole affair, and by the time the pilgrims returned to Travancore, many were convinced that the fruits of their journey would be borne shortly. And oddly enough, whether by heavenly machinations, or by Lakshmi Bayi's determined conviction or simply because of destiny, they were.

A few months after Lakshmi Bayi returned to Trivandrum, news arrived at the palace that Mahaprabha had conceived and was with child. The overjoyed Rani now went on a whole new series of pilgrimages within Travancore, so that even the local gods and divinities would collaborate with Mahadeva of Rameswaram to realise her yearning for a baby girl. In Mavelikkara, Mahaprabha was made to subscribe to a full range of religious vows and ceremonies, while missive after advisory missive arrived from her royal aunt. She was told what to eat, and what not to eat; which tonics were mandatory, and which not so much; what rituals she could omit, and what had to be performed without delay; and so on. The expectant mother merely acquiesced in all this, partly because the Rani gave her no option but also because she was conscious of precisely how important the birth of a girl child would be for her, her family, and for the state of Travancore. Nobody wanted to take any chances.

By the second week of November 1895, Lakshmi Bayi ordered Mahaprabha to find an auspicious day to move into the accouchement room at the family palace in Mavelikkara.[52] 'Think that the Lord in his mercy will bless you with a bonny female child and be happy,' the Rani commanded her. Finally, with everyone waiting with bated breath, on Tuesday, 19 November, Mahaprabha went into labour and gave birth to a baby girl: 'fair complexioned with dark large eyes and curly black hair', 'a darling little stranger'. 'How thankful we are to the Almighty,' the Rani's husband rapturously declared, 'for at last granting our unremitting prayers!'[53] It was official now. The girl born *had* to be a result of the pilgrimage to Rameswaram and of the Sethu Snanam ceremony her mother and distinguished great-aunt had performed. She was an heiress provided by the gods to the royal house of Travancore in its time of need, and to commemorate her divine origins, it was pronounced she be named *Sethu* Lakshmi Bayi. There could not be a more romantic story behind one's birth, and in the years to come, poets and mystics would make much of the heavenly origins of this daughter of providence, named after the sacred seas and her indomitable great-aunt. As it happened, though, she was destined to die faraway from her land of birth in near obscurity.

There was, of course, no question of adopting a newborn into the royal house and so, for the next few years, Sethu Lakshmi Bayi remained in Mavelikkara with her parents and surrounded by members of her extended family. The Rani was, of course, a dominant presence even in those early years and every now and then, on receiving her commands, the baby girl would be taken to Trivandrum to spend several months at a stretch at the palace. These vivid memories would remain etched in her mind, as she remembered the Sundara Vilasam Palace in Trivandrum Fort, where they stayed, next door to Lakshmi Bayi's own Sarasvati Vilasam. It was a beautiful building, full of 'huge halls and haunting passages and corridors', the girl would later reminisce. 'There was a very picturesque staircase going up to the women's quarters upstairs, where there was a single piece of rosewood called *tookhamanji*, like a swing with brass chains going up, on which you could lie or sit.' Sethu Lakshmi Bayi would remember her royal great-aunt coming to visit her here, reclining with aplomb on velvet bolsters and cushions, giving orders to her servants and retainers. It was a magical image of a stately woman that left an abiding impression on the princess-to-be early in her life.[54]

In the meantime, in early 1896 the Rani received a letter unexpectedly from a former Dewan (Chief Minister) of Travancore and a friend of Ravi Varma's called Sir Sheshiah Shastri (1828–1903). One of the earliest beneficiaries of English education in India, he had risen from being a junior clerk in service of the Madras Government to holding the prestigious Dewanships of Travancore as well as of Pudukkottai. His acquaintance with Lakshmi Bayi went back several decades to the mid-1870s, when Ayilyam Tirunal sat on the throne, but since his retirement many years ago he had not been in touch. So his message to her now came as a surprise, not least because it also appeared strangely prescient. He claimed to be 'prompted by a power, which I cannot understand' to write to the Rani about the future of her dynasty and of Travancore, 'a country which will always be dear to me'. Insisting that she should take 'measures to strengthen the Royal Family' by adopting girls, he went on to describe a curious dream he had had. In this, he claimed, he witnessed the Rani presenting to her family deity in the great temple in Trivandrum two princesses as adoptees, insuring the future of her line. 'When I awoke,' he concluded, 'I asked myself could this be only a baseless dream or was it only a foreshadowing of what is soon to happen? I felt satisfied that it was undoubtedly the latter.'[55]

This convinced Lakshmi Bayi again of divine intervention in the protection of her house. For how else could a man, unheard from for years, suddenly bring up exactly what was on her mind, especially after picturing everything in a dream? To add to it, soon afterwards it was announced that Kochukunji was now pregnant. As in the case of Mahaprabha, a whole series of religious vows and offerings followed, and on 7 November 1896, almost exactly a year after the birth of Sethu Lakshmi Bayi, yet another great-niece was born to the Rani. Like her cousin, she was duly named *Sethu* Parvathi Bayi. It appeared as though the second character from Sir Sheshiah's dream had arrived on the scene, and all that remained was to set the stage for that decisive moment in the lives of the girls and in the history of Travancore: the actual adoption. 'May the Lord save the children He has given,' the Rani prayed in all sincerity, little anticipating the tumultuous future fate held in store for them.[56]

Towards the end of 1899 Lakshmi Bayi commenced proceedings for the adoption of her great-nieces into the royal family by issuing a formal message to the Maharajah. 'I suppose you know that I am getting on in years and that I am suffering from diseases attendant thereto,' she began, before going on to recommend that the two Sethus be introduced into the dynasty. 'To propagate your family, brother, we request you to get this thing done. As the children are now old enough to be properly educated and trained to follow the royal etiquette, I request you to proceed with the adoption without further delay.'[57] Besides this, some urgency had also been added to the whole affair because one of Lakshmi Bayi's three nephews, born to the late Junior Rani, had died, reducing the number of heirs to a precarious two.[58] Adoption became all the more important because of yet another strikingly exceptional feature of the matrilineal system; if there were no male members in the royal family, its princesses were perfectly eligible to succeed in their own right as sovereign rulers. Thus, if the two remaining princes were also to pass away unexpectedly, the Sethus would be entitled, in the order of seniority, to occupy the Ivory Throne and ensure the state was not orphaned.

In a few months' time all the formalities were completed with the British Government of India and the date of the adoption announced. On 28 August 1900, thus, the children bid their final adieus to relatives and family members in Mavelikkara and set out on their journey to becoming the princesses of Travancore. Travelling by boat, they arrived in Trivandrum two days later to a fabulous reception. An escort took them to the Rani's palace, abuzz with activity in preparation of the event. Many nobles and aristocrats from all over Kerala had arrived for the function, and they paid informal calls on the princesses-to-be that evening. The town itself was brimming with people who had gathered from all over the state, lending to the whole place an air of eager celebration.

At sunrise on 31 August, the little girls were awoken by their mothers, quickly readied and taken to the Rani. Lakshmi Bayi looked as prim and majestic as ever, and with an unusual enthusiasm and energy, took charge of her wards. In a procession she escorted them for an elaborate ceremonial bath in the Padmateertham, the temple tank, where they were 'purified' and made ready to be presented to Sri Padmanabhaswamy, the royal family's deity. Then in the presence of the Dewan and all other important Hindu officials of the government, and with the Rani's youngest nephew, Prince Asvathi Tirunal, presiding, the children were led to the sanctum sanctorum of the temple. As they contemplated the inner stone pavilion called the Srimukha Mandapam, Lakshmi Bayi closed her eyes for a moment and took the name of Sri Padmanabhaswamy. She had waited many years for this day and in that instant all her worries were lifted away. And when the auspicious moment arrived, she clasped the hands of both Sethus in her own, and led them up the sacred steps.

The shrine was brilliantly lit up and kept open for Sri Padmanabhaswamy to accept the new princesses, as was traditional. Through its three doors the children beheld the resplendent image of the deity, and prostrated in acceptance of their sacred charge. At that moment, while the surging crowds outside waited, a twenty-one-gun salute was fired. As the first boom was sounded all over Trivandrum, revelry broke out on the streets. The air was filled with an utter cacophony of noises: the ululations of the womenfolk, the hurrahs of the men, the feu de joie of the soldiers, all punctuated by the occasional trumpets of the state elephants. It was a historic moment when the Sethus finally became part of the royal family, one that would shape the future of the land and the lives of its millions. They would both, in their respective rights, hold the destinies of Travancore in their hands in the years to come. And they would both leave their marks, in good ways and in bad, on Martanda Varma's kingdom.

That afternoon at the official durbar a formal proclamation of adoption was issued by the Maharajah. From an open gallery attached to the hall, and looking out at the crowds, in a booming, stentorian voice the Dewan announced:

> *Whereas it is found necessary to secure the continuation of the representation of Our House by adoption, We are pleased to declare that according to custom and usage and with the concurrence of the British Government, Sethu Lakshmi born on the 5th Vrischikam 1071 [Malayalam Era] under the star Pooradam, and Sethu Parvathi born on the 24th Tulam 1072 under the star Mulam, both of the Mavelikkara family, have this day been adopted as Junior Rani and First Princess of Attingal.*[59]

In Malayalam Sethu Lakshmi Bayi would henceforth be titled the Attingal Elaya Tampuran and Sethu Parvathi Bayi the Attingal Kochu Tampuran. These were their official titles, as the Ranis of Travancore were formally addressed as the rulers of Attingal. This was a territory within the state, which until the eighteenth century had been independent of the Maharajah's authority, directly ruled by the senior female member of the royal family. Then Martanda Varma, as part of his venture to consolidate a strong unitary state, amalgamated Attingal securely with the rest of Travancore. But the Ranis retained the title and ceremonial connections with that place, and the revenues from it continued to accrue to them. Lakshmi Bayi, as the foremost female member, was in charge of this, with her title as the Attingal Mootha Tampuran, i.e., Senior Rani, while her little great-nieces now became the Junior Rani and the 'First Princess' respectively.

With the successful performance of the adoption ceremonies, the Rani had been relieved of a tremendous weight. For years she had worried about the prospects of her dynasty, and only the birth of her great-nieces had soothed her. She seems to have been particularly fond of Sethu Lakshmi Bayi, writing for instance in 1897 to Mahaprabha as follows:

> I pass my time imagining the play of the children. How lovely it would be to see Sethukutty playing, and to hear her unformed words. I keep thinking of it. When you described it in your letter, I was obsessed with the thought that all this time without seeing her was being wasted. I consoled myself with the thought that extreme happiness comes only during periods of good fortune, and for that I pray to the Lord and wait for it to come. May God save the darling children.[60]

On another occasion, when she was lonely and missed the playful laughter of the girls, she asked her niece: 'Tell this to Sethukutty and give her a kiss on my behalf.' Yet another time on hearing of some mischief the girls had been up to in Mavelikkara, she insisted to Mahaprabha: 'Please do not scold the children on any account.'[61] It was with happiness, then, that she welcomed the two Sethus after their adoption to Trivandrum, and into her solitary life, permanently. She would finally, she thought, be able to see them for as long as she wanted, and to pamper and indulge them as fully as she had craved during all her unhappy years of childlessness.

She had had to fight her own battles to see this day, though, which contributed to her sense of relief once the ceremonies were concluded. Certainly as Senior Rani and head of the royal house she possessed the enormous privileges of that position, but adoption was anything but an uncomplicated affair. It was fraught with bitter rivalries and vehement intrigues, so worrisome that even the lives of the two girls might have been in jeopardy during their initial years in Mavelikkara. Giving heiresses to the royal house was a matter of great prestige for the Kolathiri clan in Mavelikkara. But it also provoked envy. For there were other branches of the Kolathiri family also living in Travancore at Ennakkad, Prayikkara, and Aranmula, and they all felt that they too had a right to nominate their daughters for the adoption. Since the last adoption in 1857 had been from Mavelikkara, they argued that one of their houses ought to have the next rightful claim to be considered.

But Lakshmi Bayi, after decades of exposure to court intrigues, was adept at manoeuvring through politics of this variety and ensuring she had her way. In this particular instance, she sought to bolster her proposal over others' by collaborating with the Maharajah's chief favourite. In royal families, those in palace establishments wielded much power. Especially since the accession of the then Maharajah Mulam Tirunal, a contentious 'palace bureau'[62] of favourites, sycophants, and henchmen had come into existence. This was an extremely dominant group, controlled by a principal favourite, about whom more will be said later. In any case the Rani realised that to have the Maharajah do her bidding, she would have to enlist the support of the palace bureau for her cause.[63] But the favourite was not a very easy man either, for he was conscious of his clout. He decided to bargain with Lakshmi Bayi and was prepared, he declared, to support Sethu Lakshmi Bayi's nomination, but not of Kochukunji's daughter's because the latter was, in his opinion, 'black'.[64] Instead, he recommended someone from Ennakkad, who was presumably less 'black', but the Rani insisted on having both her great-nieces and continued to lobby the palace bureau.

She could still rather easily have had her way, for the favourite was susceptible to money and flattery, had not rival branches of the Kolathiri clan also found a champion within the royal household. This was Lakshmi Bayi's senior nephew, the heir-apparent Chathayam Tirunal, who held the title of Elayarajah. This prince had over the years developed an intense dislike towards the Maharajah and the palace bureau and was, in any case, ill-disposed to the very idea of adoption. He represented, firstly, to the Madras Government under whose jurisdiction Travancore fell in the British Raj, that any adoption to the line of the Attingal Ranis, even when assented to by the senior female member, could not be valid without his consent as heir apparent. In other words, it was not the province of Lakshmi Bayi to decide these matters herself and to her personal satisfaction alone.[65] Secondly, he asserted, there was no urgent necessity at all for adoption at this time; there were three male members in the royal family and in due course it would devolve upon the last of them to introduce fresh blood.[66] As for the Rani's argument that the male members might die and lead to a crisis, he felt he might be persuaded to accept it and support an adoption, but only of older girls, close to marriageable age (i.e., about eleven years old), so that they might provide the dynasty heirs more promptly. Indeed, in his communications, Chathayam Tirunal constantly referred to the little Sethus as 'the babies', deeming them wholly unsuitable for introduction into the royal family.[67]

He also had much to say about the Rani and her excessive interest in the affairs of Ravi Varma's daughters in Mavelikkara. Lakshmi Bayi, he claimed, was unnecessarily concerned about her natal family and all her keenness to adopt the daughters of Mahaprabha and Kochukunji was to nepotistically ensure that they would have their futures safe and secure even after her time. It was her connection by blood to Mavelikkara, and not a dynastic interest in perpetuating the line of the Attingal Ranis, that made her so insistent on the Sethus. Chathayam Tirunal claimed, additionally, that the Mavelikkara stock was an inauspicious one: the previous adoption of his own mother and Lakshmi Bayi from there had been 'unfortunate and fruitless', giving the royal house no daughters. An equally troubling cause for worry was that the grandmother of the girls, Kochupanki, and one of her brothers had both been drunkards of sorts. In terms of health also, the family left much to be desired; his mother, the late Junior Rani, and her father had died of cancer.[68] In light of these unpropitious characteristics, the Elayarajah argued, it was best if adoption were sought from a better house.[69]

The Rani, thus, had met her match in her pragmatic, unsentimental nephew, who remained steadfast in his objections. No amount of emotional blackmail could sway his resolve and he insisted that his claims were in the best interests of the royal family. The Mavelikkara people, especially Kochupanki's house, were a problematic lot, and they would bring with them more dissent than there already existed in the palace.[70] He was alone in all this, though. The Maharajah made his support for the Rani known by visiting the British Resident (who at once was a kind of ambassador and watchful imperial supervisor) G.T. Mackenzie and expressing his strong approval of the Sethus.[71] Prince Asvathi Tirunal also came out to back Lakshmi Bayi's candidates, not least because he and Sethu Lakshmi Bayi's father were close friends.[72] In order to prove to the Madras Government that the girls could be adopted in spite of the Elayarajah's objections, the Dewan Krishnaswamy Rao, who was formerly Chief Justice of Travancore, approached the issue from a legal perspective. He argued that in a matrilineal family, if the majority of members were in favour of a particular act, it could be executed over the objections of the minority. In the royal household, three out of four members were in favour of the Mavelikkara children, and that was enough to carry the resolution to adopt the Sethus. Rao also made it a point to state that it would be politically unviable and detrimental to discipline in the family if junior members could flout the authority of the Maharajah and the Rani and that any decision the Madras Government took now would set a serious precedent.[73] It is also said that Raja Ravi Varma, the children's grandfather, exercised all his influence with the Viceroy in favour of the Rani's proposition.[74]

The British authorities first made an attempt to see if consensus could be built, and Mr Mackenzie even called on Chathayam Tirunal to convince him to change his stand. But the latter did not budge and made it clear that he would never support an adoption from Mavelikkara.[75] Unfortunately for him, the Resident formed the opinion that this whole problem arose because the Elayarajah, out of stubborn spite, simply wished to pique the Maharajah and the Rani and did not really have any substantial objections.[76] He thus added the weight of his own support to the Rani's proposal and by April 1900 the Government of India in Calcutta wrote to the Madras Government that 'His Highness may be informed that the adoption will be recognized and confirmed', overruling all objections to the contrary.[77]

The Elayarajah did not intend to take defeat easily, however. He offered now to personally visit the Viceroy, who was the supreme adjudicator and representative of the British Crown, to convince him to invalidate 'this illegal adoption'.[78] But the Government of India was firm in its stand. It advised Chathayam Tirunal to stop taking a narrow view of matters and made it clear that contrary legal precedents, even when valid, could not apply to the royal family as they might to private houses.[79] The matter was closed, as far as they were concerned, and no further representations from the Elayarajah were entertained. And thus, Lakshmi Bayi, after months of unpleasant, rather pedestrian, bickering and haggling won this battle against her nephew, and obtained sanction for the adoption of her great-nieces.

The Elayarajah turned out to be sore in defeat, though. Typically the entire royal family ought to have been present at the adoption ceremony and the attendant functions. But to embarrass the Maharajah and the Rani, and to make public his disapproval of these proceedings, Chathayam Tirunal absented himself from the ceremonials that day and disrupted tradition by leaving the capital ostensibly for a tour. Last-minute alterations had to be made in the ceremonies to cloak the attendant discomfiture. It was decided, thus, that at the temple ceremonies in the morning the Maharajah would not attend and Prince

Asvathi Tirunal took his place. Similarly, the Rani did not appear at the durbar in the afternoon. This, it was hoped, would evade the awkward questions that might have arisen had the Elayarajah been the only member of the family to excuse himself from the various functions of the day.[80]

The adoption ceremony went off well, despite the hint of a bitter taste, and the two children were welcomed into the royal family with euphoria and tremendous public approval. But the departing words of Chathayam Tirunal rang in the ears of Lakshmi Bayi, almost like a vengeful curse on their future. 'These babies are the children of two mothers,' he had ominously declared, 'and each will exert a most deleterious influence on the peace of the family.'[81] Mahaprabha and Kochukunji were both young and capable, and Chathayam Tirunal could foresee great rivalries and intrigues these daughters of the ambitious Ravi Varma would spawn in a contest for power, prestige and authority. It was an uncomfortable suggestion, full of forbidding potentialities. But once again the Rani simply shook such thoughts away, and taking the name of her family deity, left everything to fate.

God had given her the two Sethus. But how long would his blessings linger?

2

The Queen of the Kupakas

The careers of Sethu Lakshmi Bayi and her cousin as princesses began on an extremely unpropitious note. For no sooner had the fanfare and pageantry accompanying their adoption ceased than a grim epidemic of death descended upon the royal family. In the months that followed the Sethus' arrival in Trivandrum, three of its original four members were unexpectedly obliterated from the world by a cruel twist of fate. There was great public sensation at these happenings. The orthodox in the capital whispered of evil curses and blamed the gods, bemoaning the baneful plight of their royal house. Intelligent others offered slightly more rational suspicions, holding unholy conspiracies and a liberal use of poison responsible for these abrupt tragedies. In any case, by the monsoons of 1901, the royal family (or what was left of it) had much to mourn, with the thundering heavens and incessant rain adding visual melancholy to their gloom and bereavement.

The first victim of misfortune was Asvathi Tirunal who died quite suddenly on 10 October 1900, a little over a month after the adoption. His death was sincerely lamented in intelligent circles, for he was popularly held as the gem in the royal family. The first Indian prince to obtain a graduate degree, among other accomplishments, he had won legions of admirers across the subcontinent after an extensive study tour with Raja Ravi Varma. Even the notoriously derisive Lord Curzon, then Viceroy of India, who famously declared India's Rajahs and Maharajahs 'on the whole a disappointing study', was decidedly impressed by Asvathi Tirunal; he was, in what was one of Curzon's most flattering reviews of a 'native', 'an amiable and accomplished prince, a man of culture, of travel, and of learning'.[1] Much store, naturally then, had been laid by the day when Asvathi

Tirunal would have succeeded as Maharajah, but all such aspirations turned out to be futile. Whether by the designs of destiny or the machinations of lesser men, Travancore was denied what could have been a great rule by a great ruler in the years to come.[2]

Eight months later death called once again on the royal house. This time it claimed the haughty Elayarajah, whose loss, however, was somewhat less lamented. Chathayam Tirunal was certainly gifted and intelligent in his own right but too mulish and undiplomatic a character to claim any particular popularity with the people. He was also a diabetic who did not take care of his health, and was known more for the ample proportions of his body than his felicity. 'He has given up all exercise,' the Resident had observed, 'and round the pupil of each eye there is well marked that white circle, the *arcus senilis*, which I have never seen in so young a man.'[3] The usually upfront and fervently argumentative Elayarajah had also become strangely quiet after the death of his brother. When Mr Mackenzie met him in May 1901 at a tennis party, he appeared to be in very bad shape, and by the end of that month his diabetes worsened and he was clearly moving rapidly towards his end. This came on 6 June. 'There is now no prince to succeed to the title and position of Heir Apparent,' the Resident bleakly reported to his superiors. 'The Travancore family now consists of the Maharajah, the Senior Rani, and the two young princesses who were adopted last year.'[4]

In less than ten days, however, Mr Mackenzie would be forced to revise his list and add yet another name to his princely obituaries. For soon after the death of the Elayarajah, Rani Lakshmi Bayi too, shockingly, followed her nephews to the grave. The demise of Asvathi Tirunal had distressed her considerably and even the long-yearned company of the Sethus failed to serve as consolation. It appears that the Rani too was a diabetes patient, which diminished her fettle. By November 1900 she had already taken to bed and her condition deteriorated with each passing day. In spite of the hostility between them, it was Chathayam Tirunal's death that struck her the final blow. She had tried to placate him after the adoption, only to be scorned and ignored. 'Her Highness,' wrote her consort, 'felt this neglect.'[5] Nine days after his passing, on 15 June 1901, Lakshmi Bayi's husband painfully scribbled in his diary: 'My angel, my life, my darling, my all and all, my pride, my idol, my sweetheart—alas! and what not—expired quietly at 8 PM.'[6] And thus, in the ten months that followed the Sethus' arrival at the palace, one half of the royal line was swiftly carved out from the pages of history.

The result of these unforeseen eventualities was that little Sethu Lakshmi

Bayi was instantly pressed into the limelight. Among the male members of the family, the reigning Maharajah Mulam Tirunal survived this sinister spate of deaths, preventing a crisis of government in Travancore. But with the female constituents of the dynasty, Sethu Lakshmi Bayi now stood foremost, with a role and ceremonial prerogatives that were equal to those of the Maharajah himself. At the age of five, she was propelled into the seat of the Senior Rani of Travancore, becoming the youngest person to occupy that exalted station in all its history.[7] It was a disquieting proposition. The idea of having to fill the shoes of her illustrious great-aunt and to exercise all that was expected of her as Senior Rani was a trepidatious one. Only yesterday she had been an ordinary child, cocooned at home in Mavelikkara, surrounded by family and friends. And here she was today, plucked from her roots and installed as queen of three million subjects who looked upon her as an object of the greatest veneration. As her mother would impress upon her, she was no longer a little girl; she had become an icon and an institution, the traditions and honour of which she was bound to preserve for life. Sethu Lakshmi Bayi did not, at this time, appreciate entirely how much her individuality would recede behind the onerous charge thrust upon her. But she did realise, as her grandson later remarked, that 'playtime was over'.[8] She had become Her Highness the Rani Pooradam Tirunal. Nobody, not even her father, would call her Sethukutty again.

On 27 June 1901 the new Senior Rani was taken in procession to the Sri Padmanabhaswamy Temple where, as the sound of the conch and drums resonated through the sacred premises, she was consecrated as the Attingal Mootha Tampuran. Proclamations to this effect were issued across the state, and a durbar was held for the grandees and nobles of the land to pay obeisance and demonstrate fealty to their new queen. While for most attendees it was the ceremonies in Trivandrum that marked the commencement of Sethu Lakshmi Bayi's life as Senior Rani, what was an equally if not more important function was her installation at the temple in Attingal. It was this place, after all, that gave the Ranis their title and it was from here that generations of queens had once ruled with the blessings of their warrior goddess, Tiruvirattukkavu Bhagavathi. Unlike the benign deity of the Sri Padmanabhaswamy Temple, this was a fiery goddess who represented vigour, power and blood. Her legends were of raging anger and deadly wars, intimidating the more pious among her worshippers. She was the celebrated patron goddess of the Ranis of Travancore, and like them, she too had her roots in the lands of the Kolathiri dynasty, whence she had been brought and installed in Attingal after the first princesses of that house traversed the coast to become queens in the south.

The legend goes that long ago in the territories of the Kolathiri Rajah there was a brigade of asura savages who inflicted great suffering on the royal house and its people. The chief of these demons was Daraka, a foe so powerful and mighty that the Kolathiri Rajah was compelled to seek divine intervention to rid the land of his menace. After enduring terrible hardships, the cries of these suffering supplicants were heard and the goddess Bhagavathi revealed herself before the Kolathiri Rajah. When she discovered his troubles, she became livid with rage and assumed a frightening form, known as *roudra bhava*. With all her supernatural powers, she fell upon Daraka and his band, slaying him after a great and momentous battle. The Kolathiri Rajah was pleased. But his pleasure promptly descended into fear when it was discovered that despite bathing in Daraka's blood, Bhagavathi remained furious and deadly. With the assistance of oracles and priests, she was eventually conciliated into settling within a great temple consecrated near Payyannur, where to this day there are housed two ancient idols symbolising the goddess in her usual peaceful form as well as in that vengeful, warlike avatar. The image immediately behind the altar is regular, depicting a beautiful deity. But looming further back in the darkness is the daunting form of Bhagavathi, trident held aloft, with one foot set upon the crushed head of her fallen adversary. She could never be worshipped through Sanskritic traditions alone; she needed blood and flesh, and through the ages her temple became known for a number of gory sacrifices and fascinatingly frightful rituals, marking it as the greatest shrine in the region to the cult of the goddess.[9]

When the first adoption from the Kolathiri dynasty into Travancore took place in the fourteenth century, those early princesses, as a mark of their roots in the north, brought with them their family deity and installed her in a temple in Attingal.[10] Through the ages that followed, their successors worshipped Bhagavathi with great fervour, drawing inspiration from her gripping legends and tales of her enormous power. Every year they propitiated her in a great ceremony and it was the Senior Rani who took the lead in this. Sethu Lakshmi Bayi had now succeeded as that principal devotee of this formidable goddess, and it was to endear herself to the glorious Tiruvirattukkavu Bhagavathi that she performed an installation ceremony at her temple on 30 June 1902. She was now, in the fullest sense, the Attingal Rani, scion of a riveting legacy that had lent Kerala its identity as *pennu-malayalam*, the kingdom of women.

As principal Attingal Rani and as Senior Rani of Travancore, Sethu Lakshmi Bayi was heiress to an old line of queens, whose legends are preserved in lore and song. Their origins lay in the inceptive fourteenth-century adoption from the Kolathiri dynasty, when a celebrated ancestor of the Travancore family, King Sangramadheera installed two princesses as his successors.[11] At the time Travancore was known as the Kupaka kingdom and was not considered strictly Malayali in culture. Its rulers and people had a stronger affinity towards Tamil society, and Sangramadheera himself had married a Pandya princess, also winning his proudest victories beyond the eastern frontiers of Kerala. The Kolathiri Rajah, therefore, is believed to have been loath to send two of his sisters into a near-Tamil family, and it was through clever deception and artful intrigue that Sangramadheera orchestrated their acquisition.[12]

Perhaps as a consolation, however, it was decided to protect the adoptees in an insulated cocoon of their own, away from the Tamil influences they so abhorred. A portion of the Kupaka kingdom with its headquarters at Attingal was carved out and a miniature version of the Kolathiri country was skilfully designed within.[13] Not only was Tiruvirattukkavu Bhagavathi consecrated here as the principal goddess, but even soldiers, retainers, artisans, craftsmen, slaves and other mortal factors were brought all the way from the homeland of the princesses, instead of being recruited locally.[14] This was intended to lend Attingal an authentic Malayali feel, with familiar Kolathiri influences constantly enveloping the adopted Ranis; a northern home transplanted into the alien south. But this decision to constitute a separate demesne for the ladies would come to be gravely regretted by the heirs of Sangramadheera. For from this small territory granted them, the Attingal Ranis would spread their wings and go on to achieve a regional prominence unprecedented in India.[15] They would emerge as women to reckon with along the Kerala coast, even holding Travancore to ransom from time to time.[16,17]

Under the matrilineal system, women always enjoyed great power. In the early sixteenth century, for instance, the queen of Quilon (ruled by a branch of the Kupaka family) had considerable influence over the foreign policy of that port and enjoyed independent commercial relations with the Portuguese. In 1502 she invited the foreigners to come to Quilon and even let them build a factory in her territory. By 1519, however, relations between the Rani and the Portuguese soured, and in alliance with a neighbouring princess, also of the Kupaka clan, she mounted a vehement military campaign against them. This confederate neighbour was none other than the Attingal Rani, and together the two women had a force of 20,000 soldiers at their disposal.[18] None of these troops was enlisted by male members of their dynasty, and the soldiers vowed their loyalties to these queens independently. Their autonomy is clear also from a telling episode from some years before. In 1516, Lopo Soares de Albergaria, the third Portuguese Governor in India, signed a treaty with the queen in Quilon. Soon afterwards he approached her with a request for a religious endowment, and this is what she said to him:

> We are going to invade our neighbouring kingdom of Travancore, for which we start tomorrow. As we are now greatly pressed for money, please do not ask us about the church endowments now [sic]. As the clerks and Nairs are all accompanying me, everything has to be settled in my presence only after our return from victory. Please do not ask me about them before I return.[19]

In this campaign too, the Attingal Rani is believed to have joined forces with her cousin in Quilon.[20] Thus, the Kupaka princesses not only had independent armies under their control, but also proactively led their soldiers into battle. Moreover, the intention of this particular lady was not to subjugate just any random neighbour, but Travancore itself, which was probably ruled by her son, brother or cousin at the time. This was not the only such instance and a mediaeval ballad records a tragic fratricidal battle between the Attingal Rani and a prince of Travancore. The story goes that the prince was on a pilgrimage and needed to pass through Attingal ('a land of Amazons') to reach his holy destination. The Rani, to his exasperation, prohibited an armed escort from accompanying him, as it offended her sovereign prerogatives; only she, it was imperiously declared, could bear weapons in Attingal. And in the course of events that followed, royal egos were royally bruised, occasioning large-scale slaughter in a terrible battle, and both protagonists were killed.[21]

The Attingal Rani also had her own government and John Wallis, an English trader, in his *A Short Treatise by Way of Essay of Attinga* [sic] (1727) records how the principality was run, what its political divisions were, which among its nobles were more powerful and so on. He specifically records that 'Attinga is Governed by a Queen', also noting that this was 'an Instance peculiar only to this part' of Kerala, i.e., in the domains controlled by the Kupaka family. He also pointedly notes that Attingal was outside the realm of the prince who ruled Travancore, and names that state, in fact, as a southern neighbour of the Rani's.[22] Earlier in 1677 the Dutch commander Henrik van Rheede wrote how 'The princess of Attingah who is not alone the mother of [the prince of] Travancore but the eldest of [the entire royal family] has a territory of her own, independent of

Travancore', which was 'in alliance with the Hon'ble Company'.[23] The Attingal Ranis were matriarchs of the Kupaka family who enjoyed much authority and had an identity that was independent, if not superior, to that of their sons and brothers, the Travancore Rajahs. Only a woman could rule in Attingal and only male heirs born to her could be the Rajahs of Travancore, with each side sovereign and perfectly capable of going to war against the other despite supposedly sacred bonds of family and blood.

Attingal, in fact, had foreign alliances not only with the Portuguese and the Dutch but also with the English ('... and great was the surprise of [these] merchants,' Louise Ouwerkerk writes, 'when they found themselves negotiating trade treaties with bare-bosomed but dignified and capable Indian queens.'[24]). In 1688, the Attingal Rani granted Vettoor ('Rettorah') and Vizhinjam ('Brinjohn') to the English to establish factories, which functioned for some time until she cancelled the lease.[25] What is interesting is that these places were technically located in Travancore and the Rani made the grants while there was a king ruling there, whose consent was neither sought nor taken. Then in 1694 she would give the English the more important enclave of Anjengo, stating: 'Because the English I called hither have allways bin obedient to Mee, I do hereby grant unto them the following priviledges; I give unto them the hill of the louges that is at Anjengo, to fortify with stone and to abide there for ever; And I will send thither my officers to set forth and appoint with land marks the limitts of the Land that belong unto Mee.'[26] She also negotiated the customs due to her, as well as a somewhat forthright clause that allowed her to appropriate 50 percent of any booty recovered from shipwrecked vessels nearby. Signed by the queen herself, it was delivered to the English by her nobles ('Barrebba Poola and Mandacca Poola').

The English, for their part, received her commands with the greatest deference and agreed to carry on their trade 'without any manner of Impudence' and 'to obey Her Highness'.[27] They were compelled to toe her line, for they could not afford to have her cancel their lease on any grounds, imagined or real, again; the last time, as the queen noted, 'they were troublesome to my people and therefore I ordered that they should goe from there and make no more Contracts in my Land'. It was only after they reassured here that they had 'Intention to doe good to my Country and to bee in good ffriendship with mee' that the Rani aligned again with them in 1694.[28] It was a significant incident, and for many years Anjengo was second only to Bombay for the English East India Company, before it lost rank eventually to more lucrative centres elsewhere.[29]

The Rani, it is interesting, gave these grants of land without reference to the Travancore Rajah or any other senior male member of her house or the wider Kupaka clan. The only people she consulted and was bound by were her own nobles, showing she was answerable to her court and none other. Had she been, as was later asserted in an insecure flourish of patriarchy, a subject of the Travancore Rajah (who in those days was not even the most prominent of the Kupakas; it was the Quilon branch that was powerful), it would have been very unlikely she could confer such significant allowances and privileges on foreigners.[30] On the contrary, Dutch sources in the late seventeenth century recorded that it was the Travancore Rajah who was a vassal to the Attingal Rani.[31] Her commercial relations with European companies were exactly like those of other principalities in Kerala such as Cochin and Calicut. These foreign traders also acknowledged the import of courting the Attingal Rani and recognised no authority superior to her. She, interestingly enough, with that typical impetuosity of kings and queens, wasn't always as charitable and often did as she pleased; in 1695 she promised all her pepper to the English, only to coolly renege and give it away to the Danes.[32] When the English strengthened Anjengo's defences without seeking her consent, she attempted to unite a military alliance against them, even leaving her palace, declaring that she would 'never return to Attingal until every stone of Anjengo Fort had been tumbled down'.[33] Earlier in 1695 the Rani had already gone to war against the Dutch and destroyed their fort at Tengapattanam,[34] while in 1696 she carried an offensive campaign into Travancore as well when she felt she had been slighted.[35]

It is in fact most interesting that the Ranis treated Travancore, ruled over by their male relatives, with sneering disdain and often did as they deemed fit there. They enjoyed a position of pre-eminence among the Kupakas and when in 1693 one branch of the family became extinct, the Rani did not let the Travancore Rajah annex those lands but took it herself.[36] In another instance, in 1704 when a vessel called the *Neptune* was shipwrecked off the coast of Travancore, the queen's men hauled off all the retrieved treasure to Attingal instead of to the Rajah. 'This only confirms,' writes Leena More, 'that the Queen of Attingal's writ ran still in Travancore territory in 1704.'[37] It was an unconventional situation where the ladies of the royal house were anything but under the control of their men. Both the king and queen, whether they were brother and sister, or uncle and niece, had distinct domains, and the women appear to have been far more interesting than their brothers, arguably because of the social and political freedoms matrilineal society offered them.[38]

What is unfortunate, though, is that down the centuries, few personal names have survived of the queens of Attingal. There is, for instance, an inscription dated 1576 in a temple, recording renovations sponsored by a Kupaka queen called Makayiram Tirunal (who incidentally destroyed many Portuguese churches), but actual names are difficult to find today. The one woman who shines among all the Attingal Ranis, however, is Asvathi Tirunal, better known as Umayamma Rani or Queen Ashure. When van Rheede met her in 1677 he was struck by her 'noble and manly conduct', describing her as an Amazon who was 'feared and respected by everyone'. There was also an old injunction supposedly prohibiting Attingal Ranis from crossing the Karamana river into the southern territories of Travancore. This was presumably intended to restrict them from going into Tamil lands originally, but seems also to have been used by princes of the dynasty to prevent any expansion of the Attingal Rani's influence at their expense. Umayamma, however, happily breached this to march into Travancore proper with her armies, and 'made even the king fly before her' when she was a mere junior princess in Attingal.[39] And as she aged and took the principal title, her nerve only grew stronger.

Just as in business and war, the Attingal Ranis were remarkably unabashed in their personal lives also. John Henry Grose records that 'whom and as many as she pleases to the honour of her bed' could be taken by the Rani as lovers, adding, 'The handsomest young men about the country generally compose her *seraglio*.'[40] In addition to this, James Welsh would note that the Rani could 'change them whenever she is tired of one by sending him away and selecting another.'[41] It is quite amazing that while the rest of the world was one where sexual freedoms were permitted only to men, a phenomenon where women had it equal could be found on this sliver of India's west coast. Umayamma is said to have been particularly liberal and if Hamilton is to be believed, 'her black Majesty' even took a fancy once for a 'beautiful' Englishman who 'satisfied her so well that when he left her court, she made him some presents'.[42] The grant of Anjengo, according to some accounts, was one of those presents.[43] Regrettably, nineteenth-century Victorian puritanism and the attendant moral 'cleansing' of Indian culture would lead to a purging of these aspects of Umayamma's vibrant life. And by the early twentieth century, the poet Ulloor S. Parameswara Iyer would transform her beyond recognition into a feminine damsel in distress, the very paragon of colonial piety, in his magnum opus, *Umakeralam*. From Amazon to damsel, Umayamma's memory nevertheless remains a captivating one.[44]

The decline of the Attingal Ranis from glory to relative obscurity commenced with the death of the multifaceted Umayamma in 1698 at Valiyathura. There were no female members in the royal family and some years before she had secured an adoption from the Kolathiri dynasty to continue her line. But this princess who succeeded her and who was an aunt to the indomitable Martanda Varma, was weak for the very reason that she was perceived at court as an outsider. For her installation as Rani, she was dependent on the nobles of Attingal, and a phenomenon that had hitherto plagued only Travancore came to afflict Attingal also: the kingmakers eclipsed the rulers. These nobles began to irritate the English and for the first time the East India Company ignored the Rani and sought to directly approach Travancore for the pepper there. 'It is highly doubtful,' Leena More writes, 'if the English would have dared to open direct contacts with the Rajah if the present Queen was as strong as the old Queen.'[45] The Rajah, for his part, went out of his way to seduce the Company, even granting them the privilege of minting currency, which the Attingal Rani had staunchly withheld for decades. The Rani ('that cunning woman'), as it happened, was not pleased with this betrayal by the English. In 1721 she presided over a comprehensive slaughter of Company factors after getting them conveniently cornered at her palace during a banquet.[46] One gentleman, for instance, had his tongue ripped out and was sent floating down a river nailed to a log.[47] But they would kiss and make up and in 1722 and 1726 sign fresh treaties, again with no reference to Travancore, although the alliance was admittedly turning frosty by this time.[48]

But the power of the Ranis was on the decline ever since their nobles began to pull the royal strings. As John Wallis writes, 'since Queen Ashure's decease 30 years since, the *poolas* [nobles] have thrown off their allegiance and Severally set up for themselves and divided the Country, there being since that time a titular Queen who is only allowed annual subsistence'.[49] By 1729, her situation was even weaker and the grandees at court had a say in all her affairs, with one faction in 1721 even having, briefly, installed *another* lady as the Attingal Rani. In 1726, the Rani sought English assistance in reining in her refractory nobles, with no success, and in 1727 she had to actually flee Attingal and seek political sanctuary elsewhere, living off the charity of sympathetic aristocrats.[50] The result of all these internal dissensions was an escalation of Travancore's influence in the affairs of Attingal. By 1729, the redoubtable Martanda Varma had started bringing his own courtiers under ruthless control, using execution as an incentive to ensure loyalty, and was beginning to emerge as the sole power in Travancore. In that year he induced his aunt, the Attingal Rani, to sign a joint treaty with him and the English, drawing her decisively under his ambitious wings. Soon after this, he despatched armies to destroy the chief nobles of Attingal, winning victories and great power in that territory, albeit in the name of the Rani.

In 1731, then, the Attingal Rani sounded her death knell by signing a Silver Plate Treaty with Martanda Varma, relinquishing all her sovereign rights to the Rajah after four centuries of queenly independence. Whether this was due to her political decline or due to familial bonds is not clear, but it was most likely the former. The very fact that a formal treaty was required for the amalgamation of Attingal into an expanding Travancore shows that both the king and the queen in the royal family were political equals.[51] The treaty guaranteed that only sons of the Attingal Ranis would succeed to the throne of Travancore and that the Senior Rani would remain owner of the 15,000 acres of freehold assigned by Sangramadheera in the fourteenth century. Some years later, in 1747, Martanda Varma executed another document concerning succession in the royal family, where too these clauses were enshrined, and to which the Attingal Rani, now without any real political power, remained an equal signatory. And thus, Attingal was merged with Travancore and the Ranis reduced to a glorified impotency, living in the wistful shadows of their former greatness, even as male members of the dynasty became more and more dominating.

Despite resigning her powers, however, the Attingal Rani retained much significance at court. Until 1749 the English continued to pay her annual tribute and in 1751 when the old queen died, they fired a twenty-gun salute from the ramparts of Anjengo Fort, as they would for a sovereign, keeping flags at half-mast and shutting business for five days in official mourning.[52] When Martanda Varma asked for the tribute to the Rani to be transferred to him, the English refused until the queen gave her consent to the new arrangement.[53] With that direct relations between the English East India Company and the Rani ceased after a long history. The memory of her power, however, endured and as late as 1772 the Travancore Maharajah would be deplored as 'the usurper of her domains' and she bemoaned as 'little more than a state prisoner'.[54] Stories of the Ranis' valour continued to be told; in 1727, for example, when her nobles attempted to create trouble, the queen led a force against them and was lauded for her stirring bravery as 'She Quitted her Pallankeen and advanc'd at the Head of her people with a Sword and Targett' in hand.[55] Even as late as 1810 the British Resident in Travancore would remark that, legally, the Attingal Rani was 'the supreme authority in the State, her mandates are paramount to those of the Rajah, and her elevation to the situation of the Tumbratty [i.e., Senior Rani] is made in a manner as formal and solemn as that of the instalment of a Rajah'.[56] In 1813, he reiterated that the 'authority of the Attengerah [Rani] has continued to be revered in the country and is generally considered to be paramount to that of the Rajah and to be essential to the validity of all great Acts of the Government'.[57] In spite of losing most of her rights and her territory, thus, the eldest female member in the Kupaka family continued to command much influence and social esteem.

Two Attingal Ranis, in fact, came to rule the whole of modern Travancore in the nineteenth century. The first was Gowri Lakshmi Bayi who came to power in 1810 when there were no male princes in the royal house. She gave birth to two sons and a daughter and died in 1814, when her sister, Gowri Parvathi Bayi succeeded to the throne, ruling for a remarkably visionary fourteen years. Thereafter, however, the Ranis became more or less domesticated, not least due to subsequent adoptions where, as new entrants into the dynasty, they had to toe the lines set by the Maharajahs. Their ceremonial dignity and status, however, was always honoured, and to the people the Senior Rani remained a person equal in importance to the Maharajah. They were, after all, queens in a land that celebrated matriliny and the female, and, even though they no longer enjoyed direct political authority, their proud legacy entitled them to an 'outward state and dignity'.[58] And now, in 1901, at less than six years of age, Sethu Lakshmi Bayi had succeeded as the ninth Attingal Rani since the days of Martanda Varma, and as Queen of the Kupakas, destined to be the last of those great heiresses claiming descent from these Amazons of yore.[59]

Those who observed Sethu Lakshmi Bayi's lifestyle as Senior Rani were thrilled by the fanfare and splendour of it all. She lived in the stately Sundara Vilasam Palace in Trivandrum Fort, which was one of the handsomest buildings in the country. A bevy of ladies in waiting remained at her beck and call, day and night, and a single sneeze from the girl was enough to raise competitive uproar among her staff, as everyone rushed to comfort the child. All she had to do was lift a finger, and her bidding was done. When she went out, a posse of liveried guards marched alongside her. If she chose to go for a drive, entire streets were closed to traffic for the convenience of her entourage, while pedestrians lined up by the roadside, bowing with customary reverence as the royal carriage and mounted guards passed. When the Rani walked into a room, the whole assembly would rise and bow, beholding her with a deferential silence until she condescended to speak to them. They had to make 'a low obeisance, raising both hands and performing curious twiddlings of closing and extending of the fingers' in an elaborate namaste, and in her presence, all stood 'with the left hand on the breast and the right hand covering the mouth, lest their breath should pollute' their honoured queen.[60]

Even her father's relationship to Sethu Lakshmi Bayi, tellingly, was governed by the frivolous rules of correct decorum. Kuttan Tampuran had always to remember that he was, first and foremost, his daughter's subject, and only then her parent. She was 'Her Highness' to him, and he had to greet her with the most formal salutations, taking a seat only when permitted by his queen. As for her, whenever she sent for him, it was a 'royal summons' and not an invitation or request. If she had a question, it was never asked, but 'commanded'. 'A special language of highly artificial and conventional character,' Samuel Mateer had observed some decades before, was 'used of the royal person, property, and actions, ordinary terms being forbidden.' Sethu Lakshmi Bayi's food, thus, was 'divine nectar'; her birthday, 'a holy day'; her palace, a 'place of worship', and the exhaustive list went on absurdly about the appropriate usage and idiom when referring to royalty. While her father was ultimately allowed to sit in her presence, the Rani's poor coachman had a tougher challenge to meet. With his infinitely more ordinary origins, he was, unfortunately, expected to remain standing while driving Sethu Lakshmi Bayi about the capital, a task requiring singular agility and years of seasoned skill.[61]

But if this never-ending cycle of princely ceremonial seemed formidable and glamorous from the outside, all the protocol was quite insufferable for those within the royal household. It had to be kept up in order to preserve that aura of romance and mystique around the dynasty, but, 'as bewildered transplants' from Mavelikkara,[62] it did take Sethu Lakshmi Bayi and her cousin some time to imbibe the proper etiquette and rigorous discipline. Daily life at Sundara Vilasam was governed by an incarcerating 'Palace Manual' that ran into twelve fat, wholly despised volumes, the diktats of which encompassed even the most mundane affairs. Starting with the 'brushing of the royal pearls' (*tirumuttuvilakku*) in the morning under the supervision of court dentists, and concluding with slumbering in the right posture at night, there was no escape from the tyranny of exaggerated custom for members of the royal family.[63] The words 'freedom' and 'choice' were irrelevant and not even the Maharajah had the authority to alter these longstanding habits. Even taking a walk around the palace meant accepting a company of kowtowing household guards, called *pattakkar*s, and as late as the 1940s, on the eve of India's independence, these customs remained untouched, as a princess recalls:

In the evenings we would be taken out for a walk around 4 o'clock. There would be two pattakkars in front and two at the back and two on either side so that we couldn't run off, and we used to be taken like this round the compound. It was a great ceremony. The servants would also be there along with the pattakkars, so we were at least sixteen people going out, and of course with all these people surrounding us we were caught if we tried to run. It was great fun trying to break away but there was this feeling of being closed in, like claustrophobia. I couldn't understand it then, but I realise it now. There was no freedom. You couldn't go from one room to the next without having people following you to see what you were doing. There was not a moment to yourself.[64]

There were rigorous rules about everything. Audiences were often granted to Europeans in the capital but always early in the morning around seven o'clock 'so that Her Highness can wash off the contamination of shaking hands with an outcaste before proceeding to other business'.[65] Caste, in fact, enjoyed a constant presence and meticulous following in the palace, where menial servants were selected from respectable Nair families while personal attendants, including nannies (called *ayahammas*) were Brahmins or 'twice born' castemen. There was at court, in fact, a most farcical situation since the chief physician, a Dr Lakshman, despite his eminent medical qualifications could never touch members of the royal family because he was of low caste; a Brahmin assistant would conduct examinations and convey symptoms to him, following which the doctor, who had collected his degrees from England's most prestigious institutions, would prescribe remedies.[66] Ritual purity commanded a high premium, and in a day it was quite normal for the Rani and her royal relatives to bathe more than once (with the result that it was height of mischief to 'fudge baths').[67] On days of particular religious or ritual significance, even the bath was an elaborate affair, frequently lasting hours before its supervisors deemed it properly concluded. Attendants would carry silver bowls with varieties of oils to the bathhouse, while large copper vessels with herbal waters were heated and moved by sturdy servants in advance. Their personal staff would then escort the Senior Rani and her cousin, now the Junior Rani, to commence the *pallineerattu* ('the royal frolic in water') in all its methodical fullness:

Your hair was washed first, using green *thali* paste made from freshly-plucked leaves [and flowers], then washed and oiled with coconut oil and dried with a thin porous material called *tortu*. Then your body was washed, powder gram (chick peas) was applied and removed with a circular sort of sponge called *incha*, made from a fibrous bark, and you were washed again with warm *Nalpamaravellam* water, absolutely red in colour and made by boiling the bark of forty different [medicinal] trees. Your body was oiled and massaged, and your face, taking great care that the oil did not get on the hair because it contained saffron, which prevents hair growth. Finally, your hair was slowly dried over fragrant smoke from a *karandi*, an iron pot filled with live coals with all sorts of herbs in it. After your hair had been combed, a powdered herb would be rubbed down the parting in the middle, which was to prevent colds.[68]

Compared to this elaborate bathing ritual, dressing up was a relatively simple affair. The traditional Malayali *mundu*, a length of soft white cloth, would be wrapped around the waist, with pleats down the front. There were in Travancore old families of weavers specially commissioned to manufacture these for the royal family, with special gilt edges and a thin coloured border, giving the garment an appearance of neatness that bordered on the austere. Silk or velvet brocade bodices of colour would be worn over these, with a minimal number of ornaments on ordinary days, but including heavy, peculiar anklets worn only by women of the royal house. Another mundu would be wrapped around the torso like a shawl, and, thus draped entirely in white, with hints of colour peeking out from underneath, the Ranis would sit to get their hair done. This was perhaps what made them stand out the most; as a baffled Henry Bruce admitted when he arrived for an audience one morning, 'I had not been prepared for the arrangement of hair.'[69] After having it dried over the karandi, special attendants would comb the hair and then tie it up over the forehead in a peculiar, tight knot, shaped like 'an exaggerated pompadour roll'.[70] And, thus, dressed and ready, the Ranis would go about their commitments in the morning, before changing for lunch, and then dinner, with every day of their lives governed by this 'code of outlandish and antiquated court etiquette' that had to be followed without a lapse.[71]

The result of all this was that Sethu Lakshmi Bayi's early life became one of isolation. It was a splendid and celebrated isolation, but isolation, stark and definite, nonetheless; as her grandson would later remark, 'Being a member of the royal family was like being a favourite bird in a golden cage. You were watched and humoured and spoilt and loved. It was only when you were alone with yourself that you remembered the cage.'[72] How any other child in her position might have reacted to being denied the legitimate aspirations of a normal childhood and being conducted through each day by an infuriating manual of royal conventions, it is difficult to say. Perhaps she might have turned recalcitrant or unusually rebellious, or alternatively, reconciled to her new reality and lived with it. In the case of Sethu Lakshmi Bayi it was the latter, and she adapted herself quietly to the enormous changes that had arrested her life. Even before the adoption she was noted to have a 'reserved and serious disposition' being 'seldom vicious, with a wistful and rather melancholy look'.[73] Naturally, now, she attuned herself towards introversion rather than any other forceful expression of unhappiness. As she would later tell her grandchildren, the lesson she learnt from her mother (whose stiff upper lip could give most stony Victorians an inferiority complex) was 'to grin and bear it, and never show what you feel'.[74]

So when her old playmates and friends stood before her quietly, saluting her as they were now taught to, she met them with a regal silence of her own, and learned to behave like the queen they saw her to be. When the grandmothers and aunts who had petted her as a baby now bowed before her, she learned to acknowledge them with a little nod of her royal head. To a serious extent her mother encouraged this, for Mahaprabha laid considerable importance upon notions of dignity and stature, and wanted her royal daughter to epitomise these qualities to perfection. It was essentially a highly conservative view that Mahaprabha imbibed in Sethu Lakshmi Bayi, dinning into her that no matter what happened she should always control her feelings and patiently carry on with her head held high. She was to inspire and command, and grow into a Rani of whom the state, its people and the dynasty could be proud. It did not matter whether any of this made her personally happy. The little girl, faced with a domineering mother on the one hand, and the tethers of royalty on the other, accepted both but secretly retreated into a quiet, private world of her own inside, one that she hid from the world at large for all her life. In fact even into her late thirties, Sethu Lakshmi Bayi's most revolutionary act of rebellion against the establishment went as far as having her hair bobbed. 'Everything being so formal, and leading a life of strict protocol, when stepping out of line in the slightest was simply scandalous and unthinkable,' her granddaughter would later tell, 'she wanted to break out somehow, without, of course, deviating too much from the straight path. She thought it a refreshing change, without causing a dent in her image, so to speak.'[75]

Quietness would, in fact, go on to become a hallmark of her character into the future, equipping her with very interesting ways of dealing with and studying things. It would gift her a great deal of forbearance in the face of adversity, and her name would come to acquire a very stoic quality in the minds of her people.

Part of this may have been the result of undiagnosed ill health; decades later the Rani would be found to suffer from tuberculosis, which probably contributed to her subdued personality. But gentle reservation did not mean she was weak. On the contrary, Sethu Lakshmi Bayi had a mind of her own and was more than capable of demonstrating displeasure and disapproval where it was needed. Her general tendency towards restraint meant that little things did not unduly ruffle her (or at least so she acted). But if her larger calculations floundered, she would fight with a determination to have her way. All this came out early in life through little episodes where the Rani waged war against her tutors. While she was normally a 'mild, law-abiding and attentive student', she did occasionally challenge her teachers, as an early biographer describes:

> She liked holidays and the tutors were unfortunately ill disposed to grant as many as she wanted. The result was sometimes disastrous. There would ensue a tussle between the teachers and herself, and once her equilibrium was disturbed, no parleying afterwards would be of any avail. The thing was that Her Highness would have hopefully calculated upon using a certain day as holiday and would have provided herself with a programme of entertainments for the day, and when her teacher or *asan*, as she used to denominate her English and vernacular tutors, mercilessly called her off to business, it was no wonder that she was in a temper. The idea more galling than to have to study was that she would sink in the estimation of her prospective participators of the entertainments, when, either of the tyrants, unmoved by her reason or entreaty insisted on instant attendance to school work.[76]

Mahaprabha seems to have instructed her daughter well enough, for it was not the prospect of studying that so affected the Rani as much as the purported loss of dignity. In fact, insofar as education went, she was a model student. From the age of seven, she is said to have risen at three o'clock every morning in order to work on her English.[77] Over the years she developed an impressive vocabulary with perfect diction and the King's accent. She was a diligent pupil ('gifted with a good memory' and 'a young mathematician'),[78] did her homework properly, and scored proficiently in examinations. Some years later a report submitted to the Maharajah about her progress would happily note that she had 'been a source of great pleasure to her teachers. In emerging out of her childhood, she is giving promise of an intellectuality, a strength of character, correctness of judgment, appreciation of duty, respect for authority, and a gentleness of manner that endear her to all who come in touch with her and ought to ensure her growing into a truly noble woman and worthy daughter of Travancore.'[79] It was a review that would be repeated throughout her life.

Not surprisingly, she never went to school and was tutored in the 'school house' within the palace by a carefully chosen academic staff instead. The tutors first selected by the court for the girls' education were not, apparently, up to the mark and after a 'wild outcry in the press' a better set was commissioned at greater expense.[80] Instruction had in fact commenced shortly after her fourth birthday, with initiation into the Malayalam alphabet and then Sanskrit. A Karunakara Pisharody was appointed Sanskrit master while one Venkateswara Iyer, who also taught history, geography, arithmetic and other subjects, introduced English into the curriculum in 1902.[81] Their lessons began at eleven o'clock in the morning, with English classes first, followed by a break for lunch. Sanskrit and Malayalam lessons were then taught until four o'clock, after which the Ranis were taken for music concerts, drives or perhaps a game of tennis or croquet, always a curious sight in their traditional costumes. Visits to temples were also made daily, and in the evenings they read and embroidered, in a silly imitation of what the young ladies in Europe were instructed to do.[82] They also took piano lessons, and Sethu Lakshmi Bayi is said to have been able to 'sing and play with charming effect', although she gave it up in later years.[83] Henry Bruce witnessed the Ranis at work one day in 1908, writing about it as follows:

> The Ranis speak quite firm good English, having been at it for at least six years. They also study in Malayalam and Sanskrit. In the last language they do not try to speak, but read easy stories. I inquired about their dolls. The Senior has five dolls and the Junior, as is but right, seven. Two magnificent dolls were given to them by Lady Ampthill. The Ranis are just starting a stamp album. I heard about their little lives; how in addition to a great deal of pious ceremonial, they go out driving in the afternoon, or play badminton ... They are evidently strong and healthy. It was pretty to watch their drawing books and others marked 'Sr' and 'Jr' respectively. I saw them playing on big *veenas* seated on the floor. I also heard them, in the schoolroom, playing the piano with a good touch.[84]

For a while now in princely circles it was felt that in addition to any traditional instruction, princesses ought to also be trained in aesthetics and other aspects of that variety by cultivated European ladies. In north Indian royal families this had been taken up with gusto, and it was a regular sight to see matronly women in dull dresses marching alongside their highborn Indian wards. In Travancore the situation was somewhat different. Unlike in other principalities, here, due to orthodox views on caste and purity, foreigners could never have round-the-clock access to the royal children. As a later Resident remarked, 'none of the Tutors may stand on the same carpet' as their royal students, nor hand them books, 'nor at recreation times touch golf clubs, tennis rackets etc. at the same time as [Their Highnesses]'.[85] And a lady freshly imported from Europe could hardly be expected to fully comprehend the intricacies of local custom and the punctilious phobias about caste entertained by the royal house. A compromise between modernity and tradition would have to be found.

The choice, then, fell on a Miss Dorothia Henriett Watts, a local Anglo-Indian spinster. Described as 'a graduate of the Madras University, possessing suavity of manners, polish and great talent', she also had the advantage of being the daughter of Frank Edwards Watts, who had been Chief Secretary of Travancore during the reign of Ayilyam Tirunal.[86] Cultured, pretty ('with strawberry blonde hair'), appropriately conservative, with a thorough knowledge of the state and its ways, she seemed ideal and was appointed 'tutoress' in 1904. She would initially train the girls for three hours a week in music, painting and other ladylike skills, besides honing their English. A smattering of Latin was also added to their syllabus, and under her able stewardship, the Sethus would develop, in addition to their daily rigorous rooting in tradition and religion, the refinement and class that characterised Edwardian high society, intended to make them perfectly at ease during soirees and interactions with Europeans. Miss Watts's appointment, however, was particularly significant also because she would go on to become the only friend Sethu Lakshmi Bayi ever had in the world outside royal confines. Other teachers employed for the children, such as a Miss Yardley and a Miss Light did not enjoy the same rapport.

There were also practical aspects that were covered in the Ranis' instruction. 'The necessity,' writes one observer, 'of giving social and political as also moral and religious education was not lost sight of.' Great importance was placed on this and the Ranis were often taken out to 'visit the public institutions in the metropolis, with the object of knowing the general character of the work done at each, as knowledge thus acquired will be of practical utility in their future life'. Periodic tours were organised by the government to 'develop and strengthen their powers of observation' and 'for deriving first-hand information of the country and its inhabitants'.[87] In 1903, they went for their maiden excursion within Travancore, which was officially a religious visit where they showed themselves to the public in temple towns like Varkala, Quilon, Ambalapuzha,

Alleppey and Vaikom. This was all very arduous business. At every stop the local authorities, competing for royal favour and promotion, would put up grand receptions, with Sethu Lakshmi Bayi having to preside, cutting ribbons, receiving flowers, saying a few wise words and so on. Some events were great fun, whereas others were an invitation for pandemonium, as in Harippad where one of the government elephants decided to run off in the last minute. In good grace the Rani presented the usual dupatta to the local administrator anyway, probably lifting his spirits after all his carefully organised pageantry went awry at the whim of a mutinous pachyderm. Similarly, in 1905 the girls visited Courtallam, the 'Spa of South India', taking their first railway journey to get there, returning very excited with the whole experience.

While a generally wholesome education, was thus, imparted to the children, it was still full of restrictions, as might be expected in the case of princesses. They had no classmates because outside influences were frowned upon at court. 'It was a time of great intrigues and conspiracies,' Sethu Lakshmi Bayi would later remember, 'and they feared the influence of other factions.'[88] Every contact was carefully regulated, even within the palace, which was a hotbed of underhand machinations. No servants were permitted to get close and the children were constantly protected and cocooned. Occasionally, girls from noble families would come calling, but as the royal aura of the Ranis preceded them, there was no equality in the relationship that is necessary for the establishment of a healthy friendship. Playmates of the same age, thus, were never available to Sethu Lakshmi Bayi. 'But I had my brothers and sisters,' she would later shrug, 'so it was not a barren or lonely childhood.'[89]

She was trying to play it down when she recounted this towards the end of her life. She was characteristically averse to being demonstrative, forming a remarkable tendency towards self-effacement, letting go of the difficulties of her formative years. But it was not easy at first for the simple reason that she did *not*, in fact, have her brothers and sisters around all the time. In order to ensure that the Ranis would not become instruments in the hands of scheming relatives (a futile effort as it turned out), the Maharajah had insisted on as much distance as possible from their natural families. All the same, the girls needed maternal care, resulting, in the end, in a compromise. For six months at a time, it was decided, Mahaprabha could stay in Trivandrum, giving company to both children. Following this, Kochukunji would assume charge for the remainder of the year. During these long sojourns the mothers, whose job was to be physically present but unobtrusive, could bring their other children and husbands also, but at the end of their respective terms, they would all return to Mavelikkara. So, while for six months Sethu Lakshmi Bayi had her family near her, she spent an equal measure of time pining and counting the days before their return.

It was letters, then, that early on became an important link between the Rani and her family. Sethu Lakshmi Bayi's correspondence from these years comprises mainly of little notes sent very frequently, desperately conveying minute details of her days in Sundara Vilasam. Writing to her father appears to have been much more relaxed than to her mother, who acted a long-distance disciplinarian. Letters to Mahaprabha were normally rather formally addressed as 'For the Royal Perusal of Mother' and spoke more about her health, her studies, and other serious aspects. Occasionally, of course, Sethu Lakshmi Bayi would throw in some humour too, as on 11 August 1904 when she spoke of the Junior Rani's younger sister. 'There was a big boil on Ikkavukutty's bottom,' she impishly informed those in Mavelikkara, adding: 'At 11 'o' clock today it burst ... Please give the news to Father too.'[90] The Junior Rani too would write to her aunt and uncle, but not quite as regularly as they would have liked. 'I didn't not write because I forgot you,' she reassured Mahaprabha on one occasion. 'It's just that we have only one holiday a week, when we play around and do nothing else!'[91]

There was, to the immense relief of both mothers, however, one distinguished family member watching over the Ranis in the palace constantly, serving also as their guardian. And this was Kerala Varma, husband to the late Rani Lakshmi Bayi, with the title of Valiya Koil Tampuran (senior royal consort) at court. A man of formidable talents and ability, he is to this day considered the Kalidas of Kerala for his tremendous facility in Sanskrit poetry, and also as the Father of Malayalam Prose for his unprecedented work in developing vernacular composition as well. As consort to the former Senior Rani, he had had much time on his leisurely hands for decades, which he put to good use, maturing into an academician and scholar. He chaired the Textbook Committee for the Education Department in Travancore, revolutionising primary schooling in the state, besides winning esteemed fellowships of the Madras University and the Royal Asiatic Society in London. Into the 1890s, Queen Victoria had also dignified him into the Imperial Order of the Star of India, and he towered as an intellectual giant in Kerala society, arguably the second best known face of Travancore after his contemporary, relative and occasional rival, Raja Ravi Varma.

That is why when it was announced that the Ranis were committed to his avuncular care and supervision there was universal appreciation among all whose opinions mattered. As a later biographer of Sethu Lakshmi Bayi would write (with that mild excess typical when writing about royalty in those days), 'In the most plastic period of her life, she was placed under the tutelage of a poet-laureate and master-potter' who with all his ability 'fashioned that living soft clay into a model of culture, beautiful to behold and worthy of being imitated.'[92] To be sure, it wasn't only the girls who benefited from this arrangement. The Valiya Koil Tampuran also, recently widowed and with no children of his own, found the company of the Ranis a cheerful prospect, not to speak of the welcome challenge of moulding them into cultivated personalities. Beyond the academic implications, however, there were also more practical elements that an association with this accomplished elder provided the girls. For Kerala Varma was a seasoned, battle-scarred member of the court, who had lived through very interesting times, witnessing and participating in great intrigues and schemes, even spending five years of his life imprisoned and under house arrest. He had seen the highs and lows of royal life, enjoying sovereign favour one instant, suffering furious wrath the next. For his princely wards, he was eminently qualified, then, to guide them through all the intrigues and troubles a royal court was home to, preparing them for their tempestuous destinies ahead.

It was in 1859 that Kerala Varma married the late Rani Lakshmi Bayi. Within a brief period, he became a favourite at court, charming one and all with his charisma and talent. While to most he was to become known as 'The Symbol of Renaissance in Malayalam Literature',[93] his other achievements were equally impressive. He became after his marriage an avid sportsman, establishing the first cricket club in Trivandrum, also excelling in rifle shooting, horse riding and so on. He was also fairly talented in music, having learnt to play the veena, the sarangi, and the fiddle, and training under stalwarts like Venkatadiri Bhagvathar and Kalyanakrishna Bhagvathar Sr. He also wrote a series of Kathakali dramas such as the *Matsyavallabha Charitam*, the *Dhruva Charitam*, the *Parasurama Vijayam*, etc. Treated as a great ornament of the court, he was in those early years popular with all its factions and groups.

But that was until the 1870s. Kerala Varma, over the years, got carried away by his own confidence and charisma, and began to participate in palace intrigues of a dubious variety. The ruling Maharajah Ayilyam Tirunal was no longer on good terms with his brother and heir Visakham Tirunal by then, and the young consort of the Senior Rani appears to have been unable to resist a temptation to meddle in their affairs, little prepared for the consequences he would provoke. While the Maharajah was fond of the Valiya Koil Tampuran at first, he now resolved to put him in his place. Restrictions were placed on Kerala Varma's freedom and even meetings with his royal wife were closely regulated. This only led to more defiance on the part of the former, who gravitated towards the camp of the ruler's rival, Visakham Tirunal. But here too the Valiya Koil Tampuran was not fully at home, continuing to play one brother against the other, until in 1875 he seemed to have upset both. Things got so bad that in a letter to the Resident he wrote, 'My dear Major Hay, we are not fighting against the Maharajah when we say that you must give us British Protection. We live in the fear of life.'[94] Sometime later he was most alarmed when Ayilyam Tirunal and Visakham Tirunal, archenemies of each other, seemed en route to a rapprochement. 'The Maharajah & First Prince who used to perform all ceremonies separately have yesterday performed an anniversary ceremony together,' he worried. 'I fear they are plotting. I have shut myself here with the Rani,' he stated before ominously adding, 'I won't take the drink & mixture.'[95]

Family members would later claim that an innocent, ethically spotless Kerala Varma found himself quite by accident an unwilling pawn in great games orchestrated at court. But the truth in 1875 was that he knowingly plunged himself into a notorious controversy. By now the Maharajah was also having difficulties with his Dewan, none other than old Sheshiah Shastri, and one morning an anonymous letter arrived at the latter's official residence. 'In the other day's Privy Council,' it warned, 'there was a hint of trying to dispose of you by other means than asking you to resign ... Do resign, or take care of your cooks & men about you.'[96] Signed 'Peter III', similar letters appeared at Visakham Tirunal's palaces also. The flustered Dewan, predictably, took the matter straight to the ruler, who, having had it examined by handwriting experts in Madras, discovered that the author was none other than the Valiya Koil Tampuran. In July the Resident asked innocently whether the latter knew anything about the whole affair. Kerala Varma denied any knowledge, further implicating himself as a liar.[97]

Ayilyam Tirunal was a progressive and forward-minded ruler, but he was not a man to be meddled with. Already upset with the Valiya Koil Tampuran for exceeding his station and for squandering his reputation by involving himself in affairs that were not his concern, he decided to take drastic action. With the full endorsement of the Governor of Madras, the Maharajah had Kerala Varma arrested, stripped of his titles and rank, and deported to north Travancore where he was kept in a regular prison in horrifying conditions for fifteen months. Rani Lakshmi Bayi, who at first took a determined stand to protect her husband, had to eventually give way and beg Ayilyam Tirunal to forgive his recent indiscretions. When her consort was taken away in a police carriage, she famously ran through the streets of Trivandrum, in full public view, weeping and unkempt, her hair flying behind her, in what was one of the most dramatic episodes in the annals of the royal family. But her appeals were turned down. Following this the Rani asked to be allowed to join her husband in prison. Obviously, Ayilyam Tirunal had no intention of permitting the queen to park herself in jail and score a moral point over him. Her movements were curtailed and her allowances held back, at times forcing her to seek loans from well-wishers and friends. Indeed, she was even warned that her adoption would be annulled and she would be sent back to Mavelikkara to spend the remainder of her days in an ordinary, shamed oblivion. But the Rani called the Maharajah's bluff, aware of the legal impossibility of enforcing this threat. When one day she was told that Ayilyam Tirunal wished her to forget Kerala Varma and was looking to nominate a new consort, she coldly and very firmly replied, 'I am not a widow.'[98]

Her husband's willpower, however, was weaker, especially after being thrown into an inhospitable prison, where neither his high-caste position nor the standing of his aristocratic family aided him. Writing to seek forgiveness and clemency from the Maharajah, Kerala Varma admitted to his most 'heinous offence' in sending those controversial letters. Curiously, he confessed also to a whole host of other 'treasonous acts', which included being attracted to Christianity, corresponding with journalists, an addiction to marijuana and other narcotics, and so on, before concluding pitiably:

> ...Your Highness' humble Slave cannot possible entertain the faintest hope of obtaining a kind pardon even from so condescending and tender hearted a Sovereign as Your Highness. But feeling the most sincere compunction of conscience and most heartfelt, contrite and [illegible] remorse for all his past misconduct, Your Highness' most humble Slave begs to throw himself at Your Highness' Royal feet and with tears in his eyes most piteously implores Your Highness' kind forgiveness once for the serious offences he has committed. Whatever be Your Highness' Slave's future destiny by the nature of the arrangements Your Highness makes in disposing of him, whether to quit his native country and all relations and spend his days as an exile and a beggar, or to rove as a Fakir and perish in the snowy regions of the Himalayas, he will submit to it as his fate; but he will bear Your Highness' Command with his head bowed down and shall never deviate even a hair's breadth from it.[99]

When this pathetic letter from 'Kerala Varma, State Prisoner' failed to mute the Maharajah's resolve, the ex-Valiya Koil Tampuran attempted to appeal to the softer, aesthetic side of the ruler by submitting an elaborate Sanskrit work called the *Kshamapana Sahasra*, literally meaning, 'a thousand entreaties for forgiveness'. But when this too would not placate Ayilyam Tirunal, the (apocryphal) story goes (no doubt introduced to rehabilitate Kerala Varma to dignity after the death of the Maharajah), a vengeance arose in him and he began his *Yamapranama Sataka*, addressed to the god of death where, through barely disguised metaphor, the poet asks the latter to rid the earth of an evil king. Every day, it was later told with a theatrical flair, Kerala Varma would rise and pray to Lord Yama before composing a few verses, and on the very day he completed his work, he received, sensationally enough, news that the hateful Ayilyam Tirunal had died in Trivandrum a most painful death.

Either way, in 1880 when Visakham Tirunal came to the throne, one of his first orders was to free Kerala Varma and to reinstate him as Valiya Koil Tampuran. After five years of forced separation, thus, Rani Lakshmi Bayi was reunited with her husband, who in his gratitude composed a eulogy to the new Maharajah known as the *Visakhavijaya* (The Victory of Visakham Tirunal). In this, Visakham Tirunal is generously praised while his dead brother, to whom only recently Kerala Varma was submitting sycophantic eulogies, is cast as the villain of the piece. But perhaps because he had learnt his lessons the hard way, in the years ahead, a wiser Kerala Varma 'devoted himself to the development of the Malayalam language and literature'.[100] With a sympathetic ruler now enthroned, the sins of his past were forgotten or, at any rate, whitewashed, the blame resting solely on Ayilyam Tirunal and his notorious temper. Great works in both Malayalam and Sanskrit followed, as did honours from the British, also aiding in the reinstatement of the Valiya Koil Tampuran to favour. When Maharajah Mulam Tirunal came to the throne, he too was well disposed towards Kerala Varma; when the latter translated *Aesop's Fables* into Malayalam, the young ruler dutifully wrote to his adoptive brother in law, 'there cannot be a more elegant Malayalam composition.'[101] By the end of the nineteenth century his abilities seemingly began to abandon him, however, and he wrote in 1896 to old Sir Sheshiah:

> There was a time when [the] Goddess of Speech used to appear before me the moment I wished. At that time when the Goddess was at my beck and call, I could compose poetry instantly with the least effort ... But now the wind

> has begun to blow in a different direction. Due to the want of practice the intuition to compose Sanskrit poetry has become dull.[102]

The death of Rani Lakshmi Bayi also took its toll on him and he confessed to another prominent poet of the day, the titular Zamorin of Calicut in Malabar, that since 1901 his literary faculties had never been the same.[103] The two young Ranis kept him in good spirit though, and he remained a successful teacher, with Sethu Lakshmi Bayi once writing: 'Because *Appoopan* [grandfather, as they used to call him] teaches us *Sakuntalam* it seems easier than before.'[104] He also taught the two girls several other important Sanskrit works and even in his years of decline remained quite a formidable scholar. But in the early years of the twentieth century what was foremost in Kerala Varma's mind was not the political future or princely career of his wards but an early, comfortable settlement for them in life with suitable, well-bred partners.

Marriage was on the cards for Sethu Lakshmi Bayi.

3
Three Consorts

In November 1905, Trivandrum witnessed some very sumptuous celebrations on the birth anniversary of the Senior Rani. Palaces were lit up, colourful processions were paraded, addresses and public functions were convened, and thousands of poor were feasted at government expense. While royal birthdays were always occasions for great festivities, this one was especially significant, as Sethu Lakshmi Bayi had turned ten years old. An exciting thrill descended upon the capital, for in Travancore custom decreed that princesses must wed before the age of eleven. The court, naturally then, was abuzz with talk about the impending event, while patricians reminisced about the splendid pageantry of the last princely wedding in Travancore, fifty years before.[1] Soon afterwards the government began logistical preparations for the seven days of revelry, but nothing was too clear about who the consort would be. Even Kochukunji, who was on duty in the palace at the time, could only write vaguely to Mahaprabha that she had 'heard that the elder child's wedding will be in the month of Medam', i.e. April–May 1906 and that horoscopes had been sent for from the great families of the state. It remained to be seen which of the eligible young noblemen of Travancore would succeed in winning the Senior Rani's royal hand and queenly approval.[2]

The choice wasn't especially plentiful. Sethu Lakshmi Bayi could only, at best, pick her husband from one of ten highborn families of the realm. And precedents were such that even among these, one or two historically dominated the honour of marrying the Attingal Rani. For all of the eighteenth century, for instance, consorts were chosen from the Kilimanoor house of Raja Ravi Varma. They were lineal heirs to the Rajahs of Beypore in Malabar, originally tributary to the Zamorin of Calicut, claiming descent from martial Rajput tribes in north India.[3] It was in the days of the formidable Queen Ashure that they settled in Travancore, furnishing consorts to the Attingal Ranis, only to be toppled from their jealously guarded privilege by another house in the early nineteenth century. This was the family of the Rajah of Parappanad, who in turn had arrived in Travancore after Hyder Ali's bloodthirsty invaders ejected them from their ancestral seat in Malabar. From early in the nineteenth century down till Sethu Lakshmi Bayi's time, every Senior Rani of Travancore had been married to a Parappanad consort. While the guardian Kerala Varma married the late Rani Lakshmi Bayi, his uncle was husband to the queen before her,[4] and his uncle's uncle to the matriarch even before.[5] And through these consistent and expertly perpetuated marriages, the Parappanads had acquired tremendous influence at court and near-princely status in Travancore.

While the Maharajah requisitioned nominees from all ten houses in the state, he also granted Kerala Varma, as Valiya Koil Tampuran and caretaker of the Ranis, the privilege of recommending befitting spouses for them. Not willing to give up this prerogative and in order to preserve the longstanding influence of the Parappanads, the latter proposed an eminently suitable nephew of his called Rajaraja Varma. He was a man aged twenty at the time, studying at university, and was held to possess all the qualities the Maharajah sought in a consort to the Senior Rani. But the fact that he was over ten years older than Sethu Lakshmi Bayi did not endear him to Mulam Tirunal, and 'the Palace', Kochukunji reported, 'is more interested in the person from Changanasseri', also a member of the Parappanad house though from a different branch.[6] The Valiya Koil Tampuran, however, was determined on having one of his direct nephews marry Sethu Lakshmi Bayi and quickly sent for an alternative from his home in Harippad. On 22 February, this boy, the younger brother of Rajaraja Varma, named Rama Varma, arrived in the capital and that very afternoon they proceeded to the palace for an interview with the Maharajah.

While the brothers waited for their audience with His Highness, unbeknownst to them present in the palace was also *Her* Highness, studying them from an upstairs balcony. Mulam Tirunal had invited Sethu Lakshmi Bayi to evaluate her options and articulate a personal preference. The Junior Rani and Kochukunji, along with some giggling personal maids, also joined the proceedings, whispering their own opinions about the boys into the ears of the Senior Rani. All of them had no doubt as to which of the two candidates *they* liked more, and with a smile on her face many years later Sethu Lakshmi Bayi would remember how 'they were all saying I should marry the older one because he was more experienced'.[7] To the greatest surprise of the ladies, however, the Rani shook her head and pointed at the slightly built, timid-looking younger boy. The royal choice was made, even as the women were left baffled, and the party was promptly evacuated from the Maharajah's palace. Shortly afterwards, an emissary conveyed the Senior Rani's decision to Mulam Tirunal before he saw the boys, leaving him equally perplexed at the rejection of the popular Rajaraja Varma.

Sethu Lakshmi Bayi's selection of her second option instead of the favoured first was puzzling for obvious reasons. While the Senior Rani was not an adolescent yet, Rajaraja Varma's good looks, magnificent physique, and most imposing personality were singularly attractive to anyone who saw him. While decorum denied the women any open deliberations about his appeal—formally focusing instead on his education and experience—the fact was that he was a strikingly handsome young man. Fair to the point of appearing European, which carried great weight in Indian society, with aquiline features and proud eyes, he was rendered all the more attractive by his perfectly sculpted body. Indeed, such were his good looks that Rajaraja Varma even modelled for Ravi Varma for his famous painting, *Sri Rama Vanquishing the Sea* (1906). This depicts the epic hero of the Ramayana, his eyes full of righteous fury as he stands by the ocean at Rameswaram and threatens Varuna, god of the seas.[8] Every pleasing physical attribute of Rajaraja Varma comes to life in this work, which is why when he was cast aside by Sethu Lakshmi Bayi in favour of his 'very much more ordinary looking' brother, many thought the Rani had committed a grave nuptial error.[9]

But Sethu Lakshmi Bayi had her own girlish reasons that even at an advanced age would cause her to blush. While she generally held that it was 'the sensitive face and slighter build' of the younger boy that instinctively endeared him to her, this was not the whole truth of the matter.[10] As a reserved, largely subdued person, she may have found the less glamorous-looking candidate more fitting to her tastes. But as she would admit years later in private to her dearest granddaughter, when she saw Rajaraja Varma, she was positively intimidated by his exceptional appearance. The ten-year-old Rani suddenly found herself very conscious of her own flaws next to this Apollo whom her grandfather had selected to depict a legendary hero himself. And so she preferred the less striking and rather average-looking nominee as her consort. 'How grandmother did such a thing I could never understand,' her granddaughter would later exclaim, but Sethu Lakshmi Bayi was convinced she did right. 'You will never understand,' she would insist, 'I was so overawed that I was tongue-tied when I saw him. And so I thought it was better to go with the younger one if we had to spend all our lives together.'[11]

Now that Sethu Lakshmi Bayi had declared her decision, three days later the boys were sent to meet with the Dewan, Sir V.P. Madhava Rao, for him to officially discern if they were suitable enough to father future Maharajahs. Rao then sought an audience with the Senior Rani where he formally solicited her answer, and returned after she reiterated her liking for the younger of the two. Thus apprised of the royal choice, the government issued orders to prepare for the big event; Travancore, it was confirmed, would see its first *pallikettu* (royal wedding) in almost fifty years. In the meantime, on 27 February the bridegroom-elect, Rama Varma, was taken to Bhakti Vilas, the Dewan's official residence, where an English physician, Col. James, conducted a thorough medical examination. Once the doctor gave his seal of approval to the prospective consort, the Resident was also notified and, through him, the Madras Government as well.[12] In due course, when the Rani grew up and the marriage was to be consummated, astrologers were also involved to determine an auspicious day for that purpose, while the royal family's head priest awkwardly tutored the young consort in the dos and don'ts of lovemaking.[13] Nothing, it was clear, could be left to chance when it came to ensuring a robust supply of heirs to the dynasty, though, of course, the onus of a romantic performance fell largely on the husband; all the Rani received in terms of sex education was a pithy remark from her mother who merely stated: 'He will do certain things. Don't get bewildered'.[14]

For Rama Varma, this regal nod of approval from a little girl was about to refashion his life altogether. In spite of the urgency with which the Valiya Koil Tampuran had him summoned to Trivandrum and although there was talk about the Senior Rani's forthcoming marriage, the boy didn't dream of being considered a possible consort to the exalted Attingal Rani. He had seen her only once when she visited Harippad a few years ago on tour, and had looked upon her as a distant, awe-inspiring figure, so removed from the infinitely more mundane world he inhabited. His own childhood and life had been unexceptional, though at times difficult. He was the youngest of five siblings, and soon after his birth in 1889 his mother had died. His father, a Brahmin, had no interest in the matrilineal joint family after this, and in any case the man wasn't especially eager to contribute to bringing up his children.[15] A very spirited grandmother cared for them but the absence of parents left an indelible mark on Rama Varma. He was a demure child, constantly in the uneasy shadow of his glamorous older brother, perpetually bullied by cousins and friends, and generally not known for possessing any marks of a personality. The last thing he expected was to be chosen and commanded to marry her by the queen, over his charismatic brother, who, as it happened, was destined only for a respectable but perfectly ordinary future as a Deputy Superintendent of Police in service of the Government of Travancore.[16]

The months that followed were full of frantic activity. Rama Varma returned to Harippad to prepare for his new station in life, while in Trivandrum officials worked round the clock to ready the city for the big event. Massive crowds of people arrived from all over the principality to witness the celebrations, while at the palace Sethu Lakshmi Bayi sat in state and received congregations of distinguished visitors, including representatives of the Cochin durbar and of the Malabar grandees. But what caused a real flutter at Sundara Vilasam was the arrival of Raja Ravi Varma. Sethu Lakshmi Bayi's grandfather brought with him not only his usual bounty of fascinating stories from his life and travels beyond Travancore, but also an exquisite present for the bride: a magnificent length of silk woven with gold thread, which had been gifted to him by the Maharajah of Mysore. Half of this material was used for Sethu Lakshmi Bayi's wedding dress, with the rest assigned to the Junior Rani's trousseau.[17] In the meantime special religious observances began at all the important temples in the state for the benefit of the Senior Rani, who left by mid-March to worship personally at these shrines. She also spent three days at Attingal to propitiate their family goddess at the local temple. By the third week of April, Mahaprabha and Kuttan Tampuran arrived at the palace with her siblings, followed ten days later by bridegroom's party from Harippad.

The actual wedding ceremonies commenced on 5 May, with the Senior Rani going out to acknowledge the masses in the capital, seated in a palanquin. Heralded by trumpets and traditional piped music, a dazzling procession of elephants, cavalry and soldiers attended to her. She worshipped at the Sri Padmanabhaswamy Temple and other shrines nearby, before performing a variety of rituals at the palace. The next morning, Sethu Lakshmi Bayi arrived in the sanctified chamber where the principal wedding ceremony was to take place. An ornate chair of state was placed on a high pedestal and the Rani took her seat in this, with Rama Varma standing before her. Surrounded by family members, the high priests and the Maharajah, when the clock struck 10:30, the bridegroom placed the wedding locket around her neck before bowing so that she could garland him. The couple then walked, hand in hand, around the sacred fire seven times before proceeding to a ritual bedchamber for a few moments. Outside, the state forces fired a twenty-one-gun salute and celebrations broke out on the streets.[18]

Over the next week a number of traditional ceremonies were conducted as per convention, and entertainments were put up at various palaces in the fort every evening. Kathakali dramas, nautch performances, fireworks and more formed part of the programme, as did the giving out of presents to Brahmins and alms to the poor. Separate feasts were held for government officials according to their castes, while Mahaprabha and Kochukunji hosted an elaborate luncheon for the lady of the Maharajah and the sons and daughters of previous monarchs. Inside the palace, Sethu Lakshmi Bayi was treated to music, food and much merrymaking, until the final procession on 12 May. The Senior Rani was taken around the capital in an exquisite ivory palanquin, with her husband following in a golden howdah atop the most majestic elephant in the royal stables, attended to by the Dewan and officials of the government. Paying their respects to the Maharajah, they then returned to the palace. Just outside the gates Sethu Lakshmi Bayi emerged from her palanquin and greeted the masses that had gathered to see her. She threw a few handfuls of silver coins into the crowd, before turning to enter the palace, now not only as queen but also a wife, and participate in the final series of religious rites. The wedding was officially concluded hereafter, although banquets and celebrations continued until 15 May, after which the guests began to take their leave one after another.

In only a matter of days, interestingly, life returned to normal in the palace. The girls went back to their routine of tedious ceremonials, long hours of study, along with outings to public institutions, factories and so on. In early 1907 the Governor of Madras came on a state visit to Trivandrum, and for the first time the new consort obtained a glimpse into the kind of society he was expected to cultivate and sustain. He was practically a village boy, with a basic education in Sanskrit and Malayalam, and to provide him a more sophisticated view of the world, tutors were assigned for his study. One Subramania Iyer became the principal teacher, while Miss Watts, was in charge of training him in table manners, conversational skills and other nuances of Western refinement. Rama Varma responded to all this with creditable enthusiasm. By a twist of fate, his life was transformed altogether, and he intended to make the most of this opportunity to become a polished gentleman of learning and ability. Indeed, some would later grumble, when the boy's ambition began to exceed his station, that perhaps too much encouragement had been given too soon to this country aristocrat in his new avatar as consort to the Senior Rani, proving detrimental to the larger strategic interests of the latter's dynasty.

But it was with great determination that Rama Varma pursued his study of English, reminiscing later how he diligently memorised ten words every day from the dictionary so as to improve his vocabulary and match that of his wife.[19] He read a great deal, whether it was *Tono-Bungay* by H.G. Wells, original works by Shakespeare, or even *The Principles of Psychology*, a phenomenal academic treatise by William James.[20] He took it upon himself to go beyond the rudiments of Sanskrit and it would become a family legend how his siblings and he conversed with one another only in that layered language, because of their formidable proficiency.[21] The law was another area of interest in which he was to accumulate thorough knowledge. Like Sethu Lakshmi Bayi, Rama Varma read so much that a granddaughter would later adoringly remark how 'he knew everything about everything! One might even say that, verily, what he did not know about something was not worth knowing!'[22] He made conscious efforts to excel at sports: riding, shooting, football and more, actively following in the footsteps of the Valiya Koil Tampuran. As a later critic would remark, 'With his keenness for big game, his skilled horsemanship, his taste for amateur photography, his dignified demeanour, and his courteous affability, he cannot be considered a social failure.'[23] The consort, born in rural Travancore and now raised to regal status, endeavoured for precisely such affirmation.

Marriage, thus, in the first instance meant a good education and the moulding of a presentable personality. It did not, at least for the immediate future, connote even a remotely conjugal relationship. Rama Varma lived at the Sripadam Palace, and it was only at specified times every day that he could call on his wife. These meetings were always chaperoned either by the Valiya Koil Tampuran or one of the mothers, and he would spend precisely one hour with the Ranis. Sethu Lakshmi Bayi would remember these days as a time of 'great fun', though she was somewhat peeved that her guardian 'would never allow my husband to be with me for a minute longer than an hour!'[24] Sometimes they would play hopscotch or go out for tennis, while on other occasions he would join them in the library and read them fairytales and stories. His English might have tottered at that stage but the girls were far too excited by the welcome presence of another playmate in their cloistered environs to care for these details. They sometimes all went out, as they did to the Mateer Memorial Church, for instance, upon an invitation from the Reverend. On another occasion they sat together in a public gallery watching a variety of entertainments till almost 11:30 at night, before which they enjoyed themselves when a troupe visited the palace with seven performing monkeys. In December 1906, the Valiya Koil Tampuran even arranged a holiday together, taking them to the beach at Varkala, where palace rules took a leave of absence and they were permitted (quite literally) to let their hair down. 'What a supreme felicity,' Kerala Varma wrote, 'it was for me to meet accidentally my darling Senior Rani playing with her lovely sister and my dear nephew, her consort!' In fact, Sethu Lakshmi Bayi so took to this escape from the rigidities of palace life that she almost seems to have rebelled from her official duties. 'Had to bring an amount of pressure on the Senior Rani to make her reply to Mrs Carr's letter,' wrote her guardian disapprovingly, adding that 'the older Her Highness grows, the lazier she seems to become.'[25]

While the Senior Rani was in high spirits, news arrived from another quarter to dampen collective enthusiasm, plunging the palace into melancholy and mourning. After the wedding celebrations, her grandfather Ravi Varma had retired to his family home in Kilimanoor. While there, his diabetes took a turn for the worst and a carbuncle appeared on his body. A surgical operation had to be conducted, but he was unable to recuperate, and at two o'clock on 2 October 1906, the artist died unexpectedly. The news was received with great sadness across India, and even the international press condoled the loss of this famous painter from the subcontinent; in Lord Curzon's somewhat debatable words, Ravi Varma had with his 'happy blend of Western technique and Indian subject ... for the first time in the art history of India commenced a new style of painting'.[26] In his letter to Sethu Lakshmi Bayi's uncle soon afterwards, Lord Ampthill, the ex-Governor of Madras, also reflected a sentiment many shared with him: 'When I think I would not see Ravi Varma in this world anymore,' he wrote, 'my heart is filled with sorrow.'[27]

Ravi Varma was lauded by many as a nation builder, someone who gave India a subconscious imagery and cultural pride in its history and Hindu heritage, and he was held by most to be an unequalled genius. Not only did he initiate the evolution of modern art in India but his work also served as inspiration to the pioneers of the country's film industry, Dadasaheb Phalke and Baburao Painter. He was a visionary marketer, who despite his lack of successful business acumen executed a masterstroke by establishing a lithograph press to produce colour prints of his work. These found their way into millions of homes, where for the first time gods and goddesses could be pictured in an aesthetic fashion, even as the name of the artist became permanently etched in the public imagination. Interestingly, however, after his death, Ravi Varma's reputation took a beating of sorts, as his art was considered too steeped in Victorian aesthetics and not Indian enough: Ravi Varma was more inspired by the works of Rembrandt and other Baroque masters than by the offerings of India's indigenous Pahari or Rajput artists. The founders of the Bengal School, for instance, with their anti-colonial nationalism, took severe exception to Ravi Varma's style, although even the eminent poet and Nobel laureate Rabindranath Tagore was compelled to admit that his work was 'really attractive'.[28] Despite the controversy that had been part of his career from the onset and which only grew in the decades after his death, Ravi Varma had touched and changed Indian painting forever and earned himself a place before posterity as a trailblazer and as an exemplar of artistic excellence.

While he was widely appreciated in his day elsewhere in India, in Travancore the establishment had been relatively frigid towards Ravi Varma. When in 1904 the honour known as the Kaiser-i-Hind was bestowed upon him, the news was received with petty resentment at court, with both the Maharajah and the Valiya Koil Tampuran raising objections at his being addressed as a 'Rajah' in his commendation. It did not matter, as the artist's brother noted in his diary that 'It is the first time in India that an artist's merits have been thus rewarded.'[29] What concerned them was why he had been elevated to such glory without their approval. Rivalries, after all, were a part of life at court, and even death did not mean very much in an age when custom and protocol held greater weight that emotion and sentiment. Sethu Lakshmi Bayi did not only observe this in the manner in which life quickly returned to ordinary after the death of her grandfather. Some years later, in 1908 when the Junior Rani's sister Ikkavukutty was taken ill in the palace, the Maharajah ordered her to be removed from the capital. The reason was that owing to blood relations between the royal family and the Mavelikkara people, a death would imply a ritual pollution on Mulam Tirunal for nearly two weeks and he would be unable to visit the temple and carry out his religious responsibilities. With all his endless orthodoxy, the Maharajah had Ikkavukutty sent away so that were she to die, he would not have to hear of the news and be put to all the inconvenience. As it happened, the poor child collapsed on the way to Mavelikkara, and died on the road in a government carriage.[30]

Sorrow, then, could not overstay its welcome in the capital and soon a joyous occasion presented itself, brushing aside the gloom of death. While the distinguished Raja Ravi Varma died in 1906, six months later the Junior Rani was married to his namesake and nephew from the Kilimanoor family. This younger Ravi Varma was among five candidates displayed to Sethu Parvathi Bayi, who selected him despite the fact that he was a dozen years her senior. Lovingly called Ittamar,[31] he was a model student of high academic accomplishments, an alumnus of the Presidency College in Madras, and only the second member of the aristocracy, after the Senior Rani's father, to have obtained a graduate degree.[32] While he had studied history and Sanskrit at college, it was the latter subject that really attracted his interest, and he would go on to achieve a respectable reputation as a scholar. His age was worrying for some at court, as was his rigid orthodoxy, but he was a man of fine looks, 'very handsome, with classical features', placing him a notch above the young husband of the Senior Rani.[33] Unlike Rama Varma, he was, however, a grown man, set in his ways with most of his personality already firmly defined. He was something of a nerd (with 'less conversational powers than a flea', to quote one contemporary),[34] always with his Sanskrit manuscripts, diligently tackling one difficult verse after another, even as Sethu Lakshmi Bayi's husband was out riding or at tennis, acting more British than the British themselves. While Rama Varma was also young enough to entertain both Ranis and amuse them with his boyish charm, Ravi Varma on his visits to the palace acted his age and maintained an adult distance. It didn't matter very much at the time, although eventually an older Junior Rani and he would find their marriage not particularly fulfilling and, ultimately, rather stifling.

Sethu Parvathi Bayi, interestingly, was developing into a vibrant and energetic individual, with passionate opinions and views on everything, along with refreshing hints of a rebellious streak. In the early years after their adoption, the cousins were close and the Junior Rani was recorded to be Sethu Lakshmi Bayi's 'constant chum'.[35] But in that relationship also there was an awkward hierarchy that would considerably influence the Junior Rani's character. Early in life Sethu Parvathi Bayi understood that in their royal circumstances, so guided by convention and custom, her place was always secondary to that of her older cousin, the Senior Rani. This was essentially due to the structure of matrilineal society where age conferred precedence, even if the individuals involved were merely children. As the Junior Rani's nephew remarks, 'within the family the senior male and senior female members were equal' with a status that prevailed over everyone else.[36] In other words, Sethu Lakshmi Bayi, despite being barely a year older than the Junior Rani, was equal in rank, position, and prestige to the Maharajah himself, while Sethu Parvathi Bayi was perpetually stuck with that ancillary title of Junior Rani.

For years she would attempt to rid herself of this tag, which was more a mark of courtesy than a station of any critical consequence. The British Government also officially only addressed the Maharajah and the Senior Rani as 'Highnesses' and it would be 1935 before Sethu Parvathi Bayi succeeded in wresting from them not only the style of 'Her Highness' but also the removal of the tag of 'Junior' from her title.[37] Similarly, whenever the King Emperor of England deputed a new Viceroy of India, the outgoing as well as incoming British statesmen would send their formal greetings, known as *kharitas*, to the Maharajah and the Senior Rani separately, addressing them alike in his salutations. Indeed, Sethu Lakshmi Bayi was the only non-ruling female in all India to receive such direct communications from the Crown Representative, being a dynastic descendant of one of the earliest allies of the British, the Attingal Rani.[38] Similarly, while Sethu Parvathi Bayi was simply the Junior Rani of Travancore to colonial authorities, Sethu Lakshmi Bayi and the Maharajah had a wordy string of embellished titles to flaunt.[39] The former, then, keenly felt her lack of status and dignity, rubbed in every day by the ceremonial exactness around them.

While within the palace Kerala Varma made a conscious effort not to treat the two girls unequally, the outside world drew a clear distinction. For here they were not seen as little children but indeed as Senior Rani and Junior Rani, in their official roles. In the wider world outside Sundara Vilasam, the Junior Rani was in the shadow of Sethu Lakshmi Bayi, who as the principal Attingal Rani commanded a vastly more esteemed treatment. Whether it was on state visits, or when they went out to public institutions, or even during their day-to-day ceremonial obligations, the Senior Rani's role and prerogatives were superior to those of Sethu Parvathi Bayi. Minor incidents were enough to highlight this. Once, for instance, Zacharias D'Cruz, the well-known photographer, called at the palace and, as was customary when seeking an audience with royalty, presented gifts to the Senior Rani but did not offer anything to the Junior Rani. The Valiya Koil Tampuran quickly passed his own presents to her, but it would not be mere speculation to assume that Sethu Parvathi Bayi noticed her inferiority. Coupled with the fact that they were only children, all this is bound to have created some resentment in the only subordinate member in the entire royal house.[40]

But unlike Sethu Lakshmi Bayi, who lived up to her duties but withdrew into a shell of privacy as a person, the Junior Rani evolved into an active individual, full of zest and a great appetite for life. 'Repose is decay, and the common and unlovely spell the death of culture,' she would later declare as her motto.[41] Perhaps because of the relative lack of attention, she constantly endeavoured to excel herself in more ways than one, and to stand out on her merits, carving a place for herself where none was offered by tradition. As her son would later remark, she 'never blindly follow[ed] custom and tradition but all the same would respect them where it was desirable'.[42] Her room at Sundara Vilasam demonstrated her keen interest in the arts, its walls adorned with personally chosen paintings and pictures, its shelves full of books, music instruments like the veena, violin, harmonium, and so on.[43] Both girls were in fact instructed in music, with Sethu Lakshmi Bayi under the tutelage of one Padmanabha Bhagvathar, and the Junior Rani training under a Ramachandra Bhagvathar. But it was the latter who persisted and surpassed her cousin in the field. Into the future she would learn from such acclaimed musicians as Kalyanakrishna Bhagvathar Jr and 'Veena' Dhanammal, and such was her commitment to music that it became a matter of legend how, from the age of fourteen until she turned sixty-five, Sethu Parvathi Bayi barely went a day without six hours on the veena, honing her skills to perfection.[44]

While the Senior Rani was an outstanding student insofar as formal education went, it was Sethu Parvathi Bayi who stood out in extracurricular activities. She was irrepressible, and in 1916 the Senior Rani would write that even pregnancy did not deter her from playing her daily round of golf.[45] 'Exceptional women could subvert custom,' in royal circles, writes Lucy Moore, and the Junior Rani too flouted rules when she pleased; in 1942, at the height of wartime austerity, her guests, watching a religious procession, were surprised to find themselves served excellent Scotch whisky by Sethu Parvathi Bayi even as her son piously led the most orthodox ceremonials before them.[46] In a more amusing but equally telling story, years later in London, she met a wheelchair-bound friend who wanted to go to a flower show but felt embarrassed to go in that state. To everyone's delight, the Junior Rani decided to give her a little more than emotional support and company. She hopped into another wheelchair, and the two ladies enjoyed a wonderful afternoon together, moving about in this bizarre fashion. 'I never needed a wheelchair,' Sethu Parvathi Bayi would go on to remark, 'but it was a very comfortable way of seeing things.'[47] Equally amusingly, the Junior Rani did not in the 1930s have any qualms about 'having a footstool fitted to accommodate a dwarf to massage her legs while remaining hidden from onlookers' as she drove about in her Rolls Royce.[48] Sethu Lakshmi Bayi, on the other hand, always remained a more orthodox, stately, establishment figure that could never put one foot wrong. The Senior Rani became famously regal but decidedly staid; the Junior Rani more adventurous and interesting.

Observers did not miss this contrast in the personalities of the Senior Rani and her cousin. Henry Bruce found Sethu Lakshmi Bayi 'more reserved, more conscious of her dignity', keeping everyone at an arm's length,[49] while Kuppuswamy Aiyangar described the Junior Rani as 'quick and vivacious'.[50] While the former, encumbered by the weight of tradition, so emphasised by her mother, spent her life living up to her status as a public icon, the latter, whom custom offered no incentives, revelled in that which modernity presented a woman of talent and energy as her. As children they got along well; as the

Junior Rani's granddaughter would later tell, 'They literally grew up together as playmates and sisters. [Sethu Parvathi Bayi] was the more adventurous one, leading while the quieter [Sethu Lakshmi Bayi] followed.'[51] But as the girls grew into adolescence, taking greater stock of their respective situations in life and society, a cleavage of personality began to develop, slowly widening into a major breach. It was, to be sure, not inevitable, and they could have got along and worked together, bringing to the table their many gifts for the common good of Travancore. But the parental provenance of the Ranis was uncomfortable and such that the state was denied the possibility of cooperative action. Instead, Sethu Lakshmi Bayi would head the government and promote the cause of progress through official and carefully thought-out reforms in infrastructure, trade, education and more, while remaining largely conservative. The Junior Rani, on the other hand, exempt from the weight of office and title, could champion more radical causes like birth control and social revisionism; in the 1930s, while contemplating throwing open temples to low-caste Dalit groups, she is said to have demonstrated her conviction to the cause by herself dining with Dalits, which many would have deemed pure sacrilege at the time.[52] In their respective areas of interest, both women left unexcelled legacies; had they worked in tandem, their service to their millions of subjects would have been greater still.

Destiny, however, intended otherwise.

By the end of 1910, Sethu Lakshmi Bayi, now in her teens, was beginning to feel quite alone on account of fewer visits by her family to the palace. Mahaprabha, suffering from declining health and complicated pregnancies, was unable to travel to Trivandrum as frequently as she would have liked to, and it was the Junior Rani's mother who was present in the palace for longer durations. Letters continued to be exchanged, but at one time Mahaprabha was so indisposed that the Senior Rani suggested that perhaps she should not exert herself even to write. It was not an easy recommendation, as these letters were her only link to her distant home.[53] In 1908, when one of her little sisters, whom she was close to, died in Mavelikkara, she could not attend the funeral as tradition prohibited royalty from being seen at private ceremonies of any nature. Kochukunji had, in fact, given Sethu Lakshmi Bayi reason to believe that her sister was actually improving when a telegram arrived with bad news. Tormented by her natural desire to be with her grieving mother, yet trapped within the walls of the palace, all she could do was write, saying, 'I am sorry that I cannot be with you.'[54] Later that month the Rani sought to invite her parents to stay with her, but as it was Kochukunji's turn in Trivandrum, permission was withheld and they had to wait for a prolonged period to see one another. Visits became so difficult to arrange that at one time in the early 1910s, Sethu Lakshmi Bayi even expressed fear that her youngest sister in Mavelikkara might forget who she was because they met so rarely.[55] In words perhaps too wise for her age, she remarked: 'Through attachment, alas, people have to suffer.'[56]

The result of all this was that the Senior Rani matured quickly and reconciled to her practical isolation from her family as well as the personally difficult conditions under which she would always have to live. Part of this was due to political pressure; if the Maharajah were to die before an adult male heir could succeed him, the mantle of power would fall on Sethu Lakshmi Bayi. Already, as Attingal Rani, she felt heavily burdened, and, as her daughter would remark, 'the last thing she wanted was to rule a state. She used to say that when she went to worship our family deity, she would pray that this burden should not be thrust upon her.'[57] But here again Mahaprabha was quick to nip such self-doubt and self-effacement in its politically damaging bud. Even sitting faraway in Mavelikkara, the lady was able to instil into her daughter 'the necessity of doing one's duty, regardless of obstacles', pushing aside Sethu Lakshmi Bayi's reluctance on the subject of one day possibly governing Travancore.[58] In due course, Mahaprabha would find an ally in Rama Varma also, and together they would give the Senior Rani the confidence that would allow her one day to not only assume the reins of power, but to exercise it effectively, even if reluctantly.

But in these early years, Sethu Lakshmi Bayi remained lonely, also developing a distance from the Junior Rani and Kochukunji, taking refuge in her library, reading whenever she could after her religious and ceremonial commitments. She earned, in the process, a reputation as something of a bookworm, always engrossed in Austen and Dickens, or reading biographies of world leaders, or history, poetry, travelogues, and a whole set of foreign journals like *Punch*, the satire magazine, or the *London News*.[59] 'Naturally of a reserved disposition,' a contemporary observed, 'small talk was not her favourite pursuit and her taste for reading appeared to her as a welcome haven.'[60] To some, with her aloofness and regal detachment, she began to seem a snob. But what is interesting is that despite her vast reading and increasing knowledge of the world, the Senior Rani, with her 'inexcitable and very retiring nature', did not demonstrate any interest in actually experiencing it all; she was content with reading about things and not encountering them in person.[61] This was in contrast to the Junior Rani, who also read a great deal but not so much as to neglect her several other activities and dreams of travel. Some did attempt to get Sethu Lakshmi Bayi to take an interest in the outdoors and venture beyond her library, but at that stage, with her worries about Mavelikkara, nothing attracted her. 'Mrs Gresham is trying to get me interested in golf,' she wrote to her father. 'Though I have not the slightest interest in it, out of politeness I did not say so to them.'[62]

In the meantime, the Maharajah decided that it was now time for her to fulfil her duty to the state and their dynasty by producing children. He was by now in his early fifties without a grown heir, which became a pressing necessity with each passing day. While Sethu Lakshmi Bayi was being prepared to assume charge in the event of a contingency, Mulam Tirunal preferred the idea of avoiding such a course altogether. But only if a prince were born now could he be brought up and trained to rule, over the coming decades, by which time the Maharajah would reach his precarious seventies. Considering that all the recent rulers had not survived their fiftieth birthdays, Mulam Tirunal was naturally anxious for a sufficient and healthy line of succession to be established as early as possible. Orders were formally issued, hence, that Sethu Lakshmi Bayi, now fourteen and evidently old enough, should consummate her marriage with Rama Varma.

The storytelling and games of hopscotch were over and the two were to live together now as husband and wife, with that somewhat burdening responsibility of preserving the royal line hanging over their heads. Privacy, in such matters, was also at a complete discount and it was left to court astrologers and managers to work out the details. This was hardly an exclusive feature of the court in Travancore. In the north, in Gwalior state, for instance, when the Maharajah negotiated marriage with a second wife, she was informed that he would ride out with her on Monday mornings and spend Thursday evenings in her bedchamber, with the rest of his time allotted to his other wife and mistresses.[63] In Sethu Lakshmi Bayi's case, the astrologers studied celestial conditions and decreed that 12 February 1909 was an auspicious evening for the queen to share her bed with Rama Varma. Kochukunji wrote to her sister in what was a feeling echoed at court: 'Today is a good day for us and the people of Travancore.'[64]

No sooner had the Senior Rani started living with Rama Varma than she began to be subjected to all sorts of traditional medical treatments to augment her prospects. A dosage of tonics was ingested daily to invigorate her fecundity, even as Mahaprabha fretted and worried in Mavelikkara about their proper administration in her absence. Rama Varma too suddenly found himself facing an onslaught of pressure and public expectation about this mission to father a Maharajah. No chances were taken. For instance, by this time Sethu Lakshmi

Bayi had moved into a separate palace building known as Sarasvati Vilasam, where her childless great-aunt had lived. Adherents at court were quick to connect the late Rani's barrenness to an imagined curse on the building and hysterically prescribe another home for the current Rani. Accordingly, Mulam Tirunal ordered the construction of a new palace within the same compound for Sethu Lakshmi Bayi to occupy. She named it Moonbeam, and would spend most of the next decade here, while her husband lived nearby in a separate building, going to see his royal wife at previously calculated times and dates.

All this angst and worry were soon happily calmed when it was announced in a matter of months that the Senior Rani was with child. Exotic bath oils, incense and fruit arrived from Mavelikkara for the expectant mother, in keeping with custom, and from across Travancore delicacies were sent by well-wishers of the royal family. A great deal of interest was generated among the public also at the prospect of a new prince, and special prayers were offered at important shrines for the benefit of the unborn child. But all this excitement was in vain. For on 18 December 1909, at a little over eight months into the pregnancy, the Senior Rani lost the baby due to some undetermined internal problems. The child was a boy. Disappointment was so palpable not only at court but even among the public that Sethu Lakshmi Bayi went into a state of depression. Nobody said anything to her, but talk began to go around about curses and charms and even poisoning. 'Had the boy lived he would have been a Maharajah,' the Junior Rani's nephew remarks,[65] and it was the dashing of not only the natural instincts of mothering the baby she had carried for months, but also of the very purpose, as she had been taught, of her life. An early miscarriage would not perhaps have affected her as much as this one at so late a stage. Sethu Lakshmi Bayi shut herself from the world, only seeking her husband's companionship. This too was not permitted for some time and Kochukunji, with a hint of sarcasm at the Senior Rani's growing preference for her husband over all of them, wrote to Mahaprabha: 'I do not think she is very upset because of the miscarriage. I think she is worried because her [husband] is not allowed to come here.'[66]

Soon after this, in early 1910 the Junior Rani too consummated her marriage to Ravi Varma, and that fledgling awkwardness between the cousins began to swell rapidly into something of greater and more lasting consequence. While they were children, the business of producing heirs was very much on the backburner. But now it became a contest of sorts as to which among the adoptees would first present to Mulam Tirunal the heir and successor he so ardently desired. As the Junior Rani's granddaughter would state, 'Marriage changed the picture [and the] girls became women at a very young age.'[67] They themselves may not have cared much for this, were it not for inherited tensions from their natural home, where their respective mothers were engaged in their own squabbles. As Kochukunji's grandson would affirm, 'both mothers were responsible to a great degree' in the alienation that was crystallising now into a permanent feature in the lives of the two Ranis.[68] This was, in fact, an eventuality the late Elayarajah had predicted when objecting to their adoption, and indeed, the impending estrangement of historic proportions between Sethu Lakshmi Bayi and Sethu Parvathi Bayi had a great deal to do with the unhappy antecedents of their dominating mothers. The result was, in due course, the dissolution of all peace in the palace and the beginning of years of hateful hostility, reaching an indifferent conclusion only at a stage by when it was too little too late.

Mahaprabha and Kochukunji, it so happened, had never really enjoyed a fond sisterly affection owing to a number of reasons. They were born into a broken home, with their famous father constantly away on his travels and their furiously depressed mother living each day in wasteful misery, until she took to drinking and died young. While they had an extended matrilineal family around them, it was Mahaprabha who had to assume the role of mother and matriarch to her four younger siblings, all when she was nineteen years old. Her natural personality matched this assumption of authority, for she was generally held to have been a most imperious and seriously intimidating individual with an incandescent temper that even her husband took great care not to offend. 'When she walked into a room,' a descendant remarks, 'people would quiver and quake with fear!'[69] Even outside observers could see that Mahaprabha was made of stern material, and one writer described her in relatively modest terms as 'a high-spirited and dignified lady of remarkable personality'.[70] Indeed it is even said that her drunkard brother vanished in 1912, dying somewhere in the Himalayan wilderness, simply because she had reprimanded him vehemently for his wretched habits and told him to be gone from her sight.[71] He, this story goes on, took it to heart and departed in shame.[72]

Kochukunji, on the other hand, while equally capable and resourceful, seems to have harboured a degree of resentment towards her older sister, around whom she had never stood a chance. Mahaprabha was always the favoured daughter, with her acclaimed beauty that drew out all their absentee father's restrained attention, while Kochukunji was the dark-skinned, cockeyed middle sister. Even when they aged, family members, including Kochukunji's own descendants, referred to her sister as the *sundari amooma*, the beautiful grandmother.[73] While Mahaprabha was the favourite of their father, their mother, who by the end despised her painter husband, preferred Kochukunji, perhaps sharing with her a common feeling of neglect.[74] To Kochukunji, the adoption of their daughters and the entitlement of a superior rank to Sethu Lakshmi Bayi seemed a discriminatory repetition of her own secondary status in Mavelikkara. It also did not help that people constantly compared the looks of the two girls—with the Senior Rani, like her mother, winning appreciation generously. The memory that Sethu Parvathi Bayi might not even have been adopted because influential courtiers considered her too 'black', along with her own enduring insecurities, most likely left Kochukunji embittered. Even dispassionate officials, like the Resident, highlighted the contrast in appearance between the Ranis, with one remarking, for instance, that the Senior Rani was 'much more aristocratic in feature and complexion than the Junior'.[75] Just as Kochukunji suffered the brunt of Mahaprabha's dominating radiance, her daughter too appeared to confront a similar fate, and the situation was not a happy one for her to bear.[76]

In the matter of furnishing royal heirs, however, the two girls and their families were placed on an equal footing for the first time. If the Junior Rani were to give birth to a male child first, *he* would be the future Maharajah and her status would improve permanently overnight. Time was crucial, therefore, and it was with happiness that Kochukunji received news in 1911 of her daughter becoming pregnant. Indeed as early as 1907, after Sethu Parvathi Bayi's wedding, Kochukunji had been anxious about her daughter's future, going out, for instance, to consult mystics and others for their expert opinion. One of them, Ayyaswamy, is even believed to have gone into a minor trance and confirmed that Kochukunji's grandson would indeed become king one day.[77] As for Mahaprabha, this newfound confidence of her sister, albeit through the agency of the Junior Rani, came as an unwelcome development, not to speak of her sinister suspicion of Kochukunji, under whose watch the Senior Rani had unexpectedly lost her baby at so advanced a stage that it seemed unnatural. There were also many in the palace to fan the fire and bring about an estrangement between the two sides. As the Junior Rani's nephew states, the girls themselves were too young to have intrigued, but 'people around them began to say all sorts of things to increase mutual suspicion' until things reached a head and the relationship between the families became irreparable.[78]

While there is no evidence to show that Kochukunji ever tried to physically harm the Senior Rani, there is, however, proof of her actively conniving through less efficacious but staggeringly dubious means; years later she was discovered performing peculiar black magic against her niece and 'in this connexion', for example, 'had various objects such as a bracelet buried under the threshold of the [Senior Rani's] door at the latter's palace'.[79] Indeed in the late 1920s the British authorities would issue strict orders for the removal of Kochukunji from the palace because of her role in palace intrigues,[80] while relations of the Senior Rani would recall that the latter's rapport with the Junior Rani improved vastly, and not coincidentally, after the old lady's death in 1946. By this time, however, there was too much odium in the air for a real rapprochement.[81]

On the surface, of course, courtesy was maintained but suspicions underneath lurked on as the Senior Rani suffered two more painful miscarriages in the immediate years after the loss of her first baby. Distance and miscommunication grew and step by step the cousins began leading independent, mutually mistrustful lives. This was partly because their lifestyles were evolving in different directions but most certainly also due to other fears. For one, Rama Varma was beginning to erect a wall around the Senior Rani, evidently for her protection, though many would interpret this as overbearing control. 'His greatest nightmare was that she would be harmed,' a relative would tell, 'and he tried to keep sycophants and admirers off her alike for this reason.'[82] In the process even the Junior Rani was cut off. She too built her own walls of suspicion and fear. As late as the 1940s, when the Junior Rani's family visited Sethu Lakshmi Bayi's palace for feasts, they brought with them meals cooked in their own kitchens.[83] Similarly, while the cousins used to go out driving together earlier, since her pregnancy the Junior Rani had been making her outings separately.[84] She was already alone at Sundara Vilasam now and rarely met with Sethu Lakshmi Bayi, although Kochukunji paid her respects sometimes. The Senior Rani considered all this eyewash and wrote sarcastically that 'when she sees me, she is full of politeness'.[85] On other days she felt like a colossal failure for having let the Maharajah down and failed in her duty. In a rare moment of abject unhappiness, she admitted to her mother, 'I have never felt such depression before.'[86]

This discomfiture within the palace continued until 7 November 1912 when the Junior Rani gave birth to a healthy baby boy and Mulam Tirunal's heir. The news gave, in the account of a contemporary commentator, 'unbounded joy and gratification to His Highness the Maharajah and his dutiful subjects',[87] and Sethu Lakshmi Bayi too forgot recent disaffections and immediately went to see the child. It was she who performed the first ritual of feeding the baby gold and honey, after which he was wrapped up in silks and presented to the Maharajah, literally on a silver platter. 'There was no end to the stream of visitors who came to see the child,' she reported to her mother,[88] and the whole capital rejoiced at the happy event. A state holiday was declared and photographs show streets choked with people celebrating not only in Trivandrum but also in the far-flung towns of the state. The boy was born under the asterism of *Chithira* and six months later was given his formal name as Chithira Tirunal Balarama Varma Tampuran,[89] succeeding to the title of Elayarajah even though he was only an infant. That day, throughout the elaborate ceremonies performed in the palace, for the first time it was Sethu Lakshmi Bayi who stood in the background, eclipsed by the Junior Rani who attracted all attention from everybody present. She sat with pride and discernible joy in the midst of these proceedings, with a supremely buoyant Kochukunji nearby, and it was patent to all that much was about to change in the royal family of Travancore.

The monumental ascent of the Junior Rani had begun.

In December 1913, Sethu Lakshmi Bayi turned eighteen and orders arrived from the Maharajah handing over to her complete and unconditional control over the Sripadam Estate. This was a historic institution that originated when the last of the independent Attingal Ranis surrendered her sovereign rights to Martanda Varma. He amalgamated the region into Travancore proper but under the conditions of the Silver Plate Treaty, income from her 15,000 acres of land continued to accrue to the Senior Rani. The collection of revenue from this tract was conducted in the name of the eldest female member of the royal house, and after deducting an allowance to the Junior Rani and defraying the expenses of their establishment the remainder was placed at the disposal of the Senior Rani. Since the late Lakshmi Bayi's death the government were 'managing these lands for Her Highness [Sethu Lakshmi Bayi] as Her Highness happens to be a minor'.[90] Now that she had come of age, she was entitled to run the Sripadam in her own name, dealing directly with officials and the government. Sethu Lakshmi Bayi, in other words, had a job, if not an heir.

The taking over of the Sripadam was a significant incident and at Moonbeam the Senior Rani received numerous best wishes for her new responsibilities. She was now Attingal Rani in the fullest sense, with a treasury and a substantial organisation to manage. There were accounts to look into, decisions to be taken about the tenants and their problems, not to speak of the added religious duties she had towards the nine temples she now controlled.[91] Many entertained serious apprehensions about whether or not she would be up to the task; as a biographer put it gently, 'people who had the highest respect and admiration for her private virtues thought, however, that a bookworm like her could hardly be a successful business woman.'[92] But to everyone's astonishment, she took on her role with enthusiasm, and aided by her husband (whose role in her life grew daily as she became more and more estranged from the Junior Rani) began to demonstrate her managerial abilities. Writing to her father, Rama Varma remarked with manifest admiration:

> Her Highness takes kindly to the administrative work that has devolved on her. She has such a remarkable grasp of things and has wonderful resources to grapple with difficult problems. Except for sneering cynics we fear no criticism. Her Highness is naturally kind, considerate, and unprevaricating, qualities which are supposed to be necessary adjuncts to one in her position. You may rest assured that she will never be a failure as a woman of responsibility.[93]

A positive professional diversion from troubles in the palace was a welcome change for the Senior Rani. For peace had not returned to the royal family even a year after the birth of a son to her cousin. It was no longer about competing to produce a future ruler, for Sethu Parvathi Bayi had already succeeded in this regard. Indeed, since her son was the Elayarajah of Travancore, the Junior Rani had even demanded that the traditional residence of the heir apparent, known as Vadakkay Kottaram, be placed at her disposal. While it was unprecedented for one of her rank to move out of the Senior Rani's establishment, this was timed so perfectly that it occurred just before Sethu Lakshmi Bayi took over the Sripadam and gained executive control over their servants and palaces, and indirectly over the upbringing of the baby prince. At the end of November, days before the Senior Rani assumed power over the establishment, Sethu Parvathi Bayi departed for her new home along with her son, husband, and mother, hereafter leading her life independent of her cousin.[94]

While Sethu Lakshmi Bayi did not object to this and was possibly even happy that she needn't look forward to domestic disputes, there was much to pain her in the air. At court she was seen as an absolute letdown and even Kerala Varma, who had been very eager to see his favourite ward and his nephew bring forth Mulam Tirunal's heir could not help but express dismay.[95] On the other hand, the baby prince was kept away from the Senior Rani by his mother, whose attitude was of excessive protection. Sethu Parvathi Bayi was hugely paranoid about his safety. When the court physician offered to vaccinate the baby, for instance, she refused to allow it and the Valiya Koil Tampuran was irritated by 'the chickenhearted Rani's unwillingness'.[96] Indeed he was himself often prevented from visiting the young Elayarajah, and whenever he expressed a desire to see the boy, the Junior Rani would submit one excuse after another to avoid him. This was presumably because he was seen as a partisan of the Senior Rani and his nephew, but Kerala Varma was not pleased and blamed all this on Kochukunji and her 'insolent behaviour'.[97] Another explanation was that since the last three heirs apparent to the throne were rumoured to have been poisoned, the Junior Rani was anxious to preserve her son, including from the Senior Rani.[98] As the former's granddaughter would tell, 'My uncle [the baby prince] was of delicate health. Reports of danger to his person were rife. Grandmother guarded him like a tigress defending her cub ... afraid a lot of the time about his safety. Life at the top can be very lonely. You meet many people, but who were your real friends?'[99]

Outlandish stories were put out by the Junior Rani's adherents. One went, for instance, that Kerala Varma intended to *shoot* the baby prince, despite the fact that the old guardian's health had so deteriorated that he was being carried around by servants, unable to walk.[100] Similar accusations were also whispered about the Senior Rani whenever she showed an interest in the baby, causing her to retreat. 'There is not a moment when directly or indirectly they do not insinuate something,' she wrote to her mother only a month after the boy was born.[101] This was worsened by misleading news carried by Kochukunji about the Senior Rani's family. 'Will anyone with humane feelings say [these things],' Sethu Lakshmi Bayi complained. 'I think it is the job of some people to trouble others and make them unhappy. Not only did she not say a word about anyone in Mavelikkara enjoying good health, she said that except [brothers] *everyone* seemed to be suffering from some ailment or another. Both parents were very weak, she said. Though I know it is foolishness to believe everything she says, she gives me cause for some anxiety.'[102]

But there was, in fact, some cause for concern. Mahaprabha, ever so imperious and proud, now faced the ignominy of having to put up with talk about how her daughter was barren and that her adoption was quite a catastrophe as far as Mulam Tirunal was concerned. By 1915, in aggravation of her declining health, she was on the verge of a psychological collapse also. Envious relatives, enjoying every moment of the overbearing Mahaprabha's spectacular fall, loudly bemoaned Sethu Lakshmi Bayi as carrying a curse of bad luck perhaps, pushing the lady towards a nervous breakdown. It was the Senior Rani who eventually learned to ignore all this and gently chided her mother that she hoped she too would develop a thick skin:

> But if you grieve like this, not only will you not achieve anything, it is bad for your body and mind. Do we get upset if people say things to upset us? We will only be satisfying them then. Fortunately we have nothing to grieve about. You should only feel contempt for such behaviour and for such words, not grieve over it ... I am anxious to hear that you are not upset.[103]

Eventually, Sethu Lakshmi Bayi herself had to travel to Mavelikkara with her husband to soothe Mahaprabha, whose dreams and ambitions for her daughter had come crashing down all of a sudden, terminating her own hitherto uncontested reign in Mavelikkara as a kind of grand matriarch feared by one and all. The trip was ostensibly a general tour, so as not to upset the Maharajah, but the Senior Rani was able to spend good time with her mother before returning to the capital. It surprised many that Mahaprabha, who always seemed so undaunted and formidable, suddenly suffered such a defeatist blow, and to the Senior Rani's father and husband it seemed clear that for all her quietness, it was Sethu Lakshmi Bayi who possessed a stronger inner resolve. After taking over the Sripadam especially, it became obvious that while she might have failed the state and the Maharajah in producing heirs, she intended to do good with the responsibility and power entrusted to her in her position as queen.

But barely had a month passed since her assumption of control over the estate when a vexatious dispute began with the Junior Rani, now comfortably settled in her new palace. Typically, the latter ought to have stayed in their common establishment under the Senior Rani's control, and the move away from their joint palace buildings led to confusion about how her affairs were to be managed. The Junior Rani's son had a manager appointed for him, who forwarded to Sripadam bills for her expenses, which Sethu Lakshmi Bayi felt she was not obliged to reimburse, given that her cousin had moved out and was accumulating extraordinary costs. The Junior Rani also desired an increase in her monthly allowance, which also the Senior Rani saw no justification to grant, especially in the face of all the acrimony. As the dispute became serious, Rama Varma wrote to his father-in-law, 'Sripadam affairs now bristle with difficulties.'[104] Sethu Lakshmi Bayi gave vent to her feelings in a series of letters, most of which are now lost. 'I am not writing in every letter that it should be destroyed,' she cryptically notes in one, hoping that her father would 'destroy those that should be destroyed' to avoid their falling into the wrong hands.[105] To her mother she wrote, providing a glimpse into the state of affairs in the palace, as follows:

> It is difficult to write everything that has been happening here. It can only be communicated orally. I hope you can guess the kind of atmosphere here. Though I sometimes long to have you here, on second thought, I think that it is better you are not here now. If you were here, you too would have worried about it, but nothing would have been solved. There is a difference in hearing about it and actually experiencing it. I do not know how long it will take for some settlement to be arrived at. Apart from waiting patiently there is nothing I can do about it.[106]

Traditionally, with the Junior Rani living in the Senior Rani's establishment, she was only entitled to a personal allowance from the Sripadam. In the old days this was determined at the pleasure of the Senior Rani, but in 1876, in the days of Ayilyam Tirunal, the allowance was fixed at Rs 8,400 per annum.[107] Taking this intervention as a precedent, on 10 February 1914, Mulam Tirunal stepped into the dispute and held that Sethu Parvathi Bayi could now have Rs 12,000 from the Sripadam per annum, with Rs 48,000 allotted for general expenses, and Rs 30,000 settled on the Senior Rani for her own personal needs.[108] In the interests of peace, Sethu Lakshmi Bayi accepted this mediation, even though she was certain that there would still be cause for complaints. The whole of 1914 then passed with uncertain relations between the two palaces, until there were some unusual events that came about unexpectedly. In April that year the Junior Rani felt urged to explain her behaviour to Mahaprabha and conducted a long conversation 'justifying her conduct and procedure' over recent events.[109] Then, while the Senior Rani was still not encouraged to get too close to the little Elayarajah, on a few rare occasions Kochukunji herself ventured to bring him to Moonbeam to see her. 'He does not look like he has grown very much since I last saw him,' Sethu Lakshmi Bayi noted after one meeting, adding that '5 or 6 big teeth have come out'.[110] But none of these efforts led to a real reconciliation and the divide continued to widen drastically between the cousins and their two mothers.

Sethu Lakshmi Bayi, however, would remember the year not because of all her family difficulties, but because of a tragedy that would take her several years to come to terms with. This was the unexpected death of the Valiya Koil Tampuran on 22 September. Kerala Varma had a personal custom every year of visiting the Mahadeva Temple in Vaikom in north Travancore, and in 1914 too he bid his usual adieus to the Senior Rani and her husband before leaving. At Vaikom he went through his routine of prayers and made offerings to the deity, before going down to Harippad to spend time with his family, including with

Rama Varma's sisters: Amba, Ambika and Ambalika. Then, on the morning of 20 September, having breakfasted with his relatives at the family home, the Valiya Koil Tampuran started by car for the capital with Prof. A.R. Rajaraja Varma, his nephew and a distinguished Sanskrit grammarian. The two men were deeply engrossed in conversation as the car approached the outskirts of the town of Kayamkulam where an accident occurred suddenly.

State cars of the Maharajah in those days were rather lightly built, with broad sideboards where it was customary for uniformed escorts to stand as flanks even when the vehicle was in motion. As the Valiya Koil Tampuran reached Kayamkulam, a stray dog jumped on to the road and one of the men attempted to scare it away by kicking at the animal. This sudden movement gave the whole car a heavy jolt so much so that the vehicle skidded off the road into a ditch, injuring everyone in and on it. Kerala Varma, who was just a year short of completing seventy years and already in poor health, was badly injured and languished by the roadside for some time before a palanquin arrived and carried him to Mavelikkara for medical assistance. Whatever could be hastily arranged in terms of good-quality treatment was provided, but it was in vain; two days later the Valiya Koil Tampuran succumbed to his injuries. Writing a remembrance to the man, the master poet Kumaran Asan lamented:

> We do not think that in Kerala there is any great man other than Kerala Varma whom all Malayalis, irrespective of caste or creed, love and respect with so much sincerity, and remember with so much gratitude. When will it be possible for us to see again a combination like this of qualities such as scholarship, poetic talents, goodness, generosity, family prestige and character of the highest standard? O! Land of Kerala, thy light has gone! Thou art engulfed in darkness![111]

Whether or not Kerala was engulfed in darkness, Sethu Lakshmi Bayi most certainly was. She had always been the Valiya Koil Tampuran's pet and he had stood by her when issues arose with the Junior Rani recently, acting as her spokesperson to represent her views at the Maharajah's palace also. He had shared her sadness at her inability to give birth to a child and the consequent humiliation it had brought for her and her family. It was an injustice, Sethu Lakshmi Bayi felt, that she could not even have a look at his body before it was cremated, for as usual she was prohibited by royal decorum from going to Mavelikkara for that purpose; for all his years at court and as practically a member of the royal house, he was still not formally royal and would, inevitably, be treated as a mere consort on his death. But like before, she steeled herself together and accepted that this was how things were and she would have to live with it.

By 1914, at only nineteen, the Senior Rani had grown up and matured, both due to her natural tendency towards seriousness and also because of the circumstances she was enveloped in. Her mother's health was becoming precarious, her guardian had passed away, relations with the Junior Rani were a disaster beneath that veneer of politeness, problems were starting to arise with the Maharajah, and then in December it was also ordered that Miss Watts, whose company and friendship she looked at as a huge relief from everyday palace politics, was to have her services terminated at the Maharajah's orders, who felt that the Senior Rani no longer needed formal instruction. 'I see Madam often when I go out for drives,' she wrote dejectedly to her mother. 'Though she does not read with me, I get the opportunity to get books and discuss them with her. Now that I get books to read, you need not worry about how I spend my spare time.'[112] It was not an easy spell for the Senior Rani and books, as usual, became her escape from the troubles of the world. But for all that, she was really quite alone.

4

The Second Favourite

'Nowadays letters from the Palace are becoming rare,' Sethu Lakshmi Bayi ruminated in a note to her father in July 1915, pondering over recent convulsions that had left a deteriorating impact upon her relations with the Maharajah.[1] Ostensibly it was those grating quarrels with the Junior Rani that provoked his disgruntlement. However, Mulam Tirunal's annoyance really had other more sinister authors, lurking in the obscure shadows of his sequestered palace. The Maharajah, to be certain, was most displeased with the Senior Rani's childlessness; he had made it unambiguously clear from the onset that he viewed her adoption from the 'purely political standpoint' of procuring heirs.[2] Without those heirs, Sethu Lakshmi Bayi's position at court was precarious. While she was a child, the Maharajah is believed to have been very fond of her; every fortnight she would be heralded with the Junior Rani for an audience, and if the children impressed Mulam Tirunal, special presents would arrive for them at Sundara Vilasam. Sethu Lakshmi Bayi seems to have earned particular favour for her prodigious intelligence, and once, for instance, riotous excitement was caused when an enormous emerald arrived as a token of the Maharajah's appreciation.[3] By 1915, however, the Senior Rani's attitude presented a problem to Mulam Tirunal and his unofficial advisers, who perceived her as disrespectful of his kingly authority. Rama Varma too was unflatteringly singled out and held as a contemptuous upstart of mediocre talent, bent upon swaying his wife's better judgement, a charge that would constantly be made against him into the future as well.

While Mulam Tirunal was certainly aggravated by these considerations, the nefarious influence of what has been called the 'palace bureau' contributed explicitly towards perpetuating the growing differences in the royal household. Much of this had to do with the Maharajah's own muted personality. Born in 1857, Mulam Tirunal was left an orphan when his mother died eleven days after his birth and his father before his third birthday. His uncles brought him up, alongside an 'imbecile' brother, but despite the affection lavished on him, there was no tangible compensation for the deficiency of parental and, especially, maternal warmth. By the time he was in his early adolescence, his uncles, Ayilyam Tirunal and Visakham Tirunal, could not see eye to eye, and the then Ranis were also a 'source of ceaseless trouble' with their numerous squabbles and domestic difficulties.[4] The royal family was, in every way, an unhappy backdrop while Mulam Tirunal grew into manhood. Despite the incessant internecine feuds around him, however, the young prince was a diligent student who minded his business, once causing Ayilyam Tirunal to openly remark that he was 'the one member of the royal family that causes me no trouble.'[5] The Resident too saw in him great promise. 'He is fond of European society,' it was noted, 'dances quadrilles and such-like dances with European ladies, and joins in lawn tennis ... He is decidedly intelligent and possesses very good commonsense. In my opinion, he is likely to prove an excellent ruler.'[6]

The favour he enjoyed with the Maharajah and his consort, Kalyani Pillai, led in 1879 to Mulam Tirunal's marriage with their adopted daughter, Ananthalakshmi. But prospects of conjugal happiness were also denied him when death snatched her away in 1882, leaving Mulam Tirunal deserted again.[7] 'The loss is an irreparable one,' he wrote to Kerala Varma at that time, 'and it is more than I could bear with all my fortitude.'[8] These accumulated unhappy experiences, despite his best efforts, went a long way in moulding the man's character, even as he became increasingly dedicated to his family deity and largely preoccupied with affairs of the Sri Padmanabhaswamy Temple where he found welcome solace.

Three years later in 1885 he ascended the throne after the death of Visakham Tirunal, and his reign was decidedly remarkable, standing out as one of the best in the history of Travancore. For instance, in 1885 the government's spending on education was Rs 1,80,437 per annum, which by 1915 rose to a signally inspiring Rs 15,69,239. Similarly, the public works allotment, practically unheard of in other principalities where state exchequers were treated as personal reserves by parochial rulers, rose from Rs 9,37,118 to Rs 23,92,172 during the same period; and other departments of the administration also witnessed impressive developments.[9] The total revenue of Travancore, which was Rs 66 ½ lakhs with Rs 2 crore worth of trade when Mulam Tirunal came to power, rose to Rs 150 lakh and Rs 6 ¼ crore respectively by 1915.[10] It is also laudable that even as the prosperity of the state grew so significantly, the spending of the royal family itself increased only by a very marginal fraction, from Rs 7,57,650 in 1885 to Rs 8,12,564 in 1915.[11] Thus, Mulam Tirunal was successful in maintaining the reformist administration established by his visionary uncles, retaining for Travancore the coveted title of 'Model State of India' that the British lavished upon it among all its other princely competitors.

But alongside the revenues of the state, there also rose at the centre of power a noxious amount of corruption and vulgar self-seeking, all under the Maharajah's nose, patently inconsistent with his good record as an administrator. The situation was not at all unprecedented. Ayilyam Tirunal, for instance, despite his praiseworthy efforts to bring up the state to modern Western standards, was notorious as 'a moral wreck and a sexual pervert'.[12] He also employed a large number of henchmen who were above the law and would become forerunners of a budding 'palace bureau' that was beyond the jurisdiction of the government. The bureau itself would come to its fullest fruition during Mulam Tirunal's reign, turning Travancore, as an observer notes, into 'a land of scandals' despite impressive statistics.[13] 'It must be admitted,' the Resident wrote in a confidential note in 1908, 'that the Maharajah is weak.' He was quite 'sincerely desirous of ruling well' but 'the backdoor influence of the palace favourites appears to dominate everything'.[14] Within twenty years of his reign, thus, the original enterprise and enthusiasm that had marked his government's enlightened rule was conspicuously receding, as was Mulam Tirunal's interest in anything other than his ceremonial and religious duties. 'I fancy that he is growing more reserved and shrinks from appearing in public,' recorded the Resident,[15] who relentlessly deplored that 'sinister influence behind the curtain, which colours all his actions and perverts his best resolutions'.[16]

By this time the number of favourites had shrunk and two prominent individuals had developed rival clout in the palace. Until the turn of the twentieth century, the real force behind Mulam Tirunal was a Brahmin, Anantha Rama Iyer, better known as Saravanai or *Fouzdarswamy*. Described by one British emissary as 'the ICB (illiterate cook boy)', this son of the Maharajah's wet nurse possessed such influence over the ruler that 'the impression of the natives is that he has bewitched the Maharajah'.[17] The contemporary student activist, G.P. Pillai, was more scathing in his review of conditions in the palace:

> Soon after His Highness' accession, he raised a low illiterate menial of his ... who began life on a Rupee-and-a-half per mensem to the place of

> Palace Manager and subsequently Fouzdar Commissioner, on a salary of Rs 500 a month ... Ever since, the influence of this royal favourite has been paramount in the State. The Maharajah is a pliant tool in [his] hands, and like a marionette is being tossed about by his favourite for purposes of self-gratification. In the presence of the Fouzdar [i.e., Saravanai who was given this hollow office with high pay],[18] the mind of the Maharajah is blank and his arms are powerless. He is so completely enslaved that his very existence is intertwined with that of his favourite. In domestic as well as State matters, he is led by the nose of his eccentric adherent who always plays the Sir Oracle. The payment of bribes to him or a slavish obedience of his orders is the only road to preferment and promotion [in the official services].[19]

There is some political exaggeration in this account, for G.P. was something of a radical, but a further allegation by him that the palace bureau was responsible for Mulam Tirunal's prolonged singlehood in order to retain their control over him is interesting. Newspapers like the *Madras Standard* had already censured Saravanai for acting as the Maharajah's procurer of women,[20] and when a marriage proposal once came about, it was thwarted because the lady refused to toe the favourite's line.[21] The Maharajah, in the meantime, was recorded to 'brighten up at best upon ceremonial occasions but often lapses into a dreamy stupor', as if really under a wicked spell of some kind.[22]

Incidentally, Saravanai's fall from favour did indeed occur only after Mulam Tirunal took a second wife and new characters were introduced into this devious political saga. Sometime in the 1890s the Maharajah made his acquaintance with a certain lady known as Kartyayani Pillai. She belonged to an ordinary family in the capital but her father served as a retainer to that grand dame, Kalyani Pillai, the adoptive mother of Mulam Tirunal's first wife.[23] It is believed that it was she who, as the Maharajah's mother-in-law, suggested he take Kartyayani as his wife instead of continuing to trudge through his days as an unhappy widower. The latter dutifully obliged, the story goes, and in 1896 a son was born to them.[24] However, it was only in 1899 that the Maharajah formally 'espoused' the lady and conferred aristocracy upon her, declaring her his official consort.[25] In 1901 a daughter was born and it appeared as though Mulam Tirunal's family life was perfectly restored, and joyful days were in the offing.[26]

But if a new wife and children were expected to wean the Maharajah away strategically from the hateful influences in his palace, they succeeded only partially. Kartyayani Pillai seems to have enjoyed her sudden ennoblement into royal society, learning some Sanskrit and even 'a few polite English phrases' to fit in. 'She has a light complexion, and is short and very stout,' a newspaper profile in London chronicled, possessed of 'an excess of adipose tissue', which was seen as 'a sign of prosperity'. 'The ruler's wife, no doubt,' it somewhat mockingly concludes, 'is lucky as few women are, and she has therefore every incentive to be as fat as Nature may let her grow.'[27] But while the Ammachi inflated in bodily proportions, conditions in the palace only deteriorated, with the influence of Saravanai, as the First Favourite, being supplanted by that of a fresh entrant who was destined for even greater notoriety as the Second Favourite.

This was an infamous individual known to history as Sankaran Tampi, 'Comptroller of the Palace'. The matter would still appear to be relatively straightforward—of one shady acolyte succeeding another—except when one considers that Tampi was, in fact, the first husband of Kartyayani Pillai. In other words, when Mulam Tirunal became acquainted with his wife, she was already a married woman. Her husband in those days was known as Sanku Pillai, a low-level servant who had been a menial to Visakham Tirunal.[28] Upon relinquishing his wife to the Maharajah, however, he too was dignified with the title of Tampi, ordinarily bestowed only upon the sons of Travancore's monarchs. He would go on to marry the younger sister of his now ex-wife, but this would not prevent him from being publicly embarrassed as 'the former husband of the Maharajah's present wife'.[29] More revealingly, the episode demonstrated again the weakness within Mulam Tirunal, whose judgement could be swayed by the satisfaction of rather less lofty earthly delights, perhaps even justifying the stinging assertion that 'all the pomp and splendour associated with his rule was but a smoke screen to hide his debauchery, lasciviousness, and lust'.[30]

Into the twentieth century, Sankaran Tampi acquired unto himself a most dominating presence at court, and none other than the Chief Justice of Travancore himself acknowledged in 1906 during certain legal proceedings that he 'could be influenced by bribes to have Palace orders issued in favour of any party he wished to favour'.[31] This led to a blow on the man's considerable power and income, and 'he swore', in the words of the Resident, 'vengeance on the Chief Justice', getting Mulam Tirunal to transfer him out of Travancore.[32] Even the highest authorities in the British establishment were aware of this unsettling influence of the Second Favourite, and in 1903 the Governor of Madras had written to Lord Curzon that the man was selling prized government positions to the highest bidders. Indeed, such was the level of the Maharajah's predilection for and dependence on his favourite that there were even rumours of a homosexual romance between them, but the Madras Government seems to have dismissed these.[33] 'The state of the Court here,' a Bishop summarised, 'is very bad. Unworthy favourites rule and we hear of great scandals.'[34]

The Dewan Sir V.P. Madhava Rao made efforts, then, to rid the palace of the coterie Tampi commanded, but without success most likely because of the backdoor access the latter enjoyed through marriage to the palace.[35] The Dewan persuaded Mulam Tirunal to stop accepting petitions and official requests at his palace, so as to bypass Tampi and his channel to power, but ultimately failed and departed from the state, causing it a great loss of talent and statesmanlike ability. The next Dewan, Sir P. Rajagopalachari, more expediently chose to exude great strength but did not really upset the favourite. Instead, joining hands in many respects, they would preside over a period of 'considerable political confusion and chaos'.[36] The Dewan himself was none the better as far as moral character went (one newspaper amusingly accused him of staring at the Maharajah's wife from across a street, which was evidently the least of his sins),[37] but 'few had the courage to speak out'.[38] The arrangement worked excellently for the Second Favourite and soon he became exceedingly wealthy through his illicit enterprises, and was treated right royally wherever he went in the principality. 'Officers big and small stood in whispering humbleness before him,' which was hardly surprising since they probably owed him their jobs in return for liberal commissions and underhand fees.[39] It is even said that Tampi used to attend meetings of the state's representative organs, watching 'intently', and ensuring that no member who was likely to criticise him or the palace bureau got to speak.[40] Yet some did, to be fair, raise voices against this criminal venality passing off as royal decree. One outspoken journalist called Ramakrishna Pillai wrote a series of editorials in the *Swadeshabhimani*, courageously berating the administration for its spectacular decadence. The titles fittingly capture the situation, even as they infuriated the favourite: 'Tampuran Tampi', 'The Supremacy of the Courtiers', 'The Royal Servants and the Kingdom of Travancore', 'Why Can't We Exile Sankaran Tampi?' and so on. As it happened, it was the journalist who got exiled.[41]

When Sethu Lakshmi Bayi and the Junior Rani were still children, they knew of Tampi mainly as an important confidante of the Maharajah and as a relative of his Ammachi. But it was only after they grew up that they realised the tremendous extent of the feared Second Favourite's power, which surpassed even their traditional and ceremonially supreme status at court. To please Tampi was to please the Maharajah, and it was clear that getting into his bad books did not bode well for whoever dared; rumours persisted that that tragic succession of deaths in the early years of the twentieth century, of the late Rani and her nephews, had something to do with their having upset Tampi.[42] But, as fate would have it, the Senior Rani's consort decided to do exactly opposite of what he was advised. Rama Varma had now, with the death of his great-uncle, succeeded to the title of Valiya Koil Tampuran and treated his role as partner and adviser to the Senior Rani with self-righteous gravity, and more importantly, an unbending sense of propriety that bordered on the unreasonable. 'He recognised that the Maharajah was a weak person,' Sethu Lakshmi Bayi's nephew notes, 'and referred to Tampi in highly sarcastic terms.' He thought Mulam Tirunal was an old-fashioned character whose best days had passed, and it was no surprise that the Maharajah resented such near-seditious insubordination from a man whose sole claim to prominence and, indeed, even a personality, was his marriage into the royal house. 'It is amusing that an Edwardian individual should consider a Victorian ruler antiquated in his view of the world,' the nephew continues, 'and although he wouldn't say it in so many words, it was clear he disliked the Maharajah as well as his favourite. The Senior Rani would never say anything of the sort. She might have harboured negative feelings, but she never expressed what she felt openly.'[43]

The conflict with Tampi was precipitated over relatively minor problems. Ten years ago Kerala Varma had clashed with the Maharajah when the latter permitted Tampi to appoint one of his nominees as manager of the minor Sethu Lakshmi Bayi's Sripadam Estate. But at the time, perhaps because he feared this would land him in hot waters, he quickly withdrew, writing in his diary: 'to avoid rupture, I sent a few lines apologising'.[44] Similarly, in 1914 the Senior Rani's father recorded how an important government post meant to be given to a meritorious candidate was 'at the nick of the moment, as if by jugglery' handed on a platter to one of Tampi's nephews.[45] 'It has come to this,' he indignantly vented, 'that anything can be done now with impunity' if it had the Second Favourite's blessings.[46] For many years Tampi had been making the Sripadam appointments, but after Sethu Lakshmi Bayi took over, she began taking independent decisions, assigning positions to those she preferred. In July 1914, for instance, when her old manager retired, the Senior Rani settled the post on someone she found competent instead of one of the favourite's nominees. 'The Maharajah does not seem to have liked this appointment,' her father wrote, the implication being that although she had traditional authority over her estates, she was not meant to actually *exercise* it in defiance of the Second Favourite.[47]

There were other more serious lapses on the part of the Senior Rani as well, in effect placing her directly in Tampi's line of fire. On state occasions and ceremonial events such as Kerala's national festival of Onam, it was customary for all important officials and courtiers to call on Sethu Lakshmi Bayi and receive presents. When she was a child, Tampi was always specially invited at the Maharajah's instance, besides being treated with superior deference. Now that she was older and more aware of the kind of dubious character he was, the Senior Rani ceased to extend an invitation to him in 1914 on more than one occasion. In June, for instance, she ignored him at the time of a festival and then again in September for Onam. Mulam Tirunal was extremely agitated by this slight to his lackey, and was apparently 'anxious that the Rani should see and get his favourite's favour'.[48] The Junior Rani, perhaps bearing in mind her son's best interests, on the other hand, was more careful and worldly-wise in her dealings with Tampi; at Vishu she not only invited him to her residence, but even entertained him for an hour along with her consort.[49] What surprised everyone was that the rebellious and unorthodox Junior Rani had known not to upset the favourite, whereas the gentle and retiring Sethu Lakshmi Bayi had declared war on him. Surely, they presumed, she could not have done this had it not been for misguided outside influence. And the only person in a position to sway her was her recalcitrant consort, Rama Varma. As her father confirmed, 'The MR [Maharajah] seems to be in very bad odour with [the consort] for advising his wife in all matters.'[50]

What irked many in the palace was not only his confident personality and his increasing tendency to act superior to others, seemingly forgetting his peripheral place and humble origins in life, but also the Senior Rani's determined insistence that he be treated with more respect than was due to a mere consort. His sole legal entitlements in this role might have been Rs 200 and a few minor emoluments, but as a matter of practice, Sethu Lakshmi Bayi had been granting him greater authority. She had already disposed of the custom that prohibited him from driving in the same carriage with her, and began to go out in his company, despite screeching objections that this was not good decorum for an Attingal Rani. In the words of the watchful Resident, she 'being well educated objects to treating her husband as was customary in the old days and is anxious that his position ... should be kept as high as possible'.[51] This was in manifest contrast to the Junior Rani who had always kept her consort, now holding the title of Kochu Koil Tampuran, 'in his proper place'.[52] As a result, Rama Varma, who ought to have known that his was a subordinate role at court, began to take liberties he felt he was entitled to, irritating not only those who were more orthodox and unchanging, but also everyone on whose sensitive toes he stepped in the process. 'Heard that the MR again went down upon the consort furiously and pitiably,' wrote Sethu Lakshmi Bayi's father yet again, 'on some foolish and hateful grudge.'[53]

One of those who disliked the new status Rama Varma had assumed was the Junior Rani. Her ceremonial prerogatives were already inferior to those of her cousin, but one of the few rights she had was that of keeping the consorts standing in her presence. She exercised this power unremittingly, affronting the new Valiya Koil Tampuran, who felt he ought to have been exempted from bowing to the Junior Rani since he was consort to the Senior Rani. 'He was afraid,' it was noted, that 'she might treat him in the same casual manner as she treats her own husband,' and following age-old custom, 'exercise her right ... to keep [him] standing in her presence'.[54] This only led to an exacerbation of the jarring animosity between the cousins, for Sethu Lakshmi Bayi fully encouraged her consort's presumed precedence over the Junior Rani. The latter, in retaliation, prohibited her own husband from going to Moonbeam, where he would be obliged to bow to the Senior Rani. The episode was indicative of how unyielding and headstrong Rama Varma was becoming, with the active consent of his royal wife, much to the regret of others at court. To them, the Senior Rani had forgotten that her loyalties lay to her dynasty and not to this outsider consort. As Kuttan Tampuran recorded after a meeting with the Junior Rani's secretary, even disputes between the cousins were blamed upon Rama Varma. 'He [the secretary] was speaking to me for a long time a very elongated tissue of audacious lies and misrepresentations in justification and support of the conduct and procedure of those he serves. All the fault he would throw on the SR's consort.'[55]

The Maharajah then, backed by an irate Tampi, decided it was time now to put the consort in his rightful place and teach him a lesson in discipline and due deference to power. In January 1914, for instance, when he was seriously unwell at his family home in Harippad and Sethu Lakshmi Bayi requested a car from the royal stables to fetch him, her application was promptly refused.[56] 'For the past few days I have had no peace of mind,' she confessed in a letter.[57] In what was more hard-hitting, when Kerala Varma lay dying in Mavelikkara, Rama Varma met with the Maharajah and asked for a motor to take him there. 'But the relentless and spiteful **** did not sanction it but told him to make his own arrangements,' despite the direness of the hour. As it happened, Kerala Varma passed away that afternoon without his nephew by his side.[58] If this was meant to break the resolve of the Senior Rani and her consort, it failed miserably. Even the former's father thought it was a lost cause to try persuading them to be more accommodative of Mulam Tirunal's favourites, writing that Rama Varma was 'very firm and immovable in his attitude and character'.[59] It was to become a principal trait in his personality, and as a granddaughter would later remark, 'he never forgot a good gesture, or a bad one'.[60] Sethu Lakshmi Bayi too refused to bend before the corrupt influences in the palace. Perhaps her harshest words were elicited when Saravanai died a quick and easy death in 1912 and she wrote sardonically to her father, 'The fact that he did not suffer more can only be attributed to his luck.'[61] Her relatives too blamed all the trouble on Sankaran Tampi. 'After supper we were speaking with the Rani and the consort for a long time,' her father diarised, 'about the foolish policy of the heartless Maharajah—perhaps to satisfy the wicked whims of the scoundrel favourite.'[62]

In the years after 1915 the Senior Rani, then, interacted with the Maharajah only on occasions of state where it was essential they met and presented blissful family harmony before their people. Perhaps she encouraged Rama Varma's defiance of the Maharajah and of his favourites because she herself could not rebel, encumbered as she was by custom and her high station. Her husband, then, became the outlet of her own frustrations. But harassment from Tampi continued regularly, including upon members of her extended family, only making her more resolute in what she was certain was principled opposition. Her older brother, for instance, whom she lovingly called *annan*, had finished his studies at law school in Madras and was working as a junior with the distinguished criminal lawyer Dr S. Swaminathan.[63] But in order to be closer to his family he desired to find employment in Travancore, even expecting that as brother to the queen, he might obtain a dignified position with relative ease. Sethu Lakshmi Bayi's advice to him, however, was to stay as far away as possible from their homeland, not only because prospects were better elsewhere but also because the palace bureau stood grimacing in the way of anyone connected to her. Writing to her father, she sighed:

> Annan said that if he gets a job here it would be much better but in the present state of affairs, just as you remarked about your nephew, it is neither qualification nor worthiness that is of any account. If you want to live in honour, you have to go to some other state, because it is the speciality of the times. Even though nepotism is not a praiseworthy quality, if a person who is worthy comes, he is rejected on the ground that he is related to us, and no help of any sort is offered to him. What justice there is in this I cannot understand![64]

But she reconciled to the fact that though she was the queen of Travancore, Tampi had ordered a blockade on her authority wherever it mattered. It did not deter her, however, from seeking the best options for her siblings. 'The Senior Rani's brothers were somewhat complacent in the beginning,' remarks Kochukunji's grandson, 'because they were brothers to the queen and nobody would refuse them anything.' But 'she wisely saw the damage this could cause, taking prompt action to ensure they left the state and carved out independent careers for themselves,' not strutting about as courtly masters and royal relatives.[65] While Annan would venture into India's fledgling private sector, ultimately becoming Director of Finances for the prestigious Tata Group, the Senior Rani's second brother became a senior director with the South Indian Railways. The third was a qualified lawyer but owing to poor health lived all his life with Sethu Lakshmi Bayi, editing books and engaged in academic pursuits until his death in the 1940s. The fourth trained for the prestigious Indian Civil Services (ICS) but returned from London instead with an MA in archaeology and history, going on to become Assistant Registrar of the University of Madras. Her youngest brother, who was seventeen years her junior and practically like a son to her, followed the eldest into the private sector with the Associated Cement Companies Ltd. after his studies in London, retiring as a senior executive as well. This was in contrast to the Junior Rani's brothers, who, barring a single exception, remained in Travancore, enjoying various posts under the patronage of their royal sister.[66]

Sethu Lakshmi Bayi's brothers[67] also made excellent marital alliances, with the eldest wedding a niece of P.G.N. Unnithan, the final Dewan of Travancore before India became independent. The second married a daughter of Sir M. Krishnan Nair, a Dewan of Travancore who served Mulam Tirunal and was a member of the Executive Council of the Governor of Madras. The third, who was unwell, married a lady from the local aristocracy; the fourth the granddaughter of the titular Zamorin of Calicut; and the fifth a daughter of a member of the Legislative Council of Madras and a prominent Malabar zamindar. Most of these ladies were from historic families outside Travancore and were highly educated, and through them the Senior Rani was connected to several distinguished individuals, including among them Appu Nair, who assisted B.R. Ambedkar in the crafting of the Constitution of India; the ICS brothers, Achutha Menon and Madhava Menon; Prabhakaran Tampan, an important figure in the land reforms movement in Malabar; and even a Cochin Jew called Miss Rebecca Violet Simon. Interestingly, Sethu Lakshmi Bayi's second brother was offered the hand in marriage of the Maharajah's exceedingly pampered daughter from his controversial second wife, with a gold-plated Rolls Royce and a substantial fortune as an added incentive. But the girl rivalled her mother in the sheer enormity of her well-fed dimensions, and although her riches momentarily tempted the brother, he politely declined the offer. It was Rama Varma who again played a role in this, advising him to beware the glimmering seductions of wealth, perhaps offending Mulam Tirunal, who was anxious that his daughter should marry the Senior Rani's brother.[68] She was later wedded to the Junior Rani's sibling, Rajan Tampuran, before dying young in the 1920s, though not before Mulam Tirunal had obtained for her a decoration from the British for nothing in particular than to flatter his darling daughter's vanity.[69]

In the meantime, there was great excitement in the capital when a declaration was made that the renowned Maharajah of Baroda, Sir Sayajirao Gaekwar, was come to Travancore on a state visit with his equally illustrious wife, Maharani Chimnabai II in July 1915. The Gaekwars were, husband and wife, accomplished to formidable levels, with a most fascinating history. The Maharajah was raised as an illiterate farmhand until he was twelve, when suddenly, by a curious twist of fate, he was adopted into the royal family of Baroda and enthroned as its ruler. Tutored and trained thereafter by Sir T. Madhava Rao (who had been Ayilyam Tirunal's minister in the 1860s) and F.A.H. Elliott, he became a reformist ruler with a hotly disputed streak of rebellion and independence. During the Delhi Durbar in 1911, when King George visited India and held court for all his feudatory Maharajahs and Nawabs, the Gaekwar had refused to bow to him, literally turning his back to the mighty Emperor of the British Raj. He had since become, unusually enough for a feudal potentate, a darling of Indian nationalists. His wife, Chimnabai, was also most interesting, having broken the purdah system that kept most north Indian ladies in veiled and backward seclusion, and whose favourite sport was roller-skating around her palace corridors, with her sari flying behind her.[70] She had even authored a well-received book called *The Position of Women in Indian Life* (1911), recommending amelioration through options ranging from decorative needlework to hard farm labour. The Gaekwars were also extensively well travelled and among India's earliest princes to sojourn to Europe and America, despite misgivings of religion and caste. In every respect, then, they were unconventional visitors to the durbar in Travancore, and all in this cautious cocoon of conservative traditionalism anticipated their arrival most eagerly.

Mulam Tirunal was desirous that everything should be perfect for the reception of his celebrated guests, not least because Baroda stood higher in that jealously sustained order of precedence of Indian princely states, but also because over recent years it had made such tremendous progress under Sayajirao that it exceeded Travancore's longstanding record in enlightened governance. Sethu Lakshmi Bayi was also nervous about the visit, for she would have to play official hostess for the first time. Writing to her family, she expressed embarrassment about being forced to receive such cultivated personalities in 'this old Sarasvati Vilasam', and wondered about what she could do to beautify her unfashionable surroundings.[71] An army of chandelier cleaners, floor polishers and painters moved in for a few days, with the resultant noise carrying over to Moonbeam, where the Senior Rani worked out the minor details of the visit such as the delicacies to be offered to the guests, appropriate presents for the Maharani, and suitably urbane conversational openings that would not betray her own self-conscious experience of the world. The Junior Rani in the meantime expressed a desire to receive the guests separately in her own right instead of meeting them at Sethu Lakshmi Bayi's formal reception, but permission was not granted. It was, to her regret, considered 'bad etiquette' to have guests received by a secondary princess.[72]

On 8 July the Gaekwars and their ménage arrived in Trivandrum and were evidently impressed by the arrangements made by their hosts. 'Every house, however small, had its token of welcome to the Maharajah and the Maharani,' one of their English companions noted, adding: 'the road was hung from tree to tree with strings of flowers and leaves, neat school-houses and every village seemed to have poured out twin floods of boys and girls to line the roads, to wave paper flags, to cheer.'[73] The children were plausibly unwilling participants in this spectacle, hardly aware of who they were waving at really, but in the capital the government was all ready for the final show. The Maharajah called a special durbar for his guests and hosted a banquet in their honour, even as the state forces saluted and fired gun salutes and the majestically caparisoned elephants trumpeted and marched. The Gaekwars inspected a number of establishments and institutions, to study the modernisation of Travancore. On 9 July, for instance, they went to the Napier Museum outside the fort and to the public library. They also visited the School of Art, the Maharajah's Colleges, and the slightly newer Women's College where Miss Watts had, somewhat bizarrely, orchestrated a chorus to render the state anthem of Baroda in Malayalam, to the accompaniment of a piano and violins.[74]

The formal visit to the Attingal Rani at Sarasvati Vilasam, however, turned out to be a short affair and not entirely worth the alarm Sethu Lakshmi Bayi brought upon herself. Due to all the formality the women could not speak for too long beyond regular courtesies and the call did not last more than fifteen minutes. The Ranis followed the Gaekwars to their guest house after this, where, however, they enjoyed a forty-five-minute discussion. 'Both ladies,' the Baroda records note, 'speak English fluently and are vastly interested in affairs of the world beyond the boundaries of Travancore.'[75] The next morning they paid their formal call on the Maharajah and the Maharani, and this time sat with them for nearly two hours. Describing the whole thing to her parents, Sethu Lakshmi Bayi said:

> If you ask me what I spoke to them for so long, I would not be able to explain. It was mainly about differences in administration and caste that we spoke. They asked many questions concerning the customs here. They found it difficult to understand our [matrilineal] system. They have pressed their invitation on us to visit Baroda. I never thought they would esteem us so highly. Since everything went off so well, I must say I am very happy.[76]

Indeed, Sayajirao Gaekwar was most charmed by both the Ranis and it was at his insistence that they spent such a prolonged period of time with him and his wife. Sethu Lakshmi Bayi rose several times to take their leave, only to be persuaded to stay for some time longer and continue chatting. She would have liked to take up their invitation and visit Baroda, though as she wrote dryly to her father, 'you know the conditions here very well. I think it is better left unsaid.'[77] Nevertheless, both guests left a very good impression on the Senior Rani who was also amazed that they had 'the extraordinary ability to draw out other people's opinions and to express their own very succinctly', which she found most interesting.[78] The Gaekwars too returned very delighted by their trip and the Maharani wrote to Sethu Lakshmi Bayi shortly after she was back in Baroda: 'After seeing Your Highnesses' lovely country, we find our own part dull and ugly. How I envy living in such exquisite surroundings!'[79]

For the next few years Sethu Lakshmi Bayi would remain in touch with the Gaekwars, and Chimnabai, almost like a testy matron, wrote to her many months later asking if she had taken her advice and decided to explore India beyond Travancore yet. In 1916, writing from Kashmir, she was more nostalgic, saying: 'This month last year we were in Malabar and on our way to you and now this year we are about three thousand miles apart [sic] but the distance does not prevent my thinking of you.'[80] Later, in 1917, on hearing of the birth of a daughter to the Junior Rani, she would write to Sethu Lakshmi Bayi, wondering whether the baby looked like her mother or father; and so a friendly exchange continued between the two. But with time it slowly petered out and into the 1920s the two women appear to have lost touch. They would never meet again but Sethu Lakshmi Bayi was hugely fascinated by Chimnabai, who continued to lead an interesting life till 1939 when the death of her husband and the succession of a badly disposed step-grandson, caused her to leave Baroda for Bombay. Sadly, her marriage with the Maharajah also took a blow some years before his death, when, for all his public pronouncements on the moral necessity for monogamy in India, he took a French mistress, humiliating an already embittered Chimnabai.[81] The untimely deaths of three of her sons and the early widowhood of her daughter also took its toll, but the indomitable woman carried on until her own demise in a new India in 1958.

In Travancore, in the meantime, there was excitement on the domestic front. The Junior Rani, who had suffered a miscarriage in 1914, gave birth to a baby girl in 1916. She was named Karthika Tirunal Lakshmi Bayi Tampuran, with the title of First Princess of Travancore. But for Sethu Lakshmi Bayi happier news came in the form of permission from the Maharajah for her to leave the fort and construct a new country residence for herself. Soon after her eighteenth birthday, Mulam Tirunal had granted her a twenty-seven-acre property in Poojappura village, once occupied by his 'imbecile' brother. A token sum of Rs 10,000 was given to the Senior Rani to construct a palace there, with the remainder taken from the Sripadam treasury. Two years later the Junior Rani was also granted property in Kowdiar with Rs 45,000 to construct a residence for the Maharajah's heir. It was quite unprecedented for female members of the royal house to leave the fort, but Mulam Tirunal presumably found this an easier way to contain the disaffection between both Ranis and to remove their unhappy relations from a space he considered sacred.[82] Both Ranis, for their part, seemed only happy to leave and stay away from each other entirely.

The progress of work at Poojappura was slow, though, and it was only by 1916 that the main building was ready and the construction of the compound walls and the renovation of the old palace inside possible. 'I think it will be all over by next summer and habitable by then,' the Senior Rani wrote to her father hopefully that year.[83] But final works would be delayed for many more months and it was in 1918 that the completion of the whole palace appeared in sight. In the meantime, the talented but little known artist Mukundan Tampi was commissioned for a series of portraits and landscapes; and the final creations, especially the latter, were very well done.[84] A lot of new furniture was also crafted, based on models seen in European catalogues, and by the end of the year everything was finally ready. It was Rama Varma who took the lead in these matters. 'He was a most tasteful interior decorator,' a granddaughter would later tell. 'The many villas and mansions he designed were really excellent and the insides were beautifully furnished. He got the very best available things from abroad: crystal and porcelain artefacts, carpets and curtains from Italy and so on.'[85] The official and traditional name of the palace was Vijaya Vilasam, the Palace of Victory. But it was given a more anglicised identity by the Valiya Koil Tampuran. He took the first part of his wife's name and, considering that the palace was perched atop a hillock, devised the word 'Sethu-Lakshmi-Mound'. This was then given some more style and the new residence of the Senior Rani came to be known as Satelmond Palace. The Junior Rani's home, formally named Vasantha Vilasam, the Palace of Eternal Spring, was known simply as the Kowdiar Palace among the commonfolk.

In the first week of 1919 Sethu Lakshmi Bayi and Rama Varma moved into Satelmond after conducting an elaborate housewarming ceremony. The former's family also came down to Trivandrum for the occasion, but far from becoming a happy time of celebration, the move to Poojappura was inaugurated by dire tragedy. Mahaprabha had for over a decade now been having trouble with hypertension, and in those days there wasn't much that could be done about it even though it was one of the leading causes for premature deaths across the world. On 7 January, while at Satelmond, her blood pressure went up quite suddenly and she felt very indisposed, taking to bed right away. As this had become quite a common issue with her, nobody was unusually anxious until her condition seemed to worsen and she began to get very ill. By now doctors attached to the durbar had been summoned and were attending to her but all in vain because less than twenty-four hours later, on 8 January, forty-six-year-old Mahaprabha suddenly died in Poojappura, presumably because of heart failure.[86]

Sethu Lakshmi Bayi was shattered by the unexpected demise of her mother. While no letters or documents survive to show her exact feelings, her family members would later tell how this changed her completely and that after grieving at first, she realised that her siblings had perhaps lost far more than she had. After all, upon becoming Attingal Rani, distance and royal reservations had kept her away from her mother, giving her time to develop some inner strength of her own. But for her siblings, Mahaprabha was everything; even Kuttan Tampuran was inconsolable with grief. Suddenly twenty-three-year-old Sethu Lakshmi Bayi became the matriarch of her family, with all her younger siblings consigned to her care. 'She dared not break down,' her granddaughter tells; and she didn't.[87] She took charge quietly but almost immediately. The very memory of her mother provided her the strength she needed. There was a favourite photograph of Mahaprabha showing the grand lady posing in traditional attire, looking straight at the viewer, proud and confident as ever. This was framed and kept by her bed by Sethu Lakshmi Bayi so that every morning when she rose, she could look at it and remember the indomitable and powerful personality her mother had been.

All her courage was needed because her family was extremely vulnerable and nearly broken at this time. In accordance with the matrilineal system, with his wife's death, Kuttan Tampuran had no place in Mavelikkara now, and new arrangements were made for his children, who were entrusted into the formal guardianship of aunts and grandmothers. This was painful for all of them and Sethu Lakshmi Bayi wrote to her father comfortingly sometime afterwards: 'I know when you went there you would have had memories that would be most unbearable, but I hope that with time, when the new arrangements have become the usual routine, the mind's troubles will decrease.'[88] Kuttan Tampuran permanently moved to his own home in Kilimanoor, with only the status of a visitor in the house of his children. Sethu Lakshmi Bayi did her best to cheer him up now and then, as his health deterioriated in the years ahead, and he became afflicted by Parkinson's disease. 'Today is your birthday,' she wrote on one occasion. 'The usual custom of congratulating the birthday person and blessing him with long life can, I think, be improved. I pray that He will grant you long life and every happiness so that you may bless *us* motherless children, for a long time to come.'[89] That was not to be, and when his end came in 1926 the Rani mourned once again in silence, prohibited by convention from attending the 'private' funeral of her father.

Her siblings were not, in the meantime, faring any better either. The youngest boy, who was lovingly called Kunjunni, and who was only eight, would recount later how their caretaking relatives had neither interest nor time for any of them and that there was an enduring feeling of being orphaned.[90] There was some respite though because the Senior Rani always made sure she could have them in Trivandrum whenever possible, and her sister Kutty Amma, who was older and married by now, took charge and pulled everyone close. But there was certainly a break, aggravated by the inevitable circumstance of the older boys growing up and leaving home for their higher studies as well. Nothing would be the same again for Sethu Lakshmi Bayi's family. But, as had become a defining feature of her personality, this too she accepted with a stiff upper lip, and decided to move on.

All these changes and the sudden weight of responsibility brought about a mood of downcast melancholy over Satelmond Palace. For a whole year after her mother's demise, the Senior Rani mourned in silence, as the usual series of rituals, concluding with Mahaprabha's ashes being dispersed in the holy waters of the Ganga by her eldest son, were conducted. Sethu Lakshmi Bayi looked rather serious all the time, bottling up her feelings even more. Her husband, realising this, decided that perhaps a change in scenery would help her avoid further depression. So in the summer of 1920, instead of going to one of the usual hill stations within Travancore, Rama Varma prepared a programme for a visit to Kodaikanal in the Madras Presidency. The idea of leaving the state behind and going to a fresh location for a while succeeded in bringing some colour into the Senior Rani's life, and when the Maharajah graciously sanctioned the proposal, everyone was excited.

A house was rented for the three months they were to spend at Kodaikanal and a week before their departure, carpets, paintings, curtains, and other furnishings had been sent off so that by the time they arrived the place would be all homely. On 23 March the Senior Rani and the Valiya Koil Tampuran set out by car via Nagercoil and arrived in Tinnevelly by suppertime the next day. Having spent the night there, they boarded their train for the famous temple of Madurai the next morning but the journey turned out to be dusty and hot. By late afternoon they arrived at their destination where a Malayali called Velayudha Menon received them with a band of others, garlanding and otherwise treating them as customary, and escorted them to the palace of the Rajah of Ramnad, where arrangements had been made for their stay that night. The very same evening, having recovered her spirits, Sethu Lakshmi Bayi accompanied her husband to the famous temple of the goddess Meenakshi built in the typical Dravidian style with all its dramatic effect and attention to detail. She was fascinated by the beautiful structures she saw there: the twelve gopurams (gateways) the tallest of which was over 170 feet high; the massive tank; the very many mandapams or hallways flanked by exquisitely carved pillars and decorations, including the 'thousand-pillared hall'; and so on. The architecture seems to have taken her breath away more than the goddess's image in the main shrine, and she wrote to her father later: 'those who come to sight see [sic] would get more satisfaction from the place than those who come to worship.'[91] She reportedly also made some valuable presents to the deity, and instituted an endowment, which is said to be still in operation.[92]

The next morning a wire came in from their staff in Kodaikanal asking them to delay their arrival by one day, as everything was yet to be readied. But because it was so hot in Madurai, the Valiya Koil Tampuran decided to proceed anyway. En route their driver took a wrong turn, causing them to wander unplanned around some parts of the Tamil countryside, which became quite an adventure for the Senior Rani. But a local guide led them to the village of Vatalagundu where their two escort cars had arrived and where their meals were planned. After lunch they set off again but somewhere on the way the Senior Rani and her husband overshot the escort cars again, with the result that when they arrived in Kodaikanal by dinnertime, none of their luggage or personal attendants had reached. And in spite of sending so many things from Trivandrum in advance, the house wasn't at all what they imagined it would be. Rama Varma wrote:

> The first look around the house intended for our reception had a most disheartening effect upon us. The rooms were tiny and contained little that deserved the term of furniture and the whole house presented the appearance of long neglect and disuse. It was besides extremely cold, much more than our worst fears had pictured.[93]

This disappointment was short-lived, however, because Sethu Lakshmi Bayi immediately got down to improving their holiday home, instructing the servants to fix up and arrange the articles brought from Trivandrum according to her taste. Although the house was, in Rama Varma's words, 'small and undignified', its location offered a brilliant view of the valley below and hills in the distance. They quickly got used to the climate also, and every morning the Senior Rani would go for long walks while her husband went out riding. Miss Watts's sisters were in town at the time along with some other British acquaintances from Travancore; so very often she had company for tea. In the evenings prominent locals would come to pay their respects as well. Things were much freer and she felt a huge sense of relief as she enjoyed this break from Trivandrum and all its troubles. Her husband didn't miss this development, happily informing her family:

> During the day Her Highness walks not less than 6 miles. She is decidedly the better for the change. Her colour has returned to her and she no longer has that feeling of not being up to the mark. She is quite cheerful and likes her way of life here immensely. Though she looks more or less thin, still she is stronger and healthier.[94]

The Junior Rani had also arrived in Kodaikanal in the meantime and taken a house at some distance, which was a better place, but without a very good view. Sethu Parvathi Bayi's arrival had been rather more glamorous and through her 'triumphal progress' (in Rama Varma's sneering words) across south India that summer, she attended many reception parties. Soon after reaching Kodaikanal, then, she fell ill and the ever-caustic Rama Varma ascribed this to all her public activities en route: 'to have given thoughtful, relevant, and learned replies to the legion of addresses would tell upon the strongest of constitutions.'[95] His wife was more appropriate in her response when she heard of her cousin's indisposition and paid her several visits, which were not returned, although Kochukunji came once, complaining about the cold and giving her niece the useful information that as a remedy she covered herself in bed with her own hair.[96]

There were also many social opportunities during the season in Kodaikanal but the Senior Rani was happier visiting local schools and convents to interact with children and see the way these establishments were run. On 26 April, though, she attended her first ever Western-style party when the local club organized a fancy dress dinner. The brother of the Rajah of Pudukkottai, known as the Dorai Rajah, had even announced a prize for the best-dressed couple, but nothing could induce Sethu Lakshmi Bayi to appear in anything but her regular orthodox garments. Curiosity did take her to the party, however, but she doesn't seem to have enjoyed it much because she thought the Dorai Rajah behaved 'rather cheaply' for her standards. The Senior Rani and the Valiya Koil Tampuran then left the party by 11 p.m., early by standards in princely circles, and then heard that Sethu Parvathi Bayi had only reached by midnight, fitting much better and more smoothly into fashionable high society.[97]

The stay in Kodaikanal continued until July when the Senior Rani returned to Trivandrum where considerable changes were afoot. By this time, the Dewan was none other than Sir M. Krishnan Nair, a 'thorough bred aristocrat' from Malabar with a reputation for 'moral uprightness, correctitude and industry'.[98] He was introduced to Sankaran Tampi by the famous author C.V. Raman Pillai before being appointed Chief Justice of the High Court of Travancore in 1910. In 1914 he was promoted as Dewan, succeeding P. Rajagopalachari and initially serving the Maharajah (and Tampi) well. More importantly, it was he who steered Travancore's administration and finances during the difficult times of the First World War and in spite of tired global conditions ensured a time of 'great prosperity' for the state.[99] But by 1919 his relations with his monarch soured and T. Raghavaiah, a civil servant from Madras, was selected as his successor. Sethu Lakshmi Bayi, who carefully observed the state's politics, didn't agree much with Sir Krishnan's policies or even personality and looked forward to his replacement, writing to her father in Kilimanoor, 'we can find comfort in the thought that it is a great thing that he who was here has gone.'[100] Little did she imagine then that they would become relatives in a few years' time when her brother married Sir Krishnan's daughter, Meenakshi.

The next few years were quiet but fairly eventful for Sethu Lakshmi Bayi.

She had given up hope of having children of her own by now because her miscarriages had, according to doctors, had adverse and lasting effects on her chances. Throughout the 1910s she had tried all types of medications and even made religious offerings to remedy her condition, including at well-known Christian churches; in the late 1920s the Viceroy, on a visit to Trivandrum, would be astonished to find a large cross made of solid gold and silver donated by the Senior Rani to the Syrian church in the city.[101] To the goddess in Attingal she promised a golden flagstaff if she were blessed with a child, much to the consternation of her mother at that time. Only ruling sovereigns could, according to tradition, dedicate *kodimarams* (flagstaffs) and it seemed quite presumptuous to assume that Sethu Lakshmi Bayi would one day sit on the throne and fulfil her pledge. But after Mahaprabha's death, the Senior Rani's manner of devotion changed and a more personal form of worship replaced this outward-oriented religiosity of donations and vows. She had always been fond of the god Krishna and accepted him now as her personal deity. A silver figurine that belonged to the late Rani became her object of worship and she started dedicatedly spending hours every day in japam and prayers to Krishna. 'She loved him and had Mukundan Tampi do a series of paintings that hung everywhere in the palace,' her granddaughter remembers.[102] Rama Varma, for all his English manners and overtly Western outlook, also remained deeply religious, with his personal deity being Mahadeva. His japams were never, however, quite as long and elaborate as his wife's tended to be.[103]

In the early 1920s, Sethu Lakshmi Bayi was also doing new things occasionally. On a holiday in Ponmudi during the summer of 1921 she learnt target shooting from her husband who noted that although she would shoot only with a small rifle, she had very good potential in the sport. At this hill station the otherwise introvert Senior Rani was also having little soirees with the families of local English planters and other acquaintances like the Lights and the Prides, on one occasion also going down to visit a Mrs Marshall's tea factory to observe its working. By 1922 she showed considerable eagerness to accompany the Valiya Koil Tampuran and his friend, H.C.H. Robinson, the Land Revenue Commissioner, into the forest for a shikar where a wild leopard was frightening local tribes. 'If only I could see it once!' she wrote to her father, thrilled at the prospect of coming so close to a magnificent animal.[104] She also visited the Periyar reserve that summer, recording the experience:

> Yesterday we had been to see the Periyar dam. We started out at 3:30 in the morning and returned only at 8 in the night. It was about 23 miles from here

> to the lake. We went by car up to this point and then by steamboat to the TB [Travellers' Bungalow] where we had lunch and rested for a while. We started back in the evening. Though we could not see any wild elephants as expected we saw deer far away and I was satisfied. It was altogether a very enjoyable trip.[105]

In 1923 the annual holiday was spent at Munnar where they visited the 'Bison Valley'. Rama Varma shot one of the animals, his wife matter-of-factly reporting to family that it had a body 'not as proportionately large as its head'.[106] The Senior Rani was doing things that she would not, and most likely could not, have otherwise done if it weren't for Rama Varma. She definitely enjoyed these outside activities but a nudge from her husband was always welcome to really get her down to it; her own natural inclination was to read and read more all the time. For some time, in 1915, she had also kept pets in the form of deer that were gifted to her by her husband. But she got so attached to them that every illness or ailment they suffered would destroy her peace of mind, not helped by the fact that one of them was handicapped. And so Rama Varma decided it was better to take the animals away. The experience with the handicapped deer remained with Sethu Lakshmi Bayi forever though, and while she could understand the great thrill of hunting, she convinced her husband to engage in the sport only when he heard of wild animals troubling village settlements in the fringe regions of the state and otherwise not to go after them for the cruel pleasures of game alone.

In the meantime, in the year of 1922 two other important events had taken place. As far as the royal family was concerned, this was the birth of the Junior Rani's third child, namely Uthradam Tirunal Martanda Varma Tampuran, First Prince of Travancore on 22 March.[107] Now there were two male successors to Mulam Tirunal and for Sethu Parvathi Bayi, two prospective Maharajahs in her line. But what was closer to the Senior Rani's heart was the delivery of a son to her sister Kutty Amma in the same year.[108] Her letter to her father the next morning was full of questions: 'Was he born at a good hour? Is his *jathakam* [horoscope] good? Whom does he look like?' and so on.[109] Another letter she wrote afterwards was more emotional: 'Though this child will never experience a grandmother's petting I am sure his grandmother's blessing will be ever on him.'[110] The advent of children into the life of her younger sister must certainly have created mixed feelings in Sethu Lakshmi Bayi's mind, who was going to be twenty-seven that year. But if it depressed her with thoughts of her own enduring childlessness, she kept these feelings to herself and not a word was uttered either to her father or anybody else.

The year 1923 was ushered in quietly at Satelmond Palace and at the beginning of the year the usual plans were made about how to spend it. But most of these were thrown haywire suddenly when early in the summer the Senior Rani, while at Munnar again, started feeling very fatigued and weary. Initially this was dismissed as a consequence of her outdoor activities, but soon this tiredness began to be accompanied by nausea and her personal physician was summoned from Trivandrum. This was Dr Mrs Mary Poonen Lukose, the first female graduate of Travancore, who had gone on to study medicine in London and Dublin before returning and accepting government service. She had replaced the Ranis' old personal physician Mrs Austin in 1916 and Sethu Lakshmi Bayi was most comfortable dealing with her. It did not take Dr Mary too many tests after her arrival to determine what the issue was: Sethu Lakshmi Bayi, she declared half astonished, was with child. The news came as a great surprise to the Senior Rani and Rama Varma (and in fact to everyone else connected with the royal house). After her miscarriages between 1909 and 1913, there had been no signs whatever of her ever conceiving, effectively confirming that Sethu Lakshmi Bayi had become, as her detractors pointedly repeated, 'barren'. Now, a decade later, the news came as a bolt out of the blue, even as the Senior Rani thanked the gods for granting her unrelenting prayers.

But the mere fact of pregnancy was not particularly reassuring given her history of miscarriages and so she treated the whole thing with an almost surreal blasé, not getting her hopes too high. Draconian care was taken, and Dr Mary was specially deputed to supervise her progress, even as the Senior Rani returned to making a whole new series of religious offerings across Travancore so that the gods would not let her down at a later stage. A heavy consignment of medical books was ordered from Europe so that she could prepare herself professionally, just in case the gods did decide to dash her hopes yet again. But more importantly, she missed her mother terribly at this time and felt highly vulnerable as the pregnancy progressed into its seventh month. If this failed now, it would be more than she could bear.

On 30 December 1923, Sethu Lakshmi Bayi went into labour and was carried into her palace in the fort, where for many days special ceremonies were being conducted in anticipation of the royal birth. These had not been completed in fact as the baby wasn't expected for another month, and so it was quite unexpectedly that the chants of the priests were replaced by the cries of a baby girl. The delivery had not been easy at all but if that were worrisome, what happened after was positively frightening. In the moments following the baby's birth, Sethu Lakshmi Bayi suddenly suffered a powerful eclamptic fit. Watching the Senior Rani's weak body shake and turn so violently, her nurses felt a momentary sense of dread. But then she fell still, almost as if a curse had been lifted off her; and upon regaining consciousness, in spite of her great discomfort, felt a tremendous sense of relief: her baby was alive. Nevertheless, over the next few days, on the one hand she was severely indisposed by body aches and oedemas while on the other her mind remained full of fear.[111] The baby was premature and underweight and although she trusted Dr Mary's abilities, there was a worry that she might not survive.

> The little one was wrapped in layers and layers of cotton and flannel sheets to keep her warm. Special nurses were appointed to handle the child and her nursery was kept scrupulously germ-free and soundproof for more than a month, and again the doctor's efficiency proved successful. The baby thrived and flourished and when the doctor was satisfied that special nurses were no longer required the tension was diffused [sic] but not quite removed. The Senior Rani and more so the Valiya Koil Tampuran were constantly worried about the child's state of health. The slightest whimper from the nursery would send them both running into the room to see what the matter was.[112]

As per tradition, the baby was kept within doors for the first six months, and by March 1924 Sethu Lakshmi Bayi was reassured that this time she would not lose her child. In spite of the persistent body aches, she posed for a photograph at this point with her child because her sisters could not come down from Mavelikkara to see her. 'I look awful in it,' she self-consciously complained to them, 'so please don't show it to anybody.'[113] Six months later, Mulam Tirunal conducted the naming ceremony of his new great-niece and, for his own reasons and to general surprise, deferred to the wishes of the Senior Rani in giving the baby an unconventional name, even though it meant straying from custom. Perhaps he was finally satisfied now that Sethu Lakshmi Bayi had fulfilled the terms of her adoption. Or it might have been the look of pure happiness that had engulfed the otherwise melancholy-looking queen that caused him to be unusually gracious. Either way, he made it known that she now enjoyed his complete approval at those ceremonies.

Traditionally, female members of the royal house were named Lakshmi, Parvathi, Rukmini or Uma, but Sethu Lakshmi Bayi had selected an entirely new one for her child. And the obliging Maharajah, thus, proclaimed to their subjects the birth of Her Highness Uthram Tirunal Lalitamba Bayi Tampuran, Second Princess of Travancore.[114] That day Sethu Lakshmi Bayi posed for another photograph with her baby. Dressed all in white, with her hair in a bun at the back of her head and adorned with white flowers, a minimal number of ornaments on her person and with only the trademark *gobipottu* (long tikka) on her forehead for make-up, the Senior Rani looked down and smiled radiantly at her sleeping child as the camera flashed. And for the first time in years Sethu Lakshmi Bayi looked genuinely happy.

A month after the ceremonies, the Senior Rani and her husband went on their maiden holiday as a family with seven-month-old Princess Lalitha to Varkala. The baby had a slight fever so she was not brought out too much, lest proximity to the sea aggravate her condition. But the child recovered steadily, although back in the capital someone else's condition wasn't quite so agreeable. Sixty-six-year-old Mulam Tirunal had become rather unwell and disquieting reports were arriving daily. The matter was that he had a decayed tooth that his dentists were prohibited from extracting because of his orthodoxy, resulting in a predictable infection. By the end of July his doctors identified septicaemia but it had become too late to do anything. The Senior Rani and the Valiya Koil Tampuran hastened back to Trivandrum, while the Junior Rani who was sojourning in Ooty also rushed back. The Legislative Council was adjourned sine die and crowds from all over Travancore flocked to the fort to await news. Finally, on the night of 7 August 1924, His Highness Sri Padmanabha Dasa Vanchi Pala Sri Mulam Tirunal Sir Rama Varma Kulasekhara Kiritapathi Manney Sultan Maharajah Raja Rama Raja Bahadur Shamsher Jang, G.C.S.I., G.C.I.E., etc. etc., Maharajah of Travancore died.[115]

The funeral ceremonies took place on the morning of 8 August and the body was draped with silk cloth that was used to adorn the image of Sri Padmanabhaswamy. The flame that lit his pyre also came, in keeping with tradition, from the shrine of the great temple.[116] As his mortal remains were consumed by the blaze, with a sixty-six-gun salute booming in the background, the story of a controversial sovereign who was respected as *Ponnu Tampuran* ('the Golden King') as much as he was loathed as a debauchee came to an end. And with it closed a nearly forty-year chapter in Travancore's history. The Dewan proclaimed a period of mourning and all public establishments were shut while the royal family retreated into the twelve-day period of ritual seclusion. Those few days were solemn and quiet, and to many it seemed like the grim peace that signalled a terrible storm.

With the death of Mulam Tirunal it was the Junior Rani's elder son who would succeed as the next Maharajah of Travancore, which wasn't as promising as it sounded, for at the time the boy was not yet twelve years old. For the next six years that he would remain a minor, Travancore would need instead a Regent. In north Indian princely states in such circumstances the Government of India would appoint the minor's mother to that position along with a Council of Regency comprising distinguished bureaucrats and officers who conducted the actual administration. In Travancore, though, circumstances were different. In 1917, Mulam Tirunal himself had set the terms with regard to this eventuality when the Viceroy Lord Chelmsford wrote to him with conditions and clauses the Government of India had formulated with regard to Regencies. The Maharajah had accepted most of these, pointing out but one major exception that applied to his family:

> Your Excellency is aware that my house follows the [matrilineal] law of inheritance and custom, and that succession is on the female side. A modification is therefore necessary, and I beg to suggest that in regard to Travancore, the appointment of the Regent may be confined to the surviving 'senior female member in the ruling family'. I trust that this suggestion, which is in accordance with the customs and traditions of my house, will commend itself to Your Excellency's Government.[117]

Indeed by the law of the land in the absence or minority of a male member, power devolved upon the Attingal Rani, who might or might not be the mother of the minor ruler. As one scholar remarked, in any matrilineal family, 'In default of male members, succession devolves on the eldest female member' and there was 'nothing in the laws and customs' of Kerala 'which prevents females from succeeding to the throne or governing the country'. The 'paucity of male members does not create any interregnum at all' and the 'last male is at once succeeded by the eldest living female in full right'.[118] In Travancore there were a number of precedents for this. Asvathi Tirunal Umayamma (Queen Ashure) had reigned in Travancore in the late seventeenth century, while the nineteenth century saw two Regencies, namely of Ayilyam Tirunal Gowri Lakshmi Bayi and Uttrittadhi Tirunal Gowri Parvathi Bayi, the first of whom had ruled for nearly three years as Regnant Rani before becoming Regent, and the latter who succeeded her at the young age of thirteen. Now, nearly a century after the last Regency had terminated, it was the turn of Pooradam Tirunal Sethu Lakshmi Bayi, the last queen of the Kupakas and the final woman to hold in her hands the hallowed but dramatically contested power of the Ivory Throne.

THE REGENCY

Satelmond Palace, Poojappura

5

Her Highness the Maharajah

By June every year, Travancore would be soaked in the seasonal showers of the monsoons. The rain was always quite incessant, drizzling gently when it wasn't pouring in all its tropical luxury, adding nonetheless to the pretty charm of the coast. Rivers flowed with a majestic gush, emptying themselves lavishly into the sea, and the landscape adorned itself with the richest foliage. The jungles, lagoons, and backwaters appeared more idyllic than ever, and even the rich paddy fields of north and central Travancore would fill out into small lakes. Neat little boats dotted the horizon as people went about their business, rendering the scenery picture-perfect. The whole geography would reflect a natural abundance, every bit worthy of that appellation of 'god's own country'.[1] 'A land of beauty! A land of plenty! A land of peace!' an English grandee appropriately pronounced, enchanted by nature's liberal indulgence of this state.[2]

But the monsoons of 1924 would come to be recalled not for their romance as for the veritable terror they stirred. It seemed as if the skies had been ripped apart as the waters burst out endlessly, transforming the bountiful scene into one of violent catastrophe. 'Water! Water everywhere!' rued the famous writer Takazhi in his *In The Flood*, recording how in his village, crowded together at the highest point in a temple, stood sixty-seven children, 350 adults, and a number of pets and domestic animals, awaiting rescue. The deluge turned much of Travancore into a massive swamp and even portions of the high ranges were submerged. For weeks the heavens poured with vehemence, and homes, livelihoods and lives were washed away in its fury. Pregnant mothers and children were found adrift in massive urns, floating alongside the bloated corpses of livestock, scarring many with trauma and trepidation.[3] Panic gripped

Kerala as a whole as hundreds of human lives and thousands of animals' were lost. It was one of the greatest natural disasters to occur in south India. That year became a landmark in local history, and grandmothers would for long tell grim tales of the collective sufferings of 1099 ME (Malayalam Era).

Relief works had commenced as soon as the crisis began, with a Flood Relief Committee being urgently set up by the government. Dewan T. Raghavaiah, an accomplished civil servant deputed from British Madras in succession to Sir Krishnan, demonstrated tremendous initiative and promptly sent large amounts of money to the affected regions for preliminary assistance. In defiance of conservative opinion, while Mulam Tirunal lay dying in Trivandrum, he chose to reach out to the people by travelling to every ravaged locality, boosting public morale and personally overseeing relief activities. By early August, thousands of refugees and displaced families were being fed at different relief centres: 4,000 at Ambalapuzha, 3,000 at Alleppey, 5,000 in Kottayam, 3,000 in Changanassery, 8,000 in Parur, and so on. Mr Raghavaiah also had the sagacious sense to involve the public and it was announced to general appreciation that 'through the efforts of private citizens and Government officers, nobody was allowed to suffer from starvation'.[4] The administration was doing everything it could to ameliorate circumstances during this last major, and traumatic, event of Mulam Tirunal's reign.

There were substantial losses, however, and that year's crop was utterly destroyed. The report of the Mannar Flood Relief Deputation, which was one of the several hundred village committees constituted, noted, for instance, that 500 houses, 200 coconut gardens, 1,000 acres of land, and 6,40,000 kilograms of grain had been lost in the vicinity of that one central Travancore hamlet alone.[5] Woeful information came in from the most fertile parts of the state and it was clear that the only way ahead was to facilitate a good harvest the following season. So, by early August it was announced that in the worst affected regions, taxes would be remitted for that financial year, and a sum of Rs 4 lakh was set aside to provide agricultural loans.[6] House reconstruction funds were also constituted and the Forest Department was asked to freely supply bamboo and other rudimentary materials to the poor for temporary residential arrangements. Price stability was maintained in the market, and the government was prepared to substitute tapioca for the diminished supply of grain to prevent inflation.

It was at this stage that Sethu Lakshmi Bayi came to power. Normally, when a ruler passed away, for three days the government would cease operations at every level. But in the circumstances at hand, she agreed with the Dewan that this should not be practically done; everything was declared closed but work continued behind the scenes. Indeed, even though for twelve days the royal family was supposed to be in isolated mourning, the Rani remained in touch with Mr Raghavaiah constantly. The management of relief was left entirely to him, owing to her inexperience, but she did issue some maiden policy directions of her own. By 28 August it was announced that at the Rani's orders the amount proposed for agricultural loans was increased to Rs 5.5 lakh and all district officials were commanded 'to deal with the utmost celerity and sympathy with all applications' for assistance.[7] In due course she would also prune the rate of interest charged on these loans from 6.25 per cent to 6 per cent and less, and 10,000 applications were disposed of, with each person being granted a maximum of Rs 500 to get back on his productive feet.[8] Physical reconstruction activities were launched successfully, with the Public Works Department (PWD) allotted several lakhs of rupees to repair roads and other infrastructure. By the time Sethu Lakshmi Bayi's reign was formally inaugurated in early September, people had started to return to their homes and ordinary vocations, and normalcy was restored for most part.

Yet the Flood of 1099 ME served as something of a mental jolt to the young Rani. So far she had lived in the cocooned world of her palace and family, aloof from the everyday turmoil and difficulties of her people. Her books, her relatives, and latterly her daughter, besides the lot of ceremonial obligations, constituted the farthest extent of her horizon. Everything beyond this was an abstraction in her mind, gleaned from what she learned, heard and studied. But it was now that the burden of duty struck her with all its gravity. When agonising stories of suffering and distress reached Trivandrum during the floods, Sethu Lakshmi Bayi suddenly grasped the magnitude of what she had been entrusted with. An estimated four-and-a-half million people now looked up to her as their monarch and it became her purpose to live up to her great responsibilities.

The prospect was formidable and one evening in August, as she sat in her library, going through report after report from devastated villages, her emotions almost gave way. In many years of personal unhappiness she had rarely broken down or shed tears. But that day, when the weight of her task became clear, her mind was filled with consternation. She did not feel equipped for any of this. She was not certain she had the courage. And she most certainly did not want to fail anyone, leave alone millions. A thousand disquieting worries vexed her, but then, remembering Mahaprabha and resuming her trademark dignity, she wiped her tears and cleared her mind. Hard work alone, she decided, would stand by her during the times ahead and, with a force and determination not many imagined she possessed, Sethu Lakshmi Bayi resolved to rule.

The role of a Regent in British India was typically a limited one. He or she represented the monarch during the period of the latter's minority, and the Regency government was only an interim administration. In the conventional sense, while Regents could govern the realm, they were not permitted to make any significant changes in the laws or constitution of the country as sovereigns might; any new measures were to be consistent with the existing framework and of a nature that could be sustained when the rightful ruler came of age. Politically, what was perhaps most important was that Regents could not usually rule alone in colonial India; they were to head a Council of Regency, comprising eminent leaders of the land, usually nominated by the British after the latter were assured that they would not become impediments to the interests of the Raj. This was to safeguard that complete authority was not vested in one person during the minority of the monarch, which might be too tempting to give up when the time came.[9] The Regent could preside over the temporary arrangements, but could certainly not become a dictator.

In the nineteenth century there had been a number of Regencies in India, some of them quite noteworthy, such as of Begum Qudsia III in Bhopal, Sir Salar Jung in Hyderabad, and Sir T. Madhava Rao in Baroda. Normally, the Government of India preferred the Council of Regency to be headed by the mother of the minor prince or the senior consort of the preceding ruler. Thus, in Mysore from 1895 to 1902, for instance, the Dowager Maharani Vani Vilas Sannidhana held the position of Regent, and in the 1920s, Gwalior and Cooch Behar had two widows in power. However, these women were only figureheads whose role entailed ratifying the better judgements of their Councils of Regency. Dewans were the executive members on these bodies acting as the real rulers, requiring the Maharanis simply to sanction their resolutions. Most often, these dependent women had no other option but to comply. In Mysore, for example, the minister was told to consult the Maharani only 'as is practicable and desirable' and otherwise liaise directly with the Government of India, by now relocated from Calcutta to Delhi.[10] In other words, the Maharanis were titular heads of state, only lending royal legitimacy to the Acts issued by the Councils that really controlled interim power.

The case of Travancore, however, was exceptional. The defining aspect here was that female members of the dynasty were inherently entitled to their positions due to the matrilineal system, and did not owe their status to the accident of marriage. As sisters of the Rajahs, they carried in them the same royal blood, and were entitled to rule whenever eligible males heirs were found wanting. 'The position of [the] woman in [Kerala],' wrote K.P. Padmanabha Menon, 'is altogether different from that of her sister [elsewhere in India]. She is practically mistress of the house, whether as mother or sister of the [senior male member]. She has a recognised legal position. The principle of [Malayali] law is that the whole [estate] property belongs to her and the [senior male] is simply the manager on her behalf... Her general education is on a par with her brothers, and her intellectual capacity in the matter of special studies is in no way inferior. There have been and there are ladies of remarkable attainments in [Kerala].'[11] Thus when Queen Ashure reigned over Travancore in the seventeenth century during a minority, she did so as an absolute and supreme monarch. Later historians would refer to her as a Regent, but neither this term nor office existed in the political vocabulary of her day. By the nineteenth century, however, the concept of Regency had arrived in the state through the medium of the English East India Company, which had acquired the right to intervene in all matters concerning Travancore, including the line of succession.

It was in 1810 that Rani Gowri Lakshmi Bayi commenced her rule when there were no male members at all in the royal house. She was recognised as sovereign, but the times were unusually turbulent and Travancore was in the midst of grave internal and external crises. There had been mutinies and rebellions within that threatened the dynasty, even as the Company was becoming disconcertingly aggressive outside, annexing states and deposing rulers at the drop of a proverbial hat. Their attitude towards women also influenced matters in that the authorities could not see how a young girl of twenty could possibly manage so many difficulties in Travancore—up to the late eighteenth century, women were seen in Europe as private property, with little freedom, no rights of inheritance, and wife battering was considered legitimate domestic behaviour.[12] In essence, the female, when it came to intelligent, worldly affairs, had ineluctably to submit to the will of men. So Gowri Lakshmi Bayi, as a woman, found herself unable to claim the confidence of the British, palled perpetually therefore by the threat of expulsion.

The one thing that could secure the throne to her dynasty at this critical time when colonial chauvinists pulled the political strings was the birth of a male heir, whom the Company would recognise. For until that boy were given a chance to rule, they could be counted upon not to annexe the state. Unsurprisingly, then, when in 1813 the Rani gave birth to a son, she was asked to 'step down' from the throne, install him there, and govern hereafter as Regent.[13] In the interests of expediency and security, she did exactly that, and with this we find the first 'Regency' arising in Travancore. However, what is most vital here is that although she took the title of Regent, Gowri Lakshmi Bayi did not surrender any real powers. While the Sword of State was placed in the hands of the baby boy, she continued as interim monarch with unrestrained actual authority. All legislative Acts were issued in her name, for instance, and not in his as would be the case with normal Regencies.[14] When she died in 1814, her sister Gowri Parvathi Bayi took over as Regent, and continued to exercise full powers. The highest currency of the land carried her insignia,[15] and when durbars were held, it was she who occupied the throne.[16] Indeed, during his minority, the boy who was supposedly the real monarch, never even sat in her presence.[17] As the Resident noted at the time, 'the people were accustomed to regard her with the reverence and respect which they paid to their Rajahs' and saw her 'occupy the place of the Rajah and scarcely found any difference in the constitution of the state'.[18] Both these women, therefore, were Regents only in name. Locally, they were treated as sovereign, with all the attendant authority, and this would define Sethu Lakshmi Bayi's position also a century afterwards.

A few days after Mulam Tirunal's death, the incumbent Resident, Mr C.W.E. Cotton, called on the Rani to discuss her Regency government and other imminent affairs. For all her previous trepidation and reluctance with regard to ruling, Sethu Lakshmi Bayi now, when it came to it, more than rose to the occasion. She pointed out her anomalous position in Travancore, citing that as per matrilineal law, she was now the head of the family and ought to rule in her own name and right. Just because Gowri Lakshmi Bayi, for reasons of political pragmatism, had acquiesced in an inferior title, it was not fair to expect the same from her. Sethu Lakshmi Bayi was technically correct, and some years ago the High Court in Trivandrum had accepted that when 'a senior female takes up the management [of the family] during the minority of the male members, she does not take it up on behalf of the eldest minor male member but in her own right'.[19] Mr Cotton also accepted that while normally the senior female of the family had 'unrestricted powers' during a minority, in the royal family 'the strict letter of this law was modified in 1813' by Gowri Lakshmi Bayi.[20] By doing so, that Rani created a *new* precedent, namely of Regency, which was followed without question by Gowri Parvathi Bayi after her. Additionally, when Mulam Tirunal wrote to the Viceroy in 1917, he too referred to the eligibility of the senior female as Regent and not as sovereign ruler. So, this new tradition, though acknowledged as an invention of colonial jurisprudence and political circumstances, had to be complied with uncomplainingly, and taken to be immutable.

That said, however, the Government of India did concede to Sethu Lakshmi Bayi the rights previous Rani-Regents had enjoyed. They confirmed that 'her powers will be unrestricted as Regent' and locally she would enjoy the status of a monarch.[21] And this was ensured by the concession that there would be no Council of Regency in the state, vesting complete and autocratic control in the hands of the Rani. But there were some ceremonial deprivations. So, while the Legislative Council pledged allegiance to Sethu Lakshmi Bayi, and not the minor prince, the Rani could not sit on the throne; she had to make do with a 'Regent's Chair'. Similarly, while she would enjoy the position of monarch locally with all attendant honours, if British Governors or Viceroys visited, she would have to step back and accord precedence to the young boy. In that sense, the custom of Gowri Parvathi Bayi, which was the model emulated, was not followed to the letter. But Sethu Lakshmi Bayi did not press the matter and accepted her titular demotion as Regent insofar as it entailed no actual demotion of authority.

Once this was settled, the durbar astrologers were summoned to determine the dates for the installation of the new Maharajah and the Regent. On 20 August 1924, the Junior Rani's son performed the relevant ceremonies and took charge of the Sword of State before the shrine of Sri Padmanabhaswamy. Then came the turn of Sethu Lakshmi Bayi. Again, since in Travancore the Regent's was not merely an administrative office but a de facto monarchy, she too had to go through exactly the same religious rituals as the boy, with the exception that flowers and prasadam replaced the Sword of State. On 1 September the Rani ascended the Sreemukha Mandapam in the temple and was invested with the right to govern Travancore. As with the rulers before her, Sethu Lakshmi Bayi proceeded from the temple to the Chokkatta Mandapam in the fort, wherefrom she gave her first (customary) orders to the Dewan, commanding him to ensure the correct and meticulous management of all the temples in the country. Presents were distributed to an assembly of Brahmins and the principal ceremony was concluded. She returned, then, not to Moonbeam but to Anantha Vilasam in the Valiya Kottaram complex of the Maharajahs, which was to be her official residence now.[22] A large crowd of people waited there to pay their respects, carrying with them the *nuzzer* or *tirumulkazhcha* that was usually offered to the ruler at an audience. But Sethu Lakshmi Bayi decided to end the custom; the Dewan was ordered to let it be known that the Rani did not want any presents to be offered by her subjects who wished to greet her, opening her reign on a positive note.[23]

That afternoon an official durbar was convened to install the minor prince and the Regent. The soldiers of Travancore's nominal army (as permitted by the British) called the Nair Brigade and the Royal Bodyguard having taken their positions, at 3:45 p.m. the Junior Rani, her younger son, the new Elayarajah, and daughter arrived. The Dewan received and led them in, following which at 3:50 Sethu Lakshmi Bayi drove in a state carriage drawn by four white horses, to the resounding boom of a twenty-one-gun salute. Chithira Tirunal, the minor Maharajah, arrived in similar circumstances at 3:55, after whom the Resident, decked with his many medals and in complete formal uniform, made his appearance at 4.00 p.m. After a preliminary speech, Mr Cotton led the young boy to the Ivory Throne and handed him 'a turban plumed with the drooping feathers of the bird of paradise, held in place by an aigrette of diamonds and emeralds and two large pendant pearls'. Thereafter, Sethu Lakshmi Bayi took her seat on the right side of the throne, in the ornate Regent's Chair, and the installation proclamation was read out to all seated in court; the Rani had again broken with tradition and for the first time allowed those present to take a seat in the presence of the royal family.[24]

Once the proclamation was rendered, the dignitaries, including Chithira Tirunal and Sethu Lakshmi Bayi, moved to the balcony outside. There, Mr Raghavaiah read out the proclamation once again, and another twenty-one-gun salute heralded the inauguration of the new regime. On their return to the hall, Mr Cotton delivered a speech, announcing at the end that both the Ranis of Travancore would henceforward be styled, at the orders of the Viceroy, as *Maharanis*. This came as a general surprise and was received with thunderously loyal applause from the assembled nobility and officialdom.[25] The Resident's speech was followed by Sethu Lakshmi Bayi's inaugural address—a neat, regular affair, lamenting first the demise of Mulam Tirunal, pledging loyalty to the British Crown, and expressing the hope that she would be able to 'acquit myself of my new duties conscientiously and without passion or prejudice'. With that the durbar came to a conclusion and the Resident departed first, followed by the royal family and the other distinguished persons gathered.

In all this what was perhaps most fascinating was Sethu Lakshmi Bayi's new status as interim ruler. While the Government of India imposed the inferior title of Regent on her, traditionally within the state she was always heralded in a distinctive manner. For one, unlike administrative Regents, she had an elaborate regnal title, equal to that of a male sovereign. However, there was more. In popular parlance she would be the Maharani Regent or the Senior Maharani, similar to her female counterparts in other states. But what was distinct was that in all official documents and proclamations, she held the title of Pooradam Tirunal *Maharajah*.[26] In fact even the Resident had addressed her as Maharajah in his proclamation. This was unprecedented in India, just as the status of the Attingal Rani was also unique. For under the matrilineal system, where the sexes were equal, the monarch's gender was of little consequence. It was the position and its dignity that mattered and whoever exercised supreme authority in the state and in the royal house was held to be the Maharajah. The Government of India, with its Western outlook and cultural constraints, might have called it a Regency. But to the local people of Travancore, the reign of Mulam Tirunal Maharajah was rightfully succeeded by that of Pooradam Tirunal Maharajah, just as it would one day be relinquished to Chithira Tirunal Maharajah. To the Government of India, thus, the young lady just installed was the Maharani Regent. But to the masses, she was Her Highness Maharajah Pooradam Tirunal of Travancore.[27]

Sethu Lakshmi Bayi inherited from her uncle not just a state and a large multitude of people, but also her first political challenge. While the floods were the immediate task at hand when she came to power, her sympathetic outlook and the efficiency of the Dewan closed that chapter to genuine acclaim. But this other bequest of Mulam Tirunal was considerably more delicate, upon the smart and correct resolution of which depended her reputation as ruler. It was a matter of socio-political importance, of the kind that would be celebrated in history and long remembered by the public. In what was initially surprising, it also caught the attention of newspapers across India, propelling it as a matter of national interest. And it was patent to everybody that if the Maharani fumbled here, she would fail to win the confidence not only of her own people but also of progressive sections of society all over India.

The issue was what is famously called the Vaikom Satyagraha. The crux of the matter was the utterly vicious and deplorable variety of the caste system that was practised in Travancore. Indeed, here caste was taken to its greatest extreme so that beyond the familiar practice of 'untouchability', there was also a phenomenon known as 'unapproachability'. Certain groups were prohibited even from the *sight* of higher fellows, and none of their ilk had seen daylight without, at one point in history, forfeiting their lives. Brahmins, as elsewhere in India, had a position of primacy incongruous with their minuscule population and the native Nambutiri was treated, to quote the somewhat obsequious *Travancore Census Report* (1875), as a 'royal liege and benefactor, suzerain master, household deity' and 'god on earth'. Only the next major caste, the Nairs, were permitted to approach these Nambutiris, and all other groups had prescribed distances to maintain, which if accidentally breached would send high castes shrieking about impurity and religious violation. As the Resident had remarked in 1870:

> Roads are public to all good castemen ... but certain lower classes are prohibited altogether from using them ... lower caste men generally cannot enter—sometimes cannot approach—the courts, *cutcherries*, registry offices, etc. If the evidence of a low caste man has to be taken by a judge or magistrate, as the witness cannot come to the court, the court must go to the witness. But it must not go too near him, and the frequent result is that the witness's evidence is taken by the court, or a Goomastah deputed for the purpose, calling the questions to an intermediate peon, and the peon shouting them to the witness and repeating his replies to the presiding officer ... however desirous the higher officers may be to keep justice and show mercy, it is simply impossible for them, in such circumstances, to prevent oppression and corruption on the part of their underlings.[28]

Thus, for instance, the peasant caste of Pulayas had to keep a distance of 90 feet from Brahmins and 64 feet from Nairs. Low castes were not allowed anywhere in high-caste-dominated public spaces due to fear of ritual contamination, which in effect translated to social exclusion. They had no place in village councils, no entry to temples, no access to markets, or any other locations of socio-political importance. They were practically invisible non-entities in a deeply hierarchical society. Indeed, as late as the early twentieth century, Mulam Tirunal (and even Sethu Lakshmi Bayi for that matter) had not once seen large sections of Travancore's people, for the simple reason that they polluted the royal presence and were prohibited from approaching. Caste was such a ruthless injustice that even Swami Vivekananda was moved to decry, in an uncharacteristic display of indignation, the whole state as 'a lunatic asylum'.

Through the late nineteenth century, under pressure from missionaries and the British, some aspects of caste were relaxed, especially in the new Western-inspired education facilities.[29] This opened economic doors for one of the most sizeable low-caste groups, known as the Ezhavas, among whom a small vanguard of educated leaders emerged. The efforts of the reformer Sri Narayana Guru also united the community and made them conscious of their collective rights. By the 1890s they began to agitate for a share in government employment where merit was supposed to be the sole determinant. This battle would continue but by the 1910s, the Ezhavas had also begun to question their communal alienation in stronger ways. Convinced of its injustice, in 1919 a mass of 5,000 Ezhavas met in the village of Kanichikulangara to demand temple entry and the termination of all other social disadvantages. Nothing came of it immediately and some time later, at the Kakinada session of the Indian National Congress in 1923, T.K. Madhavan, an Ezhava leader from Travancore, proposed a movement to wholly eradicate untouchability. This received the blessings of the party and Mahatma Gandhi, and when he came home he decided to initiate the state's first-ever satyagraha against caste.

Vaikom with its great Mahadeva temple was chosen as the spot to commence the movement. That town was an important religious centre in south India with its Ashtami festival in October–November attracting up to 50,000 pilgrims every year from outside Travancore. Naturally, it was also a very orthodox place, dominated by Brahmins and other high castes bent on preserving what they perceived as the ritual sanctity of the shrine. The roads around the four outer walls of the temple were therefore prohibited to the low-born and public notice boards had for long stood there to guide polluted groups away from the sacred precincts. And the first goal of the intended satyagraha was to terminate this discrimination and have all the roads opened up to everybody irrespective of caste.[30]

The proposed movement was expertly trumpeted and publicised for several weeks so that on 30 March 1924, when it actually started, a frowning government was prepared. The local magistrate issued orders prohibiting the event and barricades were placed at the mouths of the concerned streets. Large numbers of policemen were deployed on the ground to deal with the possibility of violence and even larger crowds gathered to watch the proceedings. It was not especially dramatic, however. That morning three satyagrahis—Kunjappy (Pulaya), Bahuleyan (Ezhava) and Govinda Panikkar (Nair)—walked together towards the barricades, trying to cross on to the controversial roads. The police permitted Panikkar to pass, since he was high caste, but not the others. When they persisted, they were all arrested and carted off to prison. The satyagrahis kept coming, though, in batches of three every day. They would stand at the barricades trying to reason with the law, before being arrested, almost habitually, by lunchtime. After this, in the evenings, public meetings and processions were organised daily, which the press covered in detail.

Leaders from all communities, including from upper castes, arrived on the scene to lend their support, while others travelled the length and breadth of Travancore promoting the cause.[31] The Maharajah was bombarded with petitions to do the right thing and concede the satyagrahis' requests, but neither he nor his government budged. Perhaps Mulam Tirunal was peeved by some of the more caustic remarks made against him, such as by E.V. Ramaswami Naicker (popularly called Periyar) who dryly observed that the temple roads were 'not the property of his grandfather'.[32] But the government did take cognizance of the bad press it was receiving and cleverly decided to stop arresting the satyagrahis altogether, choosing instead to ignore them. This stole some thunder from the movement, and the agitators had no option but to squat nearby, singing patriotic songs, spinning khadi, and conducting public fasts.[33] The crowds began to thin and excitement eroded.

Then Mulam Tirunal died. This was a welcome development, breathing some fresh air into the movement. 'Let me hope,' wrote Gandhi in an emotional appeal in *Young India*, 'that Her Highness the Maharani Regent will recognise that untouchability is no credit to Hinduism but it is a serious blot on it.'[34] Through all of August the pressure of public opinion and speculation on Sethu Lakshmi Bayi's likely policy mounted. Being a new ruler and a female (which meant she was supposed to embody warm motherly qualities), there was definitely hope for progress. And the atmosphere was ripe with expectation when the Maharani offered a substantial concession at her installation ceremony; that afternoon, an unenthusiastic Mr Raghavaiah was asked to announce, at Sethu Lakshmi Bayi's orders, the release of all fifty-six satyagrahis whom Mulam Tirunal (and he) had arrested. The news was met with stirring applause, even as the Dewan's brow creased, bringing the movement back into the national spotlight. Hopes escalated that the young queen would swiftly resolve the issue to the progressives' satisfaction and bring about a happy conclusion.

However, Sethu Lakshmi Bayi's gesture of support and understanding for the cause was not met with approval either by her minister or the powerful conservative lobby. Travancore, in the words of one of its previous Maharajahs, was India's most priest-ridden country.[35] And its royal family was its most priest-ridden household. Owing to their quasi-religious character, it was not surprising that the orthodoxy was in a position of overwhelming preponderance here. To them all these modern notions of caste equality were nothing short of sacrilege. As they saw it, if today they yielded to blasphemous nonsense in Vaikom, tomorrow the clamour would inevitably reach the gates of Trivandrum Fort. And if Sri Padmanabhaswamy in the capital's great temple were exposed to 'impure' elements (and if their age-old casteist policies challenged in conjunction), it would destroy everything that was so cherished about the Brahmin paradise that was the Hindu state of Travancore.

The Dewan, for his part, was no admirer of the Congress, which was backing the movement. He saw the satyagraha as an attempt to dragoon the government into accepting the diktats of a bunch of radicals, which was not a precedent he intended to swallow.[36] What was happening in Vaikom, in his opinion, was the use of satyagraha as 'an instrument for the coercion of the government', which was absolutely unacceptable. He also stressed that it was 'the paramount duty of every government *not* to interfere with religious beliefs and the usages based upon them', which meant things ought to be left as they were.[37] It appears that the Valiya Koil Tampuran too had little sympathy for the Congress and concurred with Mr Raghavaiah in the first part. Being seen as succumbing to political arm-twisting and emotional blackmail was unwise for any government, not to speak of his opinion that interfering in religious matters was completely unnecessary.[38] And yet, Sethu Lakshmi Bayi, who had manifestly strong views of her own, decided to release the prisoners and make it known that she was not against the spirit of the movement. Given that she was surrounded by people who stood convinced in opposition, this was a move of considerable courage and resolve.[39]

But once it was done, she could not but tread with caution. Her inexperience necessitated this, besides the fact that she could not alienate others (her husband and minister included) beyond a reasonable point. So a push and pull of divergent views and opinions ensued in the palace for some time, while in Vaikom the movement simmered. The Ezhava community's leadership was proving to be exceptional, and even a number of their women came out to work hard for the cause. 'How Gandhiji would rejoice,' exhorted a participant called P.K. Kalyani, 'that the Hindu women of Kerala were piloting the Vaikom Satyagraha!'[40] These women devised some very interesting means to support the movement, such as through the *pidiyari* initiative. The word literally means 'a handful of rice', and volunteers would go from house to house, collecting grain from Ezhava women in an effort to feed those gathered at Vaikom.[41] Such innovative efforts proved very useful in spreading word about the movement even in faraway villages, so that by the end of October a fabulously sensational event could be orchestrated with public support to end the vacillation of Travancore's hesitant government.

On 31 October, with expert coordination, a number of jathas or processions, not dissimilar to but perhaps less glamorous than Gandhi's later Dandi March, set out on foot for Trivandrum.[42] From Vaikom it was heralded by

Mannathu Padmanabhan, who is best known for his efforts in unifying the Nair community, while from Suchindram in the south, it was Emperumal Naidu who led a band; and so too came regional leaders with thousands from other parts of Travancore. What is most interesting is that these jathas were of high-caste Nairs and even a few Brahmins, their intention being to demonstrate that privileged society was equally in favour of reform (with the added incentive of a Hindu consolidation, about which more will be said later). This tactic was brilliant. As the jathas passed, hundreds joining on the way, the countryside was electrified. For centuries the miserable lot of peasants and others had toiled upon the land, their invisible efforts feeding the arrogant presumptions of their caste superiors. And here was a band of those very overlords singing slogans of equality, freedom and a happier future, on their way to seek redress in the court of a compassionate queen.

By the first week of November the jathas all arrived in Trivandrum, where a series of promotional public events were successfully organised. Upon application, on 4 November it was also announced that the Maharani had agreed to grant the leaders of the movement, twelve in number and led by the fairly moderate lawyer K. Parameswaran Pillai, an audience a week later on 12 November. This was again a remarkable gesture from Sethu Lakshmi Bayi, for it was quite rare in Travancore for the hallowed monarch to receive political petitions directly from the people; the Dewan was always necessarily the first point of contact, so that the royal family would stay aloof enough and unblemished from whatever the consequences might end up being.[43] By agreeing to see the leaders of the Vaikom Satyagraha personally, the Maharani consciously discarded that convenient ring of self-preservation and once again made it known that she was willing to hear their voice and treat their cause with the utmost seriousness. In other words, she became personally involved in the matter.

On the morning of 12 November the twelve men were quietly ushered into the large state room at Satelmond Palace. There, poised in the Regent's Chair, with her husband standing at a respectful distance, the Maharani first received their customary expressions of fealty and respect, before hearing personally arguments in favour of reform. She also accepted from them a petition signed by thousands of high-caste Hindus, imploring her to do the good that her uncle wouldn't. With great patience and keenness, she listened to everything they had to say. But if the men expected the Maharani to make a momentous declaration on the spot, they were disappointed. For at the end of their presentation, when asked for her views, Sethu Lakshmi Bayi made no promises at all. An Ezhava leader known as N. Kumaran, she pointed out, had at that time introduced a motion on the topic of road entry in the Legislative Council of Travancore. This was to be taken up for discussion in January 1925 when its next session was due, and so, she said, she was inclined to observe how the legislature considered the issue before taking an arbitrary decision of her own.[44] Essentially, she wanted to see what the people's representatives felt before issuing final orders on the subject. On this note the meeting came to an uncertain conclusion. The satyagrahis left the palace somewhat disappointed by the Maharani's diplomatic stance, which seemed to contradict her several recent symbolic expressions of support and sympathy. Perhaps, they thought, she had no real intention of being the gallant crusader against caste they expected her to be. The struggle would have to continue and more pressure alone could get the government to act, it was felt.

Indeed, Sethu Lakshmi Bayi had no desire at this point to become a dramatic mascot for social reform; she had more considered designs. She genuinely appreciated the cause and its practical relevance, but while it was within her province at that time to demonstrate her support symbolically, the concrete implementation of her favour required patient engineering over time. She was sensible enough to understand this. The circumstances of the Maharani in November 1924 were complicated and she could not give assurances to anyone, for the simple fact that she was not in full possession of power yet. For unbeknown to the satyagrahis, Sethu Lakshmi Bayi was engaged at this juncture in a delicate struggle for power against the Dewan she had inherited from her uncle. The Vaikom satyagraha was a bone of contention between them and their contrasting ideals, but it had also become a critical battleground insofar as their contest for authority went. For the Maharani the movement was vital to ensure her supremacy in government, while for Mr Raghavaiah it portended the termination of his hitherto unbridled predominance. And the outcome at Vaikom, it was clear, would determine who between the two would finally prevail.

In the months that followed Sethu Lakshmi Bayi's installation, it became evident that Mr Raghavaiah and she encountered serious differences. Mulam Tirunal had for long behaved like a figurehead, allowing his Dewans (and the Second Favourite, now packed into retirement) to exercise administrative powers without inhibition. But his successor, it became obvious, wished to play a decisive role in governance and in the formulation of state policy. For a man like Mr Raghavaiah, who was dominating for the very reason that he was confident of his efficiency, this came as an unwelcome surprise. During the start of the Vaikom movement it was he who ordered the arrests, had the satyagrahis tried in court, imprisoned and then eventually ignored. His posture towards the movement was of uncompromising firmness and he had almost succeeded in crippling it when everything went haywire at the whim of a woman. Out of the blue, the very man who stood unyielding before the agitators was forced by sovereign command to release all of them and proclaim the essential validity of their cause. Mr Raghavaiah not only disagreed with this new approach but also felt deeply humiliated before what he considered a mob of delinquents; all of this because a thoughtless woman had now the authority to deem what was and was not right. He was, to state the obvious, seriously unhappy with the turn of events.

In these circumstances the Dewan did not quite understand Sethu Lakshmi Bayi and what she was doing. He viewed her, mistakenly he would realise late in the day, as an unrealistic and naive woman, who had neither knowledge nor any comprehension of the practical realities of her time. His political philosophy was that 'while he conceded the sovereign's prerogative to appoint her Minister, he would stress that her responsibility for administration would cease the moment the choice was made'.[45] In other words, she was expected to delegate everything to him and stay cushioned in the comforts of the palace, much like her predecessor. So when she made it plain that she intended to keep her minister on a tighter leash, and had no intention whatever to park herself as a mere figurehead, Mr Raghavaiah became thoroughly piqued.

The Dewan was a fighter, however, and decided that for the benefit of the government and the state (not to speak of himself), Sethu Lakshmi Bayi had to be kept in her rightful, wholly ceremonial place. The more she got involved, he convinced himself, the more damage she would do. Her alleged condescension towards him by dabbling in delicate matters such as the Vaikom movement was also evidence of her ignorance of statecraft, political finesse and of her lack of knowledge about worldly business. After all, this was a man who had kept an 'octopian grip' over the state and, in the words of one critic, had 'the spirit of a Torquemada—cold, fierce, ruthless', showing the world that he was 'strong but not sympathetic'.[46] It is not difficult to picture a headstrong and capable man like Mr Raghavaiah finding it impossible in the 1920s to reconcile to the authority of a woman whose principal occupation hitherto was temple ceremony and gentle piety; whose best friends were relatives and a strawberry-blonde spinster;

and whose excessive bookishness was only too well known. If she was suddenly asserting herself it was only because power had momentarily turned her head, and she could easily be wrenched back to where she belonged. And so the man who had once publicly proclaimed his 'absolute ownership of administrative powers' resolved to teach Sethu Lakshmi Bayi a lesson in realpolitik.[47]

His methods of doing so were insidious. Information was never given fully, his manner of dealing with the Maharani bordered on the dictatorial (perhaps in the hope that out of fear she would eventually defer to him), and her suggestions and directions were received with the greatest reluctance. All of this, however, was starkly visible to those in the corridors of government, and to Mr Raghavaiah's greatest surprise and supreme resentment, Sethu Lakshmi Bayi proved to be willing to pay back in kind. One of his innovations, for instance, was to ensure that he, as Dewan, would be her sole contact in the administration, which would leave her cripplingly dependent. It is believed that he sternly ordered all important government officers, who were so far permitted to call on the ruler to pay their respects, from meeting the Maharani. 'This attempt was interpreted as a veiled effort to keep the ruler out of touch with her subjects and to assail her customary freedom to contact them.'[48]

But Mr Raghavaiah underestimated Sethu Lakshmi Bayi's gentle demeanour and erred in presuming she could be bullied into defeat; she had stood up to Sankaran Tampi for years and had it in her to stand up to the Dewan as well. Outwardly she maintained an almost deceptive equanimity, never once raising a quarrel. But behind that shroud she retaliated more strongly than he had imagined likely. Since his effort was to keep her at a distance from her officers, she made it a point to do the exact opposite: whoever wished to meet with her was promptly granted an interview. Ostensibly to 'enrich her store of public information', Sethu Lakshmi Bayi cordially ignored the Dewan's efforts and freely conferred with government officials on state business, so that when her minister came she was always perfectly informed already.[49] Her unfailing composure and politeness towards him must also have been particularly galling, for though not obvious it was underlined by amusement, sarcasm and a pitiful resignation that a man of his ability should be so insecure. The Maharani, Mr Raghavaiah realised, was tougher than he had first imagined.

So the contest between ruler and minister spilled over from petty matters into the critical public issue of the Vaikom Satyagraha. The Maharani was obviously sympathetic while the Dewan stood obdurately against the movement. He actually had an upper hand in this matter, for high-caste conservative men staffed the state's administrative machinery for most part. They supported his views, which meant Sethu Lakshmi Bayi could find little backing within her own government, not to speak of the palace where also orthodox Brahmin dominance was compelling. Viewed from this context, her positive gestures towards the reform movement assume considerable significance beyond mere symbolic affirmations of her sympathy. They testify to a percipient shrewdness, for through these kind overtures, Sethu Lakshmi Bayi bolstered her own position (moral and political) vis-à-vis her reluctant government.

First by releasing the prisoners she made it clear that she was not going to continue Mulam Tirunal's policy and that there was definitely backing for the movement at the highest level; then by personally meeting with the satyagraha's leaders she showed she was serious in her sympathy; and yet, by not committing to anything during that interaction, she passed on the indirect message that she was constrained by her own administration, unable to do anything even when she desired to. What is also noteworthy is that after the jathas arrived in Trivandrum, she gave them an appointment only ten days later instead of wrapping up the whole affair quickly and quietly as any other reluctant leader in the hot seat might have done. This gave the agitators ample opportunity to publicise their cause in the capital, exposing those in power for the first time to the force and passion supporting them. Mr Raghavaiah was increasingly placed between the figurative rock and hard place with the satyagrahis bellowing in his ears. He registered distinctly that the Maharani's dawdling over the meeting was far from innocent, which might explain why, when the leaders of the movement went to see him after their conference with her, they met with a rebuke.[50] He did, however, have to swallow the bitter truth that just like the ruler needed her minister's support, he needed her confidence too.

Since Sethu Lakshmi Bayi had pointed out the Legislative Council's vote on the subject as a determinant in her final decision, attention turned to January 1925 and the proceedings in the house. If here the movement received support, it would mean that the public and its representatives wished to have reforms implemented, and the conservative government would have no alternative but to reconcile to change. The only person who could oppose it then, under the law, would be the monarch, which meant power would finally be in her hands alone. A positive vote would thus endow the Maharani with a clear mandate to go ahead and take an independent decision with the approval of the satyagrahis and growing sections of her people. Simply put, Sethu Lakshmi Bayi would come into her own if the Legislative Council voted for reforms. But then success for the cause would also translate into the reverberating defeat and humiliation of Mr Raghavaiah, which he had no intention of countenancing, just as he did not intend to hand over power on a platter to the ruler. He had to formulate his own strategy to win and reverse the damage the lady had done. And so even as the satyagrahis with the barely concealed encouragement of the Maharani lobbied with legislators to support their cause, the Dewan set out to foil precisely such a development. Victory, he was determined, would be his even if it meant Sethu Lakshmi Bayi falling flat on her royal face.

The Legislative Council of Travancore consisted of fifteen officials, seven nominated non-officials, and twenty-eight elected members from the public, making a total of fifty constituents. Much debate ensued in the house about the Vaikom movement but it appeared that there was enormous support in favour of the reform. However, when votes were cast on 31 January 1925, N. Kumaran's motion was defeated by twenty-two votes against twenty-one. All fifteen government officials voted against it, as did four nominated members, and three elected representatives.[51] The Dewan, it turned out, had used all his clout to ensure he got a majority, even if it was of only one vote. Seven members had either conveniently absented themselves or stood neutral, also apparently at his instigation. 'It has now become clear,' lamented a disappointed observer, 'that the Government is to a large extent acting as the real opposition.'[52] Mr Raghavaiah was lambasted openly for his unbecoming attitude and accused of 'having made himself the leader of a section with vested interests' as opposed to being 'the dignified head of all classes'.[53] And in the process he inadvertently sounded the beginning of his end in Travancore.

The episode in the legislature had a deleterious influence on the peace of the movement and reports began to be heard that there were people advocating 'direct action' now.[54] Many were asking why they could not force entry into temples, instead of trying these non-violent techniques with a government that seemed positively unprincipled. Such disquieting suggestions gave Gandhi, not surprisingly, a few jitters, but they also seem to have had an effect on the Dewan. He issued a nervous call to 'both sides' to change their 'angle of vision', assuring the people that the government was 'prepared to do everything in their power to explore the avenues' of peaceful negotiation.[55] But it was too late, for the die was cast. The satyagrahis did not repose confidence in Mr Raghavaiah any more and neither did vast sections of the masses. Sethu Lakshmi Bayi too decided that the Dewan's going out of his way to impose his policy contrary to hers was intolerable. She was willing to entertain his personality so far, but it was time now to exercise her powers and show him she meant business. Even before the vote in the Legislative Council, she had discussed with the Resident the idea of retiring the Dewan, which option was now confirmed. Citing his tendency to check her authority as absolutely unacceptable and lamenting his dictatorial practices, Sethu Lakshmi Bayi asked Mr Raghavaiah to revert to British service by June that year. His otherwise impressive career in Travancore came, thus, to a somewhat embarrassing termination for the simple reason that he refused to adapt himself to the changing tide and to his new monarch.[56]

In the meantime, after the debacle in the legislature, in February 1925 it was announced that Gandhi had decided to come to Travancore in person to resolve the deadlock (and presumably to maintain peace). He arrived with his followers, including his secretary Mahadev Desai, his son Ramdas, C. Rajagopalachari, and some others at Vaikom on 10 March. A massive crowd of 10,000 people received them there at a public function where the leaders of the Ezhava community presented an address and where he vocally expressed his complete endorsement of the movement. The very next day he commenced discussions with some of the orthodox Brahmins in the locality, which were not especially fruitful or satisfying, before driving down south to meet the Maharani and the Dewan.

At that time Sethu Lakshmi Bayi was sojourning with her family on the coast at Varkala and it was at the bungalow there that she prepared to receive the man the world called Mahatma, a Great Soul. She had made yet another positive gesture by inviting him to meet her and placing at his disposal an official car, treating him also as a state guest. Excitement was on a high and all the members of her family waited in eager anticipation, watching curiously from the windows for the car to drive up. None of them could interact with him, since the visit was official, except for Rama Varma who was present at the meeting. He was a hesitant admirer of sorts at this time, ironically, given his Western tastes and temperament. He considered Gandhi 'one of the greatest living men' with a phenomenal 'soul stirring appeal'. In *The Microcosm*, a journal edited by the Valiya Koil Tampuran for exclusive circulation, we find reflections of not only his views but also what was perhaps being discussed in the palace at the time. 'Mahatma Gandhi has at long last decided to visit Vaikom,' he announced in the February issue. 'There can be no doubt that his visit to Travancore at this time is eminently desirable in the interests of all parties. The Satyagraha movement has been mainly carried on at his instance and it is up to him to find out how much genuine support it has in the country. The caste Hindus too might get an opportunity to explain their point of view to him ... It is hoped that the Mahatma will find out the true significance of the fight. If, however, he makes up his mind in favour of the Satyagraha movement, most probably similar movements will be started in many other centres in this country such as Mavelikkara, Harippad, and Ambalapuzha.'[57]

Sethu Lakshmi Bayi was therefore perfectly aware that by welcoming Gandhi, she was courting the risk of aggravating the situation as much as the possibility of a final resolution. Still she went ahead with the plan, confident that something positive would come out of it. And when they actually met that day, it became clear that they had more to agree about than first believed. No minutes seem to have survived of that meeting but the Maharani explained herself quite clearly (and convincingly for that matter) to Gandhi, so that he left the conference as something of an ambassador for her. To the reverberating cheers of crowds in Varkala, the next morning he positively announced:

> Her Highness' sympathies so far as she is personally concerned, are entirely with those who are trying to seek redress. I am free to tell you that she considers that these roads at Vaikom should be open to all classes. But as the Head of the State she feels powerless unless there is public opinion behind her and unless therefore the public opinion of Travancore is organized in a perfectly legitimate, peaceful and constitutional manner, and unless that opinion is expressed in an equally constitutional, legitimate and peaceful manner, though ever so emphatic, she will feel powerless to grant the relief that is required. I for my part entirely accept that position.[58]

This was quite extraordinary, for Sethu Lakshmi Bayi passed a crucial message to her people through the Mahatma, which she could not do in the normal course as monarch. It was implicit in this that they ought to understand her constraints as a ruler and while she would do everything in her power, she needed overwhelming support from outside to match the pressures of conservatism inside (which remained in spite of Mr Raghavaiah's defeat).[59] She also needed Gandhi to prevent a law and order calamity arising in the state. Deducing this, Gandhi tried to help the Maharani conciliate the authorities. He assured the government that the reformers' 'objective is not to irritate orthodoxy but to win it over to their side. Their object moreover is in no way to embarrass the Government ... [but to] enlist its sympathy and support.'[60] By the end of March a temporary compromise was then finally announced after a conference between Police Commissioner W.H. Pitt and Gandhi. The Gandhi–Pitt Pact, as some called it, decided that the satyagrahis would continue with their activities to build support for the cause, but they would stop attempting to use the temple roads. And the government promised to issue orders to withdraw the police and remove the barricades from Vaikom, trusting the satyagrahis to respect the status quo until a final decision was taken. Orders to this effect were passed on 1 April, and while there were many who felt Gandhi's visit had not quite succeeded, for most part the fact that the previously severe government was willing to work with the reformers and come to a mutually agreeable conclusion was seen as a decisive development. For Sethu Lakshmi Bayi things were on track exactly as she desired and Mr Raghavaiah deferred to her wishes on the subject. In his fall, he finally decided to act with grace.

For the next several months the leaders of both sides conferred, debated, and discussed, as they ought to have been doing right from the onset. The government's persistent worry was about the consequence the reform would have. Temple entry would inevitably become the next demand and the Mahatma had himself declared that 'the opening of the roads is not the final but the first step in the ladder of reform'.[61] But as Sethu Lakshmi Bayi's next Dewan, who was considerably more empathetic, noted, old practices could not be 'dynamited out of existence' and would require slow progress, through education and debate.[62] This stand in fact hints at the continued pressure of forces within the palace, which were willing to take baby steps but would never permit a sudden and radical change of established norms. So in June 1925 when Sethu Lakshmi Bayi passed final orders, she conceded much to the satyagrahis while holding on enough to conciliate the orthodoxy and demonstrate to them that their views would also be respected.

It was decided that the roads around the Vaikom Temple on the northern, western and southern sides, would be thrown open to all Hindus irrespective of caste. The eastern street, however, which led to the main gate of the temple, remained barred, and as an alternative a new parallel road was constructed for everybody's use by November. It was also promised that a similar policy would be implemented in all other temple towns of Travancore, in consultation with local stakeholders. In some places, such as Suchindram, negotiations proved very difficult due to the powerful influence of local Brahmins, leading to agitations, so that some years would pass before success was achieved. But in others like Kannankulangara, for instance, the police were ordered to break Brahmin opposition by force and in fact open up even the eastern street to low castes.[63] One by one, public roads were opened to all subjects of the state. In other words, by 1928, infrastructure accessible so far only to the 8,00,000-odd high castes was thrown open for an estimated 1.7 million low castes also.[64] The Maharani was quick to demonstrate her own subscription of this and to lead by example; the roads around her royal abode and the temple in Attingal were declared free, and at the riverbank nearby notice boards were erected in English and Malayalam announcing that the ferry, hitherto plying only for high-caste Hindus, would now serve everyone.[65]

The news was received with great acclaim everywhere. Gandhi lauded the reforms as 'a bed-rock of freedom' and expressed his highest admiration of the Maharani.[66] Newspapers carried her character sketches and elaborate reports, while ordinary people also wrote in from distant parts of India, thanking her for the long-awaited changes. 'By humanitarian farsighted statesmanship respecting Vaikom road problem,' telegrammed one C. Vijayaraghavachari from Kodaikanal, 'Her Highness has placed Hindu religion under eternal obligation to her.' 'Man's destinies appear safer with women than men!' wrote in another admirer, while the Poona Municipality in the Bombay Presidency sent the Maharani their felicitations.[67] Many women and women's organisations also sent letters and telegrams to Satelmond Palace, and it was clear that Sethu Lakshmi Bayi had come out on top, with universal admiration at the end of the Vaikom Satyagraha. She had passed her maiden test with distinction.

In retrospect it might appear that the Maharani could have taken a more forceful stand and issued arbitrary orders right at the start. But her circumstances and disposition precluded such an option. She knew she had to rule for several more years and preside over a high-caste-dominated government. Alienating them on matters so personal and sensitive as religious sentiment would put her in a difficult position. As Gandhi himself warned, 'Let us not retard [reforms] by indiscretion or over-zeal.'[68] Similarly, while she sympathised with the reformers, she subscribed to her husband's views that she could not allow the government to be stampeded into changing its ways. In the larger perspective, in fact, consciously or inadvertently, Sethu Lakshmi Bayi's style of approaching the issue also took the right step in instilling the democratic practices of debate and discussion between conflicting groups in her state. Patience, moderation and balance were the hallmark of her policy, and through these she managed to conclude the Vaikom Satyagraha on a happy note. 'It was an act of great magnitude with far flung echoes, apart from being the first enactment of its kind in India.'[69] As a domino effect, similar movements commenced in Cochin and Malabar also, so that by the 1930s 'the climate for the introduction of social reforms of a more radical nature' (i.e., temple entry) was created with success. And thus Sethu Lakshmi Bayi earned for herself, in the words of the historian Sreedhara Menon, 'an honoured place among the social reformers of modern Kerala'.[70]

She also won some wonderful appreciation for her personal qualities and mien from none other than Gandhi himself. When he arrived in Varkala for their meeting in March 1925, little did that famous loincloth-and-shawl-clad, frugality-promoting nationalist expect he would meet such a striking young queen. Walking into the drawing room of the Maharani's residence, he was astounded to discover a handsome woman dressed in austere white who could give him a run for his money insofar as the use of cotton khadi was concerned. So amazed was the Mahatma by Sethu Lakshmi Bayi that he dedicated a generous paragraph to her in *Young India,* proclaiming to the world that he had met 'the ideal of Indian womanhood' in Travancore:

> My visit to Her Highness was an agreeable surprise for me. Instead of being ushered into the presence of an over-decorated woman, sporting diamond pendants and necklaces, I found myself in the presence of a modest young woman who relied not upon jewels or gaudy dress for beauty but on her own naturally well formed features and exactness of manners. Her room was as plainly furnished as she was plainly dressed. Her severe simplicity became an object of my envy. She seemed to me an object lesson for many a prince and many a millionaire whose loud ornamentation, ugly looking diamonds, rings and studs and still more loud and almost vulgar furniture offend the taste and present a terrible and sad contrast between them and the masses from whom they derive their wealth.[71]

Gandhi was no friend of royalty, with all their vagaries and proclivities, and it stands as a testimony to Sethu Lakshmi Bayi that India's undisputed leader looked up at her with absolute awe. It is also said that when their meeting came to a conclusion, she remarked to him, 'There is another Mahatma who resides here. I do hope you are going to pay your respects.' She was referring to Sri Narayana Guru, the spiritual leader of the Ezhavas, whom she never met but apparently respected.[72] It must have impressed Gandhi quite a bit that surrounded by so much orthodox prejudice, this fairly conservative woman still had the independence of thought and outlook to recognise and appreciate his meeting later that day with a low-caste leader who mattered so much to a large section of her people, for whom there was no other voice of expression.

All these events occurred within a year of Sethu Lakshmi Bayi's coming to power and it was widely appreciated that she could win the respect and admiration of her people so quickly and so very substantially. And it was not just Gandhi who noted her judicious and equable attitude towards political questions. The Government of India had also been keenly observing the ruler, in whom they did not really at first invest much confidence. Indeed, Mr Cotton had in September 1924, soon after her installation, made the mistake of evaluating Sethu Lakshmi Bayi at face value. He described her as being 'of the pious, orthodox and domestic type' although he conceded that she was 'remarkably well read' and possessed a 'considerable charm of manner'.[73] But when newspapers described her as 'a highly distinguished lady of wide culture, broad outlook and catholic views' who commanded the 'entire confidence of her people', the Resident was quite unconvinced.[74] He felt, like Mr Raghavaiah, that she was too inexperienced and removed from reality to make a good ruler, adding also the point that she was 'completely under the domination' of her husband.[75] In these circumstances he wondered how successful Sethu Lakshmi Bayi would be in power.

But unlike the Dewan, Mr Cotton readily confessed his error of judgement when he made one. It struck him very soon after the Maharani's reign began that a first impression could be highly deceptive. The conformism of Sethu Lakshmi Bayi's personal manners, for instance, belied her urbane and forward-looking mindset towards matters of government and state. Once this became clear he reviewed his previous conclusions, paying her the attention and respect she deserved. In a letter written to the Political Secretary in Delhi in January 1925, Mr Cotton noted with pleasant surprise and approval:

> Her Highness has now had nearly five months experience since she assumed the Regency on the 1st of September, and she has spared no pains to acquaint herself, so far as the time has permitted, with every branch of work. Her industry and intelligence are of a high order. She has a great sense of fairness and high ideals and has already shown herself on more than one occasion capable of expressing an opinion of her own and strong enough to see that her orders are carried out. The more I see of her, the more I am inclined to hold that she is not so much under the influence of her Consort, as in the first days of the Regency I feared would be the case.[76]

Sethu Lakshmi Bayi had demonstrated adequately through her work that she was set to be a success as a ruler. By her constant appraisal of the flood situation, in her manner of handling the Dewan's obstinacy, and through her effective dealings with the satyagrahis at Vaikom, the young Maharani proved to be up to the task she herself so dreaded at first. She was actually rather surprised by the ease with which she managed to apply her mind to politics, leading her to heave a sigh of relief and positively enjoy her work henceforth. By April 1925 she confidently set out on her first tour of Travancore as sovereign 'with a view to make herself personally acquainted with the wants of the people'.[77] As the Maharani's motorcade passed through the pretty hamlets and villages of the country, the awe that was conventionally owed to the monarch merged with a sincere affection for the woman occupying that position. At every major town on the way Sethu Lakshmi Bayi broke her journey to meet with her people. She personally received petitions and representations from them, often even granting interviews on the spot to those with pressing needs. Newspapers were singing paeans to the young queen by the time she arrived in the hills, recognising that her popularity with her subjects was matched by her manifest empathy for them.

And thus, the inauguration of Sethu Lakshmi Bayi's government was as eventful as it was positive. She emerged with bright colours to the applause of the masses she reigned over. The world sang her glories, with Gandhi leading the chorus, and not many rulers could claim such tremendous success so early in their reigns. But then politics was not a fairy world where things remained brilliant and sparkling forever. And the Maharani was set to unleash upon herself a wave of political fury that would not only give her nerves of steel but would also set in stone the principles by which she intended to rule.

6

A Christian Minister

When Martanda Varma died in 1758, little did he imagine how perilously close Travancore would come to annihilation in only fifty years' time. For, by the end of the eighteenth century, the horrific war with Tipu Sultan of Mysore left his distraught successor first knocking at the doors of the English for military assistance and then, having recruited their services, running helter-skelter to pay for it. During the next nearly two decades, until 1810, Travancore remained in debt with a mismanaged economy and precarious government. The English East India Company never ceased to press for payments and in 1808–09 the Dewan Velu Tampi rose in revolt against them. It was an ill-fated venture, one that would end with his dead body hanging from a gibbet, and with the complete and unabridged humiliation of his sovereign. The armies of Travancore, so masterfully assembled by Martanda Varma, were disbanded and the people were prohibited from carrying arms. The royal family began to live a ghastly nightmare, counting the days before the Company annexed its territories and relegated their dynasty to the dustbins of history.

And then, in what surprised everyone, Travancore was saved; and saved by the convictions of one man. It was not a heroic monarch or a powerful minister but a middle-aged Scotsman from across the seas who heaved the state out of its impending doom. Indeed, just as Martanda Varma forged modern Travancore from an assortment of petty principalities, it was Col John Munro of the East India Company who secured it from a premature demise at its most vulnerable moment since. The future 'Model State', which so prided itself on its Hindu identity and Brahminical traditions, became hugely indebted, thus, to the generosity of a foreign Christian.

A new chapter began in Travancore when Col Munro (popular even today among an age group of Malayalis who studied in school about 'Munro Sahib') arrived as Resident in Trivandrum in 1809. The fate of the state hung in balance before him but when, soon afterwards, a new intelligent ruler came to power in the form of Gowri Lakshmi Bayi, he realised that annexation was not necessarily the only option. The Rani, for her part, went out of her way to win him over, famously declaring: 'To you, Colonel, I entrust everything connected with my country.'[1] 'Thus, this wise Princess,' we are told, 'managed to place her kingdom which was verging on ruin and was nearly falling into the hands of the Honourable East India Company, in a position of stability,' relieving herself 'not only from the cumbersome burden of Government, but also from a world of personal inconvenience'.[2] She was a clever woman in reality, for she satisfied the Resident by practically making him the ruler while at the same time averting an actual acquisition of her domains by his Company.[3] After all, 'a line from Col Munro should have been enough'[4] to take the throne away from her successors, and Gowri Lakshmi Bayi liberally massaged his ego and allowed him to exercise real power to prevent such a development. He was successfully persuaded, then, to go that extra mile to protect Travancore from direct British Raj, shaping its modern identity in the process.

Lord Minto had made it clear in 1809 after quelling Velu Tampi's rebellion that Travancore's two options were either annexation or 'some intermediate and experimental measure' that would ensure it paid its dues to the Company.[5] Col Munro became that experimental measure, and a success at that. Residents were usually a thorn in the side of Indian rulers, but with Gowri Lakshmi Bayi giving him free rein, this one thoroughly altered the traditional administration of Travancore. Several taxes were abolished, forced labour was prohibited, a number of caste discriminations were removed, and Christians received active state patronage for the first time. Land surveys were conducted and a modern administrative machinery, modelled on the British style, was introduced into the state. The results were telling. By 1818, Travancore became free of debt, and its revenues, which had stood at Rs 17 lakh in 1810 now sat at a comfortable Rs 38 lakh. Land revenue, which had been Rs 9 lakh went up to Rs 15 lakh, while the paltry salt revenue of Rs 30,000 rose to Rs 2,30,000. It was with some satisfaction, then, that it was announced in the House of Commons in London that conditions in Travancore had 'greatly improved'.[6]

Col Munro, endearingly, also took a personal interest in protecting the state and its ruler. A popular story goes that when in 1813 the Rani became pregnant, he promptly informed the Company that she had already given birth to a male heir (for his superiors were quite uncertain about a female sovereign and the question of annexation lingered). And then he went to the Sri Padmanabhaswamy Temple and threatened to blow up the deity with a cannon if the baby were not a boy.[7] But what is perhaps more crucial than the Resident's services to the royal family is the impact of his work on Travancore's society and polity. By reforming the administration, Col Munro created for the first time in the state a class of officers and civil servants. No longer, for instance, were ancient families permitted to function as hereditary village heads; individuals, evaluated by the government, were appointed to these positions. So too at every level a bureaucracy took the place of the old feudal system, already in ruins after Martanda Varma's assaults on it, and one's ancestry began to mean less than it did before. Munro famously used to flog erring officials himself with his cat-o'-nine-tails to ensure efficiency.[8] The judicial system was revamped and courts began to be set up. Christian missionaries, who brought with them the novelty of English education, were greatly encouraged by the state. In essence, modernity (in pre-Victorian style) arrived in Travancore, bringing with it also, however, a social turbulence that would influence the state for the remainder of its life ahead.

One of the outcomes of Gowri Lakshmi Bayi's vesting so much power in the Resident was that Col Munro's successors all began to fashion themselves as chief advisors to the ruler and harbingers of progress in Travancore. While the Rani and then her sister, Gowri Parvathi Bayi (who ruled from 1814 until 1829) implicitly followed the 'judicious counsels' of the Residents,[9] the two monarchs after them found it rather galling to bear with the constant interference from above.[10] One of them was nearly driven to abdicate[11] while the other, after shilly-shallying for long, was compelled to bend to their will. This second ruler, called Uthram Tirunal, spent Rs 2.13 lakh on weighing himself in gold (which was then distributed as 'alms' to Brahmins so that His Highness might accumulate good karma) and Rs 2 lakh on the festivals in the Sri Padmanabhaswamy Temple at a time when the state was facing financial difficulties and the tribute to the Company was again in arrears. To top it, the government was operating free feeding houses for Brahmins in 1851 at an expense of Rs 3 lakh.[12] These amounts combined could have paid the tribute, and their expenditure on what the British saw as wasteful nonsense caused tempers to flare in Madras. On being admonished, the Dewan proudly announced economies of Rs 75,000 in 1852 only to later reveal that these had been 'effected by discontinuing the engineering office, dismissing 200 pioneers, reducing the number of *munsiffs* [i.e., lower level judges], and cutting the price of pepper paid to the *ryots* [agricultural tenants]'. 'By almost all admissions,' Robin Jeffrey concludes, 'Travancore was misgoverned.'[13] In 1855, then, the Governor of Madras sternly wrote to Uthram Tirunal of 'grave abuses' in his government, of the decaying revenue system, the absence of public works, and more, reviving the threat of annexation for the first time in decades.[14] This 'most dreadful'[15] communiqué shook the ruler to his senses and he realised that it was time again to curry favour with the Company and do what they desired—to enable greater efficiency, greater output, and a greater involvement in the international trade and order the Company was shaping.

The outcome was a fresh dose of modernisation in the state, on a scale considerably greater than Col Munro had perhaps envisaged. It was presided over by Uthram Tirunal's ambitious nephews, none other than Ayilyam Tirunal and Visakham Tirunal, who succeeded him and ruled for a combined twenty-five years. For instance, in 1860 the Public Works Department was officially established and where five years before a sum of Rs 38,000 only was being spent, by 1871 it was Rs 12 lakh.[16] All those departments of government that the British considered crucial to a modern state were developed, with the result that the young rulers were showered with praise. Annual reports, showcasing improvements in various sectors and in total revenue, were churned out on a large scale to highlight the 'progress' that was taking place in Travancore. But as Jeffrey reminds us, these physical manifestations of modernity (which, to be sure, were successful) were not matched with an eager programme of social change. Both rulers 'felt a tension between what they knew the British government expected of them' and the customs and traditions that maintained their exalted place in Travancore's casteist society.[17] And so they continued to modernise the state and its infrastructure, including promoting English education, while going considerably slower on reforming matters of social inequality, which they found somewhat inconvenient to tamper with, passing instead the buck (and the appurtenant headache) to the rulers who followed them.

They knew this was potentially dangerous, and there is a story that when Ayilyam Tirunal laid the foundation stone for the College of Arts in Trivandrum in 1869, he privately remarked to his brother-in-law, 'Well, Tampi, I have just laid the foundation stone for anarchy.'[18] Indeed, the spread of English education (pivoted on the Enlightenment favourites: reason and rationality) without a proportionate removal of social disadvantages caused uncomfortable questions to be asked. If a high-caste candidate were a matriculate and a low-caste one a graduate, shouldn't the better job go to the latter? Why were Brahmins being perpetually patronised at state expense when they had no educational qualifications and lived off what was now deemed superstitious mumbo-jumbo? And many more disturbing doubts arose. The balance of public life that was hitherto centred on an inegalitarian but stable caste hierarchy began to tilt unpredictably, giving birth, ironically enough, to that great bane of Indian society and politics: communalism.

English education had become a passport to success by the second half of the nineteenth century. Now that feudalism was fading, what degrees and official qualifications an individual acquired decided his employability in government (and the vast bureaucracy was the biggest employer). Competition began to mount for the limited places on offer that supplied social mobility, highlighting the inequalities of Travancore's society even more forcefully. The substantial Land Revenue Department, for example, was barred to Christians and all low-caste Hindus since it also handled the properties of government temples and shrines. Christians ventured into the plantation business with considerable success but met powerful opposition from Anglo-Indian and British planters. Besides, only very few Christians had the resources to invest in plantation, and the majority vied for state service. When such blatant injustices affected their employment prospects, the educated classes began to associate with their caste kinsmen. As communities they began to lobby and pressurise the government to open up new avenues for them. And sometimes they joined hands for common purposes while normally standing against each other.[19] But whichever was the case, in 'the rush for government appointments' and the 'scramble for offices',[20] social cohesion began to dissolve and Travancore slowly became a steaming communal cauldron.

The communalisation of competition helped get jobs, to be fair. If a Nair were appointed, he would be expected first to enable members of his extended family secure good positions, and then people from his wider community. So when Sankaran Tampi became a power in the land, even highly cultivated Nair leaders like C.V. Raman Pillai, the distinguished author, acquiesced in his predominance because his influence served their community very well.[21] But that said Nairs were not the preferred favourites of the government. The royal family being as orthodox and purity-conscious as it was, had surrounded itself with Brahmins since the times of Martanda Varma. From 1817 until 1914, for almost a century, thus, with a single exception, every Dewan of Travancore had been a Brahmin (all of them were charged with nepotism and none of them were Malayalis).[22] Tamil Brahmins, who avidly took up English education and combined the new qualifications with their ritual precedence, dominated higher government appointments in 1891.

Similarly, of the nine seats in the (then small) Legislative Council, five belonged to Brahmins.[23] In that same year, therefore, the Nairs organised a mass petition, famously called the 'Malayali Memorial', to be presented to the Maharajah, asking for a greater share of jobs for the 'sons of the soil'.[24] Travancore, they asserted, had a 60 per cent Hindu population and jobs ought to be allotted proportionately. This was rather disingenuous, for the low castes did not have as many qualified persons as they did, and by classing them all together as 'Hindus', it would be the Nairs who would benefit most. Disappointingly for them, the Ezhavas presented a separate memorial, essentially arguing against being treated as 'Hindus' and calling for reservation by community, while the Syrian Christians demanded that only the best should be employed even if they were not Hindus. It was community against community in Travancore by the advent of the twentieth century.

Through the first quarter of the century, Nairs did succeed in wresting a sizable share of higher employment from the Tamil Brahmins. They united most of their sub-castes, used their massive population to win majorities in the Legislative Council, pressed the government to their advantage and made ample use of Sankaran Tampi's reins on the Maharajah. But in keeping with the jealous communal spirit, they were unwilling to be magnanimous to anybody else, and tensions mounted. The Ezhavas, as a low caste, had several battles to fight, while castes below them were practically miserable with no voice. Among the Christians, the Syrian Christians (despite their own internal divisions) dominated while Roman Catholics, Latin Catholics and others had feeble political expression. Muslims and other minorities clamoured to be heard in what was essentially a statewide communal din, so much so that in 1916 the government decided that even students in the Maharajah's College could not be left to vote for the year's most outstanding pupil, as 'caste prejudice played a great part in the elections and ... merit was ignored.'[25]

Mulam Tirunal then made some concessions to the low castes and Christians, most notably by opening the Land Revenue Department to them by removing temple lands from its purview. But his conservatism meant that Brahmins and Nairs (in that order) were still favoured. The former tried in vain to preserve their position by appealing to the ritual sanctity of the royal family, and the latter were determined on showing Brahminism the door. While the attitude of the ruler was imperative to any development, placing one's supporters in positions of authority could make a world of difference. And so when Mulam Tirunal died, the communities braced themselves for a fresh fight in Trivandrum. For who would reign above the others and secure that most favoured status would depend on who had the ear of the new administration. Like most others, the politicians also presumed Sethu Lakshmi Bayi to be a pliable female who, like Gowri Lakshmi Bayi, would resign the burden of government entirely to her Dewan and take a comfortable back seat as a figurehead. And since it was obvious that Mr Raghavaiah had to go, the selection of the next minister became the big political question of the hour, which would determine the fate of all the factions for the coming years.

Since for over a century Travancore's premiers had been 'imported' from outside (even Sir Krishnan, while a Nair, was from Malabar) the demand for a 'native' minister was almost deafening by 1925.[26] It was a familiar call in other princely states as well, where rulers preferred loyal outsiders to possibly turbulent locals. The Nairs as the most powerful political lobby in Travancore were especially covetous of success and complete patronage now, having been denied this all these years but of which they had had an appetising slice through Tampi. That the Maharani was known to be religious and orthodox in her personal manners also raised hopes of a preference towards Hindus. If they made enough noise, it was assumed, she might be convinced to forsake the Brahmins and select a Nair.

Sethu Lakshmi Bayi, however, had a very different view on the subject. Years of bookishness, so scornfully dismissed by everybody, had in fact equipped her with a broad mind and an incisive, almost academic understanding of her political surroundings. She sought answers to address the roots of trouble, with very exact views on how to achieve this, instead of attempting to placate its immediate, superficial manifestations. Most importantly, she had no intention of playing by the communal parameters that had become the standard of public life in the state. But transforming entrenched rules was a knotty affair—one that would throw up violent resistance and precipitate intense resentment. And so when her choice of minister was announced, infuriated politicians in Trivandrum went hoarse crying foul.

Correspondence with the Government of India on how the Maharani intended to run her administration had been on since October 1924. She had already turned down their suggestion to appoint an Executive Council to assist the Dewan, noting that the politicians would insist on elections to these positions; and she was not keen to give the various communities another platform to quarrel.[27] Her decision, therefore, was to continue with the old practice of having a Dewan responsible for all affairs, allowing him to delegate authority to his de facto cabinet of the heads of departments as required. She also requested the Government of India to recommend successors to Mr Raghavaiah but none of their proposals were very appealing. So by January 1925 she put forward a name on her own after due consideration, although this was not formally proposed to the authorities until April.

The candidate in question was Maurice Emygdius Watts, a London-based barrister who was, interestingly, the brother of the Maharani's old tutor, Miss Watts. While correspondence on the subject was still confidential, news leaked out to the press in March and suddenly a whirlwind of criticism hit Satelmond Palace. 'It is notorious,' vociferated the *Jenmabhoomi*, 'that this consummation is entirely due to back-stair influence,'[28] while *The People*, under the headline of 'Unfortunate Travancore' decried the Maharani for casting an 'unwarranted humiliation' on her state by 'this unsympathetic and unwise step'.[29] Every paper, except for *The Western Star* and *The Standard* registered a protest against the ruler's choice. Politicians were up in arms against her for even *presuming* that a foreigner would be acceptable, a man about whom they knew little and whose communal affiliations (more critically) were uncertain. The general picture conveyed was that her old teacher and only friend was wickedly influencing Sethu Lakshmi Bayi to bring in her brother, which the amenable Maharani was foolishly conceding. Some newspapers even attacked Mr Cotton, for they assumed that this import from London was perhaps his idea, although Sethu Lakshmi Bayi had, having anticipated this charge, expressly written to him in February that when in due course any announcement was made, she had no qualms in letting it be known that the selection was entirely hers.[30] She would not, she assured him, shirk responsibility.

Alongside allegations of back-door influence, there were also seemingly profound expressions of shock and surprise that in a Hindu state a Christian (and an Anglo-Indian for that matter) should be appointed Dewan. The minister had certain roles to play in the Sri Padmanabhaswamy Temple, for instance, which a non-high-caste Hindu could not perform. So the politicians started offering alternatives themselves from within their respective parties. The Tamil Brahmins wanted someone from their community to be brought in from Madras while the Syrian Christians insisted on either one Mr Mathen or one Mr K. Chandy, both of whom were employed in Mysore.[31] The Nairs, who the Resident reported, had been vehemently trying for some time to 'get rid of Raghavaiah' hoped, for their part, that 'Her Highness would appoint a Nair official who would dance to their tune', and recommended the Chief Secretary Mr K. Krishna Pillai to be promoted as Dewan. Either way, the politicians were 'working up an agitation against the selection made' and protests had erupted unanimously from all communal quarters.[32]

What surprised, and perhaps even impressed the Resident, was the calm and collected manner in which Sethu Lakshmi Bayi met all the opposition, belying once again the fact that she was a new, unseasoned ruler. 'Her Highness,' he recorded, 'regards these alarums and excursions with remarkable indifference. She points out that what Travancore *needs* at the present moment is an officer who has no recent concern with local politics and is outside any factions, and free from communal bias.'[33] Indeed, while she had not anticipated so much trouble over her suggestion, she 'maintained from the beginning that it is largely artificial and engineered by partisans of those who might have confidentially aspired to the post themselves'.[34] Writing from Varkala that summer, Sethu Lakshmi Bayi made her point of view very clear, also expressing her thoughts on how the issue ought to be tackled:

> A Travancorean who is an ultra Nair is alone acceptable to the political Nair party. The Brahmin as a political factor is a negligible quantity [for in spite of all the jobs they held, they were a small minority] and is disliked by practically all the other communities. The Christian as such does not exist in politics since the different denominations under Christianity want each to be recognised as a separate community. So much so, the appointment of a Travancorean to *whatever* party he might belong, cannot and will not give general satisfaction. The only point therefore to be considered is that the holder of the post must be fit for it.[35]

The Maharani was, therefore, quite firm that in selecting her right-hand man, neither religion nor community could play any role; a 'non-party man possessing a high order of efficiency and enjoying my confidence' was whom she preferred, 'especially at this juncture when I stand in the great need of [communally] disinterested advice and help'.[36] That said, she was not unduly prejudiced against the politicians' suggestions either. For by the time Mr Watts's name was formally proposed, the Resident and she had already discussed the possibility of all local candidates. The Chief Secretary was found 'too amiable and accommodating', for example, to have the force of a minister, and so too were other candidates evaluated. In the end Mr Cotton 'entirely concurred' in her conclusion that there was 'no one who possessed sufficient force of character or general attainments to warrant his being considered for the Dewanship.'[37] As for the argument that Mr Watts was a non-Hindu, the Maharani reminded everyone that if a century ago Travancore could accept Col Munro without qualms, the objections now raised were unwarranted.[38] In any case the Resident also consulted the more orthodox neighbouring Government of Cochin, where in recent times two non-Hindu Dewans had served with no difficulty at all,[39] and was convinced that the arguments of the opposition were fallacious.[40]

This of course brings to the fore the qualifications of Mr Watts that made him, in Sethu Lakshmi Bayi's view, so eminently suitable for the position. For all the hue and cry about his being a foreigner, he was actually a Travancorean, albeit of the aloof, exclusive variety. The Watts family had a long history in the state going back at least to the eighteenth century when their ancestor, Francis Watts, was a wealthy English merchant at Anjengo. Into the nineteenth century, under his son, Vincent Watts, the family ventured into plantation and had coffee estates in Peermade and vast landed properties in Trivandrum. Mr Watts's father, Frank Edwards Watts (son of Vincent), was a student of Robert's School in the capital and for forty-three years had been in service of the Government of Travancore, becoming Chief Secretary in the days of Ayilyam Tirunal. Indeed in 1895 he was believed to have been on 'the eve of his translation from the Chief Secretaryship to the Dewanship', but that is when death snatched him away, leaving it for his son to obtain the position he never did.[41]

Mr Watts himself was born in Trivandrum in 1878 and had completed his schooling from the Maharajah's High School before going off to Madras for graduate studies at the Presidency College. Upon finishing his education in 1901, he joined the Madras Revenue Board and was quickly promoted to the political section in the governor's secretariat. Here his work involved looking after the affairs of all the princely states falling under the Government of Madras, including Travancore. By 1911 he was upgraded and sent to the imperial secretariat in Calcutta and in the same year he went to England and completed the first half of the barrister's course. Upon his return he was assigned to the Imperial Finance Service as Assistant Accountant General, a rank usually reserved for those who passed the Indian Financial Service exam but which was given to him in view of his exceptional service. Working in Delhi, Simla and Calcutta, Mr Watts had drawn a high salary of Rs 1500 per month at this time. When the First World War began, he became District Disbursing Officer for the North-West Frontier Province and by 1919 was made principal Comptroller of Military Accounts for the Government of India. But his health deteriorated at this stage causing a convalescent retreat to London, where he completed his barrister's course. In 1921, at the age of forty-three, he married Edith Malloch, an attractive woman half his age, and commenced legal practice and a new life. Indeed, during his stint in London, he reportedly became so popular that some even suggested he should contemplate standing for parliamentary elections in the future. He had thus been in England for only about five years when the call from the Maharani came, offering him the Dewanship of Travancore.[42]

When Mr Watts's name was forwarded to Delhi for approval, the Government of India performed a detailed background assessment and collected references from his previous superiors. All of them attested to his abilities and expressed confidence in his potential as Dewan of Travancore. Accordingly, the Resident was informed of Delhi's approval of the selection with the only reservation that Mr Watts should be on probation for the first six months, and his confirmation would depend on satisfactory performance during that period. The Maharani concurred with this, and backed by the Government of India, formally announced him as her next Dewan in May 1925. To everyone's surprise, the official proclamation received good press from exactly those newspapers that had first condemned the appointment.[43] Now that it was obvious that Sethu Lakshmi Bayi would not heed the loud clamour of opposition, the politicians could only hope for the best and seek to get into the good books of the new Dewan for their own interests. It was a humorous revelation of how fickle communal politics could be in Travancore of the 1920s where principles and political stands were abandoned as conveniently as they were championed.

For Sethu Lakshmi Bayi this had been a considerable battle, both political as well as of her ideals. Every morning she woke up to unabashed criticism in the newspapers, to which she could never even respond (though, as will be seen, she did have one or two plans up her sleeve for the press). Some of the papers made rather personal comments and accused her of neglecting her people. 'The Regent will be making herself open to the charges of being incapable of foresight, clear vision or sound judgment,' lambasted the *Madras States* while *The People* warned her of being toppled from power. 'Confidence begets confidence,' it thundered, pointing out that 'Her Highness cannot have any claim to the confidence of the people of Travancore.'[44] Neither the Brahmins in the palace nor the Nairs outside supported her on this one; she was going against the tide, alienating each faction in the country, which was a massive political risk. She could, as most politicians to this day do, easily have aligned herself with the most powerful camp (in this case, the Nairs) and won populist support and acclaim, as her predecessors had been doing. But Sethu Lakshmi Bayi, with all her determined idealism, only knew too well that by supporting one communal group over another, she would become party to an appalling phenomenon the state was better off without. Her intention was to downplay communalism and focus on governance; and with that conviction, she stuck by herself.

In order to drive this point home, the Maharani issued orders enunciating the principles by which her administration would consider all appointments. And the guideline was simple: equal and fair opportunity to all. In all government vacancies, candidates were hereafter selected solely on the basis of merit. Preference, however, would be given to 'unrepresented and poorly represented communities' in their position as minorities. Moreover, representation would be 'based more on the number of qualified hands available than on mere numerical strength'. It was also announced that preferential treatment to the minorities would only be in the matter of initial appointment and not for promotions.[45] 'We want our Public Service to be public and a service,' one Christian intellectual declared, lauding Sethu Lakshmi Bayi for thus terminating the domination of caste Hindus. 'Under the wise dispensation of Her Highness,' he added, 'we are getting out of the wonted rut of inequality. And the signs of the time show that the balance is being redressed. History,' he concluded, with a hint of going overboard with his admiration perhaps, 'is fond of cognomen. It speaks of William the Silent, Solomon the Wise, and Bloody Mary, to take a few instances. Let the fitting sobriquet of Her Highness be [Sethu] Lakshmi Bayi the Just.'[46]

But this was not mere flattery, for indeed the Maharani acted on her promises and opened up the government to marginalised classes. A local Christian was for the first time appointed Chief Secretary, a position second only to the Dewan, while another was made a member of the Medical Board. By 1928 an Ezhava was appointed a District Judge and another a Divisional Assistant, both of low caste but now bossing over hundreds of Nair employees. A Muslim official was promoted as a magistrate, another Christian as *peishkar*, and at lower levels too, hundreds of non-Nairs and non-Brahmins were absorbed into the state services, weakening the upper-caste monopoly.[47] As J. Devika notes, 'In a Nair-Brahmin dominated Hindu state, Sethu Lakshmi Bayi cared to listen to the minorities and seriously take them on board. It was a democratisation, something that was never done before and which would not be done after her time.'[48] In the eyes of history, the Maharani has been lauded for this, but at the time she only earned remonstrations and dislike from the leading, entrenched classes of the country.

In the meantime, the new Dewan-elect was delighted by the offer made. It was a singular honour to be appointed chief minister, especially of a state as important as Travancore, with a record of progressive rule and convincing appearances of constitutionalism. It was a glorious culmination of his career, one that was not quite expected. In his moment of elation, he wrote the Maharani a most grandiloquent letter talking of himself as a 'son of the soil who wandered far afield and is now coming back'. In almost poetic verse he added:

> My father and my sisters have given proof to the Crown of Travancore of unswerving loyalty, unstinted fidelity and God fearing integrity. These traditions permeate me; their ideals stimulate me; their devotion will be my devotion ... If, under Providence, I succeed in serving as they have served, I shall feel at the end of the day that I have done my duty by my Sovereign and fellow-citizens of Travancore and thereby have justified Your Highness' gracious selection of me as your Minister.[49]

The Maharani was not really one for flattery or honeyed writing. And, perhaps to make it clear that she meant business, she kept her response to him very tempered and clear, warning of what she expected from her minister:

> You are assuming the administration of the State at a particularly critical moment. Forces born of modern times and the present day education, accented by an unhealthy spirit of communal consciousness, which lay dormant during the reign of H.H. the late Maharajah, have suddenly been let loose, and no amount of tact and wisdom can be considered too great for the new Dewan to enable him to acquit successfully in the midst of the currents and cross currents peculiar to the Travancore of today.[50]

Meanwhile, as the new Dewan prepared to arrive, the old one decided to depart early. Mr Raghavaiah, who was previously 'desperately anxious' to continue in service,[51] had now been offered the presidency of the Council of Regency in Pudukkottai and applied to leave Travancore by the end of April. The Maharani graciously gave her permission and bid him farewell with the traditional gifts of ivory and silks. The Chief Secretary was then asked to officiate as Dewan, following which he was to be promoted as Devaswom Commissioner when Mr Watts arrived. This substantial office was in charge of all the government temples and their properties, and typically the Commissioner was responsible to the Dewan. When Mr Watts's appointment was confirmed, however, there was a call to make the office temporarily independent, and directly responsible to the ruler. The Maharani initially did not prefer this—after all, it was Col Munro, a Christian, who even created this Hindu department by acquiring 348 major and 1,123 minor private temples in 1811–12—but eventually sanctioned the proposal on the Valiya Koil Tampuran's advice.[52] It was not wise, he felt, to push the Nairs to the wall. And so a small victory was granted to them as a diplomatic device.

Mr Watts finally set foot on Travancore's soil on 18 June 1925 when he landed at Cape Comorin. He did not immediately proceed to Trivandrum, since the earliest 'auspicious date' for him to take charge was four days later. So it was 22 June by the time he was driven to Trivandrum and presented to the Maharani in the evening. The next morning he received from her the Dewan's Sword, and officially took over as the new premier of Travancore.[53] He moved into Bhakti Vilas, where a staff trained in the European style was placed at his disposal. The Maharani took a personal interest in ensuring he was comfortable, asking the Chief Engineer to make alterations to the building as the Dewan might require and ordering suitable crockery to be sent there, etc. That evening Mr Watts was also honoured with a public reception put together, oddly enough, by all the politicians of the town. 'All those who were against his appointment at first,' the Maharani's brother chuckled, 'have taken leading parts in the meeting held to welcome him.'[54] If the government was astonished at the sudden warmth of the opposition, the latter were to be surprised even more when it turned out that not only was the Dewan charmingly fluent in Malayalam, but also recognised many classmates among them. He additionally spoke Tamil and Hindustani, and had an academic understanding of Sanskrit, making him suddenly seem palatable to even orthodox Hindus.[55] An 'excellent impression', Mr Cotton endorsed to the authorities in Delhi, and Mr Watts looked like he would do just fine in the muddy waters of political Travancore.[56] His probationary period went off satisfactorily and by December that year a three-year term was confirmed by the Government of India. The Maharani had won this battle.

'The history of civilization,' wrote Sir Robert Bristow in his *Cochin Saga*, 'is written largely in the history of its ports.' And this was entirely true of Kerala, which owed a tremendous deal to trade and the gifts of prosperity it brought with it, from ancient times. The Book of Kings in the Old Testament refers to the flourishing commerce King Solomon had with the Chera dynasty between 1015 and 996 BC, importing gold, silver, ivory, apes, peacocks, sandalwood, and precious stones from their ports. From 69 BC the celebrated Cleopatra of Egypt sent her ships to Kerala, enjoying such a close alliance that upon her defeat in the Battle of Actium, she prepared to set sail and seek sanctuary here with her son. Kerala's staple produce of pepper was practically more valuable than gold, and when the king of the Visigoths besieged Rome in the fifth century, he demanded 3,000 pounds of the spice in return for sparing the imperial city a devastating raid (as it happened, he broke his promise). While most sailed hugging the coastlines of Africa and the Middle East, fearful of the open sea and its violent winds, as early as 120 BC the Egyptians were trying to beat the competition by finding a direct sea route to India. Kerala's exchanges with the East were also prominent and its ancient relations with China went beyond mere trade of goods and embraced the transfer of culture, intellectual knowledge and more. Chinese accounts in the sixth century speak of a Malayali ambassador stationed at the court of the emperor there, and when the fourteenth century Moroccan explorer Ibn Batuta came to Kerala, he discovered close to 12,000 Chinese living in Calicut, of whom about 4,800 were soldiers.[57]

But before the rise of Calicut, it was the fabled port of Muziris (now identified as Cranganore) that served as the principal gateway to India and one of the greatest commercial centres of the ancient world. The *Periplus of the Erythrean Sea* described it as being at the 'height of prosperity' in its heyday, and it placed the region on the global map so that even in the millennium before Christ, Kerala was recognised in all parts of the maritime world. Even then, it was apparently accessible and seems to have enjoyed a sterling reputation for tolerance and diversity, welcoming Arabs, Jews, Christians and many others of assorted ethnic and cultural backgrounds with open arms to contribute to its prosperity. But Muziris's vibrant life came to an unhappy termination when, unexpectedly, the River Periyar flooded and changed course in the fourteenth century, choking up all access, and reducing that historic port into a faint residue of what it used to be. One of the greatest cities of the world fell, thus, to the mandates of nature.

By now the Chera dynasty that once ruled over most of Kerala had perished and the land was divided between many quarrelling principalities claiming descent of competing legitimacies from those old kings of yore; and all of them vied to win the favour of foreign traders. Calicut emerged as an alternative to Muziris in a matter of years, establishing several centuries of dominance, both commercial and economic, over its rivals along the coast, till the Portuguese arrived and upset the local balance of power. This provoked generations of political sparring, with Cochin allowing itself to become a client state of various foreign powers, and in the process rising as a rival to Calicut in an international system increasingly being redefined by European powers as opposed to the old Arabs and Egyptians. The Dutch and the English succeeded the Portuguese as masters of the seas and of Cochin, but the whole region was reduced to a zone of military unrest. All the ports from Calicut to Trivandrum managed at best decent business in the process but none could match the sheer opulence of ancient Muziris or even the recent successes of pre-colonial Calicut. It appeared that Kerala would never again have that one major port that could make its mark on the world as a thriving cornerstone of international commerce. The princes were all battling it out, but it was a violence of desperation in an unfamiliar world and time. Commercial greatness, it seemed, was a thing of the past for Kerala.

By the nineteenth century, however, things began to look optimistic. The British were assured of their power in the land after ousting other European rivals and the bloody warfare that had characterised recent history ceased. India was united under one banner, and stability (albeit imperial) took root. The northern portion of Kerala, once dominated by the Zamorins, became the Malabar district of the Madras Presidency, while Cochin and Travancore retained their independence as tributaries. The three governments worked in peace with each other, giving rise to hopes for the first time in centuries that perhaps Kerala could resume its place as one of the great trading centres of the world. It was the Government of Madras, in fact, that first saw potential in developing a major port on the coast here at Cochin, though of course in order to augment colonial interests rather than to resurrect India's lost maritime splendour. But their ambition and imagination were not met with feasibility, and so when the idea was initially proposed in 1880 it was declared unviable. The problem was that there was a wide bar of sand out at sea which blocked access to the port for all but ships of shallow draft. Dredging was, in those days, a rather rudimentary affair and there was no way a 3-mile channel, which is what was required for deep-sea ships to sail in, could be opened. Cochin, it was regretfully concluded, would have to reconcile to continuing as a small port after all.

But into the early twentieth century more and more ships started passing by the shores of Kerala, which also acquired considerable strategic significance during the First World War. In 1914 the proposal was then re-examined, aided by the fact that recent developments in dredging technology meant that what had been rejected as impossible was now, in fact, quite possible even if still susceptible to the risk of failure. The Government of Madras began correspondence with the state of Cochin to take plans forward, and movement, at a snail's pace, finally began. Sir Robert, who was by then already a distinguished engineer with considerable experience on international harbours, was commissioned to develop the project and arrived on the scene by 1920 to commence basic preparations. He was to dedicate twenty-one years of his life to the new venture, leaving a lasting mark of glory behind.

In the meantime the Government of Madras invited the collaboration of Travancore also in the project, mainly because the expenses were far too forbidding for them and Cochin to bear alone. Besides, while the harbour itself was not part of Travancore territory, much of the land around it was, which necessitated several permissions from its government for railway lines, communications, canals, etc. Additionally, as the Governor of Madras noted, of all the goods that paid import duty at Cochin, 62.5 per cent were for consumption in Travancore.[58] So when the Rajah of Cochin objected to his neighbour's involvement in the harbour, citing material as well as 'sentimental and other objections'[59] (Cochin was always touchy about its size, squashed as it was historically between rival Travancore and the enemy Zamorin), the Government of Madras asked him to reconsider.

For Travancore, on the other hand, developing the Cochin Harbour was a worthwhile investment, as the benefits of trade were only too well known and the potential of lucrative customs was tempting. The state had its own port at Alleppey, which faced the same problem of access as the Cochin Harbour. Ideally they ought to have developed this one but it was beyond the resources of the government to do so on its own. So when the proposal to bear only a third of the expenses to develop Cochin Harbour instead came in 1919, in return for a third of the profits, Sir Krishnan had pounced like any discerning businessman would have done.

But then politicians in Travancore did not like the proposal for reasons of pride, mainly. It was believed that 'Cochin has gained a point and has inveigled Travancore into the scheme in Cochin's interest', and the whole thing became a matter of petty rivalries. This perception about what was basically a good investment plan gave Mulam Tirunal cold feet and by 1921 he was looking for an excuse to withdraw from the project to end all the criticism.[60] Thereafter the Dewan of Cochin and the Government of Madras played it carefully so that nothing would prompt Travancore to declare an exit. The Maharajah, having failed to find an appropriate excuse, grudgingly gave his consent in principle to a draft agreement by 1923.[61] Cochin still, however, had many suspicions (naturally, since it was on its territory that two other governments were getting comfortable), so nothing was finalised up until Mulam Tirunal's death.

When Sethu Lakshmi Bayi succeeded to power, the matter came to rest in her hands. The political pressure groups that were against the investment sought to exploit her unfamiliarity and get Travancore out of the proposal, even as Mr Raghavaiah worked hard to highlight its very many advantages to the state. Protests in Trivandrum continued and indeed even some members of the special committee set up to consider the project advised against it,[62] as did Mr Watts, soon after his arrival.[63] None of them was certain that the returns would be worth the investment, which was expected in four stages and could exceed Rs 50 lakh. More negotiation and discussion were suggested but Sethu Lakshmi Bayi, once again with a great deal of courageous prescience, thought otherwise. She was strongly inclined towards thinking like Mr Raghavaiah, as was her husband. And so convinced that enough time had already been wasted, and finding that Cochin and the Governments of Madras and India (who were also involved by now) only awaited Travancore's consent, she decided to go ahead. On 23 July 1925 the Maharani green-lit the agreement and realised the long-awaited Four-Party Alliance to develop Cochin Harbour, ending decades of indecisiveness. It was to become one of the best and most far-sighted economic decisions she took during her reign, the benefits of which are enjoyed to this date.

As per the agreement, both Travancore and Cochin advanced Rs 5 lakh each to the Cochin Harbour Trust to commence dredging as an experiment. This was intended as a loan and would be taken as capital investment only if the experiment were a success. Construction of a special dredger called *The Lord Willingdon*, named after the Governor of Madras, began and in October 1926 it was taken out to sea for the first time. But technical difficulties resulted in actual work commencing only by February 1927. Thereafter everything progressed well and in December 1928 when *The Lord Willingdon* dredged a 2-mile-long, 450-foot-wide channel to the inner harbour, a world record was set.[64] Earlier that year in May, a steamship from Bombay called *The Padma* became the first deep-sea ship to harbour in Cochin, picking up 'every bale of cargo, which the port could offer and which could be crammed into the vessel without sinking it'.[65] By the second stage of its development, thus, the Cochin Harbour was already set to be a success.

Over the next few years, work continued and the port grew. It slowly became clear that the Cochin Harbour was not something that would benefit two coastal princely states alone but would serve as a gateway to south India. Goods poured in from everywhere and trade became robust. The investment made by the Maharani started paying dividends so that by 1935 Travancore's share of profits from this one harbour's revenues alone stood at nearly Rs 13 lakh.[66] This was in comparison to the Rs 1,75,000 that all of the state's own ports put together yielded, marking an enormous surplus.[67] By 1946, which is when the project would finally be completed, the customs revenue would mount to about Rs 27 lakh.[68] By now the Government of India would have taken over the management of Cochin Harbour, classifying it officially as a major port of India, and using it for strategic purposes in the Second World War. A new island had also sprung up in Cochin, built from all the soil dredged and this was, quite predictably, named Willingdon Island, which is today a key location in the city. But as early as 1935, when Sir Robert was invited on the BBC, he proudly told the world: 'I live on a large island made from the bottom of the sea. And from the upper floor of my house I look down on the finest harbour in the East.'[69]

Sethu Lakshmi Bayi too would remember with well-merited pride her role in building the modern city of Cochin and returning Kerala to its rightful place on the map of the commercial world. Again, it was a serious gamble for her as a new ruler to commit such large amounts of money to be spent on what was, essentially, the property of another state. All hopes of success and profits were speculative, and given the local political opposition to the proposal, any failure would serve only to disgrace and blemish her reputation. But with commendable wisdom and vision, the Maharani saw where in history she was poised at that time. Neighbouring countries were seldom bosom friends and this was especially true in the case of Travancore and Cochin. And it was even more exceptional for the monarchs of both states to agree on matters such as this. So her choices were either to make the most of a moment like this that came but rarely in history, or to succumb to regional pride and petty grievances. Sethu Lakshmi Bayi chose the former. Joining hands with Rama Varma XVII of Cochin and the Governor of Madras, the Maharani presided over one of the most momentous developments in the history of south India, crowning Cochin as the Queen of the Arabian Sea.

With each year trade only grew here, bringing with it greater revenues and a number of forward and backward linkages: businesses, banks, hotels and more. Employment was generated in the vicinity and incomes rose for common men and women. Cochin resumed its place among the great ports of the world and became the thriving business capital of Kerala, symbolising enterprise and industry. The harbour expanded, as did its services, and eighty-five years after the signing of the agreement, goods worth Rs 5,000 crore would be loaded on to ships from here. By the first decade of the twenty-first century the number would be in excess of Rs 10,000 crore,[70] while the customs revenue in 2011 would stand at Rs 2,900 crore.[71] Nobody in the 1920s could ever have even dreamed of these gargantuan figures but they did know they were laying the foundations of a new, prosperous metropolis when they ratified that historic agreement all those years ago. Sethu Lakshmi Bayi was one of those enlightened visionaries and to her modern Kerala owes a tremendous debt of gratitude and respect.

Other economic and political reforms also made a steady headway throughout 1925. In June that year the government passed orders to establish a state-aided, joint-stock Bank of Travancore with a start-up capital of Rs 30 lakh. Within two years the public purchased shares worth two-thirds of the amount and operations began soon afterwards, with the primary focus being on improving the state's trade and industrial capacity.[72] But one innovative administrative act of the Maharani is particularly noteworthy. This idea was borrowed from the Government of India, which had passed a resolution to foster rural self-governance in 1918. Indeed as early as 1909 a Royal Commission on Decentralisation had determined that it was 'most desirable' to 'associate the people with the local tasks of administration', for which power ought to be granted to locals in basic village units.[73] Thus on 13 August 1925 Sethu Lakshmi Bayi affixed her sign manual and passed into law the Village Panchayats Act of Travancore.

This new law classed villages or clusters of villages as administrative units to be governed by panchayats (literally, an assembly of five). Each such panchayat was to consist of between five and eleven members of whom at least two-thirds had to be elected from the local population, with the remainder being nominated. These members were to be responsible for governance but were granted a degree of judicial authority also in disposing of small civil suits within their jurisdictions. Panchayats were given obligatory as well as discretionary functions with the former including maintenance of roads, communications, cleanliness and hygiene, irrigation and wells, etc., while the latter involved development of cottage industries, agricultural improvement and education. It was hoped that the panchayat system would 'accelerate the rate of progress', 'stimulate the sense of responsibility in the average citizen', and widen their horizons and perspectives towards public life. Citizens were made stakeholders in local government and the reform was hailed as a long-needed development.[74] The Act also stressed on autonomy and development, so that money collected from each village, along with grants given by the government, was to be spent 'in the village, for the villagers and by the villagers'.[75] To start with, however, due to Sethu Lakshmi Bayi's sometimes excessive sense of caution, only seven panchayats were constituted and brought under the purview of the new law.[76] These were studied for a few years to determine the feasibility of the Act, which proving positive, plans to expand the scheme across Travancore were on the horizon by 1931.

Despite the limited nature of the experiment, what is perhaps commendable is that at a time when the vote normally came with a property qualification even in advanced Western nations, elections to the panchayats were based on adult suffrage.[77] This made the Maharani one of India's earliest administrators to contemplate the vote as a democratic right as opposed to a privilege accorded to economically better-off classes of her people only. She did not, however, extend this to elections at higher levels such as of the legislature, presumably because while she was ready to experiment with smaller units having local effects, she did not want to open up the principal legislative organs of the state yet. The unceasing communal problem was one rationale for her reserve. If the current experiment proved successful on a large scale, steps to extend the right vertically could be taken in due course.

Unfortunately, when the Maharani relinquished power, her nephew's government did not share her enthusiasm for devolving power and while the existing panchayats were permitted to continue, expansion plans were not realised. Instead, in 1940, Village Unions, where representatives were nominated and not elected, and which had fewer powers than panchayats, were constituted. By 1947 there would be seventeen Village Unions and the old seven panchayats in the state, covering 1,605 sq. miles and governing a population of 1.8 million.[78] The Maharani's long-term project to decentralise the administration therefore never fully took off, and its benefits reached only a fifth of Travancore's total population. Yet the intentions of Sethu Lakshmi Bayi to grant village folk, who constituted the bulk of the state's people, a basic democratic say in how their daily lives ought to be governed, came to be highly appreciated. The Government of Kerala would take over and complete the process after Independence when the panchayat system took root with full vigour in the state, in each of its 978 villages.

One of the most fascinating social legislations Sethu Lakshmi Bayi presided over in 1925 concerned the final demise of the matrilineal system of inheritance, after decades of debate and dissent. She was hailed at the time as a progressive ruler, and indeed as a leading light among women, but years down the line sociologists and feminists would ponder whether or not, after all, the passing of matriliny was such a laudable event in history. Scholarly circles would lament that Victorian morality and the insecurity of men destroyed what had once stood out and positively shaped the very identity of Kerala. There was no doubt that in 1925 many things contributed to the inevitable fall of matriliny, but an air of nostalgia would diligently persist against the forces of modernity that withdrew from Malayali women those uninhibited rights of power and independence they had enjoyed for centuries.

There is a substantial diversity of thought on the origins of matrilineal kinship in Kerala. Some anthropologists regard it as the continuation of a system that at one time existed all over the world, while others contend that it was conceived due to some mysterious, compelling circumstances that replaced patriarchy at a historical point. There are, however, two views on this that have been passed down within the region. One is mythological and based on a Malayalam treatise called *Keralolpathi* and a Sanskrit work called the *Kerala Mahatmyam*. These refer to the creation of Kerala by the legendary hero Parasurama, who is supposed to have hurled his battleaxe from Gokarna to Cape Comorin and claimed from the sea all the land in between. He is then said to have awarded this new region (conveniently) to Brahmins after which he summoned (equally conveniently) deva (divine), gandharva (celestial minstrel), and rakshasa (demon) women for the pleasure of these men. The Nairs, the principal matrilineal caste, were, according to this theory, the descendants of these nymphs and their Brahmin overlords, tracing their lineages in the maternal line. Of course nobody of any intelligence was deceived by this version, dismissed quite pointedly by William Logan in his *Malabar Manual* as 'a farrago of legendary nonsense'.[79]

The other theory relates to the ancient martial tradition of the Nairs. Boys were sent off to train in military gymnasiums from the age of eight, and their sole occupation thereafter was to master the art of warfare. For them death by any other means than at the end of a sword on the battlefield was a mortifying ignominy and in their constant zeal for military excellence and glorious bloodshed, they had no time to husband women or economic resources. So a man would never 'marry' a woman, as in other parts of India, and start a family with their children. Instead he would visit a lady in her natal home every now and then, solely for sexual purposes, and the offspring would be her responsibility entirely. Matriliny was, as per this theory, consequent upon the men purely being instruments of war rather than householders. So the onus of family and succession was taken care of by women, who formed large establishments and managed their affairs independently in the absence of men. While the military tradition of the Nairs, famous for its suicide bands called chavers, was well known, this theory is also more circumstantial than absolute. Either way, thus, there is a lack of clarity on the origins of matriliny.

But as K. Saradamoni points out, 'None of these theories appear to have taken note of the fact that matriliny offered an identity and security to women.'[80] For under the matrilineal system, women were not dependent upon men, having control over and access to economic resources. This was something women in the more conventional patriarchal system did not enjoy; they were guests in their parents' houses till marriage; at their husbands' will after marriage; and under their sons' control in later life. On the contrary, Nair women always had the security of the homes they were born in throughout their lives and were not dependant on their husbands. Sexual freedom was also remarkable so that while polygamy was happily recognised in other parts of India, in Kerala women were allowed polyandry. Nair women could, if they wished, have more than one husband and, in the event of difficulties, were free to divorce without any social stigma. Widowhood was no catastrophic disaster and they were effectively at par with men when it came to sexual rights, with greater control over their bodies.

The marriage system itself was something that never ceased to fascinate visitors to Kerala. This was simply called *sambandham* (relationship) and as one distinguished observer noted, it was not seen as a 'sacred contract' but as a 'purely fugitive alliance, terminable at will'.[81] The bond between brother and sister was considered more sacrosanct than that between husband and wife. And with reason too, for if women were economically protected and independent in their natal homes, they needed outside men only to father their children. Sambandhams in fact even permitted remarkable interaction among Kerala's higher castes, leading to an interesting, advantageous mixing of culture and various bloodlines. Among Nambutiri Brahmins only the eldest son was permitted to take a Brahmin wife and all other men had to seek sambandhams from the high-caste matrilineal communities. This meant that Brahmin property was protected, as the issue of these younger men belonged to their mothers' families with no claims on their patrimony; and for the women, in turn, alliances with a superior caste amplified prestige. To take the Travancore royal family itself as a case, for instance, husbands were always Koil Tampurans, who in turn were necessarily fathered by Brahmins. Every Maharajah, in other words, had a Brahmin for a grandfather and a Nair for a grandson, both of whom were commoners; the Nair's father, grandfather and great-grandfather came from different rungs of the social hierarchy. The very procedure to enter into a sambandham was rather easy and simply involved the man handing the woman a piece of cloth before an oil lamp. In fact, when Sir Mountstuart Grant-Duff was Governor of Madras, he once met a lady from Travancore and the talk somehow came to the topic of textiles. He 'innocently said that he would like to send her a cloth from Madras as a specimen of the handiwork executed there' to which the lady blushed and quickly responded that while she was 'much obliged', she was 'quite satisfied with her present husband'.[82]

Relationships could be remarkably free and an anecdote from 1881 recorded by the Rajah of Cochin who ruled from 1895 until 1914 is telling. 'In the Palliyil house in Trippunithura,' he wrote, 'there was a girl who was the step-daughter of the late Rajah.' She was sixteen at the time and already had 'a regular husband'. 'I proposed,' he declares very matter-of-factly, 'to become paramour to her, and, as the husband raised no objection to this course it was done so. This kind of things [sic] was not considered improper at the time.'[83] What is interesting here is that this late Rajah's wife already had a daughter from a previous husband, (indicating that even princes married widows or divorcees) and this girl, even at the highest social station in the court of Cochin, could keep two men at the same time. In Travancore, Queen Ashure, as alluded to previously, is said to have even taken an English lover in the seventeenth century while Gowri Parvathi Bayi in the early nineteenth had two husbands. Mulam Tirunal's marriage to Sankaran Tampi's wife was preceded by his uncle's taking Kalyani Pillai as consort, when she was herself attached to a famous Kathakali actor, who in turn had several other ladies to attend to as well.[84] The author C.V. Raman Pillai wedded his late wife's sister, for whom it was the fourth marriage in a line that included two dead husbands and one divorce.[85]

Traditional Kerala society never frowned at all this for the simple reason that such sexual relations were not taboo. It was customary and made perfect sense within the historical and economic context of the land. But what did happen by the nineteenth century was the impact of Christian missionaries with their prudish Victorian notions of decency and morality, aided by the colonial enterprise to 'civilise' India. Greater interaction with other parts of the subcontinent where patriarchy was the norm also added fat to the fire. To these modern-day observers Kerala's marriage practices were a source of outrageous horror and in 1901 Augusta Blandford in her book on Travancore took exception to the Nairs and their marriage system as 'very revolting'.[86] As J. Devika records, a 'general picture of decay and backwardness' was conveyed to the world, and Malayalis as a whole came to be ridiculed for their 'peculiar system of inheritance' and their 'obnoxious system of promiscuous marriage or no marriage at all'.[87] Licentious, as a superlative, would have suited Kerala perfectly according to these modern accounts, and the 1875 *Travancore Census Report* was most apologetic when it spoke of the 'looseness of the prevailing morals and the unbinding nature of the marriage tie, which possesses such fascination for the majority of our population'.[88]

It must be remembered, additionally, that this was also the time when Nair men were out studying at the new English colleges and schools, exposed to these foreign opinions. 'The Malayalis as a class are the most idle and homesick of the whole Hindu community,' decided a Madras newspaper, 'owing to the enervating influence exercised on their character by their peculiar system of inheritance and their obnoxious system of promiscuous marriage.'[89] Hitherto local practices affected no Malayali as odd. But now he had to face derogatory comments about their repulsive 'backwardness'. 'And it became worse,' Saradamoni tells us, 'when sambandham was equated to concubinage and the women to mistresses and the children called bastards.'[90] Suddenly Kerala was told that the female ought be a paragon of Victorian virtue, which meant her rampant sexuality begged to be controlled, and that the man-wife-and-children format of family was what was eminently desirable and correct. One particularly interesting debate from these times, highlighted by Devika, pertained to the attire of women. It was quite normal for Malayali women even in the twentieth century to move around bare-breasted, just as Malayali men also wore nothing above the waist. In other words, nobody in Kerala saw covering the torso as anything worthy of discussion or special interest.[91] However, by the end of the nineteenth century, with the woman's body becoming subject to so much scrutiny, her bare-breastedness began to be condemned. Male bare-breastedness continued (and indeed still does) but suddenly women's breasts became a matter of embarrassing social concern. Nobody expressed this as well as Mannathu Padmanabhan when he declared in a speech to the Nairs, 'We need to keep our women in place by making them virtuous.'[92] Matriliny suddenly became an atrocious repository of sin and debauchery, and a national humiliation for Kerala.

Alongside all this, the economic management of matrilineal households was also deteriorating, turning them, as Robin Jeffrey quips, into 'pressure cookers'.[93] The Nairs and other high castes lived in large joint families known as *taravads* where property was owned collectively. In other words, division of land and resources on individual basis was not permitted. As the communist leader A.K. Gopalan remembered, it was much like living in a community hostel. One got fairly comfortable spaces to reside in, with food, clothing and other requisites, but that was that.[94] Cash allowances were not permitted and the elders of the family took all the decisions for everybody. It was not unusual for thirty or forty people to be living under the same roof of a taravad and in some families like that of the outrageously wealthy Paliyam in Cochin, hundreds lived together, with their own school, dining halls, hospital and other amenities. But while the taravad granted security to its inhabitants, it could not always tolerate changes. Sending young men to college, for example, was not seen as an urgent need, even if those youngsters desired it. And, what was worse, if they were sent to college and got jobs, all their earnings would go to the taravad for everyone's benefit. This created resentment and the new generation of Nairs, educated on Western lines and with a good understanding of the advantages of individualism, found it exasperating to see their money go into the coffers of an autocratic establishment of elders and half-educated cousins.

By the last quarter of the nineteenth century, educated Nairs began to call for the reform of the marriage system and for the right to claim individual shares in ancestral taravad properties. Both were very vehemently opposed by orthodox sections of society but as the political clout of these educated men grew, some legal breakthroughs were gained. In 1896 the Government of Madras allowed for sambandhams to be registered as 'proper' marriages, and the Nairs out to 'reform' the community rejoiced. The community itself, however, responded coldly; in the first fourteen months after the enactment, in the entire Malabar district only fifty-one sambandhams were registered and in the decade that followed only forty-nine were added.[95] In other words, while the young men, ashamed of their traditions, sought to emulate the 'civilised' world and cultivate women in the image of the Virgin Mary, society had far too much at stake to abandon the existing system without an alternative plan.

But pressure continued to be applied and cracks began to appear. In 1912, Travancore gave its first boost to nuclear families, modelled on the patriarchal style (virtuous wife and all) when it allowed men to bequeath part of their self-acquired property or money to wives and children instead of the taravad. More importantly (and not a little judgementally), it gave women the right of maintenance from husbands, so long as they did not 'live in adultery' (i.e., have other partners).[96] In what was seen as ideal, the man became the breadwinner and the woman and her children, his dependants. Of course, this did not mean she lost rights in her own taravad, which remained as backup, but agitation continued. By 1923 the call was final: matriliny should be abolished and individual partition was to be the weapon of choice. P. Thanu Pillai, who piloted a bill in the Legislative Council, argued as follows:

> As a result of a careful diagnosis, the disease of the taravads was traced to the evil effects of the joint family system, in which the individual has no defined right or responsibility; where the incentive to personal exertion is the happiness of other people (the sister's children, not one's own) ... The object of the bill is to eradicate once for all the evils in the [matrilineal] system with a view to better the moral, economic and industrial conditions of its followers, by giving each member full scope for individuality and personal endeavour, by holding him responsible to take care of himself and his wife and children; in short to compel him to earn his bread by the sweat of his brow or in the alternative to beg or to starve ... to give him a definite share in his taravad property as well as in his father's property. This will lead to the substitution of taravads by families in the real sense of the word, united by the bonds of natural love where children will look up to the parents with affectionate regards for support and guidance.[97]

This is most interesting, for this was the educated Nair man's reform and all the proposed gains were for 'him'. The 'individual' here is male and the call was to dismantle a system where females would be affected most. It is worth asking whether this ardent desire of men to establish nuclear families with themselves as the central characters in them stemmed from a lack of identity. In the old days, the Nair man went out to war and was always training for it. But with the coming of colonialism, he was reduced to squatting at home, under the authority of family elders, with nothing much to do. So the taravad, that had earlier created spaces for both women and men, now seemed to serve the purposes of the former only. 'Masculinity', so stressed upon by the West, became a touchy point for the Nairs as jibes from the Brahmins (who, importantly, had sexual access to the Nairs' sisters) and others began to mount. So it was most essential for the Malayali man to rehabilitate his identity by the 'sweat of his brow' and by controlling his woman, in order to gain respect in the modern (Victorian) world. And none of this was possible so long as the taravad continued to shelter women, their rights, and their 'immoral' lifestyles.

On the side, as Devika has detailed, women were also now asked to cultivate an image as humble, passive and in need of protection. 'Womanly qualities' were championed, with special emphasis on sexual virtue and loyalty to a single husband.[98] Colonial authorities actively promoted this and it is noteworthy that Queen Victoria conferred upon the late Rani Lakshmi Bayi the imperial distinction called the Crown of India to commend her moral integrity when she refused to divorce Kerala Varma Valiya Koil Tampuran at the height of court intrigues in the 1870s.[99] In the famous novel *Indulekha* by O. Chandu Menon, a landmark in Malayalam literature which became very popular with women, the protagonist Madhavi is a prototype of the new Malayali lady. She has all the qualities of a self-assured woman but (and this is crucial) she is tremendously dedicated to her one man, has the graces of an English lady, and is horrified when her virtue is questioned. Women's magazines also began to make their appearance in Kerala, promoting the domesticated, dedicated, motherly lady. 'We will publish nothing related to politics,' declared the *Keraleeya Sugunabodhini* in 1892, adding that entertaining tales, 'writings that energise the moral conscience', cookery, biographies of 'ideal women', and 'other such enlightening topics' only would be covered.[100] As late as 1926 the *Mahila Mandiram*, for instance, would strongly argue that a woman's role was as mistress of the (husband's) household, and as a caretaker and that she should leave everything else to the superior competence of men. Propaganda was at its peak.

To be fair, of course, there were serious systemic problems with the taravad as well. As families grew large they became unwieldy and domestic quarrels became the bane of every Nair family across Kerala. The senior male member, who managed affairs, could often be more partial to his immediate relations at the cost of everyone else in the taravad. Favoured nephews might get perks like an English education while others would be denied opportunities. In major taravads it was also not unheard of for impatient nephews to connive to assassinate senior kin to obtain sooner rather than later the advantages of their rank and position. Enterprising men looking for capital to start business ventures could find no support from taravads, owing to joint ownership of resources; between 1897 and 1907 alone an average of 487 suits were brought to court by nephews against the managing senior uncles of their taravads.[101] And in general, many intelligent men of the day began to see a dangerous pattern in allowing young boys to remain comfortably ensconced in the security of the taravad, wasting all productivity. By the 1920s, thus, it became quite obvious that something radical would have to be done. Some moderate Nair leaders only called for reducing the size of taravads by dividing them into more manageable branches. But as always, moderates were rarely heard and the more extreme clamour for individual partition was set to succeed.

Inevitably, the issue was raised in the legislature in Travancore and it was obvious that there was complete political support for the proposal. Any opposition was put down by moralistic arguments against which there could never be any defence; those standing in the way were admonished for holding on to antiquated, uncivilised beliefs. And so in April 1925 the Legislative Council passed a bill terminating matriliny, permitting partition of property, 'legalising' all sambandhams, and essentially inaugurating the age of the patriarchal family in Travancore. It was sent to the Maharani for her assent and on 13 April she signed the historic Nair Regulation of 1925, giving matrilineal kinship the unique distinction of being the only system of inheritance and family in the world to be abolished by law.[102] Similar Acts were passed for the Ezhava and Vellala communities also, sections of which were matrilineal. The Government of Madras would follow her lead in 1933 and do the same in Malabar, while Cochin would issue corresponding orders by 1938.

It is not entirely certain what Sethu Lakshmi Bayi's private views on the matter were. Her conservative education and outlook, shaped by Victorian characters like Miss Watts, indicate that insofar as the moral argument was concerned, she was definitely for it. For a woman whose crest celebrated *Sola Nobilitat Virtus* (Virtue Is The Only Nobility) the idea of multiple partners was abhorrent and so both polygamy and polyandry were abolished. So too she would end the practice of women walking about with uncovered breasts in public, especially in temples. As for the (patriarchal) sanctity of marriage, she was a staunch believer as clearly seen from the fact that she had no qualms in going against the head of her own taravad, Mulam Tirunal, in supporting her husband, who was technically an outsider. In other words, she clearly felt change was necessary among matrilineal communities in Kerala with regard to marriage and family. But that said, Sethu Lakshmi Bayi's policy towards women was not one of domestication. And as will be seen ahead, she did a great deal to ensure that women retained their independent spirit and power even when the taravads, that had once enshrined it, perished at the altar of patriarchal modernity.

One of the most iconic representations of these epochal social changes was that old award-winning painting by Raja Ravi Varma of Mahaprabha, holding in her arms her eldest boy. As G. Arunima tells us, *There Comes Papa* was painted in the early 1890s when the role of the 'papa' was still uncertain. 'What is the significance of the painting called *There Comes Papa* when the subject and the artist are both products of a matrilineal society?' she asks. 'The absent yet approaching papa signifies the crisis in Nair matriliny in the late nineteenth century. The fact that Ravi Varma chose to celebrate conjugal domesticity and the nuclear family at a time when these were comparatively unknown among large sections of the matrilineal population reveals his growing patrilineal sensibilities. *There Comes Papa* becomes akin to a clarion call for the end of matriliny.'[103]

And it was. If a generation earlier, Ravi Varma painted the approach of the papa, it fell to his granddaughter to open the doors and let the man in as master of the house. In the five years that followed Sethu Lakshmi Bayi's historic legislation, 33,000 taravads were partitioned in Travancore and property worth over four crore rupees was divided among the Nairs.[104] Matriliny began to fade into the memories of grandmothers and into the pages of history books. It would continue, till feminists redeemed it, to be decried as an immoral, barbarous system that served only to corrupt 'family values'. Covertly, however, women in Kerala would always remember the good old days when the taravad gave them a place and a voice against the unmistakable chauvinism that replaced attitudes towards the female, a problem that endures to this day.

In September 1925, the Maharani completed her first year in power; and it had been a year of great successes. Happily enough then, the final months of the year turned out to be a merry affair, with a train of celebrations presenting themselves one after the other. The first of these was occasioned when the Viscount George Goschen of Hawkhurst, who had succeeded Lord Willingdon in Madras, came on a state visit to Travancore. It was the norm for princely states to host such tours, packed with tiger hunts, garden parties, dazzling balls, and all other splendours associated with 'Oriental Courts'. But the present excursion was short, being chiefly to commemorate the signing of the Four-Party Alliance. After enjoying the entertainments in Cochin, thus, the Governor and his lady arrived in Trivandrum on 19 October. Sethu Lakshmi Bayi received them with due honour and following the usual courtesy calls and returns, treated them to a sumptuous banquet the next day. The Governor took the Maharani into the hall on his arm, not something she was accustomed to, but to which she happily consented in the interests of custom and good etiquette. Toasts were raised, pretty speeches were made, and unwavering loyalty, etc., to the British Crown was proclaimed. But what was more amusing was how, as the Resident noted, the Maharani was so 'greatly interested in seeing Europeans eat meat for the first time in her life'.[105] Her eyes widened as she watched, with an almost childlike enchantment, her distinguished guests carve their meat and tear it with their forks and knives. Wine was generously served, with the Hindu guests drinking plain coloured imitations. Sethu Lakshmi Bayi was in fact a little self-conscious at the banquet, for it was her first ever, but she played the hostess charmingly enough and the visit was declared a success, concluding with a picnic and shikar organised by the Valiya Koil Tampuran the next day. The Governor and his ménage took the Maharani's leave on 22 October and returned to Madras.

This was followed about three weeks later by the birthday festivities of the Maharajah on 16 November, celebrated with regular pomp. But scarcely had these drawn to a close when Sethu Lakshmi Bayi's thirtieth birthday sent Trivandrum into a thrill once again. This was her second *tirunal* (royal birthday) as ruler but since the last one had not been celebrated due to an inopportune illness, the event attracted double attention. Besides, it was rare in history for a female monarch to go out in state and so, newspapers reported, the concourse of onlookers gathered in the capital was unusually large. Feasts were organised in the Sri Padmanabhaswamy Temple for seven days and provision was made for feeding the poor. On the evening before the birthday, the Nair Brigade was called in to shoulder the responsibility of cooking and chopping (a chore one would imagine might offend their military sensibilities, but which was in fact viewed as an honour). The Devaswom Commissioner, representing the Dewan, and other senior high-caste officials cut the first few vegetables in a ceremony called *karikkuvettu*, giving them the lead in keeping with tradition.

At dawn the next morning the Maharani rose from bed and prepared for the day, surrounded by her usual bevy of maids and attendants. The inaugural ceremony was the *tirumudikalasam*, which was when she was anointed with sacred waters. In nine silver pots, water mixed with the juices of the *Ficus glomerosa*, *benjamina*, *religiosa*, and *indica* trees, was boiled and sanctified over as many fires. The priests sat before these, performing certain ceremonies and chanting assorted Vedic mantras, offering oblations to the fire. Finally, surrounded by these religious grandees, Sethu Lakshmi Bayi took her seat on a mandapam in the fort, where the holy waters were poured over her head, sanctifying her once again as reigning queen of the land. As this happened, the Nair Brigade fired a salute outside, proclaiming the news to the waiting masses. And once the tirumudikalasam was performed, she proceeded to pray in the Sri Padmanabhaswamy Temple and partook in other great rituals there, before preparing for the royal procession.[106]

The procession commenced at eight in the morning, heralded by a band of Pathans, whose ancestors were bequeathed to the Travancore durbar by its one-time overlord, the Nawab of Arcot in the eighteenth century. Playing on instruments such as the shehnai, swarbat, etc., in distinctly north Indian tunes, they carried with them flags and other regalia, including the Union Jack. The state elephants followed, each caparisoned with different colours, starting with gold and silver, moving with the inherent majesty that made them such favourite royal pets. The elephants of the aristocratic houses of the country trailed them, after whom the cavalry and troops marched by. Drummers and musicians accompanied all these components of the procession, but when the rear appeared with the Maharani, a dignified silence arrived with it as the crowds beheld their consecrated queen.

She was seated in an exquisite palanquin, with a green velvet canopy, richly embroidered and draped in gold lace, with hangings of pearls. Within it she was clearly visible, poised with her legs crossed, her back straight, and head held high, looking almost statuesque. She was dressed entirely in white, with a single string of pearls around her neck, looking, as the *Madras Mail* gushingly reported, like 'simplicity itself'. As she passed, a hush of devotion burst out in the crowds, as some bowed, while others whispered her name; and some more progressive fans even held up her photographs. With a smile and a regal nod of her head, she acknowledged the greetings of her people, adding some grace to this antiquated and rather feudal procession. And thus, she made her way in right royal style around the town and back to Anantha Vilasam in the fort, to inaugurate the birthday feasts in the afternoon.[107] At five in the afternoon an audience was granted to her sisters and their children, who presented their combined message of congratulations, after which a private banquet followed at Satelmond Palace. The culmination of the year's celebrations came then with the second birthday party of Princess Lalitha, which coincided with the new year, brightening up the palace and the town once again with joyful revelry.

The year 1925 came to a conclusion, thus, with a great deal of positive energy and enthusiasm. The pace of big and small reforms was accelerated and the work of the Maharani's government was already being lauded as exemplary. She had succeeded in appointing a loyal minister on terms that made her active hand in the administration quite clear; her relationship with the Government of India and its Resident was cordial and positive; and while her refusal to countenance communal proclivities did not impress many politicians, the people of the state saw in her an inspiring, self-assured monarch and vindicated her policy. Women, especially, began to admire Sethu Lakshmi Bayi for her graciousness, as the gates of Satelmond Palace were thrown open, in what was unprecedented, for any one of them with a grievance. Every morning when the Maharani returned from the bathhouse, scores of women would line up on the pathway with petitions and representations. A special attendant would collect these from them but each day Sethu Lakshmi Bayi listened to all these women patiently, comforting them with kind words or a warm smile.[108]

It was not an easy task, for many of the women would be distraught with emotion, telling of their indebtedness, or an impending marriage with all its expenses, or even about their difficulties in paying school fees for their children. The whole affair took up a large portion of the Maharani's time, but in spite of this, she insisted on these informal daily meetings and treated the petitioners with all the consideration and respect that was due to them. News of the sovereign of the land, a figure so revered and worshipped, personally coming down and listening to these women reverberated throughout the state. The tremendous oneness she felt with her people came to be recognised through these genuine and heartfelt gestures, and for her entire reign ahead, the Maharani always made it a point to reach out to common men and women. Perhaps that is why when Lady Elizabeth Glover featured her in a book titled *Great Queens*, there were very few who thought it was a title Sethu Lakshmi Bayi did not deserve.[109]

7
Malice Domestique

The year 1926 began with scandal. For no sooner had the new-year celebrations concluded than Trivandrum woke up to one of the most controversial pieces of gossip it had ever devoured, even with all the ribald stories that always plagued royal courts. Every tattler true to his predilections was roused into action and, to quote Mr Cotton's more gentlemanly terms, 'great sensation' prevailed in town.[1] And to the genuine mortification of the royal family and all its well-wishers, swamped in the middle of all this was Kowdiar Palace and its principal mistress, the Junior Maharani.

It all started when, within a fortnight after the new year, her husband, the Kochu Koil Tampuran, suddenly walked out of their home in a great rage. He was generally known as something of an eccentric who threw his occasional tantrums, but this time it was not a passing whim that drove him. On the contrary, he was furious and left making the wildest accusations against his royal consort, none of which were even remotely charitable or flattering. Before long it was revealed that the issue concerned a bhagvathar from whom the Junior Maharani had been taking music lessons. There was presumably nothing unsavoury about his talent, but the problem lay in that the Kochu Koil Tampuran accused the two of 'undue familiarity' with each other.[2] In what he saw as his conjugal right, he demanded, therefore, that the man be sacked. But to his great resentment, his wife (perhaps stunned) refused to do anything of the sort. The music lessons continued as did whatever familiarity normally accompanied it.

The quarrel escalated, then, and a thoroughly piqued Ravi Varma decided to stage a dramatic rebellion. No petty consort had ever done anything like this before, and everybody was shocked when he went on to broadcast his reasons. He was absolutely determined, and told the Resident, 'that he would not [return] so long as the music master was there'.[3] His pride and dignity were at stake, he felt, and he would not allow the Junior Maharani to prevail in this matter. Mr Cotton did much to sweet-talk him into his regular mood of composed submission but without success; not even the sentimental trump card of his distraught children could persuade him to go back. Uncontained, thus, the scandal burst into outrageous proportions. Liberally embellished whispers of servants reached the town and Kowdiar Palace came under a shroud of nightmarish disgrace. It was a first-class crisis; one that was for some time waiting to explode.

It appears to have been increasingly obvious in recent years that the Junior Maharani's marriage was afflicted by a malady every couple dreads: incompatibility. Sethu Parvathi Bayi was an individual of 'keen intelligence, wide interests, restless energy and boundless ambition'.[4] She was strong-minded, with a very dynamic and powerful personality that distinguished her in all the circles she frequented. Her love of travel was enormous and she profoundly enjoyed cultivating the friendship of interesting, powerful persons like herself. She hoped to 'shine in the new mixed society of cultured, progressive India', and to a serious extent was successful at this.[5] Her gregarious temperament had impressed even Mr Cotton before the commencement of the Regency, when he was still uncertain about Sethu Lakshmi Bayi. He felt that the Junior Maharani had much more spirit and was remarkably unorthodox in her views and despite an 'impetuosity which occasionally causes trouble', she was worthy of sincere admiration.[6] But to her unfortunate chagrin, it was back home in Kowdiar Palace that her myriad qualities were met with conspicuous contempt. And this fountain of disapproval was none other than her own husband.

Ravi Varma, while known to be a Sanskrit scholar of respectable standing and an intelligent man, could not make too many claims at popularity. He had little by way of personality and was a 'shy and retiring' character with 'no social graces and no wish to acquire them'.[7] While his wife was flattered as the 'accredited representative of Indian womanhood',[8] for instance, the Kochu Koil Tampuran was dismissed as a henpecked 'worm' who did not inspire even the smallest appeal.[9] He was anything but the vivacious Junior Maharani's ideal companion and as she embarked on a variety of interesting pursuits, he picked up the more mundane chores of everyday parenting. When he was not poring over his Sanskrit manuscripts, Ravi Varma was busy 'employed as a fag for the little Maharajah and nursery governess for the younger children', as Mr Cotton noted with a touch of disgust at his so-called unmanliness.[10] At banquets he ate nothing and sat with a lemon, apparently a symbol of happiness and purity, before him, feeling 'disgusted with himself at being in [the] low company' of Europeans and others.[11] His prudish lack of sophistication was often an embarrassment for his wife, and during a recent trip to Ooty, the summer capital of the Madras Presidency, he had spurred an outrage with the flamboyant Maharani of Cooch Behar, whose friendship Sethu Parvathi Bayi had recently cultivated.

Indira Devi, as she was known, was a very merry widow and a great socialite, also serving as Regent in Council of her state. A regular at some of Europe's most exclusive casinos and clubs, she was famously rumoured at one point as the mistress of Prince George of England.[12] She had far-reaching connections and many powerful friends, besides a rebellious streak that made her the object of great fascination. But the glamour that mesmerised many horrified conservative Indian society and its starched colonial masters, compounded by her promiscuous bedroom escapades that earned her the sobriquet 'Maharani of *Couche Partout*'.[13] In London she 'got into a bad gambling and drinking set' and was seen more at the 43 Club, notorious for its alcoholism and easy drugs, than at the saloons and parlours of aristocratic ladies. 'She demoralised the youth of the town and the young officers of the Household Cavalry to such an extent' one disapproving intelligence note goes, 'that the Royal House Guards (Blue) became known as "the Blacks"'. The King of England, as a consequence, was 'much annoyed' and 'owing to the notoriety she had gained by her loose style of living, her gambling, and her drinking propensities', had her practically expelled from Britain to India.[14]

As Regent too Indira Devi was profligate, spending too much of her time abroad and helping herself to her state's treasuries to fund 'tours of foreign hotels and casinos'.[15] She is believed to have initiated some developments in her state, though for most part her reputation even as an administrator was not exemplary. But notwithstanding these questionable traits, she did have an exquisite magnetism that attracted the irrepressible Junior Maharani, and they would go on to become great friends.[16] At that party in Ooty, however, when she was introduced to the Kochu Koil Tampuran by his wife, she encountered a sanctimonious individual who recoiled and publicly humiliated her by saying he would not shake hands with her. This was likely because her reputation preceded her, but the episode so embarrassed the Junior Maharani that she decided to exclude her husband from all her future advances in high society.[17]

Relations between the couple steadily deteriorated in the months that followed and their mutual discord leaked out for all to see. But Sethu Parvathi Bayi was not one with a defeatist bone. It was to prove a point that she refused to sack the musician (and it is possible her husband, with all his conservatism, was overreacting). This was her fixed attitude even after her name was dragged through the mud when the scandal broke. Sensible voices around the palace spoke of how a little discretion and maturity on both their parts could have saved the day, but there was little scope for this now. On the contrary, spurning efforts at reconciliation,[18] an unyielding Junior Maharani decided to go away instead on holiday with her children. She retreated to the beach at Varkala, ignoring the Kochu Koil Tampuran and his unceasing rants. She would not, she made it clear, be bullied, even if it was her husband on the other side. This was not an unusually striking attitude on her part; some years later when she travelled to Europe, the Junior Maharani proved herself equally capable of telling even the Pope off when his staff decided to offer her unsolicited advice about her clothes and make-up before she arrived for an audience.[19]

But then there was an uncharacteristic change of heart. Almost as if by a sudden stroke of intelligence, she realised how disastrous her situation was politically. For if the Government of India, who were sharply monitoring the situation, took exception to her 'unwomanly' attitude, which for all its sexism they tended to do, the outcome could be devastating. They could remove the little Maharajah from her household citing his moral well-being and keep him away from her for years;[20] they had done something similar with Indira Devi's son, for instance, by appointing for him an official guardian.[21] Such an eventuality was dreadful for her to envisage. And so after an injudicious posture of blasé and indifference towards her husband's frenzied expostulations, the Junior Maharani abruptly hurried back to the capital to mitigate the scandal. Mr Watts was summoned and asked to 'secure the early return of her consort' although she continued to insist that his conduct was 'most unreasonable'.[22]

Protracted negotiations followed and Sethu Parvathi Bayi sought to appeal to the Dewan's sentiments, lamenting her melancholy fate. In an 'extremely spirited review' she remembered the day when Mulam Tirunal sent her five candidates to choose a husband from and how she now regretted selecting the much older Ravi Varma simply because his BA degree had seemed an attractive bonus at the time.[23] But the Kochu Koil Tampuran was not to be outdone and countered the Junior Maharani's impassioned pleas with heated rejoinders of his own. Being of a 'jealous and suspicious temperament', he 'riposted with a catalogue of his wife's paramours or alleged paramours', prominent among whom were Yuvarajah Sir Narasimharaja Wodeyar of Mysore and Sir Vasudeva Rajah, a Malabar aristocrat.[24] Both returned fire vehemently and there was little potential for progress. Finally, therefore, with the belated consciousness that she was the one who would lose the most should the crisis continue unchecked, the Junior Maharani conceded defeat. She offered to accept whatever was decided to bring her husband back to the palace, and looked to her cousin to resolve the matter.

Through all this, Sethu Lakshmi Bayi was 'greatly upset' at the downpour of shame that had been brought upon the royal family.[25] It did not help that the Junior Maharani had, during the height of the dispute, recruited a palace doctor called Nallaperumal Pillai to help 'prove' that her husband was insane. The campaign did not succeed for, as the Resident reported, 'very slender and unconvincing is the material so far collected'.[26] This was a devious enterprise and Sethu Lakshmi Bayi was aghast. So, as head of the family who was responsible for maintaining its standing and dignity among the people (and, after Mahaprabha's tutelage she knew one or two things about the importance of appearances), she ordered disciplinary action. Mr Cotton was consulted and gave her his fullest support, and that of the Government of India, in issuing punitive measures.

The provisions of the verdict were stern. The music master was dismissed to begin with, and the Junior Maharani was prohibited from seeing him again.[27] The Kochu Koil Tampuran had also complained about Kochukunji provoking trouble, and so she too was asked to leave for Mavelikkara and allow the couple to settle by themselves. But Sethu Lakshmi Bayi's ire came out upon the doctor and his crooked exercise to establish that Ravi Varma was insane. She did not clap him in irons and throw him in jail, as she might have in the old days, but felt it necessary to make an example of him nonetheless. With a sense of irony and satire, then, the Maharani confirmed his fate. Dr Nallaperumal woke up one morning to find himself served an order appointing him head of the lunatic asylum and transferred, thus, to the treatment of 'real lunatics'.[28] Provisional peace was effected, thus, and by the middle of February, the Kochu Koil Tampuran was successfully prevailed upon to return to his wife. 'For the time being at any rate,' Mr Cotton concluded dryly, 'the voice of scandal is hushed, though I cannot myself believe in any permanent reconciliation.'[29]

He was quite correct, for by March trouble cropped up once again. This time, however, the Junior Maharani acted with greater tact and attempted to persuade her cousin through a carefully drafted representation. Noting how 'distressing the present state of things are to me' and that she had 'tried all that lay in my power' to calm her husband's 'nervous irritability', the line of argument once again was his alleged mental unsoundness.[30] A letter from his physician was also enclosed suggesting that he should 'live in entirely new surroundings, free from all conditions which are to him sources of irritation'.[31] And since the environment in Kowdiar Palace was far from sanguine, it was recommended that he move out. Simply put, a separation was sought post-haste.

Sethu Lakshmi Bayi, however, was not convinced by the direction the request was taking. She cautiously asked the Junior Maharani to make 'concrete proposals' as to what she wanted done, assuring her also that 'any proposal calculated to promote the Kochu Koil Tampuran's well-being will receive my sympathetic consideration'.[32] The Junior Maharani also tried to enlist the support of Miss Watts in pressing the matter, who in turn advised her that if she wanted a separation, she should suggest it clearly. While she was advised to keep the tone 'very moderate' without 'rancour and enmity' in it,[33] the final outcome was still quite indelicate. By the first week of April the Junior Maharani proposed that her husband be transferred to Varkala, Alwaye, Nagercoil, or Cape Comorin. If he insisted on remaining in the capital, Vadakkay Kottaram Palace could be placed at his disposal. But the crux of the proposition was that he should definitely leave Kowdiar Palace, albeit under the more dignified excuses of health this time. 'It will be desirable,' she added, 'to *make him agree* to select one of the four places above mentioned.'[34]

Sethu Lakshmi Bayi had no desire to become a catspaw in this indecorous domestic squabble. Nor did she wish to take responsibility for the state of her cousin's marriage. To a proposal that Ravi Varma should have a 'companion' imposed on him, she refused to act without ascertaining his views. As for 'making him agree' to go away, 'I must decline,' she asserted, 'to be a party to the Kochu Koil Tampuran being coerced.'[35] To the Resident, who was still observing the matter for the authorities, she wrote with incredulity about her cousin's attitude. 'It surprises me beyond measure that the Junior Maharani should be at such great pains to take my views and seek my help in a matter which is purely domestic and as such capable of adjustment without extraneous interference.'[36] It appeared to her as if Sethu Parvathi Bayi simply did not want to accept culpability for the difficulties in her marriage. But in the end the decision to refrain from undue interference helped and the Junior Maharani was compelled to settle the matter between herself and her husband, like couples normally do. The two temporarily reconciled their differences and agreed to peace for some more time; when Sethu Parvathi Bayi departed for her usual tour to Ooty that summer, her husband went with her.

This marital-crisis-become-public spectacle twirled the beginning of the year into a most nerve-wracking experience for Sethu Lakshmi Bayi. Out of the blue, the royal family, which prided itself on its dignity, and confidently professed a semi-divine status, found itself humiliatingly exposed with ghastly flaws, warts et al., which was saying something for a millennium-old dynasty, however dirty its linen might secretly have been. The Maharani was appalled. She believed that if they had to maintain their royal position, they had to inspire and stand out as extraordinary. To enjoy hereditary sway over millions meant respect had to be earned every day, through personal sacrifices and stupendous effort. The monarch and her family had to exemplify all that was best and perfect according to the culture in vogue. And if they could not live up to the high moral expectations of their people, how, she asked, could they claim to be better than them?

In a most interesting fashion, the state of the Junior Maharani's marriage served to highlight not only aspects of her own private life, but also all that was distinct and noteworthy in that of her cousin. As described previously, women and their moral character had become a subject of enormous interest in Kerala by the 1920s. In fact, had all the recent events occurred only fifty years before, they would not have prompted the slightest scandal or attracted any sustained interest locally. With a single utterance Sethu Parvathi Bayi could have disposed of her husband and banished him for good, replacing him with someone more compatible. But by the first quarter of the twentieth century, a woman in her position could no longer realistically exercise this option. A divorcee Maharani was absolutely impossible to envision, especially one confronted by unseemly (even if unreasonable) allegations of infidelity, and the lady would have faced lifelong disgrace and humiliation, no matter how cantankerous or intractable her husband might have been. The moral onus, by this time, had fallen on the woman to keep her marriage going, even if it meant being saddled with a man who could bring her little happiness.

But insofar as general gossip went, an actual divorce was not necessary and the evident drama surrounding the Junior Maharani's marriage adequately served to excite the public appetite. It is perhaps unkind to judge her but then society generally was in holding its leaders up to exceptional, even unrealistic, inhuman high standards. And so the failure of Sethu Parvathi Bayi to feature as a paragon of post-Victorian feminine virtue was all the more criticised, just as the contrasting qualities in her cousin were positively celebrated. This was most crucial, for reputations survive the events that define them, and as late as the 1940s and beyond, many differentiated between 'the good Maharani' and 'the bad Maharani' of Travancore.[37] As the Junior Maharani's name suffered, her cousin's seemed to assume an added lustre. It was most likely not a pleasing development for the former and very plausibly aggravated their relentlessly unhappy relations. For as one contemporary put it, 'that her quiet, retiring and orthodox cousin became Regent was a bitter blow to her; that she won the love and respect of her people was still more bitter.'[38]

Indeed, in the public eye Sethu Lakshmi Bayi's moral stature was impeccable. Part of it certainly resulted from the manner of her upbringing and the discipline with which she conducted herself. She did not care for fashion and was never seen except in her ascetic, almost virginal white robes. Her only concession to make-up was a long tikka on her forehead; such austerity appealed to a severely traditional population.[39] While other Maharanis of her generation, such as Indira Devi, were famed as social butterflies living lives of extravagant luxury and glamour, Sethu Lakshmi Bayi was recognised for her prodigious administrative acumen and exceptional ability. While they concerned themselves with the haute couture and grand monde, she grappled with issues of communalism and unemployment. She was never seen hobnobbing with the who's who, spending all her time instead in ceremonious religiosity, which won over the orthodoxy, or at work. In other words, she stood apart from the rest, and eminently so. The unassuming, simple yet commanding Maharani became, thus, an ideal monarch in the conception of her times and to those whose opinions mattered.

In what was more appealing to the masses, she also retained an endearing innocence and private reservation in spite of daily interacting with so many different people at so many levels. As late as 1929, for instance, when a Dutch woman, appointed to a lectureship at the Women's College, was presented at Satelmond Palace, she noticed a 'a very shy little woman who was really more interested in her children quarrelling in the adjacent room than in her visitor'. It did not offend Miss Ouwerkerk in the least, for the Maharani had a disarming charm about her even as she sat in a chair of state and received her. Instead she left with the happy impression of 'a very human couple behind all the pomp of bowing attendants and the luxurious little reception room'.[40] This positive impression also passed through to the public who were glad to see that for all her majesty and prestige, the ruler was still a 'homely' figure. She had all the 'queenly', 'womanly', and maternal qualities that the common herd appreciated.[41] And so she rose in their esteem, even as the Junior Maharani, despite her individual accomplishments and fascinating social unorthodoxy, was left somewhat diminished.

But in perhaps what was most important, Sethu Lakshmi Bayi took the greatest care to maintain her sterling reputation as a woman of almost Catholic good character. One of her more interesting habits, which she adhered to diligently for much of her life, was of never receiving any men alone. Whether it was the Dewan, the Resident, or even her brothers-in-law, Sethu Lakshmi Bayi insisted on having Rama Varma in attendance whenever she met them. 'Unless he is present to act as chaperon,' it was recorded, 'Her Highness does not give personal interviews to anyone.'[42] And, if he intended to go away somewhere, she would make an announcement to that effect so that those who wished to see her could seek an audience before his departure or wait until his return.[43] This often served to irritate Mr Watts and the Resident, for she would not be available for consultations at urgent, unforeseen moments. But the Maharani sternly forbade all objections. Perhaps the most amusing testimony to her excessive regard for moral propriety was that poor Mr Cotton, who at fifty-one was a confirmed bachelor, finally had to shake hands with matrimony. The Maharani considered it bad form for the Resident to be unwed when stationed at the court of a female monarch and in 1925 he had to belatedly find himself a highborn spinster.[44] Thus, next to her cousin trying to prove her husband was insane and battling charges, however bizarre, of 'undue familiarity' with musicians, Sethu Lakshmi Bayi prominently rose as a dignified and honourable lady of unimpeachable personal, albeit conservative, integrity. As O.M. Thomas, usually sharp-tongued, wrote of her 'spotless purity' in a review typical of its times in its tone:

> Her crystal virtue lifts her from modernity to the Golden Age of a forgotten past. Julius Caesar laid down a dictum which Her Highness has taken to heart. Her place is with Sita and Savitri, Draupadi and Damayanti, and those other pristine patterns of primary virtue that, I hope, will save us from the inroads of flaunting flappers and blatant bobbed hair. Her Highness has a peculiar way of averting her eyes from those who are admitted to her audience ... Her Highness is a pearl among Princesses and a Princess among pearls, so to say. May she be long spared to us to shed her radiance all round, to live amongst us as a shining example from another age and another world.[45]

Such moral power was politically most advantageous. 'The people,' as her cousin's nephew would remark with resignation, 'saw things in black and white and there was no grey area of nuance or detail. So they said wonderful things about the Regent Maharani and not as many wonderful things about the Junior.'[46] Sethu Lakshmi Bayi was able to harness this perfectly for matters of reform and policy. As an icon of grace and moral virtue enjoying a maternal sway over her people, she could do away with a lot of social ills that previous rulers did not have the courage to touch. There was, for instance, a practice in some temples of north Travancore of singing *poorapattus* on festive occasions. Originally sung to celebrate fertility and the power of the goddess, these had evolved over time into vulgar songs involving the liberal use of expletives and astonishing obscenities about women. Sethu Lakshmi Bayi decided it was time to abolish this, even though a decade ago her predecessor had conveniently decided to 'leave the matter alone'. 'Orders were issued to the police and the magistracy,' the *Travancore State Manual* reports, 'to take the necessary steps to enforce [her] command.'[47] Similarly, she terminated the violent custom of animal sacrifice in the state's temples, although such rituals were once necessary to venerate her own Tiruvirattukkavu Bhagavathi. To be sure, the Brahmins fussed that she was interfering with religion when she really ought to stay aloof. 'But once having decided upon her course,' *The Baltimore Sun* reported in faraway America, 'she stood firmly and soon the grumbling ceased.'[48] Humorously enough, when anyone insisted on the need to offer sacrifices at temple altars, Sethu Lakshmi Bayi recommended the beheading of subsidised cucumbers instead. The suggestion was reluctantly accepted.[49]

The contemporary French writer Maurice Dekobra who visited Travancore during these years made a perceptive observation of the Maharani's influence over her people. He noted that even the ordinary conservative 'preferred not to stand in the way of the will of a Maharani Regent who devotes her entire time and intelligence to the good government of her subjects'.[50] The strength of her maternal power combined with her hard work was such that all those in the public who objected gave way and withdrew in the end, much like recalcitrant children do before their mothers. It was a clever and an acknowledged political instrument employed by women in power across the world. In India no one would exemplify the political mother as well as Indira Gandhi at the peak of her career in the early 1970s. So too would the celebrated Evita Peron accumulate almost legendary influence as the Mother of Argentina in the late 1940s. In perhaps more modest circumstances, but not less shrewdly and sagaciously, Sethu Lakshmi Bayi too became the Mother of Travancore. It endowed her, as if by a moral imperative, not only with inspiring love and admiration but also with the deference and immensely useful obedience and loyalty of the masses. To quote O.M. Thomas again, she swayed the rod of authority with 'generous maternal affection' and a 'gentle, firm majesty' that installed her 'not so much

[as] an individual as [much as] an institution' in the eyes of her people.[51] And, wisely enough, Sethu Lakshmi Bayi ensured it stayed that way.

None of this adulation meant, however, that the Maharani was herself, despite appearances, in the most blissful of marriages, leading a life of great personal happiness unlike her cousin. Given the isolation Sethu Lakshmi Bayi had felt for years at court, she had certainly grown accustomed to depending on her husband, thereby allowing him considerable personal and political ascendance. And to be sure, she did not have a bad marriage. But it was still at best only a regular marriage, with a degree of formality to make up for its romantic awkwardness. For, after the initial phase of their life together, the Maharani and the Valiya Koil Tampuran discovered they had entirely different world views and personal traits, and would have to live together in acceptance of this. As their granddaughter would later tell,

> Yes, she was of an austere temperament, courtesy her mother's training, but she loved romance. Grandfather was not a romantic, so there was disparity there, no doubt. He was much in awe of her beauty and her intellectual capacity, but he confided to me during his last years that he refrained from expressing his admiration to her because he thought it would all go to her head. He was even afraid that with all the attention and eulogies she was getting, she would be tempted to go astray! He never truly understood her temperament, her commitment, and her integrity, but he was very much in love with her. His nature was cold and precise and practical, while grandmother, by her own confessions to me, was idealistic and a dreamer. Such a pity that he was unable to communicate his real feelings to her, because she was warm-hearted and generous to a fault. It is truly sad that though they both were fond of each other, they could never succeed in letting the other know it. Neither believed in the other's affection.[52]

Here again, then, it was Sethu Lakshmi Bayi's ability to stick to the figurative rule book of good behaviour that her mother had saddled her with that endeared her to the public. She always defended her husband before the world, even if it meant that many, mistakenly, believed her to be under his thumb. And he too diligently referred to her always as his queen and as 'Her Highness', so that neither let their guard down or allowed that façade to slip. It is also likely that to some extent he was reassured by her determined deference to him, given his fears that she might 'go astray' and actually had the power and position to discard him if she ever wished. The Maharani, for her part, was conscious that there was more at stake here than personal feelings, sacrificing the latter at the altar of what she believed was her duty. She must have, as her granddaughter remarked, loved her husband in order to make such an effort to give him a sense of security, but, as will be seen ahead, such stubborn idealism and discipline could also have its disadvantages. To the people, however, Sethu Lakshmi Bayi was a most perfect wife, a most perfect mother and a most perfect queen.

Perhaps it was fitting then that 1926 was the year in which the Maharani gave birth to her second and last child. In April it was declared that she was once again with child and that the baby was expected in October. It was a momentous announcement, because the last instance of a ruling princess giving birth was in 1813 when Swathi Tirunal, the famous musician prince, was born to Gowri Lakshmi Bayi. Preparations began in full gusto for the event and Dr Mary was brought in to oversee everything like the last time, assisted by nurses Miss Martin and Mrs Alwin. By July parts of the palace grounds were cleared to erect sheds and other temporary buildings for the medical staff. Excitement mounted and the months passed in a flurry of preparatory activity. By 18 October soldiers of the Nair Brigade arrived at the palace, ready to fire a salute as soon as the baby was born. There was also some romantic anticipation that just like over a century before, this time too the ruler might give birth to a heroic male heir. It would, it was felt, be such a wonderful, fairytale setting.

But that was not to be, even though the rest would still befit a fairy-tale. At 1:57 on the morning of 23 October, Sethu Lakshmi Bayi gave birth to a healthy baby girl, her second daughter. She was brought into the world to the booms of a twenty-one-gun salute and Travancore celebrated the occasion with a state holiday.[53] A 'wave of public rejoicing' broke out throughout the state, the *Madras Mail* reported, and large crowds of people flocked to Satelmond Palace to see the child later that morning. It was unprecedented in the royal family for a baby to be shown in public before the age of six months, but the Maharani decided to break with this custom, like the several others she had agreeably put to rest. Under her special command the little girl, asleep and wrapped in silks, was taken to the principal gallery of the palace and held up by her exuberant father for the crowds to see.[54] Across the land it was then proudly proclaimed that Her Highness Pooradam Tirunal Maharajah had safely given birth to a new Attingal princess. She was in due course named Karthika Tirunal Indira Bayi Tampuran, Third Princess of Travancore.

Sethu Lakshmi Bayi's family portrait was now complete.[55]

When Queen Victoria married Prince Albert in 1840, her counsellors and friends all issued dire warnings to her. He was a man, they said, and no man would remain peacefully for long under the authority of a woman, whoever she might be. Staunch royalists insisted that he should have nothing at all to do with government and that he ought to be purposefully kept away. Some others, like Stockmar, felt the queen could devolve power in degrees to him over a substantial space of time. Albert himself was uneasy at first. 'In my whole life I am happy and contented,' he wrote, 'but the difficulty in filling my place with proper dignity is that I am only the husband and not the master of the house.'[56] As a man who owed everything to his wife, he was naturally quite powerless before her. Yet, by the time of his death, scholars concurred that Albert had influenced the policy of the queen discreetly but very successfully.

In Travancore, the Valiya Koil Tampuran was in very similar circumstances. As one contemporary remarked, 'His position no doubt is not an easy one for he appears in the conflicting roles of husband and subject of Her Highness at the same time.' He had to be 'ever conscious of the line of demarcation between his privileges as royal partner and his duties as loyal citizen. This perplexing situation,' it was felt, 'will tax any man's mental alertness.'[57] But Rama Varma was not all that perplexed. For right from the onset, he appears to have desired to play more than a peripheral or merely advisory role in the Maharani's administration. Owing to her caution about public appearances, it is not certain what the entire reality of their relationship during this period was when it came to his political involvement. But insofar as all the evidence goes, Sethu Lakshmi Bayi usually stood by her husband and his actions. One can assume that she did not object to his interest.

At the commencement of her reign, interestingly, she had handed over the management of the Sripadam to him, which was 'generally regarded as a hint that she does not want him to interfere in affairs of State'.[58] But this was really done in order to reduce the burden on her shoulders and not to sidetrack him. Mr Cotton knew this, which is why he was so concerned at first that the Valiya Koil Tampuran might hijack his wife's authority. That did not turn out to be the case, yet he remained nervous. He imagined that the amount of power Sethu Lakshmi Bayi had inherited could turn the man's head, and informed Delhi that he was 'watching him carefully'. His feelings about Rama Varma were mixed at this time. On the one hand he felt he was 'not a bad man' and that there was 'much that I like in him', but on the other, he was also 'strong willed, somewhat mulish and like most Malayalis [!] avaricious and mean'.[59] But if there was any tendency to interfere in appointments, as Sankaran Tampi used to do in return for lucrative amounts, or to provoke quarrels with his old enemy, the Junior Maharani, the Resident promised to 'carpet him in and in the last resort threaten to report his misconduct'.[60]

In the initial phase of Sethu Lakshmi Bayi's administration, the Valiya Koil Tampuran did give some legitimate cause for concern to Mr Cotton. In November 1924, for example, when Chithira Tirunal celebrated his twelfth birthday, the entire royal family was supposed to meet for a feast. But nobody from Satelmond Palace attended, mainly because the Junior Maharani had, justifiably, written to say that since Rama Varma had not once called on her son since his installation as minor Maharajah, she would not receive him.[61] Sethu Lakshmi Bayi too therefore decided against going, seeing how her husband was unwelcome. It took a year for some rapprochement to be effected when during Lord Goschen's visit in October 1925, Rama Varma met and engaged in friendly banter with the Junior Maharani's husband at a garden party. The Kochu Koil Tampuran then took the initiative and called at Satelmond Palace, following which his counterpart paid his first ever visit in years at Kowdiar Palace.[62] But then another quarrel broke out and everyone was back at starting point. 'Nothing will,' Mr Cotton bemoaned, 'terminate the feud between the Junior Maharani and the Valiya Koil Tampuran but the death of one of them.'[63] And so long as they did not see eye to eye, chances of the two cousins reconciling were also slim.

Similarly, two months after the Maharani's rule was inaugurated, it turned out that the Valiya Koil Tampuran was covertly financing an editorial series in the *Hindustan Times* that warned against Mr Cotton's interference in the administration.[64] When the editor of the *Princely India* visited Trivandrum, Rama Varma also had him put up as a state guest and reportedly paid him a large amount of money when threatened that he would 'expose' his clash with the Junior Maharani. The Resident's information was that while Sethu Lakshmi Bayi was unaware of these transactions, Mr Raghavaiah, who was pandering to her husband at the time for his retention as Dewan, was privy to it.[65] Since Mr Raghavaiah was sacked anyway, it appears that the Maharani did not heed her husband's advice and went her own way, which contributed to Mr Cotton's confidence in her. Additionally, she also summoned the editor of the *Hindustan Times*, none other than the future diplomat K.M. Panikkar, and gave him 'a good dressing down' for the misleading articles being published.[66] Thereafter, when in

January 1925 the paper was still printing false reports of altercations between her and Mr Cotton, she personally issued a firm press note denying the rumours, without consulting anyone on the matter.[67] Rama Varma, consequently, had to give in to his wife's resolve and in a conversation with Mr Cotton he admitted to having mistrusted him in the past and sought to now become friends.[68] This inconsistent behaviour combined with his mischievous conduct continued to render the Valiya Koil Tampuran suspect in the eyes of the Government of India. If there were a dark figure in Sethu Lakshmi Bayi's administration, people mumbled, it looked very much like her husband.

The concerns continued and by February 1926 a grievance arose from Mr Watts regarding undue interference by the Maharani's husband in state matters. The Dewan was said to be 'fed up' with Rama Varma over his intrusions in 'administrative questions and particularly in the matter of patronage'. It appeared that there was a vacancy in the Law College and Mr Watts selected a Nair to fill it, while the Valiya Koil Tampuran recommended a Christian candidate. The Resident's information was that the Dewan had threatened to resign (although from private correspondence with the Maharani it does not seem to have gone that far) before Rama Varma backed off. He was, in Mr Cotton's opinion, 'not venal' but had a 'passion to play King, and withal so short a time for its indulgence'.[69] Again, it appears that the Maharani made her final decision independently and went with the Dewan. Moreover, in spite of the dispute between her husband and Mr Watts, she was happy to consider the latter's application for a raise solely in recognition of his excellent service to her.[70] Power might momentarily have gone to the Valiya Koil Tampuran's head, but common sense had not abandoned Sethu Lakshmi Bayi.

Then again, in April that year the Land Revenue Commissioner also registered a protest against Rama Varma. This time he had involved himself in the business of transferring certain officials, and one A.R. Subramania Iyer, 'one of the laziest and most corrupt' tahsildars, who happened to be an acquaintance from Harippad, was shown special favour. In addition to all this, the Valiya Koil Tampuran spent most of his mornings in 'giving audiences to subordinate officials seeking to avoid unwelcome transfers or obtain undeserved promotions'. Hitherto, the Resident warned, people only accused the Maharani's husband of being greedy for power. But if he continued to hold court for so many petty government servants, it would only be a matter of time before he was charged as Sankaran Tampi's heir in the business of corruption too, whatever the truth might be.[71] And predictably, it did take one unnerving experience for the

Valiya Koil Tampuran to learn the tact and discretion requisite for a man in his position, and to rein in his ambitions.

It all started when late in 1925 the *Jenmabhoomi*, a prominent vernacular newspaper with considerable circulation, published a vehement attack on Rama Varma. Calling him corrupt and unscrupulous, this article even shocked the hawk-eyed Resident with its colourful variety of insinuations. He recorded, to the Valiya Koil Tampuran's credit, that the article was 'not only scurrilous but without a shadow of justification', adding that for all his other flaws, the Maharani's husband was 'certainly not a rake' and could not be accused of corruption.[72] The gravity of the false allegations was severe enough for Mr Cotton to write to Rama Varma personally, 'as your friend', about how 'disgusted' he was by the piece, assuring him that that such 'recklessly made charges of venality and incontinence' cut no ice with anybody of intelligence.[73] And to Sethu Lakshmi Bayi he sent his sincere sympathies against 'the most disgraceful, false aspersions' cast upon her husband by 'this mischievous rag' of a newspaper. 'The editor probably hopes,' he added indignantly, 'that if he only throws enough mud some of it will stick.'[74]

The Maharani, however, no matter what her disagreements with her husband, was not willing to take this attack on him lying down. This one article would set into motion a series of events that would bring down the iron hand of the government not just on the *Jenmabhoomi* but on the entire Travancore press. It helped that for some time now a need was being increasingly felt to regulate newspapers in order to restrain the communal tensions they blatantly promoted. The fact was that even the press in Travancore was divided along communal lines. As a commentator in the *Madras Mail* noted in 1905, 'we have the Brahmin interest, the Nair interest, the Syrian interest, the Ezhava interest etc., and ... there are journals to support each one's cause' in what was a 'social civil war'.[75] In the legislature on two occasions, therefore, non-official members had already called upon the government to control the 'systematic propagation of misrepresented and ill-represented reports'.[76] The Maharani too had been 'anxiously observing' a 'reprehensible laxity' in the quality of the press.[77] The fact that a newspaper had without fear, openly launched itself against none other than the monarch's consort became the last straw, regardless of the substance of its allegations. The Resident, reflecting the attitude of the colonial state on the matter, informed the Maharani of his fullest support to 'stay the pens of the ink slingers' and called for the 'very early introduction of a Press Regulation'.[78] Sethu Lakshmi Bayi decided, therefore, to take up the matter and issue yet another reform that her predecessor's government had not felt the courage to pass. It was, however, a perilous move, one that would scorch her husband seriously and bring about the first concerted effort to topple her from power as well.

The business of printing is very old in Kerala. It arrived with foreign missionaries at the end of the sixteenth century and about two hundred years later, in 1772, the first printed Malayalam book was published from Rome. Newspapers and journals took some more time to make their appearance and in 1847 the *Rajya Samacharam* was published in Malabar, with the distinguished linguist and scholar, Hermann Gundert, as its editor. In 1876, the *Satyanadam Weekly* commenced circulation and in 1881 the *Kerala Mitram* followed. The *Deepika* was set up in 1887 and then, perhaps the most celebrated of all, the *Malayala Manorama* was born in 1888.[79] Very many more journals and newspapers established themselves in Travancore and in the early 1920s there was an unusual surge in numbers. On an average there were three newspapers and six magazines per taluka, a considerable statistic compared to other parts of India.[80] By the end of the decade there were seven prominent dailies with large-scale circulation of 16,000, and twenty-two weeklies with a circulation of 20,000 in the state, not to speak of smaller, more local players and papers from Cochin and Malabar.[81] In addition to this, for every 1,000 of the population, 289 were literate, according to the coming 1931 census of the state, and as education continued to reach out to more and more, the attendant appetite for news only swelled the business's market.

It was in 1903 that the government first imposed a very moderate regulation under which all newspapers were ordered to register with local authorities. This was followed by another step in 1917 binding them to deposit copies of their publications immediately after printing, with default inviting a fine of Rs 50.[82] Thereafter, during the Dewanship of Mr Raghavaiah, thought was given to a more serious, qualitative regulation of the press in the interests of communal harmony.[83] For it was a time when 'different communities began to struggle tooth and claw for scraps of offices', and the press started to manifest these rivalries. Officers from one community could have their reputations maligned by the newspapers of a competing group, and 'scurrility, obscenity, vilification, and vituperation' were rampant in the press.[84] As a European professor in the Women's College would write, the papers in Travancore 'live by collecting exciting rumours and then denying them—else how would they fill their columns and the Editors' pockets'?[85] The government definitely had an interest, thus, in controlling the free rein of the Fourth Estate.[86] Nothing was done about this during Mulam Tirunal's time, however, as it was bound to cause enormous uproar as an illiberal clamp on the freedom of expression.

Sethu Lakshmi Bayi, nevertheless, decided to go ahead with the idea in spite of the potentially fiery opposition and foreseeable unpopularity. For one, in her determined effort to weed out communalism, the elimination of such a powerful political weapon from her opponents' armoury had its obvious strategic advantages. In fact, communalism became the declared moral justification for the regulation. 'Every schoolmaster in our three thousand and odd schools,' the Dewan argued, 'is the centre of a political group and as every Nair and most Ezhavas and Syrian Christians are prone to politics and evince a keen interest in affairs generally, you can well imagine that the demand for newspapers is great.'[87] And if the press were communal and denigrating in nature, it was dangerous to allow it to seep through to villages, where communalism was not yet entrenched, or to schools, where young minds were moulded. The Maharani was determined, therefore, to impose restrictions on the contents of newspapers in order to arrest any further divisive drifts in Travancore's society. Or so the official line earnestly proclaimed.

That said the royal family had always had an awkward relationship with the concept of the freedom of expression. The Maharani's guardian, Kerala Varma, for example, had all the subscriptions in the state to the *Keralapatrika* cancelled when it carried unflattering critiques of his Sanskrit works. Earlier in the 1870s when Ayilyam Tirunal ruled Travancore, the *Santishtavadi* was shut down for being 'outspoken in its criticism' of the government. So too during Mulam Tirunal's reign the *Malayali* was forced to move base to a British enclave fearing royal wrath, not to speak of the infamous expulsion of the editor of the *Swadeshabhimani* in 1911. There was, thus, a history of the government and the royal family not tolerating the press beyond a certain point; that point normally being the preservation of the halo around the royal family.[88] In 1926 too what finally triggered the Maharani's decision to impose a comprehensive blanket regulation was (notwithstanding her avowed position against communalism) the jolt she received from 'the most atrocious calumnies published about my husband'.[89] This was the latest in an exasperating series that included attacks even against Mr Watts, whom one newspaper sourly called 'The Mussolini of Travancore'.[90] Sethu Lakshmi Bayi perceived these as personal attacks on her, and it is quite likely they were. She believed that this 'pronounced tendency to attack highly placed persons' began to be 'noticed only from the commencement of the Regency', indicating that some politicians had an axe to grind against her authority exclusive of their long-standing communal battles.[91] For while they could not directly vilify her owing to her standing with the masses, what they *could* do was traduce her adherents and diminish the credibility of her regime. It was time, the Maharani therefore felt, to use her sovereign power and make a point, both moral and political.

But forcing any kind of control on the press has always been universally resented. And Sethu Lakshmi Bayi was severely criticized for her draconian policy on this count by most in the business. A peculiar circumstance that opened her up to direct liability was that she personally and independently took the final decision. For, by the middle of May 1926, when it became clear the new law would be promulgated, both Mr Watts and Mr Cotton had to go away to England for private reasons. Some suspected, therefore, that the Maharani was taking advantage of their absence to issue a directive they did not really support. And to add to it, she intended to do so by royal decree and not through the legislature. This prompted the loudest protests in the press, for they were confident that politicians would never allow the regulation to pass if they were allowed to have a say in it. A delegation of journalists desperately called at Satelmond Palace to appeal against the decision but they were told the Maharani would not receive them. Members of civil society also expressed that while 'some restrictions on the Press were necessary, they should not [take] the form of "judgment without trial".'[92] Nevertheless, unwavering and resolute, and in a rare admission that despite constitutional concessions, Travancore was, ultimately, the inherited fief of a single family, on 22 May Sethu Lakshmi Bayi affixed the sign manual to the Newspaper Regulation, imposing upon the press a series of qualitative standards and a number of stringent political restrictions as well.

No newspaper could henceforward publish without a licence available from the government at a price of Rs 500. This was intended to ensure that no Tom, Dick or Harry could at a whim start up a newspaper solely to defame someone, and shut it down once that objective was achieved, as was apparently being done. Only those with the necessary capital could hereafter invest in the business, and it was hoped that at least out of the fear of forfeiting the expensive licence, they would toe the government line. Similarly, the press was prohibited from publishing anything that would 'excite disaffection or bring into hatred Us or Our Government or His Majesty the King Emperor of India or the Government established by law in British India'. Criticism of the royal family was strictly banned as was anything that would 'promote feelings of enmity or hatred between the several classes of people' in the country. In case newspapers erred, the government was authorised to revoke licences forthwith. The former were permitted, however, to approach the High Court and appeal against the authorities for a reversal if they so desired.[93]

At the time this proclamation was issued, Sethu Lakshmi Bayi was sojourning in Peermade. And when she returned to Trivandrum on 1 June, a number of protest demonstrations and political marches greeted her, voicing their opposition to her policy. Writing to Mr Cotton in England, clearly unmoved, she referred to this 'burning topic of the hour'. 'The Newspaper Regulation has been promulgated,' she informed him, 'and it has naturally evoked trenchant comments here and in a few outside papers. Meetings are being frantically held all over Travancore and truculent resolutions passed. It is worthy of mention,' she added, 'that the agitation is mainly carried on by the party which conducted the Anti-Watts campaign a year ago.'[94] Sethu Lakshmi Bayi, in her characteristic style, ignored the disgruntled politicians and their protestations, remaining adamantly impassive. As the Acting Resident Mr H.A.B. Vernon noted, she was conspicuously 'offering prayers for her safe confinement' at various temples at the time (for all this had happened when she was pregnant) instead of expressing any alarm at the political turmoil.[95] This sustained, deliberate disregard for criticism seemed almost bizarre to many, and once again the finger of suspicion was pointed at the unpopular Valiya Koil Tampuran.

It was alleged that the Newspaper Regulation was Rama Varma's brainchild, given his recent troubles with the (largely Nair) press, which had also baited him ('without an iota of justification', Mr Cotton had remarked) when many Christians were given high appointments after the Maharani came to power.[96] Besides, he was the one to first bring up the issue in 1925 when he wrote in the *Microcosm* about a 'hope' that the press in Travancore, where 'sobriety of views and moderation in language' were absent qualities, and which acted more 'in the light of brigandage than a useful institution in the polity' would be restrained.[97] It did not help that as Sethu Lakshmi Bayi's accouchement approached and she was increasingly unable to transact too much daily government business, he began to indulge himself once again. In early June when some officers went to visit her, for instance, the Valiya Koil Tampuran asked them to 'deal directly with him'.[98] It was found that owing to her incapacity, he was giving independent orders to the government and 'in other ways standing between the Maharani and her people'.[99] 'The Maharani in her present state of health,' Mr Vernon concluded, 'seems to be entirely in his hands. The position may develop further if he is allowed a little more rope.'[100] Rama Varma suddenly had all the heat and hostility turned on him, partly also because nobody believed the gentle, serene Sethu Lakshmi Bayi was capable of behaviour that bordered on the dictatorial.

In the meantime the Nairs had constituted a 'Newspaper Regulation Repeal Committee' that put forth their grievances (and surprise at the Maharani's attitude) in a resolution in late June:

> Since the Travancore Newspapers Regulation V of 1101 has been promulgated otherwise than through the Legislative Council and kills the liberty of free public opinion, veils the evils of administration, prevents the means of redress of the grievances of the poor and the helpless, and is prejudicial to the welfare of society, this meeting with feelings of regret at the absence of any action on the part of the Government even after noticing the volume of popular agitation against the measure, appeals for the immediate repeal of this Regulation.[101]

By this time the crucial budget session of the Legislative Council was about to begin in early August and Mr Watts had returned from London. Different measures were contemplated to compel the government to heed the politicians' demands. K. Parameswaran Pillai, who had led the Vaikom deputation to the Maharani, suggested that 'all members should observe complete silence without participating in the general discussion' to bring the Dewan to his knees.[102] But as was characteristic of Travancore politics, there was no consensus and in the end the legislature was allowed to function because of a fragmented opposition. A motion was moved, however, to repeal the regulation and the Dewan, taking a considerable risk, permitted it. He was not obliged to do so, since the Maharani's diktat was final, but she was certain the government would be vindicated. And to the genuine surprise of all those opposing the Newspaper Regulation, the repeal motion was indeed defeated, and by a non-official majority for that matter.[103] Thirty members of the Council supported the Maharani's action and only sixteen voted for a repeal, delivering a resounding victory to the authorities. The regulation, it became clear, was here to stay until the ruler chose to repeal it.

Effects of the restraints had in fact already begun to be felt by now. On 29 June, for instance, the *Navashakti* published an article about the Dewan claiming he was incapable, inefficient, partial to some communities and disrespectful of the legislature. The Maharani was incensed by the piece. Much like a disciplinarian schoolteacher, she decided to give the paper a chance to 'express unreserved regret' at its conduct. An apology was duly published but it was found to be 'not sufficiently reflecting a repentant attitude'. The *Navashakti* lost its licence. Indeed, while in 1926 there was a total of fifty-seven newspapers and eighty-nine periodicals circulating in the state, the stern hand of the Maharani cut down the number to forty-four and fifty-six respectively in a matter of twelve months. By 1930 the Travancore Press (Emergency Powers) Act would come to be passed under which newspapers suspected of mischief were asked to deposit Rs 1,000 with the government and pay up to Rs 2,000 for publishing 'unacceptable' articles. This was passed through the legislature where once again thirty members supported it against fourteen in opposition. And it was the *Prabodhakan* that became one of the earliest to fall before the law thereafter when it published a caustic editorial about Sethu Lakshmi Bayi's regime entitled 'Heaven or Hell' in September 1930.[104] But the larger purpose of the Maharani was achieved in that journalism became more responsible in its tone, and open communal propaganda was contained. Indeed, despite the loud denunciations of the 'oppressive' policy of the government, by 1930 Travancore's press would be flourishing once again with a record sixty-three newspapers and ninety-five periodicals.[105] None of them breached the law and all of them maintained a bare minimum of standards, which included, however, publishing nothing against the royal house.

Nevertheless, the Newspaper Regulation remains one of the most controversial edicts of the Maharani during the time she held the mantle of power. Many argued that she muzzled the progress of larger, cherished ideals of the freedom of expression, even if she sincerely intended to control unhealthy communal forces. But much like killing two birds with the same stone, it was certainly also designed to protect the monarchy at a time when the royal family was under amplified pressure to give up more and more power. As one historian notes, until the 1920s Travancore's politicians were in the habit of dishing up elaborate memorandums and proposals to the state as they sought more responsible, democratic governance. Rulers could then generously concede some favours, earning a reputation as constitutional monarchs. But in that decade, 'which was socially and politically very turbulent', a new era of 'agitational politics' was initiated and politicians lost their patience with wordy memorandums. For the first time it was made clear that communities could wage open war to win their shares of power.[106] And, as the Maharani noted, 'the knowledge that the present administration is only for a specified period', emboldened many to stand up to the state, without fear of long-term retribution.[107] Challenged by a phenomenon unseen so far, Sethu Lakshmi Bayi did what she deemed necessary to exercise control. And curtailing the powers of the press was one considerable step in the direction of keeping the balance of power in the monarch's autocratic favour.

Newspapers were a critical part of this ongoing political struggle. As early as the 1890s, officials began to recognise that the press was becoming 'a power in the land' that threatened the existing structure.[108] The high rate of literacy in Travancore, fashionably showcased for most part by the government, backfired in that by the early twentieth century every village had a handful of people who could sit by the roadside or in local coffee shops and read the news out loud for general benefit.[109] Editors began to enjoy widespread influence, which they utilized completely in laying pressure upon the government. Needless to say, communal politics seduced the power of journalism into a formidable union; some of Travancore's firebrand politicians were also journalists. Often this anomalous communal marriage led to curious situations. During the tenure of one Dewan from 1892 until 1898, for example, Syrian Christian papers asserted that the state had gone 'from bad to worse' even as their Nair competitors insisted he ruled 'faultlessly'; all because he had supported the latter community.[110] By the 1920s, as Mr Watts put it, there was probably 'no part of India so given up to public meetings, resolutions, representations, deputations as Travancore', in all of which newspapers were involved. Whether as 'vehicles for the expression of views' or as 'actual participants', they were all 'vigorously engaged'.[111] The press was turning into a kind of non-state political actor, causing a good amount of restlessness in the corridors of royal power and of the absolute monarchy that headed it.

Sethu Lakshmi Bayi was therefore not merely trying to prevent the menace of communalism from becoming deep-rooted in the minds of the rural masses. While that was a definite goal, a more long-term objective was to prevent politics itself, as it was then practised, from reaching the villages. For if the many literate people in rural Travancore also began to clamour for rights from the royal family, the situation would become very precarious. This was aggravated by the fact that rural Travancore was already producing the vast bulk of educated youngsters, all eager to compete for the limited opportunities the state had on offer. The Unemployment Enquiry Committee the Maharani would appoint in 1928 highlighted this growing danger of unoccupied youths in the state's villages, all prone to political activism. And it was to forestall the politicians from recruiting a vast army of discontent against the monarchy that she decided to control the most powerful medium of information that carried their propaganda, along with their growing irreverence for royal authority, to the remotest corners of her country. The leaders of the Nair community recognised these larger, strategic implications of the Newspaper Regulation. M. Govinda Pillai, a lawyer of legendary fame, summed up the issue succinctly when he claimed that the new law would not merely restrain the press. It would, he warned, 'crush the Nair community' and its political aspirations in the process.[112]

Previous governments in Travancore had, in fact, readily tolerated communal propensities and cleverly played groups against each other. In fact, P. Rajagopalachari during Mulam Tirunal's reign had openly declared that there had been 'a systematic effort to conciliate the Nair community by employing men of that community more largely in the public service'.[113] The strategy was to win the most important party on to the government's side, with the dubious carrot of special rights, while using the stick on the rest if needed. And in this way the last many governments had continued to hold on to all the powers that mattered while keeping the growing political movement conveniently distracted with communal issues. But Sethu Lakshmi Bayi decided, with all her quiet grit and determination, to put an end to such an approach. She would not bribe one community against another and soil her hands; she would not take sides. Instead, she aimed to change the rules of the game entirely. The first step in this direction was taken in 1925 by announcing equal opportunity to everybody regardless of communal affiliations. And a decisive second aimed in 1926 to demolish the power already accumulated by political factions thanks to the short-sighted carrot-and-stick policy of her predecessors.

It is also likely that given her own idealistic outlook and political conservatism, the urbane Maharani viewed the politicians and their petty communal rivalries with a kind of righteous condescension. A later Resident, for instance, declared most local politicians 'as lousy a lot' as possible, who were 'lying, mean, cowardly, conceited, intriguing, and packed full of envy, hatred, malice, and all uncharitableness. I wish,' he added, 'they could be deported en masse to Abyssinia and have a taste of real repression and oppression by a really totalitarian government.'[114] Sethu Lakshmi Bayi herself, more tellingly, had a very poor opinion of political journalism in Travancore. She saw it largely as 'a nefarious trade' and a 'newspaper tyranny' run by 'men of straw and no education' for the 'intimidation and blackmailing' of the government. No moralistic arguments about the Freedom of Expression could convince her to change her mind because what was at stake here was more serious, in her opinion, than the right of a few to write what they pleased. Indeed, she would stubbornly defend the Newspaper Regulation, happily pointing out some years later that it had had a 'most salutary effect' on the 'moral atmosphere' in the country, and was lauded by all but a 'refractory minority' who were out to make trouble.[115]

And so it looked as if the Maharani had declared war against the existing state of affairs. It was a can of worms, however, and she was cautioned to stick to the tried and tested methods of her predecessors instead of stepping on the toes of such powerful factions. P. Rajagopalachari, for instance, warned of how the 'fanatical' Nairs 'once roused, will be difficult to pacify'.[116] In the short time she had to rule, others quietly counselled, it would do her better to placate that most potent political group in the land, however unabashedly communal its agenda might be, and win its approval. Problems of a larger, irreversible nature would inescapably emerge in the long run, but they could be addressed at that time by whoever was in charge. Sethu Lakshmi Bayi, however, stuck to her obstinate scheme of political and moral reform. With no compromises, she insisted on the need for local politics to champion values superior to communalism, and with as much single-mindedness, she was determined to preserve the power of the monarch during these years when Travancore increasingly seemed to veer towards the uncertainty that precedes democratic, free rule.

The Nairs, though, had to defend their own objectives against the Maharani's resolve. In the initial aftermath of the Newspaper Regulation they were somewhat confounded as they went about arranging protest marches and demonstrations. But they recovered soon enough to realise that a strategic policy needed to be met with calculated tact in equal measure. While loudly lamenting the demise of free speech in a language laden with moral rhetoric, they too prepared to hit the Maharani where it hurt most. They knew that all other Regents in India had only limited powers that prohibited them from altering longstanding policies. But Sethu Lakshmi Bayi ruled with the full powers of a sovereign because the Government of India had recognised her as a 'unique' Regent. If they withdrew that status, however, she would be reduced to a mere figurehead and all her executive acts could be declared illegitimate, including the latest. And so if they could cripple that basic foundation of her regime and bring her down, the rest of the struggle could be won with ease. In the desperate throes of the times, therefore, the Nairs came together and decided to inflict upon their Maharani a political blow she would never forget.

While within Travancore its politicians' patience with memorandums and petitions had long been exhausted after decades of cumbersome dealings with the royal family, in attempting to win over the Government of India they were still prepared to make use of such ostensibly constitutional methods. The feeling of a pan-Indian nationalism, with the British Raj as its sworn enemy, had still not arrived in the state. The result was that local politicians were willing to implore and beseech the powers that be in Delhi instead of going down the path of anti-colonial demonstrations and Gandhian satyagraha that sought to construct an Indian nation. Their agitations were against their monarch and in achieving their goals, which were more local than national, they were happy to pose as the very embodiments of moderate virtue before authorities they knew to be superior to the royal house. Accordingly, on 20 July 1926 a group of Nair politicians, amid considerable fanfare, submitted a lengthy political memorial against the Maharani to Mr Vernon. Ambitiously titled a 'Representation from the People of Travancore' it was duly transmitted to the Political Department of the Government of India for their consideration and counsel to the Viceroy.[117]

The principal objective of this memorial was to strike at the roots of Sethu Lakshmi Bayi's status as de facto ruler of Travancore. She enjoyed the position of Pooradam Tirunal Maharajah because under matrilineal law she had succeeded as head of the royal house. And in that capacity she was vested with full powers that allowed her to supersede the legislature and command all customary authority. The title of Regent was only one that was imposed by the Government of India, which had no practical relevance in that her authority was internally absolute and unrestricted. But the memorialists decided to challenge this. They conceded that indeed matrilineal law guaranteed uninhibited power to the senior female member of the royal family. However, they argued, Sethu Lakshmi Bayi could not personally claim to benefit from this owing to certain peculiar precedents. She could only, instead, do what appointed Regents in other states were permitted to do. And this was, simply, close to nothing.

The Government of India was reminded that at the time of the Maharani's adoption, the then Elayarajah had objected to the proceedings citing his own right to do so according to custom. As per the strict letter of the law, thus, the adoption ought not to have been recognised since there was no consensus in the family. But Mulam Tirunal and the Government of India had brushed aside his protests arguing (a) that the royal family was not an ordinary matrilineal household and so the regular law did not strictly apply and (b) that the adoption was an Act of State that did not require sanction under matrilineal law anyway. If the adoption were an Act of State without connection to matriliny, the memorialists conjectured, the Maharani, as a product of the adoption could surely not claim rights under the law. In other words, the 'contention that Her Highness the Regent rules by inherent right is opposed to the facts and circumstances of the adoption'. Indeed, they went to the extent of suggesting that 'any other person', a complete alien, could have been appointed Regent in Travancore. Similarly, there was nothing to stop the Government of India from instituting a Council of Regency, which they felt ought still to be constituted to check the tyranny of the Maharani.[118]

The memorial then did itself a disservice by listing an exaggerated assortment of grievances against Sethu Lakshmi Bayi's reign. Mr Watts, it stated, was selected as Dewan only because he could be counted upon as an accomplice in the ruler's evil designs. She herself was not acting in the best interests of the state, an example being that she was restructuring Satelmond Palace using public funds. 'Favour or disfavour having become the bases of action,' it went on to say, 'efficiency of the state services has considerably suffered.' But then, after haphazardly beating around the bush with a plethora of random complaints, the memorialists came out with their second major grouse: the Valiya Koil Tampuran.

> We are far from suggesting that Her Highness the Maharani Regent is personally responsible for this state of affairs. Her Highness is a devoted wife, and the influence of Her Highness' consort is an irresistible force to be reckoned with. Wise, just, and impartial advice is hardly available to Her Highness whose sex, inexperience and peculiar position make the need of such advice absolutely indispensable. We have reason to believe that any proper advice that may be offered in the present circumstances would get refracted through the medium of influence that surrounds Her Highness.[119]

It was contended that Rama Varma no longer 'disguises the part he plays in the destinies of Travancore' and that though he had no formal authority, he was helping himself generously to power, 'taking undue advantage of his position of trust and confidence'. Ceremonially also, sycophants had started addressing him with the Malayalam titles and honorifics used only in the case of sovereigns. He had secured an income-tax exemption, which was a concession denied him by Mulam Tirunal during the last government. He consistently slighted young Chithira Tirunal and was alleged to be the source of the 'unseemly squabbles' between his wife and her cousin, whose reputation he deliberately always attempted to malign. In every sense, Rama Varma was, therefore, a negative influence not only on the Maharani but also on the administration, and needed to be shown the door.

> The Valiya Koil Tampuran has practically usurped the reins of power. He has become the only channel of communication between the Maharani Regent and her officers. He controls admissions to the royal presence. It is suspected that Her Highness is allowed access only to such channels of information and organs of public opinion as he deems fit that she should have. The Maharani spends most of the year outside the capital and no responsible officer, not even her own Private Secretary, is allowed to accompany her in camp on such long sojourns. The position is peculiarly dangerous when it is remembered that all important papers have to receive the sanction of the Maharani Regent and that all such sanctions have to be communicated over the signature of the Private Secretary. What passes behind the scenes is no longer a mystery; and it is suspected with some reasons that sanctions and orders emanating from the palace have not always been personally approved of by the Maharani Regent herself.[120]

The memorialists then went on to alert the authorities that Rama Varma and his tendency towards 'power without responsibility' even threatened to disturb 'public tranquillity' in the principality. They also listed some more miscellaneous grievances regarding appointments that were 'unfair' (interestingly enough, these positions were all those recently given by the Maharani to Christians and Brahmins). The lengthy representation ended, then, with a plea that the Viceroy should correct this state of affairs in Travancore and politely put Sethu Lakshmi Bayi in her rightful place as a powerless figurehead, just as it did elsewhere. In that, it was dramatically concluded, lay the salvation and future happiness of Travancore.

There was some serious hope among the memorialists that the Government of India would swiftly swoop down on the Maharani after receiving their representation and throw out her 'dictatorial' government. Disappointingly for them, however, the authorities did not share their enthusiasm. It was noted that of the mere thirty-four signatories to this petition, twenty-eight were Nairs, four Tamils and two Brahmins. Neither the Christians, nor the Ezhavas, Muslims or other minorities were involved. 'The petition,' Mr Vernon dryly commented, 'can hardly be called representative of the people of Travancore.' He felt it was 'merely a verbal expression of the age-long feud between the Nairs and Christians aggravated at the moment by the apparently pro-Christian tendency of the present regime'. He did, however, feel that there was a 'very considerable substratum of truth' when it came to the 'unlawful activities' of the Valiya Koil Tampuran and the disaffection surrounding the Newspaper Regulation (and this certainly seems to have been the case). But beyond that the memorial was all stuff and nonsense.[121]

There was, in fact, a reason why Rama Varma suddenly seemed to enjoy too much power. Since the inauguration of her government, the Maharani suffered from an occasional illness that caused her to collapse into a febrile state and take to bed in great distress. After convalescing for a few days, she would recover just as suddenly and resume official business again with a zealous tenacity. This would continue for a long, positive stretch before that debilitating fever returned to immobilize her for yet another brief span. It was initially dismissed as induced by stress, but soon afterwards, having observed an uneasy pattern, Dr Mary decided to run some more tests. She had a vague suspicion what the ailment might be, but it was too dreadful to articulate until further investigation. It did not help that despite her illness Sethu Lakshmi Bayi chose to carry on with her interminable tours among the people. Indeed, while Dr Mary's suspicions were aroused as early as March 1925, it would be July before the Maharani was convinced to find the time for an examination by two experts in Nagercoil.[122] And when results came back in September, Dr Mary's worst fears were confirmed: Sethu Lakshmi Bayi was suffering from tuberculosis. However, Dr Mary's timely suspicions permitted its discovery before things got out of hand and the correct treatment was initiated promptly.

Owing to the social stigma attached to the disease, though, Sethu Lakshmi Bayi's illness was kept a carefully guarded secret, so that even many in her family were deliberately kept in the dark.[123] Her medical files were very possibly destroyed, and even successive Residents, who usually had a good network of informants in the palaces, found only ambiguous information on exactly how far the disease had progressed. While Mr Cotton knew about the initial diagnosis in 1925, by December 1926 he was no longer certain of where things stood. The Maharani, he thought, now 'looked well' and 'had grown stouter' which suggested the disease was in remission.[124] She would, however, suffer from the distressing effects of carrying the infection for at least a decade ahead, and the disease would subside fully only into the 1940s. But for the entire duration that she had to bear such severe bouts, nobody ever articulated the word tuberculosis; it was always referred to it as simply 'the illness'. And the Maharani never acknowledged having the disease and positively made it a point to go about her ordinary routine as though all was well, despite the protests of her physicians. As her future specialist Dr Noble would complain in 1930, when she had a particularly serious outburst of 'the illness', the problem was definitely 'aggravated by Her Highness' strict orthodoxy and temple observances', which she was unwilling to relinquish even temporarily.[125] Sethu Lakshmi Bayi was determined that her illness should not handicap her responsibilities, both temporal and religious.

But having to live with a deadly disease as a perpetual companion was not an easy affair. As one survivor from Sethu Lakshmi Bayi's times would recount, having tuberculosis 'changed my entire life'; people 'pitied me, stared at me, and treated me differently'.[126] And while the Maharani was spared social opprobrium, mental anxiety could not have evaded her. To have tuberculosis, for which no real medical treatment was available until the 1940s, was to come to terms with living with the persistent possibility of an unexpected, untimely death. Naturally, therefore, the Maharani had to bear with considerable mental stress, notwithstanding the anxieties of government. Supporters of the Junior Maharani were quick to capitalise on the situation too, and as early as 1925 Mr Cotton had recorded 'sensational rumours' being 'broadcasted to create the impression that she was too ill to continue' and to 'strengthen the demand for the immediate creation of a Council of Regency'.[127]

It was thus perhaps that Sethu Lakshmi Bayi turned a blind eye or even let her husband exercise power deliberately. Decisions had to be taken, and during her illness she could only turn to her husband, even if his judgement on matters of state did not always match her own assessments. In 1926, however, they were lucky, for in the matter of the 'Memorial from the People of Travancore' there were no harmful repercussions. With news of the memorial leaking out to the public, a second one was despatched from Trivandrum, which, however, was a show of support for the Maharani's government. With 184 prominent signatories from all classes and communities, including the Nairs, Christians, Brahmins, etc., this new memorandum more than evened out the stakes as far as Sethu Lakshmi Bayi was concerned.

> From the clandestine manner in which the [other] memorial has been prepared and presented, it will, we feel sure, be clear to Your Excellency, that the memorial does not in the least represent public opinion in Travancore, but that it is only an attempt on the part of a few designing individuals to bring discredit to Her Highness the Maharani Regent and Her Highness' Government, and we beg most emphatically to protest against the action of the memorialists. As the Travancore public is kept in the dark about this memorial we are not in a position to refute these allegations or insinuations, if any, contained in it. Our object in submitting *this* memorial is to acquaint Your Excellency of the whole-hearted loyalty and devotion of the people

of Travancore to Her Highness the Maharani Regent, and their entire confidence in the present administration of Travancore.[128]

Having received these two contradictory petitions, the Government of India took some months to arrive at its conclusions. But meanwhile in Trivandrum, a rattled Rama Varma was shocked by the sheer quantum of antagonism the Nairs harboured against him. While his indiscretions and carelessness were the undeniable cause for all this, he also realised that he had unwittingly become a scapegoat for politicians to mount attacks on his otherwise highly popular wife; he, of all people, had given cause for the public to doubt their monarch, against whom few had anything but good to say. His desire to gratify his ambitions had been the provocation for all this and it was his conspicuous swagger and misguided indulgence that aroused resentment in many. This patently injudicious, even presumptuous conduct had played right into the hands of the Maharani's adversaries and he was completely despondent at having let her down.[129] 'He had authoritarian tendencies,' his nephew notes, 'and an eye for detail. While the Maharani was concerned with policy and the broad canvas, she took his advice on the nitty-gritties of implementation. In that sense they complemented each other. But he was action-oriented and where there is action, there are bound to be repercussions. Some liked it, but many did not, and so in some circles he was always unpopular.'[130]

But he was not one to repeat his mistakes. And so, almost instantaneously, he began to make amends and saw to it that his shortcomings and blunders would never again embarrass his wife, setting himself on a whole new course. Having learned the hard way about the necessity for subtle discretion and tact, he decided to consciously recede into the background, never again to be seen interfering in the administration. 'He may take a leaf out of the book of Prince Albert and Queen Victoria,' recommended O.M. Thomas, adding that 'Of all the subjects of the Maharani Regent, he must be the most interested in the unqualified success of Her Highness's rule; we can rely on that interest to steer him clear of the rocks and shoals which beset her course.'[131] And indeed he did. He would continue to advise the Maharani but unobtrusively so, within the private confines of the palace, bound by the limits of his role as a consort.[132] His eagerness to participate met with political maturity, and he learned to show himself more properly in the eyes of the public.[133] When, for instance, an official press note drafted by a sycophantic secretary declared that Sethu Lakshmi Bayi was 'fortunate in the company of Her Husband Prince, who is every inch a king in word, deed, and mind, and in whose qualities of head and heart there is hardly a parallel in the history of the State', Rama Varma had the common sense and wisdom to strike it out.[134]

Soon enough he won the respect and approval of the Government of India. By November Mr Cotton happily reported that the Valiya Koil Tampuran was behaving 'much more correctly' and that Sethu Lakshmi Bayi, having delivered her child, was 'once more taking an active part in the administration'.[135] The authorities began to sympathise with Rama Varma's complicated position now that he backed into the shadows, and as a later Resident stated, 'the fact that Her Highness consults him, her own husband, is only reasonable'. It would have been much worse if she had some favourite like Sankaran Tampi, and her husband was nowhere as bad. 'My experience shows,' the same Resident would continue, 'that Her Highness is by no means unduly swayed by the Valiya Koil Tampuran ... [who] is a good husband and father ... [and] bears an excellent character morally.'[136]

Similarly another representative of the Government of India would add that there was no need in the least to worry about him secretly dictating Sethu Lakshmi Bayi's decisions. 'The Maharani Regent,' he pointed out, 'is a stronger character and has more ability than her husband.' Though in small matters she conceded him space, wisely not hurting his masculine ego, 'in important questions of policy she is capable of taking and does take her own line'.[137] The Valiya Koil Tampuran thus found himself an uncontroversial niche in the administrative arrangements of the country and henceforward consistently steered clear of trouble. In the years to come, 'his critics would find it difficult to prove any definite interference in State affairs,' as yet another Resident put it, and that was that.[138] The only downside of all this good behaviour was that the Maharani's opponents now lost their favourite enemy. Indeed, as early as December 1926 Mr Cotton informed the Political Department that as Rama Varma already kept 'very much in the background', the 'coterie of disgruntled Nairs' were forced to discover new vistas, and were now concentrating on attacking the Dewan instead.[139] Rama Varma began to appear rather harmless and to the Dutch lecturer who met him in 1929, he even seemed simply bored with not enough to do. At her audience at the palace, 'somehow the [consort] and I got arguing heatedly about the prospects of a religious revival in Russia', and she thought he was just a 'quick witted, argumentative Indian man who was overjoyed at having someone to listen to his pet theories'.[140]

As for the infamous memorial, it met with an inglorious end at the hands of the Government of India. The political grievances contained therein were neither given official cognizance nor real consideration. The Maharani was adjudged free to govern Travancore as she had been doing for nearly two years with enormous success and much acclaim. As for the renewed demand for a Council of Regency, the Political Department had already expressed that since Sethu Lakshmi Bayi was 'a very remarkable lady' who was 'perfectly capable of carrying on the administration', a rare ruler who was 'industrious, intelligent and devoted to the interests of the state', she would 'do her best if given full responsibility'. There were many inefficient princes in India whom the authorities had to worry about, but Sethu Lakshmi Bayi was not one of them. And so they had no intention of standing in her way. 'Without a Council,' it was concluded, 'the State would get her best output. With a Council it will not.'[141] The Government of India thus clearly held the Maharani in high esteem and their dependable support became her pillar of strength, reinforcing in her time of need that umbilical bond that existed between the princely states and their colonial masters. Reassured, thus, that she could always rely upon those in Delhi to back her, Sethu Lakshmi Bayi continued her reign with confidence and courage, issuing reform after reform in Travancore, and working tirelessly to improve the lives of her five million subjects. Nothing, it seemed, could shake her in this endeavour.

That is, until she introduced her next project.

8

Tea and Troubles

Legend has it that during the heyday of the Pallava emperors in south India, there was born in the sixth century a prince destined not for mighty conquests and military vigour as for legendary piety and spiritual resolve. Dharma, as he was called, was not an adherent of the Hindu creed, choosing instead the light of the Buddha, already flickering in the land of its inception. It was perhaps thus that he departed the realms of his forefathers, renouncing his patrimony for the shimmering court of the Liang emperor of China. Buddha's teachings were still a powerful force here and Dharma acquired much fame and standing as a great master in this foreign land. One day, however, he decided to seek ultimate spiritual salvation, the path to which lay in deep, unwavering meditation. He began a nine-year penance, vowing to deny himself sleep during all this time, seeking to conquer desire and comfort, and to discover for himself the inner peace that the Buddha had achieved.

For five years, Dharma stoically sustained his austerities, not once closing his eyes, staring constantly at a wall within his shadowy cave. But then his body started to rebel. A tremendous yearning to shut his eyes began to overtake him, even as his intellect realised this would mean compromising his sacred oath. He needed something to compel his defiant body to heed the commands of his mind, and in desperation he leaned forward and quickly grabbed the leaves of a nondescript plant growing nearby. He stuffed his mouth with as many leaves as he could, and swiftly began to chew. And there! Suddenly Dharma felt enormously refreshed. His fatigue retreated, his body surrendered to his mind, and he was able to finish the next four years of his unsleeping penance without a single hassle. At the conclusion of his stupendous effort, however, the monk realised that he had discovered a little more than just inner peace. For Dharma's penance had inadvertently introduced the world not only to another inspiring story of spiritual deliverance, but also to something more earthly, something it was to savour with delight for all of time ahead. The renunciate prince, folklore tells, had discovered tea.[1]

Over the years, Dharma paled into history, first as an exotic memory and then as legend, but the plant he found flourished. From beginnings in his hill cave, it spawned a very industry and economy of its own, slowly seducing the entire world with the steady march of time and trade. By the era of the Tang emperors in China, cakes of tea were being transported across the empire, where those who could afford the luxury cut, powdered and happily consumed it as their 'liquid jade'. Indeed, such was the opulence associated with tea that in 1391 the Ming emperor decreed that his trembling vassals could pay him their tribute in tea leaves! Europeans who travelled in China told alluring stories of this fine drink, but it was not until the Portuguese established a trading station at Macau that Dharma's plant began its journey to conquer the West. By 1618, tea was an international delicacy, and when the Chinese emperor sent presents to the Tsar in Moscow, it was a beautifully carved box full of rare tea that he despatched. In 1660 King Charles of England received as the dowry of his Portuguese bride not only the islands of Bombay but also huge mountains of tea, popularising the drink in Britain. Soon his subjects were demanding massive imports, and fearing too much silver was being drained from the economy by an addictive beverage, the king imposed a ban on tea. But the fiat was short-lived, for it provoked such outrage that the government was forced to capitulate and revoke its restrictions in merely six days. Tea, it was clear, was here to stay.

By 1766, over six million pounds of tea was being imported into Britain annually, despite stringent protectionist terms imposed by the Crown. Taxes were as high as 119 per cent but far from sobering demand, it only led to a thriving business for smugglers, who catered to an estimated half of the market. This victory march of the beverage, the king and his court soon realised, was now irreversible, and finally taxes were trimmed. Tea even found a place in politics, and to defy the colonial state in 1773, nationalists in America organised the sensational Boston Tea Party, sending shivers down the back of the British establishment. By the early 1800s, the Duchess of Bedford provided tea a proper place in the cultivated Englishman's daily routine by introducing 'afternoon tea', destined to become one of the favourite pastimes of the British. Concerns, continued, however, about the smuggling of cheap Dutch tea into the country;

so finally the English East India Company decided it was time for them to start actually cultivating the crop in their colonies and obtain a steady supply.

In 1848, Robert Fortune, the botanist, was deputed in disguise into China to try and collect as many specimens of tea as he could, and to ascertain the precise formula for its correct manufacture. For two-and-a-half years he wandered in China, until finally he succeeded in smuggling out 20,000 saplings across the border into India. He even persuaded a number of experienced Chinese cultivators to accompany him to virgin estates in Assam. Wild tea, in fact, had been identified on these hills some time before but, as demand remained strongest for China tea, it was this that replaced the indigenous Indian plant. The British, controversially, produced opium in India and had been exchanging it for tea from China, but now they began to develop their own tea, boosting trade in the process.[2] Soon tea spread into other parts of the subcontinent, notably into the Nilgiris in the south, and then onto the hills along the Kerala coast, where a new and happy home was, in due course, found for it.

For many years it was not tea but coffee that grew in Kerala. The roots of coffee are placed by legend in Koffa in Ethiopia, wherefrom sometime in the early seventeenth century a pilgrim called Baba Budan brought it to India. He is believed to have planted seven seeds in a garden in Chikmagalur, from where the crop spread to other parts in the south. But it was only into the nineteenth century that coffee estates were set up along the coast, again at the instance of the East India Company who had taken over Malabar from the Zamorin, and established supremacy over Travancore. To the Maharajahs of the latter region, the towering mountains guarding their eastern frontiers were resources of exotic forest produce and elephants, but all so mysterious and frightening that they were content to accept pledges of allegiance from local tribes, and otherwise leave the hills alone. The people here had no roads, no houses and not even the rudimentary semblance of an infrastructure. The ancient tribes of the forest 'lived and died in primitive simplicity, unconcerned by any knowledge of, or contact with, the millions who lived below on the plains'.[3] They ventured out occasionally to exchange their cardamom and honey for salt and textiles, but for the most part the high ranges, with their wild jungles and treacherous heights, remained an enigma.

The English, however, were determined to convert these hills into a plantation district. 'The story of the transformation of the hills of Central Travancore,' it is said, 'is well worth the telling, for it is a story of enterprise, courage, and self-reliance.' It was not officialdom that enabled cultivation in the virgin hills of Travancore. On the contrary it was through private initiative that this was achieved. It was in 1849 that the Government of Travancore first gave up 6,400 acres of land to one Mr Huxam to set up an estate, and by 1862 the sale of government land for plantations at the giveaway price of Re 1 per acre led to a precipitous explosion in commercial agriculture; within three years Travancore had forty-five new estates covering over 9,000 acres.[4] In 1878, the old Rajah of Poonjar, a feudal chieftain at court, surrendered 1,37,000 acres of land to a British planter for a measly one-time payment of Rs 5,000, and an annual rent of an equally pitiful Rs 3,000. The Kannan Devan Hills Produce Company later acquired this lease, and continued to maintain estates in that tract. For decades taxes on these plantations were kept low and even when increased, yielded only a pittance in returns to the local government. The profits all went to foreign planters while benefits to the people of Travancore were largely inconsequential.

To be fair, however, it was these foreigners who opened up what was until then an acutely inhospitable terrain. They built the first roads here, as well as schools, hospitals and other modern amenities, opening a whole new avenue for economic advancement. Christian missions were established, drawing substantial numbers of converts from local tribes, and the high ranges emerged as something of a state within a state, with its own economy and way of life, largely untouched by the Maharajah's government. 'The early planters were plain practical men, who came to the hills to make a living.' Some died of disease, while others gave up. But numerous 'remained where they first settled and gradually accumulated land around them. A few became rich.'[5] It helped that for many planters, Travancore's hill ranges offered tempting incentives of social mobility also. One Richard Tweson, for instance, departed from home in England 'with no particular regrets and few academic distinctions', only to arrive at an estate here and become 'monarch of 450 acres of tea and sahib and arbiter of a labour force of some 500 souls'.[6] It was a giddying rise, albeit in an alien land.

The earliest planters preferred coffee on account of the fact that it required less capital than tea and the process of cultivation was simpler. 'The soil,' one testimony went, 'is everything that can be desired and it only wants capital and energy to bring a large portion of this fine tract into cultivation.'[7] Remarkable successes followed and whereas in 1860 less than Rs 9,000 worth of coffee was exported out of Travancore, by 1880, the value stood at Rs 8 lakh.[8] A global economic boom also contributed, as a result of which demand was on an all time high. The opening of the Suez Canal in 1869 made trade even smoother, and 'the accumulated wealth of Britain was poured into capitalist enterprises overseas', including into Travancore.[9] Even new companies flocked to obtain virgin territory, developing it with their own servants, and making phenomenal profits. Perhaps due to pressure from their colonial superiors, the royal government preferred to hand over tracts to foreigners than to Indians, and officials went out of their way to remove bureaucratic obstacles from the paths of these valued European investors.[10] Such was the new-found preoccupation with plantations, in fact, that by the 1870s, old Ayilyam Tirunal himself wished to acquire some estates, only to be dissuaded by his humourless Dewan who sneered that engaging in such business was 'hardly consistent with his dignity'.[11]

The cultivation of coffee, however, began to decline when a disease of the leaf swept Ceylon and south India and laid waste to old estates, paving the way for tea to finally arrive in Travancore. It entailed more complex processes but was so lucrative as to justify that effort. Indeed, in a matter of one decade, tea became such a prized crop that exports were valued at nearly Rs 7 lakh in 1891, and by the turn of the century rose to an eminently more agreeable Rs 12 lakh.[12] The government eagerly welcomed foreign investment in the new sector, and this reflected well in the balance of trade for the state, although outsiders cornered actual profits. Even labour for tea cultivation was imported from the Tamil districts of the Madras Presidency, and slowly the public in Travancore, latterly aware of the benefits to be obtained from their hills and natural resources, began to voice disapproval. In 1907 the *Malayala Manorama* fulminated that it was simply 'unpardonable and shameful' that nothing was being done to enable locals to 'undertake this profitable venture'. Legislators also issued impassioned pleas about how 'capital, labour, and everything is foreign', with 'neither the state nor the people' benefitting in a palpable manner.[13]

At the time there was little the government could do, partly because European planters were backed by the Government of India, but also because officials, mainly Nairs and Brahmins, had no interest in plantations themselves and couldn't care less about who did what with the distant hills of the principality. Naturally, then, it was the traditionally entrepreneurial Christians who lobbied for gains in the sector; indeed as late as 1925, of the seven Indian-owned estates in the state, Christians held five.[14] In fact while tea remained elusive, they did venture with greater success into rubber. By the 1920s, of the 48,000 acres under tea cultivation, almost all was dominated by Europeans, while Travancore Christians held 50 per cent of the 52,000 acres of rubber.[15] Tea, however, continued to enjoy the leading position among all the exports of the state. In 1921–22, 9,000 tonnes of tea worth over Rs 1.2 crore were exported compared to only Rs 25 lakh worth of rubber.[16] 'The policy of the Travancore Government has always been to encourage the [foreign] tea planter to settle in the state,' it was declared, 'and the generous and sympathetic treatment he has consistently received has resulted in a large amount of capital being sunk in the country in opening tea estates'.[17] While the government received incomes through rents, income tax from resident planters, and export duties, these were only minor compared to the advantages captured by investors. And this made local entrepreneurs and planters unhappy.

It was in 1926, when Sethu Lakshmi Bayi was in power, that her government announced that the policy of allotting valuable real estate and resources at throwaway prices to outsiders was being reviewed. It was felt that land, at this rate, would only be alienated into foreign hands, with no enduring benefits to the state. That is why when in 1926 a major buyer approached the government with the grandest proposal yet to purchase and develop an enormous 1,00,000 acres, the Chief Secretary was asked to make it clear that the Maharani was 'unable to assent to a monopoly concession in the form proposed'.[18] The old policy, it was informed, had been rescinded. Nevertheless, it was also made known that the Maharani was willing to examine schemes if they incorporated tangible, long-term benefits to Travancore in the process. Any proposals for concessions in the plantation sector, in other words, were to demonstrate exactly how locals of the state would benefit from these ventures.

Soon after the new policy was enunciated, the chief executive of 'a certain very big company' approached Mr Watts in London for purchasing land in the state. The Dewan immediately rejected the offer but suggested that a potential joint venture with locals might be more acceptable to the Maharani. In July, then, this company, Brooke Bond, officially put forth a proposal for the consideration of the government.[19] The idea was to clear hitherto unused forest land in Travancore, if it were found suitable for cultivating tea, dividing it into units of 1,000 acres. Of these units, the company would hold 600 acres, with the rest divided among small 'native' planters. Each unit would also house a modern factory, set up by Brooke Bond, for manufacturing tea.[20] Other general terms of the proposal were as follows:

> The smaller [local] owners will be supplied with tea seed. They will also have the benefit of the experience of the company during preparatory cultivation, and, until the lands begin to yield tea, the company will help the small holder with money. When the time comes for gathering the leaf, the company will undertake to manufacture tea for the small holder, and after the manufacture, the holder may take the tea himself and sell it wherever he likes, or the

> company will purchase it from him or will send it to England on his behalf to be sold there in auction.[21]

Mr Watts was very keen on the project and, with the Maharani's consent, had the offer submitted to the Economic Development Board of Travancore for expert evaluation. The EDB looked at the gains and losses from such a scheme, which for the first time offered reciprocal and meaningful terms to the state. Considerable debate ensued. One advantage was that a significant area of land would be brought under profitable cultivation. Capital required per acre was £20, and it was evident that the government would be unable to embark on such a scheme single-handedly. Economically, to begin with, the proposal appeared sound. Fears were, of course, aired that if the company were to exit the scheme midway, the state would be in a fix. However, an assurance was offered that if the project were to be proceeded with, Brooke Bond would float a subsidiary for the purpose, registered under the local Travancore Companies Act, subject to the laws of the Maharani's government. An institutional framework could also be set up to formulate rules and obligations of all parties, so that the enterprise might not be abandoned midway.[22] The Chief Secretary also reminded the EDB that

> ...if this opportunity is missed, one like it may never recur. It is not often that a business concern established all the world over with vast financial resources and backing like that of Messrs. [sic] Brooke Bond will come this way to offer generous terms to the middle classes of Travancore in cooperating for their mutual advantage. If the Board will approve the scheme in principle, no assurance is necessary that the Government will in their future negotiations keep steadily before them the prime need for safeguarding the interests of the State and of the middle class smallholders who may enter into the scheme.[23]

The EDB gave its consent in principle to the proposal being taken to the stage of an official negotiation, with only one member objecting on grounds that foreign investors should not be allowed to purchase land in Travancore (even though the proposed company was intended to be registered locally).[24] But by now rumours had begun to spread in the capital, and it was put out that the Maharani had already signed something with a foreign company, alienating huge areas of land. The Resident mused that no matter what the benefits might be of the scheme, entering into agreements with Europeans was a highly emotional matter, 'bound to meet with great opposition'.[25] And indeed when the Legislative Council met on 24 November 1926, a member moved a motion of adjournment to discuss Brooke Bond. Mr Watts disallowed this, but invited questions. The member for Chirayinkil demonstrated how politicians had based their information on rumour, asking whether it was true that land between 1,00,000 to 2,50,000 acres was being sold in entirety to a foreign corporation. The Dewan clarified this was untrue and that only a discussion for a smaller area on a basis of partnership had been initiated. When the member for Pathanamthitta confronted him with hearsay again the next day, he responded with some annoyance:

> To begin with, you seem to know more than everybody else. You seem to know that 200,000 acres of cultivable land exists in Travancore. I do not know. Nobody else knows. You seem to know that 100,000 acres has been assigned to some tea company. I do not know. No member of the Government knows. Nobody else of any responsibility knows. But you from Pathanamthitta seem to know.[26]

In reality the proposal was for an area of 25,000 acres, as a larger bloc of land was in any case not available in Travancore.[27] Out of this, only 15,000 acres was to be registered in the name of the company registered by Brooke Bond, with the remainder assigned to local planters. The land was also far from the prime 'cultivable' property that rumour alleged. A survey team deputed to study the area found it 'absolutely devoid of roads or paths except such as have been made by elephants and sambur'; it was in the heart of the forest.[28] The Dewan also assured frenzied politicians that at this stage he could not, due to plain business ethics, divulge *all* the details but they could rest assured that no decision would be taken unilaterally, and only with the backing of the Legislative Council would the scheme be ratified *if* negotiations were to prove successful.[29] The 'final verdict', he emphatically announced, 'will be with the representatives of the people'.[30]

Rumours, in their usual way, however, remained unrelenting. In March 1927 the Dewan was pressured into mentioning the scheme in his speech to the Sri Mulam Popular Assembly, the advisory upper house of the legislature, to assuage worries. In their response to him, its members insisted that the matter should be discussed jointly with them and the Legislative Council, continuing to believe that 1,50,000 acres of land was being isolated for an outright sale. They argued that their government really ought to be supporting local planters instead of a foreign company, which would hurt the interests of the state, unwilling to entertain the idea of a foreign direct investment in the state. They went on to add that

> [t]he proposal has created a good deal of unrest among the people. The law of diminishing returns has begun to operate in several portions of the cultivated tracts in this state and the evils of unemployment are manifesting themselves in direct proportion to the steady growth of population. In the circumstances, wisdom and statesmanship would point to the absolute necessity for preserving all available lands intact for the exclusive use of the present and future generations of the people of the state.[31]

Mr Watts continued to reason with the politicians, as did the chairman of the EDB who pointed out that 'the large majority of our people could not take up tea cultivation for the want of sufficient capital and technical knowledge'. And now here was Brooke Bond, who despite the proposal being unusual and 'contrary to the policy of the ordinary producing company, who only spend capital on their own interests', was happy to offer a mutually beneficial agreement that would bring with it capital, technology, as well as terms to benefit small planters in the state.[32] By now news of political opposition to the project had reached London, however, where Brooke Bond, sensing risks of this nature in the future as well, decided to withdraw the scheme. In June they wrote to Mr Watts stating that

> [t]he great natural differences to be overcome in road-making in what, to begin with, would prove an unhealthy area, is an obstacle which might be overcome, but we feel that an active opposition on the part of the Travancoreans themselves, even of a somewhat unintelligent minority, would prove an insuperable obstacle to the scheme, which, for its success, must depend on the active cooperation of these very elements.[33]

And thus came to an unsatisfactory conclusion the proposal to set up twenty-five tea factories in the state, bring 10,000 acres of land under the control of local planters, 15,000 in the hands of a locally registered company, with potential to create 75,000 jobs in the coming years.[34] As the legendary journalist Mammen Mappillai lamented, this 'immensely profitable agreement' had to be put aside because 'people who were ignorant' of its merits 'created a lot of heat stating that a foreign company was attempting to make a lot of profit. It is indeed a great pity,' he added, 'that the great majority of people could not see the brighter side; and what is more, they refused to see it even when it was pointed out to them by others!'[35] Another journal lamented that the whole subject had been 'attacked with a virulence worthy of a better cause'.[36] Brooke Bond, incidentally, proceeded to sign their agreement with the Maharajah of Mysore instead, and the proposed venture was implemented in that rival state. Mr Watts, frustrated as he was, remained, however, sincerely unapologetic despite all the criticism. 'Safe cooperation between the experienced English capitalist and the untrained man of Travancore, whereby both may work for the commonweal as well as for individual advantage,' he declared firmly, 'was the ideal I had in view.'[37]

The scheme was projected to offer 'new and attractive avenues for profitable employment to a growing number of intelligent young men of the middle classes'.[38] In fact, it would not only have benefited the middle classes but also lower sections from marginalised castes. In 1921 the largest number of estate workers in Travancore, leaving aside Tamil labour, were Parayas, Shanars, Sakkiliyans, Ezhavas, Maravas, Pulayas, Kuravas, Kammalas, Muslims and Vellalas, numbering 12,000-odd, all of whom were from backward communities. The opening up of an estimated 75,000 new jobs would have benefitted *them* most, offering cash incomes, as well as access to schools and amenities set up in the high ranges by Christian missions.[39] It was a great blow to Mr Watts that the scheme was abandoned merely because of shrill, hysterical propaganda. Much opposition was simply ridiculous, with one politician claiming he dreaded the desecration of hill temples and another proclaiming haughtily that 'the native planter did not stand in need of tutelage' from Europeans.[40] 'Are we to pour the enervating tonic—tea—into the mouths of the starving people of Travancore?' yet another critic thundered melodramatically. 'What they want,' he insisted, 'is *kanjee* [food] ... Bitter experience has shown the atrocities of foreign settlers in Travancore—women hood-raped [sic], murder, assault etc. on poor and helpless people ... If Mr Watts is an honest man let him drop the mater ... Dewans will come and go,' it was ominously threatened, but 'The Maharani herself will come down from her exalted position and there will come a time when future generations will curse our Maharani.'[41]

And so the matter was dropped.

Right from the onset of her reign, Sethu Lakshmi Bayi had been uneasy with what she perceived as a lack of enterprise and initiative in her people. It was one thing that the British exploited India and confined its economic potential to two principal functions, namely the supply of raw materials to their industries followed by the consumption of resultant foreign manufactured products. But even within these limited parameters, there were spaces that resourceful Indians could fill and capitalise to their advantage. Since the First World War, for instance, demand for rubber had been on the rise, and cultivation of cash crops were giving substantial returns to agriculturalists. The Syrian Christians, famously 'dynamic and flexible', paved the way in making use of these opportunities, but the old-fashioned Nairs, who controlled most economic resources, looked down at unconventional agriculture and commercial undertakings with 'lordly disdain'.[42] Ensconced within the bubble of self-sufficiency provided by their (rapidly diminishing) ancestral holdings, they sneered at trade and anything involving 'vulgar' notions of profit. As early as 1820 it was noted: 'However poor the Nair, his pride makes him unwilling to work for anyone of an inferior caste; he may perhaps act as an overseer to an opulent Christian farmer, but invariably smooths [sic] the concession by receiving a certain extent of land, not pay, as remuneration.'[43] What this feudal mentality blinded the Nairs from, however, was that the winds were blowing in a new direction now, portending the speedy demise of their inherited financial security. And unless viable alternatives were found, and they dispensed with what an early nineteenth-century diarist called 'the most exalted notions of their own nobility', they would all be left high and dry.[44]

While Travancore was one of the most prosperous states in India, its economic circumstances were unsound in the long run. It relied for most part on an agro-based export system that worked perfectly so long as industries in Britain demanded its raw output. In other words, it was a system that gained by complying with the colonial formula, never seeking therefore to overcome it even marginally. And naturally, then, wealth generated from its foreign trade, which in 1927 stood at a handsome Rs 17.5 crore, was quickly expended in the consumption of imported goods instead of being invested in profitable new endeavours; that same year the government revealed that while imports of rice, salt and other primary goods was slowly declining, demand for motor cars, foreign liquor, garments, tobacco and other such luxury items was on the rise.[45] While, for example, 17,928 gallons of liquor were brought into the state in 1925, only two years later it jumped to a staggering 28,357 gallons, demonstrating precisely how Travancore was spending its money.[46] Capital accumulation was abysmal, and people remained content with shipping preprocessed agricultural output abroad instead of manufacturing and creating capital and wealth indigenously. This latter development is very crucial, however, for any economy to progress into an advanced and more reliable state of prosperity. And the Maharani's endeavour was to facilitate the creation of a viable framework that would bolster capital formation while encouraging her people to graduate from being accessories in profitable production to becoming such producers themselves.

But commercial enterprise and capitalism cannot manifest out of the blue. They require, to begin with, an entrepreneurial mentality that hungers for material success with unabashed self-confidence and spirited courage. And in this Travancore seemed to be singularly deficient. There prevailed here, to quote the Maharani's husband, 'a ruinous feeling of complacence',[47] so that the population was by and large content with the status quo, disdaining to imperil it by taking the risks that entrepreneurship entails necessarily. In a predominantly proletarian society, aspirations were unexceptional for most part and as long as modest everyday hopes were fulfilled, most were satisfied.

Even great families were perfectly happy to hoard ancestral riches than to invest them gainfully by welcoming minor insecurities. Sethu Lakshmi Bayi's hopes, therefore, were to bring about a transformation in this conventional approach to economic matters. While official policy towards plantations and attendant transfers of land were reviewed, the Maharani also turned her focus to developing the primary sector. For one, since the export-led income of the state was dependant on agriculture, it was pivotal to sustain its prosperity in the foreseeable future. In addition to this, 50 per cent of the population subsisted on agriculture, and their interests needed to be improved as well as secured. The Ezhava community and its rising clout were living proof of the importance of this. Traditionally cultivators of coconut palms, they suddenly found that demand for their produce had multiplied due to manufacturing needs in the West. While earlier they supplied to feudal masters, by 1922 copra exported from Travancore was worth over Rs 1.2 crore in the global markets, incomes from which reinforced the rising political and social leverage of their community.[48] Sethu Lakshmi Bayi realised that economic independence was the only sustainable formula for social change among the quarrelling classes of Travancore. And since agriculture was the principal economic activity, steps were taken to enhance growth here. The results were admirable, especially in certain critical spheres. One of the most compelling successes of the Maharani lay, for instance, in the development of credit facilities. This enabled thousands of families to progress from mere subsistence farming into commercial agriculture, boosting incomes, standards of living and the socio-economic prospects of their children, who were able to afford more promising futures and come into their own politically as well.

Banking as an organised business had taken off in Travancore under a handful of prominent Syrian Christian families in the late nineteenth century. These initiatives were all registered as joint stock companies, and in 1900 there were twenty-six such ventures in the state, including non-banking concerns. Nearly twenty-five years later the figure rose to only 134 but the most extraordinary progress was yet to come. For it was after Sethu Lakshmi Bayi came to the helm that the number of joint stock companies began to multiply at an unparalleled pace, reaching a record 653 by 1931. Their paid up share capital totalled Rs 1.76 crore while working capital stood at an impressive Rs 2.7 crore.[49] The vast majority of these companies (at 529) were engaged in banking and insurance services, catering to farmers and local cottage industries. While few could be credited as 'big' enterprises, they were, nonetheless, legitimate and strong enough to 'withstand even the severe shocks of the Great Depression' that would commence in 1929.[50] And all of them successfully fulfilled their most important function in that innumerable farmers in Travancore, where 90 per cent of the landholdings were smaller than 5 acres and therefore prone to be commercially unviable, were able to access valuable institutional credit. The easy availability of funds at rates of interest much lower than the oppressive levies of traditional moneylenders provided a substantial impetus to agriculture.[51]

Organised banks were not, however, the only sources of credit that flourished under the Maharani's regime. The local, informal banking system known as the *chitty* also progressed. From 1,037 funds worth Rs 15 lakh in 1924 their numbers went up to 1,656 worth Rs 45 lakh by 1928.[52] Similarly, the cooperative movement in the state received a stimulus so that from 1,002 societies in 1924 it increased by 1929 to 1,688 societies. During the same period, membership rose from 74,076 to 1,77,824 (one fifth of all the hands employed in the primary sector),[53] including nearly 20,000 women. And the working capital of these societies mounted from Rs 16 lakh to the more significant figure of Rs 42 lakh.[54] It is also noteworthy that the movement was not confined to higher castes alone, for by 1928 there were 222 societies dedicated especially to aiding deprived castes find their economic moorings.[55]

It must be said, however, that none of this caused the traditional moneylender too much anxiety, for his influence remained largely unaffected in the short term; of the nearly 56,000 loans taken in 1928–29, over 92 per cent were furnished by the traditional sources. That is, while the total demand for credit was worth Rs 1.7 crore, the new banking system could supply only Rs 22 lakh, with the remainder being furnished by traditional channels.[56] There was still, therefore, a great way for institutionalised banking to go, and to look into this the Maharani would in 1930 constitute a Banking Enquiry Committee. In pursuance of its recommendations, a Central Land Mortgage Bank was established by 1932, alongside a number of other policy initiatives, all of which facilitated a thriving banking sector in the region. This was a most significant achievement considering that even to this day, in the second decade of the twenty-first century, there are pockets in India where proper banking has not arrived. Travancore was, even in the 1920s, decades ahead of much of the subcontinent.

The impact of the effective and steady network of credit that developed under Sethu Lakshmi Bayi on agriculture was slow but increasingly decisive, while in the future it was expected to play an even greater role. Indeed, while in the short and medium term the banks would cater mainly to the primary sector, they were planned to aid other spheres of the economy as well. Just as in Japan in the 1880s, in Travancore too the idea was that some years down the line, when the banks matured and expanded, they would diversify from agriculture and finance the processes of industrialisation. The ultimate goal, thus, was to secure the industrial future of the state, where the credit facilities set up today would act as foundations of that later stage, when the time came. It was a long-term view, one that was wise and would prove to be most gainful for generations to come.

The Maharani was, in fact, remarkably cognizant of the long term and many of her contributions were oriented towards setting the stage for crucial future happenings. This far-sightedness previously manifested itself in her endorsement of the Cochin Harbour Scheme, which proved to be a great success. Similarly, her resolution of the Vaikom Satyagraha became a historic prelude to the even more momentous Temple Entry Proclamation a decade later. While these were some of the more significant examples of her visionary pre-eminence, there were smaller instances too where she rose to tackle specific issues, paving the future path for critical developments. One pertained, for example, to a dispute between the government and the aforementioned Kannan Devan Hills Produce Company. For twenty years before she came to power, the two sides had been locked in acrimony over water resources inside the hilly tracts leased to the latter. The company claimed unabridged rights over all the water passing through its property, including that of generating power. The government, however, was prepared to recognise rights only for ordinary purposes (irrigation, cultivation, etc.), claiming authority to charge a recurring fee for any other use. The two sides sparred bitterly until the matter reached an impasse that lasted decades, which is when Sethu Lakshmi Bayi came to power.

The Maharani instructed the Dewan in 1925 to commence fresh negotiations with the company, and what had been a generation-long deadlock was settled to mutual satisfaction within the year. And early in 1927 Mr Watts announced that the company recognised 'without qualification' Travancore's rights over the disputed water, agreeing also to pay a royalty for every unit of power they generated from it. They also withdrew a previous claim that only they had a right to set up a power plant, with the result that the state was now in a position to build a hydroelectric station in the hills, 'if and when the need arises'.[57] In other words, the Maharani successfully cleared the path for the establishment of the state's first power station. And indeed when the Pallivasal Hydroelectric Plant was opened in 1940, Sethu Lakshmi Bayi would look back with satisfaction at having persuasively closed that old battle with the company, something her uncle had failed to do, without which the project could never have taken off, delaying the desperately needed supply of electricity for the industrial advancement of Travancore.

Much of her work was of a foundational nature, thus, whether it pertained to banking, ports, infrastructure, social reform and more. She could see the flow of time and did not try to obstruct it normally, even if, like the good old-fashioned conservative, she did not always appreciate the direction of that flow. And in laying the bedrock for so many progressive schemes lies the Maharani's particular significance in history. But engineering for the future is never an easy task, and with each year, opposition from politicians and all others, who had a stake in the existing entrenched social conditions that favoured one class or caste above another, only got louder. But as the Resident noted in a report to the Government of India, Sethu Lakshmi Bayi had 'the courage of her convictions' and guided by her idealism and intelligence alike, did her best to firmly overcome all these obstacles.[58]

'The death of a Ruler,' Sethu Lakshmi Bayi would observe, 'always leaves a legacy of troubles to his successor.' And in her particular case, 'the knowledge that the present administration is only for a specified period' tended to 'prolong the unsettlement and unrest'. In other words, as it was obvious to her opponents that she would hold power only for a short duration and not for all her lifetime, fear of royal displeasure was at its lowest, and politicians were more ambitious and forthright than in a regular reign. They were also aware that the Government of India scrutinised princely states closely during such interim periods, and even if an impression of instability could be conveyed, they might swoop down and clip the Maharani's wings. 'If,' she explained, 'the present administration had not been a Regency, the movement would long ago have fizzled out.' But this was not the case, and whenever she was 'found to be disinclined to dance to [the] tune' of her rivals, petitions and complaints were quickly dispatched to Delhi to have her government discredited.[59] So far none had succeeded, however, because her achievements in only a couple of years were numerous and the respect she earned from the general public far surpassed the ceaseless objections of local politicians from assorted communal backgrounds.

Sethu Lakshmi Bayi's principal opponents were the Nairs. Historically, with an axe to grind against the Brahmins, they did not take too kindly to the introduction of Christians also as rival elements in Travancore's political equation. The Maharani, whose effort was to curtail that overdependence of the privileged classes on the state and to promote a new spirit of independent entrepreneurship, was constantly accused of favouring minority communities at the cost of the Nairs, who had lost their most powerful votary, Sankaran Tampi, after she assumed control over the administration. The Newspaper Regulation was perceived as a direct blow to their community; social reforms diluted the prestige of their class and enhanced the standing of Ezhavas and other lower castes; and economic reforms again aided largely the Christians and those with business ventures. The Nairs, essentially, were used to being part of the establishment, but now were being asked to fend for themselves, even as their share of the economic pie was diminishing by the day. As the *Madras Mail* reported in 1898, 'Syrian Christian merchants are getting the trade of the country into their hands. In the villages the hard-working Syrian is ousting the [Nair] and the [Brahmin].'[60] Agitation, naturally, was their recourse, to preserve their position. And if there was any additional inducement necessary to get them to stand up to Sethu Lakshmi Bayi, it came in the form of an ally within the royal household.

Since 1925 the Junior Maharani had begun to concern herself with matters of state, where she technically had no locus standi and which she could never have contemplated during the previous administration. But as mother of the minor Maharajah, she now felt herself entitled to a hand in government, which when Sethu Lakshmi Bayi refused to allow, she resented. Her first association with the cause of the Nairs came at the time Mr Watts was appointed Dewan, and the Resident noted how the opposition had 'obtained a valuable recruit' in her.[61] She was persuaded to write to him that the successor to Sethu Lakshmi Bayi was her son and that he should be protected from being 'handicapped by new policies' when 'no necessity has arisen to make this departure' from custom in appointing a Christian as Dewan.[62] She felt it abominable, she claimed, that old traditions were being breached, affronted by the fact that this was happening 'without even so much as being mentioned to me and my views ascertained'.[63] Mr Cotton was not convinced about the sincerity of this concern. The Junior

Maharani was famously unorthodox and the fact that she was 'quite ready to pose as a pattern of orthodoxy and conservatism' now was suspicious. 'I regard her,' he inferred, 'merely as the catspaw of the Nairs,' adding that no 'real weight need be attached to her contention that the appointment of Mr Watts does violence to the religious susceptibilities of the people.'[64]

What was more interesting was that the Junior Maharani also utilised public uproar among the Nairs about Mr Watts to pitch certain proposals of her own. 'I think the time has come,' she proffered, 'for the creation of a Council of Regency.' In other words, she wanted the uninhibited powers her cousin enjoyed under matrilineal law and tradition, revoked, and wished the Government of India to implement their regular policy of conducting the administration through a council. It was amusing to the Resident that whereas the Junior Maharani claimed to be a protector of tradition in the matter of the Dewan's appointment, she was anxious to contravene custom completely when it came to her rival. 'In my opinion,' she elaborated, 'the Council should consist of H.H. the Maharani Regent, *myself* (the mother of the minor Maharajah), and one experienced officer with good reputation and character.'[65] The proposal bemused Mr Cotton, for before the start of Sethu Lakshmi Bayi's reign, he had consulted the Junior Maharani on ideas she might have about the administration. At the time she had declared that any notion of a Council of Regency was simply 'repugnant' to her. 'I do not recollect,' he wrote testily now, 'your hinting that these objections would vanish if there was a change in the Dewanship.'[66]

Rebuffed by the Resident thus, the Junior Maharani decided to go above his head and submit a memorandum directly to the Viceroy. Through her confidante Sir Vasudeva Rajah, with whom her husband had linked her romantically, she placed before the Government of India a representation arguing that the 'position attaching to the mother of the heir-apparent is considered to be one of great dignity and the fact that the Junior Maharani attained to this led to a strained relationship between the cousins'.[67] In other words, the suggestion all at once was that her opinions ought to be treated with respect since she was the Maharajah's mother, and that she should not be held inferior to her cousin, who might be prejudiced by their unhappy and historic rivalry. It was quite another matter that matrilineal law did not promise any such status; only the senior male and senior female members of the family enjoyed rank, no matter what their mutual connections might be, and the mother of the senior male member did not inherently gain rank because of the birth of a titled son to her.[68] However, the Junior Maharani felt keenly that she was 'entitled to a voice in the administration of the state as mother and guardian of the minor Maharajah and that the establishment of a Council of Regency is indeed all the more necessary in view of the divergence of interests' that existed between her cousin and herself.[69]

Much to her abiding regret, however, Delhi refused to treat this representation transmitted through Sir Vasudeva (notorious for 'interesting himself in political affairs which are not his concern')[70] as proper conduct. They promptly consulted Mr Cotton and were told that 'There is no doubt that the [Junior] Maharani has only lately become a convert to the idea of a Council of Regency,' when she realised she could gain from it. Additionally, he added, 'I do not think she is entitled to any voice in the administration of the state as mother of the minor Maharajah. Nor is she,' he clarified, 'according to the [matrilineal] law governing the ruling family, the guardian of her son.'[71] This was indeed true, for as per tradition her son was a ward of the head of the family, namely Sethu Lakshmi Bayi, and not his own mother. To dilute the Junior Maharani's claims, the Government of India also received intelligence at this time that the only reason Sir Vasudeva was championing her cause was that he had been promised a 'substantial loan, of which he is in urgent need' if the scheme were successful and a Council of Regency instituted.[72] Even sympathetic factions perceived the Junior Maharani's actions as a 'tactical mistake' for she had only made herself more unpopular.[73] Soon enough a telegram arrived from the Viceroy's office curtly stating: 'His Excellency has been fully acquainted with all aspects of the case and does not consider further representations would serve any purpose. In any case,' it added, rebuking the Junior Maharani for attempting to supersede Mr Cotton through Sir Vasudeva, 'representation can be received only through Agent to Governor General,' i.e., the Resident.[74]

By 1927, the Junior Maharani found the controversy around Brooke Bond ripe for another interjection, even though her opinions too, like those of the politicians, were based on misinformation. 'It has come to my notice quite recently, and also very casually,' she wrote, 'that there is a proposal to assign about a hundred thousand acres of cultivable land in the Travancore State to a British syndicate for tea cultivation.' While political implications of all this did not really concern her, she did feel that such a proposal should 'neither have been mooted nor pursued' during the minority of her son and when the country was under a Regency government. 'I would therefore urge,' she ended, 'that this question be left over till the majority of the Maharajah is attained.'[75] In response, Mr Cotton informed her that the plan was 'much more modest', and in any case, it would have to pass through the Legislative Council and obtain the sanction of the Government of India before it became reality. Her grievances would, he assured her, be considered, if deemed necessary, at the appropriate moment.[76]

Once again, in other words, Sethu Parvathi Bayi was politely asked to desist from venturing advice in the name of her son. The fact that all this came only shortly after the controversial domestic spat with her husband also did not earn her favour with the authorities, in whose mind she was out simply to make trouble.

However, the most chafing dispute between the Junior Maharani and Sethu Lakshmi Bayi pertained to the allocation of funds. Every year a certain sum was set aside as the royal family's Civil List, but this straightforward task was now rendered peculiarly complex owing to the situation where the minor sovereign and the ruling Maharani belonged to rival camps. In 1923 Mulam Tirunal's Civil List stood at Rs 7,31,000,[77] which by 1924 increased to Rs 7,57,000.[78] Out of this, the majority was earmarked for so many wide-ranging expenses, from religious obligations to the payment of palace pensions, that only a surprisingly small amount of Rs 60,000 was spent on the personal outlays of the Maharajah. His pocket money was also as little as Rs 500 per month, and despite all his legendary frugality, he left behind savings of Rs 18 lakh, all of which would be inherited by the Junior Maharani's son when he came of age.[79] Indeed, such was the relative simplicity pervading the royal household that Mulam Tirunal did not claim most of the income from his Crown lands, preferring to donate an amount of more than Rs 2 lakh from that source every year instead to the general funds of the state for the benefit of his people.[80]

The Civil List also included allowances to subordinate members of the royal house. The Junior Maharani received Rs 19,000 per annum, of which Rs 6,000 was meant as a personal allowance, Rs 5,000 for tour expenses and the remainder for any religious donations she might desire to make. But the recipient of the largest sum after Mulam Tirunal had been Sethu Lakshmi Bayi who as Attingal Rani had more serious expenses. She had Rs 46,000 per annum of which Rs 33,000 was exclusively for her religious commitments in that position, Rs 6,000 for tours and the rest for costs of her establishment. The Sripadam treasury met her private expenses, where also she had a separate fund for religious obligations.[81] But with her succession as Pooradam Tirunal Maharajah and as Regent, an additional Rs 2 lakh had been granted her, with the sanction of the Government of India, as a special income. This was not an especially generous sum, for in smaller (and badly run) states, her counterparts often enjoyed similar or better incomes. But by Travancore's standards it was a most liberal amount and the Maharani accepted it. There was also another reason for the allocation of a special purse to Sethu Lakshmi Bayi. As Mr Cotton wrote to the Government of India:

> The Regency has devolved upon her under a law of succession peculiar to this and the neighbouring state of Cochin, and her enhanced position necessitates both now and after the Regency has terminated considerably greater expenditure than if she had continued merely as Senior Rani. And a further reason for treating her generously now is that as she is not the mother of the minor Maharajah, she is unlikely to receive any special consideration upon the latter attaining his majority.[82]

The Junior Maharani too, however, had her eyes set on a better financial position. She was, to begin with, unhappy with the practicality that her cousin controlled the Civil List, suggesting instead that as much as Rs 3,12,000 be assigned to her every year 'for my branch of the family'.[83] This was completely unprecedented, for the head of the house controlled all funds, and Sethu Lakshmi Bayi saw no reason to revoke custom and deposit such large amounts into the hands of the Junior Maharani simply because she was the Maharajah's mother.[84] She did allocate the Rs 58,000 sanctioned for the Maharajah and Rs 35,000 for the general expenses of Kowdiar Palace to her cousin to defray, but other requests were declined.[85] To her friends and in representations to the authorities, the Junior Maharani attempted to present this as an example of her cousin stinting her grievously in the matter of money. But, as Sethu Lakshmi Bayi noted, 'Her grievances viewed with reference to the style of living of the Travancore Royal Family and the age long customs obtaining in the family, will deceive no one, but when examined in relation to the conditions prevailing in the households of the Northern Indian States, may appear very real.'[86]

At the same time, a somewhat tired Sethu Lakshmi Bayi also admitted that she had 'not thought it necessary to go out of my way to heap coals of fire on the Junior Maharani', and that wherever possible, she had tried to make things easier. But there was no question of any special favour being shown, 'her attitude being what it is'.[87] She described the Junior Maharani's posture towards her as one of 'militant antagonism'[88] right from the commencement of her administration. To remain above board and to preserve objectivity, however, Sethu Lakshmi Bayi channelled all negotiations on this subject through the Resident. And Mr Cotton supported her decisions, for they were grounded in law and the established practice of the royal family. But the Junior Maharani never ceased to press for greater provisions. She even took the opportunity that discussions on the Civil List presented to have her own personal allowance raised to Rs 30,000. But here, at first, Sethu Lakshmi Bayi tried to draw the line:

> ...I have regretfully to express my reluctance to move in the matter, so long as she maintains her attitude of wanton hostility to me and open defiance of my authority. I have suffered no end of humiliation and indignities as a result of her misguided activities and my present unwillingness to comply with her request is to be construed merely as an attempt to chasten her and not to retaliate.[89]

Sethu Lakshmi Bayi was referring to the growing impasse on numerous counts with Kowdiar Palace. Mr Cotton too had observed that the Maharajah's mother was difficult and stubborn, never compromising while always expecting her cousin to bend backwards on so many real as well as imagined grounds. 'I have never seen,' he wrote to the Government of India, 'any indication of her willingness, even in the most petty matters, to defer to the wishes of the Maharani Regent.'[90] When he went on leave, the Junior Maharani attempted to have the Acting Resident advocate for her, and through similar methods kept the issue of financial allocations unsettled for years. Her memorandum to the Viceroy also alleged that the reason Sethu Lakshmi Bayi did not treat her charitably was plain jealousy that she was the mother of the Maharajah. A clearly irritated Senior Maharani again had to point out that while outsiders accustomed to patriarchy might hold the status of the mother of a Maharajah as high, in Travancore there was no such precedent.

> [It is] a stern reality that the Junior Maharani, despite her relationship to the Maharajah, has no voice in the direction of the general palace Civil List or the State funds ... However unpleasant or unnatural this position may be, it has to be reconciled to. All the world over there are conventions and customs which are so many anomalies and in Travancore, for instance, the fact that a Maharajah's son has no locus standi in his own State may very likely outrage the sentiments of a person imbued with the more common patriarchal system of inheritance ... Very often we have to face things as they are instead of worrying about what they should be.[91]

The indefatigable Junior Maharani was determined to fight on, however, and submitted yet another memorandum to Delhi. It met a similar fate as the last one, but Sethu Lakshmi Bayi was so troubled by all this that in December 1926 she agreed to settle 'the formidable and vexatious question of the Civil List' for once and for ever, giving her cousin the personal raise she so ardently desired. This along with the Rs 12,000 she received from the Sripadam treasury increased her total income to Rs 42,000, which, Sethu Lakshmi Bayi pointed out, 'in normal times even the Senior Rani could not [have found] for her personal expenses'.[92] In other words, it was despite tradition and existing fiscal customs of the royal family that this raise was provided. The Junior Maharani had won this point. But there was no gratitude in the picture and early in 1927 Mr Cotton was disappointed that while Sethu Parvathi Bayi wrote to thank him, she had not sent 'even a line of appreciation' to her cousin, who had granted her this raise 'unasked' and despite confirmation from the Government of India that she was not obliged to do so.[93] Sethu Lakshmi Bayi was not perturbed, only hoping instead that the Junior Maharani would 'bring about a change in her attitude towards me' and allow for peace in the family.[94]

Far from contemplating gratitude or peace the Junior Maharani's supporters continued their offensive. Attempts were made to defame the Valiya Koil Tampuran on a regular basis; when he shot a bull bison in the jungles near Peermade it was put out that he had brutally murdered a tribal woman. This was, in Mr Cotton's words, 'pure unadulterated fiction', but it went some way in tarnishing Rama Varma's name, already suffering.[95] Soon afterwards when a forest officer accompanying the Valiya Koil Tampuran died of a heart attack while on the job, it was declared again that he was a sadistic murderer. 'Of course,' sighed the Resident, 'the Kowdiar Palace set on foot the rumour that he had been shot.'[96] Later in January 1927 Sir Vasudeva resurfaced in the state and 'paid a clandestine three day visit' to the Junior Maharani at Cape Comorin. He promised her that the Viceroy was set to visit south India soon and 'great changes' could occur in Travancore if they obtained a memorial against Sethu Lakshmi Bayi.[97] Promptly news was heard that the Junior Maharani wanted a fresh petition prepared and was offering a reward of Rs 500 to anybody who might initiate this among the public. Even some months later, though, nobody approached to undertake this had 'shewn any great alacrity' in accepting the commission, and the Resident noted that the scheme had proved to be a flop.[98]

Surrounded by intrigue and machinations of this nature, peace of mind was in no way part of Sethu Lakshmi Bayi's life at this time. But if there was stress, she never revealed it. Quite to the contrary, she seemed to be at her best with the odds stacked against her, and for all her troubles in 1927, at a state dinner thrown for the visiting Commander-in-Chief of the Indian Army, Sir William Birdwood Bard, the Resident noted that he had 'never seen the Maharani Regent more vivacious'.[99] She enjoyed herself thoroughly, letting down her reserve, and circulating among all present that evening with unusual enthusiasm. The Valiya Koil Tampuran was also very relaxed, exuding bonhomie and humour with the guests. A jungle shikar he had organised for Sir William had been a great success and he was lauded for taking care of all the details at this 'admirably designed' shooting camp.[100] In October none other than Mahatma Gandhi had also returned to Travancore and met with the Maharani at Satelmond Palace, expressing to Mr Cotton 'his highest admiration' for her.[101] To the regret of her opponents, she remained popular both with high dignitaries as well as with common men and women. As Mr Watts declared in his demonstrative and grandiloquent manner:

> Circles though small, are yet complete. That is what we proudly feel of Travancore. Set in the centre is our Maharani, radiating wisdom, courage, goodness, and a warm love to all her peoples. The patient light is to me, her Minister, a beacon ever showing the way to justice and to righteousness. Her Highness rules. And so a blessing lies upon this land.[102]

For all its embellishments and extravagant rhetoric, however, behind this veil of dedicated cooperation and loyalty too cracks had started to appear. The relationship between the Dewan and the Maharani, in reality, was reaching breaking point.

9

The Boudoir Dewan

In the eighteenth century as the mighty Zamorins confronted their inevitable decline, Martanda Varma in Travancore was carving out a centralised, modern state, vesting all power in the monarch. He crushed the petty princes of south Kerala, many of whom were his relations, and defanged the Nair aristocracy, until a military behemoth headed by his house reigned supreme in the region. But for all his remorseless ambition and brutal exercise of force, Martanda Varma was also a compelling strategist. While he expanded the borders of his state and annexed a number of regions, he realised that the people here regarded him merely as an invader and an alien brute. In fact, though their vanquished rulers fled before his mighty armies, the people consistently rebelled, refusing to capitulate, constantly questioning Martanda Varma's legitimacy over their ancestral lands.[1] Something, naturally, had to be done to quell this dangerous hatred for the new king. It was here that Martanda Varma's shrewd genius unearthed a weapon more formidable than any other from the chronicles of history, deploying it masterfully to render all resistance to his power morally impotent. The Maharajah discovered the power of faith.

In January 1749, a decade before his death, Martanda Varma performed a fabulous, visually stunning ceremony in the great Sri Padmanabhaswamy Temple in Trivandrum. It was loaded with religious meaning, making a tremendous statement to the world at large. That morning the Maharajah laid his sword before the sanctum sanctorum of the temple, and through a number of elaborate and awe-inspiring rituals, dedicated his freshly forged principality to the presiding deity in perpetuity. Travancore, as it existed on that date, now belonged not to Martanda Varma or any of his family, but to

Sri Padmanabhaswamy. The Maharajah assumed the ostensibly humble title of *Sri Padmanabha Dasa*, Servant of the Lord, hereafter claiming to rule over Travancore as the earthly representative of his dynastic deity. In an ingenious stroke, thus, the newly conquered territories went from being the rightful property of their dispossessed Rajahs to becoming the sacred estate of Sri Padmanabhaswamy. Any action against the ruler or the principality was now *swamidroham*, a crime against the almighty. Travancore, a state built over the debris of ancient houses of lords and princes, and despite the breaches of local law and canon in its very founding, acquired overnight a holy character.[2]

To question Martanda Varma was now tantamount to violating the sanctity of the hallowed deity in Trivandrum. This was the worst abomination for his orthodox, albeit reluctant, Hindu subjects, and a sure highway to hell. They were now bound to respect him as their sovereign and liege lord by religion. It was a masterstroke by the Maharajah who understood the importance of engineering public imagery and social perception. It created a welcome new narrative, painting Martanda Varma as a great devotee and supremely fervent protector of the faith, selling him and his house as exemplars of unparalleled devotion and spiritual surrender. Arguably, however, it was a calculated political move that sought to shroud the injustices of Martanda Varma's conquests and dress the bloodshed of war in a cloak of religious mystique.[3] He was hardly being original here, for sensible monarchs before him had always used faith as an instrument of power; even the Muslim Sultan Balban of Delhi had himself declared Allah's Vice Regent on Earth in the thirteenth century in order to secure his power in an unstable political environment.[4]

If this were not enough, Martanda Varma proceeded to augment the standing of his family also in the eyes of the public, investing them with a semi-divine social personality. This may have been the result of bitter experience. A generation ago, powerful lords of the realm had few reservations about drawing blood from members of the royal house. They were not seen as sacred in the least, existing in a formal state of primus inter pares among other nobles and barons of the land. But this was about to change now. For, in June 1751, Martanda Varma, through means of another extravagant and inventive ceremony known as the *hiranyagarbha*, upgraded his own dynastic line in caste and social status. As early as 1739, in fact, the Dutch recorded that the Maharajah was anxious to perform a ceremony by constructing a 'golden cow through whose mouth he was to go in and come out again at the tail in order to bear the title of Brahmin, which one of his ancestors held for himself through such a ceremony, while acquiring for his family, which was before of a lower kind, the elevation to the

Kshatriya caste, His Highness wearing the thread on this account'.[5] This too was hardly an original strategy: for the last many years the hiranyagarbha was being performed by *poligar* chieftains in the Tamil country, while closer home the Zamorin of Calicut had also undergone the procedure a generation before. In 1659 the ruler of Tanjore had passed through a golden cow into the arms of the wife of his chief priest, the lady playing 'the role of midwife, rocking and caressing him while he cried like an infant'.[6]

Hitherto, the royal family were held to be superior only by a minor degree from others at court and were by and large considered Nairs themselves.[7] However, for a good period of time they had been aspiring to propel themselves from the taint of being relatively ordinary in origin to a greater dignity; as early as 1683 Father Vincenzo Maria, one of the four Carmelite friars deputed by the Pope to Kerala, noted that the king of Travancore 'is by caste a Nair or soldier, but desirous of ennobling himself, with a ridiculous invention he made himself a Brahmin'.[8] Indeed, at one time, the Travancores were forbidden even from sitting in the presence of the Rajah of Cochin, who, despite his uninspiring military talents, was respected as the foremost legitimate Kshatriya prince in Kerala.[9] The device to obtain superior status, then, was the hiranyagarbha, and Adriaan Moens, the Dutch governor recorded its execution in the reign of Martanda Varma's successor some years later: 'It is true he is not of noble birth, but he caused himself to be made a noble following the example of his uncle [Martanda Varma] who first caused himself to be ennobled. This is called by the people of Malabar "to be reborn" ... It is derived from the droll ceremonial which the ennobled person goes through viz. passing through a big cow made of gold; after which the golden cow is beaten to pieces and divided among the Nambutiris or priests; and this king [i.e., the heir to Martanda Varma] was also so raised to nobility but with this difference that the ceremonies performed in his case were more complete and costly than those of his uncle, on account of which not only has he himself been made a noble but his posterity also have been ennobled once for all.'[10]

This status having been obtained, successive Maharajahs performed a slightly amended version of the ceremony where they sat in a golden urn, representing a golden womb, while Vedic mantras for pregnancy and then birth were chanted, after which they emerged, 'reborn' and having, in the words of Kosambi, 'acquired a higher caste, while the obliging Brahmins acquired the vessel of gold as part of their fee'.[11] They all remained, nevertheless (though perhaps revealingly) very touchy about their new-found Kshatriya status, and one royalist historian would go to great pains in the late nineteenth century to 'prove' that the Travancore royal family had always been highborn and that hiranyagarbha had nothing to do with a caste upgrade.[12] The fact, however, was that it had ennobled the dynasty, providing them, if not equality with Cochin, at least the pretensions of higher prestige and all the public ascendancy that accompanied it. All this concerted deification of the monarchy had, in the words of a staunch nineteenth century royalist,

> ...the desired effect, for since that time the people of Travancore have had a devoted attachment and sacred regard for the royal house ... This religious regard for the sovereignty is so great that the people of Travancore, both high and low, would not dare to speak ill of the Maharajah or the royal family ... Thus this wise [Martanda Varma] strengthened the position of his heirs with every support, religious, political, or military ... so that the position of the Travancore sovereign has become somewhat parallel to that of the Pope in Rome; and therefore neither the people nor the servants of the State would dare to disobey the king or act against the wishes of the sovereign, whether royalty was represented by an ignorant minor, or an educated sovereign in his dotage.[13]

Thus Martanda Varma, once hounded and harassed by his nobles and people, established for himself and his successors an unassailable position as socio-religious dignitaries. He secured a permanent insurance against any challenge to royal authority through inventive ritual devices and through theatrical customs that could camouflage their lack of historical pre-eminence.[14] In 1673 van Rheede had recorded that the subjects of the ruler were 'not bound to observe any orders, commands, or whims and council decisions of the king which are not in conformity with their [own] laws, welfare, or privileges, and have not been approved in their own district and ratified at the meeting of their district assemblies'.[15] As a scholar would remark, in the past:

> The princes were never above the laws laid down by the [people]; they were as accountable as everybody else. On their part, they also never aspired to rise extraordinarily beyond the average citizen. Thus it is that one encounters a total absence of any carefully constructed self-image of royalty in Kerala literature, whereas the rest of southern India and India witnesses the same in ample measure in most royalist literature, including the *prasastis*. The overriding theme of these kind of writings was to construct a superhuman royal image of the kings based on origin myths, dynastic traditions,

> genealogies, etc. to legitimise their right as hereditary rulers. Even this aspect of divinization of monarchy to invoke religious symbolism and thereby legitimise political power was absent in Kerala. The first such instance came about in the late eighteenth century, when the Maharajah of Travancore attempted to legitimise his rule as Padmanabha Dasa.[16]

After Martanda Varma, thus, people began to 'look up the Rajah with a degree of respect bordering on devotion' and he began to be considered, in the words of a traveller, 'the sacred representation of the tutelary divinity of the country ... to whom the country is dedicated and belongs'.[17] He, additionally, backed it in real terms by obtaining complete control over the army and divesting Nair lords of the final vestiges of feudal power. He began to import Tamil Brahmins to aid his government and to work closely with the royal family; owing to their own recent social promotion, they mingled less with Nairs as in the past and more with 'twice born' Brahmins, who were happy to recognise their new claims in return for economic rewards. As Susan Bayly notes, 'it had come to be accepted that the king must have Brahmins to receive his largesse', for without them 'he could not make the transformation from blood-spilling warrior to divinely mandated king'.[18] Much like he defeated rivals by commissioning mercenaries from outside, Martanda Varma began to replace the traditional influence of the Nairs, thus, with alien assistance. This too was a universally recognised political policy; throughout Central Asia and the Middle East, there were slave warriors called *mamluk*s brought in from outside by great emperors, 'due to a deep-seated suspicion' towards local powers and nobles whose loyalties were at best dubious.[19] Martanda Varma also assumed unto the government the estates of the old princes and barons he had destroyed so that 75 per cent of all agricultural land in Travancore was hereafter classed as *pandaravaka* or state land, giving him direct control over vast economic resources.[20] Altogether as Robin Jeffrey points out, 'non-Nair influences and institutions' were created around the Maharajah, reducing that class into a crippling state of dependence and a force incapable of challenging the pseudo-Kshatriya and imported-Brahmin centre.[21]

The Nairs were not, to be sure, however, completely ejected. They constituted most of the military; and leading officers and servants of the state, though no longer hereditary claimants, had to be invariably selected from their caste, at least until enough Brahmins were procured. Unlike in the past when wealthy and ancient houses claimed power, hereafter individuals even of humble backgrounds could rise by merit to serve the Maharajahs. As the Dutch governor Julius Stein van Gollenesse would remark, 'All the great men of his kingdom called

"Anavies" are men of common Nair origin and their rank is not inherited by their descendants; accordingly they depend entirely upon the ruler, they owe everything to him and they obey him with a slavish submission; and as their welfare depends entirely on the favour of their master, the king is served with great promptitude and from them he never need fear conspiracies against his person or possessions.'[22] Their princely patrons could, thus, count upon their loyalty. For instance, Martanda Varma's successor's most highly valued general and minister was a Nair of obscure and impoverished origins, not from the recently divested traditional aristocracy. It was this man, Kesava Pillai,[23] who led Travancore against the invading armies of the Sultan of Mysore and forged treaties of protection with the English East India Company, through all of which he remained steadfast in his loyalty to the Maharajah and to the enterprise that was modern Travancore. Of course, homilies were paid to the Nairs in general and they continued to be celebrated in official accounts as 'the lords of the country' and as 'guardians of the public weal'. But in reality their power had reached its lowest ebb, and they knew it.[24]

A final, desperate effort to recover their lost prestige was made shortly after a young, indolent prince succeeded to power in 1798 and surrounded himself with a coterie headed by a 'stupid and unprincipled' Brahmin. His cabinet, a 'triumvirate of ignorance, profligacy, and rapacity',[25] offered in the guise of economic reforms such tyrannical measures that a rebellion was provoked in the state, showing that the Nairs still had enough fight left in them. Its leader, Velu Tampi, was a Nair of superior family standing, who camped outside Trivandrum with a vast militia (something that Martanda Varma would never have allowed, and which was a sign that the royal family's grip was slipping).[26] He orchestrated an easy coup by which the cabinet was dismissed (and brutally punished) and Tampi himself took over the office of the Dewan of Travancore. As an administrator he was ferocious, and his adherents liquidated those who made the mistake of standing in his way. 'His utmost merit,' we are informed, 'lay in the fact that he was a strong man and inspired dread.'[27] A formidable dispensation began to exercise power, and Velu Tampi slowly even had the Maharajah quivering before him. A single Nair leader, it seemed, was on the cusp of undoing all that Martanda Varma had achieved for his dynasty, reclaiming power for the old feudal class of the land.

But attempting to reverse the course of history was an initiative doomed to fail. By now the English East India Company had secured considerable ascendance over the internal affairs of Travancore owing to the fact that the state owed large sums of money to them from the war against Tipu Sultan of

Mysore. Their Resident in the capital, Major Macaulay, initially saw in Tampi an able man who could help the Company recover its dues, and therefore boosted the Dewan with his own support, all at the cost of the Maharajah who could only fret and fume. But when Tampi attempted to raise funds by reducing the pay of the army, he found a mutiny on his hands, and 10,000 soldiers marched to Trivandrum to demand his dismissal. He was seen as working for the British and not for his Nair comrades and for the people of Travancore. He promptly obtained help from the Company's forces and had the insurrection quashed. One particularly unfortunate rebel had 'his legs tied to two elephants and the animals were driven in opposite directions, tearing the victim to pieces'.[28] The Maharajah in 1805 was then made to give his blessings to a renewed treaty with the Company, doubling his tribute to them, and imposing fresh financial liabilities on the royal treasury. Supported by the British from the outside, emaciating the monarch on the inside, Velu Tampi became the most powerful man in Travancore, little realising, however, that these happy days were all a prelude to the cruel fate that awaited him ahead.

By 1808 Tampi's honeymoon with Macaulay was mouldering, since the latter pressed for payment of arrears incessantly. While he was an efficient and exacting man, the proud Dewan was not used to being threatened, and decided to cast off the Company's yoke now. He assorted a number of allies. He had the Resident's Brahmin assistant murdered through some aides, while the consort of the Maharajah gathered for him palace secrets through pillow talks with her royal husband.[29] The hereditary Nair minister of the Rajah of Cochin, known as the Paliyath Achan, joined forces with him and together they sought to capture Macaulay. The Resident escaped by boat, but a full-fledged rebellion, with the Nairs at its head, broke out in Travancore and Cochin, while in Malabar the titular Zamorin, now an impotent pensioner of the Company, was also invited to participate.[30] Then, in what was the most momentous aspect of the revolt, Velu Tampi issued a proclamation to the people of Travancore. 'It is the nature of the English nation to get possession of countries by treacherous means,' he thundered, before going on to list a litany of grievances. 'If Velu Tampi was the most unscrupulous in his designs,' one historian notes, 'he was undoubtedly also the ablest man of his time. He knew how to lead his countrymen like sheep and how to work upon their fears.'[31] Charged with betraying his country only a few years ago, Velu Tampi was now the undisputed leader of its Nairs.

The rebellion, like numerous others against the British in India, however, was destined for spectacular failure, even if it earned for Tampi retrospective distinction as a martyr. Cornered in a temple and surrounded by the enemy troops, he cut his throat before the goddess, really going down in history as the final of the great Nair heroes of the past. Never was one of them to rise again in such a forceful manner. And the British made sure the Nairs had learnt their lessons. 'Several men of position were hanged and banished from the country for being implicated in the insurrection,' and Tampi's own kin were exiled or killed.[32] The Nairs lost their military vigour in the years that followed, not least because the army was disbanded, leaving behind a faint skeleton force called the Nair Brigade, and the Company assumed complete control over the defences of Travancore. 'I never beheld a more dastardly crew,' wrote one observer, adding that 'they did not deserve the name of soldiers' any more.[33] By the third decade of the nineteenth century, the Nairs were reduced into an agrarian class and 'that warlike, refractory, and turbulent temper for which the Nairs of Travancore were once so remarkable' had 'totally disappeared'.[34]

Following the quashing of Velu Tampi's rebellion, the influence of the British Resident grew by leaps and bounds. It was Col. Munro who followed the irritable Major Macaulay in Trivandrum, and while he had the full cooperation of the royal family (for their very survival now depended on keeping him pleased), he practically assumed all power, even serving as Dewan for some years. By 1814, however, the Company decided to withdraw from the direct administration of Travancore, and the Resident was informed to merely offer, 'invariably in terms of conciliation and respect, the reasonable assistance of good counsel' to the ruler, 'with a view to the permanent interests of the alliance, and to the progressive improvement of the country'.[35] This meant, in practice, however, that nominees of the British were appointed Dewans, so that they took their orders not so much from the Maharajahs as much as the Company. Munro, for instance, sent his candidate with a reference to the then ruler 'suggesting the propriety of appointing him' as Dewan.[36] And naturally 'friendly' guidance thus offered was followed without question.

The rise of the Resident cost Nairs most in terms of power. Company officers often brought with them Marathi Brahmins ('Raos') who were English-educated and served as their assistants. And over the years, these protégés were 'ensconced in many of the cosiest niches the administration had to offer', all at the instance of their British masters.[37] Some were individuals of respectable efficiency, but the sole qualification of many was merely a slavish loyalty to their sponsors. Despite the express orders that the Resident 'will carefully abstain from an open interference in the administration', this was complied with only on paper.[38] One particularly colourful individual, General Cullen, was notorious for so many libidinous activities during his twenty-year tenure, even as he became a permanent headache to the Maharajah. He insisted on reports and updates from government departments, and devoted such attention to harassing officials, that the administration became a 'tyranny of the Resident'.[39] He too brought with him a Rao whom he placed into a plum position in the state service on a handsome salary, before the latter, with Cullen's active connivance, went on to intrigue his way into the Dewanship itself. Martanda Varma, who had spent decades accumulating power for the monarchy, would have turned in his grave, if he had one. The Maharajah was by now largely a cipher in the hands of the Resident, who emerged as the sole fount of all meaningful promotion and patronage in Travancore. As for the Nairs, all this was another blow, having lost in a century their traditional influence, and now even claims to senior positions in the state machinery. As the *Madras Mail* would caustically remark some decades later, 'Whenever any vacancy occurs, one need only refer to the long list of Rows [sic] to choose the right person, and it is only a question between one particular Row and another.'[40]

This propensity of outside Dewans to serve the Resident caused such trouble and humiliation to the Maharajahs that one of them during Cullen's tenure prepared to abdicate, before he was dissuaded from executing this dire threat.[41] Even as late as 1871, when the popular Ayilyam Tirunal was in power, the Resident could find a way to throw his weight around. By now, however, things were not as *easy* for the British as before. Ayilyam Tirunal and his precocious Dewan, Sir T. Madhava Rao (the most prominent in that train of Marathi Brahmins), understood early on that the pretexts inviting hated British interference were indebtedness of the government or reports of maladministration. As late as the 1850s the threat of annexation had been openly employed, and to avoid a repetition, both were determined to exceed all expectations of the 'Paramount Power', as the colonial state was pompously known. Madhava Rao 'knew what the British wanted and he was able to give it to them; he played them successfully at their own game'.[42] He also understood the 'art of self advertisement' and was soon churning out reports of his government's administrative schemes and their successes, even as revenues mounted. The British endorsed all this and called Travancore a 'Model State', as schools were opened, roads built and reforms proclaimed (even if not implemented with the same enthusiasm always). But there was a reason why this particular Rao was more loyal to the Maharajah than to the Resident; his first job in Travancore had been as tutor to Ayilyam Tirunal, and during those years both men had developed an excellent rapport, allowing them to cooperate in a manner that none of the previous 'foreign', British-deputed Dewans and Maharajahs had managed.

In 1871, however, the British quite unexpectedly secured a handle to interfere in Travancore when it became known that Ayilyam Tirunal and Rao were no longer on amicable terms with one another. The Maharajah was determined to send his Dewan packing after twelve excellent years together, but such was the reputation built up by the latter, and his importance to the smooth functioning of the administration, that the Governor of Madras was aghast at the prospect. He promptly despatched a mediator between the quarrelling prince and his minister but Ayilyam Tirunal was 'unalterable' in his position. And if there were any intentions to compel him, it would, he pointed out, be so 'very painful' that he would be forced to contemplate abdication. While this was not something the Governor desired, the Maharajah was reminded by the Resident of the relevant provision in his treaty with the British where it was explicitly implied that he would always follow the 'friendly' advice of the Paramount Power.[43] For the time being the Maharajah had to hold his fire, even as the Dewan wrote him an ostensibly conciliatory letter. But behind the scenes, both negotiated a clandestine deal under the terms of which Rao might depart from Travancore quietly with a handsome pension for life and other terms settled in advance. In terminating their relationship too, thus, the two men attempted to cut the nose of the ubiquitous Resident, something the latter did not obviously appreciate.[44]

Dewans like Madhava Rao were extremely useful in implementing schemes in benefit of the state. They were products of English education that was making its way around India, and perfect examples of that famous 'class of persons, Indian in blood and colour, but English in taste, in opinions, in morals, and intellect'. Subscribing to this British ideal had its benefits. Rao was aware, for instance, that great opportunities awaited him on the all-India stage, and Travancore was but the beginning of his career in that wider framework of colonial patronage. His 'personal object was not money ... but Fame'.[45] However *success* was necessary for this, as was the building of a loyal network of supporters. In Travancore, when he embarked on modernisation and attendant projects, hitherto unknown in the region, he needed qualified men to support him. The local Nairs were hardly able to implement new, British-style state policies on education and trade, still steeped in their old feudal ways. So Western-educated bureaucrats were sought, no matter what their origins. And thus continued the stream of Marathi and Tamil Brahmins, with a critical distinction; the first tide of immigrants were sponsored by Martanda Varma in his state-building project that could not be entrusted to the suspect loyalties of Nairs; the second arrived with Residents as their agents; but this third proceeded at the invitation of the Maharajahs and their Dewans who needed them to pre-empt British interference by sustaining good governance.

Thus, 'under cover of the need for outside expertise, a number of the Dewan's relatives and castemen became established' in the Travancore service.[46] In the late 1880s, for instance, the Rao in power employed his son as his private secretary, his brother as a palace officer and the uncle of his daughter-in-law as a judge.[47] These men rose swiftly within the nepotistic ranks so that even as more Nairs obtained educational degrees to rival them, giving up the sword for the pen, the former had the advantage of experience and years in service. The fact that they were Brahmins allowed them to socialise freely with the royal family, and in 1857 it was openly stated that a Nair could not become Dewan due to the handicap of his caste.[48] While Nairs enjoyed access to lower-level jobs, the cream of the government positions was monopolised by Brahmins. In 1890, the Dewan was none other than a cousin of Madhava Rao's; of the four subordinate Dewan Peishkar positions, Tamil Brahmins occupied three; out of eighteen judgeships in the state, foreign Brahmins, who comprised 145 of 231 licensed lawyers and pleaders, held a majority of ten; fifteen out of twenty-nine tahsildars, and seventeen out of thirty English schoolmasters, were also outside Brahmins.[49] Indeed, in all these decades the only Nair to have obtained the Dewanship was Nanu Pillai, the immediate successor of Madhava Rao. But the sole reason Ayilyam Tirunal chose him was that he was afraid that any outside Dewan or a Rao would somehow be connected to his last Dewan, whom he despised.[50]

The Nairs were not willing to take this lying down, however, and by the end of the nineteenth century were bombarding the Maharajah with petitions. As the most famous of these, the Malayali Memorial, would note, the Nairs as 'the most loyal portion of Your Highness's subjects, as they are in point of intelligence, general culture and attainments not behind any other class in the country, as they were from the earliest times till within the last few years the ruling race in the land, as it is they that mainly contribute to the resources of the state ... their claims on Your Highness's Government are far stronger than those of any other class in the country'. Foreign Brahmins, they added, 'regularly and systematically ... without exception not only introduced their relations, castemen and friends into the State, but tried their best to oust the Nairs', which was 'all the more deplorable when it is remembered by Your Highness that they were from time immemorial till within the last few years the chief administrators of the State'.[51] One fiery activist would directly accuse the Maharajah: 'to serve the royal man as his menial ... Malayalis alone are wanted and Malayalis alone could be found. But to enjoy the comforts of the country, to fill all the higher appointments in the State, to obtain the highest honours of the land, to deserve all the gifts, donations, and rewards, foreign Brahmins alone are wanted and Brahmins alone are sought.' The Nairs, he vociferated, were 'held in subjection by a class of foreigners who have not conquered them by the sword ... who are not intellectually their superiors nor physically their betters ... can Travancoreans never expect to rise', he thundered, 'to that personal distinction and that political influence which were the glory, the pride, the richest heritage, and the brightest possession of their ancestors'?[52]

With Nairs raising voices against these imported premiers and the prejudice it caused them, the Brahmin Dewan in the early 1890s arrived at an accommodation with them, offering them better and higher positions in the government. But this did not put an end to the predominance of foreign Brahmins, what with even the Maharajah's then favourite, Saravanai, being one of them. It was the rise of Sankaran Tampi that gave, then, the next fillip to the Nair cause, and by 1903 an observer would write how 'Brahminical interest is latterly much on the decline, the Nairs having organised themselves in what are really anti-Brahmin clubs all over Travancore to resist the Brahmins everywhere, believing themselves to have been victimised by the Brahmins for centuries'. It was also, he added, significant that 'The all-powerful favourite, Sankaran Tampi is a Nair and not a Brahmin,' who 'uses his influence against Brahmins.'[53] Yet the highest office of Dewan eluded Nairs, until Mulam Tirunal appointed Sir Krishnan in 1915. But he was, after all, an aristocrat from Malabar, where the Nairs were different in culture and outlook from those in Travancore. And in any case, another Brahmin, the despised Mr Raghavaiah, followed him, and for his entire term Nair politicians were hard at work to boot him out.[54] To their great discontent, when Sethu Lakshmi Bayi finally disengaged him, she brought in his stead not a Nair or even, more predictably, a Brahmin, but a Christian, upsetting the calculations and the forty-year-old campaign of the Nairs to recover the highest executive office in Travancore for themselves. As the Maharani herself had reported with surprise, 'The vigour of the opposition put up against the proposed appointment and the manner in which the Nairs and Brahmins, setting aside their traditional enmity, applied themselves to the task are without a parallel in the history of Travancore.'[55]

Writing about the political currents a typical Dewan of Travancore would have to navigate, a later Resident would note that the people of Travancore

> … have two weaknesses in a marked degree, namely communalism and the worship of power. To them the community is everything and the State very little … Again their worship of power makes it essential for Travancoreans to be ruled by one who is seated firmly in the saddle with no fear of being ousted at any moment … It is a fact that no Dewan in the past has ever been able to enforce obedience for a single day after the security of his tenure has been seriously threatened. Once the idea gets about that the Dewan intends to retire or has lost favour, he must either go at once or be confirmed in his post by the Ruler emphatically and for a definite period. There have been cases of Dewans fallen from favour who, though still holding the appointment, have been unable to get [even] transport to take themselves and their families out of Travancore.[56]

Projecting power and authority, thus, had to be an article of faith for Dewans in Travancore. And unfortunately, insofar as maintaining discipline through this went, Mr Watts proved fairly disappointing. One of the reasons for all the turbulence and political agitation that Sethu Lakshmi Bayi's reign witnessed was not only that hers was an interim government, but also that her Dewan was eager to please *everybody*. Even before his appointment the Maharani had informed Mr Cotton that the purpose of having a Dewan who did not pledge loyalty to any of the warring communities in Travancore was to strengthen executive power. But in his usual manner, Mr Watts appeared more a magniloquent *talker* than an undaunted leader who could command authority in the choppy communal waters of Travancore politics. Some called him modest, which was not really a compliment for a Dewan of Travancore. At the time of his appointment, he called for cooperation from all sections, stating (ominously) that 'Were it not for such cooperation, whole hearted [sic] and sincere, my task here would be futile and it would be best that I lay down my office and quit.' Further, he added, 'if I am to achieve anything, do anything, leave anything behind me to be remembered by, it must be, and shall be due wholly to the cooperation of the people of this State.'[57] He continued:

> There will be many difficulties which I may have to face here, and never before having been Dewan, I shall make mistakes. I am sure I shall blunder at times. But do not for a moment believe that I will pretend that I have not made a mistake. Do not think I will throw the blame on somebody else. I shall own up my mistakes and trust to the goodwill of the people of Travancore to help me correct the mistakes.[58]

This was a gentlemanly attitude to take, but surrounded by politicians who had made life even for the gritty Mr Raghavaiah difficult during his tenure, Mr Watts revealed himself as a soft target. It was no surprise, then, that even his smallest mistakes were blown up for 'correction' by his numerous opponents. In an interview to Reuters he spoke of how his appointment would serve as an opportunity to bring about greater cooperation between the European and Indian races. Many naturally complained that this demonstrated an attitude of condescension towards Indians. At his first budget session in the legislature he had not been as thoroughly prepared as he ought to have, so that, in the words of one observer, 'The President of the Council whose duty it is to call "honourable members" to order, had to be called to order by Members!'[59] He had a 'disarming naivete' about him, and was genuinely concerned about the welfare of the people, but could not assert himself for the actual implementation of the causes he assumed so fervently. On one instance he promised to reverse a government decision when he heard first-hand from a public deputation about the difficulties it would cause, only to vacillate on its execution, no doubt due to pressure from his officials. 'Has he again bent his knee,' asked a critic, 'to the paladins of the Secretariat?'[60] Reviewing the first six months of his tenure, O.M. Thomas decided that

> Mr Watts is a namby-pamby, shilly-shallying sort of man. He has good intentions, is accessible, kind, considerate. But he cannot make up his mind. The capacity to come to right and swift decisions is the chief asset of an executive in any sphere of responsibility. It is a quality in which Watts sorely lacks. He allows himself to be the sport of conflicting views and rival disputants ... If he keeps a firmer hold on the reins of his office, he would be hailed as an agreeable contrast to his immediate predecessor ... Mr Raghavaiah had the spirit of a Torquemada—cold, fierce, ruthless. His grasp was simian, his execution thorough. Such a man does Mr Watts succeed. Raghavaiah was strong, but not sympathetic; Mr Watts is sympathetic, but not strong. Raghavaiah respected public opinion by flouting it; Mr Watts flouts public opinion by respecting it. Raghavaiah revelled in swimming upstream; Mr Watts floats with the current and gets into eddies. That is the difference.[61]

In other words, the Dewan was not perceived as powerful, partly due to his own attitude of accommodation. This was to an extent the reason why the government could be coerced and dragooned in the matter of the Brooke Bond scheme by a group of hysterical politicians. But it was also feared that it would all reflect rather badly on Sethu Lakshmi Bayi. As O.M. Thomas, who was unusually generous in praise when it came to her, noted, the Maharani was 'unfortunate in her constituted adviser'. For 'If administration were only a matter of making sentimental speeches, Mr Watts, the Dewan, would be hard to beat. The art of government is a trifle more severe an exercise; and in that art he, by common consent, has not impressed us with more than indifferent abilities.'[62] 'All that the people of Travancore desire with unanimous sincerity,' he alerted, 'is that Mr Watts should not cause a "rift in the Lute" which will make Her Highness' "music mute". Let him but talk less, act more, and keep his temper; and he will yet not fail, though he may not quite succeed.'[63]

What with Mr Watts's tendency towards bombastic and demonstrative expression, there were few signs, at the commencement of his tenure, of his relations with Sethu Lakshmi Bayi being anything but satisfactory. He was extravagant in articulating his loyalty and avowed devotion to her, and in a newspaper interview admitted that he regarded his appointment 'as due purely and solely' to the 'personal considerations' of the Maharani.[64] She too, for her part, went out of her way to make him comfortable, not least because everyone else in the state seemed hostile to him and she had to make it clear that he enjoyed her fullest confidence. In 1926, when his mother died, both she and the Valiya Koil Tampuran treated him with considerable kindness, and he wrote to them thereafter how eager he was to 'prove my deep appreciation of your large heartedness' and to serve as a loyal and efficient Dewan.[65]

But as his critics noted, his sentimental words did not match his actions and sometimes Mr Watts displayed an almost childish petulance. His first conflict of sorts with the Maharani emerged when only months after his arrival he desired a revision of his pay, and to raise it from Rs 2,000 per month to Rs 3,000. When Sethu Lakshmi Bayi expressed her reluctance to move in this matter so soon, he had his sister press upon her. Miss Watts was careful to add, however, that whatever her decision might be, 'it is not going to make any difference in my brother's attitude or loyalty to you, nor in mine'.[66] 'I am very sorry at the distress this affair is causing you,' she added. 'I understand only too well the feelings on both sides—how you feel tied down by public opinion and how hurt my brother feels at being less than those former Dewans and less too than some of the officers under him.'[67] Eventually, seeing how delicate the matter was for Mr Watts, the Maharani raised his salary to Rs 2,500, before he had completed even a year in service, telling a somewhat disapproving Mr Cotton that the desire was entirely hers and there had been no application from the Dewan.[68] 'Two friends may have a difference of opinion and [yet] remain friends,' Miss Watts noted awkwardly, betraying her own discomfort at being put in the middle of all this.[69]

Despite this unusual favour being shown to make him comfortable in the state, the Dewan proved to be perpetually sensitive about his position. When he heard an 'absurd story' that Mr Cotton wrote to the Government of India that there would be no peace in Travancore while he was in office, Mr Watts took it as a personal affront and asked him to 'tell me the truth and not beat about the bush or try to do the diplomatic stunt'. He was, he dramatically declared, prepared to 'pack up my trunks and make room for a better man' if the Resident found him wanting as the Dewan. Mr Cotton was somewhat amused by this overreaction, confirming to Mr Watts that the only thing he had told his superiors in Delhi was that as 'the Nairs have become tired of baiting the Valiya Koil Tampuran', they were now focusing on the Dewan, demanding his 'immediate removal' from the state. He, as Resident, was 'more than satisfied' with Mr Watts's service so far.[70]

By 1927, however, the Maharani began to tire of her Dewan's infantile moods and Mr Cotton recorded that she was 'less well disposed' towards him than before. It also did not help that within the government too Mr Watts, with his inability to assert himself, was allowing coteries to develop. There was, besides the ever-present network of Nairs, also an unfavourable 'Syrian Christian Triumvirate' comprising the Chief Secretary, Dr Mary, and the famous writer O.M. Cherian who were 'for the moment in high favour' with the Maharani, according to sources of the Resident.[71] She did not, however, allow them to supersede the Dewan and when efforts were made to suggest a Syrian Christian nominee as a possible replacement to Mr Watts, the group were swiftly put in their place. And soon the Chief Secretary who was deplored for representing communalism 'in its extreme form' against the Nairs, apologised to the Dewan for trying to 'short circuit' him.[72] But these internal government manoeuvres leaked into the public domain and were blown out of proportion as always, and before long it was out and about that Mr Watts was retiring to London as 'Stores Purchaser' for the government, even as 'local prophets' sprang up predicting the next Dewan.[73] The rumours did, however, have an effect on the Nairs. Partisan newspapers that had 'hitherto shown no respect' for Mr Watts were now 'actually urging his retention' while their more extremist affiliates 'prophesy communal riots and even revolution if a Syrian Christian succeeds to the Dewanship'.[74] Everyone in Travancore, it seemed, had an amiable penchant for the dramatic.

By April that year, however, the Maharani and the Dewan were again having trouble on account of the fact that she did not support him more openly with his pet Brooke Bond Scheme. Another administrative project on which they disagreed more seriously concerned the extension of railways in Travancore. Mr Watts had plans to extend the existing railway line from Quilon to the Cochin Harbour to facilitate easy movement of goods, and from Trivandrum to Nagercoil for southward connectivity as well. The Maharani had given her consent in principle to this and a survey had been conducted under a special railway engineer.[75] But when it came to implementation, Sethu Lakshmi Bayi did not think it wise to commence work during her regime. She felt that the project, which 'involves heavy borrowing of capital', might or might not be successful. 'Just now to embark on it looks like a leap in the dark,' she pointed out, adding that since her administration was to last only a few years, whereas liabilities would weigh on the treasury for longer, constraining the hands of her successor, 'I do not wish to take the risk.'[76] Again, as a result, Mr Watts felt aggrieved and the air was full of rumours about him having threatened to resign upon 'finding no support for his ambitious railway programme from the Maharani'.[77]

In June 1927 Sethu Lakshmi Bayi confirmed to Mr Cotton that the Dewan no longer appeared up to the mark.[78] 'Mr Watts and the Palace have exchanged cordial letters,' recorded the Resident, 'but there is no doubt that he is no longer in favour and that if he threatened resignation, [he] would be taken at his word. He seems to realise this,' it was added, 'for he has decided not to make the railway programme a question of confidence.'[79] The fact was that for quite some time the Dewan had been hinting at resigning every time he and the Maharani disagreed, and Sethu Lakshmi Bayi had had enough of this game. The Nairs, however, sensing a rift between the Maharani and her minister jumped at a potential opportunity to win him over now, and in what was a hilarious incident, 'asked him to believe that they were now convinced that he was the Nairs' best friend and assured him that they would support him in and outside the [Legislative] Council', if he wanted to pass anything despite the Maharani's objections.[80] Of course, as in the usual way of politics in Travancore, this friendly façade did not last, and by August that year the very same Nairs were 'concentrating in a mass offensive' against him, seeing how he and the Maharani had resolved their differences.[81] Indeed, by September the Dewan clarified both to Sethu Lakshmi Bayi and to the Resident that he was eager to serve beyond his original three-year tenure, giving the impression that things were better between him and the Maharani.[82] By early 1928 she confirmed that she was happy to grant him a one-year extension of service, and newspapers speculated that it was 'probable that he will in fact be Dewan until after the Regency.'[83] Whatever quarrels they had had, both appeared to be able to handle them professionally.

But Sethu Lakshmi Bayi had reasons other than satisfaction with Mr Watts's output and competence for granting him this extension. The extent of tension in their relations was actually extremely severe, and although the Dewan himself had at first requested a second term, when the Maharani formally offered it to him, he first turned it down somewhat impulsively. In a curt letter, he declared that 'my decision must be against remaining in office after the close of my present term'.[84] The Maharani then invited his sister for a discussion and impressed upon her the necessity that the Dewan make a rational choice, so that the very next day Mr Watts changed his mind. He had not been happy that he was again offered the same salary and terms, but claimed he was willing to overlook this. 'In view of the generous sentiments Your Highness was pleased to express to my sister last night, I shall be glad to stay on as Dewan so long as I command Your Highness' confidence in my judgment, trust, and fidelity, and belief in the disinterestedness of my advice. All that I hope for is that Your Highness will open your mind to me more freely in official matters.'[85] The Maharani accepted his change of heart and typically ostentatious pledge of devout loyalty, making it clear in response, however, exactly why she had not been able to see eye to eye with him recently and what he needed to do to make amends:

> I shall send you a copy of the memorandum left by the late Maharajah for the guidance of the Dewan in his dealings with the Ruler, with a few supplementary clauses, which I shall add, and think that with this at hand for ready reference the difficulty of knowing which of the papers passing through your hands need to be informally submitted to me, will be obviated, and consequently the possibility of a misunderstanding will be greatly minimised. Something has to be done to prevent long delays in the disposal of papers, which at the present moment have become a subject of general comment. I hope you will be able to tackle this question and suggest measures that will ensure a reasonably quick disposal.[86]

The matter was that Mr Watts had not been referring matters to the Maharani as she expected to be done, and had been slow in his pace of conducting government business. The allegations of 'shilly-shallying' and not being able to make up his mind, were not unfounded, and the Resident was compelled to ask whether 'Mr Watts has given any undertaking that he will work more methodically in future, and not issue orders without obtaining Your Highness' prior approval?'[87] As it happened, the Dewan did not quite improve in his ways and by September 1928 the Resident had to again report that while he was on decent terms with Sethu Lakshmi Bayi, 'it is said that his interviews with the Maharani Regent have not been as frequent as formerly was the case'.[88] Both sides were making their best efforts to create an impression of blissful harmony and understanding, despite relations deteriorating with every passing month. The extension of tenure to Mr Watts in fact even led to protests by the Nairs in the capital, and for quite some time two newspapers were engaged in an outstanding public battle for and against the Dewan. Their disagreement was not so much a matter of principle, however, and the only reason the *Daily News* was anxious to support Mr Watts was because its owner had recently received a government contract, while *The Express* vociferated against him for having lost that very contract.[89]

The real reason, however, for the Maharani's decision to retain the Dewan in spite of difficulties in working with him was that Mr Cotton's term as Resident was soon to end, and a new British representative was to arrive in Travancore. 'You will doubtless appreciate,' she wrote to the incumbent, 'that in making this proposal [to continue with Watts] a desire to avoid anything like an unsettlement in the country which the appointment of a new Dewan usually creates, especially after it has nearly returned to tranquillity, and a consideration of the unwisdom [sic] of having a new Dewan when the Resident is also new, have considerably influenced me.'[90] She, in other words, would be placed in an extremely vulnerable situation if both the Resident and her minister were men inexperienced in tackling sharks in the political waters of Travancore. But this was a temporary measure. When asked if it was possible that Mr Watts would continue for a period beyond the already approved one-year extension, the Maharani clarified that 'save under exceptional circumstances' she had no plans of the sort, adding somewhat dryly that while he was able, 'perhaps due to indifferent health, there is [still] a delay in the disposal of papers'.[91]

In August that year the new Resident conferred with Sethu Lakshmi Bayi on the problem that Mr Watts had become. 'I had an interview with Her Highness last evening,' he wrote to his superiors, 'and she tells me that Mr Watts's manner towards her savours of dictation; that in spite of her orders, he frequently sanctions estimates for works which she has distinctly told him she does not approve of; incidentally, she mentioned that he had told the inhabitants of certain villages that he would give them new schools, and this without consulting her.'[92] In a written communiqué to him, the Maharani expressly stated that she could not help but pull up her Dewan for 'his easy irritability, growing tendency to import personal prejudices into official actions, and fondness for initiating measures not only without my previous concurrence but sometimes contrary to explicit instructions'. It was all 'making it increasingly difficult for me to get on with him' and what worried her particularly was that 'Mr Watts's intransigence and unfriendliness would appear in a particularly lurid light when it is remembered that in appointing him Dewan, I went against the wishes of the entire people of Travancore ... not to speak of the fearfully scurrilous attacks I was subjected to in the newspapers here and elsewhere.'[93]

The straw that really broke the camel's back, then, was a jarring dispute over the selection of the new Director of Public Instruction. The officer-in-charge had been unwell for much of 1928 and was unlikely to continue for much longer. Mr Watts desired to appoint the European principal of the Science College to the post, while the Maharani had in mind Rangaswami Iyengar, the principal of the Arts College. While ostensibly the Dewan opposed this on the grounds that the confirmation of 'a very orthodox Brahmin' would result invariably in complaints from other communities,[94] the Maharani knew that in reality his grudge was personal. He in turn insisted that her endorsement of Iyengar was 'the job of a Brahmin Clique that had gotten hold in the palace'. But what Sethu Lakshmi Bayi really wanted was a real confrontation with Mr Watts to put an end, for once and forever, the simmering, underhand resentment on his part. 'I could perceive,' the Resident put down, 'that Her Highness was very anxious to bring matters to a head between herself and Mr Watts, and that the latter should resign.'[95] In other words she had had enough of his defiance of her authority, and had been especially agitated by 'a letter or rather a memorandum from Mr Watts to her, in which he stated that if this appointment was made, he would be unable to continue his duties'.[96] The Dewan had even written a similar letter to the Resident, stating that this 'appointment is a trial of strength between him and his political opponents'.[97]

It was patent, however, that the real issue was that the Dewan had had a longstanding quarrel with Iyengar, which began with his sister who, sometime ago, had such a falling out with the man that she had resigned from her post in the Department of Education, refusing to serve 'even three months' under him.[98] Sethu Lakshmi Bayi, despite her friendship with Miss Watts, did not interfere, and stood by her officer since he was not at fault in all this. The grudge, then, was transferred to Mr Watts from his sister, which again the Maharani failed to countenance. Writing to the Resident she made it clear that she was unwilling to 'sacrifice Iyengar on the ground that the Dewan has taken a prejudice against the man', fearing that 'it might create an impression that the criterion of a man's competence lay not so much in his merits, as whether he is in the good graces of the Dewan or not. So in the interests of the state,' she concluded with unusual vehemence, Mr Watts's challenge of resignation 'has to be accepted'. She was not, however, blind to the possible problems this could create. For she continued:

> You are quite right in saying that his sudden resignation would create a sensation and give food for undesirable talk and newspaper scribbling, but if I yield to his protest for fear of facing a situation of the kind, whenever in future I am unable to see eye to eye with the Dewan on State matters, he might carry the point with the threat of resignation. It is certainly essential in the interests of efficient administration to maintain the prestige of the Dewan, but when this cannot be done without imperilling that of the Ruler ... you will doubtless agree that the former should give away. In any case Mr Watts has concern with the administration of this country only for a few months more, whereas mine extends a few years longer. Also his resignation, if ever it takes place, will be attributed by the intelligent people to pique rather than to just indignation born of a genuine sense of wrong.[99]

Sethu Lakshmi Bayi was obviously determined in this matter, revealing again the occasional staunchness that lay behind her normally gentle exterior, latent until it was provoked out of its state of regular composure. 'I know in his heart [he] desires to remain on as Dewan,' noted the Resident, aware that even Mr Watts was taken aback by the Maharani's decision to put her foot down on this occasion when he threatened to resign.[100] She, in the meantime, had even decided that in the event that he did carry out his distasteful threat, the Devaswom Commissioner would be placed in charge of the administration till a suitable candidate was found, even if the fact that he was an 'ultra orthodox Brahmin' would offend the Nairs. Asking the Dewan to contemplate the writing on the wall, she noted:

> I am extremely sorry that you should have brought matters to a head by your threat of resignation in the event of Rangaswami Iyengar succeeding to the post of the Director of Public Instruction. If you consider that to continue in office after Rangaswami Iyengar's appointment would be incompatible with your honour and principles alike, I shall say no more, as I have decided to give Rangaswami Iyengar a real chance to prove his competence. I am

> perfectly sensible of the direct and indirect consequences of your threatened precipitate action, and perhaps the most humiliating and painful of them all would be to face the inevitable taunt that the very man in supporting whose nomination I went out of my way and raised a storm in the country, unprecedented in its violence and extent, eventually fell out with me. If you are still determined to resign and are not going to be influenced by any other consideration, than that which has so far weighed with you, I request I may be informed when you propose relinquishing your office, so that I may instruct you as to whom to hand over charge.[101]

This letter was not only an admonishment and clear articulation of her lack of trust, disfavour and her more than evident disappointment at having backed such an unreliable person in the face of loud opposition, but also a clever manipulation that steeped the Dewan instantly in guilt at having forced her to the wall. He had acted churlish and cantankerous for far too long and while she was accommodating at first, he had carried it too far, compelling her to put her foot down, no matter what the implications to her own government and her reputation. The Government of India also backed her and a telegram from Delhi made it clear that the Dewan had to be induced to 'moderate his attitude' and realise that he was, after all, an employee, and not the source of all authority in the state.[102] The Resident's suspicion that he really desired to continue as Dewan and that he had not quite expected this forceful response from the Maharani was now confirmed. For soon after her verbal dressing-down to him, Sethu Lakshmi Bayi received from the Dewan an apology, again couched in words of great loyalty and the usual flair for histrionics:

> The possibility of Your Highness being exposed to humiliation and painful taunt leaves only one course open to me. I should be something less than man did I not stand between your Highness and that. Dissociating myself from my office, I find I have strength and the courage to bear my cross, humbled and shorn of pride. Therefore, I surrender my position to Your Highness. I am prepared to give Mr Rangaswami Iyengar another chance, as desired by Your Highness. The safeguarding of the prestige and authority of the Dewan will, I am sure, be safe in Your Highness' keeping, so long as the incumbent commands Your Highness' confidence. I have caused Your Highness more pain than I thought. I am sorry. I too have suffered over this incident.[103]

A rapprochement was, thus, effected, and as it happened, Iyengar proved to be a success as Director of Public Instruction, uncovering major irregularities in the Department of Education the following year, and putting an end to a great deal of inside corruption.[104] But peace between the Maharani and her Dewan was not to last, for soon they were to argue about a similar appointment of a judge to the High Court. 'I cannot help observing that I am becoming increasingly nervous when I am obliged to take an opposite view to yours on public questions,' she wrote to him, afraid that he might continue this tendency of making a public spectacle of all their disagreements.[105] By 1929 their relations were so fractured that it had become 'impossible and Her Highness has become altogether unwilling to give him an interview as she informed me she was afraid he might be rude to her'.[106] As it happened, the Dewan was quick to lay the blame for all his troubles with the Maharani at the door of none other than the Valiya Koil Tampuran, whose earlier indiscretions seemed to have invited for him the misfortune of being everyone's favourite scapegoat. But it did not convince many, and as a future Resident noted,

> The trouble between Mr Watts and 'the Palace' lay not in the big question of policy but was due to the fact that Mr Watts considered that he alone, as Dewan, was the actual Ruler of the State and that Her Highness should blindly follow his advice. If this advice was not always taken, he lay the blame on Her Highness' Consort, the Valiya Koil Tampuran, and talked of him as 'the Boudoir Dewan'.[107]

Indeed, when Mr Watts left the state at the conclusion of his term, there were even rumours that he had in his possession letters of recommendation given by Rama Varma to various candidates to enable them to get government jobs, and that he had plans to publish these in newspapers to discredit the Valiya Koil Tampuran.[108] Nothing of the sort really transpired, but it was clear that by the end the Maharani's husband and her Dewan could not agree. 'The position in 1925-26,' it was reported, 'was that the Valiya Koil Tampuran and Mr Watts were great friends.' But soon afterwards, the Dewan was 'beginning to become swollen-headed and undoubtedly hoped to become the uncrowned king of Travancore.' With the passage of years, and with the Maharani making it clear that she and not he was the head of the government, and that she had no intentions of sitting quietly at the margins, allowing him to run the state all by himself, 'Mr Watts became more and more headstrong, and took upon himself to pass orders in cases where it has always been the custom for the Ruler of the State to do so. Thus started the gulf which thereafter became wider and wider between the Dewan and Her Highness the Maharani Regent. The Maharani

Regent began to demand explanations from Mr Watts, and in some instances, I understand, she cancelled his orders. Mr Watts ascribed these actions by Her Highness to the interference of the Valiya Koil Tampuran and instead of being a great friend ... he became his bitterest enemy.' Such was the hatred, in fact, that the Dewan now harboured for Rama Varma that by 1929 'he was unable to say anything bad *enough* about the Valiya Koil Tampuran'.[109]

The Maharani, however, did not make too much of this. It had become a force of habit for those who opposed her to target her husband. But with the termination of the loyalty and friendship of Mr Watts, she was genuinely pained. She could discern a pattern in his behaviour, oscillating between overblown claims of fealty and absolute recalcitrance, but this did not mean she could not appreciate his positive qualities, including a drive to do good and to improve the lives of her people. Writing at the height of her dispute with him, she seemed unhappy and resigned at the turn of things, even though she was determined in her stand.

> I am only too glad to testify to his great powers of initiative, drive, and general parts, not to speak of the facility and virility of his speech and writing. If his intolerance of restraint had been less pronounced, if he could have viewed public questions with greater detachment and calmness, if he could have brought to bear upon big questions more judgement than passion, it would have been difficult to beat him as an administrator. He has besides rendered considerable personal services to me. If he does go, I shall be genuinely sorry. [However,] in accepting Mr Watts's challenge I do not regard the issue as between Watts and Rangaswami Iyengar, but as between my sense of fairness and his prejudice.[110]

In 1925 Sethu Lakshmi Bayi fought a veritable battle of principles against the orthodoxy to appoint Mr Watts her Dewan. And in 1928 it was precisely those very principles she defended again, this time battling the man she had once protected from insult and opprobrium, even if it meant losing him and facing humiliation and ridicule from all her jeering opponents in Travancore.

10

Black Magic

In the early nineteenth century, when Col Munro arrived in Travancore, the state had just emerged from the violent throes of the revolt of Velu Tampi. His comrades and he had been utterly routed but the British were yet to decide whether or not the principality, with its finances and administration in such spectacular chaos, deserved retention as an autonomous unit. Annexation was a perfectly real possibility. The Maharajah was supremely incompetent, marked 'by imbecility, caprice, and other qualities' making him 'wholly unequal to the task of Government'.[1] Real power was then entrusted to the grandson of a long-dead prince, Ummini Tampi, who now held the position of Dewan.[2] He was a capable man like the redoubtable Velu Tampi, keeping the monarch on a tight budgetary and political leash, working closely with the British authorities. But in 1810 when Rani Gowri Lakshmi Bayi came to the throne, he met in her his final match. While she acknowledged the supremacy of the English East India Company, she refused to tolerate further humiliation in the form of Tampi's dictations, finding an artful way to eliminate him from the state altogether.

In a manner that distinguished her relations with Munro, she played up her ostensible helplessness, projecting herself as a vulnerable female in need of protection from the vile intentions of all the evil men around her. Playing a damsel in distress was a cunning strategy to dissociate herself from the foolish reign of her predecessor, and win sympathy from the new Resident and his masters. 'As I consider the gentlemen of the Company in the light of parents, and myself as their daughter, I have committed my cares and services to them, and expect the comfort and happiness of myself and my country from their justice and protection only. If the Company do not protect and assist me,' she asked with dramatic poignancy, 'who will protect me?'[3] Gowri Lakshmi Bayi, thus, having touched a chivalrous nerve with Col Munro, the latter decided to play a knight in shining armour to this helpless Indian princess. The Rani then went on to state categorically what she desired. 'My representation is this, that I do not require the services of the present Dewan. As I am a woman, it is not becoming to write more but I earnestly trust that my wishes may be taken into serious consideration, and that the present Dewan may be removed from office.'[4] It did not help that the incumbent had embezzled property belonging to the demised Velu Tampi, and this became the crime for which he was to be expelled. Col Munro gallantly shouldered the Rani's cause and ordered the 'harsh and vindictive' Dewan's removal.[5] Following this, the Rani conveniently informed him that since she regarded him as her brother, nothing would please her more than if he took up the position himself.

Ummini Tampi, after some retaliatory seething and intriguing against the Rani and Resident, was banished to Chingleput. By all accounts he was an unpleasant man and the previous Maharajah had openly declared that if he had had a chance, he would have liked to himself shoot him. Tampi also likely deserved the punishment imposed on him. But at the time of his departure, Gowri Lakshmi Bayi revealed herself to be so vehement in her hatred that she was prepared to inflict on him a low, personal blow. The Dewan, it so happened, had a lover called Umayamma, who was a dancing girl attached to the government *natakasala*. It was customary for officials of the state to select women as paramours from this establishment, but as the Rani wrote to Col Munro, 'they are invariably recalled on the death or dismissal of those officers'.[6] The banished Dewan's only request in his defeat was that his darling of fourteen years be allowed to accompany him. The Rani, in her vengeance, however, refused. It was Ummini Tampi's fate to languish alone in prison until his dying breath, pining for his beloved, who also, presumably, spent her days in romantic misery, cast from the embraces of one official to the next.[7]

The Umayamma in question here was perhaps a regular courtesan. But there was an older institution in Travancore, and indeed in other parts of India, where women were dedicated to deities and temples, their lives committed in service of god, dancing and singing and preserving high culture in great Hindu temples of the land. Indian history and tradition resound with stories and legends about these devadasis, maidens of god. A two-thousand-year-old inscription at the Sitabenga Cave tells the tale of a painter, Devadinna, and Sutanaka, the beautiful devadasi he loved. The *Meghadutam* of the legendary poet Kalidasa portrays a vivid picture of the great shrine of Mahakala in Ujjain, which 'resounded with the sound of the ankle-bells of the dancing girls'.[8] An eighth-century king of Kerala went on to dedicate his own daughter to the deity at Srirangam, while in the thirteenth century a Kupaka prince enjoyed a heady romance with another devadasi serving in the temple of Siva at Kandiyur.[9] These women enjoyed a high position in society and 'they were honourable invitees in all important festivals and ceremonies, such as the coronation of kings'.[10] They were educated women of wealth and means, instituting endowments, building temples and more.

Indeed, even in the colonial nineteenth century, devadasis remained dedicated to their vocations, some winning fame as musicians and actresses. The 'queen of theatre', for example, in Madras was a Kumbakonam-based devadasi called Balamani, and trains passing through the station would halt for fixed periods there to allow passengers to attend her shows.[11] She donated liberally to temples in the region, and her Balamani Ammal Company was a haven and refuge for abandoned and homeless women. She never married, and as irony would have it, died in poverty, but during her heyday she was tremendously influential, rumoured at one time as the mistress of Mulam Tirunal in Travancore.[12] Devadasis were also among the earliest brand ambassadors for Indian art and culture abroad; as early as 1838 a troupe travelled West becoming 'the first indigenous artists to perform all over Europe', even dancing at the French court in Tuileries and becoming, reportedly, 'instant celebrities'.[13] Even M.S. Subbulakshmi, the doyenne of Carnatic music in the twentieth century, who arguably did more to popularise Indian music around the world than anyone else, was descended from a line of accomplished and highly talented devadasis.[14]

Nineteenth-century Victorian values that were imposed by the British in India and latterly embraced by local elites, however, began to alter the position of the devadasi. Ancient Indian texts like the *Natyasastra*, remarks J. Devika, classed women into categories such as *kulina* and *veshya*. The former was a chaste householder, one to provide heirs and a womb to preserve the purity of her line. The latter, on the other hand, was 'the vessel of culture, the provider of pleasure—aesthetic, intellectual, and bodily pleasure—to men of a certain social standing, at a price'.[15] Veshyas were not in any way judged or considered low for being 'vessels' of culture. On the contrary, they had serious social contributions to make, and money earned by them was poured into a number of public ventures of one kind or another. There was the possibility of oppression, as in every field. But the stigma attached to their dance and art and music, intertwined as it was with sexuality and expression, was new-found and a consequence of Western cultural attitudes that frowned on women's bodies, and the use of these without a badge of marriage. While on the one hand women were being liberated and sent to college and asked to take up vocations, on the other, their sexual personality had to fit the patriarchal model of a daughter, sister, wife or mother, and cease to exist outside these catholic parameters. Indeed, as Girish Karnad notes, even M.S. Subbulakshmi's 'spectacular career had much to do with the way she managed to shed all traces of her devadasi past and transform herself into the perfect image of a Tamil Brahmin housewife'.[16]

The art of the devadasis, though, was valuable, and would be cast in a more 'acceptable' mould by reformers so as to correspond with the new sensibilities of upper class Indians. Rukmini Devi Arundale, for instance, stripped the Bharatanatyam dance drama, once performed in temple mandapams, of its eroticism and adapted it to the Western-style stage, giving it respectability, even while wrenching it from its ancient custodians, the devadasis. In Kerala the Mohiniattam was stigmatised because of its overtly sexual tenor but Kathakali, which was more dramatic, retained patronage.[17] While ancient Indian painters did not shroud the flesh and sought to celebrate sexuality, Raja Ravi Varma made even his voluptuous female figures 'sensuous but not seductive, forthcoming but not coquettish'.[18] The devadasis did not take all this lying down and in Madras efforts were made to unionise and resist this attempt to impose Western moral codes on their ancient religious and artistic practices. A memorandum submitted by one devadasi association made it clear that they ought to be treated as a minority and their rights and privileges jealously guarded from 'the autocracy and high-handedness of the more powerful' who had 'no right to impose their views and fancies' on their community.[19] They pointed out that as women 'enjoying special rights of property, legal status, religious honours, and recognised independence sanctioned by ancient scriptures, traditions, and customs', they resented now being asked to fit into the mould of kulina householders by 'a very small section' of pseudo-puritan Hindus. They also, interestingly, pointed out that 'we are women not having the disadvantages of [most] Hindu women but possess, on the contrary, all the privileges of males in regard to property, special laws of inheritance, rights and privileges in temples'.[20] Asking them to transform into kulina ladies was also a means for taking away these rights they had enjoyed since time immemorial.

It was unfair to abandon them to 'wolfish' reformists, they argued, and made it clear that it was inappropriate to equate an Indian devadasi with a Western sex worker who sold her body for personal economic reasons. How, they asked, could they 'be judged from the angle of western culture,' passing 'judgment on Hindu Society without understanding the genius of its construction'.[21] It was clear that Indian zealots in an effort to purge Hinduism of anything that a Victorian might hold as immoral, were determined to divest the devadasis of their culture, and revise it without these women. But it was a battle they were destined to lose, and reformers were determined to succeed. As early as 1853 when Tanjore was taken over from its princely ruler by the British, the devadasis had realised that their final bastion of royal patronage had collapsed. In a desperate bid to salvage their art and their positions there, they took to singing '*God Save the King*' in English, but history was against them, and so continued the decline of their ancient, somewhat decayed world.[22]

In Travancore the movement against devadasis had caught on early in the twentieth century, with first the dedication of girls before puberty to temples being disallowed, and then, in 1921, *all* recruitment prohibited by an absolute decree.[23] One cannot help but note in this a parallel with the demise of the matrilineal system that existed in Kerala, where also women were suddenly told that their breasts were meant to be covered, and not doing so meant they were unchaste; that the patriarchal ideal of the dutiful wife and mother was the pattern to live by; and that stoic widowhood was more becoming than the old polyandrous custom of taking, if they so desired, more than one husband. Nair girls did not dance and sing, but like the devadasis they too had enjoyed a social framework that offered them economic resources and freedoms; institutions that the new code of morality was determined to destroy.

It was Sethu Lakshmi Bayi who passed that historic legislation in the state by which matrilineal families were abolished and patriarchal nuclear households given a boost as an intellectual ideal. The Maharani herself was something of a reformer who had adopted Western codes regarding the 'proper' behaviour of women. While she had grown up watching nautch performances by devadasis and others at court, by the time she came to the throne this was disposed of and a more austere, Victorian ethic given the place of honour. She had imbibed notions of womanhood that were now celebrated and, in fact, became an exemplar of the ideal Indian woman. This was why the Valiya Koil Tampuran was allowed a status superior to what custom decreed him, and as one Resident noted, 'It is a matter of common knowledge that in the lifetime of the late Maharajah, he much disapproved of the Maharani Regent allowing [Rama Varma] to sit in her presence and to drive in the same carriage.'[24] On another occasion when she was informed that her husband did not enjoy precedence at court and would have to be excluded from certain functions, she refused to accept it, stating that 'the fact that he is my lawfully wedded husband and that our children are heirs to my family is all that is relevant to the question'.[25] Sethu Lakshmi Bayi was the epitome of the 'good' and 'devoted' wife, which is something even her worst critics admitted. One newspaper editorial that was otherwise ungenerous in holding her government to be full of 'administrative blunders' conceded that 'the people had genuine and natural love and loyalty towards [the Maharani] on account of her womanly virtues.' She was 'always a loyal and dutiful wife first and foremost' who 'subordinated everything else to her unfailing duty to her husband'.[26]

It was not especially surprising, then, that in 1930 Sethu Lakshmi Bayi during a visit to south Travancore balked at the prospect of being received at a temple by the local devadasis, who were now akin to prostitutes simply because their sexuality did not come with a marriage badge. She was 'vexed' to an extent that she 'commanded on the spot that the system should go'.[27] While her uncle proscribed the dedication of *new* devadasis in 1921, he had allowed existing participants to continue in service. The Maharani, however, put an end to even this, and no longer were these women to be seen in temples of the state. Their last day in that vocation was to be 15 August 1931, but in what was lauded as a generous move (by the puritans, since this was little consolation for the devadasis themselves), Sethu Lakshmi Bayi did not divest them of their incomes. 'Her Highness,' it was reported, 'especially commanded that the women should continue to enjoy all the perquisites and allowances due to them' during their lifetimes, so that they would not be forced to take to the streets.[28] As in Madras, here also the devadasis objected and tried their best to prevent the Maharani from actually terminating their way of life. It was unfair, they argued, 'to abolish their profession at the very moment in which women were being encouraged to enter the public domain through state support' by the very same Sethu Lakshmi Bayi.[29] But she was resolute and the reform was carried out, so much so that the forthcoming census report proudly, albeit somewhat indelicately, advertised that 'no woman has been returned as a prostitute' and that the abolition of the devadasi tradition had 'contributed to this happy circumstance'.[30]

She most likely thought of these women, in what was the general opinion those days, as sex workers. This explains why she did not otherwise mind women taking part in the performing arts; in the 1940s she would train her own granddaughters in dance and music. In 1928 the first Malayalam feature film, *Vigathakumaran*, was released in Trivandrum. The lead actress was P.K. Rosy, a Dalit woman, whose duties included not only acting but also 'cleaning up the kitchen and vessels' on the sets. However, when the movie was released, high-caste audiences were incensed at having to watch a low-caste woman on screen. 'They created a ruckus in the theatre, even burning down the screen.

Rosy was heckled and her family ostracised. Once, Rosy even survived an attack against her when she went with her mother to the Chala market.'[31] The Maharani promptly ordered police security for the actress, shocked at the horrific treatment to which she was being subjected.[32] While Rosy never acted again, Sethu Lakshmi Bayi's encouragement of cinema continued. She offered the makers of *Vigathakumaran* financial assistance for their next venture, a biopic on Martanda Varma. 'However [they] put forward only one prayer before the ruler—that [they] be granted the opportunity to perform the puja of the film box of *Martanda Varma* at the Sri Padmanabhaswamy Temple.' The Maharani 'not only sanctioned it, but assigned a portion of the cavalry to escort the film box, which was carried by an elephant, to the Capitol Theatre after the puja'. She also presented 'a sword with the royal emblem' to the lead actor, which became, apparently, 'the first award in Malayalam cinema'.[33]

If in the times of Gowri Lakshmi Bayi it was customary to grant government officials not only salaries and pensions but also female companions; by the days of Sethu Lakshmi Bayi even the last vestiges of this had been uprooted. But the cultural conservatism of the Maharani did not mean that she desired women to remain at home and withhold from participation in public life. While they were expected to be 'ideal' receptacles of the new morality, within those parameters she opened up spaces for them to occupy and to prosper. She herself, as successive Residents noted, always walked a step behind her husband and ensured that in all her meetings with men, he acted as chaperon. But in reality, she was more intelligent and capable than he was, and successfully negotiated that tightrope of running the government on the one hand, seeking his counsel on the other, but never offending his masculine ego. It was no surprise then that the cause of modern (patriarchal) women received an extra momentum during the Regency in Travancore, and unprecedented advances were made in a number of areas, including education, law, employment and more.

Perhaps the simplest indication Sethu Lakshmi Bayi gave of her support to the cause of female education was a plain but unusual incentive. In the mid-1920s much excitement was aroused in Trivandrum when it was announced that all girls who went to college in the state would automatically be rewarded with an invitation to join their queen at her palace for tea.[34] It was an attractive inducement, one that had its charms in a princely state with a popular Maharani who was perhaps the only 'celebrity' available at the time. However, Sethu Lakshmi Bayi backed such symbolic gestures by actual proof of her commitment to female empowerment. Only months after her succession, the Maharani had elevated Dr Mary Poonen Lukose, Travancore's first woman graduate and a product of one of the best medical colleges in the West, from being surgeon in charge of the Women and Children's Hospital and her personal doctor, to the head of the Medical Department of Travancore. The news was printed in the *Madras Mail* under the heading of 'Feminism in Travancore', not least because at the same time Dr Mary was also nominated by the Maharani as a member of the Legislative Council, becoming the first woman to a take a seat in the house. It was the first time in India that a woman was being appointed the head of a major department, and also the first instance of a 'Lady Legislator'.[35] When she took her seat at the next session of the Council, 'she was accorded an enthusiastic ovation and even after that there was a chorus of praise about the liberal and wise step' taken by Sethu Lakshmi Bayi in opening these doors to educated women.[36]

By 1928, the Maharani would nominate another woman to the legislature, one Mrs Elizabeth Kuruvilla, who would champion a motion to give equal chances to women in government appointments with men by the following year.[37] By 1931 the Sri Mulam Popular Assembly, which represented local needs of the various classes of people in Travancore to the government, saw its rules revised so as to allow women to become members and to vote. As many as five women were immediately nominated into the Assembly, but 'it is hoped', announced the Dewan, 'that at future sessions *elected* women will take their place', fulfilling the Maharani's 'solicitude to advance the cause of women and to give them their rightful place in the political life of the country'.[38] It was noteworthy that these five women belonged to various castes, high as well as low, in order to represent the needs of their respective sisters.[39] Earlier in 1927 the Maharani opened up the study of law to female students, despite adverse comments, so that in a few years the state had in Miss Anna Chandy 'the first woman judicial officer not only in Travancore but also in the entire Anglo Saxon world'.[40] She began practice at Kottayam, stood for elections to the legislature (and lost), and went on to become a criminal lawyer in the High Court in Trivandrum by 1930. The idea of a woman advocate drew much attention and also some scorn; in one amusing incident an ignoramus Brahmin was so astonished that he went around insisting that Chandy had to be a man in women's clothing 'since no woman could possibly argue cases with such ruthless vigour'! Yet there were also jealous remarks that she made use of her femininity to win cases, with one disgruntled colleague claiming: 'If I also wore a blouse and a sari, I would have won.'[41]

In 1927, Sethu Lakshmi Bayi raised the Women's College in Trivandrum from second grade, where it taught intermediate and 'ladylike' but professionally useless courses, to first grade, obtaining affiliation with the University of Madras and starting classes on history, natural science, languages and mathematics.[42] Trained lecturers and teachers from Europe were also acquired at considerable expense and brought down to Trivandrum. Not only were salaries high, but these professors were also given a number of other perks so as to induce them to stay on; a Dutch lecturer discovered to great happiness that she was entitled to a large bungalow ('the bedroom suite has three rooms'), one butler, one cook, one cook's assistant, two gardeners, one sweeper, one chauffeur, two personal servants, and even an ayah.[43] Soon there were 232 women going to college in Travancore, with over 9,500 girls in English schools. Two women were undertaking legal studies, and fifteen were studying medicine in Madras. Indeed such was the explosion in women's education that by 1928 about 450 qualified women were being churned out each year, and the Unemployment Enquiry Committee that the Maharani would constitute had, to the surprise of its members, to carry specific studies on the problem of female unemployment in Travancore.[44] 'A degree', it would note in its report, 'makes a daughter as valuable in the parents' eyes as a son', also expressing some amazement that women 'look for employment as eagerly as men do'.[45] By now the capital also witnessed the inauguration of a Travancore Lady Graduates' Association, which became a lobby group for educated women. In an address to elected representatives Mr Watts had to announce:

> The other day a deputation of young ladies waited upon me and unfolded their tales of woe. It would appear that there are no less than 30 or 40 qualified but unemployed women graduates in the State. The seriousness of the position is apparent from the fact that some have even migrated to fill appointments *outside* the State. It is true that women are freely employed in the service of the State as teachers and school inspectresses; as nurses, doctors and vaccinators. But it would seem that the time is come when other avenues till now monopolised by men should be thrown open to women. Women in Travancore hold a position of their own and so the Government have decided to throw open certain other appointments to them ...[46]

The promise was promptly acted upon. Women were soon being appointed as clerks, typists and secretaries in the posts, accounts and revenue departments, as well as at the High Court and in the government secretariat, hitherto the preserve of educated men with narrow communal loyalties. Earlier, in 1925 the Maharani had opened a special class for typing and shorthand in Trivandrum, so that even matriculates could pick up an employable skill, and indeed, by 1931, her government had on its payrolls not less than 412 women in the

Maharajah Ayilyam Tirunal. Though lambasted as a 'moral wreck and a sexual pervert', he was a great moderniser and patron of the arts.

Maharajah Mulam Tirunal of whose reign a bishop reported: 'Unworthy favourites rule and we hear of great scandals.'

Rani Lakshmi Bayi, of whom a French writer said: 'it is only in old Indian miniatures that I have had a glimpse of such princesses.'

Lakshmi Bayi's husband, Kerala Varma, the poet and scholar who was once jailed for treason, 'an inclination to Christianity' and a desire for 'stronger narcotics'.

Mahaprabha, Rani Lakshmi Bayi's niece, whose beauty and imperiousness spawned a family feud that would last generations.

Kuttan Tampuran, Mahaprabha's husband, a quiet, scholarly man, whose diaries castigate the Maharajah's slavish deference towards his favourites.

Raja Ravi Varma, the painter, with his attendant. Ravi Varma's unhappy marriage provoked a battle royale with political repercussions decades after his time.

Kochukunji, Mahaprabha's less attractive sister, with her husband, Bhagavan Tampuran. With a tendency to dabble in black magic, she and her children were considered a 'thoroughly bad lot' by the British.

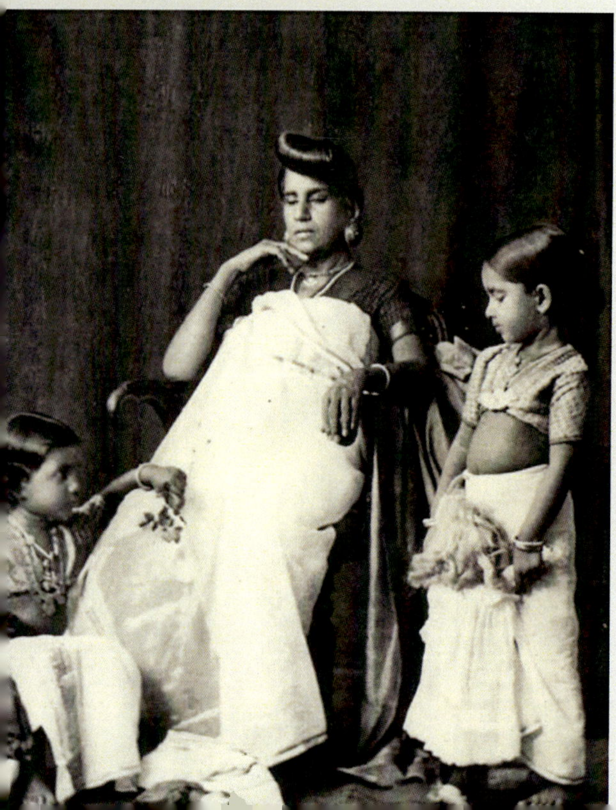

(Above) Sethu Lakshmi Bayi with her brother R.M. Varma, who features in Ravi Varma's famous painting, There Comes Papa *(1893), with their mother Mahaprabha.*

(Left) Sethu Lakshmi Bayi (standing) and Sethu Parvathi Bayi, daughters of Mahaprabha and Kochukunji respectively, before their adoption into the House of Travancore by Rani Lakshmi Bayi.

Kartyayani Pillai, after she was ennobled overnight as royal consort, in which role she had 'every incentive to be as fat as Nature may let her grow', a London magazine joked.

The Second Favourite, Sankaran Tampi, notorious as the 'former husband of the Maharajah's present wife' and the most powerful man in Travancore.

The scene before the adoption durbar in 1900 where Sethu Lakshmi Bayi and Sethu Parvathi Bayi became princesses of Travancore.

The Sri Padmanabhaswamy Temple in Trivandrum, the vaults of which hold fabled treasures beyond imagination.

Sethu Lakshmi Bayi with her husband Rama Varma, the Valiya Koil Tampuran, in a wedding portrait by N.N. Nampiyar.

Sethu Lakshmi Bayi after her installation as the Rani of Attingal, 'a land of Amazons' once ruled by a line of warrior princesses.

Sethu Parvathi Bayi with her husband Ravi Varma Jr, the Kochu Koil Tampuran.

Sethu Lakshmi Bayi in a 1910 portrait by Mukundan Tampi.

The Senior and Junior Ranis in their teens, on the eve of their great rivalry to produce the heir to the Ivory Throne.

Mahaprabha, in her later years, in a portrait by Mukundan Tampi.

Dorothia Watts, the Anglo-Indian spinster who became 'tutoress' to the Ranis.

Gowri Parvathi Bayi, the previous Regent of Travancore in the early nineteenth century, seen here with her nephew and niece.

Sethu Lakshmi Bayi, seen here with her daughter, came to be 'held in the greatest reverence and esteem throughout the State' during her Regency in the 1920s.

Sir C.P. Ramaswami Iyer, the famous Madras lawyer and one of the 'cleverest men in India' was a loyal supporter of the Junior Maharani.

The British Resident C.W.E. Cotton, who observed sharply happenings at court and the war between the Maharanis.

Mr M.E. Watts, the Christian Dewan in a Hindu state, whose appointment by Sethu Lakshmi Bayi provoked considerable agitation.

Rama Varma, his archrival the Junior Maharani, and the latter's son, Maharajah Chithira Tirunal. 'Nothing will,' bemoaned the Resident, 'terminate the feud between the Junior Maharani and the Valiya Koil Tampuran but the death of one of them.'

The Senior Maharani with her family in 1928. The British considered her 'a real little grande dame' and the 'best of the lot' in Travancore.

The Junior Maharani with her daughter and son, the Maharajah, in 1933. A 'more amiable Catherine de Medici', she emerged as the power behind the throne by 1932.

The Senior Maharani and the Valiya Koil Tampuran after the conclusion of the Regency in 1931. They went into retirement and led largely private lives with their daughters, the Second Princess Lalitha and the Third Princess Indira.

Princess Lalitha and her husband, whom she first saw on a street during a temple procession, in 1938.

Princess Indira with her first husband in 1945.

The Senior Maharani and her family in 1945, by which time they were entirely isolated in the corridors of power.

As the 1940s passed, the 'notoriously simple' Senior Maharani became disillusioned with the drama at court, and immersed herself in family and children.

The Junior Maharani remained at the helm of affairs in Travancore, though the British Resident remarked that she was really the 'villain of the piece'.

Princess Rukmini, Sethu Lakshmi Bayi's favourite grandchild, as an infant.

Rukmini (centre) with her sisters Parvathi and Uma in the late 1940s at Satelmond Palace, where their parents (below) spent their final years of royal life.

In Kodaikanal the princesses were sent to school for the first time.

By 1949, Lalitha, seen here with her family, transformed herself from Her Highness the Second Princess of Travancore to Mrs Kerala Varma of Bangalore.

In 1952, Indira left the 'golden cage' in Trivandrum and moved to Madras with her second husband, K.K. Varma, an industrialist and lawyer.

Lalitha's house on Richmond Road in Bangalore, which became a scene of many parties, Sunday gatherings and domestic bliss.

Lakshmi, Lalitha's fourth daughter, with the family pet, Rex. She would become the first member of the former royal family to carve out her own career.

Parvathi, Rukmini, and Uma in their teens in Bangalore in the 1950s.

In the late 1950s the Senior Maharani and the Valiya Koil Tampuran also relinquished the palace and moved to Bangalore. The Maharani gave up her string of titles, effacing herself into an old, story-telling great-grandmother.

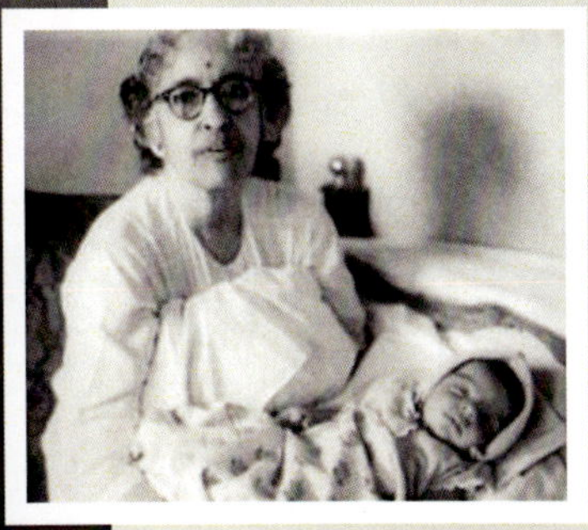

By the 1960s the Varma family was westernised and indistinguishable from the 'smart set' of Bangalore. Rukmini, Uma, Lakshmi and Parvathi grew into attractive young women, going on to lead independent lives. Their brother, Balan, was Lalitha's favourite, to whom the palace and life there were merely stories hesitantly told in the family.

Sethu Lakshmi Bayi and the Valiya Koil Tampuran after one of the Maharani's later birthdays.

Lalitha and Indira in the 1960s, which was perhaps the happiest phase of their lives.

Rukmini in 1976 at the opening of her London exhibition by Lord Mountbatten.

Sethu Lakshmi Bayi towards the end of her life, when she spent most of her time in a small room 'watching the dusk slip in and out of a series of windows'. (Below) From Satelmond Palace to No 7 Richmond Road: her final home.

The Junior Maharani on one of her birthday ceremonials at Kowdiar Palace, where she and her family (below) continued to live after Independence, largely in the old regal fashion.

Sethu Lakshmi Bayi and Sethu Parvathi Bayi, with the latter's children, in 1979 when they met after nearly twenty-five years of silence. They would never see each other again.

administrative machinery, excluding those who served as teachers and nurses.[47] It was not a large number in absolute terms; there were only twenty-five women for 1,000 men. But it was 'considerably better than in 1921 when there were no women employees at all', and a tremendous figure considering that other parts of India were yet to wake up to the potential of employed women.[48] Women's health also concerned the Maharani and two classes of midwives were opened so that by 1927 their services were being requisitioned 'even in remote villages' and one-tenth of all births that year could be handled in a professional and safe manner.[49]

Scholarships were granted to girls for advanced studies outside the state, but the proliferation of women's education under Sethu Lakshmi Bayi resulted in demand always surpassing supply of funds. One Janaki Amma wrote a moving letter to the Dewan stating that unless she could find money, she would be forced to return from the Lady Willingdon Medical School in Madras to her village and discontinue her education. The authorities could do little, as 'there are already two [girls] in the Madras Medical College and two in the Vellore Medical School for Women' and allotments had run out. Indeed, by 1929, there was such a surplus of lady doctors in the state that the board for scholarships 'do not consider it necessary to recommend any scholarships for medicine at present', since it would only add to the list of unemployed doctors in due course.[50] Yet applications came in, and one eighteen-year-old called V. Mary 'on bended knees' approached the Dewan to ask for a grant later that year. She was a Mukkuva girl, from the fishing community, demonstrating that across the board, interest in female education was steadily increasing.[51] Muslims, Ezhavas, Christians and others applied eagerly and it was telling of the kind of diversity in terms of caste as well as economic background when a typical board recommendation read how a certain applicant could receive funds 'similar to the one already granted to Amina Bee Sahiba or Miss N. Lakshmi'.[52]

Of course none of this was easy for the Maharani to champion, for there was a great deal of resistance also to progress being made. 'Our women who have received modern education are usually found negligent,' ventured a *female* columnist, 'in the performance of domestic duties. If a woman who has the fortune to be a wife and the mistress of a home surrenders the welfare of her spouse and children to servants and the preparation of food to hired cooks, then the home will itself suffer badly.' Another critic was even more vociferous: 'Respected sister! Have you ever contemplated on why we fuss so much over this totally meaningless higher education?' It was, in the view of this writer, also female, that 'As women, our god-ordained duty is the care of the home and service towards our husbands. Government service and political activity are beyond its purview.'[53] It was again merely a repetition of the new cultural outlook that women were meant to be devoted little homely creatures, caring for their husbands and children, their minds not meant to tackle any superior intellectual challenges. Officials too, despite the Maharani's policy, were unprepared when it came to conceding actual space in jobs to women. By the end of her reign it was universally lamented that 'the great majority of girls' regarded their education 'not as something of cultural value in itself but as a direct means of securing employment and competing with men in the open market'.[54] But even the most chauvinist male officers had to quietly adapt to the changes unfolding in their plain view, and affirm how it was 'quite in the fitness of things that this expansion of the scope of women's work in the public service should come while the country is being ruled by Her Highness the Maharani Regent'.[55] They may have cursed Sethu Lakshmi Bayi behind her back, but as always, once having made up her mind, there was no turning back and the cause of female education and empowerment continued ahead in full steam.

While Sethu Lakshmi Bayi was, thus, fully immersed in issues of state and policy, the Junior Maharani was not partaking in the forces of social and economic liberation her cousin was unleashing to such acclaim in the state. She was, to be sure, an ardent feminist and in 1928 presided over the Travancore Women's Conference, which Miss Watts had begun with her cousin's encouragement. But these were activities carried out on the side, for her singular purpose during these years was, one way or another, to secure the creation of a Council of Regency (with herself on it) or, were this not possible, discrediting Sethu Lakshmi Bayi till the British authorities compelled the latter to resign. Relations between the cousins had barely improved in the previous year, although at one point it came close enough. In October a venerable friend of the family, Nilakantha Iyer, arrived from Madras to negotiate a reunion between the two Maharanis. The Junior Maharani was prevailed upon to call on Sethu Lakshmi Bayi, her first visit in years, and the cousins spent an hour together. 'It remains to be seen how long these much to be desired relations will endure,' mused the Resident.[56] They did not, as it happened, last long. In November, for the Junior Maharani's birthday, she invited Sethu Lakshmi Bayi for dinner but 'omitted to invite the Valiya Koil Tampuran', essentially clarifying that her 'gesture of friendliness did not extend to the consort'. The invitation was declined, and the Junior Maharani 'has therefore become more bitter against the Regent and her consort'.[57] Peace between the palaces had lasted precisely one uneasy month and sometime later the Resident would report that while it was 'difficult to say who is most in fault' the 'Junior Maharani loses no opportunity now of backbiting against the Valiya Koil Tampuran'.[58]

Earlier that year the Junior Maharani had also left Travancore on a tour, ostensibly to find a new tutor for her son (and the expenses of these trips were another subject of disagreement between her and Sethu Lakshmi Bayi who never left the state during all her years in power). While the Resident had intelligence that she was again making an effort to submit a memorial to the Viceroy,[59] what interested him more were details of a meeting she had in Madras with some influential individuals who, she felt, might aid her in her mission. At a garden party thrown by the Junior Maharani, she met with two newspaper editors, Rangaswami Iyengar of *The Hindu* and one Mr Ramaseshan of the *Daily Express*. Sethu Parvathi Bayi began by lauding the latter for the interest his paper had been taking in Travancore, adding that she 'hoped he would not hesitate to criticise the present state of affairs'.[60] When the man said that everything was 'all that it should be' as far as he could see, the Junior Maharani darkly observed how 'From a distance that may be so, but at close quarters, from the inside, things have never been so bad.'[61] She then made an attempt to 'exact a promise of adopting a policy to attack the present administration and press for a drastic change' from both editors. Iyengar, reportedly, did not show any interest, while Ramaseshan refused to join because of his 'lofty sense of duty and responsibility'.[62]

As it happened, it was Ramaseshan himself who conveyed all this information to the Dewan and the Resident at the first opportunity he got, hoping that a financial contribution to his paper might follow as a reward. That was not to be, but his claims were 'singularly corroborated' by other sources, so that some worry was caused about what transpired. The idea was allegedly to project the Regent as 'gentle; wrapped up in home and children; practically gone into retirement; and wholly uninterested in the world or the State—and more absurdities. The stupidity,' Mr Watts remarked, 'I have made clear to Ramaseshan.' Then there was the Valiya Koil Tampuran who was the 'actual Ruler of Travancore' who had 'bought up the Dewan, who terrorises the officers; and so on.' Then came Mr Watts who was to be painted as quite 'unfitted for a big job' who 'meekly submits to the Consort' and was 'nothing more than a signing machine'. Even Mr Cotton was not spared and was accused of being 'hand-in-glove' with the

Valiya Koil Tampuran, while humiliating the Junior Maharani and her son.[63] The intended memorial recommended that Mr Watts should not be given an extension of tenure and that a Council of Regency ought to be set up as soon as possible in Travancore. Evidently, the conspirators even discussed names of potential members on the Council, with old Sir Vasudeva Rajah and the brother of the editor of *The Hindu* being offered for duty.[64] As usual, however, nothing came of these intrigues and although the Junior Maharani was 'very well pleased with the success of the tour', the Regency carried on and she was not a step closer to attaining her goals.[65]

Perhaps it was failure with political schemes that prompted partisans of the Junior Maharani to embark upon an unusual and positively bizarre strategy next in 1929: black magic. This was not the first time that such means were contemplated in the Travancore court. It was through black magic, many held, that Sankaran Tampi obtained his arresting control over the late Mulam Tirunal. Others whispered that Sethu Lakshmi Bayi's miscarriage in 1909 and subsequently also had sorcery behind it. The Junior Maharani's mother, Kochukunji, was known to dabble in black magic against Sethu Lakshmi Bayi, and the Resident recorded how she had 'had various objects, such as a bracelet, buried under the threshold of the Maharani Regent's door at the latter's Palace'.[66] This had occurred when the Junior Maharani was on tour recently, and although Sethu Lakshmi Bayi knew of this, neither she nor the Resident made much of it, dismissing the whole thing as first-class nonsense. But employment of black magic to destroy enemies was evidently popular enough as to deserve fairly generous descriptive space in the *Travancore State Manual* (1906):

> A very favourite form of *kshudraprayogam* (working evil with the aid of the low genie) is the burying of an earthen pot under the threshold of the house of the person who is the object of hatred. The pot is filled with human hair, flowers, charcoal, bones &c., and a small silver, brass, or copper plate inscribed with a diagram containing mystic letters to which *puja* has been made for a number of days, is always added, and sometimes an effigy of the victim as well. If the victim crosses or recrosses the threshold a number of times, it is believed that he will either be destroyed or paralysed for life or subjected to other incurable maladies.[67]

Kochukunji may well have consulted this official publication, and apparently the procedure could cost as little as Rs 28, with prices varying according to the extent of harm intended for the victim. However, the incident with the bracelet under Sethu Lakshmi Bayi's door was merely the understated initiation of a more elaborate scheme. It began when the Junior Maharani was in Calcutta where she evidently received a newspaper cutting stating that the Regency was expected to continue for another six years, which meant her son would receive his full powers only in 1935. 'This is believed to have decided her to try to put an end to the present Regency' through these sinister and remarkably dubious methods. She ordered Rs 2,000 to be wired to her brother in the palace, raising suspicion among her staff; generally the Junior Maharani was tight-fisted towards her siblings and the order now 'was so contrary to [her] parsimonious disposition'.[68] Around the same time intelligence was also received that Kochukunji was in correspondence with certain Brahmins in north Travancore who specialised in dark magic, spurring the initial gossip on the subject, even before the Junior Maharani had completed her tour.[69]

Soon after she returned to the capital, however, the aides de camp of the little Maharajah, one Kalinga Rayar and Goda Varma, reported that 'something sinister was afoot' and 'about a dozen' priests had been summoned to the palace for a twelve-day ceremony.[70] Through the palace physician, Krishna Pillai, it was found that precisely Rs 2,000 had been paid to the head priest, and that an additional (and princely) Rs 50,000 was promised by an unwritten 'contract', with the honour of a courtesy call to the priest's home by the Maharajah, should the ceremonies prove effective.[71] All of this, however, was little more than outlandish hearsay for the Resident, until the Junior Maharani herself brought it up in conversation. She told Captain Harvey, her son's tutor, how she had arranged for a religious ceremony to 'counteract the influence of certain stars' in her horoscope, and that during the twelve days of the puja, she would be unable to see him. And then, just as suddenly as she brought up the topic in the middle of their discussions on a completely different subject, she dropped it too.[72] The ceremonies commenced and details were reported to the Government of India:

> Either nine or eleven Nambutiri Brahmins have been housed in the Palace in strict secrecy for some 10 days past; their names are not known even to the Palace servants, and their wants are administered to by only two servants, one of whom is the servant of the [Maharajah's] uncles. The granite floor of the old Palace has been lifted and a square hole has been made in the bare earth. Ghee has been specially imported from North Travancore in far greater quantities than would be required for consumption. A maidservant has admitted to [Dr Krishna Pillai] that daily some 20 to 25 rats have been caught and handed over to the Nambutiries. The orthodox ADC [Goda

Varma], himself a Sanskrit scholar and philosopher, knows of no Hindu puja which demands this sacrifice, unless it be for some sinister purpose.[73]

Incidentally, the Dewan received information around this time that for black magic of this variety, 'a human sacrifice was a desideratum,' and that there could be 'attempts to procure a child for this purpose'.[74] Coincidentally, only two days later the child of a servant employed by a certain Narayana Menon suddenly went missing, but was quickly traced with three unidentified men on the road to Kowdiar Palace. Upon being apprehended they gave flight[75] but the boy mentioned how he was beguiled by a promise of sweets if he went with them.[76] To add to these mysterious happenings, it was then reported by Captain Harvey that the Maharajah had, during lessons, raised a few questions about the effects of black magic and 'his almost excited belief in its efficacy is not to be doubted'.[77] On questioning the Maharajah why he was suddenly so interested in such a subject, Harvey discovered that he was aware of the puja and displayed 'some fear' and it was clear 'that he knows it is sinister in some degree or other'.[78]

The 'orthodox' ADC Goda Varma also overheard some of the mantras being recited and promptly reported that 'either madness or death is intended for the person against whom the puja is being held'.[79] The manager of the Maharajah's retinue, Subramania Iyer, was also perplexed; normally he was informed about functions in the palace, and indeed it was he who made necessary arrangements. But this time he had been kept entirely in the dark.[80] It was also a matter of suspicion that the Junior Maharani, 'never backward in making demands of money', did not this time apply to use Civil List funds, using instead her personal money.[81] All in all, it was clear that something peculiar was transpiring at Kowdiar Palace, and it had little to do with maligned stars in the Junior Maharani's horoscope. 'Whatever we Europeans may think about "black magic",' the Resident noted, 'there is no doubt that what has been going on has very seriously affected the Palace' and, in what was worrying, 'is beginning to be known outside that circle'.[82]

By this time Mr Cotton had retired as Resident in Travancore and it was a Lt Col Charles Gilbert Crosthwaite who took up the post, with the current happenings being his maiden initiation into local intrigues. He was not, however, a novice, having previously been the Resident in Gwalior. Here too there were two warring Maharanis with a minor Maharajah; the Senior Maharani was the childless widow of the last ruler, while the Junior Maharani was the mother of the heir. The former was a 'warm and engaging woman, popular alike with officials and sardars' while the latter was 'a strong-willed woman, prickly over questions of protocol, and given to fits of temper and prolonged bouts of sulks whenever she felt that her wishes were thwarted' and who resented the Senior Maharani.[83] Mr Crosthwaite, then, was no stranger to the machinations when royal women set themselves against each other, and could take a clear view of things. His concern about happenings in Kowdiar Palace, thus, were not about the effects of the sorcery under way but other more human possibilities:

> ... there is not unnatural fear lest the very heavy reward [of Rs 50,000] for favourable results might lead to poison being administered or other direct actions taken by the priests to implement the [promises made through] magic rites. In fact the responsible officers of the Junior Maharani's palace are afraid of some terrible catastrophe for which they may be held partly liable, and His Highness' Private Secretary, a retired Brahmin Dewan Peishkar [Subramania Iyer], has suddenly taken leave of absence, which is ascribed to a fear of these doings. I understood from Harvey and Kalinga Rayar that Mr Watts has had an interview with the Maharani Regent and has informed her of what is taking place.[84]

The information received from palace sources was that the precise objective of the ceremonies was 'to end the present Regency by the death of Her Highness the Maharani Regent' and to keep the young Maharajah 'in temperamental subjection to his mother and her family as long as possible' by causing 'mental derangement' so that he could be dominated and 'his mother may become the Regent'.[85] 'A precedent of the efficacy of such pujas,' mentioned Mr Crosthwaite, 'is alleged in the case of the Junior Maharani's husband, who is somewhat mentally deficient,' with his condition being 'ascribed to the Junior Maharani's machinations'.[86] While this was all held to be irrational nonsense, what concerned the Resident, the tutor and the ADCs was the unusual nearness of the Maharajah to his maternal uncles, for these brothers of the Junior Maharani 'bear by no means good characters'.[87] It was also clear that they were the 'instigators of the puja' and the boy had to be somehow extracted from their negative influence.[88] To Mr Crosthwaite there was 'no doubt' at all that 'the Junior Maharani's family—her mother included—are a thoroughly bad lot'. The 'Junior Maharani herself,' he added, 'I am afraid bears none too good a character and there are more than one or two scandals regarding her, which, however, I perhaps need not repeat here.'[89]

It was then decided to expel the uncles of the Maharajah from Kowdiar Palace and for this, the Resident asked Mr Watts to arrange for them to be sent to meet with him in Peermade. This alarmed the Junior Maharani who sent her secretary to see Mr Watts and find out what Mr Crosthwaite had in mind. He reassured the secretary that he probably merely wished to speak to them in person so that things could be settled 'quietly and informally'.

> I also told [him] that the Junior Maharani might seriously consider terminating those secret ceremonies ... immediately, and even before they would ordinarily conclude. To this he remarked that it was not at all impossible. Similarly, I also said Her Highness might consider whether it would not be advisable for her to forestall any formal advice or instructions to that effect by spontaneously preventing her brothers from going to Kowdiar Palace or otherwise having access to the Maharajah ... [The secretary] agreed with me that it is very undesirable that these Uncles should associate with His Highness ... [Even the ADCs] were emphatically of the opinion that the three brothers who had practically taken possession of Kowdiar Palace should be kept out of the place, and should not have any access at all to the Maharajah.[90]

But despite instructions from the Resident for the brothers to see him as soon as possible, it took a number of days and another set of urgent telegrams for them to at last arrive on 25 February. In his report on the meeting to the Dewan, Mr Crosthwaite included minutes of the conversation he had had with all three men. In rather firm words without beating too much around the bush he made it clear that

> I do not wish to trouble the Junior Maharani by having to write for definite instructions to the Government of India that you are not to go to the Palace, and I hope you will carry out my wishes. This is a serious matter and if I have to bring it to the Government of India's notice, it then remains on record, and I am sure that the Junior Maharani would not wish any record should remain with the Government of India, that you or your mother or your sisters should not go to the Palace, and particularly the old lady, your mother. I hope you quite understand that you are not to go to the Palace without first of all getting an invitation from the Junior Maharani, and my approval.[91]

Through all this Sethu Lakshmi Bayi, despite being one of the alleged victims of the ceremonies being held, had not betrayed too much concern. She may not have been surprised, given the previous attempts at black magic by Kochukunji, and all the stories she had heard for years. But in this particular case, she was happy that the sixteen-year-old Maharajah was not involved in scheming against her. 'Her Highness does not seem to be unduly worried about the matter' and in fact 'seemed pleased', noted the Resident, 'when I informed her that His Highness the Maharajah in all probability was unaware of the exact object of the puja'.[92] She was, however, perturbed by the attitude taken by Mr Watts. Despite express orders that the Junior Maharani's brothers be sent to see the Resident before 23 February, so as to prevent completion of the puja, the Dewan, who had also thought it acceptable to go on holiday to Ponmudi, arranged for them to reach two days late, by which time all the ceremonies had concluded. Later when the Junior Maharani wrote to the Resident to ask if one of her sisters could continue to stay in the palace, Mr Watts sympathised officially, so that Sethu Lakshmi Bayi curtly wrote to him how 'I can think of no instance in the past when the Dewan interceded with the [Resident] in a personal matter of the Junior Maharani's'.[93]

The Junior Maharani, in the meantime, was incensed by the order to have her family expelled from Kowdiar Palace, and came out with a vehemence against all of her staff who had passed on information to the Resident. Her principal grievance was against the tutor, Captain Harvey, asking in an interview with Mr Crosthwaite if he would put up with such insubordination and backstabbing by one of his staff.[94] The Resident, who had decided to close the black magic episode without a formal inquiry, consequently found himself in a difficult position to discuss the reason for Harvey's concern openly with the Junior Maharani. It was she, in fact, who decided to bring up the subject and in her conversation with him 'she mentioned the "rumour" of the Black Magic Puja and pooh poohed the idea, saying how could such things be in the twentieth century!'[95] She also admonished the Resident with a polite threat for taking action against her brothers. 'I feel confident,' she elaborated, 'that on reflection you will perceive the wisdom and expediency of personal and confidential discussions on such matters with me before advising or acquiescing in any action. I therefore have purposely refrained from formally addressing [the Viceroy].'[96] It was an empty threat, as Delhi was already contemplating action that was to be hugely unpalatable to Sethu Parvathi Bayi.

But Captain Harvey was to suffer as were both ADCs. The servants 'are being prompted to be insolent to them in the hope of some retaliation', and when soon the Junior Maharani and her son left for their annual retreat in Ooty, they were informed 'somewhat discourteously' by a house servant 'that they are to enter only one room in the house taken by His Highness and the Junior Maharani i.e. the dining room, and to wait there until they received their orders'.[97] Captain

Harvey, however, was willing to pick a fight if necessary and when reproached by the Junior Maharani, listed a number of his own grievances about her, including about her visit to the home of a male friend with the Maharajah and staying there for hours without the ADCs.[98] Not that this meant anything but 'in my opinion,' wrote the tutor, 'it simply won't do with a man of his reputation and the stories that have been so long current'.[99] Concerns of this nature had troubled the Resident also and on the eve of the Junior Maharani's departure for Ooty, he wrote with some exasperation to the Government of India how the friend in question 'will probably be in and out of their house all day', adding: 'I regret to say that his name has been, for some 18 months past, coupled with that of the Junior Maharani, and a good deal of scandal has been caused thereby.'[100]

The incident of black magic and these reports about the Junior Maharani caused the authorities in Delhi to take stock of the situation. The Political Secretary wrote secretly to the office of the Governor of Madras, essentially with a request to spy on the Junior Maharani and her friend. 'Reports,' he began, 'which we are receiving couple his name with that of the Junior Maharani of Travancore, which appears to have caused a certain amount of scandal.' It was probably a friendship, for the Junior Maharani was unorthodox and did not subscribe to old-fashioned notions of keeping a distance from male company. 'Unfortunately, the young Maharajah of Travancore, who is the son of the lady in question, is in the position of "ward in chancery" so far as we are concerned, and we may have to take somewhat drastic measures in order to protect his moral and material welfare,' if there was really a fire behind all the smoke of gossip about Sethu Parvathi Bayi.[101] In other words, the Government of India held themselves responsible for the Maharajah's upbringing, and while his mother was free to have friendships were she a private individual, as a Maharani, it was unbecoming of her to be so careless and in allowing indiscreet rumours to surface.

Within two weeks the Governor's office responded stating that the gentleman and the Junior Maharani had definitely been seen walking together and driving in the same car, but beyond that there was nothing to worry about. He did have something of a reputation, because of which the Maharajah's mother being seen with him caused a little scandal, but 'There appears to be no reason to suppose that the liaison between [the man] and the Junior Maharani is having any evil influence on the Maharajah—in fact it is understood that he dislikes it.'[102] Either way, however, the Viceroy and his advisers decided that perhaps it was time that the Maharajah was removed from the company of his mother. Writing to Mr Crosthwaite they pointed out that 'it seems desirable that he should leave the

State for some period' and that 'the question of his administrative training', which would ordinarily have commenced in the following year, 'be considered *now* instead of next year'.[103] This would also mean that a special tutor would need to be found so that in addition to lessons given by Captain Harvey, the Maharajah could have detailed training in administrative affairs also.

It was a can of worms waiting to be opened. Musing on what was inevitably going to happen, the Resident remembered the words of his predecessor on the same subject, which succinctly expressed what concerned him as well:

> When it comes to the selection of a suitable tutor, the chief difficulty will, I fancy, prove to be the Junior Maharani's anxiety (however cleverly she may attempt to camouflage it in conversation) that the officer appointed shall have no influence whatever over her son. It was Mr Dodwell's inability [he was the tutor before Harvey] to secure any such influence that reconciled her for so long to his continuance as tutor. Her antipathy to the Maharani Regent has become an article of faith with her, and she is afraid that the Maharajah, if disinterestedly advised, may recognise the futility of the feud between the two Palaces, and realising the greater virtues of his aunt, end by sending his mother to Coventry.[104]

And this, they felt, was something the Junior Maharani would never allow.

11

In Letters of Gold

Despite the bitterness in Mr Watts's relations with the Maharani, in April 1929 the Resident noted how the former 'hopes against hope' that, by some change of heart, he would be offered another tenure as Dewan.[1] It was a deep sense of denial about the inevitable; Mr Raghavaiah too had harboured such thoughts after his fallout with Sethu Lakshmi Bayi. To put an end to wishful speculation, the Maharani made it clear that she had already decided on her next minister and that there was no question whatever of Mr Watts continuing beyond June. The man was, Mr Crosthwaite said, 'considerably chagrined', and 'inclined to look upon the termination of his time of office as an injustice'.[2] Furthermore, he 'ascribes the termination of his Dewanship as being due to the Valiya Koil Tampuran'. Indeed the latter's opponents 'allege that unknown to Her Highness, he takes money for appointments made in the State'.[3] In some quarters it was rumoured that the new Dewan-to-be, in fact, owed his confirmation to Rama Varma alone, with one (Nair) canard telling how another (Nair) candidate missed out simply because he was an hour late in showing up with a suitcase bursting with cash.[4]

Resigned to his fate, then, Mr Watts spent his last weeks in Travancore receiving addresses from the public and well-deserved encomiums, including, ironically, from his worst enemies. They were not moved by sympathy at his fall but saw in supporting him yet another avenue to manifest their displeasure with Sethu Lakshmi Bayi. In the words of the Resident, 'Meetings were held and addresses given to Mr Watts, not so much from admiration of the latter as in order to demonstrate against the Maharani.'[5] Curiously enough, these were by 'the very same people who were most hostile to Mr Watts and "the Palace" on

Mr Watts's first appointment, and who, since Mr Watts's differences with Her Highness became well known, have allied themselves to Mr Watts. The latter,' he commented, 'should have known better than to encourage these demonstrations, but in spite of his decided astuteness and ability, he allowed his vanity to get the better of his commonsense.'[6] Mr Watts, once lambasted as the Mussolini of Travancore, was now lauded as a 'people's Dewan' mainly because in his unhappy relations with and subsequent departure from Sethu Lakshmi Bayi's court, he offered ample resources of political capital to be reaped by her rivals.

But the Maharani did not contest that, despite his headstrong propensities, in Mr Watts she did have a good public servant, with his heart in the right place, even if his mind and overblown eloquence sometimes carried him away. He too, on the eve of his departure, realised that while acrimony had raised its head in his relations with Sethu Lakshmi Bayi, on the whole his term in the state had been rewarding and that together, they had been able to achieve much for Travancore and its people. He was in a sentimental mood as he boarded his ship from Bombay, writing to the Maharani a most gracious letter of thanks:

> Your Highness did me a very great honour in selecting me for the Dewanship, and that I can never forget or fail to appreciate at the fullest. Your Highness trusted me and believed in me, and I have throughout in thought and deed sincerely tried to prove myself worthy of that trust. In serving Your Highness I have never given self a thought but have always striven to conduct the administration under Your Highness' control, so that Your Highness' people may feel, now and for all time, that the period of Your Highness' reign is one signalised by justice, sympathy, and single-minded effort to ensure the well-being of Your Highness' country. Of Your Highness personally, if I may say so without offence, I have never abated my admiration. So too my goodwill and high regard for Your Highness will never weaken. I pray that peace and health and happiness may be with Your Highness and Your Highness' family. ... And I can never forget the deep concern and sympathy Your Highness and Your Highness' Consort have extended to me when trouble overwhelmed me and when illness befell me.[7]

Sethu Lakshmi Bayi too was considerate in bidding Mr Watts well and convinced the Government of India to allow her to settle on him the highest pension possible at £300 per annum. This delighted Mr Crosthwaite who wrote her a warm letter stating how 'I have always felt sure that you would do that which was right'. 'Your Highness' decision showed,' he added, 'a most forgiving and noble hearted, sweet disposition, as I am well aware that Mr Watts during his last year of office behaved in an impossible manner towards his Ruler.'[8] Life in England did not promise to be easy for Mr Watts. His much younger wife had left him for someone else and afflictions of illness were starting to show. To help him, the Maharani then granted a bonus of £1,000, which again surprised everybody. This latter gift was also, interestingly, proof that for all the incessant gossip, when it came to real decisions, her husband did not possess as much influence, as was ordinarily believed. 'I know,' confirmed the Resident, 'the Valiya Koil Tampuran would never have allowed her to give it if he could have helped it.'[9] A grateful Mr Watts picked up his life in London, but his health deteriorated, until a few years later, in 1933, he died of his illnesses. All public offices and institutions in the state were that day closed as a mark of respect and in memory of the contributions he had made to the progress of Travancore.[10]

And indeed, Sethu Lakshmi Bayi and her Dewan had achieved much in only a few years' time. Plain numbers, more than anything else, revealed the extent of their accomplishments, establishing Travancore as one of the most prosperous and leading principalities in India. When the Maharani succeeded to power in 1924, the treasury commanded revenues of Rs 199 lakh; by 1929 this mounted to Rs 256 lakh, which was a 28 per cent increase, or a little less than one-third, in only five years—an unprecedented rate of progress.[11] The value of trade in the same period rose from Rs 13 crore to Rs 21 crore, while the government's cash balances escalated from Rs 74 lakh to Rs 170 lakh.[12] Prosperity was conspicuous even in the daily lives of ordinary citizens who had better roads, more amenities, higher incomes, new conveniences and so on. 'In the fullness of time,' lavished one tribute, 'Her Highness can look back with pride on her disinterested labours for the country and its people, the results of which she could, by the grace of God, see the people themselves reaping.'[13] The Maharani deserved 'special congratulations in so far as at no period in the history of Travancore were so many schemes launched with so much grit and boldness as at present'.[14]

Whether it was the opening of all but the temple department to all castes and communities, or in creating spaces for women to prosper, or even in matters of religious or social reform, Sethu Lakshmi Bayi had shown herself, with the assistance and energy of Mr Watts, as exceptionally able. Specific sectors attracted her especial attention, in all of which she left enduring legacies. Infrastructure was one such area. While in 1924 it had a budget of Rs 30 lakh, in 1930 over Rs 62 lakh would be invested in roads, bridges, irrigation and more.[15] While Travancore altogether had about 5,000 miles of roads, the length of main roads jumped from 2,874 miles in 1925 to 3,252 miles in 1930.[16] The Maharani built two particularly important highways during this period, namely one from Quilon to Cochin and another from Cochin to the plantation district in the east. The former for the first time provided a land route from Cape Comorin, at the tip of India, along the coast to Cochin,[17] but it was the latter that had even more economic advantages. Hitherto tea, coffee and products from the high ranges left Travancore by going east into the Madras Presidency; the new Neriamangalam–Pallivasal road allowed it to be transported instead to Cochin Harbour, another of the Maharani's accomplishments.[18] A bridge of superior technical quality was built at great expense across the Neendakara Bar, and numerous similar, smaller projects were taken up as well. Existing roads were widened and new ones built so that in 1926 alone 200 miles were constructed and in 1928 another 135 miles added. By the end of her regime, leaving aside reserved forest lands, Travancore had at least one mile of modern roads for every square mile of territory.[19]

The idea of bringing rail transport to the coast had first come up in the 1880s, but orthodox Brahmins decried the 'fire carriage' as the instrument of the devil, raising a shrill hue and cry so that it would be 1903 before a train chugged into the state. Even then the late Mulam Tirunal 'refused to allow it to desecrate Trivandrum'[20] and it was left to Sethu Lakshmi Bayi to erect the Central Station in the capital and to extend the line into the city.[21] Even though the Maharani did not undertake further expansion to avoid indebting the state during an interim administration, she did allow groundwork to proceed and surveys were conducted to extend the railways south into Nagercoil and north towards Cochin, and by 1929 special staff were constituted to formulate estimates and plans.[22] The policy of spending large sums on repair works of buildings was terminated and allotment under communications swelled in general, so that from Rs 10.2 lakh in 1925 it would rise by 162 per cent to Rs 26.7 lakh by 1930.[23]

Telephones, in what was a novelty, were made available to the public, especially to the benefit of traders and merchants in Alleppey, Cochin and Trivandrum. It was early in 1910 that the Indian Telegraph Department set up the state's first connection, but under the Maharani services were thrown open to the people. In collaboration with the Chicago Telephone and Radio Company, eighty initial connections were set up in Trivandrum.[24] Similarly, the implementation of a water and drainage system in the capital had been pending for half a century, until in 1928 it was finally implemented, after the Maharani gave it the stamp of official approval.[25] Experts were deputed to study similar schemes in other major Indian cities, and construction would begin in 1931 with the Willingdon Water Works inaugurated by 1933. Built at a substantial cost of Rs 50 lakh, and to cater to the estimated population of 1961, this was a major achievement of the government.[26] As one press eulogy went, 'the Regency period will ever be remembered for [the] amenities of civilized life' introduced to the people by Sethu Lakshmi Bayi.[27] Along with the bridges she built and highways she laid, they would emerge as 'monuments of keen political farsightedness and high statesmanship of a lady' who got 'these begun and completed as early as possible, with a view to facilitate [sic] trade and commerce' and a better standard of living for her people.[28]

In February 1929 while Kowdiar Palace was deep in the darkness of black magic and sorcery, Trivandrum was illuminated in light when, for the first time, electricity arrived in the state. On 25 February, when the Resident was admonishing the Junior Maharani's brothers in Peermade for their misdoings, in Trivandrum the lights were switched on for the first time 'in the presence of a distinguished gathering', with 541 street lights and two maiden private consumers receiving six hours of power in the evening.[29] By 1930 the power station would be capable of handling greater demand and the capital had nearly 1,000 street lights, and 375 private and 113 government consumers with twenty-four hours of supply.[30] Visitors were surprised to see even small alleys well lighted, and by 1931 electricity projects commenced in Kottayam, with plans drawn up for other major towns like Alleppey, Nagercoil and Quilon also. The blueprints of what would later become the Pallivasal Hydroelectric Scheme were also initiated at the same time.[31] The onset of electricity in Travancore, in addition to the other modern facilities made available now transformed the capital. 'The immaculate cleanliness of the city with its red sand streets, its well-kept houses, its inhabitants dressed entirely in white, the parks of its palaces, and the brilliant gardens' impressed Maurice Dekobra,[32] while Louise Ouwerkerk thought 'the people looked prosperous and contented' with their lives under a well-run government.[33]

Medical facilities in the state were also improved under Sethu Lakshmi Bayi, with expenditure under this heading nearly doubled. Dispensaries proliferated the country and a new cooperative scheme was initiated, where the government contributed the medicines and other supplies, while villagers offered the necessary infrastructure. 'In all these places' one report states, 'the local people came readily forward and gave requisite furniture and suitable buildings for the dispensaries.'[34] By 1929 not less than 1.65 million of the total five million subjects of the state were in a position to access the government's health amenities and the modern medicines they supplied.[35] In addition to the existing Medical Department, the Maharani also created a Public Health Division that was to deal especially with epidemics, maternity, child welfare and other broader issues that were not so far given due importance. In 1928 this was begun in collaboration with the Rockefeller Foundation, and two officers were sent to train in the United States, later to return and take over the new section.[36]

Agriculture, on which 54 per cent of the state's population depended, also witnessed an impressive scale of developments. The cooperative movement flourished at an unusual pace and it was 'gratifying', the Dewan declared to the Sri Mulam Popular Assembly, that 'the *ryot* and the small industrialist have begun to appreciate its advantages'.[37] By the end of Sethu Lakshmi Bayi's reign there were nearly 2,000 cooperative societies at work in Travancore, with one for every 2,245 of the adult population of four million.[38] The number of joint stock banks in the state catering mainly to agrarian families grew to 275, by the end of the Maharani's reign, so that in 1932 Travancore accounted for 20 per cent of all banks in India.[39] While the idea of bringing 25,000 acres of virgin land under tea cultivation through the Brooke Bond Scheme did not succeed, between 1925 and 1932 what did succeed was the husbanding of a tremendous 87,000 acres of forest land due to the efforts of the Maharani's government.[40] Revisions in the law were implemented to make things easier for farmers in these tracts allowing them to 'cultivate land assigned to or acquired by them without fear of eviction or harassment from collecting officers' through protective clauses.[41] Although since 1904 taxes were no longer accepted in kind, when floods occurred in Kuttanad, the Maharani first reduced the commutation rate from twenty-four chuckrams (a denomination of the local currency)[42] to twenty chuckrams, and then to eighteen chuckrams. However, when stressed farmers conveyed that it was easier for them to pay in paddy, despite objections from officials that this would be inconvenient administratively, 'No considerations of such difficulty were allowed to stand in the way of affording relief to the people,' and they were permitted to remit taxes in whatever form possible at the already discounted rate.[43]

On the other hand, a reversal of taxation in kind was proclaimed on the Crown lands of the Maharajah and on the Sripadam Estate of the Maharani, which together covered 35,000 acres, having thousands of tenants. Although government revenue had for decades been collected in cash, due to customs and tradition, rent on these private lands of the royal house continued to be required in kind. The system, however, was fraught with corruption and difficulties, and farmers were often forced by tax collectors to give them commissions and cuts over and above due rents. Eight hours before the birth of Princess Indira in 1926, Sethu Lakshmi Bayi had put an end by a special proclamation to this, therefore, and a money rent, well below the market rate, was fixed in place of paddy. In taking this decision she was 'fully aware of the loss' to the royal family's coffers, especially to the Sripadam treasury that covered her personal expenses. But she was 'not actuated by a meticulous balancing of profit and loss' as much as by the goal of giving relief to her tenants, and the new measure was promptly implemented.[44] 'This great agrarian reform,' one fortnightly would remark, 'has been reckoned as an achievement of far-reaching importance and is the best evidence of the sympathy and beneficence of Her Highness the Maharani Regent' who was hailed for her 'large-hearted and broad-minded policy' for mass welfare.[45]

Education was another department that received special focus. Already in 1925 it was noted that there was one primary school for every 1.9 square miles of the country, and for every 1,000 heads of the population.[46] The allocation for this rose from Rs 35 lakh in the first year of the Maharani's government to Rs 49 lakh by 1930,[47] so that 'of all the provinces and states of India, Travancore' commended the Resident, 'spends the largest percentage of her revenue on Education'.[48] The 'special' schools that existed for backward castes and communities were brought into the mainstream by 1928, and a new policy was formulated where schools received aid only if they freely admitted students irrespective of social background. 'The rapid growth of literacy in Travancore and Cochin began only after the complete removal, in the late 1920s, of the caste restrictions on admissions to primary schools.'[49] Midday meals for children from poor families was implemented and this was responsible 'for the rapid increase in the voluntary enrolment in primary schools', also giving a boost to literacy and its spread along the coast.[50] Since 68 per cent schools in Travancore were privately run, a system of grants-in-aid was put in place where any expenses above incomes of upto 50 per cent for boys' schools and 75 per cent for girls' schools was provided by the state. To ensure that the teachers taught well, lesson plans were sent out regularly from the capital, and teachers' organisations were encouraged. Salaries were increased, so that headmasters received anywhere between Rs 200 and Rs 300 per month, while teachers made from Rs 25 to Rs 120 per month.[51]

In Mr Watts's words, 'The Government begrudge no money to the schools, for nothing but good can come of universal literacy in the State and there can be no question but that a widely spread middle school education operates to the advantage of every branch of human activity in a civilised State.'[52] Indeed, such was the degree to which education had caught on and become a medium of social and economic advancement that

> ... the cult of the shirt [of the educated man] is an inexorable bar to manual labour. Every boy fixes his eye on a college degree or a school final certificate; and fond parents are ready to sacrifice all, thus, to equip their sons for Government employment. So we have an army of graduates and certified youths besieging the Government for appointments. Hence the cry of unemployment.[53]

Unemployment was not a problem with educated men alone, but also with rising numbers of women, and soon after the Maharani opened up the legislature to women, the ladies were also 'agitating for the gates of the Municipal Councils' to be thrown open, 'as also the offices of Bench Magistrates in the Village Panchayat Courts'.[54] But because Travancore was hideously communal in its politics, unemployment only led to greater divisions in society, and distributing opportunities and vacancies in the state administration had to be done as fairly as possible. The Maharani had already been practising this policy, despite its unpopularity with dominant castes, but in 1931 work began on constituting a Public Service Commission, which would go on to be established in 1932 for a proper system of job allocation.[55] Sethu Lakshmi Bayi, however, protected the minorities, who reciprocated with gratitude. 'We have only to say,' one eulogy went, 'that the rights and privileges of all classes of Her Highness' subjects are safeguarded, and justice between man and man [is] meted out by Her Highness most fearlessly.'[56]

The Maharani also enabled a greater democratisation of the manner in which the government functioned, involving as far as possible members of the public in running even important departments. In 1926, for instance, she reorganised the Economic Development Board (EDB), which was hitherto a panel of bureaucrats, into a body with five officials and seven non-official members, of which four were elected by the legislature from among the people's representatives, and three nominated by the government from among distinguished members of the public.[57] The Medical Department, similarly, was also reconstituted by 1927 so that two official government doctors led it alongside one non-official doctor with the aide of a bureaucrat secretary. This way, one member could always travel, inspecting health facilities even in rural parts of the state, while other affairs of the department did not suffer.[58] It was a rather bold experiment at the time, with many critics saying that such a way of running the government was unheard of. But it proved a success. 'The association of a non-official in the management of an important department,' the Dewan would proudly declare, 'is an innovation in Travancore.'[59]

Similarly, since Sethu Lakshmi Bayi was widening and improving infrastructure in the state, it was felt that the system of sequestered bureaucrats in the capital taking decisions from afar needed to be ended, and the public allowed to guide them in using scarce resources as best as possible. By 1927, a Central Road Board was constituted in Trivandrum, with 108 subordinate local boards, all of which included on them private citizens.[60] The principle behind this was to marry 'official experience and local knowledge as well as wishes of the people's representatives' in determining where the people wished to have roads and bridges built.[61] Local councils and other bodies were encouraged to construct small roads on their own, 'the department merely advising alignments and constructing bridges and culverts'.[62] But cooperation between the public and the government was the ingenious rule, and 'The question of future road development' would depend on these 108 boards and their studied 'deliberations and recommendations' that enabled the government to spend its public works budget as wisely as possible, while satisfying local needs.[63]

A number of important legislative measures such as the epochal Nair Regulation, the Ezhava Regulation, the Nanjanad Vellala Regulation and the Malayala Brahmin Regulation were passed by Sethu Lakshmi Bayi, 'calculated to advance the social and material interests of important sections of the people'.[64] Counted with economic and other reforms passed by the 'socially enlightened' Maharani, these would all become part of a 'long list of liberal changes' that 'influenced and enforced schemes that became catalysts for vast changes in social structure in the successive generations'.[65] For all this, Sethu Lakshmi Bayi's name rose to tremendous heights in India as an exemplar of good administration and wise public policy, not to speak of fearless social reform. That is why when late in 1929 the Viceroy Lord Irwin came to Trivandrum, in what was also an endorsement of the Government of India's staunch support to the Maharani, he declared in an open address his pleasure that he was visiting 'at a time of unexampled prosperity in the state', adding:

> I think, I may safely say, that during Your Highness' five years of Regency, the highest proportion of advancement has been seen [in the entire history of Travancore]. Your unflagging devotion to State affairs, your personal attention to every detail of the administration, and your constant desire to treat all communities in the State alike with fairness and impartiality have borne the richest fruit in the contentment of your people.[66]

He then invested the Maharani into the Order of the Crown of India, an honour that was 'given but rarely and only given in cases of outstanding achievements' to the leading female dignitaries of the British Empire by the British King Emperor.[67] It was, in its day, the highest decoration for women, counting among Indian recipients the Begum of Bhopal and the Maharani Regent of Mysore, both distinguished women administrators, and in Europe a number of members of the British royal family as well as illustrious ladies who had excelled themselves in public service during the Great War. But Lord Irwin was not the only Viceroy to sing Sethu Lakshmi Bayi's praises; years later India's last Viceroy and the final representative of His Britannic Majesty, Lord Mountbatten, would extol the Maharani's 'quiet elegance, her innate dignity, and the fact that she endeared herself to one and all. No one who had ever met her,' he would say in London, 'could ever forget her. She stands as a shining example to womanhood as a great queen and as a great woman.'[68]

Sethu Lakshmi Bayi, with all her old-fashioned modesty, did not make more of such praise or imperial baubles than necessary; as her adoring daughter would later tell,

> She was truly a person of high thinking and gracious living. She used to be praised for her extraordinary beauty, her position, the power she had then wielded in just the correct way—the list seemed endless, but all this did not impress her in the least. She never thought there was anything out of the ordinary about herself. It was as though she were asking, 'What is there to be praised because one is not a bad individual?'[69]

But those around her thought it eminently well merited in recognition of her hard work and untiring efforts to rule well. 'She deserves it,' wrote a Women's College lecturer in a private letter. 'For sheer devotion to husband, children, and country, it would be hard to find her equal.'[70] A prominent journal circulated among princely states similarly remarked how the Regency, far from being 'a period of marking time, which most people feared it might be', had been one of 'quiet but incessant activity, calculated to forward the welfare of the people in every way'.[71] That is why Ulloor S. Parameswara Iyer, the poet laureate of Travancore and a leading intellectual of the times, was believed when he declared that the days of Sethu Lakshmi Bayi's government would 'be recorded in letters of gold by the future historian of Travancore'.[72]

A few months before Lord Irwin's visit to Trivandrum, a Dutch lecturer called Louise Ouwerkerk was appointed to teach at the Women's College in Trivandrum. A lady of impressive personality, with an incisive approach to local politics, she took an interest in chronicling contemporary Travancore, which she would later compile into a stimulating manuscript. With no reservations in expressing inconvenient opinions about the state, she would fall out of favour with the government when the Junior Maharani's son came to power some years down the line. But early on, she was to record her first impressions about the land and its feuding royal family. Her views about Sethu Lakshmi Bayi were positive, but writing about the Junior Maharani after their first meeting, she expressed more mixed feelings in a candid letter to her mother:

> I was going to tell you about my visit to the Junior Maharani and the Maharajah. She is the younger cousin of the Regent, on whom I have already called, and owes her prestige to being the mother of the Maharajah. What rivalry exists between the two is obvious from the nature of the case; the Junior Maharani has no power now but oh! Won't she get her innings in a couple of years' time when the little boy comes of age! So she is carefully tying him to her apron strings in preparation for those glorious days. She is an ardent feminist, lively, well read, talkative; and she pinned me down in my chair and fired question after question at me concerning the State of Things in England. She pumped me from 7:45 am to 9:15 am, and sent me away longing for my breakfast and horribly conscious of having talked a lot of drivel in order to satisfy her thirst for blood. And all the time the poor little Maharajah was sitting fidgeting on the edge of his chair listening to his mother saying simply dreadful things about men. I caught his eye once or twice and he smiled weakly, but he is used to that sort of thing. She tries it on everybody she can get to talk about the subject. Nonetheless, I did really enjoy that interview, being brought up against a remarkably lively and penetrating mind, and getting a chance moreover to discuss the College with someone who will have immense power in a couple of years' time. Miss Gomey, freshly returned from Oxford with a large crop of Western ideas, had an interview with her the next morning and said exactly the same things I had been saying ... the little Maharajah himself is highly intelligent when Mama is out of the way.[73]

While the Junior Maharani's electric energy and enthusiasm made an impression on Ouwerkerk, the latter's remarks about her rapport with her son were not flattering. But it was a view that corresponded with opinion even in high places, and many felt the Maharajah for his mother was merely a means to satisfy her own ambitions. The occurrence of black magic, with the alleged objective of making the boy as dependant on her as possible, did not help her case, and both his tutor, Captain Harvey, as well as his private secretary informed the Resident of their judgement that 'the Junior Maharani is obsessed by the idea that she must maintain control over His Highness, not so much from the point of view of a mother's desire to control her child, but from the view of a woman of the world determined to maintain her control over a future Maharajah of Travancore'.[74] This was not entirely outlandish, and elsewhere in India also, the British had to grapple with women in the zenana attempting to control minor princes for purposes that could be antithetical to those of the Paramount Power.[75]

For over two years now the Junior Maharani had been attempting to obtain some clarity on her son's future political position, and when the galling Regency might end. In August 1927 Mr Cotton had noted with amusement how the Nairs were 'cock-a-hoop' with joy because the Maharajah's mother had successfully secured a meeting with the Viceroy in Ooty and, reportedly, 'got all she wanted out of him'. Rumour at the time had it that it was 'only a matter of weeks' before the Government of India ordered Sethu Lakshmi Bayi to relinquish absolute power and accept a Council of Regency.[76] As it had really happened, however, the meeting between Lord Irwin and the Junior Maharani had been strictly formal, with Mr Cotton present. 'She only had almost a quarter of an hour with His Excellency,' he reported, 'and spoke about her son's education and the date on which the Regency was likely to terminate.'[77]

She also submitted a memorandum with ideas on his administrative training in the future, but more importantly, received considerable bad news from the Viceroy. The Government of India had enunciated a policy along with the body known as the Chamber of Princes that young Maharajahs ought not to receive full powers at the age of eighteen. As Mr Cotton was informed, the authorities were 'averse to giving powers to a young prince before he is 19 ½ at the earliest'.[78] So when Sethu Parvathi Bayi asked Lord Irwin whether she could presume the Regency would terminate in 1930 when her son turned eighteen, 'I told her she could not,' noted the latter in his minutes, 'and that the general policy of the Government of India was to defer grant of full powers till 19 ½ or possibly 20' years of age.[79] In other words, the Regency was to continue in Travancore beyond 1930, at least until August 1932, when the boy Maharajah turned nineteen-and-a-half-years old.[80]

This information troubled the Junior Maharani, for it extended her cousin's reign by nearly two years, and she argued that it could lead to friction between her son, who would resent his powers being withheld, and the Regent. But the argument was not accepted. 'Regencies are seldom if ever popular,' Mr Cotton observed, 'and when as in Travancore, the Maharani Regent is not the mother of the minor Maharajah, the Junior Maharani, who is without any authority, is not unnaturally impatient to see her son invested with ruling powers, and encouraged by those interested in widening the breach between her and the Regent, to exaggerate the anomaly of her position and the disabilities under which she and His Highness labour.'[81] Moreover, before the Maharajah could assume control of the state, he had to become independent and obtain sufficient training in matters of governance. This would mean removing him from the Junior Maharani's household once he grew up, and 'If [she] protests, as she almost inevitably will, the obvious retort is that a Maharajah who cannot be allowed out of his mother's sight is obviously unfit to be entrusted with the responsibilities of a grown man.'[82]

Accordingly, in January 1928, the Junior Maharani was officially informed, further to the Viceroy's verbal confirmation, that her son would be installed and the Regency concluded, only in August 1932 after he had turned nineteen-and-a-half 'as the experience of the Government of India has shown that the earlier age of 18 puts too severe a tax on youthful discretion and capacity'.[83] Confidentially, Delhi also informed the Resident that after the Maharajah's administrative training began, 'he should be provided a separate establishment and [should] no longer live with his mother'.[84] By August 1928 the Resident conveyed both these points to the Junior Maharani, and informally also let Sethu Lakshmi Bayi know.[85] This is a crucial point, as years later partisans of the Junior Maharani would insist that it was intrigue on the part of Sethu Lakshmi Bayi that led to the extension of the Regency, whereas the fact was that both women were informed at more or less the same time about this decision taken unilaterally by the Government of India in pursuance of a general policy.

The Junior Maharani, however, was determined to try and do what she could to prevail, and to bring about her son's installation at eighteen. While individuals like Sir Vasudeva Rajah, and later even K.M. Panikkar, had been assisting her in representing her views to the Government of India, in 1927 she had formed a friendship with a phenomenal lawyer and luminary of that generation, Sir C.P. Ramaswami Iyer. And it was he who, more than anyone else, proved to be of real service to her. In the words of a future Resident, he was a genius who would 'talk the hind leg off a horse' and one of the 'cleverest men in India'.[86] Born in

1879 into a Tamil Brahmin family in the Madras Presidency, he followed in the footsteps of his father and entered the legal profession, where his rise was 'breathtakingly meteoric', allowing him to become one of the wealthiest and most sought-after lawyers of the Madras High Court.[87] 'Forty-two minutes, my Lord,' he once announced to a judge who asked him how much time he would need to finish a case.[88] Soon he was elected to the Legislative Assembly and also became a member of the Executive Council of the Governor, and such were his first-class brain and formidable intelligence, that in the future he would be nominated as a member of the Viceroy's Executive Council on two separate occasions.[89]

Sir CP, as he was popularly known, had several old connections with Travancore. He had fought high-profile cases for the government and the late Maharajah, but his interest now in championing the cause of the Junior Maharani was seemingly triggered by a combination of mutual friendship and personal ambition. As early as January 1928 it was revealed that the Junior Maharani had secured his assistance 'in preparing a fresh memorial' against the Regency, and there were rumours that he was 'anxious to come to Travancore as Administrator [i.e., Dewan]'.[90] In the words of a biographer, 'prolonged, intense lobbying and long, complicated manoeuvres' commenced soon after he became interested in the Dewanship at some point in the 1920s.[91] It seems likely, for Sir CP was extraordinarily rich in this period, and his 'weakness', in the words of a contemporary, was 'for power and fame, and not money'.[92] With his shrewd far-sightedness, he might have perceived a better opportunity in becoming Dewan when the Maharajah came of age, than now, when an interim administration was in place. Either way, he accepted the Junior Maharani's cause with pleasure and applied his formidable energy to realising her wishes. In fact so allied had the two become in recent times that in 1928 and 1929 the 'friend' connected by uncharitable gossip with the Junior Maharani, and to whom Captain Harvey had taken exception while the Government of India clandestinely ordered a report, was none other than Sir CP. And indeed, throughout their association, scandals and rumours about there existing a romantic liaison would hound them. These were probably 'completely unfounded' but as the aforementioned Louise Ouwerkerk would remark, 'the political fact was not their truth or untruth but the fact that they were universally believed'.[93]

In 1929, after the black magic episode, it was decided to remove the Maharajah from 'the somewhat doubtful influences prevailing in his mother's Palace'.[94] While ordinarily he would have commenced his administrative training towards the end of 1930, this was now brought forward, and detailed plans began to be drawn about how his time would be employed until 1932. There were not inconsiderable fears that the Junior Maharani would 'object most strenuously' and 'try to enlist aid from whatever quarter she can'.[95] But the Government of India had made up its mind, also clarifying that there was 'no question' of the Maharajah's mother accompanying him during his period of training.[96] Several pros and cons of the proposal, however, had to be borne in mind seriously. The points in favour of sending him away were, in official records on the subject: '(1) the recent "black magic" affair; (2) the liaison apparently existing between the Junior Maharani and Sir CP [Ramaswami] Iyer; (3) the general desirability of giving the boy a new outlook on life'.[97] On the other hand, there were also concerns that the Maharajah was not yet seventeen, and removing him from his familial environment could backfire. But in the end, whatever was to be decided, 'it seems clearly desirable', noted the Political Secretary, 'that the Maharajah should be separated from his mother's influence for a time'.[98]

The Junior Maharani, embarrassed and aware that the black magic incident had really pulled her down in the estimation of the authorities, tried now to present a good and positive impression, so that during her meeting with Mr Crosthwaite to discuss her son's training he noted, sarcastically, that she was 'affability itself'.[99] She promised to send him in writing her views on the subject within ten days. But this, incidentally, was merely an attempt to buy time. For at the same time plans had been made for Sir CP to travel to England and raise the Junior Maharani's case with none other than the Secretary of State, the British Cabinet minister responsible for India, who was, in a way, the Viceroy's boss. Since Lord Irwin was not amenable to her representations, it was hoped that his superiors could perhaps be persuaded otherwise, and to grant a verdict in favour of the supplicant. As it happened, news about this reached Sethu Lakshmi Bayi through one of Sir CP's aides in Bombay who claimed to know 'what has transpired in Ooty and Bangalore [where meetings had been held between the Junior Maharani and Sir CP], and what is likely to happen in England'.[100] The Resident too received information that a withdrawal of Rs 50,000 from the Junior Maharani's bank account when she was in Bangalore was in order to fund this commission to London and back.[101]

While all this occurred at the end of August 1929, on 5 September the Junior Maharani wrote to Mr Crosthwaite asking for another ten days to allow her to convey her views on her son's administrative training.[102] This was granted, but the Resident reported to the Government of India that the request was mainly due to the fact that she wished to consult Sir CP as to what she should say; her letter had reached him just as he was leaving for England and she had to wait for his response to be posted from Aden when his ship, the SS *Cravocia*, docked there.[103] By 17 September, Mr Crosthwaite had still not heard from the Junior Maharani, and after a gentle reminder, she finally sent him her memorandum on the Maharajah's education. She felt that while there was no 'insuperable objection' to his going away from Travancore for some time, it must be temporary, extending only two months at a time, and altogether not lasting more than six.[104] She claimed to have more ideas, which she promised to express in person to the Viceroy when he was to visit later in the year, but she did point out, aware that a separation from her was in contemplation for her son, in the interim that

> ... I must insist that there should be no break in the continuance of family and maternal influences and company on His Highness at a time when deleterious and extraneous influences are likely to be prevalent and harmful. I must also make it quite clear that without motherly watching over his health and welfare and moral upbringing, anything may happen to him between now and his assumption of Ruling powers.[105]

In other words, the Junior Maharani very much intended to be with her son while he trained outside the state so as to prevent bad influences affecting him, even as the Government of India held her to be a source of such influences. The Resident thanked her for her views, without committing to subscribe to them.[106] In the meantime Sir CP's mission in London had proved to be a comprehensive flop, and the Secretary of State did not reverse the Viceroy's decision. 'All the influence he could exert in New Delhi and Whitehall could not effect a speedy termination of the Regency,' in the words of a biographer,[107] and far from putting a speedy end to Sethu Lakshmi Bayi's rule, the Viceroy, who was also in London at the time of Sir CP's mission, visited Trivandrum later that year and publicly endorsed her work and her government, besides investing her with the insignia of the Order of the Crown of India. As for the Junior Maharani's views on her son's training, 'little or no consideration' was ordered by Delhi to be paid to it,[108] and her demand that he should not stay away for longer than six months was turned down.[109] Permission, however, was given for him to be able to visit his mother now and then, but certainly not at the two-monthly intervals that the Junior Maharani had in mind. And even decisions regarding these meetings would be taken in Delhi.[110]

As the mission to London had failed, and since it was now official that the young Maharajah would receive his powers only in 1932, Sir CP and the

Junior Maharani in haste began to devise other measures to somehow prevent the Regency from continuing beyond 1930. In November 1929, therefore, another memorandum was prepared by the former 'at the instance of and under instructions from Her Highness the Junior Maharani' and given to Mr Crosthwaite.[111] Beginning with a description of the adoption of the two cousins in 1900, it told how the Junior Maharani had two sons and Sethu Lakshmi Bayi none, 'so that it may be said that the future succession would normally be in the line of [the former's] descendants'.[112] Pointing to Hindu law, it was argued that the Maharajah had actually already attained majority at the age of sixteen, but since eighteen was now universally held as the age of adulthood, the Junior Maharani acquiesced to this. However, when he did turn eighteen, the Maharajah would be the senior male member of the royal house in effect, and 'will be entitled to the rights and privileges appurtenant to the headship' of his family, 'this being quite irrespective of any conventions or rules that may be formulated by the Paramount Power with reference to the conferment of powers of administration on a young Ruler'.[113]

In other words, while the Government of India had decided to withhold the grant of power till 1932, the Maharajah would in fact become an adult in 1930 and was to take over rights of headship in his family from Sethu Lakshmi Bayi, even if he did not enjoy sovereignty. This being the case, it was argued, 'arrangements might be and should be made by which, the Regency being terminated, a transitional system should be devised whereby, while the Maharajah's legal position is recognised, yet in actual administration he does not exercise plenary powers, but acts either through a Council of Regency or in such other manner as may safeguard those wider interests which the Paramount Power has been accustomed to keep in view'.[114] Sethu Lakshmi Bayi, it contended, ought not to have objections, as in any case she initially expected to rule only till her nephew turned eighteen. Besides,

> One cannot ignore the disequilibrium and embarrassment, to say nothing of other practical consequences, that would flow from the fact of one branch of the family, with no immediate or prospective reversion to the throne, exercising ruling powers, while in strict theory of law and by long usage, such powers inhere in a person belonging to another branch.[115]

This was something of a bizarre proposition, as while Sethu Lakshmi Bayi did not have sons and, therefore, no immediate successors to the throne (after herself) she did have daughters, whose sons would in fact be prospective heirs.

That is why the Political Secretary in Delhi in any case did not bite the bait and refused to entertain hopes of a 'transitional system' or a Council of Regency. It seemed to them that since efforts to secure an early succession for the Maharajah had failed, the Junior Maharani was again attempting to have a Council constituted. By January 1930, then, the authorities wrote to the Resident about the lines along which their decision was to be conveyed to the Junior Maharani:

> I am to explain that the ordinary rules of succession under Hindu Law do not apply in the case of jurisdictional States, and His Excellency has accordingly decided that the existing Regency arrangements in the State should continue until the Maharajah himself is invested with powers in August 1932. His Highness should, however, be assured that the delay in granting him his powers after he has attained the age of 18 years is not due to any action or influence on the part of the Maharani Regent, but is in pursuance of the general policy of the Government of India not to grant powers to young Princes until they have reached the age of at least 19 ½ years.[116]

This decision was despite the fact that yet again a memorial by a group of Nairs had been submitted against the Regency. Nothing new was stated in this, so that it too would meet the fate of previous representations in being thoroughly ignored. The gist, however, was that the ever-hectored Rama Varma was 'an impecunious adventurer' whose 'towering ambition' and 'passion for official recognition' had entirely disabled the government. With 'spying watchfulness', he coerced his wife, who was always frightened and careful not to 'make any statements beyond what she is tutored to make' during meetings with the Dewan or the Resident.[117] Mr Crosthwaite, who was already tiring of intrigues, dismissed it as another ploy by 'these Nair agitators' to make trouble just before the Viceroy was to visit the state.[118] Moreover, the memorial seemed to him particularly mischievous in its timing, for it was in many ways an expression of support to the Junior Maharani's own memorandum, also claiming that after the Maharajah turned eighteen the Regency should be ended and that a Council of Regency appointed in its place.[119] As usual, then, the Resident exonerated Rama Varma, simply stating that he was an honourable man targeted always on account of there being no other legitimate handle for airing imagined complaints and grievances against the Regency. Far from being the tyrant he was painted to be, the hawk-eyed Ouwerkerk too would remark, if there was 'one person worth a brass button' between officialdom and the Resident in Travancore, it was the Valiya Koil Tampuran.[120]

12

Mother and Son

The rise of Travancore in the eighteenth century was received first with shock across the Kerala coast, followed by inconceivable dread. The Portuguese and Dutch had drawn the wind out of the Zamorin's sails, leaving him a wistful shadow of his former glory in the north. In the centre, Cochin had become 'less a dependency than a mere proprietary estate' of its consecutive European sponsors.[1] The south was, until the first quarter of that century, a mishmash of chiefdoms of the Kupaka family, when the fearsome Martanda Varma overwhelmed them. Their lands were subsumed into his modern state of Travancore, which for the first time marched armies trained in European style, with mercenary support from outside, firing English weapons, and trained by Dutch deserters. Old Nair chieftains were disempowered and robbed of real power, and a bureaucratic network designed by Tamil Brahmins was developed to run this unprecedented political enterprise. Martanda Varma had a remorseless tenacity for success, before which the listless Rajahs and aristocrats of Kerala could but gasp and crumble.

But the storm of war had inevitably to be followed by peace and conciliation, where also that founding Maharajah of Travancore proved a genius. Save for some distant (though by no means unique) glory of descent from ancient kings, this dynasty had little, beyond recent and brutally unleashed violence, to boast. The old nobility of the land had suffered under its military excesses and the kingdom was cloaked in the blood of the ancien régime Martanda Varma vanquished. The much-touted dedication of his conquests, then, to Sri Padmanabhaswamy, offered for the first time a singular identity to Travancore in a day and age when nationalism was not yet conceived. 'Like most of the other new rituals of state, [this too] was,' Susan Bayly remarks, 'essentially a new event in which fragments of traditional Malayali ceremonial were blended with the ruler's own inventions, and with symbolism borrowed from the Tamil country and from the Maratha domains.'[2] Even as the Zamorins helplessly squandered their ancestral pre-eminence in Kerala, an emerging Travancore overcompensated through its excessive demonstrations of piety and theatrical ceremonial, cementing their new-found primacy at the apex of the coastal polity.

Legitimacy, as always, necessitates recognition from the highest social ranks, and in Kerala this meant the acknowledgement of Travancore as a lawful, sanctified principality by Brahmins. In the Deccan, the great Maratha warrior Shivaji had obtained such sanction from the 'twice born', and Martanda Varma too secured it through expensive ceremonies such as the hiranyagarbha. As a *class*, though, Brahmins required more inviting incentives to invest Travancore with their socially rewarding blessings. Since migrant Tamil Brahmins had been invaluable to the construction of the state, primary benefits were offered them, first by the opening of numerous feeding houses, maintained at public expense, serving free meals. In 1842 it was estimated that some twelve lakh meals were disbursed from these *oottupura*s, and by the end of the nineteenth century these establishments would cost nearly Rs 4.5 lakh to maintain. In 1909 some 8,000 Brahmins were being fed daily by the state.[3] Slowly, but steadily, positions in the administration also followed as a more tangible reward. Travancore became famous as a 'Land of Charity', which of course meant charity for Brahmins and not for the general needy. And little over a century later this would cause much discontent among other classes, who found that the free provision of meals to Brahmins amounted to something of a government subsidy, freeing them from the punishing difficulties under which others languished unfairly. 'By Brahmins,' the *Madras Standard* would vehemently note in the 1880s, 'we simply mean those classes which are sucking the life blood [sic] of the country,' adding that it was a mistake for the government to 'encourage a class of indolent and unscrupulous Brahmins ... to fall back upon it for support and existence'.[4] This disgust towards the Tamil Brahmin had emerged even during the lifetime of Martanda Varma, with one of his court poets composing with undisguised revulsion:

Rice and curd and plantain fruit,
Are mashed into a pulpy mess.
With this they stoke themselves,
In a squelchy, slimy, ghastly way.[5]

Unlike *foreign* Brahmins, however, the Malayali Brahmins demanded a rather more refined strategy than such obvious charity, for they were a landed class, affluent and without need for money in a conspicuous fashion. To satiate them and to win the badge of being ardent protectors of the Hindu faith, a number of public ceremonies were then instituted. It was a fact that the most distinguished Brahmins of Kerala resided not in Travancore but in Malabar, in the dominions of the Zamorin, and so Martanda Varma worked hard to attract them to him. He first convened a conference of 'all the learned Brahmins of Malabar, Tinnevelly, and Madurai', and at their recommendation instituted the *murajapam*.[6] 'It was not only a religious expiation for the atonement of sins involved in the spilling of human blood, the conquering of less powerful neighbours, and robbing them of their land and goods; it was also in the manner of a peace offering, a political concession to the barons and the landlords of the subdued principalities and a bid for the transfer of their allegiance and fealty to a better king on more favourable terms.'[7] Beginning in 1751, once every six years Malayali Brahmins were invited to Trivandrum to recite Vedic mantras at the great temple there for a stretch of fifty-six days, during which time Tamil Brahmins were kept out of their way. They were feasted and feted, and with corresponding expenses to the exchequer, championed the cause of Travancore as an ideal Hindu state with a most devout royal family.[8] Sins of the past and the inadequacies of pedigree were cast aside, thus, through a 'new court culture and new rituals of state, which served to assert and dramatize' Travancore's monarch and his newly cemented principality.[9]

It is no wonder, then, that nineteenth-century state patronage was most readily disbursed among Brahmins, for the very founding of Travancore was married to such policies. In the words of one historian, the state was 'in fact a Tamilian conception and its advancement towards the north was the victory of Tamilian over Kerala culture', promoted by Martanda Varma 'in the interests of his dynastic ambition'.[10] A creature of Brahminism, that class were the natural beneficiaries of the Government of Travancore. On a wider scale, though, due to its claim as a generally Hindu state, the Nairs too were granted secondary benefits within the system, though nothing like their past status. The demilitarization of Travancore following Velu Tampi's rebellion and the imposition of British supremacy, however, meant the Maharajahs were forced to, all the same, implement a modern meritocratic administration and dish out welfare schemes so as to keep the English East India Company at bay. Indeed, at one time it was openly proposed that the Brahmin feeding houses be converted into 'open workhouses' and that the murajapam be transformed into a 'Grand Exhibition of products, arts, and manufactures' of Travancore.[11] Such schemes did not materialise, and Martanda Varma's defining rituals were to continue, even though by the end of the century, English education, which officially qualified individuals for state patronage, began to spread outside the elite Brahmin and Nair communities, with results that could not at first have been anticipated. Robin Jeffrey describes the position succinctly in a comparison between the situations in the nineteenth century and in the early decades of the twentieth, by which much had changed in local society:

> In Travancore in 1847, it was as if the various groups were seated at a table with stacks of poker chips in front of them. Nairs had more than most others, while Malayali [and arguably Tamil] Brahmins had so many that the ensuing 'game' lacked interest, and they disdained to play at all. For others, however, there was no option but to play. In the course of the game, new rules were made, new chips came into play, and the value of some of the old chips was drastically reduced. By 1908 when the players looked up to take stock, they found that the chips in many cases had been redistributed. Some groups [like the Ezhavas and Christians] had gained from others or had won some of the new counters. Other groups found that not only had they lost chips but some of those they still held were either worthless, or, indeed, carried a penalty.[12]

Behind all this were several forces. The Maharajahs, whose ancestors had fought hard to elevate them to semi-divine status, desired to sustain that position; the British wanted to see modernisation and progress, with all its physical manifestations; and all at once, Christian missionaries from elsewhere were educating the lowest caste groups and telling them they deserved better. Society was simmering, with the royal family swaying atop this wobbling edifice that was officially determined to continue as a 'good' Hindu state. The global economy also began to change the dynamics of caste and politics. The Ezhavas saw the value of their coir products more than double in the last decades of the nineteenth century. In 1870 the Resident would record how they were in the past 'prevented ... from keeping milch cows; from using oil mills, metal vessels, umbrellas; from wearing shoes and any but coarse cloths and ornaments'.[13] As late as 1884 the Ezhavas would complain that they 'are not allowed to come near any public office whether it be of the 1st Class District Magistrate or [the lowest] of the tax collectors. They are put to the greatest inconvenience whenever they use any of the public roads, inasmuch as they have to move a considerable distance away from high caste men whom they meet on the roads. They have, in speaking to people of higher castes, to use certain technical expressions, which if they do not, they are taken to task for it. There are many [Ezhavas] in the state but not a single one of them has ever had a situation under government.'[14]

Yet, 'By the turn of the century a few Ezhavas,' despite being an inferior caste technically, 'owned coir factories, while Ezhava women who collected and sold coconut shells for fuel earned more than enough to feed their families.'[15] The activist C. Kesavan would remember how his mother in the 1890s employed three or four weavers and joined them herself; along with a little farming and the incomes brought in by her two husbands (who were brothers), they had enough to raise a family of eight children in relative comfort.[16] Into the twentieth century, an economic and socio-religious movement made them strong enough to demand more rights. Their cultural magazine, *Vivekodayam*, had as its motto, 'God helps those who help themselves,' marking out their aspiration and optimism. In 1905 they would organise an industrial exhibition in Quilon, attended by 3,000 people, to showcase the products their community brought out and to stimulate pride in their economic potential, also throwing in a Sanskrit recitation contest.

> The exhibition had a wide impact. C. Kesavan, then a boy of thirteen, wrote a vivid four-page account in his autobiography nearly fifty years later. He recalled the dress of the leading men: their dark suits, long coats, and turbans. It was rare then, he wrote, for an Ezhava even to wear trousers; the honourable dress was a single cloth around the waist and another draped around the shoulders. He remembered also the typewriter, which he saw for the first time, the skilful exhibits of the Ezhava craftsmen and agriculturalists and the resentment of [upper caste] Hindus at such Ezhava pretensions. As a result of the meeting and exhibition, he wrote, Ezhavas began to awaken.[17]

Such was the electric mood created by this movement that in the same year riots were provoked between the Nairs and Ezhavas when the former objected to the women of the latter, with their new-found confidence, covering themselves above the waist in the upper-caste fashion. But the Ezhavas were undaunted. They became the driving force behind the satyagraha in Vaikom in 1924–25 and in the future would push the government to open even the gates of the most hallowed temples to them on a basis of equality. By Sethu Lakshmi Bayi's time, there were over 27,000 workers employed in coir factories in the state, most of whom were Ezhavas, not to speak of the nearly a quarter million people who were connected to the industry through forward and backward linkages.[18] As Jeffrey continues,

> While Nairs acquired BAs and BLs [i.e., degrees], scrambled for the [state] services, formed genteel associations (usually, one feels, with Cobden and Bright strongly in mind) and *preached* about the dignity of labour and the need for social reform, without doing much about either, necessity forced the Ezhavas into more practical organisations. In spite of their crumbling institutions, Nairs could still afford to *play* at social reform; Ezhavas could not.[19]

Syrian Christians too prospered at the same time, while resenting official state policy of denying them many rights. Their faith gave them an affinity with the British masters of India, and through modern education and by taking enthusiastically to new economic opportunities, their wealth and influence grew each year. Yet when one of them in the early 1870s returned eminently distinguished with degrees from England and sought a job in the government service, he was turned down. Officials, it was made clear, had 'duties connected with temples' and so only high-caste Hindus could be appointed.[20] In 1895, similarly, it was shown that of the eighteen magistrates appointed in the previous eight years, only five were Christians, all of whom drew not more than Rs 70 per month, while Nair and Brahmin magistrates were paid not less than Rs 125. Of the 5,850 jobs listed on the government rolls, only 174 belonged to Christians, while of the ninety-one prized positions that offered more than Rs 200 per month, they only held five. In 1898 when the head of the Medical Department appointed two Christians who had returned following advanced studies in Scotland, he received a stern note from the Dewan asking him to cease all further hiring.[21] Since official patronage was not a reliable option, trade, plantation, business and so on brought to the Christians higher incomes and aspirations for a better social status. By the beginning of the twentieth century, Nairs, with their relentless tendency to persist within 'the unyielding shell of custom'[22] were selling land injudiciously to maintain their old way of life in a socio-economic system that could no longer sustain it. This in turn benefitted affluent Christians and, to a smaller degree, Ezhavas. The Nairs were horrified and,

> ... for the Syrians to point to their prosperity merely alarmed western-educated Nairs and made them cling more tenaciously to their remaining privileges under the [state]. Where Nairs were losing land, Syrians were

> acquiring it; where Nairs were plagued by litigation, indolence, and [problems of the matrilineal] taravad, Syrians were experimenting with banks, joint stock companies, and cash crops.[23]

With Sethu Lakshmi Bayi's passage of the historic Nair Regulation of 1925, a longstanding demand from the Nair community itself, ancestral property could now be partitioned. But if it were expected to free Nairs from the grip of custom and give them the wings to flourish, it did not succeed entirely. Unable to come to terms with their diminishing social position, alienation of property continued; in the fifteen years that followed the Nair Regulation, 45 per cent of all property sold came from Nair hands, while most buyers were Christians and Ezhavas.[24] This was a culmination of a long process. Early in the twentieth century, a Nair leader noted with resignation how travelling in north Travancore, 'I was surprised and not a little concerned, to observe that not a single patch of wasteland was being cultivated by a Nair. From one end to the other, the hillsides, from top to bottom, were all aglow with cultivation. But it was the hand of the industrious Native Christian or Ezhava that was at work, and the Nair—he was nowhere. I was informed that all the land once belonged to him. But now it has flown out of his hands into those who deserve to keep it.'[25] 'The Nairs: Do They Rise or Sink?' asked a 1905 headline of the *Malabar Herald*, and as Robin Jeffrey notes, while they 'did not plunge to the bottom of some social and political sea', it was apparent to the Nairs by the beginning of the twentieth century 'that they could no longer regard buoyancy as their birthright; in future like Christians and [low-caste] Hindus, they too would have to swim'.[26] As a prominent Nair of that generation remarked with resignation,

> Whenever you see a person that is strong in physique, smart, and of good bearing, you may infer that he is either a Syrian Christian or an Ezhava; and if you see one that is weak in physique, pale and listless in bearing, your inference that he is a Nair will not often be mistaken. Similarly, if you see a garden—land with a good hedge and first-rate coconut palms in it, you can infer that the owner is a Syrian or an Ezhava—if hedgeless and unattended, you can be sure that the land belongs to a Nair.[27]

By the 1920s, the Nairs, psychologically withdrawn and depressed, were in dire straits as a social class and the battle of the many communities in Travancore was inching towards its final stages. The people, in any case, as Samuel Mateer put it, were 'not a nation, but congeries of artificially and widely-separated, for the most part mutually opposing, sections of the population'.[28] Among them, the Nairs still held much land, but the burden of history prevented progress and stagnated their existence. Once political powerhouses of the land, they were first fleeced by the rise of a monarch who centralised authority, before being emaciated by the British following their uprising. Brahmin dominance in the nineteenth century and sneering debates on matriliny, the 'chastity' of their women, and the failing system of joint families plagued them, even as Christians and Ezhavas, perceived as socially inferior, flourished and chipped away at the few social privileges and prestige the Nairs still enjoyed by virtue of caste. By the 1920s, the bleeding of power and economic influence continued not only unabated, but more painfully than before owing to the new official policies of Sethu Lakshmi Bayi. As they continued to live in an erroneous fallacy of their own 'glorious past' and 'refused to change with the times', they found that the new ruler was more than happy to let them go, and champion those whose efforts were more dynamic and oriented to the future.[29]

In 1929 although the Maharani presided over the murajapam ceremony and ensured everything was conducted according to tradition, this was despite vocal discontent expressed in newspapers across the state.[30] Many called for the whole thing to be banned altogether, but as the head of an interim government, who was accused consistently of being too favourable to the minorities, this was not possible for her. It also does not appear that Sethu Lakshmi Bayi wished to tamper with old customs in any case, even though for the first time as ruler of Travancore she adopted a policy of fairness towards all communities in the state. She seemed to persist in pro-Brahmin traditions and did not seem to cause that community as much angst as she did Nairs, while also initiating policies that were pro-Christian or pro-Ezhava. As J. Devika points out, 'She really took the minorities on board and recognised that they had contributions to make, which they had been making for long, fighting their own battles in a Hindu state.'[31] For her it was a policy of fairness; for the Nairs, a first-class betrayal by the monarch, to promote nouveau riche classes and a still-powerful clique of Brahmins. The Maharani herself would put the matter in plain terms:

> Another and perhaps the immediate cause [of Nair agitation] is the change in the Government's outlook on the question of recruitment to the higher ranks of Government Departments. This [new policy] has done away with the inequalities under which the non-castes [i.e., lower castes and other minorities] have for generations past laboured. The giving of practical proofs to the policy, long since foreshadowed, of throwing open all the

> temporal appointments as the gift of the Crown to *all* classes of subjects of the State, gave umbrage to the most vocal among the privileged classes, who had hitherto regarded the higher appointments in the State as their exclusive monopoly. The discontent and disappointment arising from these circumstances have expressed themselves in an organised effort to create troubles for the Government in various ways.[32]

In other words, the Nairs, beset with pressures from everywhere, looked to state patronage as their only hope to withstand the traumatising changes around them, since rivals already took other, better-yielding avenues. But now even this was declared fair game for everybody. The Christians and Ezhavas ought to have stayed within the business and entrepreneurial sectors of the economy; why hanker for the state services and jobs, that final bastion of Nair pride, where Brahmin competition was in any case a longstanding factor? From Sethu Lakshmi Bayi's point of view, however, this was an emotional rather than rational plea, and the Nairs were still in a position of power. The right of franchise in Travancore, for example, was based on ownership of landed property, which favoured them. In the Legislative Council elections of 1931, of the twenty-three seats available, Nairs won a majority of fifteen, while Syrian Christians got only four and Ezhavas and Muslims none.[33] By 1933 the Public Service Commission she had formulated would declare that Brahmins and Nairs held 75 per cent of all government jobs, high and low, which was three times their share of the total population.[34] And of the 24,534 jobs, Nairs specifically held 54 per cent at 13,435 offices, while Christians, Muslims and Ezhavas together held less than 5,500 jobs.[35]

So, for all the crisis of identity among Nairs, labouring under a psychological sense of loss of power and prestige, Sethu Lakshmi Bayi was convinced that they were not worse off than other communities in the state. She thought it eminently fair to create an environment where minorities also had as promising as possible a shot at success if they worked hard, and that the government could no longer act as a purely Hindu concern. That is why when Changanassery Parameswaran Pillai, a Nair leader she had appointed as a judge (besides appointing also a Christian judge, Joseph Taliath), spoke at a public forum in a communally provocative manner, he was promptly admonished. Writing to him at the Maharani's orders the Dewan made it clear that,

> Government consider that it is of utmost importance that all Government servants, particularly highly placed officers like Judges of the highest judiciary

> in the State, should not act in a manner likely to create communal friction or engender in the minds of the public doubts regarding their impartiality. In the circumstances, Government direct that in future, you should not take part in any public meeting of whatever character without their previous sanction.[36]

The Nairs were not pleased by this presumption to tell their leaders off, and in 1930 yet again a representation was made to the Government of India with numerous old and new complaints about the Maharani's administration. Led by G. Sankaran Nair who claimed that 'large bodies of people' were anxious to convey these views to the authorities, he called for constitutional government to be implemented in the state (presumably since direct calls for a Council of Regency had been declined).[37] His main grievances were that there was excess dilatoriness in the government; that the Maharani had a pro-Brahmin policy; and that the Valiya Koil Tampuran and his supporters enjoyed too much power. 'I do not consider,' wrote the Resident, that these allegations 'amounted to a very serious indictment of the Travancore administration and much of what he said I had heard before.'[38] Rama Varma, as usual, was decried as a 'half-educated usurper'[39] with Mr Nair going on to say,

> As I told you, the people of Travancore have nothing but respect for the person of the Maharani Regent. ... But they feel convinced that she, being too good a wife, has abdicated her functions in favour of her husband, the Valiya Koil Tampuran, whose influence on the administration is found to be unwholesome. This Valiya Koil Tampuran has a Brahmin favourite named Kulathu Iyer and the general impression in the State is that both together are running the administration ... Here I would like to point out that, in a talk I had with Mr M.E. Watts, the late Dewan of Travancore, just on the eve of his retirement, even he admitted to me that the impression referred to above was fairly correct and he himself was forced to resign office on account of the unwarranted interference of the Valiya Koil Tampuran in state matters.[40]

The Kulathu Iyer named was the 'Palace Special Officer' and was to serve the Maharani and her husband for many years as their man Friday. His especial talent lay in ferreting out useful nuggets of information through a vast network of friends and agents of his own. As Sethu Lakshmi Bayi's nephew would later tell, this man, in his bandhgala, mundu, with a shawl always tied around his waist, and his kudumi ponytail swinging as he trotted about humming Carnatic tunes, was 'shrewd, not dishonest. He wouldn't antagonise anybody, and he wouldn't cross swords with anybody. But he would still get his work done and do that which the Maharani and her husband could not directly do. He had no permanent enemies and no permanent friends, only a network of officials deep in the government that gave him information on who was whispering what and why.'[41] The vagueness of his role came across in his very denomination as 'Palace Special Officer', and it is no wonder that to Nair opponents of Sethu Lakshmi Bayi, he seemed a most sinister character and a typical, wily Brahmin. As for Mr Watts's claim that he had resigned because of undue interference by Rama Varma, successive Residents had dismissed this, not to speak of the truth that he had not, in reality, resigned, but on the contrary entertained hopes of serving another tenure as Dewan, till the Maharani effectively asked him to leave.

In any case, Sankaran Nair deemed it 'highly essential' that the Regency should be at least modified, with a Council of Regency being imposed, if the authorities found themselves unable to take a more drastic decision. To him the Maharani's rule was 'a complete failure, and it is not an exaggeration to say that things never went so bad in Travancore within the last fifty years as they have done now'.[42] The Resident did not give the representation more credit than necessary, pointing out that if there was any existing dominance of Brahmins in high positions, it was an inherited condition and not one of Sethu Lakshmi Bayi's creation, adding that 'in these days recruitment is freely made from non-Brahmin communities, and I believe that if the matter were impartially investigated, it would be proved beyond doubt that the Maharani Regent has pursued a more liberal policy in this respect than any of her predecessors'.[43] The appointment of Christians as the Dewan, Chief Secretary, and a judge; of Ezhavas and Muslims as magistrates, not to speak of hundreds of job openings made available to minorities at lower levels, was unprecedented in ostensibly Hindu Travancore. It was this, after all, that caused the Viceroy also to praise the Maharani for taking a fair and impartial stand in the matter of appointments. Allegations against her husband were also dismissed as vague and unfounded.[44]

As for the claim of Brahmin domination and dilatory administration, this arose because in selecting her new Dewan after Mr Watts, Sethu Lakshmi Bayi had placed her trust in V.S. Subramania Iyer, a Brahmin of Tamil origin. Previously a judge in the High Court, he had 'an unbiased and dispassionate' view of affairs of state, something that had apparently been found wanting in Mr Watts. He was also, however, a 'cautious man' who 'lacked the tremendous drive' of his predecessor, as a result of which in the final years of the Maharani's reign, new projects were not taken up with as much gusto as before. Instead, completion of existing ventures became her principal focus.[45] Mr Iyer was 'a pleasant man to deal with', accordingly to the Resident, 'and I believe him to be conscientious and well-meaning'. However, 'he is not a trained administrator, and I think he is naturally slow'.[46] It is likely that having taken something of a risk in choosing Mr Watts, with results that scathed her when he no longer accepted her orders, Sethu Lakshmi Bayi now preferred a more orthodox executive, who would not stand in her way. As one commentator would note, the Maharani wanted a 'look-wise-and-nod-assent' Dewan, after the near-debacle with Mr Watts.[47]

The administration, as a consequence, suffered and became somewhat tardy, causing at one time the Resident to wonder whether an Executive Council ought to be formed under the Dewan to ensure speedier transaction of business. This would remove the load off his shoulders and decentralise the top-heavy system. On reflection however, it was felt that this could be misconstrued as a Council of Regency in another garb, with the risk that Sethu Lakshmi Bayi's 'feelings would be hurt and she would inevitably be disturbed in mind, which is just what the Government of India desire to avoid'. Things were definitely slow under Mr Iyer, but 'the Travancore State on the whole is fortunate in its Government' and so, concluded the Resident, 'I think we should leave well alone.'[48]

By the end of 1929 Mr Crosthwaite's term as Resident came to a conclusion and one Mr A.N.L. Cater arrived in Travancore in his stead. This was precisely the kind of situation that gave Sethu Lakshmi Bayi cause for worry. With an unseasoned Dewan in office, the onset of a new British representative opened up the possibility of compelling lobbying and propaganda being put up by rival factions. And as expected, an effort was made in this direction when Sir CP and Sir Vasudeva Rajah appeared in the capital together, with the latter calling on the new Resident on 1 January 1930 to discuss the Regency, and problems current in it.[49] He also hinted, not very subtly, that Mr Cater should be careful about which 'side' he picked, for soon he would have the ear of none other than the Viceroy on a visit to Baroda. The threat backfired when the Resident reported its details to the Government of India, recommending that the Viceroy entertain no complaints from Sir Vasudeva if he saw him.[50] For what could be called damage control, Sir CP then met with Mr Cater and had a long conversation with him on everything else but Travancore. Reportedly, this was under instructions from the Junior Maharani who was 'very annoyed' with Sir Vasudeva for 'having made a false move in approaching me prematurely'.[51]

The Maharajah's mother was trying to do all she could to thwart plans being made for her son, vexed also by the failure of her latest efforts in London and Delhi. Her insistence that 'motherly watching' be permitted while he underwent administrative training was also turned down, and it was actually her cousin who had a greater say in deciding details of the Maharajah's future education, along with the Government of India. Sethu Lakshmi Bayi had at first suggested the name of none other than old Mr Raghavaiah as administrative tutor for her nephew. He was almost uniquely qualified, she felt, for this, having been Dewan of the state.[52] But at the time the authorities were 'loathe to lose his services' in Pudukkottai, and she was asked to make alternative suggestions.[53] Writing in reply, Sethu Lakshmi Bayi wisely laid the onus of finding a good tutor on the Resident and his superiors, anxious to avoid allegations later that she tried to influence the process and have an acolyte of hers appointed to a position of influence over the Maharajah:

> I do not know many who could be thought of for the appointment and naturally I am unwilling to recommend one about whose fitness for the responsible and important office I cannot speak with a certain authority. The prospective tutor should have large administrative experience, a high character, and a sober general outlook. As regards Mr Raghavaiah, his close knowledge of local conditions in Travancore will be an added advantage, as his claim to the other requisites cannot be challenged [and this praise despite her bad relations with him in 1925]. I therefore am of the opinion that one more fitted for the post than Mr Raghavaiah would be difficult to find. If, however, for other reasons, Mr Raghavaiah's services cannot be made available, I would request that three names may be offered to me from which to select one. I have no doubt that you will understand that the reason for my attaching so much importance to the selection of the man proceeds from my realisation of the fact that the training His Highness is to get now may largely influence his later career as Ruler.[54]

Indeed, despite poor relations with the Junior Maharani, Sethu Lakshmi Bayi does not seem to have harboured anything but good feelings towards her nephew, whom in any case she barely knew. During the black magic incident, she was pleased to hear that he had had nothing to do with it; she frequently sent him presents on his birthday and other festivals, and he too reciprocated.

Sometimes, however, there were ruptures. After the black magic episode, when relations between the Maharanis were 'as strained as ever', Sethu Lakshmi Bayi sent her nephew, as usual, certain gifts on Onam day. But this time they were 'returned by the Maharajah on the score that the cloth sent was inferior in quality'. While indeed the cloth was found to have faults, the Resident opined that this was still no excuse for 'His Highness' rudeness' to his aunt.[55] On other occasions such as Vishu when it was traditional for junior members of the royal family to call on the eldest, neither the Junior Maharani nor her son paid visits to Sethu Lakshmi Bayi to receive presents. In 1928, for instance, both went away from the capital, as the Maharajah's mother 'does not wish him to be in Trivandrum on Vishu day, while the Maharani Regent continues to dispense' gifts to all others, including government officials.[56] For their part, they resented that the Valiya Koil Tampuran, although he participated in processions on the Maharajah's birthday and on other ceremonial occasions, failed to call on them and pay his respects as was expected of a consort.

With regard to the Maharajah's education, however, Sethu Lakshmi Bayi showed herself willing to go out of the way to find a suitable man. Recommendations came in from the Governor of Madras and other dignitaries, but none of them was deemed suitable; so the Maharani asked Delhi for their preference.[57] Since Mr Raghavaiah was not available, her own choice now was for an older, retired official with no previous connections to Travancore. This, she felt, would remove the possible risk of the tutor later attempting to influence the Maharajah for high offices in the state, or of seeking other favours; a concern the Resident felt was 'quite correct'.[58] The Maharani added that she was prepared now to waive her previous conditions that the individual should be a south Indian Brahmin, and that he could not enjoy a salary higher than the Dewan's. She now offered a princely sum of Rs 3,000 per month so as to acquire the best individual for the job.[59]

> It appears that there would be a distinct advantage in securing for the purpose an officer of proved ability and character, who has retired from British Indian service by superannuation. Firstly, he will be in a position to discharge his duties with detachment and uninfluenced by considerations of self-advancement, as his age would, on the face of it, preclude his entertaining much hope of getting any fat employment in the state in the years to come. Secondly, the influence of a sober, disciplined gentleman of mature years would, I believe, be a wholesome accession to the training the Maharajah is to get.[60]

It was finally Mr Cater who suggested one P.C. Dutt, an ICS officer then serving as Collector of Madras. Heading one of the most important offices in India, and with wide experience in various departments, he was thought a perfect candidate. However, Dutt was not a Brahmin but a north Indian Kayastha, but since the Maharani had waived her demands on these counts, they were not considered disqualifications any more. In December 1929 officials of the Madras government called on her for a conference, after which she gave her official approval to the nomination. She only insisted on one specific condition, that despite higher pay, the tutor would not have precedence over the Dewan.[61] M.V. Subramania Iyer, the old private secretary who had resigned, shocked by the black magic incident earlier, was persuaded to return; even at the time of his resignation Sethu Lakshmi Bayi had lamented the loss (stating how 'a man of his age and sobriety might be regarded as some kind of moderating influence on the Junior Maharani').[62] His reinstatement was, therefore, happily welcomed.

The first part of the Maharajah's training was scheduled in Bangalore, with Sir Mirza Ismail, the Dewan of Mysore, assisting in finding suitable houses and making other arrangements for the use of the Travancore party. The Maharajah's retinue was to include forty-five servants, including cooks and drivers, along with his private secretary and one ADC, while Mr Dutt was to be provided twelve servants and every convenience he desired.[63] At this point the Junior Maharani again entered the picture, for though it had been decided that she was to play no part in her son's administrative training, and that he would not live with her, she forwarded to the Viceroy a second appeal asking for leniency. A compromise was then reached, whereby the Political Secretary wrote to Mr Cater as follows:

> With regard to the request of the Junior Maharani to be allowed to take a house at the place where the young Maharajah is undergoing his training, I am to say that His Excellency recognises the natural anxiety of a mother to watch over her son at a critical period in his life, and is prepared to agree to her request as a tentative arrangement, on the understanding that the Maharajah will visit his mother at definite periods, say once a week, to be arranged beforehand. His Excellency, moreover, must retain full discretion to advice the Junior Maharani not to live in the same station as His Highness, if it is found that the young Maharajah is thereby prevented from gaining a sense of responsibility and ability to stand on his own feet, or if for any good reason the arrangement proves inconvenient.[64]

In other words, while the Government of India were prepared to be lenient to the Junior Maharani, it would depend on her proactively not interfering in the routine and programme envisioned for her son. But either because she was upset by these terms or perhaps hoping to utilise Mr Cater's newness to the scene, fresh complaints were then raised through Sir Vasudeva. In January 1930 she again wrote to the Resident expressing her disapproval at being excluded from planning the Maharajah's training, also complaining that she had not been consulted before Mr Dutt was confirmed as the tutor. Once again, she stressed the need for maternal watch over the Maharajah during this time, and made it clear she was unhappy at being asked not to go with her son during the period of his training.[65] Nothing came out of this, however, and it was calmly pointed out that these decisions were taken by the Government of India, and that even previous appointments, such as in Captain Harvey's case, were decided at higher levels, with no input from the Junior Maharani.[66] They were, however, happy to have her views on members of the Maharajah's household, his date of departure, management of finances and so on. The Resident also informed the Junior Maharani that the period of training was provisionally fixed for one year in Bangalore, with an interval at six months, and permission to visit Travancore for religious ceremonies at which the Maharajah's presence was mandatory.[67]

The Maharajah was to leave the capital on 20 April 1930, but as the date for his departure approached, the Junior Maharani became 'rather cantankerous and obstructive'.[68] But tantrums were ignored and by 23 April her son reached Bangalore and commenced the final stage of his education, for the first time removed from his mother. In the meantime, instead of taking up the offer to stay separately in the city and to see her son on regular occasions, the Junior Maharani proceeded to Ooty. Soon a new set of requests were submitted through Sir CP, asking for progress reports that were sent to Sethu Lakshmi Bayi to be despatched to the Maharajah's mother also, and a special amount for rent should she decide to maintain a residence in Bangalore.[69] Both requests were accepted, but what pleased everyone more was that the training seemed to be doing the Maharajah good. In only a matter of days it was reported that 'in a small but significant way', the boy had 'shown his relief at being released from the bondage of his mother's apron strings'.[70] A preliminary assessment of his progress was also forwarded to the Government of India by June:

> Dutt reports that he is attentive and ready to learn, though without showing great keenness, and both he and Harvey complain that he lacks initiative and healthy inquisitiveness. I ascribe this chiefly to the repressive nature of his upbringing and perhaps in part to his poor physique, and I have advised his

> Tutors not to expect or aim at too rapid a development of character. Some difficulty has been experienced in finding suitable companions of his own age, but through the good offices of the Dewan [of Mysore], two or three boys were found and have been invited to tennis parties, etc. The Maharajah has, however, shown little desire to cultivate their acquaintance. His social manners and behaviour are excellent and in this respect he seems to create a favourable impression upon all whom he meets.[71]

This review was not surprising, and in the previous year Louise Ouwerkerk also expressed a similar opinion in private. Even while in Trivandrum, under Captain Harvey the Maharajah was encouraged to play as many sports as possible, and to take an initiative in inviting many people for such activities, since he had no friends of his own. Writing after her first game of tennis with him, Ouwerkerk noted:

> I suspected the boy would come out of his shell when Mama is not about; these tennis parties are his own show entirely and Mama does not appear, and he is quite a different person, a lively little cricket. The whole affair tickled enormously; he being a high caste ... may not eat in the presence of outcastes (which white folk are, of course!) so we had a good tea and drank deep of lemonade at intervals, while he ate not a crumb and must have got horribly thirsty in the course of the afternoon! And as soon as he had shaken hands with his departing guests, he rushed off to get a bath to wash off the pollution! And yet he has had an English tutor, is surrounded by English influence, and appears in his manner and speech like any normal English boy of sixteen. You wonder what will happen to him in the end.[72]

By August 1930, less than four months after his departure from the palace, the young Maharajah appeared to be a vastly different individual. When Mr Cater went to Bangalore to witness first-hand his development, he was evidently pleased by the changes he saw, and

> ... it is satisfactory to be able to report a definite advance in his progress. Physically he is much stronger and has put on nearly a stone of weight. In other ways he has also changed for the better. Instead of being the rather silent, reserved boy that he was at Trivandrum, he has now, so to speak, come out of his shell and is talkative and cheerful, and altogether more natural and boyish than he was. He is thoroughly happy in Bangalore, and I have no doubt that his stay there and contact with all sorts and conditions of people

> whom he would never meet in Travancore is doing him a world of good, apart from the administrative training which was the principal object of his going to Mysore State.[73]

But if the Maharajah was thriving, his *mother* seemed to be in a state of high panic. Although Sethu Lakshmi Bayi had allocated money for her to take up residence in Bangalore, she had preferred to go away to Madras instead, for her own reasons. In July the Resident then received intelligence of yet another conspiracy being hatched by the Junior Maharani there with all her 'fondness for intrigue'.[74] It seemed that like before, the Maharajah's mother had approached a journalist from the *Pioneer* to help her 'rectify her grievances' and to put an end to the Regency, and the separation from her son.[75] When the journalist in question spoke to Mr Cater about this, and he in turn questioned the Junior Maharani, the latter issued a firm denial. The journalist then, one A.S. Menon, wrote to the Resident claiming to be 'outrageously betrayed'. By informing the Junior Maharani of their conversation, Mr Cater had, he said, let him down.[76] Despite this, however, he went on to give more information about this latest intrigue, which involved the Cochin durbar as well.

Like the royal family of Travancore, Cochin too was split with factions, not least because there too existed two power centres. From 1895 till 1914 the state was ruled by a widely popular Maharajah, who decided, for personal reasons of health, to abdicate.[77] 'The Cochin which His Highness picked up in 1895 in a state of chaos in many respects and which, through his faithful and watchful stewardship for a period of nearly twenty years, he raised to a unique position' in both 'political independence and material prosperity', was ruled now by a cousin, who was next in line.[78] But the old ruler remained head of the royal family with the status of Valiya Tampuran. The new ruler, however, was 'entirely swayed by his Consort', a dominating Nair lady of renowned ability and personality, known as Parukutty Neithiyar Amma.[79] The ex-ruler resented this outside influence, since his successor's wife had no locus standi to exercise power, and consequently difficulties arose in relations between Abdicated His Highness and Reigning His Highness.[80] It so happened that Sethu Lakshmi Bayi and her husband were close to the former, and in 1927 even had him visit Trivandrum as a state guest,[81] while the Junior Maharani was friendly with the all-powerful Neithiyar Amma of Cochin.

It was now revealed that just before the Maharajah left for Bangalore, his mother, completely agitated at the impending separation from her son, met with the Neithiyar Amma to request her assistance in preventing this, and to help in putting an end to the galling Regency. Reportedly, in a somewhat hysterical mood, the Junior Maharani 'flourished a revolver and threatened to shoot herself if her grievances were not redressed'.[82] The Neithiyar Amma promised to do what she could, and 'the result was the employment of an agent who is well-known in Cochin for fishing in troubled waters'.[83] The name of this individual was not revealed but a copy of a letter handed over by Mr A.S. Menon, the journalist from Madras, to the Resident clarified the commission given him by the Junior Maharani:

> I have been authorised by Her Highness the Junior Maharani of Travancore to do all that is legal and constitutional in getting the order of the Government of India revised in respect of the extension of the Regency in Travancore, the guardian tutorship of Captain Harvey, and Her Highness' enforced separation from His Highness the young Maharajah during the period of His Highness' administrative training, and to incur in this behalf all reasonable expenses.[84]

Despite the Junior Maharani's vehement denials, Mr Cater had reason to believe Mr Menon's information was accurate.[85] This was partly because Menon had already tried to express the Junior Maharani's 'sad circumstances' to the Government of India, only to be rebuffed and told to approach the Resident first.[86] In any case, the Junior Maharani was utterly frustrated by the turn of events and her son's removal from her authority, and wanted, more than ever, for the Regency to come to an end. Such was her aversion to being in Trivandrum that she refused to visit even for her son's eighteenth birthday, when he himself was in town, preferring to see him in Madras instead where he went for Christmas. To the Resident it appeared to be a simple case of the Junior Maharani, long accustomed to using her son as 'a kind of shuttlecock' in 'her endeavours to get the best of the Maharani Regent and myself',[87] no longer having him available for her calculations.

Sethu Lakshmi Bayi, in the meantime, had matters of state pressing her. The Great Depression of 1929 was beginning to take a toll, and revenues were beginning to drop. Expenditure on public works and other ongoing schemes remained high, leaving a relatively small surplus of funds. 'At no time in recent years have the prices of staple articles of local produce such as paddy, pepper, coconut, rubber and tapioca fallen so low,' reported the Dewan. 'Our economic revival depends to a large extent upon the increased buying capacity of our foreign customers and no action taken by ourselves alone can accelerate the economic revival of the foreign countries which buy our goods.'[88] To find a way to guide the state through these economic doldrums, the Maharani constituted an Economic Depression Enquiry Committee, and sanctioned a preliminary sum of Rs 3.5 lakh in loans to the agriculturists of the state, who would have to bear the worst effects of the crisis. Trade still remained fairly buoyant, and there was no deficit, but it was clear that a difficult tide would have to be weathered for a few years, after the enormous boom of the 1920s that had enabled Travancore to progress at such an unequalled pace. As the Committee would report, only when prices returned to their original levels would the situation improve, without which the exports of the state would continue to be undervalued, and income even of ordinary people would diminish.[89]

All over the world hysteria broke out, and in some parts things were to become extremely difficult. Travancore, with its record of good governance and benevolent state policy, was able to navigate the storm. It would emerge from the throes of the Great Depression relatively unharmed, resuming its course of high growth in a few years' time. But it was not easy. Prices dropped 40 per cent in only fourteen months between 1929 and 1930, and the total value of India's trade fell from Rs 330 crore in 1929 to Rs 132 crore by 1932.[90] While countries like Brazil, where one crop dominated, suffered the worst, India with its internal diversity of cultivation was in a better position and a total catastrophe was, therefore, averted. Protectionist policies were imposed, custom duties increased, the defence budget curtailed, and government salaries cut down. In 1930, while the Government of India's budget suffered a deficit of Rs 11.5 crore,[91] Travancore's reduced revenue of Rs 247 lakh still left a surplus of nearly Rs 7 lakh after all expenses. Even the drop in the government balance from Rs 170 lakh to Rs 165 lakh was relatively minor given global conditions.[92] The Maharani, in hindsight, probably heaved a sigh of relief for having firmly refused to sanction Mr Watts's Railway Scheme, which if under way at this time would have bankrupted the state. But as she worked harder than ever to tackle what John Maynard Keynes considered a 'first class disaster',[93] another one, political in nature, was afoot in Simla—that 'pleasant hill sanatorium' where, regretted John Kaye, 'our Governors-General, surrounded by irresponsible advisers, settle the destinies of [even] empires without the aid of their legitimate fellow-counsellors, and which has been the cradle of more political insanity than any place within the limits of Hindostan'.[94] The partition of Bengal was designed here, as were the disastrous invasions of Tibet and Afghanistan. And in 1931, on a decidedly minor but still problematic level, loomed an intervention in Travancore, destined to bring to a premature conclusion the reign of the Pooradam Tirunal Maharajah.

13

La Revanche

'British policy in India,' remarked Sarvepalli Gopal, 'was, in essentials, determined by governments' but there were 'times when what was seen as the personal touch of understanding' made a world of positive difference.[1] While general policy directives were issued from London, a great deal depended on attitudes of imperial emissaries as well—whether Viceroys and their votaries decided on conciliating and understanding the people they governed, or in dividing and manipulating them instead. Lord Ripon in the 1880s, for instance, 'testified by his actions that British rule was not always wholly unprincipled', just as decades later India's last Viceroy, Lord Mountbatten, did enough good to depart 'to resounding cheers' from masses of Indians themselves. 'But perhaps the most substantial contribution by any individual to the building of goodwill between India and Britain,' continues Gopal, 'was made by Lord Irwin', who was the Viceroy from 1926 until 1931, protecting the interests of the Crown he served in South Asia to the best of his understated abilities.[2]

Irwin arrived in Delhi after Lord Reading's unpopular tenure and the general impression was that 'no man in English public life was better fitted than [him] for the political climate and situation in India' at the time.[3] A devout Christian of 'sincerity and religious dedication', he made a 'marked impression' on an equally pious Gandhi and several other leaders of the nationalist movement in India, opening the doors to work with rather than against them. He presented to the Indian people 'his credentials as a Viceroy who was concerned with more than mere execution of [British] policy, and management of the administration'.[4] In the beginning mistakes were made when he tried to force the Mahatma down to his terms, but very quickly Irwin 'saw what all his successors, except

Mountbatten, failed to see, that it was in Britain's interest to win Gandhi over'.[5] By 1929 he famously declared that his goal for India was dominion status and autonomy within the British Empire, causing such umbrage among conservatives back home that Churchill privately lambasted him as 'Lord Worming and Squirming' and publicly accused him of 'drinking tea with treason'.[6]

But Irwin was determined. He told horrified critics it was simply inconceivable to expect India 'to occupy a permanently subordinate place in an Empire of white nations' and that as far as possible, they would have to reconcile to local aspirations.[7] Gandhi too reined in more extremist voices within the Congress and was prepared to confer with Irwin, so that even at their worst times, they could reach agreements such as the historic Gandhi–Irwin Pact of 1931. While the Viceroy had no intentions to inaugurate the beginning of the end for the Raj, he did concede space to Indians, and do his best to bring the opposition on board. 'I do pray,' Irwin expressed in his farewell note to the Mahatma, 'that history may say that you and I were permitted to be instruments in doing something big for India and for humanity.'[8] It was a genuine sentiment and the man retired with his conscience clear.

But Irwin's hopes were dashed to the floor with spectacular effect by his successor who had not the least inclination to do anything for India other than to grip it in Britain's hardened imperial clutches, and put Gandhi in his rightful place. Lord Willingdon, who arrived in April 1931, considered his predecessor a 'simple man' who had been unfortunately 'deluded' into doing business with Gandhi.[9] The new Viceroy had 'the appropriate imperial arrogance and requisite contempt' for Indians, so as to undo all that Irwin had achieved, and go back to the days of ruling India as a personal fiefdom of the King Emperor.[10] To Churchill's delight, he condemned Gandhi as 'the most Machiavellian bargaining little political humbug I have ever come across', and decried the outgoing Viceroy's 'mistaken hobnobbing' with this Father of Indian nationalism.[11] In hindsight, Willingdon's selection as Viceroy is considered 'among the major misjudgements of the National Government in London', since he was 'so limited a man', determined to obliterate all demands for freedom, blinded by his firm conviction in Pax Britannica.[12] Succeeding Irwin was not easy, and Willingdon made blunder after historic blunder in the following years. 'Irwin sought cooperation and conciliation. Willingdon, on the other hand, sought conflict and confrontation. Irwin befriended Gandhi; Willingdon imprisoned him and banned the Congress Party.'[13] Even Muhammad Ali Jinnah, the Quaid-i-Azam of Pakistan and no admirer of the Congress, would refer to the man as 'that wretched Viceroy'.[14]

Willingdon had some experience in India, having served a term as Governor of Bombay and then another in Madras, before going to Canada as Viceroy there. He had no particular gifts as such and was best known as 'a minor Liberal politician and a county level cricketer' at first.[15] General opinion was that he 'would have remained a parliamentary backbencher had it not been for two things—tennis partner to King George V, and his pushy spouse'.[16] Having become Viceroy, however, he was 'hell bent on finishing off' the Congress, 'took to a policy of suppression', and 'encouraged communal and feudal forces with a view to creating a wedge in the struggle being waged against the Imperial Government'.[17] He 'seemed to prefer India's princes to its politicians'[18] for no other reason than to employ them as a bulwark in that traditional colonial formula of divide and rule, against Gandhi. Where Irwin circulated notes on good governance to the Maharajahs, and tried to persuade them to relinquish petty despotism in favour of enlightened rule, Willingdon desired to cultivate them as imperial allies, lavishing titles, flattery and favours in pursuit of his goals. Irwin contemplated self-rule for India and 'succeeded to a degree not even he had anticipated' in ensuring participation of the princes in this grand scheme, while Willingdon had every inclination to keep India as divided as possible.[19] While Gandhi thought Irwin 'an honest Viceroy with decent impulses', Willingdon was, he felt, 'bereft of all grace'.[20] The latter was decidedly rude to the Mahatma; during their conferences in Simla, the Viceroy refused to relax rules prohibiting cars from plying the town's roads except his own, forcing Gandhi to walk 6 miles every day to see him, often in drenching rain.[21] 'Combining ostentation with repression, Willingdon's regime aroused bitter enmity among nationalists' and was set to become one of the most notorious viceroyalties in a long time.[22]

While Irwin, who admired progressive statecraft, professed Sethu Lakshmi Bayi's reign as perhaps the best in all of Travancore's history, Willingdon too had concerns with the state, though less with its administration and more with the royal family. It was when he was Governor of Madras in Mulam Tirunal's days that he first visited Trivandrum and met both the Maharanis. His arrival as Viceroy now, however, was to prove a godsend for the Junior Maharani in particular, and a positive nightmare for her reigning cousin. His installation in Delhi was one among several other changes happening at the time. Mr Cater, the Resident, had departed the state after a relatively short stint in that role. One Lt Col H.R.N. Pritchard succeeded him in October 1930, and had only half a year in overseeing affairs for the Government of India. The Junior Maharani herself, meanwhile, showed no inclination to return to Travancore, dividing her time between Madras and Ooty. By April 1931 she went up to Delhi and

Kashmir, and later in the summer arrived in Simla, the 'hot weather' capital of the British Raj, where the Viceroy was getting on with tackling Gandhi and his other imperial headaches. But for the Junior Maharani, this visit was to become momentous and turn the tide in her favour for the first time in years, finally providing her the sympathy of the Paramount Power that had so far proved elusive.

The story, which has since gained such currency that it is widely accepted as the true historical narrative, goes that Sethu Parvathi Bayi was utterly vexed by the delay in granting her son his ruling powers. She feared that the Regency of her cousin 'might be converted into a permanency' and that the Maharajah's fate would be to languish forever as a prince without a throne.[23] It was critical, therefore, for him to be 'moved out of his perilous minority', putting which off was detrimental not only to him personally but also to 'the State at large'.[24] While Sethu Lakshmi Bayi herself was acknowledged as popular, and though she held warm affection for the Maharajah in her heart, there were certain individuals with vested interests (in other words, Rama Varma and associates) who were making every effort to prolong the Regency and perpetuate their own wicked hold over power.[25] Uncharitable rumours were spread regularly about the young Maharajah, which had reached even the ears of the previous Viceroy that the boy was 'unfit' to succeed to the throne.[26] The efforts of these men were to extend the Regency 'indefinitely by convincing the Government of India that the young Maharajah was not mentally up to the mark, [and was] in fact something of a moron, and hence incapable of assuming ruling powers'.[27] This vile propaganda was the only reason Sethu Lakshmi Bayi's rule had continued beyond 1930 and the Maharajah was prevented from claiming the throne on turning eighteen. In order to resolve this shameful injustice, a gallant Junior Maharani, devoted to her son, proceeded to Simla and magisterially demanded of Lord Willingdon thus:

> You are the representative of an ancient royal house that continues to be revered as rulers of a great empire. Please consider whether you should postpone the legitimate investiture of a prince merely because of rumours. Is there justice or law in taking a one-sided decision without direct knowledge of such a serious matter? After talking to my son, whatever decision you take shall be accepted.[28]

Another rendition of the fable, recorded in the memoirs of the younger son of the Junior Maharani, presents her in a more defiant tone. When told by Willingdon that her son was not fit enough, she replied coldly that she was not aware the British Crown appointed as Viceroys 'people who do not apply their minds'. This baffled Willingdon, who indignantly asked what she was suggesting. In return the Junior Maharani directed him to meet the Maharajah first, instead of succumbing to 'selfish, ulterior motives', and form a personal opinion on his fitness.[29] We are then told that a now wiser Viceroy realised the great merit of the Junior Maharani's argument, and wrote to the Resident, demanding to see the young Maharajah himself. And when the boy arrived, they spent many days together, dining and playing tennis, until Willingdon, impressed by his many qualities, was moved to exclaim, 'If this young man is of unstable mind as alleged, so am I!'[30] He then decided that a grave prejudice had been perpetrated in denying the Maharajah his legitimate rights, and with a stroke of his pen terminated the Regency, and in the process, the hideous and hated tyranny of the Valiya Koil Tampuran and his favourites. 'In this way justice was meted out to my brother,' the Junior Maharani's younger son would declare, sealing the story with a fittingly dramatic climax.[31]

This erroneous but compellingly woven sentimental tale has some serious problems that become clear by a simple perusal of official documents. There was, to begin with, no possibility whatever of the Regency becoming a 'permanency', for its date of expiry in August 1932 was decided as early as 1928. Similarly, the claim that the Regency was extended because of rumours put out about the Maharajah by jealous detractors, is a convenient fallacy, when the reality was that as early as the summer of 1927 the Junior Maharani was told that, as a matter of *general policy*, she could expect her son to receive his powers only when he turned nineteen-and-a-half. Furthermore, in 1930, the Maharajah had again been assured that this decision had nothing to do with Sethu Lakshmi Bayi, who was apprised of the extension of her rule at the same time as the Junior Maharani. As for the story, almost definitely apocryphal, that the Viceroy expressed dramatic surprise at seeing that the Maharajah was not mentally unstable, no official record exists of this. The real papers show his response as rather regular, with not the remotest allusion to the boy's psychological state. The only sources where the aforementioned story is found, then, are the memoirs of the Junior Maharani's son and a biography of Sir CP written by his granddaughter, both arguably deficient in objectivity.

The true course of events, then, was different. Early in 1931 the Resident and Sethu Lakshmi Bayi were in the midst of correspondence about a proposed all-India tour for the Maharajah upon the conclusion of his training in Mysore later that year. This was planned to cover many British Indian provinces and numerous principalities as well. Following this, the Maharajah was to return to

Trivandrum by March 1932 and commence training in the local administration, before being formally placed on the throne with full powers on 16 August, a date deemed especially auspicious as it was the Malayalam new year.[32] It was then that Lord Willingdon arrived and took control of the Government of India in Simla, soon after which the Junior Maharani also made her appearance in the hills. Following this, in June 1931, the first intimation to the Resident was made that 'it has recently been suggested to His Excellency the Viceroy that His Highness the Maharajah of Travancore should be granted ruling powers in March 1932'.[33] The headspring of these suggestions was not difficult to guess, for the Junior Maharani had with her the ever-resourceful Sir CP, famous for many years now as 'the blue-eyed boy' of Lord Willingdon.[34]

Sir CP's influence over the Willingdons was legendary. When the Viceroy was Governor of Madras a decade ago, Sir CP was 'the uncrowned king of the Madras bar' and they had worked closely together, forming a lasting friendship.[35] In the words of the latter's biographer, 'CP had always struck Willingdon as a remarkably adroit administrator',[36] while his own granddaughter would tell that the Viceroy, who was at first hesitant to entertain the Junior Maharani, 'did so as a good friend of *Thatha's* [i.e., grandfather's]'.[37] It was in fact Sir CP who convinced Lord Willingdon that August was somehow not a good month for the Maharajah's investiture, and that March, only slightly earlier than scheduled, would be better.[38] There were also stories about the kind of sway Sir CP possessed over the Viceroy's wife. As one biographer remarks, albeit disapprovingly, 'Much was said about Lady Willingdon's extraordinary interest in CP. Any honour or distinction bestowed on CP was attributed to Lady Willingdon's influence.'[39] Indeed, there was much talk about the Viceroy's famously imperious wife being positively obsessed with the man. Khushwant Singh noted how Sir CP, 'a strikingly handsome man, as fair skinned as any Kashmiri, with aquiline features and large drooping eyes' had many female admirers 'because he also had the gift for words'.[40] Lady Willingdon was supposed to be positively 'besotted with him',[41] while a more exaggerated memoir claims that he enjoyed 'long, loving conversations' with her over the telephone too.[42]

It was well known that Sir CP, despite an 'ugly reputation as a womaniser', probably merely had platonic friendships with these women, including the wife of the Viceroy.[43] She, however, was notorious for interference and personal domination over her husband, and a popular joke told that while Lord Willingdon was born to govern India, his wife was born to govern him.[44] She had a bizarre love for the colour mauve, which was evidently the secret to winning her favour, with one Maharajah even supplying her appropriately coloured toilet paper as a token of his appreciation.[45] When Kasturba Gandhi met her and offered to send her khadi cloth spun by the Mahatma, the Vicereine expressed delight before insisting it should be mauve in colour.[46] Lady Willingdon was, moreover, infamous due to her propensity for giving (and taking) favours (and more). When she joined the Viceroy on his visits to princely states, with rulers famous for owning magnificent baubles and gems, 'Aides carried around a capacious bag with a yawning mouth' so that she could conveniently appropriate whatever she set her eyes on and liked.[47] 'An expensive gift to Lady Irwin would invite a rebuff,' one north Indian royal would comment, 'while Lady Willingdon would drop not very subtle hints about how much she admired the ropes of Basra pearls around the Senior Maharani's neck. Promptly, but discreetly, the next morning it was sent to Lady Willingdon's room.'[48] With bizarre energy she set out to propagate her family name, having roads, gardens and whatever else she could find, named after an assortment of relations, including her son and a grandfather who never set foot in India. Together, husband and wife happily named and renamed so many places and streets that 'it took more than half a century for independent India to get them renamed'.[49]

There is more than a fair possibility that it was the intimate association between the Willingdons and Sir CP that finally lent the Junior Maharani, hitherto snubbed due to intrigues of her own concoction, the ear of the Viceroy. When the Resident was, therefore, asked for his views on advancing the installation of the Maharajah to March instead of August 1932, he responded with some surprise and expressed concern at what seemed to be careless tampering at the hands of a hasty Viceroy uninformed about the antecedents of the Travancore case. In his response he pointed out that several issues would need to be addressed before confirming such a decision. He also noted: 'When Lord Willingdon was appointed Viceroy, it was freely said in Travancore that with the assistance of [Sir CP] Ramaswami Iyer, the Junior Maharani would succeed in persuading Lord Willingdon to revise Lord Irwin's decision.'[50] No matter how many declarations were made that this had nothing to do with the merits or demerits of the Regency, 'The credit for what will be styled the downfall of the present regime and of achieving a complete victory over the Maharani Regent, will undoubtedly be given to the Junior Maharani.'[51] Sethu Lakshmi Bayi, he warned, would feel 'her face has been blackened' and though 'Her dignity and courtesy will, however, possibly prevent her from divulging her true feeling,' she would most certainly be hurt.[52] 'The Maharani Regent,' Mr Pritchard opined, 'has given her best' and had trusted the Government of India all along, and 'I consider it is up to us to do what is possible to soften what is bound to be her complete eclipse when His Highness gets his powers.'[53] Revising the date of termination now would, he felt, be a betrayal of her longstanding faith in and goodwill towards the Government of India.

Mr Pritchard also felt that a change in plans at this late stage would upset the schedule already prepared for the Maharajah's training. But the Viceroy, it was told, had become 'very anxious' to personally carry out the investiture ceremony, also wishing to inspect Cochin Harbour in the course of the same trip (where his wife and he would name the reclamation 'Willingdon Island').[54] Since the last stage of the Maharajah's training programme was a tour, he did not feel cancelling it would have any serious impact.[55] But the Resident did have a point in that the Maharani's feelings merited serious consideration; as the Political Secretary put it, she was 'a lady of great charm and high character' who had 'done admirably in circumstances of considerable difficulty', and so the Government of India were obliged to 'consider her feelings and position as far as reasonably possible'.[56] However, while she had several times been told that her rule would terminate in August 1932, all the same, it was felt that at no point was a guarantee given, and she could be expected to acquiesce in the new decision of the Viceroy ungrudgingly. To protect her sentiments, though, it was suggested that Lord Willingdon pay her a high tribute at the installation durbar. All this having been considered the Viceroy decided that Sethu Lakshmi Bayi's feelings or expectations ought not to prejudice a decision pertaining to her nephew's inherent rights.[57] It is quite noteworthy that while these discussions were occurring in Simla, the Maharani herself had no clue about what awaited her, and it would be some more days before the Resident gave her the information on 8 July.[58]

Throughout all this, Sir CP and the Junior Maharani remained with the Willingdons, and the Viceroy formed the opinion that the only matter pending was to ascertain, through a personal interview, whether or not the young Maharajah was trained enough to take over from his aunt.[59] It is this decision that was later recast in that popular story about summons to the Maharajah to determine whether he was fit in his mind and psychologically sound, a twist that was intended, arguably, to discredit his aunt. By this time the investiture was moved further up the calendar by a few months, so that it could occur as early as November 1931, i.e., in a matter of about three months, and nine before the Regency was originally intended to conclude. This was because Lord Willingdon apparently just realised that he would be unable to leave Delhi after January 1932 due to a session of the Central Legislative Assembly commencing that month.[60]

Mr Pritchard was therefore asked to arrange for the Maharajah to reach Simla as soon as possible so that a final decision could be reached, and the Viceroy could thereafter formulate his tour programme to visit Travancore and south India in November that year.[61]

It was on 2 July that the Resident was asked to send the Maharajah to Simla post-haste. But instead of doing so immediately, he responded on 6 July with his previously stated concerns about the Maharani and waited for further instructions. This was followed by a second telegram from Simla on 7 July noting that his views were being considered but that the Maharajah should be sent right away in any case. The following day Mr Pritchard informed his superiors that as the Maharajah was engaged with the *bhadradeepam* ceremony in the Sri Padmanabhaswamy Temple, he would not be free to leave until 17 July. This caused much annoyance to the Viceroy, for his information (presumably from the Junior Maharani) was that this function was not very important.[62] Lord Willingdon was not pleased by the delay in the Maharajah's arrival and even suspected that perhaps 'adverse influences' were at work in Trivandrum.[63] But the Political Secretary vouched for the integrity of the Resident, informing the Viceroy that Mr Pritchard was perhaps unaware of the great 'personal interest' taken by him in this matter.[64] It was also soon confirmed that indeed it was not possible for the Maharajah to leave in the middle of the bhadradeepam and that he would arrive as soon as possible later in the month.[65]

The Resident was duly informed by the Political Secretary that 'the proposed change of date for investing the young Maharajah is due entirely to Lord Willingdon's own convenience [owing to the impossibility of going on tour after January 1932]' and 'owing to his friendship with his [the Maharajah's] father'.[66] This was somewhat unusual, as the Kochu Koil Tampuran, held to be a 'worm', 'mentally deficient', and lacking in all social respects, was unknown to have any highly placed friends, leave alone the Viceroy. But what was clear was that his decision was one based on personal discretion. In the meantime he convened a meeting with his advisers and Sir CP to discuss Sethu Lakshmi Bayi and her reaction if an early investiture were finalised. Lord Willingdon, despite entertaining the Junior Maharani's wishes, was apparently keen, nonetheless, to ensure her cousin was not hurt, owing to her tremendous standing. 'His Excellency understood,' the Political Secretary recorded, 'that the reputation of the Maharani Regent, both as an administrator and as head of the family, was of the highest and he was unwilling to do anything that might make it appear that Govt. was dissatisfied with her rule.'[67]

Sir CP noted the Viceroy's concerns but pointed out that the Maharani's high position and enlightened administration had already been recognised through the conferment of the Crown of India and, like the Political Secretary had suggested, it was possible 'to safeguard her position by high encomiums in His Excellency's speech' at the investiture.[68] It was further suggested that the Viceroy could write her a *personal* letter explaining his reasons for investing the Maharajah with powers sooner than later so that she might rest assured that it was not due to lack of confidence in her.[69] Sir CP also added that 'in any case the Regent will continue to be the head of the ruling family in Travancore. She has also a high position as the Rani of Attingal, a large estate which she will continue to enjoy even after the Maharajah is invested.' In fact, he claimed to be in favour of her 'continuing to receive all her existing privileges and allowances even in retirement'.[70] Thus, the Viceroy was made to understand that there was no reason to worry about the Maharani's concerns at this time and that she would be well taken care of, thereby strengthening the case that the Maharajah's fitness to rule was the only aspect to be taken into account.

In retrospect many found it odd that Sir CP, an avowed advocate of the Junior Maharani's, was permitted by the Viceroy to act as spokesperson for her cousin, who had never foreseen the need for hiring lobbyists in Delhi, again pointing to the personal influence Sir CP exercised over the Willingdons. In any case, on 23 July, the Maharajah arrived in Simla where it was arranged for him to meet the Viceroy that very day. At the end of their meeting, Lord Willingdon announced that the Junior Maharani's son could indeed be given powers sooner than previously proposed and noted down in his official records of that meeting the following:

> I have now met him and feel after conversing with him and reading the reports of the administrative training he has already undergone, that it would not be fair to defer giving him his powers later. I have made some deviation from the general policy laid down by my predecessor, but I think each case has to be treated on its own merits and I consider the young Maharajah's training has reached a point when it would not be profitable to pursue it further.[71]

Thus, the Viceroy's response was a far cry from the popularly told, righteous exclamation of wonder that the boy was not mentally unstable, clarifying that his own discretion was the reason for this departure from the general principle enunciated by Lord Irwin some years ago. By the end of July, thus, it was finalized that the Maharajah would be installed in November 1931 with full powers, and the Resident asked Sethu Lakshmi Bayi to ascertain an auspicious date for the event. She, however, chose to defer planning of this durbar wholly to the Maharajah's staff[72] and it was thereafter confirmed for 6 November, two days before his nineteenth birthday. Additionally, the Viceroy decreed that 'there is no longer any necessity to keep the Maharajah from the society of his mother' and that 'His Highness will in future live with her'.[73] The Government of India, however, realised that this new arrangement was perhaps embarrassing for Captain Harvey due to his disputes with the Junior Maharani, and that it would be best, to avoid friction, if he be permitted to leave before the end of the Regency.[74] Sethu Lakshmi Bayi agreed and accordingly he was relieved from service and departed soon afterwards.

By now news broke out in Travancore of the Viceroy's decision. Mr Pritchard anticipated that with most of the newspapers in the state being 'out for sensation', the Maharani ought to prepare to have her feelings 'gravely hurt' by the press.[75] He was not let down and these newspapers, he wrote, made 'little attempt at disguising the editors' pleasure on account of the early termination of the present administration'.[76] The Junior Maharani too was rejoicing. On her way back with her son she arranged all the way in Travancore addresses, receptions and celebrations.[77] The capital was abuzz with talk about who the next Dewan would be, with the names of K.M. Panikkar, Sir V.T. Krishnamachari, and Sir CP standing out as most likely. There was general euphoria among the politicians in Trivandrum, their joy as much due to the termination of the Regency as it was about the investiture of their Maharajah. As for Sethu Lakshmi Bayi, she suffered a relapse of tuberculosis, which, doctors informed the Resident, was due to 'worry owing to the unexpected curtailment of the Regency period'.[78] Her thoughts at the time are glimpsed in a letter she wrote Mr Pritchard:

> I feel grave misgivings about my future but my consciousness that all through the stressful period of the Regency I have done the exacting duties of my position according to my lights and that I have done nothing forgetting God or my conscience, will, I hope, make me endure with fortitude, the troubles the post-Regency period may hold in store for me.[79]

To assuage her concerns, which were natural, the Viceroy sent the Maharani as decided in Simla, his personal assurance that the early termination of the Regency had nothing to do with any faults found with her government but was determined by other factors entirely. On 18 August the Maharani received the

Viceroy's letter in which Lord Willingdon, after explaining how he found the Maharajah to be capable enough to take over the administration, wrote:

> In coming to this decision I would assure Your Highness that I do not differ in any way from my predecessor's opinion regarding the manner in which you as Regent have ruled the great State of Travancore during the minority period. The appreciation of the Government of India has already been given public expression by the conferment upon Your Highness of the Crown of India and all that I have seen and heard makes me realise with increasing force how richly Your Highness has deserved that high distinction. I have since my assumption of office learned nothing but good of Your Highness' administration and all praise the admirable manner in which, under conditions of considerable difficulty, you have discharged your responsibilities on behalf of the minor Maharajah. In deciding therefore that he should receive his ruling powers in November, my one regret has been that this may cause some disappointment or inconvenience to Your Highness, since you had reason to suppose that your tenure of office would extend until August 1932. I am sure however that you will realise the weighty reasons underlying my decision and will believe me when I say that if I had felt it consistent with my conscience to postpone the date in your interest, I should in view of your great services to Travancore have been anxious to do it. I feel, however, that when a minor has become competent to assume the duties and responsibilities of his inheritance it is my bounden duty to invest him without further delay.[80]

As it happened, it had by now turned out that the Viceroy would not, after all, be able to personally install the Maharajah. The Second Round Table Conference in England was scheduled to commence in September and the Government of India were in constant touch with London on this account already; the Viceroy could barely go on tour at such a critical time.[81] The decision about the Maharajah, however, remained and it would be up to Mr Pritchard to perform the ceremony in November, with a message from Lord Willingdon read out in public. The Viceroy also informed the Maharani personally of his regret at being unable to perform the investiture and hoped to visit Travancore 'and renew my old time friendship with Your Highness' at another date.[82] For her part, the Maharani acted with decorum and, with her stiff upper lip, showed herself satisfied with the Viceroy's letter. The following day she replied:

> If I had any misgivings about the *raison d'etre* for revising a decision repeatedly affirmed by successive British representatives in Travancore, Your Excellency's assurance that the revision was necessitated by the considerations stressed in Your Excellency's letter and that it meant no reflection on me or my administration, has dispelled them. I am deeply gratified by the eloquent tribute Your Excellency has been pleased to pay to my work in the State and I am happy at the thought that I can go into retirement conscious that the Regency Administration has all along been well received by the Suzerain Government.[83]

The months passed quickly thereafter, and November arrived with frenzied haste. Aspects of the investiture durbar on 6 November had all been planned at the Kowdiar Palace, and were to be followed two days later by the Maharajah's first birthday revelries as a monarch. But when the final draft of the programme was sent to Sethu Lakshmi Bayi, she felt unhappy on seeing that she was to be received at the function with a twenty-one-gun salute and other honours, but would depart with none, as though she were merely an ordinary member of the family, not a retiring ruler. The Maharajah, however, was firm and refused to permit the firing of a salute for the Maharani once she had resigned powers 'even as a special courtesy for the occasion'.[84] It appears she considered not participating in the durbar at all, but the Maharajah 'expressed a wish that Her Highness should be present at the function so that he could take over the administration from her directly with her blessings'.[85] Therefore, so as not to be called churlish in laying down the reins of state, she decided to waive her objections and to personally hand over power to the Maharajah. And as promised, at the installation durbar, a message from Lord Willingdon was read out before the assembly, in which high praise was reserved for Sethu Lakshmi Bayi.

> Your Highness is fortunate in succeeding to the inheritance of a State which has been administered in a most statesmanlike fashion not only by your predecessors but also by Her Highness the Maharani Regent during your minority. The debt which Your Highness and the Travancore State owe to Her Highness the Maharani Regent is one which it is difficult for me to estimate or for Your Highness to repay, but I feel sure that you will leave nothing undone to maintain Her Highness' dignity and welfare in retirement.[86]

With that, the Maharajah was proclaimed sovereign ruler with much fanfare and splendour, and Sethu Lakshmi Bayi 'resigned her powers with great dignity' and relinquished the Regency after ruling for a period of seven years.[87] When she left the durbar, she found waiting for her an ordinary carriage, devoid of those marks of state that she had enjoyed for the last several years as ruler. As the guns boomed in the capital, celebrating the rise of a new monarch and the emergence of a new power centre, Sethu Lakshmi Bayi returned quietly to Satelmond Palace and collapsed into bed, unwell, with her heart full of unspoken resignation.

The eclipse Mr Pritchard forewarned had begun.

As Regent of Travancore, Sethu Lakshmi Bayi had enjoyed an unparalleled position in India, with more power than any other ruling Maharani. Though, in 1924, at her own installation durbar she was declared an appointed Regent, in the subsequent years the position was clarified and the Government of India accepted that as per matrilineal law, she had actually succeeded to power.[88] She was not handicapped by a Council of Regency, despite persistent demands by detractors, and conducted the government in the manner of a Regnant Maharajah, also enjoying all marks of sovereignty within the state. That is why, when the decision was taken to invest the Junior Maharani's son with ruling powers sooner than initially anticipated, she was asked to submit 'in accordance with the State and family custom' proposals for her future in retirement.[89] Sethu Lakshmi Bayi had every reason to hope for an honourable settlement; after all the previous Regent in Travancore, Gowri Parvathi Bayi, who ruled from 1814 until 1829, received 'all the honours appertaining to a reigning sovereign' even in retirement,[90] and at the time of her death some years later, 'all the funeral ceremonies and other observances on the demise of a sovereign' were duly performed.[91]

The most important ceremonial honour Sethu Lakshmi Bayi desired to have continued was the twenty-one-gun salute she enjoyed within the state. She also wished to have a personal nineteen-gun salute granted by the Government of India, were she ever to travel into British Indian territory or to another principality. The request by itself was not unprecedented, for in 1895 the Maharani Regent of Mysore had received this honour, and Sethu Lakshmi Bayi too expected the same in 1925.[92] But by then the attitude of the Government of India regarding personal honours had changed significantly and the 'tendency in modern times' was strongly 'in the direction of restricting all such honours'.[93] The authorities viewed that indeed in Travancore the Maharani held a very unique position and was 'a Regent in a more real sense than the Rani Regents [elsewhere] usually are'.[94] But if such an honour were granted to her, there would be similar inevitable demands from others too, opening a can of worms Delhi preferred to avoid.[95] So, in 1925, the decision was against the grant of a personal salute but the Government of India concluded that 'when a suitable opportunity offers itself' in the future, combined with her unique status, an exception from the rule could perhaps be justified.[96] For the time being, since the Maharani was enjoying a full twenty-one-gun salute within the state and all the dignities of a sovereign, the authorities felt that the matter ought not to be pursued.[97] She repeated her request in 1929, however, wanting also to discuss her retirement, but was again told that it was too early to negotiate these.[98]

So, in 1931, when the Maharani was finally asked for a proposal pertaining to her settlement, she repeated her request for a personal salute, and asked for the continuation of the local twenty-one-gun salute to her for life. As for allowances, she desired to continue receiving the Rs 2 lakh she had per annum for expenses as also the Rs 15,000 allotted for tours within the state. For ceremonial honours the Maharani requested continuation of her subhedar escort, with fifer, drummer and colours, besides a contingent of the Royal Body Guard of five outriders, including one non-commissioned officer (NCO), to act as her escort when she went out driving. At Satelmond Palace she expected the existing police guard to remain, as also the usual force of special constables that accompanied her when she toured the country. On her birthdays she desired the same ceremonials that she had been enjoying for the past seven years. As for her office, she wished to have a staff of one secretary, two clerks, one typist, and twenty peons, in addition to the peons she had as Attingal Rani. Finally, the Maharani wished the state to provide her a good limousine for her personal use and a cheaper car for the use of her entourage, with two drivers and two cleaners, all maintained at state expense.[99]

The Maharani was keen to have her settlement decided by the Government of India before the termination of the Regency owing to 'fear that the Maharajah may not accord her just treatment' and 'by her uncertainty as to how far the Maharajah will be influenced by his mother'.[100] While Mr Pritchard appreciated these fears, he did not deem it wise to settle the matter without consultations with the Maharajah, and suggested that the Government of India wait until after the investiture. The matter of the Maharani's honours and allowances, he opined, were 'exclusively the prerogative of the Ruler' and the authorities could intervene only if the Maharajah failed to behave 'wisely and justly'.[101] In 1829 also, when the last Regency terminated, from the record of a conversation the then Resident

Col Morrison had with the young Rajah, it appeared that it was up to the latter to decide the future of the ex-Regent; at that time Rani Gowri Parvathi Bayi was provided 'through life the same honours and marks of respect to which she had been accustomed as Queen Regent'.[102] From this it appeared that the present Maharani had a 'substantial' claim to existing privileges continued for life but the Government of India would have to see 'the extent to which the Maharajah is prepared to go to satisfy Her Highness' and could only 'use their good offices' in convincing him to provide a dignified settlement to Sethu Lakshmi Bayi.[103]

As for the request for a salute, Mr Pritchard was personally in favour of this owing to her exceptional status and position. Regarding her allowances, however, he was against the continuation of the existing sum of Rs 2,15,000 but pointed out that the Maharani would nevertheless require a 'large annual allowance fixed on her for life' because her financial position merely as Attingal Rani did not befit her status any more.[104] In her capacity as senior female member of the family the Maharani received an average of Rs 40,000 per year from the Civil List, which, however, was 'intended to be disbursed solely on religious and charitable purposes'.[105] Then she enjoyed from the Sripadam Rs 54,000. Out of this, Sethu Lakshmi Bayi paid Rs 12,000 to the Junior Maharani, Rs 16,000 for costs of her establishment, and another Rs 12,000 towards religious charities. This left her a slim figure of only Rs 14,000 a year for her personal income, which was deemed too inadequate for a woman who was practically sovereign in a wealthy state for years.[106] Mr Pritchard felt, thus, that if an aggregate pension of Rs 1 lakh were provided to the Maharani, she would be satisfied and 'there would still be ample margin for savings'.[107]

The Government of India again declined the request for a personal salute but took note of the Resident's views and agreed that the matter could be decided only after the Maharajah's investiture. Accordingly, Mr Pritchard opened the topic with the latter promptly following his installation and birthday celebrations. There was some urgency in reaching a decision, it was felt, as the Maharani's own birth anniversary was fast approaching and ceremonials on the occasion would depend on the Maharajah's orders. To general shock, however, the Maharajah issued a notice that on the Maharani's birthday she would be given the same honours and dignities that she had enjoyed before the Regency, when she was simply Attingal Rani.[108] Sethu Lakshmi Bayi immediately protested and Mr Prichard had to himself approach the Maharajah and remind him that the last Regent had received a full twenty-one-gun salute on her birthdays, with all honours of sovereignty, which ought to be the precedent in the present case also. He also requested Sir CP to put together a formal note containing what exactly was proposed for the Maharani's future, which he could then forward to the Government of India before final orders were issued on this subject.[109]

Sir CP, however, wrote to the Viceroy complaining that the Resident was being unnecessarily pushy in pressing the new Maharajah for an early decision on the matter, stating that

> ... His Highness is naturally anxious to go into the matter carefully in consultation with me having regard especially to H.E.'s statement [in the message at the investiture paying a tribute to the Maharani]. The solution that I propose to suggest is that His Highness should pass orders to the effect that he will shortly examine the question and decide on the honours and dignities due to the [ex-]Regent, the Junior Maharani and the other members of the family, but that, for this year pending such decision and without prejudice to it, the ex-Regent will get the same honours as last year (when she was actually Regent) except that she will get a salute of 2 guns less than the Maharajah.[110]

This was acceptable to the authorities and thus at the Maharani's birthday she received, for what would be the last time in her life, all the dignities and honours due to a sovereign, minus two guns from the twenty-one-gun salute. But the tone of Sir CP's letter was not propitious, for it seemed to suggest that the Maharajah viewed her as just one among other members of the family and not with any special consideration as ex-Regent who once held ruling powers herself, or as head of the royal house. In any case, in the months after her birthday, the new government as well as the Resident became busy due to a number of reasons, and it was February 1932 before Mr Pritchard spoke again to Sir CP about the pending matter. The latter responded that the promised memorandum was still not ready but offered a vague idea about what he would try to persuade the Maharajah to provide. This was that the Maharani be granted a seventeen-gun salute within the state, an allowance of Rs 1 lakh, and 'that for the rest the precedents in connexion with Rani Gowri Parvathi Bayi should be followed'.[111] Mr Pritchard was agreeable to this and felt that Sethu Lakshmi Bayi, who was 'getting very restive' and was 'anxious that the matter should be settled with the least possible delay', would also accept it.[112] Now that Sir CP knew what to propose, he could, it was imagined, move forward and finalize matters. But, for obvious reasons, the Resident suspected that 'unless His Highness and Sir C.P. Ramaswami Iyer are pushed a bit they will still further delay the decision on the case'.[113] Since the Maharajah was scheduled to go to Delhi soon, he suggested that the Viceroy too put pressure on him to settle the matter promptly.

On 3 March, Lord Willingdon wrote to the Maharajah asking him for a report on the Maharani's settlement, insisting that it ought to be finalized without too much delay.[114] The Maharajah duly replied stating that he himself was 'quite anxious' to settle the question and had instructed Sir CP to 'go into the matter fully' and acquaint the Viceroy with its progress when they met.[115] This meeting took place eventually and Sir CP made the same suggestions as he had to Mr Pritchard. But on 1 April 1932 when the Maharajah issued orders, they appeared to Sethu Lakshmi Bayi as an absolute travesty:

> Her Highness will receive an aggregate annual allowance of one lakh of rupees, the said sum being *inclusive* of the income from the properties, allowances and other emoluments set apart for the senior female member of my family. She will be entitled to the privileges and dignities as set out in the papers relating to the 1840 [sic] precedent ... her Salute being fixed at 17 guns. It is to be remembered that this order deals only with the personal perquisites of Her Highness and does not deal with those of her children whose cases will be similar to those of other junior members of the family.[116]

The Maharajah's decision, when it was communicated to the Maharani, was at once received as insulting and unbecoming. For one, his decision that the Rs 1 lakh was to be inclusive of her existing allowances was massively disappointing; as the Maharani sourly wrote to the Resident: 'Surely the term one lakh in itself possesses no peculiarly pleasing sound unless it stands for its accepted value.'[117] She pointed out that in Pudukkottai, which was a small neighbour of Travancore and an inferior in the precedence of princely states, the ex-Regent received in retirement half the allowance enjoyed in power. Her own standing as Regent of Travancore had been much higher than the former's. Besides, she argued, 'the receipt of any allowance less than Rs 1 lakh would be quite incompatible with the status of the ex-Regent of an important State like Travancore whose position the Government of India has declared to be on a higher footing than that of appointed Regents'.[118] She expected the decision to be in keeping with 'the spirit of Sir CP's oral communication', which had appeared more generous, rather than this present parsimonious interpretation.[119]

As for ceremonial honours, the Maharajah's order was unclear. The Maharani was informed that only on her birthdays would the salute of seventeen guns be fired and not on other occasions. Besides, the order did not speak of questions such as her birthday ceremonials, her escort and so on, and she wanted 'a statement in unambiguous terms showing in detail every item under honours and dignities' she was to enjoy.[120] From the present order it appeared to her that she was to have 'none of the customary honours of the Ruler in ordinary times but all [of them]' on her birthdays, a situation that would be 'nothing short of a mockery'.[121] Having expressed her protest in writing Sethu Lakshmi Bayi concluded:

> ... I am really much worried and unhappy at my future position not being settled even after all these months and would earnestly request you to kindly represent to the Government of India that I feel deeply distressed at the thought that for the faithful and unselfish discharge, under exceptional difficulties, of the onerous trust committed to my care the reward should be the kind of treatment that is being meted out to me.[122]

The Maharani also wrote to the Dewan, asking for clarifications and pointing out that the allowance proposed earlier was meant to be exclusive of existing receipts, unlike what was actually ordered, and that she 'would strongly protest' if the present decision were considered final.[123] Mr Pritchard also was very disappointed by the Maharajah's orders. He reminded the Government of India of a meeting the latter, Sir CP and the Junior Maharani had with the Viceroy prior to the investiture when it was agreed that Lord Willingdon 'should be the final arbiter as to the nature of the honours and dignities to be enjoyed by the Senior Maharani'.[124] Sir CP had also earlier promised to submit a memorandum with proposals for the Government of India's consideration before passing final orders. None of this had been done and the Maharajah had directly issued unilateral instructions in breach of this understanding.

The Resident pointed out that the Maharani, who had at first asked for all her allowances and dignities to be continued in retirement, accepted Sir CP's proposal for a more modest settlement not because she was satisfied by it 'but simply because she wishes to do everything reasonably possible to avoid bickering and haggling'.[125] Then, when Sir CP suggested the figure of Rs 1 lakh there was not 'the faintest suggestion' that this was to include existing allowances. This would mean that the Maharani would actually receive only Rs 46,000 a year as pension for her services, which was seriously below what was suitable and dignified.[126] While he knew that in claiming Rs 2 lakh at the start Sethu Lakshmi Bayi was 'preparing the ground for a compromise', she could not reasonably be expected to accept anything less than Rs 1 lakh, and he could therefore understand why she was 'incensed' by the present decision.[127] This order itself,

Mr Pritchard felt, was 'actuated by vindictiveness' on the part of the Maharajah and his mother. Indeed, he asserted, ever since the termination of the Regency was announced, both had 'gone out of their way to hurt Her Highness' feelings and generally make her a lot unhappier'.[128] This was all in contravention of the hopes expressed in the Viceroy's message that the Maharajah would treat his aunt with dignity and honour in retirement.

Besides the question of the allowances, there were the items of honours such as strength of the outriders, escort, a permanent subhedar guard, etc., 'which are of the highest importance in the maintenance of Her Highness' dignity'. The Resident had already informed Sir CP about the urgent need to settle this as well.[129] But in deciding this matter, excessive reliance could not be placed on precedents, for papers available were scarce and incomprehensive. The only records pertaining to the former Regent Rani Gowri Parvathi Bayi's life in retirement were some orders to the state forces, which only showed that she was 'accorded the highest honours on the occasion of her birthday', including a twenty-one-gun salute.[130] In view of this, Mr Pritchard felt that it was not 'unreasonable to assume that in the matters of guards, escorts, etc. about which no documentary evidence is traceable, the ex-Regent was treated with equal generosity'.[131] Now, however, the Maharajah was determined to stick to the letter of the old documents and provide honours only on birthdays, ignoring the Maharani on other occasions and treating her not only as any other member of the family, but also withdrawing from her the high position she ought to enjoy as head of the dynasty.

Sethu Lakshmi Bayi, in the meantime, further scaled down her expectations and expressed them more precisely. As Attingal Rani she enjoyed a *jemadar* escort and now 'what I want is only the substitution of the subhedar for the jemadar and the addition of a fifer and drummer'.[132] Similarly, as against the two mounted soldiers who escorted her as Attingal Rani, she wished to have four outriders and one NCO when she went out driving. She was similarly entitled to one NCO and three privates at Satelmond Palace as her official guard, and she now wanted the addition of three more privates to this number. As for her salute, these, in keeping with her position, were to be fired not only on her birthdays but also when she left and arrived at the capital, as they would be for the Maharajah and were for her for the past seven years. The number of peons she wished to have for her office was reduced to eight and she hoped to retain the police guard as before. As for personal staff, she was willing to forfeit this request. And on her birthdays, the Maharani wished the state forces to carry colours in honouring her, for her information was that existing records showed the last Regent as having enjoyed this.[133] But on further perusal no such information was found in the records and hence she withdrew that stipulation too.[134] This revised claim was, she noted, more than reasonable hoping that at long last the Maharajah would agree and take a final decision.

But the Maharajah was unrelenting and in the last week of May, Mr Pritchard expressed his regret to Sir CP that he had not agreed to provide Rs 1 lakh exclusive of existing allowances to the Maharani.[135] Sir CP's words in response were: 'I will tell you what it is Colonel Pritchard. I could not get either of the parties to view the matter dispassionately.'[136] By 'either parties' he meant the Junior Maharani and her son, and further stated that their ill feeling owed to their bad relations with the Valiya Koil Tampuran.[137] Mr Pritchard argued that while Rama Varma might have given offence to the Maharajah and his mother, that was no reason to distress Sethu Lakshmi Bayi who had ruled with widely lauded dedication. He also asked Sir CP why the time-honoured process of going through the Government of India before passing final orders had been flouted, which question, however, the latter evaded.[138] Sir CP insisted that he personally thought of Sethu Lakshmi Bayi as 'a most estimable lady' affirming that her claims were 'by no means excessive', then ascribing the delay to hangers-on and relations who were supposedly influencing the Maharajah against being generous towards his aunt.[139]

In any case, Mr Pritchard decided to meet the Maharajah personally. At first Chithira Tirunal attempted to ward him off, stating that he would express his views privately to the Viceroy.[140] The Resident then put his foot down and insisted that this would entail further delay. At first, he pointed out, the Maharajah evaded a decision claiming there was not enough time. But now 'it could not be denied that it was not for the want of time that the question ... remained unsettled' after so many months.[141] But the Maharajah made it clear that he had no intention of furnishing a proper memorandum with proposals that could then be sent to the Government of India, suggesting instead that Sir CP would write a private letter to the Viceroy explaining his views on the subject. This raised an objection from the Resident who explicitly stated that there was nothing 'private' about all this and that it was entirely official and had to be channelled through the Resident and not through Sir CP or any outside agents, no matter what their personal connections with Lord Willingdon.[142]

With regard to the substance of the settlement, the Maharajah made it clear he had no inclination to 'go out of his way' to give the Maharani 'anything extra' than what was proved to have been received by Rani Gowri Parvathi Bayi.[143] The Resident once again asked the Maharajah to reconsider because there were only a few military orders extant and 'it would not be just to refuse certain dignities and honours to the ex-Regent merely because papers a century old, if they ever existed, cannot be traced'.[144] Chithira Tirunal then came to his principal objection against giving the Maharani such honours, for her demands, he claimed, showed that 'she wanted to be on an equality with him'.[145] When Mr Pritchard asked him to give one example of such a desire on her part, the Maharajah pointed out that a subhedar escort was the ruler's privilege, which she wished to claim. The Resident responded that there was sufficient distinction, as his guard would carry colours and the Maharani's would not and that he would have two fifers and drummers and she one each. Some more petty discussion in this vein entailed after which, surprisingly, the Maharajah informed Mr Pritchard that he had not actually so far seen any of the papers repeatedly submitted by Sethu Lakshmi Bayi regarding her claims.[146] The interview, therefore, did not take the matter at all forward as the Maharajah was unacquainted with important aspects of the case, and had not found the time in all these months to even glance at her representations and appeals.

Mr Pritchard found Sir CP's behaviour also quite distasteful, for he had consistently stated that 'he was most sympathetically inclined towards Her Highness and that he was in favour of her being treated magnanimously'.[147] And yet, there was this insistence to take a few existing military orders as a definite precedent and granting the Maharani a salute and other honours only on her birthdays, which had 'nothing sympathetic or magnanimous about it'.[148] By June, matters were still pending at the palace and the Resident realised that the Maharajah was not serious at all about fulfilling his duties towards his aunt. Papers regarding the Maharani's claims were available with the Dewan, but the latter had not received any orders to forward them to the palace.[149] Indeed, stated Mr Pritchard, 'not a single reference' had been made to the Dewan by the Maharajah in connection with the Maharani's settlement, almost as if it were a non-issue for him.[150] It was clear that the question was not being considered by officials but by influences in the palace. It was also seen as disrespectful of him towards the Viceroy, for five months previously in April he had assured the latter that the subject was receiving his full attention. From his attitude since then, however, 'it would not appear that the Maharajah is troubling himself very much'.[151] Mr Pritchard felt that it was time for some plain talking now, and to insist that the Maharajah settle the issue within a fixed period of time. Additionally, he informed the Government of India that

> ... Her Highness has been seriously ill for weeks and is really ill now. I am told, and I believe it, that she is fretting very much indeed on account of the delay

in the settlement of her claims, and that if her anxieties were removed the slow progress she is now making might be accelerated. This is an additional reason why, in fairness to Her Highness, the case should be decided without further delay.[152]

Sethu Lakshmi Bayi, despite her illness, was constantly troubled by stress and angst about her future, which did not seem at all promising, given the open hostility of the Maharajah. Writing on 20 June to Mr Pritchard, she made her grievances against the Government of India's acquiescence in Chithira Tirunal's lack of sympathy known while also appealing for a speedy decision:

> I am sorry that nothing has so far resulted from my writing to the Dewan about my allowance etc. in accordance with your suggestion. I hope that you will not now think that I am fretting myself without cause, seeing that over seven months have passed since the termination of the Regency. When first I requested a settlement of my post-Regency position the Government of India said that since the Regency was to terminate only in August 1932 they did not find it necessary to decide the question so far in advance. I reopened the question a year or two later and they said in reply to my representation that the matter would be decided at the time of the Investiture. Afterwards when the determinative of the Regency was decided upon before the time originally fixed for it, I requested you to have the question settled if possible before the end of the Regency. The Government of India's order then was that they would be settled after the Maharajah was invested with powers. Now the Investiture has taken place and, as I have already stated, seven months have followed and yet there appears to be no early prospect of the settlement of my affairs. I dare say the matter is still pending with the Government of India. May I request you kindly to convey to the Government of India my sense of acute disappointment and humiliation at the matter still hanging fire and to pray for early orders. If a telegraphic message can be sent I shall be deeply obliged.[153]

But none of this worked and eventually the Maharajah's personal connections with the Viceroy appear to have been more important than the Maharani's record as Regent or official propriety in deciding these matters. And Lord Willingdon got away with praising Sethu Lakshmi Bayi but not backing those sentiments with material proof of his commitment. It was the middle of August before the Viceroy had a conversation with the Maharajah. The latter then informed him that the Maharani was entitled already to nearly Rs 1 lakh as

Attingal Rani (not adding that only Rs 14,000 of this accrued to her personally and that the rest were religious and other costs), and so Lord Willingdon decided that a further allowance of Rs 75,000 would be a fair settlement. As for dignities and honours, he held the Maharajah's ideas as 'quite sound' and preferred, ominously, to leave those aspects to be decided by him, 'relying as I do on Your Highness' sense of fairness and generosity'.[154] Interestingly, at the end of the letter, the Viceroy stated that the matter was 'a private and personal one' between himself and the Maharajah and had been treated as confidential. Therefore, Chithira Tirunal was to formally write to the Resident and the Political Department for their official records to finalise matters.[155] In other words, Lord Willingdon was corresponding behind the back of his own officers in discussing these issues with the Maharajah in private. In response Chithira Tirunal expressed his gratitude and how he was 'fully conscious' that he could 'rely implicitly on the sympathy and kindness' characterising Lord Willingdon's dealings 'with my house and me in particular'.[156] Once again, it appears, the influence of Sir CP in providing the Maharajah private access to the Viceroy, circumventing official procedure, helped avoid unpleasantness with the Resident at the Maharani's expense.

The final orders of the Maharajah issued the same day granted the Maharani Rs 75,000 a year exclusive of existing incomes but the allotment was 'to include any sums that may be necessary for a Private Secretary and clerical staff in case Her Highness decides to employ such staff'.[157] The Maharani was to continue with her jemadar escort, only that a fifer and drummer would be added to it 'although ordinarily', pointed out the Maharajah, 'a jemadar escort does not include a fifer and drummer'.[158] The mounted escort would be provided one NCO and the Maharani would receive a guard only at her official residence. Similarly, the firing of a seventeen-gun salute was to be confined to her birthdays 'in accordance with precedents', while four peons would be added to her existing staff.[159] This, it was finally decided, was to be the settlement in retirement of Sethu Lakshmi Bayi after seven years of ruling Travancore.

It did not impress her much and writing in October from Nagercoil, where she was convalescing following treatment under her tuberculosis specialists, the Maharani pointed out sarcastically that the order still did not 'appear to err on the side of excessive lucidity' and would need many clarifications.[160] She further stated:

> Apparently the decision of His Highness as now communicated has received the blessings of the Government of India in which case I cannot help feeling

> that I have been badly let down by them. I am accepting the decision under strong protest and reserve to myself the right to request the Government of India to revise the present decision on more generous terms at any time in the future. The contrast between what is now offered to me and what was allowed undoubtedly on the Government of India's advice to my ancestor in similar circumstances is painfully striking.[161]

Indeed, it had been Col Morrison who had first suggested to the then Rajah in 1829 the provision to the ex-Regent of all honours in retirement also. But at that time relations between the Rajah and his aunt were closer and the former even referred to her as his mother, perhaps explaining his readiness to accord her the highest status possible.[162] He is also described by a granddaughter of the Junior Maharani as a 'grateful nephew' who felt it necessary to bestow on his 'decidedly deserving' aunt all honours in retirement.[163] Now, however, that was not the case as relations between the Junior Maharani and the Maharajah on the one hand and Sethu Lakshmi Bayi on the other were anything but cordial and the latter was perceived as not 'decidedly deserving'. And this influenced the question of her settlement in a significant manner. But the Maharani was not alone in resenting the attitude of the Maharajah in all this. As Mr Pritchard ruefully wrote to the Government of India,

> A fact which I do not think he [the Maharajah] realises and to which his mother's intense and unreasonable antipathy towards the ex-Regent blinds her, is that the latter is held in the greatest reverence and esteem throughout the State, and, unless the Maharajah's final orders are in keeping with the high position of the ex-Regent—not to speak of his own dignity—they will be received by his people in silent resentment.[164]

And they were. Writing in November 1924 the then Resident, Mr Cotton, had warned that the Junior Maharani was already 'like the French after Sedan, counting the days for "la revanche" as soon as her son is vested with ruling powers'.[165] And no sooner had Sethu Lakshmi Bayi resigned authority than the Junior Maharani had her revenge. Lord Willingdon rewarded the Maharajah with power after years of his mother's efforts while his aunt received lofty words of admiration and praise, but little else. Even as he plunged India into an era of political chaos seated in Delhi, little realising it the Viceroy also abandoned Sethu Lakshmi Bayi to an uncertain fate. But she reconciled to this. 'I emerge a wiser woman from the Regency,' she ruminated in a pensive letter to the Valiya Tampuran of Cochin, 'and have learnt that often in this world one gets kicks for honest, selfless work, while the canting self seeker wins half pence.'[166]

RETIREMENT

Lalindloch Palace, Vellayini

14

A Real Little Grande Dame

'Thank God the Regency has terminated,' sighed Sethu Lakshmi Bayi in a letter to Mr Raghavaiah, 'and I am experiencing now the comfort of retirement and freedom from the worry and cares of office.'[1] It was a decorous and formal response to his homage to her work in Travancore, but the reality was that the Maharani had a great deal to be anxious about. The niggardly manner of deciding her settlement hardly heralded an untroubled retirement, and the attitude of the new regime so soon after gaining power suggested little that was propitious. All varieties of harassment were to be inflicted upon her, and it did not matter that she was the head of the royal house, its matriarch or even an ex-Regent who had ruled by inherent right. The authorities were determined to drain even the last vestiges of influence she possessed in that position. A letter, then, to the Valiya Tampuran of Cochin was more honest, where she expressed how 'After seven years of strenuous work performed under very difficult conditions I am naturally sighing for that quiet and peace, which I fondly *hope* may be my portion in retirement.'[2]

While the Junior Maharani took pleasure in travel, socialising and a diversity of entertainments, Sethu Lakshmi Bayi retreated, partly also for reasons of health, into a quiet, more relaxed but charmingly refined style of living. Perhaps in anticipation of difficulties emanating from the Maharajah, towards the conclusion of the Regency she acquired a number of private properties for the use of her daughters and herself; from her retirement till 1938 she tried to literally stay away from the centre of power. 'My parents,' Princess Indira would later remark, 'seemed to specialise in finding unknown but beautiful spots'.[3] Rama Varma would then assume responsibility over planning the structures, having something of a talent for elegant architecture, while the Maharani designed the gardens and general landscape in partnership with her expert brigade of gardeners. In the late 1920s, for instance, a vast rural estate was purchased by the Vellayini Lake, 8 miles outside the capital, and a country house, 'far removed from the active concerns of the town though near enough to command its conveniences',[4] was constructed there. With 'a forest of palm trees all about the lake, and glimpses of the vivid green of paddy fields, a more pleasant site could hardly be found,' pronounced a contemporary travelogue,[5] and for Sethu Lakshmi Bayi this became a favourite abode surrounded by simple villages and much peace and quiet.

Unlike Satelmond Palace, where the premier structure contained several wings and housed all the members of her family, the abode in Vellayini had separate stately buildings. The Valiya Koil Tampuran and his attendants occupied a large premises of their own; all of the Maharani's official establishment and servants had buildings unto themselves; while she herself resided in an exquisite bungalow, with large, airy rooms and 'surrounded by excellent rose gardens with a very well done arbour, about 9 or 10 feet high, covered in greenery and flowers and very soothing to look at'.[6] Her sisters and their families, who normally accompanied her, had a bungalow at a distance and 'after supper every evening we would walk up to the main palace and spend time with the Maharani'.[7] There was also a large patch of shared gardens, beside which Sethu Lakshmi Bayi had a granite pavilion constructed, with a black-and-white chequered floor. It was here that she received visitors in the late hours of the afternoon, with fresh coconut water served them in traditional copper tumblers, while members of the royal family sipped out of silver glasses. 'She also had a tall silver plated Krishna statue here, which was installed in such a manner that she could view it from her own part of the grounds on the other side.'[8]

As her daughters grew up, Sethu Lakshmi Bayi had another palace building constructed across the gardens from the pavilion for their use. Rama Varma called it Lalindloch Palace, with the first part of the name ('Lal-Ind') being a mix of the children's names (Lalitha and Indira), and the second a Gaelic term for 'lake'. Surrounded by vast verandahs on all sides, it had enormous apartments with high, vaulted ceilings and huge windows. One section with all its suites of rooms was allotted to Princess Lalitha and the other to Princess Indira. 'There were maids for everything we did: one pair to bathe us, another to dress us, another to watch over us while we played, all of whom slept on mats around our beds at night. Now that we think of it, it feels like we lived on another planet altogether!'[9] Every year the family would spend months at a stretch staying at

Vellayini, wandering out for picnics, going rowing in the lake, riding around the countryside, or merely exploring the vast grounds around the palace, which were very nearly a dense tropical forest. 'The mosquitoes here these days are simply beyond conception,' Princess Lalitha complained to her father on one occasion. 'I mean the awful nights when they bite and suck one's blood till I verily believe we rise up each morning perhaps ounces of blood less than we went in!'[10] But for all that it was a very calm lifestyle, and 'we all just lounged about all day, with everything taken care of'.[11]

All of the Maharani's establishment of about 300 servants would attend to the family even in Vellayini. 'They were not all deployed at once, and every ten days a new set of about 100 would take over, and the previous 100 would go on leave.'[12] They were paid modest salaries, and the palace guaranteed meals, clothes, and other needs. 'It was absolutely amazing, the logistics of managing the whole place, and there were clear hierarchies; we never even saw all the classes of servants, or knew them, because there were too many, spread across departments and parts of the estate.'[13] None of them came from poor backgrounds. On the contrary, the menials and maids hailed from respectable Nair families, who considered it an honour to serve in the palace, while cooks and serving staff were all Tamil Brahmins or castemen of the royal family. There were 'inside servants, outside servants; upstairs servants, downstairs servants; kitchen staff; garden staff; garage boys; the sweeping staff; the laundry staff; the official staff; the valets and menservants; the liveried guards; and heaps and heaps of people in general'![14] Besides these servants, there were special men to maintain the stables, the tennis courts, the palace dispensary, the palace electrical substation, as well as the chief royal carpenter called Kesavan Moothassari, 'a dour, quiet person' who took his orders from the Maharani and her husband.[15] The manager would, every time vacancies arose, select men or women and Sethu Lakshmi Bayi and others in the family would pick their individual choices after the Valiya Koil Tampuran had finished conducting his extensive background checks. And then, of course, there were 'so many drivers who lazed around pretty much every day and invariably got into scraps over a pretty housemaid'![16]

This very substantial establishment, including the soldiers on guard duty, was catered to from the huge palace kitchens. Known as the *madapally*, it was housed in a separate building altogether, 'always so smoky, with delicious aromas, although we rarely saw the inside.'[17] This department of the palace alone employed twenty-four cooks, and every afternoon attendants would carry massive copper and silver vessels, full of hot food, on their turbaned heads into the great hall where the royal family dined. 'It was such a procession, with lines and lines of these men coming out of the madapally, and each meal was a great ritual.'[18] The head of all this was considered one of the 'unsung heroes' of the palace. 'He was the finest vegetarian cook we knew,' the Maharani's nephew would tell, 'and was innovative and experimented with new dishes that he tasted elsewhere.'[19] There was a large green marble hall at Satelmond Palace used for lunch, and a long plantain leaf would be laid before the Maharani, with silver bowls and plates placed on them. To wash hands there would be 'a servant holding a basin, another standing by to pour water out of a pitcher, and yet another attendant with a towel on the arm'.[20] While Brahmin servants cooked and served the food, 'once you finished eating they wouldn't touch the plates, which had to be removed by lower-caste Nair ladies'.[21] For all the Brahmin influence, though, the best item on the menu was a certain black, spicy *teeyal* mix, the recipe for which the Valiya Koil Tampuran acquired from a tribal settlement in the forests.[22] As for the rest of the meal, as Sethu Lakshmi Bayi's granddaughter would remember:

> [The Maharani] had to have a certain number of dishes in front of her. For lunch she would have two curries cooked in a certain manner with curds as the base, one *dal* curry, two vegetable curries with gravy, and one dry vegetable, plus a silver bowl with rice in it, from which she would help herself. For tea there had to be ten things, six salty and four sweet. For sweets there was *apam*, made of bananas and rice flour fried in ghee, and a kind of a *halwa* made of arrowroot, sweet but very bland. Among the salty dishes there was a variety of *bhajiyas* and *pakoras* (a type of fritters) fried in batter, and varieties of *dosas* (savoury pancakes) and *idlis* (steamed rice-cakes). The whole family would assemble for this ritual, but not [the wives of male relatives]. They couldn't come anywhere near us when a meal was being eaten, and if by accident they did, then the whole meal had to be sent back—because if anyone below caste set foot in the room while the meal was in progress, it would have to be cooked again [for these wives were all Nair women]. Dinner was always a bit more relaxed, because that was after sunset, when everything is more relaxed.[23]

The palace would always have guests coming in and out, all through the year. Sethu Lakshmi Bayi's sisters were always close; Kutty Amma did not accompany her to Vellayini because her children went to school in Trivandrum, and instead moved to the royal residence in the Fort when the Maharani withdrew from Satelmond Palace. The other sister, Kochu Thankam, however, acted as Sethu

Lakshmi Bayi's principal companion, who also brought up her children during the Regency years. And *she* moved around with the Maharani during her long sojourns everywhere. Her younger brother, known as Uncle Chodhi, who was unwell, also stayed on the palace premises, taking a keen interest in the studies of his royal nieces. Other brothers, who were employed in Madras, Bombay and at other places in upper India, visited now and then with their wives and children, on all of whom the Maharani lavished presents. If they visited Satelmond Palace, they would stay at The Hermitage, a guest house on the grounds, but at Vellayini they occupied a part of the Valiya Koil Tampuran's large building, and servants would be allotted to care for them during the duration of their holidays.

Meals were the only instances where caste came into the picture with the Nair sisters-in-law of the Maharani; their food was *sent* to their apartments and they could not be invited to join the royal family in the dining halls. 'It was not that she herself cared for these customs,' tells a granddaughter, 'but life in the palace had a number of guidelines and traditions she was expected to uphold.'[24] That perhaps explains why once meals were out of the way, the Maharani interacted quite freely with her Nair relations. When one of her brothers married and introduced his bride for the first time at the palace, Sethu Lakshmi Bayi made the usual presents of gold jewellery and gilt mundus to the young girl. 'Normally,' her niece remembers, 'she would not have touched my mother, but to everyone's surprise—and it was very unusual for them—she herself draped the mundu around my mother, touching her freely and without inhibitions. My maternal grandparents were so astonished that the Maharani was treating their daughter as one of her own. That was besides the fact that they were already stunned by her very presence. They had never seen anyone so fair-skinned and beautiful, and all she wore for make-up was her black tikka!'[25]

Sethu Lakshmi Bayi invested an unusual degree of interest in her nephews and nieces. The husbands of her two sisters served as her private secretary and manager, and received salaries from her treasury. All their expenses—meals, clothing, stay and more—were taken care of by the Maharani, as were the academic expenses for their children. She encouraged them to study, so that Kutty Amma's son and younger girl were both educated at the Madras Medical College and then in England, going on to become renowned names in their fields,[26] while one of Kochu Thankam's sons also pursued medicine, and the other two studied in the United States.[27] The six children of her two sisters grew up around Sethu Lakshmi Bayi, and although their parents always referred to her as 'Her Highness', she would have none of it from the younger ones in the family. 'We used to refer to them as Valiyamma (senior aunt) and Valiyachan (senior uncle),' one nephew recalls, 'but it was customary not to address them directly when in their actual presence.'[28]

> We used to play around in the palace compound and in the late afternoon the Maharani would come out for her walk in the garden. There would be the household guards and a dozen servants, with someone holding up a large parasol, all walking silently behind and around her at a distance. I would join her and I still cherish the conversations we had. She loved gardening and would tell me the finer points about how to grow different plants. She was very knowledgeable about a lot of subjects and often corrected me if I said something wrong. The relationship was easy and free of reserve with us, and she laughed and behaved with effortless informality. Of course we held her in very high esteem, and all of us thought of her as our guardian angel. According to the *acharam* (custom) of those days, though, we would not sit in front of her, and always stood with folded arms. About an hour later, this procession would return to the palace and I would go back to play.[29]

While her sisters were always close to her, she saw the children of her brothers less frequently. But even with them, she was always concerned and anxious to help. In the 1940s when her youngest brother's daughter was afflicted by polio, 'my parents were devastated', the latter remembers. 'But then the Maharani started reading more about it, ordered medical books and journals and advised my father on exactly how he should care for me. She recommended a lot of ayurvedic treatments, and made sure they were all performed. She was very sad that one of her nieces should suffer something that could not be cured. She also prayed. She vowed to offer a leg made of pure gold to the Muruga Temple at Palani if I got better, and as I did, she had a solid piece crafted as promised, which, as you can imagine, cost quite a bit. When someone asked her about the expense, she simply told them, "It is my wish, it is my money, and I want to do this."'[30] Years later after an operation was conducted on her niece's leg, her brother and his wife needed a big car to take all their belongings from Madras back home to Coimbatore. 'The Maharani would hear nothing of hiring a car, and she sent her imposing Humber all the way to her [other brother's] Harrington Road bungalow, fetched us and had us driven to Coimbatore. It was only after this that the driver returned to her.'[31]

When her youngest brother, with youthful remiss chose to go on a leisure trip shortly before his examinations in London, and got into a car accident, he was 'very scared and very sad that he might disappoint her, because she had financed his education. But she said it didn't matter, and what did was that he was safe. That was the effect she had on the rest of her family; nobody feared her temper, for she rarely got angry, but they were all very upset if they disappointed her in any way.'[32] Anger did, however, reveal itself in Sethu Lakshmi Bayi on the odd occasion, as Princess Indira remembers. 'The grounds [at Satelmond Palace] were quite vast. Stray dogs managed to sneak in and wander about. After lunch my sister and I used to give them food placed on banana leaves. One day, mother learnt that some of the cooks were in the habit of chasing them away by pouring boiling water on them. She was a very gentle person, but cruelty was something that never failed to arouse her ire. I saw her really angry that day, her beautiful and expressive eyes flashing fire.'[33] The rest of the time, however, she remained perfectly unflappable, something like, as her grandson would remark, a 'benign presence' at the pinnacle of the rest of her family.[34]

Yet the majesty of royal life pervaded everything she did. The pattakkars were the highest class of palace servants, and it was 'deemed the greatest honour to serve as a household guard'.[35] With their scarlet tunics with silver braids and decorations, and huge, flat turbans ('like Tipu Sultan's, with silver hangings'), the royal family's crest emblazoned on their chests, these men would always be marching around the palace, escorting members of the family from one room to the next or accompanying them on walks and drives. 'Everywhere you'd turn there were always these characters hovering around,' one of the Maharani's granddaughters would later laugh, 'and the maids were in awe of them in their excellent uniforms and looking like soldiers.'[36] Whenever Sethu Lakshmi Bayi came downstairs, 'they would greet her by doing a *namaskar* with folded hands, starting at the top of their heads and then bowing right down to touch the ground, with a lot of fluttering and waving of their hands in between. They had to do this seven times and it was quite an amazing sight.'[37] When her brothers arrived, they too first called on her formally, in what was called 'temple dress', with a mundu around their waist and the upper shawl never draped across the torso but tied around the midriff. They would then greet her by throwing their sacred threads over the shoulder to the elbow, 'and then first doing a namaste and then moving both hands outwards and in again in a fast motion, meaning "Many, many greetings"'.[38]

Sometimes, however, uproarious laughter rang in the palace halls when these customs went spectacularly awry, usually at the irreproachable hands of very young children who hadn't the faintest clue about the correctness of decorum in the presence of their queen. One recorded instance tells of a little Christian boy who came to pay his respects to Sethu Lakshmi Bayi with his distinguished grandfather. 'He was told when he saw [the Maharani] he should fold his hands in a greeting form and bow seven times, not six, not eight, since those numbers were not auspicious, and it would be considered an insult.'[39] Rehearsals were administered and the child was prepared by his punctilious warden for the grand event. But when eight-year-old Thomas Phillippose actually arrived at Satelmond Palace, he was so awestruck by its stately magnificence that he forgot to count the numerous salutations he had to offer. The result was that he 'got a little spanking on his buttock with a command, "stop it", from his grandpa', right in the little durbar hall. Sethu Lakshmi Bayi 'found it hilarious' and was so charmed by the oblivious innocence of the boy that she asked, enthroned in her chair of state, for him to be sent up to her. 'When grandpa showed some reluctance, [the Maharani] commanded the boy be sent. The good-looking Rani sat him in her lap and embraced him tightly' (where he reportedly felt 'the cool comfort of her ample bosom'). Later, when he took her leave, she rewarded him with presents, 'including a gold sovereign'.[40]

Living in a world like this, Sethu Lakshmi Bayi was never unescorted, and the perennial presence of obsequious and kowtowing servants added to that picturesque aura about her. 'She disliked pomp, ostentation, and being in the limelight,' Princess Indira would remember, 'but in her position they were hard to avoid.'[41] She had eight personal maids, of whom four were in constant attendance, even inside her bedroom. They were the ones who dressed her, got her bath ready, and oversaw all her personal affairs. In turn, to supervise them, there was a Brahmin lady ('a large, domineering lady called Chella Ayahamma' and later one Paru Ayahamma),[42] who always brought Sethu Lakshmi Bayi her breakfast in bed and remained in attendance while she bathed, dressed and had her hair done. 'The hair in itself was such a fascinating sight to watch and took quite some time,' it would later be recalled. 'Someone would hold up a mirror and there was a peculiar comb, while the other maids stood around. And if they didn't get it done perfectly, Kochu Thankam used to show them how.' [43] Her clothes for the morning would be laid out by then. 'She used to wear these crisp mundus; so crisp that they rustled when she walked. She changed them thrice a day, and every new set had to be fresh and laundered. She'd wear one in the morning, and discard it for the next three hours later by lunchtime. But each one of them was very simple—a plain *puliyalakara* mundu, with a black-and-gold border. She used to wear pale blouses with these, and it all somehow offset her personality. She seemed to have this dovelike quality, dressed always in white, and we thought she looked stunning; slightly on the plump side, but absolutely stunning.'[44]

Through all this, the other personal maids merely sat in the anteroom 'lolling about all day with nothing to do really other than gossip and wait to flirt with their favourite pattakkars as soon as they had a chance'![45] If Sethu Lakshmi Bayi had messages to deliver to the Valiya Koil Tampuran in his part of the palace, she would command one of the anteroom maids to do so, and they would immediately run this and similar errands. When she finally left her apartments for her library or the dining hall, these women were left in charge of her room, arranging her clothes and other belongings and overseeing the sweepers who could only appear when the Maharani was nowhere in sight. 'There were lots of valuables, no doubt, in her room, but she barely wore jewellery, and expensive clothes were only worn on state occasions.'[46] There were cupboards and cupboards full of mundus—'satin, brocade, silk, and so on, for various occasions'—and one entire section devoted to the gold- or silver-threaded tissue shawls she preferred to use. The shawls were really the only marks of luxury as far as dress was concerned, but as Gandhi had noted in 1925, she did not derive her queenly aura from dress as much as from her natural appearance. Even servants at Kowdiar Palace invented a Malayalam catchphrase—*Lakshmi Bayi Maharani, Lakshanam Othoru Tirumeni*—essentially praising her impressive countenance.[47] As a granddaughter states:

> I always thought her the most beautiful woman on earth. She had such a great, regal bearing and she looked every inch a queen, from head to toe. Grandfather always complained that, despite his best efforts, no painting or photograph could do justice to her looks and persona. She seemed almost flawless. She had enormous eyes, heavily lashed, and her long, black tikka. Her lips were beautifully shaped. Her nose was a little prominent, but it didn't look defective; it's length actually fit in with the fact that she had once been a ruling monarch. Her movements were all steady and majestic, like she pondered about each and every step. Everything! If she wanted to pick up a book, she would take it in a slow and elegant manner. She had a grace for every single thing she did. This was probably the most amazing thing about her as a woman of presence. I can't describe it. I have never met anybody like that in all these years.[48]

When the Maharani moved about in the palace, her four personal maids, and often the head Ayahamma, followed her, albeit at a slight distance, always with their backs somewhat hunched in a half bow, and their hands folded across the chest, with a palm covering the mouth. 'It was really a procession that trailed around her all day,'[49] waiting for instructions and orders. The Valiya Koil Tampuran would call on her at specific times, decided in advance and communicated through their respective valets and attendants. They would discuss affairs related to the Sripadam or any other official business, transact finances, and give relevant orders to their secretaries and others, before returning to their respective routines following lunch. 'I can remember mother having very many hours of prayers in the day,' Princess Indira recalls, 'and she spent a great deal of time in her worship room, praying to the small, silver Krishna figurine that she had inherited from the previous Rani.'[50] This was the only time Sethu Lakshmi Bayi could be alone during the day, even though her maids and attendants waited outside, ready for her call. She had these meditations ('there was no chanting or loud worshiping, and she merely sat in silent prayer for long stretches of time') in the mornings as well as evenings, with her time in between dedicated to teaching her children. In a letter Princess Lalitha sent her in 1932 aged eight, she says:

> My dear Mother, I hope you are quite well. Today my little sister went at the same time when Miss Poulose came to teach. Please I want to [know] whether is there [sic] any lesson at *pallivetta* [a festive day] with Miss Poulose? She wants to [know] that is there any lessons on Monday. I think today we cannot walk because today is a rainy day. I would be very, very glad if you allow me to walk in the heavy rain. Today I am very glad because I have only two lessons, that with Mister Krishnayer [Krishna Iyer] and with you, but sister has with bhagvathar and with Mister Asan and with Miss Poulose. Today Mister Krishnayer brought a book and it was very good to look at, but really it was very easy to read, and I read it in a few hours. Mister Krishnayer said when he brought it here that it was a very good book, but when I showed it to father, he said that it was a very bad one to teach me, then I showed it to Mister Krishnayer and said it was a very bad one to teach me, then Mister Krishnayer said that it is a very bad one to teach me; ha ha ha! Please allow me to stop my letter now. I am stopping my letter. Your faithful daughter, Lalitamba.[51]

When Sethu Lakshmi Bayi was in power, much of her time was consumed by affairs of state. Kochu Thankam and a battalion of nannies took care of the girls at the time, and early on Princess Lalitha had formed a habit of writing little notes for her mother. She would even get an obliging clerk to type them up and send them neatly in envelopes along with files and official papers. 'My dear Mama, I hope you are doing well,' goes one. 'I fired a few crackers this morning. Your beloved Lalitamba Bayi.'[52] Yet another was more profound: 'Please pardon me. I am very very very very very sorry for vexing you. I hope you did not think that I want to vex you, but do not think that I never think!'[53] As she grew, Princess Lalitha became a little bit of a tomboy, who was closer to her father than her mother, in appearance as well as personality. The Valiya Koil Tampuran indulged her, and they spent much of their time together, cracking jokes, playing football, or going rowing, with the former later introducing her to his pet hobby of photography. 'He was an excellent prankster, and one of his favourites was to craft little cockroaches and leave them around, especially near artefacts he knew visitors were bound to touch,' Princess Lalitha's daughter would chuckle, 'and mother became his natural ally in these practical jokes! They loved seeing people's reactions, and he often made fun of them without their realising it. Only mother, with glee, spotted his sarcasm, her stomach hurting as she tried to control her laughter.'[54] On another occasion, Rama Varma shot a crocodile in a river during one of his hunting expeditions and decided to leave it rolled up in the sleeping mat of one of his attendants. 'When Iyengar unrolled his mat preparatory to sleeping, he yelped and jumped several feet in the air and forever after that was wary when he approached his mat!'[55]

Once, at Princess Lalitha's unbending insistence, Rama Varma yielded and presented her a pair of khaki shorts similar to the hunting attire he wore on his shikars in the jungle. 'The Maharani was one day holding court for some extremely pious, orthodox guests in the east drawing room, and suddenly they were treated to the bizarre spectacle of the Second Princess of Travancore prancing about in khaki shorts in the corridors, utterly thrilled with this latest addition to her wardrobe! "My god," she thought, "what has happened to this child's sense of decorum?"' On other occasions, she would dress up her maids 'as all sorts of funny characters and have them accost the footmen and stewards, who would be completely fooled'![56] Princess Lalitha's letters to the Valiya Koil Tampuran were also remarkably informal. 'Well now for some home news,' one of them goes. 'As I've heard somewhere, if aunt's beautiful new maid takes it into her head to come into our study or any place where there is a clock, I won't be surprised if the clock stops suddenly! For she is so good looking! Anyone will be enamoured of her for sure. And though she must be surely past forty, she's still going strong!'[57] A discussion followed on the merits of the name Malcolm ('I can't believe any stupid blockhead LOVING that awful hideous name') before she admitted being in a spot of trouble for having taken a calf 'away from his shed and planted him in the main cowshed. Suppose the little darling benefitted by its change and was glad to be near to mummie?'[58] Another letter from 'yours ever truly loving tiny totty Lalitamba Bayi'[59] to her father when he was away warned him to 'expect a nice family invasion tomorrow afternoon'.[60]

The Valiya Koil Tampuran did not always, of course, understand or agree with his daughter. Years later, on one amusing occasion, Princess Lalitha, who would go on to become the mother of seven children, found herself served a stern notice of summons from her father, as her daughter recounts:

> Grandmother [Sethu Lakshmi Bayi] was ecstatic each time a grandchild was born, while grandfather frowned upon the inordinate number. Mother told me that after the birth of her third child, a shocked and disapproving grandfather ordered her to his presence and admonished her, pointing out that this sort of prolific reproductive habit was normally common to the canine and feline species, which are prone to the litter pattern, and should scarcely be followed by members of august royal families. You can imagine the state of his mind when the seventh baby was born. By then he had probably given up on mother! But in spite of grandfather's continuous disapproval of mother's rebellious and unorthodox outlook on life, she remained his favourite. He never stopped censuring her, and she never stopped flouting his orders.[61]

Princess Indira, on the other hand, was closer in personality and even features to her mother. 'Very pretty and extremely fair' in complexion,[62] with gentle and quiet manners, she preferred reading to sports like football, and early on began to write poetry and would often put up song-and-dance performances with her maids for her parents. 'She was always more dignified and reserved, compared to Lalitha's chummy personality, but had an extremely good sense of humour that could leave even the Valiya Koil Tampuran in splits.'[63] Where Princess Lalitha had to be counselled that she ought to behave in a more ladylike fashion ('No, I want to be a boy!'), Princess Indira was always a very feminine child, and had much of her mother's grace and aristocratic bearing. Yet she too disclosed a temper now and then. Once, for instance, she took a vehement dislike to her despotic Sanskrit teacher, whom she called asan. Knowing that her ever-enterprising sister would conjure a solution to get rid of him she sought her counsel and Princess Lalitha, then twelve, told her nine-year-old sibling of what was meant to be an infallible strategy.

Mother told aunt Indira she would find a way to send the man packing, and came up with what she thought was her cleverest plan. When Indira returned after yet another boring class, mother declared that at her next lesson with the asan, she should wear a side parting of her hair, and not a centre parting. The idea was that a curious asan would ask why she had changed her hairstyle. Indira was to stubbornly refuse to tell him, and this, it was hoped, would get him into a rage till he huffed and puffed and left! On the day in question, asan arrived and started dictating grammar and making her write. He didn't notice anything about aunt's hair. She was so thoroughly agitated that she literally went and put her head right under his nose. When he still didn't bother to ask, she stood up and indignantly demanded that he ask her about her hair. The man was so stunned that he asked her what on earth was wrong to which Indira replied imperiously, *ineem asan pokko* (asan, you may go now)! When mother heard of this she was so afraid the man would really resign, that she found a maid called Kunji, who participated in many of their childhood pranks, and told her to chase down asan and bring him back at any cost. And when he refused to return to class, Kunji went and lay down in his path, refusing to let him leave until he returned![64]

For most part, however, Princess Indira was a studious, law-abiding child, as her mother had been, and often sent the Maharani cards and pictures she had drawn for 'the world's best mother'.[65] She even painstakingly typed up short stories she had written for her mother, whose old-world qualities and refinement she adored and would remember late into her life with almost a degree of awe:

> The world knew her variously as a Maharani, as someone who ruled the former state of Travancore for seven years as Regent and brought in many progressive reforms; as a very beautiful, cultured and learned lady who demonstrated by her own life all the virtues of Indian womanhood, and at the same time, held very mature and progressive ideas on many subjects. To me, however, she was just Mother, with all the connotations the word evokes. She was a very warm and loving person, and a very understanding one, so that one could go to her with all one's problems, sure of a patient hearing and sensible advice. She was broad minded and tolerant. One notable quality of hers was that, though she was scrupulous in her own morals, she never set herself up as a judge of those of other people ... She was [a] very gentle person and tried her level best not to hurt anyone's feelings ... but she was not meek. She was spirited in her own way and always refused to yield to injustice.[66]

The Valiya Koil Tampuran took Princess Indira too along on some of his adventures, and on one occasion Sethu Lakshmi Bayi was thoroughly nettled when she discovered her daughters, after a shikar in the jungle, had been fed breakfast atop a rogue elephant he had just shot. The 'Breakfast Elephant' was one of few such incidents, however, and for most part he preferred to involve his children in less dangerous activities on the palace grounds. When they went to their beach resort at Kovalam, he would take them out a great many times. 'My father insisted on daily morning walks,' Princess Indira would write, 'which we enjoyed because we walked all around the grounds, with the sea surrounding us. On these walks we would visit the cowsheds, which were a delight to us, for often there would be calves frolicking. On these walks father would stop at various places to talk to people working there.'[67]

Kovalam was in fact a personal retreat for Rama Varma, who foresaw its great potential for tourism in the years to come. Land was purchased here from the Bishop of Quilon and for decades, the beach was practically the private estate of the Valiya Koil Tampuran. Over the course of the years several dignitaries, including Lord Mountbatten, were entertained here, and the Mountbattens held it to be 'among the best [beaches] they had seen anywhere in the country'.[68] Most guests simply sought access to the sea to bathe, but many joined the Valiya Koil Tampuran for tennis, arc lights shining brightly around them. Sethu Lakshmi Bayi and her children spent charming vacations by the sea here, in the privacy of their home. A Romanesque bungalow was constructed, entirely of granite, and it 'seemed so much a part of the cliffs that it looked as though part of the rocks had risen up to form a house'.[69] A tower, with a high-powered telescope atop it, was constructed with the building, and Rama Varma, with his typical tendency to surpass even the British in their Britishness, called it Halcyon Castle. His hunting trophies, favourite books, as well as exquisite rosewood furniture with his personal emblem carved on it, were kept here, and while Sethu Lakshmi Bayi enjoyed long, relaxed stays at her country residence in Vellayini, the Valiya Koil Tampuran often retreated to Kovalam when he felt the need for some 'alone' time. As the little Princess Lalitha wrote,

> How I love to come to Kovalam and see you! Is the sea very rough? Has the keeper Govindan got over his illness? You remember he said he was ill the day we went there. Oh! How I miss you! I spent the night—that is—slept in your giant bed. And there is a particular aroma which reminds me of you. It is a very good smell. I love it.[70]

The Maharani did often proceed to Kovalam with the children, and a number of buildings sprang up around the principal 'castle' for their use and for the retinue and guards that invariably accompanied them. And on each such visit, Rama Varma would welcome his royal wife and daughters by firing a small cannon into the sea.[71] Sethu Lakshmi Bayi took an active part in designing outdoor aspects of this house too. Soon a 'fabulous' rose garden embraced the whole place, and a 'sea of roses' wafted 'their glorious perfume all around'.[72] The tower room offered a breathtaking view, and the family often sat there and watched the 'splendid vision' of the sun 'sinking slowly, inch by glorious inch, into the sea' after which they would watch 'the shifting, entrancing colours on the water.' The building was designed specially to fit in with the natural aesthetic of the sea. 'The windows had glass, shaped like long petals. The glass was of an unusual shade of green, similar to the under-side of the huge waves. When the windows, with their wooden Venetian blinds were closed, one felt that we were under water beneath the sea,' Princess Indira would fondly remember.[73] Fisherfolk would also often bring them 'treasures from the sea, such as sea anemone, coloured shells, and once even a sting ray's tail,' which would then be stored in an attic that was accessible only through a tiny door that was 'more magical than the door in *Alice in Wonderland*'.[74]

Outside, a part of the grounds was cleared and a dining area, complete with a granite dining table and chairs, was constructed from rocks hewn off the beach. 'Even better was the "drawing room" they constructed. The ground was covered with square granite slabs of alternate black and light grey, resembling a large carpet, and there were granite chairs fixed at strategic points, and a round granite table in the middle.'[75] A flight of similar granite steps led down to the cliffs and the beach, and very often the princess would 'get up early in the morning and sit on the steps, gazing at the sea, the wind roughly caressing my face', while on other times one of her 'chief delights was to stand in the water, waiting for each wave to come near and then duck below it, and feel it breaking over my head'.[76] Sometimes the Valiya Koil Tampuran would arrange for the girls to join local fishermen when they went out to sea on small rafts of wood. 'My sister and I loved these rides. It was an exciting experience. We would be drenched to the skin when we returned.'[77] Their parents, in the meantime, would wait back at the beach with hampers of food spread out on a sheet over the sand, welcoming their daughters for a quick bite when they returned.

When the 'hot weather' arrived, the whole family would travel to Peermade, which became a favourite sanctuary from the formality of life in and around the royal capital. The highway to Kottayam, and then the road to the high ranges were cleared of all traffic, and with a pilot car and an elaborate entourage, the family would arrive in the hills. It was the principal highlight of the year for locals. 'The staff was always smaller on these trips, and so everyone let their hair down to some extent. Only the secretary and manager, the four personal maids, four or five pattakkars, the head cook and two assistants, and some menials would join her. Not more than twenty-five servants. Of course the others had their own staff as well, but it was still on a smaller scale altogether than in the palace.'[78] Sethu Lakshmi Bayi purchased a grassy hillside here, and a beautiful house, with stone walls and wooden rafters, was built, surrounded by the usual ancillary buildings. The house commanded a striking view of the valley below, and Rama Varma often rode to the local club to play golf at Travancore's highest course with the Resident, who too maintained an official residence here. Meanwhile, the children and the Maharani took long walks and picnicked by the brook passing through their grounds. There was also, nearby, the old, traditional summer house of the royal family, but Sethu Lakshmi Bayi was no longer certain she had access to it now that the Maharajah was in power and since he used it often with the Junior Maharani.

In due course the Valiya Koil Tampuran also constructed 'Villa Manimala' at Pothencode, set amidst vast rubber estates. At the centre, atop a hillock, stood a large, proud stone bungalow 'that had vistas of the rolling countryside from every window', with the gardens full of fountains and pink Edward rose shrubs;[79] 'on a clear day one could even see the sea in the far distance from the terrace'.[80] 'I was fascinated by the leopard-skin carpet on the floor as soon as you entered,' one of his grandchildren would recall, 'and the different animal heads on the walls.'[81] The whole place was maintained in a very English fashion, and was 'very stately looking' with orderlies all over the place as late as the 1970s. 'There were pile carpets and heavy furniture all around,' a great-granddaughter would say, 'and stuffed animals and trophies in the lobby and living room. Some of them were so scary and almost alive. We kept a safe distance from them while walking past.'[82] The prize of the collection was, in fact, a stuffed bear, one on which the girls often enjoyed climbing as a mission of childish grit! Sometimes they read by the fireplace, while the Maharani reposed in a rocking chair, 'resting her eyes'.

After visits to Coonoor, another summerhouse called Aspect Lodge ('of sweet and pleasant memories,' Princess Lalitha remarked)[83] was purchased there, and years later the family would sometimes holiday in Ooty as well, where the Junior Maharani maintained an estate of her own. 'A part of the journey was made in trains and there were lovely carriages reserved for us,' the Maharani's nephew recalls, 'with a sitting area and a bedroom, and perfect furnishings. It was great fun and whenever the train stopped at stations, soldiers would present arms and guard the carriage. A lot of vendors and people with all kinds of interesting wares would be squatting on the platform, and if the Maharani wished, they would be allowed inside and we would all choose what we liked.'[84] Each year, thus, Sethu Lakshmi Bayi and her family would divide their time between these beautiful homes they built for themselves, returning to Satelmond Palace in time for religious ceremonies, state banquets or whenever the Maharajah demanded their presence. 'Every few months,' Princess Indira recalls, 'a message would arrive from Kowdiar Palace that we had been away from the capital too long, and must now come back.'[85] Promptly, then, everything was packed and the family would make its way back to dear old Satelmond for months of temple visits, processions and religious ceremonies, eagerly awaiting their next 'escape' to the privacy of their other beloved homes.

These moves in themselves were always sensational affairs. Writing to Rama Varma from Vellayini in 1933, Princess Lalitha recorded how 'Yesterday evening the bus came here bringing the new soldiers. I do not know why, but I know they are going [back] this evening. This evening the other set of maids are coming with the soldiers so that all the maids here are very excited.'[86] Arrangements had to be made to transfer hundreds of servants and members of staff to whichever house the Maharani had chosen to spend that part of the year. Soldiers would arrive in advance to take up their positions at the gates and around the perimeter. In special buses, chattering maids were driven up to ready the place before the royal family arrived. By the time Sethu Lakshmi Bayi vacated Satelmond Palace everything would be wound down. A bare skeletal staff of caretakers, sweepers and others would stay back, always unhappy at missing out on these great excursions to the hills or the countryside. The bedrooms, libraries, stores and other important wings of the palace were shut down, and bagsful of clinking keys would be carried to the next location. And when the royal motorcade drove up the gates of Lalindloch Palace or Halcyon Castle, the military forces would be waiting to blow the trumpet and welcome the Maharani in state to her chosen home for the season.

> The limousines used by the Maharani and her family had the State emblems where the license plate was normally located. Whenever the Maharani, her daughters, and [later] granddaughters were riding in the car, each end of the front mudguard would fly the State flag (depicting a conch shell in the middle with two elephants on either side in gold, on a red silk background). If the

consorts were travelling on their own, the flags were not flown. Again, when the car passed the main gate where a unit of the State Force was on sentry duty, the soldiers would come out, present arms, and sound the bugle. The consorts were entitled to a simple rifle salute by the sentry if they were not accompanying members of the ruling family.[87]

There was, in this lifestyle, something very quaint and old-worldly, and while the Junior Maharani embarked on world tours and travels, Sethu Lakshmi Bayi remained in Travancore, living the laid-back life of a country aristocrat (though many saw it less romantically as a kind of self-imposed exile from the capital). She took her children out for picnics and drives, viewed motion pictures at their little private palace theatre, watched her daughters put up plays and dance performances, admonished Princess Lalitha when she fell off trees or hurt herself at football, and generally enjoyed a slow, retired pace of life surrounded by her extended family. With the aura of royal bodyguards, legions of servants and so many others constantly bowing and curtseying before her, a great princely ambience, however, informed every aspect of this. 'Everything about her,' the writer Nihal Singh had written in an American newspaper, 'bespeaks refinement, kindliness and intellectuality.'[88] She also retained that famous charm when entertaining those who came to pay her their respects, despite the formality that always encompassed all her interactions with people outside family circles. As late as 1936, five years after she had given up power, Sethu Lakshmi Bayi continued to leave a lasting impression on all whom she met. 'We like the Senior Maharani and her family,' recorded the then Resident.[89] He thought the Maharajah was 'boyish and pleasant' and the Junior Maharani 'charming, gay, and lively.'[90] But the 'best of the lot' in Travancore was Sethu Lakshmi Bayi, 'a real little "grande dame"', and her husband and 'very nice' girls.[91] 'Pity,' he concluded, 'we don't have more to do with them.'[92]

While the Maharani made every effort to lead a peaceful, quiet life, there were others who were determined to ensure that her retirement was not quite as tranquil as she hoped. Having relinquished power in November 1931, it took almost a year for her pension and settlement to be resolved, soon after which Mr Pritchard's term as Resident concluded, and one Mr D.M. Field arrived in the state. It was a perpetual fear she entertained that successive British representatives, who had had no direct experience of her rule, might be less inclined to rein in the Maharajah if he chose to harass her unnecessarily. Small incidents had already begun to show that no sympathy was forthcoming from the new regime. In the summer of 1933, when the Maharani wished to import two cars (since her request for official cars had been turned down), she wrote to the Dewan asking for the courtesy certificates Indian princes enjoyed as a privilege so as not to pay custom duties. But she was told that this could only be given to the Maharajah or to 'members of the family' who 'reside with and are dependant upon him'.[93] She, in other words, would not be granted the courtesy certificate and would have to pay import duties. Indeed, only a matter of months after her 'exiguous settlement' was confirmed, Sethu Lakshmi Bayi, who was in Ponmudi at the time, was compelled to write to the new Resident of the evolution of her nephew's attitude towards her from 'one of unkindness into one of determined and violent hostility'.[94]

Leaving aside the fact that not even the peons she was promised had been made available, the Senior Maharani wrote that she was facing 'several deprivations, including privileges and honours' enjoyed even before the Regency. Normally her permanent royal guard was stationed at her residence in the Fort, and whenever she was in camp elsewhere, fresh guards were provided. This was regular practice even in the time of the last Maharajah, but now she was told that she would have to make do with existing soldiers, and, moreover, pay for their transport from her own pocket.[95] During her stay in Ponmudi, she received information that the guards at Satelmond Palace, including the police, were summarily withdrawn from duty. In addition to this, unprecedented expenses were being charged to her account; government servants deputed on duty with her were hitherto paid their travelling allowances from public funds, as was the medical officer who visited every day to check her. Now, however, their TA bills were being forwarded to her. Similarly, while in the past she received maintenance grants for all the buildings she controlled under the Sripadam on the Malayalam new year, she had not, since 1932 received any money. All of this was, she felt, 'arbitrary and humiliating', compelling her to engage in petty squabbles, 'but perhaps', she added with resignation, 'it is late in the day for me to complain about humiliation'.[96]

If these were more official concerns, there were also growing quarrels of the domestic kind, which, due to the Maharajah's attitude, she found exceedingly galling even as it was embarrassing for her to ask for the Resident's intervention. One of these came up when the Maharani received a letter from Kowdiar Palace asking for the return of an old necklace she had in her possession. This was a present from Mulam Tirunal to her when she was a child, and she had been using it for over thirty years. Naturally, she protested the demand for its return to the current Maharajah, but was told that Chithira Tirunal himself desired to wear it, and she would have to surrender the item. Reluctantly, she forwarded the old ornament to Kowdiar Palace.[97] But if this were not already an effort to hurt her feelings, soon afterwards Sethu Lakshmi Bayi received a second communication from the Maharajah's office. One of the small rubies in the locket, it stated, was broken and an 'enquiry' had been, therefore, ordered.[98] Moreover, the Maharani was instructed that henceforth, every six months, all the ornaments used by her and her two daughters were to be sent to Kowdiar Palace for 'inspection'. 'The stipulation', a humiliated Sethu Lakshmi Bayi wrote, 'can only be regarded as a ruse substitute for a direct demand for the return of all articles now with us since the impracticability of keeping them subject to the [new] condition is patent.'[99] The damage to the ruby in a thirty-year-old necklace was made to seem as some kind of impropriety on the Maharani's part, and with great indignation she returned all the jewels she and her children had in their possession. Decades later when the personal ornaments of the royal house, valued in 1924 as worth over Rs 10 lakh,[100] were partitioned between the two branches of the family, the story goes that Sethu Lakshmi Bayi's heirs arrived in Trivandrum and discovered that all that was left was a single pair of large, old earrings that belonged to the previous Rani.[101]

Other pretexts were also found by the new regime to blow out of proportion in order to insult the Maharani. At the commencement of the Regency, certain watches were found among Mulam Tirunal's belongings. His staff had them brought to her for safekeeping, and for being regularly maintained and wound. Sethu Lakshmi Bayi had all the pieces sent to the little Maharajah so he could select some for his own use, and the six that remained were kept in working order at Satelmond Palace. When she resigned power, she promptly had all of these forwarded to Kowdiar Palace so that Chithira Tirunal could use them if he wished.[102] It then turned out that one of the watches was registered with the Chellamvakai, where all the royal family's valuables, leaving aside private possessions, were maintained. When that particular watch was submitted to the treasurer at Satelmond Palace, the latter issued a receipt for it. Now it appeared that the description (as brief as it could be on a slip of paper) did not 'match' that of the watch despatched to Kowdiar Palace. The Maharajah's secretary ordered the treasurer, then, to pay the full price of the piece, amounting to Rs 500, for evidently misplacing the original. Sethu Lakshmi Bayi, upon inspection, however, was convinced it was the same watch that had been shown to her seven years before, and vouched for her employee. When Kowdiar Palace would not relent, she asked them to recover the price from her own account, hoping that this would be the last she heard on the subject.

> But no. The Palace office is apparently afraid to let the matter rest there, since to do so would deprive it of a handle for further bullying me, a view supported by the unnecessarily indignant language used in the letter sent after the recovery of the price of the missing watch [from her account] compared with the even tone of the previous ones.[103]

This last letter was one stating that another inquiry would be constituted, even though the money had been paid in full, 'as a check against a repetition of similar mistakes in future'.[104] Once again, the tone of the letter suggested the Maharani was somehow personally responsible for allegedly mislaying the watch and needed to be disciplined for this error. As usual, Sethu Lakshmi Bayi put up with the insult, hoping that ultimately the Kowdiar Palace would run out of reasons to treat her in such a bizarre, vindictive manner. But while she bore these insults, there was one personal issue that was contentious, where the Maharani proved highly unwilling to comply with orders from the Maharajah.

Early in 1932 correspondence commenced on the subject of Sethu Lakshmi Bayi, Rama Varma and their two daughters paying courtesy calls to the Maharajah on, as his secretary informed them, the first and fifteenth day of every Malayalam month.[105] The Maharani agreed to the suggestion but pointed out that with regard to herself and the Maharajah, the precedent of the late Rani Lakshmi Bayi and Mulam Tirunal should be followed. This was because, as in the present case, the Maharajah then was also younger than the Rani and it was he who called on her and she 'only rarely went to call on the Maharajah herself', as she was head of the royal house, giving her premier rank in the dynasty.[106] Nothing was heard about visits due to the Maharani from the Maharajah but the princesses were sent accompanied by their father to Kowdiar Palace on one occasion. But at that time the Valiya Koil Tampuran was asked to wait outside while the Maharajah met the girls in private.[107]

This thoroughly upset the Maharani and on the next date, two weeks later, the children were not allowed to go. Again on Onam day, when the princesses went to receive presents from Chithira Tirunal, Rama Varma was asked to wait outside. This provoked a firm message from the Maharani that if this were the code of conduct on these courtesy calls, she would 'be reluctantly obliged to give up the idea' of sending her children to the palace altogether.[108] The response to this from Kowdiar Palace was that 'His Highness the Maharajah as the Sovereign and the Guardian has the right to demand interviews with the Princesses unattended by anybody.'[109] Unwilling to accept this, Sethu Lakshmi Bayi simply said her views had been explained clearly in her previous communications, and if her husband were not allowed to be present when the Maharajah interacted with her daughters, she would, not due to any disrespect or 'spirit of contrariness' but owing to 'practical difficulties', find it difficult to send the princesses.[110] She was equally firm in writing to the Resident:

> My children (daughters) are only nine and six years old, and the Maharajah is a practical stranger to them. My proposal, which to me seemed eminently reasonable, was that they should go in company with my husband, but His Highness insisted that no one should be present when the visit was being paid—a proposition to which I have the strongest objection and to which I could never persuade myself to yield. Once they grow up I would certainly withdraw my objections, but not till then.[111]

Upon receipt of the Maharani's complaints, Mr Field spoke to the Maharajah and the latter agreed to get the promises confirmed in her settlement fulfilled and even showed him papers proving that he had already passed orders to the effect.[112] The Resident then advised the Maharani to contact the Dewan to get the arrangements made accordingly, since it appeared that they were only pending implementation. As for personal complaints raised by her, he felt it would be difficult for him to intervene, as this was a family matter outside the purview of his position as British representative. Nevertheless, he invited the Valiya Koil Tampuran to meet with him in June to discuss these concerns of the Maharani soon after the family returned from their stay at Ponmudi.

Accordingly, Rama Varma called on Mr Field on 9 June and engaged in a long discussion. The latter informed the Maharani's husband that the Maharajah objected to him personally and perhaps he would be conciliated if the princesses were sent along with their aunts instead.[113] Rama Varma, who was 'friendly and reasonable' at this interview, could understand why Mr Field could not intervene and also informed him that in reality the principal objection of the Maharani was not about her pending honours or dignities but about her children having to see the Maharajah alone.[114] As for their two aunts, they led 'secluded lives' and were themselves averse to visiting Kowdiar Palace.[115] The interview ended with the Valiya Koil Tampuran assuring Mr Field that nothing further was necessary regarding the complaints, if the settlement were really to be implemented, and the Maharani would not insist that he interfere in the family dispute. But she did want the Resident to 'bear the matter in mind', as it demonstrated yet again exactly what she had to put up with in her relations with the Maharajah.[116]

Mr Field had already by now guessed that the Maharani's grievance was about the courtesy calls her daughters were expected to pay and remarked that the trouble arose 'in consequence of the wide difference in outlook and mode of life of the two Maharanis' who were 'incompatible'. He further noted:

> I suspect that the Senior Maharani does not approve of the conditions now prevailing at the [Kowdiar] Palace, and she both dislikes and fears the idea of her children being introduced to these conditions. While I think that the Senior Maharani would do better to be more diplomatic and worldly-wise, I think she should in fairness be treated with greater consideration and respect, not only as a member of the ruling family, but by virtue of the excellent service which she rendered to the State during the period of the Regency. A little give and take on both sides would settle the matter, but it is a difficult and delicate subject for intervention.[117]

The Resident was right in suspecting that the Maharani was averse to exposing her children to the environment at the Maharajah's palace. This was because the Junior Maharani's siblings and mother, against whom disciplinary action had been taken during the Regency after the black magic episode, were once again frequenting Kowdiar Palace. Besides, the new palace manager was none other than Dr Nallaperumal Pillai, the very man who had been expelled in 1926 after he ventured to have the Kochu Koil Tampuran medically declared insane—he would shortly hereafter be honoured with the title of 'Rajabhakta' (faithful servant).[118] In any case, with Mr Field unable to intervene, Sethu Lakshmi Bayi had to make her peace with Kowdiar Palace, and let her daughters see the Maharajah by themselves, even as her husband waited in an adjacent chamber. 'I knew there was a dispute,' Princess Indira would later remember, 'but never knew the details.' With state guards and an escort, she and Princess Lalitha would be driven to Kowdiar Palace every two weeks, the Valiya Koil Tampuran following in another car, since he was prohibited from sitting in the same limousine as his daughters on these visits.

The Maharajah did not trouble the girls at all during his meetings with them, and on the contrary gave Princess Indira the impression of being 'very sensitive' and a fine individual personally. 'He would give us toffees and ask routine questions: Where are you coming from? Is it raining there? What have you been studying? And more in that vein.'[119] She got the impression that it was the Junior

Maharani who insisted on these courtesy calls, but she herself was rarely present in those days. In fact, she seemed quite a formidable prospect for the children, and Sethu Lakshmi Bayi's nephew would remember times when she came to Satelmond Palace with her sisters and Kochukunji in tow. 'They used to treat us very nicely, as if we were their own children, and pet us and take a great interest in this side of the family. It was as if the disputes vanished, as nobody spoke about it openly, and behaved with great courtesy when face-to-face. But while the Maharajah, his sister, and brother, were all wonderful, the Junior Maharani always looked very stern. She only spoke to the adults, and never said anything to us children, and there was no petting or cuddling at all. Her sisters, however, would love to sit and chat.'[120]

The Junior Maharani had really come into her own after her son obtained his powers. Her high-spirited appetite for life was married to opportunity in its great fullness, and she became the mistress of her own destiny. No longer was she compelled to apply to Sethu Lakshmi Bayi for tour funds, or furnish answers about her activities, as she had been forced to during the Maharajah's minority. No longer, also, was she officially 'the *Junior* Maharani' as the Viceroy had allowed her to be addressed with a 'Highness' at last, and declared her simply 'the Maharani Sethu Parvathi Bayi'.[121] Her reviews remained, however, quite a contrast to her splendid, regal cousin. The very Resident who referred to Sethu Lakshmi Bayi as the 'grande dame' of Travancore, considered the Junior Maharani 'a Bourbon if ever there was one, learning nothing and forgetting nothing',[122] although his first, positive impression was not inaccurate either:

> What a clever, naughty, vivacious, humorous woman she is! Very much 'all there'. Diplomatic too. Gets what she wants 'across' to you without seeming to express an opinion. Though I don't altogether approve of her, I must admit she has that vitality I admire so much in women...[123]

John Paton Davies, the famous 'China Hand' of the United States, considered the Junior Maharani 'a lively conversationalist' who could slide from one topic to the next with the greatest ease and comfort. 'She told me about a visit she had made to Bali and the racial and religious ties between the island and Hindu India. She worried about how the Japanese might be treating the Balinese. Somehow we got onto the subject of a room that she was having done over at the palace, and her conviction that "modernistic" furniture was unliveable. Then a discourse on Indian painting. Inevitably we came to the matter of elephants. They have near-human intelligence, the Maharani declared. One of hers accidently injured a mahout, whereupon it burst into tears. Travancore, she went on, had a game sanctuary where no shooting was allowed. This brought to mind the Maharajah of Bikaner: "Poor Bikaner, he is not happy unless he is being photographed with his foot on the head of some unfortunate animal he shot."'[124]

Indeed, having explored much of India already during her son's tours, her first expedition, only months after the Regency concluded, was to travel to Europe, a long-cherished dream, with her daughter. Together, the Junior Maharani and the First Princess became the earliest members of the royal family to venture across the 'black waters' that orthodox Hindus shunned, breaking taboo after taboo. She spent several months in Europe, leading to some grumbling at home about the expenses at a time when the state confronted the Great Depression. On her return, however, a grand reception was arranged in Trivandrum but the Junior Maharani so dominated affairs that day 'that it was generally considered inappropriate for the Maharajah to have been present', entirely in his mother's shadow.[125] The Resident also found the whole reception 'almost completely devoid of sincerity', stating that it was 'engineered' by the government so as to shut out the orthodoxy and their complaints.[126]

In 1933, the Junior Maharani again headed West for a second time, with the Maharajah accompanying her on this occasion. Official publications waxed eloquent about the triumphal progress they made from one European capital to the next. Back home, however, 'the gossips murmur that some temple treasures were sold to defray expenses, and this has given terrible offence in certain quarters'.[127] Indeed, by 1934, the Maharajah would plan a visit to Ceylon and the East Indies, only to cancel it on being advised against the serious expenses involved, so the tour was accomplished a few years later.[128] Other innovations were also occurring. The Maharajah and his mother, for the very first time, began to appear at private parties and receptions thrown by the Dewan and others.[129] Indeed, when it was revealed that their hostess at a function organised by a Muslim associate was to be in purdah, the Junior Maharani refused to accept the invitation, until 'the curtain had to be lifted temporarily and be dropped again when the reception was over'.[130] In the late 1930s she would upset very many conservatives in Travancore by inviting to the capital, despite protests, none other than Margaret Sanger, 'the family planning crusader', to propagate the cause of birth control.[131] There was great initiative in her and she championed even unusual causes, for which she was lauded, even as other aspects of her personality invited criticism.

The travelling, however, continued unabated, so much so that shortly after his succession, the *Princely India* was advising the Maharajah not to become an absentee prince. 'Since his Investiture with Ruling Powers just ten months ago,' the Resident reported, 'the Maharajah has been away in Simla and Delhi for over half that period, and this is strongly deprecated in Trivandrum.'[132] 'Your work,' lambasted the paper, 'demands your presence in your own capital, and not in the capital of the Indian Empire.'[133] The response from Kowdiar Palace was to order the police to go to the post office and seize all copies of the *Princely India*, which continued to condemn several aspects of the new administration. The Resident deemed the confiscation as illegal under both British as well as Travancore law, and the Maharajah was forced to release the papers.[134] Shortly afterwards, the Newspaper Regulation was made more stringent than before, and as a historian states, those papers favouring the government and its position on various topics were promoted, while those that expressed opposing views became victims of the law, silenced or banned.[135]

The Junior Maharani was unusually suave when it came to public perception, however. Even in the days of the Regency she saw the value of cultivating the press and trying to manipulate the tone of its discourse. She not only foresaw objections to her maiden foreign tour but also ensured precisely for that reason a grand, ostensibly supportive reception to din out grumblers. Later, in what was an equally canny move, to make sure that her son and she received adequate and positive press coverage on the all-India stage, one the earliest acts of the new regime was to establish, with a government subsidy, a branch of the Associated Press of India in Trivandrum that 'gave a lot of publicity to the doings of the ruling family'.[136] With 'a mania for self advertisement', and aware that the law alone was barely an adequate means to mould attitudes in the press, proper strategies to deal with the media were employed.[137] Sir CP, who was in the words of a future Viceroy, an 'expert propagandist', gave his generous advice in these matters,[138] and in the future would himself declare that the Junior Maharani and her son 'made regular propaganda for advertising Travancore', 'constantly talking to European friends and Indian Princes' all about their state so as to make it 'fairly well-known' in circles that mattered.[139]

It was a very wise strategy, for the Maharajah and his mother had in mind for the state and its people certain very bold schemes and reforms, some of which would have been impossible to even articulate only a decade ago, and which many felt were truly inconceivable even in the 1930s. Only this tremendous combination of clever management of public relations, the shrewd force of personality, and a determined refusal to capitulate or to change their course of action despite great pressure, could bring to fruition what was to become known as, and was always intended to be, the greatest act in the history of Travancore: the Temple Entry Proclamation.

15

A Palace Coup

When Col Munro first arrived in Travancore in 1809, he discovered himself in the midst of the most staggering financial and political chaos. Velu Tampi's rebellion had been violently struck down, bleeding the entire principality. The royal treasuries were barren. But what was perhaps most astonishing was the degree of malice and spite that divided the court into a number of warring factions. Indeed, such was the nature of affairs at the time that the unforgiving saga unfolding in the 1920s and 1930s between the Junior Maharani and Sethu Lakshmi Bayi pales spectacularly by comparison. These two twentieth-century princesses were no match for their crafty ancestors a hundred years ago; if now cousins were gripped in an epic contest for authority, the decades before Munro's time witnessed the sordid episode of a treacherous mother turning against her own daughters. So intoxicated did this woman become with the enticements of power that she presided over great intrigues and illicit manipulations in pursuit of her goals, even, allegedly, seeing to the death of some of her own flesh and blood who had the misfortune of standing in her way. To those shocked by the battle between the two royal women in the twentieth century, these antecedents of their forbears proved that this was all perhaps a natural component of the troubled heritage of the ruling dynasty.

The story began in 1788. In that year, the line of the Attingal Ranis was to go extinct due to want of females in the royal house. Two princesses, then, were adopted in keeping with tradition from the Kolathiri family and installed as Senior and Junior Ranis. These were the daughters of a Kolathiri princess by the name of Chathayam Tirunal, who was the mother of five girls. The youngest was none other than Princess Arya, the ancestress through whom Sethu Lakshmi

Bayi and her cousin claimed membership of the Kolathiri line before their own adoption in 1900. But the daughters adopted in 1788 were the second and third children of Chathayam Tirunal, the former of whom begot a long succession of rulers starting with Gowri Lakshmi Bayi down to Maharajah Mulam Tirunal who died in 1924. In 1789, shortly after their adoption, Chathayam Tirunal was forced to abandon her ancestral home in Malabar and seek refuge in Travancore when the armies of Tipu Sultan ravaged their lands. In exile, the mother and her three other daughters were permitted to take up residence at Attingal with the Ranis. It seemed like a happy family reunion, but as fate would have it, was an arrangement destined to become 'most unfortunate in its consequences'.[1]

It so happened that Chathayam Tirunal was a masterful lady of terrible ambition, 'a woman of violent, profligate, and sordid character', in Munro's words.[2] Having lost all she had in her homeland, she now set her eyes on her daughters, living in great state and comfort in Travancore, a large and impressive kingdom which alone had been able to withstand the invading hordes from Mysore. It did not, evidently, take the lady long, then, to become 'jealous of the superior dignity of her daughter', the Senior Rani. Soon she commenced a sequence of intrigues and schemes against her own more exalted offspring, persecuting them 'with a malignity and rancour that embittered her subsequent life'.[3] Two factions were born at court, 'one consisting of the two [adopted] Travancore Princesses, and the other of their mother and three sisters' till 'their quarrels became so frequent that the Rajah was obliged to remove the latter to a separate Palace.'[4]

But Chathayam Tirunal was not one to accept defeat or to contemplate chastened retirement; she was determined to regain what she had lost in the north, and more. Knowing that the reigning Maharajah, the successor of Martanda Varma, was disappointed by the character of his own heir (whose reign would thoroughly weaken the position of the state and provoke Velu Tampi's rebellion), this lady suggested in 1795 the introduction of a male member from the Kolathiri dynasty, presumably a confidante of hers, into the royal family. The Maharajah, apparently, did not outright reject the proposal, alarming the Senior Rani who 'earnestly resisted that design as hostile to her rights' until the ruler 'abandoned it in consequence of her remonstrances, and his own conviction of its entire illegality'.[5] Its illegality was on account of the rule that only females could be brought into the dynasty by adoption, and their naturally born sons alone were entitled to succeed to the throne. In 1798, however, the Maharajah died, paving the way for the singularly unpropitious reign of his heir, 'a young man of 17 years of age, without experience, principles, or morals—sunk in debauchery—at once cruel and weak—jealous of his power and ruled by a set of profligate wretches.'[6] Soon after this, the Junior Rani died in childbirth giving birth to a boy. And in this situation the clever and perpetually scheming Chathayam Tirunal found a fresh opening for the pursuit of her own ambitions.

In 1788, there was a reason why this lady's second and third daughters were adopted into the Attingal line, and not her eldest. This was because the latter was at the time already married, whereas custom in Travancore was to acquire unmarried females. By 1799, however, this eldest daughter of Chathayam Tirunal had a son, and his cunning grandmother determined that he offered the most perfect conduit for her forthcoming intrigues. When the Junior Rani died, she tried to have this grandson of hers, technically a member of the Kolathiri family, perform her funeral ceremonies. But the Senior Rani, aware that this would result in a problematic acknowledgement of dynastic openings between an Attingal Rani and a Kolathiri prince, resisted, and had the infant son of her late sister conduct the ceremonies under her own guidance. 'The child did not,' however, 'long survive his mother, and the successive deaths of all the children who stood in the way of [the eldest grandson of Chathayam Tirunal] have excited strong suspicions against [her] whose character attracted suspicion,' Munro would record some years down the line.[7]

Luckily for the indefatigable old lady, in the new regime of a weak, easily swayed ruler, the Senior Rani did not enjoy much power and was increasingly cornered. All influence was vested in the Brahmin Dewan, resented as 'the associate and minister of his debaucheries' whose 'most flagrant extortion and tyranny' would provoke Velu Tampi's ascent shortly.[8] The Dewan, it was also reported, had 'a passion which he is said to have entertained' for the eldest daughter of Chathayam Tirunal (the mother of her stooge grandson),[9] and exploiting this and 'by presents and promise' the old lady persuaded the man to orchestrate the adoption of her grandson into the royal family and his installation as Elayarajah or heir apparent.[10] She was evidently 'incited to this proceeding not only by the implacable enmity which she cherished against her daughter', the Senior Rani, but also 'by a hope of succeeding *herself* to the dignity' of Attingal Rani 'if she could procure the adoption of her eldest daughter's son into the family of Travancore'.[11] In other words, Chathayam Tirunal could not care less for tradition and custom; her endeavour was plainly to obtain for herself and her own faction and chosen heirs future power in Travancore, her home in exile.

When she heard of what her mother was conniving to do, the Senior Rani 'sent for the Rajah and in a tone of authority and dignity enjoined him to desist from their prosecution'. But the monarch was entirely in the hands of his Dewan and so he 'promised whatever [the Rani] desired', but promptly went back and 'immediately afterwards sanctioned all that she had inhibited'.[12] Disgusted by this weakness and treachery of not only her mother but also the ruling prince, the Senior Rani next 'summoned the [Dewan] to her presence and commanded him to relinquish his intentions, but he treated her with disrespect and insolence'.[13] Pushed to the wall, and powerless against the combination of her mother, the minister and the ruler, she then approached her last resort: the authorities in the temple without whose cooperation the proposed adoption could never take place. To her great relief, '*they* considered it to be their duty to obey her orders' and 'solemnly promised to refuse' the adoption and 'adhered faithfully to their engagement'.[14] The Dewan and Chathayam Tirunal, however, had no intention of giving up and the former himself took the grandson of the latter to the temple 'where he made some offerings and then conducted him to the [Senior Rani] to receive her benediction in the character of his mother'.[15]

> She refused to see him or to give any sanction whatever to the proceeding. The [Rani] was then far advanced in pregnancy—two other [princesses], her daughter and her niece, were alive—the reigning Rajah was in the prime of his life and there was no pretence or excuse for the illegal and arbitrary measure which he sanctioned. The unfortunate [Rani] tore her hair, refused all nourishment for three days, and lamented with expressions of poignant sorrow the cruelty of her fate in being separated from her own house, and rejected by that into which she was adopted. Nor was her grief unreasonable: the adoption [of Chathayam Tirunal's nominee] by the single authority of the Rajah if permitted to pass into precedent would be effectually subversive to all the rights and privileges of the [Attingal Rani]. The succession to the Musnad would not then be conferred to the offspring of the [latter] but be regulated by the caprice, the affections, or the enmities of the Rajah and his ministers. The [Rani] deeply sensible of these considerations sedulously avoided any measure that would indicate her concurrence in the adoption...[16]

Her spiteful mother, however, was unrelenting. The grandson now began to claim for himself the title of Elayarajah while Chathayam Tirunal, barely concealing her glee, 'threw aside all disguise and openly wrote letters and issued orders in the character of [the Attingal Rani]'.[17] This, however, was treasonous, and 'formed the Rajah to banish her and her three daughters' to Mavelikkara. The Elayarajah, in the meantime, tried on every occasion possible to obtain some semblance of acceptance from the Attingal Rani. On completing the ceremonies and wearing the 'twice born' thread, he approached the latter to seek her blessings as his adoptive mother. But the Rani 'indignantly repulsed him, desiring him to go to his real mother'.[18] Sometime later, when she fell ill and it became clear she would not survive, Velu Tampi, by now Dewan, ordered the customary ceremonies in the Sri Padmanabhaswamy Temple, asking the Elayarajah to represent the Rani. But 'rejecting with disdain his Ministry in that capacity, she rose from her couch to offer the [rituals] with her own hands' and returned from the temple and 'expired the same day'.[19] Even as she went to the grave in 1808, thus, the Attingal Rani withheld recognition from her hateful mother's chosen heir, preserving for her own descendants the title to the throne.

It was after this that the ruling prince died and a succession dispute broke out between the pretender Elayarajah and the eldest surviving daughter of the dead Rani in 1810. She carried on her mother's campaign to have the former's so-called adoption nullified and declared illegal. Munro decided after a thorough investigation that it was 'universally admitted that according to the established Law and usage of Travancore' only the sons of the Attingal Ranis were 'legal heirs to the Musnad'. He established 'beyond controversy that the mother of the person styled [the Elayarajah]' had never been an Attingal Rani, and though he might have himself been, through some ceremonies, made a member of the royal house, he could not claim the throne unless he was the son of an Attingal Rani.[20] Travancore, then, was entrusted into the hands of the late Rani's eldest daughter, none other than Gowri Lakshmi Bayi, and her pretender rival was expelled to Chingleput. Chathayam Tirunal herself spent the remainder of her days in Mavelikkara, thwarted ultimately in her vendetta against her daughter and her issue, dying there in obscurity in 1832, decades before descendants of her line from her youngest daughter, Princess Arya, were absorbed into the royal house and installed as Attingal Ranis, a title she herself had failed to obtain.

The court in Travancore, thus, was often all about potent combinations that could even prevail over the strict letter of tradition and custom, though ultimately it was the law, after several twists and turns, that triumphed. Once the Attingal Ranis had been great queens, but by the end of the eighteenth century, influential factions thwarted them in their own households. In the years that followed, the power of the senior female member in the royal family became more diluted than ever before. Sethu Lakshmi Bayi, in what some deemed her idealism and others her naiveté, always looked to the law and to the correctness of custom to protect her position. The Junior Maharani, who understood the lessons of history better, on the other hand realised that power could never be exercised without strong allies. And no sooner had her son's reign begun, than she attached to herself perhaps the greatest single ally and loyalist in all of Travancore's history, one who was to not only bend the letter of the law to his own advantage but cleverly ensure that this time round, the Attingal Rani would not triumph at the cost of his sponsors.

It was rather telling that in 1932 when the Maharajah deemed it sufficient to offer his aunt a pension in retirement of Rs 75,000, after seven strenuous years of running the administration, he also created a post of Legal and Constitutional Adviser, granting the candidate a princely Rs 72,000 per annum.[21] It was an unprecedented office in Travancore, more exorbitant than even the Dewan, and was created specifically to retain the valuable (and inordinately expensive) services of the 'trusted friend' of the Maharajah's family, Sir C.P. Ramaswami Iyer.[22] In the long run it was a beneficial investment, for numerous schemes for the benefit of the principality and its ruling house could not have succeeded without the brilliance of this man. Some other schemes like an ill-fated bicameral legislature, however, saw lesser success. The appointment in itself, though, instigated much resentment among the public and the press. 'Life in Indian States is intolerable,' began the *Princely India* with its undisguised sarcasm:

> Take for instance Travancore. The people of the State were post haste to see the young Maharajah on the [throne] when the Maharani Regent was managing the affairs in a quiet way. People believed blindly and foolishly that the Junior Maharani and her son would remove all maladies of the people ... But the maladies which the Junior Maharani herself was subjected to were greater than those of the people. She first of all realised that without a Constitutional Adviser she couldn't pull on. And Sir CP's stars were in the ascendant. Rs 6,000 a month as salary and various other allowances! Sir CP could be the Constitutional Adviser [whether] he remained in Simla or Sylhet, London or Lausanne. What a nice job to boot! ... But who invented and wanted a Constitutional Adviser? The late Maharajah Sri Mulam Tirunal managed the State administration a thousand times better than all his contemporary ruling Princes without a Constitutional Adviser. The Maharani Regent never went in for a Constitutional Adviser. But the

> Junior Maharani, from the experience she gained in her free, itinerant life, discovered that with the aid of a Constitutional Adviser the State could be converted into a Paradise. Yes, a Paradise to her, and hell to the people.[23]

While the *Princely India* was prone to exaggeration (in another piece it went on to indelicately compare Sir CP to 'a squeezed lemon' and suggested that the Junior Maharani, who had 'been trying to become a perfect actress', lacked 'what the Senior has in abundance—that [which] can be had only by the grace of God'),[24] there was a significant quantum of truth in that the institution of such an inflated title for Sir CP was not received well. His presence in the state by October 1932 was 'becoming more and more unwelcome', noted the Resident, and there was 'no doubt that his appointment' had been 'all along exceedingly unpopular'.[25] His superior salary and precedence over the Dewan, his residence in the Vellayambalam Palace, as also the glaring fact that his official contributions were deemed 'totally incommensurate' with his high pay and that such work 'has always been carried out by the Dewans' in the past, all placed Sir CP into a singularly inauspicious setting, further convincing many that he was merely being rewarded for services to the Junior Maharani.[26]

Some of the resentment was also due to his unusual friendship with the royal family, i.e., the Maharajah and his mother, which is perhaps why he was not given an official bungalow but a whole palace for his use. 'His friendship with the Maharajah's mother had given rise to gossip for decades,' wrote Louise Ouwerkerk,[27] and the fact that when in Simla the Maharajah actually stayed with him caused, on account of his 'unenviable reputation', 'much adverse comment'.[28] The royal family had 'stood out among other Ruling Houses for its simplicity of life, purity of morals, and devotion to duty; and the people were saddened by the blot on its reputation.'[29] Indeed, persons like Malcolm Muggeridge believed that Sir CP ('famous for his lechery and debts') enjoyed 'great power nowadays in Travancore' by the simple virtue 'of being the Junior Maharani's lover'.[30] Extravagance as well as association beyond formal necessities of the new regime with Sir CP caused great anguish not only among the orthodoxy but also the public in general.

It also did not help that the Dewan, seemed wholly powerless. Soon after the Regency, Mr Iyer had resigned and a British ICS officer called Thomas Austin was appointed (for all the criticism in 1925 about selecting Mr Watts, also a Christian, to the post). But what was meant to be the highest executive office in the state suddenly found itself answerable to more than one overriding authority in the form of the Legal and Constitutional Adviser. The Maharajah himself was, of course, never blamed, for 'it was widely realised that his mother had a dominating influence over him and interfered in matters of state where he ought to have been acting on his own initiative'.[31] And Sir CP, as the source of power behind the Junior Maharani in turn, was considered the real problem, as the Resident noted:

> This was, in the first instance, due to the fact that he was considered to be nothing more or less than an adventurer, whose relations with the Junior Maharani were not above suspicion, but I think that the present mood, and it is, I believe, the mood of the bulk of the intelligentsia, is largely due to the indisputable fact that the State is being run by him and the Junior Maharani, with the Maharajah, who is completely dominated, and is likely to remain so until he marries, well in the background, and Austin, the Dewan, almost out of the picture. It is Austin's influence which the people would like to see brought out to bear on the Maharajah and not of Sir C.P. Ramaswami Iyer, and that Austin has, through no fault of his own, cut comparatively little ice has, I know, been a cause of keen disappointment. I am quite confident that Sir C.P. Ramaswami Iyer interferes in matters which do not come within his province, and Austin must know this.[32]

By 1934, a thoroughly vexed Dewan handed in his notice and departed. Sir M. Habibullah was then chosen, also fated not to last very long in Travancore, due to the same difficulties that haunted his predecessor. For 'any advice he gives is criticised by the Legal and Constitutional Adviser'.[33] 'Both Mr Austin and Sir Muhammad Habibullah have complained to me bitterly,' reported the Resident, 'of the influence and interference exercised by Sir C.P. Ramaswami Iyer' and 'complained that Sir CP's influence often works against that of the Dewan, who is held responsible by public opinion for resultant action.'[34]

> It is unpleasant for me to have to record anything against Sir C.P. Ramaswami Iyer, for I must admit that my relations with this man have always been cordial, and he has, so far as I am aware, been of material assistance to me in my relations with the Palace. I respect Sir CP's mental attainments and I like him personally; but I am forced to face the fact that he is exceedingly unpopular in South India; it is clear that nobody trusts him, and that his present association with Travancore tends to make His Highness' administration suspect and unpopular. More than this, it is obvious that we shall never get a reliable and capable Dewan to stay long in Travancore while

> a Legal and Constitutional Adviser, acting with no public responsibility whatever, is able to influence all [of] the Maharajah's decisions.[35]

By 1935, Sir Muhammad had confided to the Resident that 'we cannot depend on his services for more than a few months longer' since he was 'very dissatisfied with the existing conditions'. He was a man of great ability and had all those qualities that Mr Watts had once shown. 'He is just and impartial, courteous and accessible to all, and there is no doubt that he has hitherto commanded public confidence to a large extent, but the public are losing faith in him through no fault of his own, and I think he is sensible of this.'[36] This was mainly because the palace now wished to execute a pro-Hindu policy, replacing the Regency-era decision to be above board in communal matters. Sir Muhammad, on the other hand, was inclined to be fair and unbiased. Communal trouble was naturally provoked, then, and the Resident sided with the Dewan in warning that 'The remedy lies in an impartial yet firm administration.'[37] 'The present regime,' he added, 'does not inspire confidence, for the Travancoreans are quite intelligent enough to see that though they have all the trappings of constitutional and popular Government, there are concealed behind these trappings influences they dislike and mistrust, and which sometime operate in opposition to justice and fair play.'[38]

In the meantime, efforts were devised in Delhi to somehow extract Sir CP from Travancore. Lord Willingdon promptly nominated him to the Government of India's Secretariat Committee, popularly known as the Wheeler Committee that was to help revitalise the Indian bureaucracy. Sir Muhammad, as a result of his rival's forecasted departure from active involvement in the state, was persuaded to stay on as Dewan. But by the end of 1935 in the three months that followed his move to Delhi, Sir CP made three separate visits to Travancore, demonstrating every intention to continue intervening in local affairs. 'I should like His Highness to be very clearly given to understand,' wrote an irritated Resident, 'that these continued visits of Sir CP are not beneficial to His Highness' interests and the sooner they are stopped the better for His Highness and the State.'[39] Additionally, he pointed out,

> ... the difficulty in present Travancore politics ... is the existence of a 'trinity'— His Highness, Her Highness his mother, and Sir CP; and it is almost like a three-card trick in trying to 'spot the knave' ... What they want is [for] Sir Muhammad to resign. [A decision to give him] a few days ago the title of 'Nawab' was just a manoeuvre in that direction to forestall criticism

> that the Ruler has treated his Dewan badly. I may remark that the decision to bestow this honour on him was only arrived at at the eleventh hour on the very day of the birthday durbar, [and] its bestowal has deceived no one, except Sir Muhammad himself. This view may seem an uncharitable one to take, but I am afraid it is the correct one. Sir CP having got what he wanted can afford to be generous.[40]

As usual Sir CP employed his personal influence to persuade Lord Willingdon that he would stop interfering in Travancore. He expressed how he hoped to derive a 'great advantage' from his place on the Wheeler Committee. It would, he emphasised, 'give him an opportunity of gradually severing his connection with Travancore'.[41] The impression evidently created was that there was nothing more Sir CP wished to do than leave the state. But behind the curtain, great intrigues were afoot, which even shocked the Dewan. By the end of the year Sir Muhammad looked 'ill and tired' and 'confessed to feeling done up'.[42] He had even been forced to issue a press note that he had no difficulties at all with Sir CP, when news of what was happening leaked out to an indignant public.

> At present there is full scope and opportunity for palace intrigue and, as I think you are already well aware, Her Highness (His Highness' mother) and Sir CP are universally credited with being its leading joint authors. His Highness, young and inexperienced as he is, continues, I have observed, to be completely under the sway and domination of his mother; and in the background there still persists that self-seeking influence of his 'Eminence Grise' Sir CP. I am persuaded that it is palace intrigue which was responsible for the position of Sir Muhammad ... As Sir Muhammad said to me himself, he was tricked into giving Sir CP a 'clearance certificate' of non-interference. He was manoeuvred into being compelled by the express desire of His Highness to issue a lamentable note to the Associated Press on the 27th September 1935 ... Sir Muhammad felt [the insult] keenly. 'Colonel Garstin', he said to me, 'in the 42 years of my service, I have never had to do such a thing as this.' I do not think he was acting a part: he looked miserable.[43]

The plot finally reached consummation in August 1936. Unable to implement a policy of fairness to tackle communal problem and appalled by Sir CP's unrelenting influence running counter to everything he did, Sir Muhammad resigned and left. But if the Government of India expected to find the state a new, able Dewan who could resolve these issues and perhaps stand up to Sir CP, they were to be stunned. For 'a minor coup, engineered by the Palace itself, with the knowledge of Sir CP' was in the offing.[44] On 31 August, the Maharajah communicated to the Resident about the selection of his new Dewan, stating how he felt an urgent need to have a candidate 'in whom I have full confidence'. And apparently after 'bestowing anxious thought on this matter', he had decided to appoint none other than Sir CP himself as Dewan.[45]

The Government of India were taken by outright bewilderment at the news. They instantly objected to this unilateral decision, arguing that their sanction and consent were required for the appointment of a new minister. The Maharajah calmly responded that the Paramount Power had recently granted him the right to make all appointments with salaries over Rs 500 a month himself, without reference to them; the Dewan received well above this sum and he could therefore appoint whomever he wanted. Furthermore, even when he chose Sir Muhammad, he had offered him the post first and then written privately to the Viceroy who commended his choice. Now he was merely repeating that custom and saw no reason to consult Delhi.[46] 'Never before in the history of Travancore' notes one writer, 'had a Dewan been appointed in defiance of the official opinion of the British government.'[47] The 'private' door that Lord Willingdon opened to the Maharajah in 1931 through Sir CP to put an end to the Regency had now come to stab an utterly astonished Government of India in its own back.[48]

There was no doubt that this coup to install Sir CP in power would strengthen the hands of the Junior Maharani. 'CP's appointment as Dewan,' states the former's biographer, 'had been the climactic conclusion of a long-drawn power struggle between the Senior Maharani, who enjoyed the support of the Christians, and the Junior Maharani, who was backed by the Nairs.'[49] As for the man, the Governor of Madras wrote, amused that the Political Department had not seen this coming: he 'obviously prefers to be a dictator in Travancore to one of a crowd in Delhi' on some obscure committee the Viceroy gave him as a distraction from Travancore.[50] The Maharajah himself seemed unable to stand up to this formidable union of his mother and this new Dewan who were destined to rule all of Travancore in his name in the years ahead. 'That His Highness is at present very subordinate to those behind him is quite obvious,' the Resident had noted. 'I believe there is much good in him and a sincere desire to rule well, but he is naturally reticent and timid.'[51] Successive Residents, therefore, tried to win him over so that he would realise he had the support of the Government of India and need not succumb to the influence of those in his palace. But as a frustrated Mr Garstin, the latest British representative, recorded, these attempts to counter-manipulate the Maharajah did not succeed:

> My predecessor Field did his best to try and counteract this palace intrigue by attempting to win the confidence of the Maharajah, but he told me that whenever he made any move in this direction, the Maharajah, always studiously polite and courteous, listened to all he had to say but could not be persuaded to express any opinion himself, merely remarking that he would consider the matter: in the result nothing would be done. I have [myself] found this attitude of stony reserve whereby one is made (very politely) to feel that the friendly discussion with the [Resident] is not welcomed—indeed almost resented: His Highness is ever on his guard as though he has been carefully tutored beforehand and is afraid to say anything ... Apparently this attitude is inculcated by Her Highness, his mother. There is no doubt at all that the treatment Her Highness received during the Regency years (I do not impute any criticism of that treatment) still rankles in Her Highness' mind and accordingly influences the overmastering hold she has over her son.[52]

At the time of the Regency, Nairs complained habitually that Sethu Lakshmi Bayi was under the domination of her husband and never said anything beyond what she had been taught to say. Residents, who as always maintained a hawk's eye over the royal house, consistently rejected the accusation. Now, however, they watched with disbelief, as the Maharajah seemed entirely withdrawn under his mother's overpowering wings. In Bangalore it was stated with great relief during his training and the attendant separation from the Junior Maharani that he was finally emerging out of his shell into a fine young man. Now, five years later, he seemed to have gone back right in, beating a disappointing retreat. It was reminiscent of an episode in 1928 when one of Chithira Tirunal's tutors asked him, after saying goodbye before his departure, if he would write to him sometime. The sixteen-year-old Maharajah innocently responded: 'I must ask my mother first.'[53]

In 1925 at the climax of the Vaikom Satyagraha, when Mahatma Gandhi met Sethu Lakshmi Bayi, they discussed not only the topic of opening public roads to all of Travancore's Hindu subjects, but also the larger abomination of untouchability. Prolonged discussions on this continued at their subsequent meeting in 1927, where he expressed his admiration of her deepest conviction 'to see that this wrong is removed at the earliest possible moment'.[54] Eradication of the evil, however, would correspond to opening the hallowed gates of temples in Travancore to all its Hindu faithful. When the Maharani was asked if she was prepared to allow this, she responded: 'I agree this should be done, and it will be done.' But as the head of an interim government, with a Christian Dewan and other senior officials also from minority communities, she would offend the orthodoxy by embarking on so sweeping and historic a step at that point. Temple entry, she therefore announced, would have to wait for her nephew when he came of age.[55] And, true to that belief, in November 1936 the Maharajah, on the occasion of his twenty-fourth birthday, passed the epochal Temple Entry Proclamation, throwing open all Hindu shrines in Travancore to all its hitherto low-caste subjects:

> Profoundly convinced of the truth and validity of Our religion, believing that it is based on divine guidance and on all-comprehending toleration, knowing that in its practice it has throughout the centuries, adapted itself to the needs of changing times, solicitous that none of Our Hindu subjects should, by reason of birth or caste or community, be denied the consolation and the solace of the Hindu faith, We have decided and hereby declare, ordain and command that, subject to such rules and conditions as may be laid down and imposed by Us for preserving their proper atmosphere and maintaining their rituals and observances, there should henceforth be no restriction placed on any Hindu by birth or religion on entering or worshipping at temples controlled by Us and Our Government.[56]

The import of this declaration, passed in a matter of months after Sir CP took over the administration, cannot be understated. Indeed, it remains the single greatest reform for courageously executing which the Maharajah is remembered even today, becoming also the greatest highlight of Sir CP's own phenomenal career. Champions of the Hindu cause celebrated it as 'heralding the birth of a new conscience in the Hindu world',[57] while C. Rajagopalachari considered it perhaps 'the greatest religious reform in India after the time of Asoka'.[58] Gandhi saw it as 'a people's charter of spiritual emancipation' and it was altogether a tremendous act, earning for Chithira Tirunal 'an immortal place among the social reformers of modern India'.[59] The day temple entry was proclaimed the iron gates of Kowdiar Palace were thrown open for the masses to express their overwhelming gratitude to their monarch. 'The guards withdrew,' the Maharajah's brother recorded, 'and the people just kept pouring in. The palace grounds resembled a pin cushion, only heads!'[60]

While Sethu Lakshmi Bayi, in conceding the Vaikom demands and terminating disabilities of many kinds afflicting low-caste communities, set the stage for temple entry, credit for taking it to its rightful conclusion is due to the Junior Maharani, Sir CP, and the Maharajah in equal measure. Travancore now had a male ruler with a Dewan who was not only a Brahmin but also possessed the courage to weather any political storm unleashed by the orthodoxy. By 1937, even the venerated Azhavanchery Tamprakkal, the highest sacerdotal Brahmin dignitary in all Kerala, was persuaded to declare 'unequivocally' his support, despite pressure from other factions that were 'greatly disturbed' by these happenings.[61] Cochin prohibited Travancore priests from entering shrines within its domains, and the Zamorin too exercised all his feudal influence in Malabar to reject the principle of temple entry. The Maharajah and his mother and the minister carried on unfazed, however. Earlier in 1934 they had openly demonstrated their abhorrence of untouchability when they welcomed at the wedding celebrations of the First Princess all their subjects, without prejudice of caste.[62] Gandhi too praised the Junior Maharani for staunchly supporting her son in this groundbreaking reform, declaring how the proclamation was 'due to the influence of one woman' who was 'determined to do what was the purest act of justice'. The Maharajah 'could not,' he concluded, 'have done it without the support of his mother.'[63]

But no great reform occurs in a vacuum and consciousness of the injustices of old social practices is married to changing opinions and calculations on the ground, when especially they threaten social order. Travancore was no exception, and behind temple entry in 1936 lay decades of agitation and social pressure applied masterfully by low-caste groups in one way or another. It is also significant that all three principal players behind the proclamation were concerned by the political implications of Hindu casteism and the weaknesses it engendered in the wider community. While the Junior Maharani was 'a declared sympathizer of the Hindu cause' who had gathered Hindu forces during Sethu Lakshmi Bayi's allegedly pro-Christian administration,[64] Sir CP would some years down the line remark 'that Travancore would cease to be a Hindu State if the Christians are allowed a free hand'.[65] He also harboured very serious suspicions, reportedly, that the latter, from time immemorial, were attempting to capture and transform the state into a Christian dominion.[66] As for the Maharajah, his devotion to his family deity, and to pious Hinduism in general, was legendary, and he was hugely concerned by the loss in Hindu numbers in Travancore.[67] Even as fringe tribal groups were steadily absorbed into the mainstream Hindu fold, the 1931 census reported that from nearly 70 per cent of the population in 1901, Hindus now stood at less than 62 per cent, while Christians increased their standing from about 24 per cent to nearly 32 per cent during the same period.[68] As his brother stated, 'the Maharajah wanted to bring about a consolidation of the community and growth of self-respect among all its members'.[69]

Shortly after succeeding to power late in 1931, the Maharajah's administration had therefore revealed itself as having a stern Hindu bias, with the Nairs forming their principal base of support. As the historian Sreedhara Menon remarks, the Christians had 'incurred the displeasure or wrath of the Junior Maharani' so that now there was a 'backlash' against them.[70] Even as late as the 1940s Christian groups would see the new pro-Hindu policy as a repercussion of the feud between the Senior and Junior Maharanis. With reference to the first memorial submitted against Sethu Lakshmi Bayi, mainly by Nairs who championed the Junior Maharani's quest for a Council of Regency, the corresponding support of Christians and other groups of minorities to Sethu Lakshmi Bayi was cast in a negative light. While Nairs 'who foresaw that the Regency is to last only a short time' supported the Maharajah's mother, the Christians 'were falsely regarded as opponents of the Maharajah' primarily because 'they did not oppose the Regency regime' and further the Junior Maharani's agenda.[71] With her son's succession, then, it was no surprise that the state had a vendetta to gratify by means of 'an anti-Christian policy' that was 'started with the able assistance of Sir CP'. He was rather imperious a Hindu himself, and in his *World Religions: A Study in Synthesis* (which he defended as 'purely a personal enterprise') he allegedly ridiculed Christian ideas openly, including Immaculate Conception and the divinity of Christ.[72]

By 1936, Hindu social organisations of a somewhat controversial variety were boldly encouraged, while Christians missions were locked into a tough grasp by the authorities. The administration evidently blessed the reactionary Hindu Mahasabha with official funding, and by 1941 it would proudly be reported that 80,000 people had been reconverted through its exertions.[73] Preachers from the Christian, Muslim and even Ezhava communities complained, on the other hand, that they were prohibited from making even speeches on religious matters. 'Shelter is taken under the possibility of disturbance of the public peace by District Magistrates,' it was protested, 'to prohibit evangelists and preachers from propagating their faith' even as the Hindu Mahasabha and its allies published pure virulence freely, with official patronage. One aggressive publication, for example, represented the missionary as a 'modern Ravana loathing what we long for, holding in contempt what we respect, and destroying everything which we will attempt to protect even by pledging our lives'. The chief enemy of Hindus, it went on, was the Christian evangelist, who was 'the murderer of Hindu culture and the destroyer of *Sanatana Dharma*', an 'angel of death' who was 'engaging himself in untiring efforts to convert India into a land of sin'.[74]

Much of this was provocative rhetoric, but what rankled the minorities was that the administration not only turned a blind eye to it, but also sometimes actually went out of its way to promote it. This was all a departure from Sethu Lakshmi Bayi's policy. When Mr Watts was appointed Dewan in 1925, for instance, the Christians 'looked upon his arrival as the birth of a new power' and the Hindus 'as the break of an old one'. But the Maharani wisely counselled him not to succumb to taking sides. He showed, therefore, a sober sagacity in living down both expectations 'by his great level-headedness and sense of fair-play' while Sethu Lakshmi Bayi handled communal issues 'with consummate tact', earning praise for her unprejudiced impartiality.[75] The new regime, however, as the Resident reported, was more than happy to play the communal ball and favour one community over another, like in the old days. Trouble was already brewing by 1935 and 'I think it is likely to grow worse, and indeed have serious consequences, unless the administration can see its way to pursue a policy of strict fairness and impartiality between the warring communities.'[76]

While he believed that the Maharajah was 'personally disposed to be fair and impartial', he was 'nothing like a free agent' and influences behind the curtain thwarted hopes of his exercising policy in the famously even-handed manner of his aunt.[77] Communal trouble, in the meantime, got worse, and the 'Christians, Ezhavas, and Muslims are beginning to assert that the good which Sir Muhammad has done to remove the unfair Nair predominance' had led to a situation where the latter were determined not to allow him to survive.[78] The Maharajah himself then seemed to be taking sides in favour of the Hindus; in Quilon there was a mosque that had reached an understanding with local Hindus that temple processions passing by their premises should play softer music. 'His Highness took a different view and after personally coming to the Residency to see me, he adhered to his opinion that it would be a mistake to order the Hindus to give up an old prescriptive custom.' The Dewan disagreed and thought that both sides would have to compromise and not just the Muslim minority, which did not go down well with Kowdiar Palace. 'I can now say that His Highness does appear to be anxious to get rid of Sir Muhammad', and it was after similar disagreements on communal policy that the old Dewan had left.[79]

It was no surprise that the government reverted to the old game of playing one community upon another after Sir CP came to the fore. As a previous Resident had stated during Mulam Tirunal's rule, 'To put the matter crudely, the sovereignty of the ruler is secured by the factions among the people, rendering any combination against the Durbar improbable in the extreme.'[80] But while the Junior Maharani and Sir CP rewarded the Nairs with patronage for their support during the Regency, and openly promoted Hinduism, the time had long passed when others who faced the brunt of this approach would quietly pray and hope for better days. Travancore of the 1930s was a different place. The impartial policy of the Regency rule had allowed 'the Christian elite' to enjoy 'an unusual degree of official favour' after decades of overtly Hindu state procedure[81] while the low-caste Ezhava community found doors of high employment opened to them for the first time, with even a general secretary of their strongest organisation and mouthpiece (the Sri Narayana Dharma Paripalana [SNDP] Yogam endorsed by Sri Narayana Guru) appointed a magistrate by Sethu Lakshmi Bayi.[82]

To close doors now and repossess them into high-caste Hindu bastions was a move the minorities were determined to frustrate. For the first time low-caste Hindu groups, Christians, Muslims and others would rally together into a united front to rival Nair dominance. Inadvertently, thus, the Junior Maharani and the Maharajah would, by returning to communal state patronage, allow their opposition to unite into a singular, potent force, which was to herald the end of communalism itself, demanding instead a responsible government of the people, for the people and by the people before the end of the decade. Sethu Lakshmi Bayi had, through her fair policy, set the wheels in motion, to remove from Travancore the idea of communalism and replace it (unwittingly) with one of nationalism. Temple entry was, then, a desperate attempt to fracture the alliance between the Christians and the Ezhavas, at a historic crossroads where the latter, with all their influence, could either join forces and march alongside the former, standing up to the communal regime, or be won over by a drastic and far-reaching reform to back the Hindu cause against the Christians by that very regime.

In 1932, in what was trumpeted as a revolutionary reform, the Maharajah inaugurated a bicameral legislature in Travancore, which was hoped to temper communal rivalries among politicians. The lower house, the Sri Mulam Assembly, was to have forty-eight elected members (with five from special constituencies) while the upper house, the Sri Chithira State Council, had twenty-two elected members (six of whom represented special interests). Franchise was extended to all owners or registered landholders paying not less than Rs 5 in tax per annum.[83] 'The liberal nature of this measure of reform was the result of the bold initiative of His Highness the Maharajah,' lauded a state publication, 'and the scheme and the details benefited a great deal by the advice of Sir C.P. Ramaswami Iyer, whose mastery of the underlying principles of modern constitutions and his long experience of the working of representative institutions are so widely known and appreciated.'[84]

But while the size of the electorate was effectively doubled by the Maharajah, the franchise was not as liberal as it pretended to be, with only 1,56,797 individuals in a state of five million being eligible to vote in the first elections of 1933.[85] What was also disappointing to the minorities was that the franchise qualification of landholding or ownership advantaged the Nairs most, for Christians and Ezhavas who held land often did so on subordinate tenures, and not in their names, so that even those lands cultivated by them qualified tax-paying Nair or other Hindu landlords in the eyes of the law.[86] 'In a country where it has to be admitted with regret that even highly cultured men hardly rise above communal considerations in public affairs,' it was lamented, 'it is essential that no single community should possess a dominating influence in the Legislature and the Public Service.'[87] The new rules did nothing to temper Nair dominance, and it was argued out that contributions of others, through commerce and industry, ought to receive consideration, where due to historic reasons their control over land had always been minimal.

What the minorities wanted, instead, was communal reservation, to which the government was entirely opposed, despite the fact that this was also now the agreed formula even in British India, accepted by Gandhi as well. In their defence the administration argued that reservations would only widen existing communal cleavages. The minorities, however, 'contended that the reforms proposed by the government actually placed all other communities under the dominance of one group, the Nairs, and that this unequal distribution of power was the basic cause' of communalism to begin with.[88] If, they articulated somewhat naively, each community were given its rightful share, it would 'have the beneficent result of gradually *obliterating* communal discord' since every section would become 'satisfied that it has its due and nothing more' and the 'raison d'être of the communal struggle vanishes'.[89] The government, however, refused to respond to these concerns, let alone arrive at a compromise. It was then that the inconceivable occurred: the Ezhavas, Christians and Muslims came together to constitute an All-Travancore Joint Political Congress (ATJPC, not allied to Gandhi's Indian National Congress) to ventilate as forcefully as possible their united opinions and ideas.

As early as 1914, a Dewan had noted how Christians, Ezhavas and Muslims, who for generations had complained of Nair predominance, could one day unite to seek redress and cause serious damage to the monarchy.[90] And indeed, the combination was a formidable one, which nobody had ever before seen in Travancore, so beleaguered by petty communal divisions. While the Nairs and other high-caste Hindus together comprised 22.3 per cent of the population, the union of the Ezhavas (at 17.1 per cent), the Christians (at 18.9 per cent Syrians and 12 per cent non-Syrians), and the Muslims (at 6.9 per cent) created an unprecedented behemoth in terms of sheer numbers.[91] In order to retaliate against an unresponsive government, the ATJPC decided to boycott the 1933 elections so that when results were announced they came as 'a severe blow to the administration'.[92] In three-fifths of the constituencies, no opposition was put up, and the Nairs won thirty-five of the fifty-nine general seats in both houses, while Christians, Ezhavas and Muslims, whom the government expected to receive nineteen seats, won fourteen. But these victors were not prominent members of their communities, who all sided with the ATJPC, and were instead government minions,[93] or as another source put it, 'government sponsored nobodies'.[94] This did not please the Maharajah who had hoped the elections would be a sensational affair to showcase Travancore's advances towards constitutionalism. 'I am glad to inform you that the constitutional experiment that has been started,' he had announced, 'is being watched with sympathy and interest by many outside the state' including the Secretary of State in London.[95] The boycott took the sheen off the exercise, and the results proved the ATJPC right when Christians with a population of 16.04 lakh won ten seats; Ezhavas with 8.09 lakh won three; but Nairs with 8.68 lakh won a phenomenal thirty-five seats.[96] Nothing more was needed to prove firsthand the undue influence of the Nairs.

As it happened, 'with some encouragement from the Paramount Power' the Maharajah was compelled to make amends and revise the new system.[97] By 1935, the franchise was reduced to a tax payment of Re 1 instead of Rs 5, which alone tripled the electorate to half a million, and one-sixth of the adult population in the state.[98] Fourteen seats in the Sri Mulam Assembly were reserved for Ezhavas, socially backward Christian sects and Muslims, so that by the elections of 1937 the ATJPC was in a position to capture twenty-six seats in the Lower House and eight in the Upper House, cutting Nair preponderance to almost half, overnight.[99] They also succeeded in having the government implement a system of reservations in the public services, even though most important positions were still handed to high-caste Hindus.[100] Yet, on the whole, the Nairs had to face 'a painful loss of influence' by the time of the 1937 elections, which were 'free of the more extreme manifestations of communal tensions' on account of the fact that the principal low-caste group and the Christians and Muslims were now firmly united against the Hindu state and its high-caste supporters.[101] There was some grumbling about this, but as the Resident noted, 'the Nairs will be very ill-advised to attempt to get the recent electoral reforms altered, as it will only once more revive communal jealousies and misunderstandings'.[102] And due to a whole host of new problems that had emerged, the government could not afford to offend the Ezhavas in particular any more.

But these reforms on the part of the state had to be positively wrested out, and it made every effort to engineer the dilution of the ATJPC and its influence following the debacle in the 1933 elections that left the government fuming. Known at the time as the Abstention Movement, it had 'as its backbone the unprivileged sections of the Hindu community' sharing an 'excellent rapport' with Christians and Muslims.[103] The Nairs were quick in denouncing the whole enterprise. 'At no time in the history of Travancore,' decried one leader, 'did communalism stride like a colossus over the whole country and inflame baser passions and encourage fissiparous tendencies.'[104] This was despite the fact that the Nairs seemed the only purely communal group now, with the others having united into the ATJPC, setting aside their differences. It became clear that this union was achieved by casting the Nairs, with all their overwhelming control over the state, as the common enemy. The strategy to counter it, then, was to find a new enemy and bring back the Ezhavas, who had equal numbers, not to speak of a powerful political presence, into a united Hindu bloc against Christians, resented equally by the Nairs and the regime. The contest transformed into one between the Nairs and the Christians. And the Ezhavas became both the clinching factor as well as the reward.

The Nairs were the first to react and cast the ATJPC as a Christian movement that 'desired to convert Travancore into a Christian country' by 'seeking to destroy the power of the Hindus by creating splits among them'.[105] This seems to have matched the outlook of Sir CP and the Maharajah as well, with paranoia exacerbated by the actions and statements of prominent Ezhava leaders themselves, who began to threaten mass conversion to Christianity. The very fact that this community of low-caste but statistically Hindu subjects of the state were willing to forsake the Hindu cause (justifiably, of course, since the Nairs had not shown any generosity in accommodating them so far) shook the government and its supporters. With nearly a quarter-million Ezhavas engaged in industry, they were fast becoming class conscious also, and as early as the Vaikom Satyagraha the Dewan had noted that they were 'imbued with strong ideas of some form of communism' and had begun to 'talk of the equal rights of men'.[106] To a crowd of 2,000 one leader had even declared: 'Just as the Russians managed to obtain freedom by putting an end to their royal family, so the Ezhavas must also fight to the very end without caring [for] the guns of the sepoys, batons of the police, or even the Maharajah.'[107] The Ezhavas seemed to be heading down a route that could prove disastrous for the establishment, all the while seemingly cheered on by their Christian allies.

The Ezhavas in the meantime had also turned into a tightly organised society, and in a space of thirty years their internal subdivisions had almost completely vanished. They also had a 'long tradition' of 'flirtation with Christian missionaries' and by the 1920s there was even talk of embracing Buddhism to escape the tyranny of the Nairs and other high-caste Hindus.[108] As far back as 1905 the Ezhava paper *Sujanandhini* would state: 'Many are contemplating a change of religion. It is under discussion whether Christianity or Mohammedanism will afford the necessary relief.'[109] The community was perfectly aware of the effect that talk of rejecting Hinduism had on the Nairs, so that during the Abstention Movement, C. Kesavan declared openly at a meeting that 'The Nairs are making monkeys of the Ezhavas' by talking of a united Hindu cause against Christians. 'We are not Hindus,' he proclaimed, telling his fellowmen: 'Renounce this Hinduism.'[110] Then at a factory strike in Allepey, Ezhava workers shouted slogans like 'Destroy the Nairs, destroy Nair rule, destroy capitalism.'[111] When the government sometime later asked their principal organisation, the SNDP Yogam, to show cause for getting involved in political affairs when its charter promised to confine its activities to education and economic welfare, its general secretary quietly informed Sir CP that the government were free to dissolve the SNDP Yogam if they wished but he would ensure that its thousand branches were turned into a thousand platforms for the opposition party. Sir CP had no option but to back down.[112]

The question of the Ezhavas turning against the Hindu cause seems to have even concerned Gandhi who remarked that while he didn't mind that 'Christian missions are flirting with the Harijans [i.e., low-caste communities]', the great truth was that for the latter 'there is no social equality, no real freedom anywhere except when it is *first* obtained in Hinduism'.[113] Rameshwari Nehru, who visited

Travancore, also expressed similar views when she said, 'I am amazed to find missionaries of every religion rushing to Travancore thinking that the Ezhavas can be converted to one religion or [another]' which was 'a sad, humiliating spectacle'.[114] Something had to be done, then, to prevent further inroads into the politically vital Ezhava numbers being made by Christians, even if it meant that the high-caste factions would have to reconcile to losing their longstanding religious privileges in the process. The Ezhavas had themselves already clarified that the 'right to worship in temples was the test of their acceptance' into the Hindu mould, and that no matter what other reforms the state passed, 'as long as they were excluded from the temples, they were not fully accepted' and would not embrace Travancore's Hindu identity.[115]

'The Christian threat to the character of a Hindu state could, in Ramaswami Iyer's view,' then, records Robin Jeffrey, 'be overcome by uniting all Hindus into a single, devout community without distinctions of caste.' It would serve the ATJPC a death blow and put an end to the first non-communal, organised opposition in the state. And, 'Throwing open the government temples at the right moment could be a vital step in the process of consolidation.'[116] By 1935, Sir CP was clearly awake to the perils of the situation, when C. Kesavan openly criticised Nair supremacy, declaring in no uncertain terms that Ezhavas might soon withdraw from the Hindu fold altogether.[117] Added to their political alliance with the Christians, it was no surprise that the state began to pursue an anti-Christian policy through a series of efforts, causing the officialdom and government to be deplored as the 'Engine of Oppression' for victimising Christian communities.[118] By August 1936 the Resident also noted that there was a clear flow of Ezhavas into a religious union with the Christians:

> There is, I am convinced, no doubt at all that the Ezhavas will not any longer put up with their present condition which for many years past they have found intolerable. They are determined to effect a change. If the caste Hindus will give them political and social privileges and grant them temple entry, large numbers doubtless will be thereby induced to remain in the Hindu fold; but among the humblest and the poorest the tide has begun to flow, and if allowed free play, will gather force.[119]

The government were already acting desperate and the Resident further stated that a notice in July 1936 insisted that public peace was threatened by conversions through Christian missions. 'This notice is regarded by the various missionaries as a very disingenuous move by the Government to put a stop to the present conversion movement,' he added. 'It is pointed out that it is a plain encouragement to district and police offers to take action to prohibit conversion activities on the ground ... with the sure and certain knowledge that their actions will be officially supported.'[120] But these were all moves to buy time and it was clear that a leap would have to be taken before the situation got even further out of hand, and the Ezhavas were forced to effect their threat of renouncing Hinduism. And thus, in November 1936, was passed the Temple Entry Proclamation. As Gandhi himself declared, 'believe me, Travancore will go down in history as the saviour of Hindu religion which was in danger of perishing.'[121]

Even as well-deserved praise for ending another conspicuous proof of social inequality was won from across India, there was no doubt of the political advantages of the proclamation at a very vital time in the state's history. As a Christian memorial to the Paramount Power in 1946 would plainly remark, 'Government unsuccessfully tried several methods, and finally as a last measure to counteract the wave of conversion, decided to open all Hindu temples to Ezhavas and other non-caste Hindus.'[122] And indeed, as Jeffrey confirms, 'From the government's point of view, the proclamation had many of the desired effects. The movement for conversion ceased abruptly, and there were stories of recent converts returning to Hinduism.'[123] The attitude of the Ezhava community towards the Dewan and the high castes was also 'dramatically changed' as a result.[124]

While Gandhi and Rajagopalachari celebrated the proclamation, the all-India leader of the low-caste movement, Dr B.R. Ambedkar himself expressed a more lukewarm response. He was not, he made it clear, convinced that spirituality or emancipation were the real intentions of the Maharajah's historic proclamation. Instead, it was knowledge that the 'cessation of so large a community would be the death-knell to the Hindus' and the fact that Ezhavas by their recent actions had 'made the danger real', that compelled the state to act in a substantial manner.[125] If it were not for these political pressures, Travancore might never have changed. Gandhi himself revealed his awareness of the uncomfortable political background of the case by playing it down. 'I regard it,' he would remark, 'as the performance of a purely religious duty of the State. And it should be taken and so treated by all ... To give it any other colour will be to destroy its great spiritual purpose and effect.'[126]

Even though temple entry was intended to wean Ezhavas away from Christian influences, the ATJPC would endure, becoming the single largest party in the legislature in the 1937 elections. By 1938 it would rechristen itself, with a number of prominent Nairs joining the movement, as the Travancore

State Congress (TSC). It was 'the beginning of a new phase in the state's political development; one in which the politics of pragmatic nationalism overlaid the politics of caste and community'.[127] The ATJPC had won representation in the Assembly and Council, but realised that neither could really contain the autocracy of the government, which held on to all powers that mattered. Responsible government, then, became the stated objective of the party, and into the 1940s the Maharajah would face serious troubles through the Travancore State Congress, which also allied with Gandhi's wider Indian National Congress. In 1944, for instance, one of their leaders would have the temerity to state openly in the legislature: 'Sir, I want to assure the government that our attitude will not be dictated by a spirit of opportunism or sycophancy. We are not here to sing the panegyrics of the head of the administration.'[128] It was not a tune that pleased the princely government very much.

In the beginning demands for responsible government were brushed aside under the excuse that the Government of India would never allow it. But when it was declared in London that the Paramount Power 'would certainly not obstruct proposals for constitutional advance initiated by a Ruler',[129] the administration had no excuses except the retention of power unto itself, not to speak of the old return that 'Travancore was a Hindu State and it would not be possible to concede Responsible Government without diluting its Hindu character.'[130] The Travancore State Congress became alive to the idea of a greater India and its struggles against British rule. The despotism of the Maharajah's government, no matter how benevolent in its intentions or effects, was seen as merely an extension of the absolutism of colonial rule. The people no longer wanted generous monarchs; they wanted power for themselves. Their aspirations were given a fillip by Sir CP's retaliations when, for instance, he 'crushed' a Christian banking concern and launched 'Operation Sabotage' against its influential owners, who opposed him politically, 'at the behest of the Palace'.[131] But after the initial shock, the only result was that communalism, once the bane of local politics which aspired at best for greater patronage from the state and thereby allowed the monarchy to sustain its overbearing authority, was forcefully 'swept away on a tide of patriotic enthusiasm and Travancore was swept into the national movement', one where the monarch had no place at all.[132]

'I hope,' expressed Gandhi shortly after the Temple Entry Proclamation, that 'the Senior Maharani is rejoicing over the great change that has come over

Travancore and over the fact that the Proclamation is being welcomed by all and sundry.'[133] But when the Mahatma presumed Sethu Lakshmi Bayi was celebrating, the truth was in fact to the contrary. Shortly after the Regency, the Maharajah retired Mr Iyer as the Dewan and asked him to head the Temple Entry Enquiry Committee, which placed its report before the government in 1934. It's general thrust was that while indeed the public were more amenable than before to the idea of temple entry, a strategy of going step by step would be most advisable, commencing with the relaxation of basic rules by permitting low-caste groups to first approach the temple gates and flagstaff, and ultimately, opening the gates when the time was correct. In the meantime, a council of Hindu pundits could be constituted to determine the most uncontroversial way to execute temple entry, and adjust religious ritual accordingly.[134] 'But the Maharajah and his advisers,' we are told, 'did not believe in half-measures'. With their innate 'courage strengthened by genuine conviction, and an outlook which no Indian monarch had been able to entertain for a couple of thousand conservative years,' they decided to implement absolute temple entry in 1936.[135]

Eleven years earlier when Sethu Lakshmi Bayi had met Gandhi, she had made it clear that while she was sympathetic to the movement, 'it was still necessary to sound [high-caste] opinion and to convert it to the reform'.[136] She was not, it is said, inclined to taking autocratic, unilateral decisions on such far-reaching subjects merely because she had the power to do so, and instead held a *progression* of reforms to be the appropriate method of implementing such ideas (though, of course, in the matter of the Newspaper Regulation she had proved perfectly capable of autocracy). Now, in 1936, the Mahatma was of the opinion that such progression had been achieved, even meeting the Maharani on his visit to Travancore the following year,[137] and publicly expressing his thanks that she 'did not remain idle' in her years in power. It was, he declared, due to her 'sustained efforts' to 'arouse both [low-caste] and [high-caste] public opinion', that the reform had succeeded now, without which backing 'even the Maharajah with all the goodwill in the world would have found it impossible to issue the Proclamation'.[138] Sethu Lakshmi Bayi, for all this suspiciously conciliatory praise was not, however, convinced.

To be fair, as Gandhi pointed out, had the Maharajah and the Junior Maharani 'reasoned out the pros and cons of the Proclamation', they would have found several compelling reasons for postponing its promulgation.[139] But this was one of those times in history where a leap had to be taken. Given the Junior Maharani's personality it is not surprising that she was prepared to take that leap. Sethu Lakshmi Bayi, on the other hand, largely so ponderous and cautious, was not. She opined that the ground was not prepared yet to embark on something as revolutionary as this, and that there would be a severe backlash.[140] And indeed, there was; though Sir CP obtained an endorsement from the Tamprakkal in Malabar, the decision was 'entirely resented' by 'the large majority of Brahmins in Cochin, as well as in Calicut,' according to the Resident.[141] In hindsight, this was misguided opposition, but at the time it was nothing short of outrageous that the highest Brahmins in Kerala (who resided in Cochin and Malabar) were prepared to boycott the state altogether. Temple entry was all good, but not at the cost of upsetting entrenched power interests across the coast.

Besides, it has been argued that Sethu Lakshmi Bayi was unable to reconcile to a unilateral decision of this nature simply because the administration felt threatened that its own partisan policy had backfired and endangered Travancore's identity as a Hindu state. Ironically, Sir CP too had expressed similar views only a few years ago in 1931 arguing that the 'problem could only be gradually solved' and that 'Shock tactics will not answer the purpose' of preserving the 'solidarity of the Hindu community'.[142] He now did a volte-face, and even Ambedkar considered this more due to political expediency vis-à-vis the Ezhavas than to spiritual conviction.[143] Either way, Sethu Lakshmi Bayi decided she would not be a part of the movement and never again, after 1936, set foot in the Sri Padmanabhaswamy Temple or any other shrine. Her family members would justify this controversial decision as due to personal humiliation ('She was kept in the dark about temple entry, and her views as head of the family were not sought')[144] or as a result of a general withdrawal from outward religiosity ('She wanted to live as a recluse, and stopped going to all temples').[145]

Reasonable whispers persist, however, that it was conservatism that prevented Sethu Lakshmi Bayi from blessing the proclamation. 'Although the Maharani Regent had carried out many reforms,' noted Louise Ouwerkerk, 'she remained strictly orthodox.'[146] She certainly was extremely conservative even in the recent past. In 1927, for instance, when the son of one of the Junior Maharani's sisters died within Krishna Vilasam Palace in the fort, her chamberlain was upbraided severely, 'as no natural deaths except of members of the Ruling Family are allowed to take place (and none have within living memory occurred) within the palace precincts. It is said that he should have made arrangements for the removal of the child before the end.'[147] This was perhaps because the Maharajah's *tirumadampu* ceremony, where he was invested with the sacred thread of the 'twice born', had just been concluded, though it was reminiscent of a painful episode from the Sethu Lakshmi Bayi's own childhood when the late Mulam Tirunal had the Junior Maharani's sister sent away in similar circumstances, just before her death. In what was another mark of her unbending personal conservatism, her doctors complained to the Resident during her treatment for tuberculosis in 1930 that she could have been nursed better if only she did not insist on meticulously fulfilling her religious obligations. The disease, they felt, was 'aggravated by Her Highness' strict orthodoxy and temple observances' that were invariably at odds with judicious medical counsel.[148] Their pleas, however, fell on deaf years, and she would simply not listen.

What also strengthens the argument that it was disapproval of permitting low-caste groups access to holy spaces which moved Sethu Lakshmi Bayi is that she was not the only one to cease visits to temples. As the Junior Maharani's nephew states:

> There was an entire generation at the time that did not approve of temple entry. They were sympathetic to the aspirations of those who demanded equality and freedom from social prejudice, and individuals like the Senior Maharani did a lot to make things better for large numbers of people. But breaching the ritual sanctity of a shrine was akin to breaking a thousand-year-old law that had passed down so many generations. Temple rituals and the precise ways of worship they entailed were not to be tampered with. When it became inevitable that temples would have to be opened, they accepted it. But they chose to stand aside from the tide. For instance, in 1948 the Maharajah of Cochin would bow to the will of his people and implement temple entry in his state. He had his own Temple Entry Proclamation. But after making it public, he never went to temples again. This group included the Senior Maharani, the Maharajah of Cochin, the Zamorin of Calicut, and a number of other personalities in Kerala.[149]

As a strong establishment figure Sethu Lakshmi Bayi had, during her reign, sustained every tradition and custom connected with her family and the monarchy. But her traditionalism had sometimes contradictory layers: on the one hand she would freely touch Nair and Christian relatives and associates, despite injunctions of caste, while on the other she clearly held extreme convictions about low-caste communities expecting sacred shrines to extend similar liberties to them. What did, however, stand out even in this situation was her lack of hypocrisy. While she personally refused to sanction the Temple Entry Proclamation, she had no qualms a year later about her daughters praying at the now 'defiled' family shrine; as the Resident noted, 'it remains to be seen whether the Senior Maharani shows her approval of Temple Entry by herself worshipping [there] and by throwing open her own temples'.[150] As Attingal Rani she controlled nine shrines, and the Maharajah's proclamation was not allowed to extend to these. The decision was entirely hers, since the Valiya Koil Tampuran did not care much for caste, and not only interacted with all manners of people but even dined with tribal communities in the forest, caring little for issues of ritual and ceremony.

In essence, the Maharani was happy to champion the cause of Dalit groups when it came to access to infrastructure, opening up secular opportunities such as jobs and universities, etc. However, in the matter of literally opening up the highest ritual spaces of the Hindu community, she went against the trending mood. Perhaps, as her nephew tells, it was due to the fact that 'after the Regency, when she lost power, it was the orthodox elements that formed her support base. As her influence in real terms became more and more diluted, it was they who buttressed her moral position, which was a kind of consolation. The Junior Maharani was making too many changes at once, and such traditional circles related more to the Senior Maharani. And given the hostility she faced within the family, she needed that support.'[151] This might explain (though not convincingly enough) why while she made a statement by personally staying away from temple entry, she let her family follow the Maharajah's course. Altogether, then, there is something of a paradox in Sethu Lakshmi Bayi's reaction to the Maharajah's most lauded, most widely celebrated, and Travancore's most popular Act of State, despite the fact that she knew she was in a dwindling minority of opponents at a historic moment.

It was a fact, however, that her visits to the Sri Padmanabhaswamy Temple had declined several years before the proclamation was issued. 'She never said why she stopped visiting the temple, but aunts and relatives mentioned that the Junior Maharani had changed a number of rituals, and she did not approve of this,' remarks one granddaughter. 'And years later when we asked her about it she would simply say Padmanabhaswamy was in her heart and she didn't particularly miss looking at an image in a shrine.'[152] It was after the Regency that Sethu Lakshmi Bayi was told that though she was head of the royal house, she could only visit the shrine after the Maharajah, like juniors in the family.[153] There was also a general withdrawal on her part from public activities because the Maharajah did not treat her, as she had already placed on record, in a befitting manner; as late as 1939 she would again observe that not even the peons promised in her settlement had been given,[154] while the Resident noted that it was in 1938 for the first time that she was given 'her proper precedence' at a state banquet.[155] Till then, the Maharani had been avoiding such banquets. The Maharajah also altered the general warrant of precedence; where the Elayarajah had once been subordinate to the Senior Maharani, Chithira Tirunal now ordered that his adolescent brother had precedence over his older, customarily higher-ranking aunt.[156] Sethu Lakshmi Bayi found herself treated as a subordinate member of the dynasty, with no regard for her position as an ex-Regent or as matriarch of the royal house, not to speak of existing traditions being amended by the Maharajah to boost his side of the family at the cost of hers.

The Maharajah found the Senior Maharani's attitude taking the sheen off the act that would place him in the highest league of Hindu monarchs. In the legislature in Madras, for instance, it was openly stated that after initial enthusiasm, low-castes had stopped going to temples. It was also, more embarrassingly, asked whether it was true that Sethu Lakshmi Bayi's private shrines had been excluded from the Temple Entry Proclamation's purview.[157] And since it was a fact that they had, something had to be done to correct this. A rather old dispute between the Senior Maharani and the Junior Maharani, then, offered the perfect pretext, and in 1938 the authorities would move unexpectedly to compel Sethu Lakshmi Bayi to toe their line and reluctantly, in her powerlessness, fulfil the scope of the Temple Entry Proclamation, whether she liked it or not.

16

The Ultimate Eclipse

In December 1937, Princess Lalitha entered her fifteenth year and the Valiya Koil Tampuran decided that it was time for her to marry. It was plausibly due to reasons of state that such an early marriage was sought. The Maharajah's sister, after two past miscarriages,[1] was declared to be with child earlier that year, and in January 1938 would produce a male heir. 'The infant will succeed,' recorded the Resident, 'to the [throne] after the Elayarajah, and there is now no question of the succession reverting to the family of the Senior Maharani after the Elayarajah's death, as would have been the case had one of the latter's daughters anticipated [the First Princess] in giving birth to a son.'[2] In other words, the Junior Maharani had two sons and a grandson in the line of succession, while Sethu Lakshmi Bayi had none yet. It was also not particularly reassuring, as a future Resident would remark, that the 'Junior Maharani is very strong minded in the pursuit of her own purposes, which is chiefly to ensure the [throne] to *her* descendants, as opposed to those of her rival, the Senior Maharani.'[3] Only if Princess Lalitha married early would she be able to add numbers to this side of the family, and so Sethu Lakshmi Bayi welcomed her consort's advice on the matter, and the question was taken up in all earnest.

This also meant certain strategic concessions on the Senior Maharani's part in the interests of conciliating her cousin. 'The birth of a son to the Maharajah's sister,' wrote the Resident, who was now one Mr C.P. Skrine, 'may result in a rapprochement between the Senior Maharani and Maharani Sethu Parvathi Bayi. The former has twice come into Trivandrum to perform certain ceremonies connected with the infant in the presence of its grandmother, and it is understood on good authority that the two Maharanis got on quite well together.' Mr Skrine had 'reason to believe that the Maharajah and his mother were apprehensive lest the Senior Maharani should refuse to perform the ceremonies. The Senior Maharani on her part has more than once expressed fears to the Resident lest the Maharajah should refuse to assist at the marriage of her daughters, the elder of whom is now of marriageable age. The anxiety of Maharani Sethu Parvathi Bayi lest one of the Senior Maharani's daughters should give birth to a son before her own daughter having been removed, there is every hope of a reconciliation between the two houses.'[4] In private, however, Mr Skrine proved he could see through what was happening, hinting that current expediencies more than any desire for a real rapprochement lay behind the ongoing cooperation:

> You know how important, even vital, the religious ceremonies are in connection with a birth or wedding; well the Senior Maharani 'played up' generously and cooperated in the birth and other ceremonies following the birth of a son to the Junior Maharani's daughter last January, so in return the Maharajah and his mother agreed to celebrate the marriage of the Senior Maharani's daughter with exactly the same magnificence as they celebrated that of the First Princess in 1934. Hence the rapprochement.[5]

In the meantime certain proposals had been made for Princess Lalitha, neither of which she fancied. 'One of the candidates,' Princess Indira would recall, 'was the son of our father's sister Ambalika, and there was another who I remember was called Unni Chettan. But my sister didn't want to marry either, and since she was just as strong-willed as father, she set herself against it stubbornly till she had her way.'[6] The Valiya Koil Tampuran wasn't awfully pleased at his nephew's rejection, but perfectly aware of his daughter's determination made his peace, and joined the Maharani in evaluating alternative proposals. In the meantime, in October 1937, Princess Indira celebrated her eleventh birthday, and as was usual on such occasions, she and her sister were taken in procession around the fort with the usual parades of soldiers, officials and others. At one stretch of the route, then, they came across a crowd of young men waiting dutifully to view the royal procession. The boys bowed as the sisters passed them. But seated in her palanquin, Princess Lalitha spotted amidst them one particularly striking face. And there and then she made her choice: that, she decided, would be the man she married.[7]

On her return to the palace she walked into the study where her parents were poring over photographs of eligible suitors, and declared to them that she had found her consort. 'To say the least,' her daughter now laughs, 'grandparents were both stunned at first and then aghast at the prospect of their child selecting a stranger off the city streets.'[8] 'No, no! We don't do things like this!' a predictably outraged Rama Varma vented, while the Maharani tried to convince her daughter that at her age, she couldn't possibly take a serious decision that could affect her whole life.[9] 'He could have been a Christian or a Muslim or someone below caste who didn't come from the aristocracy. He could have been anybody really!'[10] Princess Lalitha stuck to her position adamantly, though, even as her parents would have none of it. Eventually one day a photograph was brought to her. 'Grandmother said, "Now look, we have a very nice proposal here, and this is the person we think you should marry." Mother wouldn't entertain them but they insisted she at least look at the picture. And that is when she got the biggest surprise of her life when she realised that it was exactly the man she had seen during the procession!'[11] What happened was that Princess Lalitha saw the boy near the townhouse of the Kilimanoor clan, to which the Maharani's own father and illustrious grandfather had belonged. And by a happy coincidence he was a member of the same family, which had a historic tradition of marrying into the royal house.

The boy in question was a twenty-one-year-old called Kerala Varma, and was something of a unique contender within the wider Kilimanoor family. It was because of this that his horoscope and photographs had reached Sethu Lakshmi Bayi's hands as a potential consort for her daughter in the first place. 'His uncle, you see, was a judge in Trivandrum, and one of those anglicised gentlemen who kept his favourite nephew close,' remarks Princess Lalitha's cousin. 'And so compared to the other Kilimanoor boys, he had a different upbringing after high school. I think the judge intended for him to marry one of his daughters! It was then that they heard the Senior Maharani was looking for a son-in-law, and, as he was not one of the usual, orthodox crowd, the uncle thought he stood a reasonable chance at becoming a royal consort.'[12] Kerala Varma himself would recall the way in which he was quite unexpectedly told about his impending exaltation. 'My uncle called me into his chamber and asked me if I had anything in mind about marriage. When I said I hadn't any plans, he asked me, "So how would you like to marry the daughter of the Senior Maharani?" I said I had no objections at all and that it would be my privilege!'[13]

In January 1938 then, once the preliminary discussions had concluded, Sethu Lakshmi Bayi forwarded the proposal officially to the Maharajah, requesting him to commence preparations for the wedding. But permission from Kowdiar Palace was immediately denied. A young girl of fifteen, decided the Junior Maharani, could certainly not select her own husband (even though she herself had taken her pick aged ten). The Maharajah's mother even offered to make some suggestions of her own, but Princess Lalitha wouldn't hear of this. 'Mother declared that if she were coerced to marry against her will, she would throw herself off the third floor balcony. It was a clever touch of drama, and it worked.'[14] Mr Skrine was asked to mediate between the two houses on this, and help secure permission from the Maharajah. He called at Lalindloch Palace and after discussions with the Valiya Koil Tampuran and the Senior Maharani, Princess Lalitha was invited to meet him. 'Young lady,' he asked, 'are you quite determined on the person whom you are going to marry?' When she responded positively, he decided to play the devil and added, 'Or have you any doubts at all; are you even a little undecided?' That is when the princess made it clear precisely how unwavering she was in her choice. 'No, none at all,' she replied, with as purposeful an expression as she could muster to match her conviction.[15]

The Maharajah, though, refused to sanction the wedding until Sethu Lakshmi Bayi personally visited him on a courtesy call. She agreed and thus, finally, Princess Lalitha's wedding was confirmed for 12 September 1938.[16] In the meantime the bridegroom-elect, in the rush and excitement of the proceedings, promptly failed his final exams at the College of Science. His plan, before the royal proposal changed his life forever, was to become an engineer. 'He once made a water clock for mother, with a drop falling for every second,' his daughter would recall. 'It was a fantastic contraption and he would have made a good engineer if he had pursued it.'[17] Instead his destiny was to live in a great palace and spend his future time mastering music and playing the veena, learning to paint from the favourite court artist of his royal mother-in-law, N.N. Nampiyar, enjoying the pleasures of riding and sport, and engaging in other princely recreations in the company of a doting princess. Though at the time, failing his exams came as a disappointment, it was not *as* daunting as being ordered to meet with the forbidding Valiya Koil Tampuran for an interview. 'Our first meeting was supremely formal,' he would recall, 'and it was really an interrogation. For example, he asked me questions about my reading habits and then suddenly demanded, "Who was the author of *Ivanhoe*?" I hadn't a clue and blurted the first thing that came to mind for no specific reason: Rip Van Winkle!'[18]

Shortly after this minor catastrophe began his professional instruction in royal etiquette. The Maharani's brother-in-law was in charge of grooming her prospective son-in-law, and he took Kerala Varma under his wing. Along with a number of the official staff, they proceeded to Madras to high-end stores of the day for purchasing suits and other products on a reasonably lavish budget. While there, they stayed at Ramalayam, the sprawling mansion of the Junior Maharani in Adyar, who often herself visited the city as an active patron of the famous Music Academy there. Once the necessary purchases were made, they returned to meet the family priest who, as was traditional, gave the consort-elect an awkward overview of the gentlemanly and proper methods of lovemaking.[19] Soon old Miss Watts, 'large, dark, Eurasian, advising everybody, ordering everybody about, sympathising with everybody, the very hub of State and Society' arrived on the scene in her enormous, equally imposing yellow car.[20] She was to ensure that Kerala Varma's table manners and other social skills were up to the mark, teaching him how to dress well, how to tie the perfect bowtie, and so on.[21]

Princess Lalitha in the meantime carried on with her routine. 'Lessons became a joke,' her sister would tell, 'and we barely studied anything. They were classes in name. All we did was to sit around and chat with our teachers. I remember once a pet cat of ours climbed atop an almirah and I got the asan to stand up and bring it down. And that was one lesson! Then Miss Poulose came and again all we did was chit-chat until the end of the hour. It was a very exciting time and all the talk was about silks and jewellery and hairstyles and that sort of thing.'[22] The bhagvathar who taught Princess Lalitha music had decided unilaterally to terminate classes. Or in her sister's words: 'She studied for a little while and then the bhagvathar himself said, "My dear child, it is better if you stop." So Appu Bhagvathar and Ranga Bhagvathar stuck to teaching me.'[23] While Kerala Varma would make up for his future wife's disastrous advances into the world of classical music, Princess Lalitha would give up much of her boyishness and turn into a still gregarious but considerably more feminine little thing. Only months before her wedding she wrote a letter to an imaginary friend in an imaginary world of her own. She was, of course, Miss Molly Gardner of 'Rosewood Manor, England', and her friend, whose cartoon she drew with bobbed hair and a pink frock, was Vera Rattler of no particular location:

> Darling Vera, Gee, thanks for a very charming letter. Old thing! I was so pleased to get it. Vera, my sweetheart! I am now, dear, going to be fourteen—next month on the fourteenth. Oh Vera, mum is calling me. So sorry but I can't write any more now. Yours ever, Molly.[24]

Before long August arrived and grand temple rituals and ceremonials in both Trivandrum and Attingal replaced the routine of this girl who was still very much a child. On the pre-decided 'auspicious day', the wedding took place, followed by a week of festivities in the capital. Vast masses of people came out once again to celebrate not only the princess, but also their Senior Maharani who drove in state and showed herself to her subjects officially after many years. As part of her understanding with the Maharajah, she was also given her correct precedence at events, so that altogether it was a happy few days. The Resident was welcomed on a tour of the 'astonishing temporary buildings attached to the 16th century palace in the Fort' and wrote:

> Really vast halls, with lofty richly-decorated roofs and endless colonnades of solid looking round pillars, exactly copying the old style of architecture and most impressive. At the further end of the biggest hall, which must have been at least 200 feet long and 40 high, were two magnificent thrones, golden chairs on pedestals with canopies over them, side by side, with fairy lights outlining them and powerful flood lights illuminating them (the whole hall was artificially lit and had no windows). In contrast to this and three other smaller halls which were used for the receptions and feastings and theatrical performances and dances, which had been going on for 6 days, the rooms in which the actual ceremony had taken place was tiny—just space enough for a canopied dais and about 30 or 40 near relatives to stand around it, the ceremony consisting merely of the 'giving of the cloth' and garlanding each other in the presence of witnesses.[25]

The Resident also, in the meantime, had worries about raising a toast on behalf of the Paramount Power to the newly-weds, as he later wrote:

> The festivities have been going on all week on a tremendous scale, the whole town being en fete ... I had to make the speech proposing the health of the happy couple ... and you have no idea how difficult it was to find something to say on such an occasion when you know nothing whatever about the bridegroom except that he has failed to pass his exams and is going to do nothing all his life except be the Princess' consort, and the bride, though charming, is only just out of the nursery! He is 20 [sic] and she 15. However, the party went very well and we all enjoyed the very good food provided, and afterwards ... I found myself, after the regulation, 5-minuted with HH sitting on quite a small sofa between the bride and her cousin, the First Princess, attractive girls both of them in their quite different styles, chatting away merrily about the wedding and the saris and the bride's jewellery (she had some perfectly lovely earrings and clips on).[26]

The wedding celebrations concluded with a durbar where Princess Lalitha and her husband appeared at court and paid their respects to the Maharajah. The next day they left for their honeymoon at Halcyon Castle in Kovalam. They were destined for a long and unusually happy marriage together, their personalities complementing each other. Sethu Lakshmi Bayi was also jubilant when she returned to Vellayini, now eagerly looking forward (in that typical Indian fashion) to the prospect of grandchildren. The year 1938 proved to be a greatly satisfying year for her—almost too happy to be true—with Kowdiar Palace cooperating generously in every respect, despite continued disagreements about temple entry and other matters of policy. The public also responded to peace that year between the two branches of their royal family. 'The popular rejoicings,' reported Mr Skrine, 'were all the greater because the wedding signalised a long-hoped-for rapprochement between the two Maharanis.'[27] But, in what was the curse of their clan, amicable relations were not fated to last, and less than six months later Sethu Lakshmi Bayi would confront her greatest battle yet with the Junior Maharani, one she was destined to lose, and which was the climactic culmination of her eclipse in Travancore.

In 1934, shortly after the wedding of the First Princess, the Junior Maharani notified the Sripadam for an allowance for her daughter who was now eighteen. The Senior Maharani rejected the application on two grounds. Firstly, she clarified, the Sripadam was meant only for the two eldest Ranis (Senior and Junior), and not for all female members of the royal family. If every girl had a claim, such a claim would have existed from birth onwards, and the late Maharajah had rightly not charged expenses of the First and Second Princesses during his reign to the Sripadam, instead making allowances from the Civil List. The Senior Maharani also sought to quash the claim that reaching eighteen years made a female eligible for an allowance. Both she and the Junior Maharani had their expenses borne by the Sripadam from the time they were only children of five and four respectively, which negated this argument. In fact, the Senior Maharani stated, that their expenses as children were borne by the Sripadam, while the First and Second Princesses' were not, proved the establishment was for the Ranis only and had nothing to do with age.[28]

Secondly, the Senior Maharani pointed out, the Sripadam did not command adequate resources to offer allowances to every female in the dynasty. For one, with each newcomer, its limited funds would have to be redistributed, and this was not viable. For it would be she who would stand to lose the most in such an arrangement. The Junior Maharani had all her expenses taken care of by the Civil List and even an extra allowance from it, not including her personal allowance of Rs 12,000 from the Sripadam. The Senior Maharani, on the other hand, had only religious expenses covered by the Civil List and her other expenses, which included more religious and ceremonial obligations, and costs of her establishment, not to speak of personal allowances, were entirely from the Sripadam. Junior female members also received allowances from the Civil List, unlike the Senior Maharani, and as her manager put it,

> ... if it is suggested [that] every female member of the Royal Family were to [also] be granted allowances from the Sripadam funds, it would lead logically to an absurd position namely that while the junior members would be receiving steady incomes consisting of allowances from Sripadam and the Palace, the Senior Rani would be left with a progressively *diminishing* income with *no* separate allowance from the Palace, the Senior Rani's allowances being merged in the Sripadam funds.[29]

The Maharani thus rested her case stating that as per precedent, it was only the Senior and Junior Ranis who were entitled to the Sripadam, and that there were not enough resources to distribute among other female members. But the Maharajah's manager was not convinced and informed her that merely because Mulam Tirunal had allocated the Sripadam solely for the Ranis, it did not tie the present Maharajah to any tradition. It was also conveyed that in over a hundred years, at no time were there more than two females in the royal family, who were automatically therefore Ranis, and hence there was no precedent to go by with regard to other female members.[30] This was untrue for in the early 1920s there were four females in the royal house, and logically the fact that at the time the First and Second Princesses had never drawn from the Sripadam ought to have been considered a precedent. But Kowdiar Palace denied this. As for the fact that the Senior Maharani would consistently lose income if the new proposal were effected, the manager dismissed it as 'totally irrelevant'.[31] The Maharani was also instructed, since she claimed an insufficiency of funds, to forward the Sripadam's accounts for three years so that they might be inspected.[32]

Soon after this the Maharajah found cause for dissatisfaction with the accounts because an auditor, Mr C.S. Krishnaswami Iyer, was sent from Kowdiar Palace in 1936 to review the books for a longer period. The audit was performed and a report was submitted to the Maharajah's office by April 1938, but no information was passed to the Maharani thereafter for many months. However, inconclusive correspondence continued. The government were also corresponding with the Maharani since 1933 regarding the ownership of the Sripadam lands. She had been enfranchising certain properties classed as Erayali, which were given to families that provided traditional services to the Sripadam. But in modern times this had become a difficult problem for both sides. At this stage the Chief Secretary questioned her manager as to who had authorised the proceedings[33] and on being informed that it was the Senior Maharani, he responded as follows:

> These lands are really *pandaravaka* or [government] lands and appertain to the Government of His Highness the Maharajah as in the rest of the State. The revenues of the Sripadam tract which have been, or which may be, settled by the Government of His Highness the Maharajah from time to time as being the revenue derivable therefrom, have *alone* been assigned to the Sripadam. As against His Highness the Maharajah and his Government, Her Highness the Senior Maharani can have no rights in respect of the lands in the tract, Her Highness being entitled *only* to enjoy the revenues referred to above.[34]

The claim being made, plainly, was that the Sripadam lands did not belong to the Maharani and she was only entitled to the revenues assigned by the Maharajah. A point in favour of this argument was that it was the government, under the seal of the Dewan, which collected Sripadam revenues and not Sethu Lakshmi Bayi's private officers.[35] The latter, however, calmly directed the Chief Secretary to study the records and declarations of previous Dewans and governments, also pointing out that it was the Sripadam itself that had requested the Revenue Department to take care of its collections many years ago, before which it was independently administered.[36] The argument, therefore, that it was government property simply because government officials undertook tax collections was declared fallacious, and a blind ignorance of the Sripadam's history.

'Simply because Government have undertaken management of these lands', a former Dewan had stated, 'it does not follow that the revenue derived from them belongs to the *sircar* or that the rules applicable to sircar lands can be applied to them.'[37] He also stated that the government could only act as per directions received from the Attingal Rani. Similarly, yet another Dewan also affirmed that the Sripadam lands 'are the property for Her Highness the Senior Rani' though the 'management being in the hands of our officials, it proceeds practically on the same lines on which the administration of the Government land revenue proceeds'.[38] Enfranchisement of the Erayali lands had in fact commenced in the early years of the twentieth century when it was summarily stopped because the government felt that their position was that of 'a trustee for Her Highness' and it was not justified, therefore, 'in making any material changes, during Her Highness' minority'.[39] This suspension, interestingly, was at the instructions of Mulam Tirunal, for he felt that it would prejudice the minor Sethu Lakshmi Bayi and could wait until she reached majority and took a decision in this regard on her own.[40] It was thus that in the 1930s she continued the process.

But the present Maharajah took a different view of matters. In 1935 a revised version of the *Travancore Land Revenue Manual* was published and in this the very definition of the Sripadam Estate was modified to suit the new regime. Thus while the previous manual of 1915 had stated that Sripadam lands were the 'private domain' and 'private property' of the Attingal Rani,[41] the new publication defined the lands as 'private property of the *Sovereign*, the Attingal Ranis having only the right to appropriate the revenue from the lands'.[42] Overnight, thus, the Sripadam went from belonging to the Senior Maharani, whose ancestral claim over it was repeatedly affirmed in the past, to the ownership of the Maharajah.

The Maharani had objected to this new definition but then the Sripadam dispute petered out for a while, before making a fresh appearance in 1939. In February that year her manager received from Kowdiar Palace a new letter, with extracts from the legal opinion of Sir Krishaswami Iyer, the Advocate General of Madras, and a notice that the Maharajah had, in its light, been pleased to suggest an amount for the First Princess's allowance.[43] The Maharani, having perused the dossier, requested the Maharajah's office to forward the full legal opinion of the Advocate General, as opposed to snippets and extracts, and also the records and documents that had been supplied to him in reaching his conclusions.[44] But the palace manager was unwilling to oblige, and wrote back stating that the Maharani's request to see relevant documents was 'somewhat unusual' and could not be entertained.[45] In the face of the Maharajah's refusal to let her have records so as to prepare a proper rejoinder, the Maharani had to make do with whatever she could gather from the extracts.

Her manager wrote to Kowdiar Palace, then, pointing out that when Attingal was amalgamated with Travancore, the Rani resigned sovereignty but retained fiscal control of the tract, along with a condition that only the children of the

Attingal Ranis could succeed to the throne of Travancore.[46] That is how the Sripadam came into existence and remained under the control of the eldest female member in the family. The claim of the Advocate General that all female members had an equal right in the Sripadam was dismissed, with the explanation as before, that in that case the previous Maharajah, 'who was eminently qualified to appreciate at once the obligations of Sripadam and the rights of the members of his family', would have taken an initiative and given instructions, which were not done in the case of the First Princess and then again the Second Princess.[47] It was also telling that Mulam Tirunal had left absolute control of the Sripadam with Sethu Lakshmi Bayi in spite of their personal differences at the time, and even as difficulties were created for the latter, her ancestral estate was never touched, with respect for her position as the matriarch of the royal house.

The Maharani's manager also rejected the Advocate General's suggestion that matrilineal law, under which all members of a family had claims on its estate, applied to the Sripadam. The claim of the Maharajah essentially was that the royal family *was* the Sripadam. But, in return it was pointed out, if the Sripadam were a matrilineal taravad, as claimed, its management would have always vested with the Maharajah and not the eldest female constituent of the house. In reality, then, just like the eldest male member of the dynasty had 20,000 acres of Crown lands, the eldest female had the 15,000 acres of Sripadam. Similarly, Sir Krishnaswami's claim that all females had an equal share was negated, as precedents demonstrated convincingly that Junior Ranis throughout history received only a small portion, with the vast majority of the revenues going to the Senior Ranis who were the principal Attingal Ranis and whose ceremonial status and attendant expenses were upheld by the Sripadam.[48]

It was at this juncture in July 1939, while the matter was still disputed, that the Maharani received a notification from Kowdiar Palace, stating that the audit of the Sripadam's accounts showed irregularities, proving its management to be inefficient, and that in the interests of the other female members of the royal family, the Maharajah had decided to appoint a new manager.[49] It was also informed that this new person would report to Kowdiar Palace and not to the Maharani, and that he would take over from her manager, none other than old Kulathu Iyer, on 17 August, i.e., the Malayalam new year.

By now the Maharani had already broached the issue with the Resident, one Mr G.P. Murphy, but had not raised the subject formally. With the receipt of this notice, she finally wrote to him, pointing out that the Sripadam was 'a comprehensive term for an institution which administers my ancestral estates, controls my domestic and office staff and has charge of all the moneys I receive in my capacity as Senior Rani', i.e., the Sripadam was basically her establishment, the control of which if passed to the Maharajah would mean that her 'personal servants, money for current expenses and provisions' would all rest in 'unfriendly hands' and 'completely paralyse' her ménage.[50] She also brought up the question of the ownership of the Sripadam lands, before registering some other long-standing complaints.

> From the time of the termination of the Regency, the treatment I have received from the State has not been of a kind which one might expect by virtue of my standing in the Ruling family, the position I occupied during the minority administration and, above all, the recommendation contained in His Excellency the Viceroy's letter to His Highness the Maharajah. I have suffered much, and once or twice I made an attempt to obtain redress by seeking the intervention of the British Representative, but the times were peculiarly unpropitious for the purpose and I had resolved to possess my soul in patience unless and until conditions were made intolerable. I am afraid that stage is being reached now.[51]

Sethu Lakshmi Bayi listed some of the troubles she had been facing with the Maharajah. One irritant was a change in the arrangement of guards provided for her. It was customary for every member of the royal family to receive, wherever they stayed, a guard of four men and one NCO. These used to be changed every week and the Maharani paid for the conveyance of the guard from Trivandrum to Vellayani or wherever she was residing. That is when the Maharajah issued new orders that the guard would need to be changed every day and that she would have to pay a daily fee for their transport.[52] The Maharani's objections had no effect and in fact an additional bill was inflicted upon her, because now an officer would also come every day in order to 'inspect' the guard, for which also she was to pay daily.[53]

She then wrote to the Maharajah's office requesting them to cease providing a guard altogether, even though it was an obligation of the state, because she could not afford to spend money every day on their conveyance. But this was also not acceded to and her personal finances were bled continuously.[54] Similarly, while the state was obliged to provide a guard to Princess Lalitha who was living at Kovalam, by virtue of her membership in the royal family, this was not done, and instead soldiers from the Maharani's permanent guard were removed and placed at Halcyon Castle, their daily fare, along with that of the inspecting officer, also being charged to the Maharani.[55] The Maharajah, in other words, had become determined ever since she rejected his Temple Entry Proclamation to drain not only her finances but also harass her in general till she submitted to his ruling.

It was around this time that the Maharani decided to go to Peermade on her usual tour and requested the conventional three men and one NCO for her escort. But the Maharajah's office insisted that she take an exorbitant posse of two NCO's, one officer, and nine soldiers, or else the tour would be prohibited. Once again the Maharani proposed that an escort be cancelled altogether, since the costs to her would prove cripplingly extortionate, and she would go without protection, which was, on this occasion, readily accepted. 'This I think,' she later wrote, 'is the first time a member of the Ruling Family of Travancore has been refused a military escort.'[56]

After her tour when she returned to Vellayani, she found that a new guardhouse had been constructed there, despite it being her private property, and that costs, as was usual by now, were debited from her account. Once again, her objections were not entertained in the name of security and the money was charged.[57] 'It passes my comprehension', an exasperated Maharani wrote to the Resident, 'why they should be so frightfully anxious that I should have a guard when I am at Vellayani or Kovalam, while very determined not to let me have it while on tour. The only difference I see is that the former is more expensive to me.'[58] Having thus given instances of the difficulties she faced in her dealings with Kowdiar Palace, and requesting Mr Murphy to prevent the Maharajah's imposition of his own manager to control her establishment, the Maharani concluded as follows:

> You can easily imagine how distasteful should be the role of a petitioner to one in my position. I have endured much ill usage these years in the fond hope that, with the lapse of years, either through a change of heart or for want of new openings, the present policy of the authorities might undergo some change. But that was not to be ... I have no desire now to fight for right for right's sake. When aggressions on my rights and privileges occasioning loss of dignity and prestige, and material loss assume unconscionable proportions and continue with impunity, I feel obliged to resort to the last and only course open to one in my position, namely an appeal to the Paramount Power ... I have stated my case. I have the unique distinction of receiving, among non-Rulers, from incoming and outgoing Viceroys kharitas in which I am assured of their interest in my prosperity. I cannot therefore think that when I am subjected to such indignities and humiliations as to make life a

> hideous nightmare, my appeal for redress would fall on deaf ears. My request is that if an enquiry establishes that I have been badly treated, I might be assured conditions of life, which would enable me and my children to live in peace without fear of constant victimization.[59]

Mr Murphy promptly despatched the Maharani's representation to Delhi and secured an assurance from the Dewan that while the matter was sub judice, no action would be taken by the Maharajah.[60] An assurance was also sent from the Viceroy's office that the matter was being studied. But while the authorities did not take over the Sripadam on 17 August as planned, they initiated a new policy that was meant to coerce the Maharani into accepting their stand on matters, and to chastise her into submission, no matter what the Viceroy or anyone else had promised her.

On 30 August the Maharani wrote again to the Resident complaining that since the new year, the Maharajah's office were refusing to have any dealings with the Sripadam. Letters sent from the Maharani's establishment were, for instance, returned unopened. In more real terms, the Rs 2,500 she was supposed to receive that month for religious and other expenses had not been given; her daughters' allowances were withheld; provisions supplied for day-to-day consumption had been stopped; and provisions for certain daily religious rites, being conducted for Princess Lalitha, had all been discontinued.[61] The Maharani could not comprehend this malicious attitude and appealed to Mr Murphy to ensure that the status quo that existed before the dispute began should be restored, and she should not be dragooned in this manner by the powers in Kowdiar Palace.

Whether the Resident attempted to correct matters is not known, for a month later, on 25 September, the Maharani wrote to him once again stating that the Maharajah's manager continued to withhold allowances, and that communications from the Sripadam were still 'taboo in the Palace Office'.[62] More importantly, the government and its officials now refused to collect Sripadam revenues, and from the lands in Trivandrum, nothing had been received so far.

> The bulk of my estates lies in the Taluk of Chirayinkil. Here the revenue officers, since my writing to you last, like their confreres in Trivandrum Taluk have been displaying a mysterious attitude of *non-possmus* in regard to the collection of revenue due to Sripadam. With my income from one source wholly, and from others partially, cut off and my own obligations

> regarding disbursements remaining intact, the difficulties of my position have been increasing. The suspension of my daughters' allowances is also creating difficulties since the salaries of their establishments are paid out of these.[63]

Interestingly, at this point the Maharajah, despite assurances to the contrary to the Resident, appointed his nominee, T.S. Sankaranarayana Iyer, as Sripadam manager. On 26 September his secretary wrote to this gentleman, addressing him with that title, stating 'notwithstanding the removal of Mr Kulathu Iyer from his position as Sripadam Manager under commands, the late Sripadam Manager, Mr Kulathu Iyer, is still retaining the keys of the Sripadam Treasury. This is an irregularity which may be pointed out immediately and rectified.'[64] In keeping with these instructions, Mr Sankaranarayana Iyer visited Vellayani and sought an interview with the Maharani to 'rectify' the error. But she refused to see him, and did not recognise his appointment, which was in complete contravention of the Dewan's promise.[65] On hearing of this, the Resident promptly took up the matter and was once again assured that the status quo would be maintained, and the Maharani needn't worry.[66]

But barely a day after this reassurance was given, military officers who were in charge of the Sripadam office in the fort received orders to prevent Kulathu Iyer from entering and opening the Maharani's treasury, and to permit only the new Mr Sankaranarayana Iyer to do so.

> These fresh bans [have] put the cope-stone [sic] on my trials ... It was inevitable that the normal functioning of my ménage should be rendered impossible with the sources of income stopped and access to available money [in the treasury] cut off, and that business in my office should be paralysed with the Palace and State officials either refusing to receive or taking no notice of communications from my office. Payments to my servants and contractors, which are already due, could not be made owing to the ban on the opening of the treasury. There are many menial servants and pensioners on my establishment who are clamouring for payment of their dues, which it is impossible to disburse in the present circumstances.[67]

An urgent telegram was sent to the Resident to which he did not respond, after which another reminder was despatched a week later in which the Maharani called for immediately ceasing 'the latest phase of the campaign' against her, 'namely the employment of naked force'.[68]

> How mortifying my present position is you can well imagine, since you must by now be thoroughly conversant with all the facts. Any one of the coercive and other measures directed against me during the last few years would ordinarily have been regarded as worthy of condemnation, if it had been an isolated case. But the fact that there has been a *succession* of these seems to have given to the aggregation an air of normality, though each is bolder in conception and more stinging in its effect than its predecessor, with the result that its inherent iniquity is likely to be lost sight of ... I do not know what further steps designed to bring me to my knees are in contemplation [but the] present situation is imposing a terrible strain upon me, not to speak of the inconvenience it involves.[69]

By now the Maharajah had consulted more lawyers and the opinion of Sir Tej Bahadur Sapru, the famous advocate who had great clout in Delhi, was forwarded to Satelmond Palace, in order to let the Maharani prepare her defence. This gentleman rejected statements made by previous Dewans and others regarding the ownership of the Sripadam, pointing out that those were not legal in nature and were untenable, therefore, even as he relied on similar statements by others that fit the Maharajah's argument. He also noted that in the last century there were precedents to show various Maharajahs directing Sripadam affairs, demonstrating that they could indeed go over the head of the Attingal Rani and take unilateral decisions, the last instance being in 1914 when Mulam Tirunal intervened to determine the Junior Maharani's allowance.

He also affirmed that the Sripadam was a matrilineal entity and not the Attingal Rani's Crown lands, and that both male and female members had a corresponding claim on its resources, although the Maharajahs had traditionally permitted females to control revenues derived from it. The present Maharajah was moreover justified in his intervention because the accounts of the Sripadam had errors. Finally, Sir Tej Bahadur concluded that the Senior Maharani was subordinate to the Maharajah in all family matters and could not 'ignore or disregard' his rulings, which 'must be treated as final so far as such family matters are concerned'.[70] This was despite the fact that under matrilineal law the eldest member, male or female, was the head of the family; and in this case it was Sethu Lakshmi Bayi who presided over the dynasty. It was also completely contrary to Sir CP's promise to Lord Willingdon during negotiations in 1931 that she would remain head of the dynasty and enjoy all her revenues as Attingal Rani.

One repeated argument against the Maharani's position pertained to the so-called irregularities in Sripadam accounts. Already in August Sethu Lakshmi

Bayi had told the Resident that the Maharajah should have sent her the auditor's report, in which there was damaging testimony to her management, and sought an explanation before taking the decision to appoint a new person as manager.[71] When this report was finally sent in October, Kulathu Iyer had answered each of the concerns one by one. The principal offence was that from 1924 onwards, until 1933, the annual accounts of the Sripadam had not been written up. This was indeed true but Mr Iyer pointed out that as soon as he had taken over as manager in 1933, the mistake was corrected. It was also informed that although annual accounts were not kept, daily and monthly accounts were in order, which is why the annual audits could be completed after 1933 without any problems.

Another issue the Maharajah's auditor took exception to was the removal of Rs 1,07,594 from the Sripadam funds. To this the manager responded stating that this was done when the Senior Maharani was a minor, and hence her management could not be held liable. In any case the money had far from vanished. The Government of Travancore held it as a deposit and interest that accrued was annually being paid to the Sripadam as an income.[72] It was therefore an investment and not an irregularity, and the amount was in the government's possession. Similarly, certain 'extraneous' expenses were found going back to 1918 and before. It was found that the Maharani's sisters had received about Rs 10,000 from the Sripadam, and for the education of her brothers, she had spent over Rs 10,000. A sum of Rs 86,640 had also been withdrawn during the construction of Satelmond Palace while Rs 13,000 worth of furniture was purchased at the time, and so on. All of these were now determined as inappropriate expenses.

Kulathu Iyer clarified that all these expenses were incurred during the lifetime of the late Maharajah, who would have objected had they been irregular. Indeed, it was pointed our, even the late Senior Rani incurred such expenses on Sripadam funds for her nieces and nephews (who were mothers of the present Maharanis), and they were not objected to either. As for the use of funds for construction and expenses of Satelmond Palace, this was in keeping with Mulam Tirunal's notice dated 05 Meenam 1090 ME wherein he granted Rs 10,000 for the building, and ordered that any further funds should be drawn from the Sripadam.[73] Thus there were no 'extraneous' expenses as alleged, and all the instances pointed out enjoyed the sanction of the last Maharajah as well as of precedent. The only irregularity was with regard to the arrears in maintaining annual accounts for many years, but this, as the Maharani noted, 'was detected and rectified long before the audit [by the Maharajah] was contemplated'.[74]

In any case, the Maharani was now preparing her own defence but this was also rendered very problematic. It had now been two weeks since the Maharajah had physically banned her manager from access to the Sripadam office and treasury, with military force, and the resultant difficulty was that the Maharani did not have access to records she needed to vindicate her position in this dispute. 'It is an intolerable situation', she wrote to the Resident, 'the full implications of which no words can adequately describe.'[75] She also made it known that if this ostracism she was facing continued, she would be left with no option but another direct representation to the Viceroy in New Delhi. It was blatant bullying for the Maharajah to use soldiers and force against the Maharani and she was appalled by the levels to which Kowdiar Palace seemed to stoop.

In the meantime the Resident, after consultations with the Dewan, found out that the main issue was that Kulathu Iyer was a '*persona ingrata* with the Palace', perhaps because of his reputation as the Valiya Koil Tampuran's favourite, and that if he were removed from office 'all difficulties could be solved'.[76] The Maharani was shocked by the suggestion that she should remove her manager merely because the Maharajah took to him an unreasonable dislike, especially in the light of the former's 'meritorious discharge of his official duties and deep personal devotion' towards her.[77] But knowing how she, in spite of being Senior Maharani had to deal with so much trouble from Kowdiar Palace, she acquiesced for she feared that Mr Iyer, who was only a government pensioner, might fare worse, even though asking him to vacate office was 'a painful and distasteful task' for her.[78] In keeping with the Resident's instructions, she then appointed a new person as manager, in the hope that the Maharajah would be more reasonable, now that the individual he disliked was gone.

The new man was accordingly sent to Kowdiar Palace with a letter of introduction. But then she was told that 'the letter could not be received as the Palace had already appointed a Manager' namely Sankaranarayana Iyer![79] When a protest was lodged with the Resident, he asked the Maharani to send the name of her person to him, so that he might ask the Maharajah to recognise him. This statement from Mr Murphy thoroughly agitated her, for the solution 'simple as it may sound, strikes at the root of the principle for which I have suffered no small amount of indignities and hardships during the last two months', namely that the Sripadam was hers and that she, not the Maharajah, had the right to recognise and appoint managers to it. Even in the heyday of Sankaran Tampi when Mulam Tirunal did not like her appointments, he had never thought of imposing someone on her. 'So I am extremely sorry,' she wrote to the Resident,

'I cannot accept your suggestion.'[80] In the meantime the domestic crisis at Satelmond Palace had reached horrific levels and the Maharani pleaded with a strangely unperturbed Mr Murphy to ensure a dignified status quo at the very least. But this time she took a stronger stand:

> The payments to contractors and my servants should have been made from yesterday. Provisions in the store have run out. I cannot take money from the treasury to meet current expenses on account of the orders given to the military in charge to let no one other than the Palace nominee open my treasury. I am in a really desperate plight ... After all that I have suffered from the time the Sripadam affairs reached a climax two months back, I am sure I shall not be liable to the charge of hasty action ... If the authorities do not raise the bans before this evening I shall send a wire to His Excellency.[81]

As she helplessly expected, the authorities did nothing at all and the Resident, who was plausibly tied down too, did not do anything either. So in her distress the Maharani sent a telegram to Delhi, enumerating her troubles and then appealing as follows:

> These improper measures have accentuated hardships & inconveniences already being experienced as is natural when sources of income stopped & access to available money cut off. Coercive measures of this nature to make me submit to wanton aggression on my rights together with instances of ill usage already submitted impose insupportable strain. Pray respectfully for immediate relief since inability to meet urgent financial obligations & current expenses have rendered my situation desperate.[82]

It was quite something that a woman who had once ruled over millions, and ruled admirably for that matter, was today forced to a point of cringing desperation by her relatives. There was, of course, a legal dispute, but the Maharajah's ostracism of the Maharani and her daughters by coercive measures such as suspending incomes and blocking access to the treasury, in order to force her under his authority, spoke a great deal about the extent to which, as previous British representatives had affirmed, vindictiveness had coloured actions. Ever since 'la revanche' had commenced, Sethu Lakshmi Bayi had put up with much, but this Sripadam dispute was the most serious blow yet from her cousin and her nephew.

Even as she was preparing her defence, the Resident sent an explanation to the Government of India. The crux of the matter, he felt, was regarding who had the right to appoint the Sripadam manager. The Maharani claimed it was her prerogative that was independent of the Maharajah, whereas the latter insisted that he could overrule his aunt, especially in light of the irregularities in account keeping. For his own reasons the Resident felt that the Maharajah was well within his rights in claiming that the manager should be appointed and approved by him. All the same, he rejected an argument the Dewan had recently made that this was purely a private family matter and not within the Viceroy's scope to intervene. He also made it clear that while the Maharani, in his opinion, could not claim independence from the Maharajah, she should be treated with consideration not only because of the 'peculiar relations' she enjoyed with her cousin in Kowdiar Palace but also because she was once Regent, an antecedent that threw 'an extra obligation on the Paramount Power to see that the lady obtains fair and justifiable treatment in conformity with her position'.[83]

At the same time, he did not accept the argument that the loss of control over the Sripadam would cost the Maharani much of her income. She was receiving Rs 75,000 as pension (although what this had to do with her ancestral right is unclear), about Rs 6,000 to Rs 7,000 every month from the Civil List (which was, however, for maintaining her position and not as a personal allowance and included moneys paid for her daughters quite independently), and Rs 70,000 from the Sripadam, of which only Rs 12,000 went to the Junior Maharani. Even though the remainder included the costs of her establishment and her personal allowance, there would still be funds to provide for junior female members of the family, in the opinion of the Resident.[84] It was obvious that Mr Murphy saw the case as one of distributing incomes, whereas in reality it was about precedent, custom and the fact that in the royal family it was the Senior Maharani who was the head of the house, and not the Maharajah, as was the case in patriarchal dynasties. As the Junior Maharani's own nephew would remark, 'in matrilineal families age is the determining factor' and that 'in family matters the opinion of the senior female member is always taken and accepted by the senior male member'.[85]

By December, the Maharani's lawyer, Kuttikrishna Menon, an expert on the matrilineal system, who would go on to himself become Advocate General of Madras, prepared her defence. In this it was pointed out that Sir Tej Bahadur Sapru, who was no specialist on matrilineal law, had approached documents placed before him from a patriarchal perspective, uncertain of the intricacies of Kerala society and of practices obtaining in other aristocratic families. He also seemed to have given an opinion 'not for the purpose of ascertaining whether the proposed action is legal but for the purpose of justifying the action already taken by the Maharajah'.[86] He then stated that while the royal family was a matrilineal family, it did not imply that the Maharajah was the sole manager of its properties. Indeed in many Malabar families, the right to manage lands was vested in ladies, as in the Zamorin's family where the senior women of the three branches of the house controlled its lands. He also argued that the Sripadam was not a taravad and that male members of the family could not claim a share in its properties, as attested to by several documents and declarations in the past.

He also found it noteworthy that the Attingal Tampurans were always female and no male member in the royal family had ever been called an Attingal Tampuran. As for precedents in the last century showing the Maharajahs' control over Sripadam affairs, most of these were simply *neetus* or notices issued when the Ranis appointed managers. This did not mean the Maharajahs were ratifying those appointments; it was merely custom. Thus, for instance, the Maharajah always issued similar neetus when bishops were appointed. But this did not mean he had any power over the appointment of bishops. The only instance when a Maharajah actually took over the Sripadam was in 1885, due to a situation of indebtedness.[87] He found issue with two points assumed by Sir Tej Bahadur Sapru, namely that in matrilineal houses it was the senior male member who managed properties, which was shown to be wrong through the example of the Zamorin's dynasty. He also explained that the irregularities were not irregularities at all, with the exception of a lapse in drawing up annual accounts.

This rejoinder to the Maharajah's case was submitted to Delhi and a decision from the Viceroy was awaited. But at the same time the coercive conditions that had been created were not lifted and on 19 December the Maharani was forced to send another telegram:

> I beg to inform Your Excellency that despite my repeated appeals my grievances remain unredressed. Owing to stoppage of all my allowances payments to my servants and others are in arrears for three months. In my previous representations I have said all I have to say. Since conditions are daily becoming more and more distressing I respectfully request early decision.[88]

By now Sethu Lakshmi Bayi was in such a harried and desperate plight that she urgently wanted the harassment terminated, no matter how just or unjust the judgement from Delhi would be. A week later, the Government of India finally reached a decision, bringing to an end this very vexatious question. There appears to have been a consensus in Delhi that they should support the Maharajah even before the rejoinder was received there, for in a personal letter the Political Secretary wrote Sir CP (the usual 'inside' man to link Kowdiar Palace to the Paramount Power) on 9 December, he stated that it was 'distinctly unlikely that the view provisionally held at present will be altered', which was the view that had been endorsed by the Resident that the Maharani could not be independent of her nephew.[89] Then on 26 December the Viceroy himself communicated his final decision to the Maharani:

> I have carefully considered Your Highness' letters of October 2nd, December 4th and December 7th, and the legal opinion of Mr Kuttikrishna Menon, a copy of which was enclosed with your letter of December 4th. I cannot find in the arguments adduced by your Counsel or yourself or in the practice followed in the past any ground of objection to His Highness' action in assuming the management of the Sripadam Estate, for which there are several precedents during the last century, or any reason why suitable provision from it should not be made for the First Princess ... Your Highness may rest assured that there is no intention on the part of His Highness the Maharajah of preventing you from enjoying that share of the revenues of the Estate which is your due, or of invading your legitimate privileges.[90]

Thus came to a conclusion the most serious dispute between the two palaces, in a victory for the Maharajah, whose manager controlled not only Sethu Lakshmi Bayi's money and allowances now, but also her domestic establishment and aspects of her everyday life. Although this had received the blessings of the Government of India, it is telling that when the Regency terminated in 1931, a lesser pension of Rs 75,000 had been sanctioned precisely on the grounds that the Maharani already had income from the Sripadam. That promise was now forgotten. Similarly, at that time it was assured that even in retirement she would remain head of the royal family, as per matrilineal law, but a treatment befitting that position had never been accorded her and the whole basis of the Maharajah's present action was that he was the head of the family, and not the Maharani. In any case, neither of these contraventions were raised, and the Sripadam dispute finally came to an end, with Sethu Lakshmi Bayi in dire straits and entirely abandoned to the authority of Kowdiar Palace. The temples of the Sripadam were shortly afterwards opened, and the Temple Entry Proclamation enacted in its fullest scope.

The Maharajah's assumption of control over the Sripadam Estate was, in fact, the final milestone in the Attingal Rani's spiral towards oblivion. Her decline had really begun soon after the time of the redoubtable Queen Ashure. In her day the Dutch had recorded how Travancore was politically 'under the sway of the Rani of Attingal' and could not even keep treaty relations 'without her approval'.[91] Indeed, even after her rights of sovereignty and supremacy in Travancore were surrendered by the Silver Plate Treaty, in 1810 Col. Munro recorded that the Attingal Rani was still 'regarded as the supreme authority in the State' whose 'mandates are paramount to those of the Rajah'. Her succession rites and the attendant ceremonies were 'made in a manner as formal and solemn as that of the instalment of a Rajah upon the Musnad'.[92] In 1813 he would again remark that the 'authority of the [Rani] has continued to be revered in the country, and is generally considered paramount to those of the Rajah and essential to the validity of all great Acts of the Government'.[93] By 1938, however, this was all wistful history. The obliteration of the final vestige of authority enjoyed by the royal family's matriarch was achieved at the Maharajah's behest, and leave alone acts of state, not even allowances and the enjoyment of her ancestral estates could be determined without the grace and favour of the ruling male monarch.

Such incidents were not isolated to Travancore alone. In the first half of the nineteenth century, 'in the pursuit of its traditionary ideas of inheritance, neither Eastern nor Western' and 'in the true European prejudice against woman [sic]', the East India Company had tampered with the rights of the begums in Bhopal, unwilling to permit them their traditional position on account of their sex. 'This,' lambasted a critic, 'is British wisdom and liberality—this repeated denial of the right of the female sex to rule.'[94] By the 1890s a case occurred in the principality of Indore, with striking similarities to Sethu Lakshmi Bayi's treatment by the Government of India in 1938. Like the senior female member of the royal house in Travancore had the Sripadam, the Senior Maharani in Indore was traditionally the owner of an estate known as the Khasgi. In the last decade of the nineteenth century, however, the Maharajah, a son of the Junior Maharani there, did not get along with his late father's Senior Maharani. He ordered the taking over of the Khasgi from his stepmother in order to reduce her influence at court. As in Sethu Lakshmi Bayi's case, when the Senior Maharani refused to give up her traditional rights over the Khasgi, her allowances were cut and provisions to her household withheld in order to compel her to submission. The Senior Maharani in 1899, therefore, wrote to the Viceroy for his protection, stating:

> The Khasgi Estate is in the nature of a *jagir* in the Indore State and the possessor has inherent rights like any other *jagirdar*, chieftain, or landlord, which cannot be tampered with. The ruling Rani exercises supreme revenue and judicial powers, subject to an appeal to the Maharajah in respect of serious offences alone. The Rani holds durbars for the transaction of business. There is a separate throne, a separate seal, a separate establishment; separate [tributes] are paid to her on solemn and festive occasions; and the Rani at the time of her accession is placed on the throne and receives a salute in the same way as the Prince does ... Further, the Khasgi has a treasury of its own. It has independent jurisdiction both in matters civil and criminal.[95]

The position was almost entirely similar to that of the Attingal Rani, who in fact enjoyed even greater privileges. But as in Sethu Lakshmi Bayi's case, the Senior Maharani of Indore was also let down and the Maharajah was permitted to coerce her into toeing his line.[96] In Travancore, however, the Maharani's plight was the culmination of a long process, and the Government of India felt justified in sanctioning this due to a number of historic and cultural factors. To begin with, the arrival of the British and the commencement of colonial rule had altered some very basic principles of the old matrilineal system. In the past, as one anthropologist noted, the senior female member in a family was its head, with the next in line her 'Prime Minister', and the senior male essentially acting on their behalf and in consultation with them.[97] As Saradamoni remarks, 'Until the early nineteenth century, power within the [matrilineal joint family] was more a generational privilege than a gendered right. In other words, the elders in the family—women and men—would make decisions in matters pertaining to property, authority, inheritance or residence, and often women had special entitlements within the household.'[98]

The colonial state, however, began to recognise only the senior male member as the rightful exerciser of power in the family. The 'steady singling out' of the eldest man 'as the figure to make settlements with by the Company in the early decades of the nineteenth century created a "sexual contract" between the state and men', with the British 'treating "headship" as a gendered right available normatively to men' alone. By doing so they were 'altering the existing equation' where the eldest female had tremendous influence, over and above the eldest male.[99] It was not as though the British were unaware of the changes they were making. As late as 1830 it was stated in the House of Lords that the 'senior male of the family is generally considered as the manager, although, properly speaking, the senior female is the lawful proprietor. The Cannanore Beebee, for instance, also the Ranny or Queen of Travankore, under the name of Attingal Umma Tamburattes. Treaties, everything of importance is or should be done in her name, though the Rajah, her son, is the ruling Rajah.'[100] But this was all in theory. In practice now, as Saradamoni concludes, 'the senior woman was no longer the head of the family, having given place to the eldest male'.[101]

One of the reasons for this Western tendency to vest the male, rather than the female, with power was plain Victorian prejudice. In royal families particularly, the British viewed with enormous suspicion any hint of influence being granted to women. Females in royal households were determined, they were certain, to thwart their best intentions and the forward march of what they were convinced was 'progress'. As Viceroy Lord Lansdowne declared in 1890, 'In all cases where a very young ruler succeeds to a Native State, the widows of his predecessor give an infinite amount of trouble. Their object is of course to get hold of the boy and to bring him up under conditions, which in a few years will convert him into an imbecile and leave the power in their hands. Our object is to prevent such a state of things arising.'[102] Thus, in Mysore, when a Regency commenced in that decade, the Maharani was dismissed as 'a lady of domestic tastes who has not concerned herself with events beyond the range of her family and the palace walls. The palace is, as it ever was, a hotbed of petty and mischievous intrigues, and a lady living in seclusion might with the best of intentions be moved by evil influences to exert her authority in a wrong direction.'[103] Having given her a chance, however, the Government of India were surprised to find that she was really 'a woman of decided opinion and of considerable strength of character' and 'anyone who supposes she is going to prove a puppet is likely to find out his mistake'.[104]

Almost exact words were also employed in describing Sethu Lakshmi Bayi at the beginning of the Regency as being of 'the pious, domestic, orthodox type' before successive Residents realised she was, behind all that, a singularly capable woman. But the Government of India were never compelled to take a kinder view of women in royal families, because intrigues did transpire: in Travancore, for instance, courtesy the Junior Maharani. But intrigues and factions were features of courts and palaces across the world, with the only difference in India being the wholesale application of imported Victorian prejudices upon the situation so as to justify constant interference by the British. As Caroline Keen remarks, 'rules of descent could be and were manipulated' by the colonial state to fit their own needs, and powerful Residents held 'the balance of power' to determine which course the future would take.[105] Under the same policy, internal traditions and customs, as in the case of the Sripadam dispute in Travancore or the Khasgi Estate in Indore, could also be dispensed with and replaced by what the Government of India deemed best in the interests of the state and its own influence over the ruler. By interfering with and amending the internal affairs of a family, promoting one group over another, and then doing just the opposite sometime later, Indian Maharajahs were not only taught that the British had the power to do so, but that their own royal authority was 'a favour, not a right'.[106]

In Travancore, to be fair, however, the decline of the Attingal Rani had begun even before the British assumed supremacy. It was Martanda Varma who first commenced the process through the Silver Plate Treaty, and though Munro would, decades later, recognise that the Attingal Rani still sustained great influence at court and in the state, her power was really much reduced. He would specifically point to the intrigues of Chathayam Tirunal in the 1790s and the illegal adoption of a male heir despite the Attingal Rani's opposition as proof of the latter's diluted status. So while she was still revered, her 'authority appears to have gradually been weaker and less respected'.[107] Munro then unilaterally decided that instead of resuscitating the Attingal Rani and returning her to her original glory, since the involvement of the British now was with the Rajahs, 'it appears to be expedient that we should continue the same constitution of Government'.[108] At the same time, however, it was essential not to relinquish too much authority to male members in the dynasty. So, he added, 'it may also be expedient that we should endeavour to augment as far as may be possible the dignity and consideration in the State of the [Ranis]; as their influence may be expected to temper the rash and inconsiderate resolutions of the Rajahs'.[109] It was, in other words, the maxim of divide and rule implemented within a royal house.

It was held that since the Attingal Rani resigned her powers officially in 1731 through the Silver Plate Treaty, and because by 1810, despite theoretical primacy, she had no actual influence at court, any future position she enjoyed would be the gift not of tradition but of the East India Company. That is why when Gowri Lakshmi Bayi gave birth to a son in 1813, it was within Munro's province to decide whether or not the Attingal Rani should be allowed to continue ruling. He recommended, for the reasons mentioned above, which would 'be in part accomplished by vesting Her Highness the Rani with the charge of the Government during the long minority of her son',[110] the constitution of the first Regency rule. His superiors agreed that the 'influence of the [Rani] in the State should be upheld to a certain extent with a view to temper and moderate the Proceedings of the reigning Rajahs', and gave their blessings to the new arrangement.[111] They were perfectly aware that under matrilineal law there was no concept of Regency, and that the senior female member of the dynasty was free to rule in her own name. They were also conscious that Queen Ashure, in a similar circumstance over a century before, had exercised full powers. But that letter and spirit of the law were changed. In 1814, thus, when Gowri Parvathi Bayi came to the throne, she too was denied the title of a reigning ruler (though she was styled 'Uttrittadhi Tirunal *Maharajah*'). For, it was felt, 'although perfect reliance might be placed on the natural affection of the [Rani] for the children of her deceased sister, yet it must be kept in mind that in the event of their decease, the right of succession would devolve on Her Highness or her offspring'.[112] In other words, they would let the Attingal Rani rule, but only in theory as a trustee of the minor ruler, and on terms determined by the East India Company.

It was a similar consideration that the Government of India entertained when the Regency of Sethu Lakshmi Bayi (albeit as 'Pooradam Tirunal Maharajah') began in 1924. The Maharani apprised the Resident that were it not for these peculiar historic considerations, typically under the law she ought to have been ruling as a regnant queen and not as Regent. But this claim, though only mentioned in passing, was promptly quashed, stating that ordinary 'Hindu Law does not and cannot apply to regalities', i.e., princely houses, whose destinies had to be guided by the Paramount Power alone.[113] Besides, as in the case of Gowri Parvathi Bayi a century before, it was 'at once manifest that a system by which the senior lady of the family, who (as in the present case) is not necessarily the mother of the minor Ruler, conducts the administration in her own right and not as a trustee of the minor's interests, is liable to abuse and is not one to which the Government of India could readily accord its approval'.[114] Queen Ashure might have ruled in her own name. But a 'safe precedent' to be taken into account now was the one created by the British in the last century.[115]

That said the Government of India could not, all the same, ignore the unique position custom and traditional law granted the senior female member of the royal house in such a position. In 1814 when Gowri Parvathi Bayi came to power, she was only recognised as a Regent. But, as it was informed to Munro, 'You will observe that the Governor in Council has not ... assumed the power of *appointing* the [Rani] to the office of Regent of Travancore; but on the ground of your report, has acknowledged her right of *accession* to it, as the senior member of the reigning family. Her Highness has accordingly been addressed as if she had actually *succeeded* to the Regency.'[116] In other words, while they did not accept the right of the Attingal Rani to succeed to full powers, she could succeed (as opposed to being appointed by the British) to the title of Regent (a British invention), as a compromise entirely of colonial vintage. Her powers were not curtailed, and as Munro stated, 'the people were accustomed to regard her with the reverence and respect which they had paid to their Rajahs' and 'saw her occupy the place of the Rajah and scarcely found any difference in the constitution of the Government'.[117] In Sethu Lakshmi Bayi's case too, she explained that while she was willing to accept she could never claim the title of regnant ruler, she wished for recognition that 'the right of Regency is *inherent* in her and that she has as good a right to succeed to that office in the event of a minority ... as has a natural heir in the direct line to succeed to the [throne]'.[118]

It took nearly four years of deliberations on the subject before the Viceroy in consultation with the Secretary of State in London reached a decision in 1928. While Mr Cotton was sympathetic to the Maharani's claim, the Acting Resident, Mr Vernon, in 1926 advised the Government of India against it. He agreed that Sethu Lakshmi Bayi was the head of the royal family, with her own sign manual, and was 'looked on in consequence in the State as holding ruling powers.'[119] He also confirmed that 'a hereditary right of succession [to full powers] on the failure of male heirs, and of Regency during a minority, is vested in the [Senior Rani] of Travancore, and that right was acknowledged and a precedent established' in the nineteenth century. But now in the 1920s, he felt, this should not be allowed and the Maharani ought to be treated like all other 'appointed' Regents elsewhere in India and not 'in her hereditary position as head of the Ruling Family'. For 'the consequence,' he declared in what was brazenly sexist, 'will ensue that at any time the reins of power in Travancore may pass into the hands of a lady, totally inexperienced in statecraft, liable in the course of nature to be incapacitated for months together from attending to the business of the State, and not infrequently predisposed to lend too ready an ear to the advice of a husband whose position as consort of the Ruler is at best an anomalous one'.[120]

The Government of India, however, decided against tampering any more and creating a new precedent, not least because by this time Sethu Lakshmi Bayi had proved her administrative capabilities. And so late in 1927 the Viceroy wrote to London for permission to sanction the Attingal Rani's right to succeed as regnant ruler when there were no males at all in the dynasty, and 'to exercise by *right* (unless disqualified) the powers of Regent during a minority'.[121] The Secretary of State gave his consent to this, and it was confirmed early in 1928 that she was 'recognised as Regent by right and not by appointment' in Travancore.[122] But while the British were somewhat generous to Sethu Lakshmi Bayi during her rule in the 1920s, the crux of the matter was that all precedents and rules could, and were, altered and modified by the Government of India as they deemed fit at any moment. That is why in 1938, less than a decade after she relinquished the Regency, she found, like the Maharani of Indore, the Paramount Power sanctioning the Maharajah's assumption of control over her estates, placing her firmly under his control. As a telegram from the Resident to the Government of India shortly after the dispute was settled noted, the 'Maharani has now informed Maharajah that she will act in conformity with his directions in Sripadam affairs and matters relating to the family.'[123]

After battling Kowdiar Palace for nearly a decade, Sethu Lakshmi Bayi was by now simply exhausted. And so she accepted defeat.

17

The Villain of the Piece

'Darlingest, dearest, *omanest* mummie,' rambled Princess Lalitha to her mother from Kovalam. The newly-wed was evidently missing her family and sought some maternal sympathy from the Maharani, who did not, she protested, write as frequently as she ought to have. Scribbling in her unladylike scrawl, she went on to ask for some eminently more ladylike advice about her wardrobe:

> Won't you write a letter to me? I simply dance with excitement and do the famous stunt of standing-on-my-head and waving-my-heels when I receive letters from you *Omane* [i.e., dear one] ... Now to come to a little business. Tomorrow we are supposed to present ourselves at KP (Bless it!). And you said that the light pink georgette will do. But I think it is too dull. I mean its colour. So why not the blue French sari or the dark green affair? Or the orange georgette with its heavy black border? Don't you think it will suit?[1]

Sethu Lakshmi Bayi is bound to have been amused by her daughter, so happily acting the carefree bride, whose sole concerns in the world were clothes and her adoring new husband; at her age, the Maharani herself was coming to terms with having lost her baby son and venturing into her early battles with the palace bureau at Mulam Tirunal's court. Now that Princess Lalitha was married and had come of age, as it were, she was expected to make separate courtesy calls at 'KP' to the Maharajah, along with her husband. Her rebelliousness had not abandoned her altogether after marriage; soon she would provoke a minor scandal in the Sri Padmanabhaswamy Temple. She told bewildered priests, who wouldn't treat her husband in the exalted fashion they did her, that she wouldn't accept their obeisance until they welcomed Kerala Varma also in an equally befitting manner.[2] 'Like mother, like daughter,' they probably mumbled since Sethu Lakshmi Bayi too in her day went out of her way to honour Rama Varma with an eminence higher than consorts could traditionally claim.

At Kovalam, days passed in a romantic breeze. The couple rode beside the waves in the mornings, played tennis and spent hours talking about their favourite topics as they walked barefoot on the beach—with the ubiquitous household guards in tow. Visitors called often to pay their respects. These included members from Kerala Varma's family who were 'completely overawed' by Princess Lalitha and her sunny energy and zest for life.[3] She could not visit them in Kilimanoor, due to court conventions, and so she welcomed them with all her warmth at Halcyon Castle. 'She could ignite joy in any gathering,' a cousin recalls,[4] and she employed her famous charm to its fullest in a bid to win over her husband's relations. 'She encouraged father to take the front role, and made him feel rather more important than he was traditionally meant to be,' their daughter tells. 'In fact, she quite spoilt him!' And realising how she had no desire whatever to act the haughty princess, Kerala Varma's family also became considerably more comfortable with her after an early phase of reverential obsequiousness.

Then in April 1939 Sethu Lakshmi Bayi heard from her daughter that she was unwell and nauseous with what, she presumed, was a reaction to being so close to the sea for many months. The Maharani knew better, and immediately commanded Dr Mary to examine the Second Princess. To her great elation, her suspicions were confirmed when it was announced that Princess Lalitha was expecting a child. The Maharani promptly wrote to her 'to be very careful and not to allow her exuberant high spirits free rein so as to endanger the life of her baby'. A lot of bed rest, a healthy diet, and a suspension of dangerous outdoor sports were sternly advocated. She need not have fretted, though, for the young girl had severe bouts of nausea 'and nothing was further from her thoughts than exuberance or high spirits'.[5] Three months later an entourage arrived from Vellayini to escort her to the Maharani, under whose direct supervision she spent the remainder of her pregnancy.

It was around the same time that the Sripadam dispute reached breaking point. And this was precisely why Sethu Lakshmi Bayi was vexed by the suspension of her allowances, of household provisions, with even access to all her money barred by intimidation. With a pregnant daughter to care for, the problems that naturally followed this rancorous policy of the authorities assumed an added gravity. 'Another anxiety which weighs heavily on my mind,' she informed the Resident, 'arises from the continued cessation of religious rites which used to be performed daily for the well-being of my daughters, and which as a result of the new Palace attitude, have been suspended. This is particularly regrettable at this juncture when special rites are customary owing to my elder daughter being an expectant mother. To a devout Hindu these rites possess great significance, and therefore their neglect causes me much uneasiness.'[6]

Throughout all her disputations with Kowdiar Palace, Sethu Lakshmi Bayi had always carefully insulated her children, never letting her own tribulations affect them. 'We barely knew what was happening,' Princess Indira would recall, 'and the little bit that we did hear were whispers from aunts. Mother never uttered a word about these things, not then and not later.'[7] Even the quarrel over the Sripadam, perhaps the Maharani's most exacting trial, was kept away from her daughters, who lived in the happy cocoon that was Vellayini. 'It was all so malicious but she didn't want to pass any of that to her children. She always thought that at least they could lead their lives in peace, without worry.'[8] That said even Sethu Lakshmi Bayi never expected the authorities to be so inconsiderate as to the extent of trying to drain her finances and cutting even the supply of kitchen vegetables, with a pregnant princess awaiting confinement in the palace. The Valiya Koil Tampuran was, of course, not remotely shocked.

As the time for certain critical prenatal ceremonies approached, the Maharani despatched a personal appeal to the Maharajah asking for their commencement. In return Chithira Tirunal wrote how pleased he was to hear of the good news, and that arrangements for the ceremonies would be made on the receipt of 'the usual formal communication' from the Sripadam.[9] Sethu Lakshmi Bayi, accordingly, asked her manager to forward the traditional notification. But it was merely another handle to prosecute the dispute, for she was told that since her manager was not recognised by Kowdiar Palace, a communiqué sent under his sign and seal was not acceptable. Only a note from the manager the Maharajah had appointed could be received. 'I fail to see how the arrangements for the Princess' confinement,' cried a crestfallen Maharani, 'should be made to depend upon my recognition of the Palace nominee.'[10] It appeared to her that not only were she and Rama Varma out of favour with the Maharajah, but hostility extended even to her daughters who had little to do with these quarrels other than being her natural heirs and family.

Nevertheless, Sethu Lakshmi Bayi remained stoically hopeful that Chithira Tirunal would have a change of heart and relax the siege on her and her children. The latest auspicious day to conduct the relevant ceremonies was 15 December but as the days passed, it became patent that the Maharajah would not make any arrangements at all for the rites to be performed. Somehow, then, 'at the eleventh hour,' wrote the Maharani, 'I had to conduct them quietly, without the customary pomp or pageantry'.[11] Where the senior male member of the family was meant to preside, owing to the deaf ear turned by the Maharajah, it was her sister Kutty Amma's son who stood in and performed the duty. It was a substantial breach of custom to perform a ceremony of this nature, normally a state affair, privately, but there was no option at the time other than giving in to the Maharajah vis-à-vis the Sripadam dispute.

When on 15 February 1940 Princess Lalitha went into labour and gave birth to a baby girl, the Maharani was overjoyed. And by this time the Sripadam issue had also been settled in favour of the Maharajah. She informed the Resident about the news, who in turn noted, however, that the official notification that was usual at such times had not oddly arrived yet.[12] This was because, it turned out, the Maharajah had not 'recognised' the birth, since he had not given his consent to the prenatal rituals during the pregnancy! In other words, since Princess Lalitha's pregnancy had not received his blessings during the Sripadam dispute, the advent of her daughter was also treated as a non-event. As far as Chithira Tirunal was concerned, nothing of import had occurred that month.[13] Weary of such bizarre turns, Sethu Lakshmi Bayi offered to implement whatever the Maharajah desired by way of redress so that six months later, at what was meant to be the naming ceremony of the newborn, Princess Lalitha found herself again, for official purposes and in order to satisfy the Maharajah, 'pregnant'. Laughing about it now, the controversial baby in question tells,

> I was wrapped up in lotus leaves, which served as a make-believe womb, and held against mother's stomach. I presume our priests recommended this peculiar 'remedy' to the problem that I was born but wasn't supposed to be born without permission. Anyway, I was packaged like that, and the Maharajah performed the ceremonies he was meant to do months before my birth. And then the leaves were opened and I was laid on the ground. The maids and women there were all instructed to come forth with these joyous ululations and loud exclamations, and so there was a great hoo-ha about my so-called 'birth'. Then the Maharajah 'recognised' me and proceeded to the naming rituals. To her dying day mother couldn't stop laughing when she told us this story, though on that day itself she was firmly instructed not to betray any emotion lest offence be taken.[14]

What did not, however, amuse Princess Lalitha was that she did not have the permission to name her own baby. As per tradition the head of the royal family chose the name and the senior male member performed the naming ceremony. Since Sethu Lakshmi Bayi as the matriarch and head had no remaining powers, it was the Junior Maharani who named all the children through her son.[15] And in this instance the Gazette Extraordinary issued that day announced the official name of the baby as Her Highness Bharani Tirunal Rukmini Bayi Tampuran, Fourth Princess of Travancore. For all the tribulations, whether it was the difficulties her grandmother faced during her mother's pregnancy, or her stunned mother having to put up with an unofficial and apparently official process of childbirth, not to speak of being unable to name her 'Sharada' as she had hoped, Princess Rukmini was born at a time astrologers deemed beautifully exotic. It was at 4:30 in the morning, known as the *brahma muhurtam*, that she arrived into this tumultuous world of palaces and politics, of temperamental princes and princesses, and of eccentric rituals and ceremonies, on *kumbha bharani*, the festive day of the great goddess.

In the years that followed the birth of her eldest child, Princess Lalitha had three more girls, all of them princesses and successors to the lineage of the Attingal Rani. Though the absence of a male heir delayed any chance of a member from Sethu Lakshmi Bayi's branch of the royal house succeeding to the throne, the Maharani is said to have been relieved at the onset of her granddaughters. 'It was generally remarked in those days that the Junior Maharani was anxious to keep the title in her branch of the family,' tells a relative, 'and frightening rumours abounded that the doctors had been given clear instructions that if a male child were born to the Second Princess, it should not survive birth.'[16] This was most probably sensational nonsense, for the Resident, who had vigilant eyes and ears everywhere, would have smelled out any such sinister plot. Either way, Sethu Lakshmi Bayi and her family welcomed a number of girls at Satelmond Palace. Towards the end of 1941 arrived Princess Uma, followed in 1943 by Princess Parvathi, and in 1946 by Princess Lakshmi.[17] Each time, the babies were wrapped in silks and presented on silver trays to the Maharajah who would visit specifically for the purpose and return after inspecting the infants.

Kowdiar Palace too saw the birth of more children, and in 1942 and 1945 two princesses were born there.[18] However, tragedy struck in 1944 when the only grandson of the Junior Maharani died of heart failure. The Maharajah and his mother were in Bombay on account of some medical treatment the latter was undergoing, but chartered a plane back to Trivandrum. The whole state was palled in official mourning. The young prince was unhealthy for all of his six years, but his sudden passing came as a shock, and the Resident reported that 'the Maharajah has taken the death of his little nephew terribly to heart—as indeed have the whole family. Apart from the personal bereavement the death, of course, reopens,' he added, always conscious of political implications, 'the possibility of the [throne] passing over to the Senior Maharani's family, as her two daughters may be able to produce a son before the bereaved daughter of the Junior Maharani can replace the dead heir presumptive.'[19]

At the time of the death the weddings of both Princess Indira and the Junior Maharani's younger son had been planned for later that year. Now, due to a prolonged period of state mourning, they were postponed by twelve months. On 9 May 1945, then, Princess Indira was married to her father's nephew, Rama Varma, who was lovingly known as Kuttan.[20] Coming as it did only a year following the demise of a prince, celebrations were not as splendid as in 1938, though *The Indian Express* was still able to report how the 'entire route was thronged by spectators and the procession was a very imposing one. Her Highness the Third Princess was seated in a palanquin followed by her consort seated in a golden howdah on a gaily caparisoned elephant.'[21] The wedding of the Junior Maharani's younger son was a less spectacular affair, since marital alliances of male members were immaterial to the dynasty, and their brides were not formally welcomed into the royal house or received at court. On 9 September, in the presence of the Senior and Junior Maharanis as well as the Dewan and senior government officials, the Elayarajah married Radha Devi, a Nair woman of extraordinary beauty, and an adopted daughter of Lt Col K.G. Pandalai, a legendary military man who was 'one of the best surgeons in Madras'.[22] In keeping with custom she was never destined to be a 'Highness'.

While all these marriages were occurring in the family, it had, in the meantime, become a matter of public gossip why the Maharajah had not taken a consort. He 'ought to marry', reported the Resident, 'and have a home of his own'. During a discussion with Sir CP, the latter asserted that despite 'unkind rumour that charges Mother and Dewan with an unholy pact to discourage' marriage so as to keep Chithira Tirunal under their thumb, the truth according to Sir CP was that the Junior Maharani was 'always urging the Maharajah to marry' and had even, reportedly, 'threatened to leave the Palace and go and live alone if he persisted in his bachelordom'. Apparently, the 'trouble was that the Maharajah disliked the matriarchal system; the idea of his wife being only the consort and his children being excluded from the privileges of his dynasty were most repugnant to him'.[23] Several marriage proposals were, at various points in the past, from 1932 until 1944, considered, even though none came to actual fruition.[24]

Politically, however, it appeared that Chithira Tirunal was really still very much subordinate to his mother and minister. As the Resident, Mr H.J. Todd stated:

> He is now 32 and still unmarried, living with his pervasive and capable mother, the Junior Maharani, his brother, and sister. Impresses one as shy, rather lacking in confidence, and still quite over-powered by his mother. Very pleasant manners, an easy facility in light conversation, kindly, would certainly flinch from, and probably abhor, association with grievous misrule or injustice, although his masterful and jealous mother might easily persuade him to countenance any safe strategy to preserve the succession in his own family. Having to function at the temple every day, he seems reluctant to take much part in other public functions although under his mother's tutelage he carries out his public duties with a certain simple dignity. With such a purposeful mother and such an all-powerful and all-absorbing Dewan, he has no chance whatever of developing a personality, already timid by nature.[25]

There is no doubt that he was personally very popular, with a tremendous effect on all who encountered him, much like Sethu Lakshmi Bayi during her years in power. Describing him in 1939 one traveller noted: 'The graceful face of this twenty-seven year old Ruler of five million souls was a study in itself. Sweetness and quiet dignity radiated on his countenance. Seldom have I seen such a winsome face in all India. The man himself is a darling and the more I looked at him, the more I felt a great affection for this talented and wise young man, the qualities of whose head and heart could be elaborately written in a thousand printed pages.'[26] John Paton Davies's review was that the Maharajah was 'a handsome, strong-looking fellow' and seemed thoroughly imposing as he led a temple procession.[27] His own family members in the future, however, would go a step further to sustain the image of Chithira Tirunal as a *pratyaksha* Padmanabha or god incarnate, which to this day many in Trivandrum reverentially believe because of his matchless (some said eccentric) devotion for his dynastic deity.[28] But these were all impressions of the man as a devout Hindu and religious functionary in a great temple. As a *ruler*, his political superiors in Delhi entertained a completely different view, far from one of awed admiration. For them the real monarch of Travancore was not this amiable, disarmingly charming, even if exceedingly reticent, prince. The real power here was his domineering minister: Sir CP.

In 1938, the All-Travancore Joint Political Congress had dissolved to form the Travancore State Congress, their declared objective being the attainment of responsible rule. 'We all knew,' wrote the Resident, 'that the victory of the [Indian National] Congress in 7 of the Provinces of British India would have "repercussions" in the more advanced Indian States, and these came last spring in Travancore.'[29] He was referring to the new policy of the Government of India to inaugurate *elected* Indian-run governments in territories under their control, subject, of course to the authority of British Governors. Naturally, the Maharajahs were under public pressure to concede similar schemes to their people as well. In Mysore 'the rather weak policy' of its Dewan, Sir Mirza Ismail, had committed that state to responsible government, while closer home, Cochin 'introduced a mild form of "diarchy" last January'. The visit of a former Undersecretary of State from London, Lord Lothian, added fat to the fire, when he declared that Indian princes would have to surrender power to the elected representatives of their people. This 'encouraged the politically-minded in Travancore still more'.[30]

The State Congress understood that Sir CP was the principal adversary in the realisation of their aspirations. But the man was 'too clever and experienced a politician and too forceful a personality to lie down' and let a group of what were perceived as 'second-rate place hunters and demagogues ride roughshod over him. Moreover,' it was added, 'the strong-minded and ambitious Junior Maharani whose word is law at the Palace, has no intention of letting her son's powers be curtailed.'[31] Accordingly, the Maharajah stood firmly behind his Dewan, whose term of office was extended by five years. 'The idea is, as Sir CP puts it,' recorded the Resident, 'to stabilise the position and obviate ill-directed manoeuvres and agitation' and the 'announcement is a clear indication to the popular party [i.e., the State Congress] that His Highness is behind his Dewan in his disapproval of this movement'.[32]

The agitation continued but was not destined to last. With the Junior Maharani and Sir CP presenting a 'strong combination' against them, the Congress 'found their campaign not going at all the same way as in Mysore and certain other States further north'.[33] Later that year, with Gandhi's blessings a disastrous civil disobedience campaign also began in Travancore. Mr Skrine termed it a rebellion, 'For that's what it has been—a rebellion against CP and the Maharani he serves.'[34] Leaders of the Congress were arrested and imprisoned wholesale and at certain places the agitation even turned violent, with clashes between the police and demonstrators. In Alleppey a general strike of factory workers paralysed the region, while in Neyyattinkara police opened fire and killed an agitator. By October the police again came down heavily on a 'mammoth public meeting'.[35] In a private letter, the Resident who was no fan of popular movements wrote:

> They [the Congress] started agitating on thoroughly seditious lines among the more inflammable masses in certain districts, held meetings in defiance of the Government, put up speakers who volunteered for jail and told the villagers and workmen that the Government was afraid of them, the police weak and cowardly, and the troops undisciplined and armed only with blank ammunition. The result was that at four different points in one week, the mobs incited by the State Congress leaders attacked the police with stones and brickbats and when the troops were sent to overawe them, attacked the troops too![36]

Though the Congress was originally an organisation of Christian, Ezhava and Muslim sections of the population, it had won support from a number of prominent Nairs as well. The principal leadership of the Nairs, however, formed a rival Travancore National Congress with Sir CP's backing, though when they tried to visit Gandhi for his blessings they found 'The Mahatma was good at separating sheep from goats' and only 'gave them polite words'.[37] With the government retaliating with equal violence, an appeal was made to the Paramount Power from 'All Subjects of Travancore' through a long memorial. Its primary demand was the immediate removal of Sir CP 'so that peace, security, and communal harmony may be rehabilitated in Travancore, which is today considerably disturbed on account of gross misrule and repression by the Dewan'. They called it a regime of 'personal absolutism' stating how the Maharajah's man had no 'scruples or hesitation to ride rough-shod over the rights and liberties of the people'. He was nothing more than a power-hungry despot who, owing to his old connections with the Maharajah, took advantage of a friendly, generous monarch to impose his own rule on the people. He had 'special relations' with Kowdiar Palace and great influence over the Junior Maharani. 'The mother's influence over the young Maharajah and Sir C.P. Ramaswami Iyer's influence over the Maharani are notorious,' the memorialists alleged.[38]

Testimony from Congress workers that reached Gandhi disconcerted him. The account of a doctor who was imprisoned at the height of the campaign revealed that the police were authorised to inflict even torture. 'I was told that I would be released,' he claimed, 'if I resigned from the State Congress.' He alleged that while in custody he and his compatriots, were all beaten up ruthlessly till he had to be hospitalised.[39] 'The problem now facing us in Travancore,' declared G. Ramachandran (or 'GR'), a leading Congressman, 'is far more fundamental than political reform. The question is whether peaceful citizens are to be persecuted for the exercise of fundamental rights by organised hooliganism.'[40] Evidently, a right-wing organisation called the Hindu Loyalist League was involved in the violence, siding with the government, and Sir CP even defended them in a telegram to Gandhi. The claim of 'no provocation [from the Congress was] not accurate', he insisted, adding that the 'Travancore Government have no desire to interfere with *legitimate* political activities'.[41]

By the end of 1938 the government and the Congress negotiated a truce by which 188 political prisoners were released in return for the suspension of the movement for civil disobedience. But peace was short-lived and 'Direct Action' was contemplated against the regime by January 1939.[42] To pre-empt this, prominent leaders like GR and Pattom Thanu Pillai were arrested, so that those who remained outside lost their nerve and called off the proposed action. This led to a split in the party's support and a lowering of morale among its rank and file. On Gandhi's suggestion, they returned to negotiate with the government, which again, inevitably, broke down, and agitation resumed, with corresponding retaliation from the government—almost like a pattern. Gandhi wrote to Sir CP stating he was aware that 'you want the State Congress to give up altogether the idea of responsible Government' and that 'You want them also not even to consult the National Congress leaders or be under their influence. I suppose it means that you resent even their consulting me.' He then declared that 'if you will insist in robbing people of their self-respect, there is nothing left for them but to engage in a fight for honour, however hopeless and unequal the fight may be.'[43]

In his response Sir CP, extremely politely, argued that the Mahatma had been 'misinformed' by the Congress, adding that 'it is true that the Travancore Government do not propose to inaugurate Responsible Government in the sense of the Executive being responsible to and liable to removal by the Legislature'. But this did not mean he would not welcome a 'thorough association' between the people and the state. He welcomed Gandhi's advice and guidance on this, 'But if what is involved is the direct leadership of Gandhiji or his direct intervention in the matter of *agitation* in Travancore, then of course, the position is very different; and entirely unwillingly the Travancore Government will perforce to [sic] resist such intervention.' Painful as such a confrontation would be, 'there is no alternative but to proceed on our course, relying on the justice of our cause and on Providence'.[44] This matched the Dewan's position also, reportedly, that the Congress was merely a hooligan gang of 'proven liars, men of no standing, with no stake to lose, most of them unemployed or briefless barristers' whom he would never permit to stand in his way.[45]

In other words, Sir CP warned Gandhi from raking up trouble in Travancore. And soon enough, realising that indeed the Dewan meant business, with all the state's coercive machinery at his disposal, the Mahatma advised the Congress to lie low. As the Resident recorded earlier, 'CP and Gandhi have been exchanging statements in the Press, a wordy war in which the Mahatma is no match for his adversary and from which he seems to have retired. But verbal victories over Gandhi will do CP no good with the general public, to whom Gandhi is a saint and CP an arch-villain.'[46] And it didn't, for soon even such stalwarts as Rabindranath Tagore were lamenting the initiation of 'a regime of fascism' in Travancore.[47] Mr Skrine then advised them that instead of locking up Congress leaders, effectively turning them into martyrs for a greater cause, and impulsively retaliating with brute force, the proper thing would be to hold 'full dress' trials against them with imported judges from British India. They would be impartial, and the state and its government could recover its prestige as a proper institution.[48] While Sir CP was in favour of this idea, the Junior Maharani 'who is a regular Bourbon and is also so fanatically proud a Travancorean that she hates any suggestion that Travancore can't settle its own problems without outside assistance, is blocking the scheme. She is all-powerful in the Travancore Government, as you know—which is one argument in favour of the introduction of responsible government in Travancore!'[49]

Frenzied agitation continued, and Mr Skrine reported that 'mobs of hooligans and students organised by the Travancore State Congress have destroyed six culverts and otherwise completely blocked the roads between Kottayam and the capital'.[50] The state was full of protests and 'the prisons are getting fuller and fuller of Congressmen. The wordy campaign of calumny and hate against Sir CP continues unabated, and the schools and colleges are seething with student discontent, expressed in many cases by "hartals" against their authorities.'[51] His suggestion to deal with the problem legally was still not accepted. The Resident, privately, vented how neither side displayed any decency, which was perhaps more a scathing review of the government, since it was meant to set an example, and not come down to the level of agitators. He was highly astonished by the 'crookedness of the fighting' and the 'characters of the combatants'. 'I've great admiration for CP's brain and many of his qualities, but at best he's a Jesuit and a Machiavelli, while the [political] Travancoreans whom he tries to govern are as lousy a lot as I've come across anywhere—lying, mean, cowardly, conceited, intriguing, and packed full of envy, hatred, malice, and all uncharitableless.'[52]

A brief truce was negotiated between the government and the Congress during Princess Lalitha's wedding, which the agitators honoured, presumably due to respect for the Senior Maharani.[53] But then conflict resumed, till Gandhi himself advised the movement to quell its passion, following his exchange of letters with Sir CP in 1939. For the next several years, until the end of the Second World War, the State Congress would languish for most part at the periphery of the state's politics, resuming its activities after this hibernation at a more auspicious moment. The Dewan would obtain some respite through a 'Defence of Travancore' proclamation, by which all political activities during the Second World War were heavily repressed. Even the legislature became a government body, and as one leader of the Congress declared, was comprised of 'wooden hands, which will rise to support government policy at a word from government'.[54] A number of Congressmen took to Cochin, and when complaints were made to the Dewan there, the latter cuttingly responded to Sir CP: 'The Rule of Law is established in *this* State and His Highness the Maharajah has never exercised his powers in an arbitrary manner.'[55] The exiles, in other words, would not be sent back to face the government in Travancore, and Sir CP received a proverbial slap on his ministerial face.

It is noteworthy, however, that during the reign of Sethu Lakshmi Bayi, though there was a great deal of agitation against her from the Nairs, they were never crushed using force by the administration. The police instead deputed spies at their meetings and conveyed information on their proceedings to the Maharani, beyond which the state permitted such demonstrations. As Gandhi himself had noted with wonder at the time, the Maharani's government 'will not only tolerate but welcome agitation' since they demonstrated the mood of the public.[56] Even on the day of the Viceroy's visit in 1929 to commend her work in Travancore, while she prohibited a procession by the Nairs, the attendant protest meeting was allowed to continue and at no point were the police forced on the agitators even though the whole affair was embarrassing to the Maharani.[57] Now the tables had turned, for the demonstrators found that the government would not sit quietly and allow them free rein, and was willing to hit back and pay them in kind.

The Maharajah, of course, paid the price for his minister's autocracy by a dip in the popularity of his regime. As early as 1936, when Sir CP was appointed, the Political Secretary in Delhi had warned that despite his 'undoubtedly great ability', the new Dewan was not trusted by the people of the state, and that he 'would weaken the Maharajah's position with his subjects'.[58] And by 1938 Mr Skrine only confirmed this when he pointed out that the monarch and his family were no longer beheld on a high pedestal, even though nobody would openly criticise the royal family, and focused instead on hating the Dewan. 'The most striking feature of the situation,' he wrote, 'is the intense, almost hysterical, hatred shown by the educated and semi-educated classes for the Dewan. With a few exceptions, everyone in the State seems to long for his removal, and many yearn also for his ruin and disgrace.'[59] Indeed, such was the fear of this man that it is said people were afraid to even walk on the road outside his official residence, Bhakti Vilas.[60] Again, this was quite a serious contrast from Dewans like Mr Watts who remained accessible always, even inviting ridicule and criticism for not being overbearing enough with the politicians who then perceived them as weak. Sir CP, on the contrary, took no chances, and made it clear he was the only power in the land, whether they liked it or not.

It did not help that Sir CP strutted around as a most 'superior person' and was 'domineering and contemptuous of the common herd, incapable of suffering fools gladly'. To his credit, though, he was 'incorruptible by money and therefore hated by the race of politicians, wire-pullers, shady financiers, blackmailing journalists and others among whom corruption is universal and taken for granted. His weakness is for fame, not money,' felt Mr Skrine, who thought that he sincerely desired 'peace and prosperity for Travancore, fame and success for the present Ruler and his mother as well as for himself'.[61] But his *means* were not quite as noble as his intentions. 'His methods are Machiavellian; he rules by dividing, he bribes with office and other favours, he sets traps for his critics, and plays on the weaknesses of his enemies. It is no wonder that the man in the street does not love him.'[62] Instead of building strong institutions, the Dewan developed a power-serving patronage network with himself as its presiding epicentre.

But his crafty personality alone did not account for the hatred against him or for the 'widespread revolt against his administration', as the Resident continued:

> He is handicapped by the necessity for carrying out and justifying the ideas and ambitions of the Junior Maharani. Among those who know, this lady is the real 'villain of the piece'. She is arrogant, uncharitable, egotistical, bad-tempered, insular, and vindictive. This would not matter so much if

> she did not meddle in affairs of State, but she presses her favourites on the Dewan for appointments and promotion, listens to tales against those who are not her favourites and insists on action (often underhand) against them, suggests this measure, vetoes that, and otherwise interferes arbitrarily in the administration. Her influence over her son is so strong that for all the world can see, he and she act as one. Sir CP is so loyal to her that it is impossible to elicit from him the slightest hint that a particular action has been dictated by her; but I am absolutely certain that some of his most unpopular and (as has since turned out) mistaken ideas have emanated from the Junior Maharani. He is thus the target of much odium, which should rightly be aimed at his exalted mistress. In fact a great deal of it *is* directed at the Junior Maharani, for there is no doubt that she is cordially hated, partly for the unpleasant characteristics mentioned above and for her complete lack of pity and sympathy towards her son's subjects; partly for the feud which she carried on for years against the popular and respected Senior Maharani; and last but not least for her almost hypnotic influence over the young Maharajah and her usurpation *sub rosa* of ruling functions which he ought to be exercising on his own initiative. Sir CP as I have said bears a great deal of the odium for this state of affairs, because loyal Travancoreans dare not voice such sentiments towards their Ruler's mother. They abuse the Dewan instead; and perhaps they are right in demanding his removal as an alternative to getting rid of the Junior Maharani. For without his brains, his driving energy, his immense capacity for work, his skill, and above all his unswerving loyalty, she might easily have taken a back seat long ago.[63]

That said, though this controversial trinity controlled Travancore, the Resident felt there was to them no viable alternative. 'Not only is communalism rampant, but discipline, civic sense, mutual goodwill and cooperation, and genuine respect for authority are notably lacking in public life.' Nobody was pleased by anything and the education system required significant reforms. 'Sketchy, book-crammed education sadly deficient on the character-building side has spread all kinds of raw, undigested ideas, yearnings, and discontents, which are aggravated by the parlous economic state of the country due to gross over-breeding,' he added with palpable disgust. No matter what Sir CP did, he would receive 'nothing but jealous hostility from political rivals, abuse from profiteers whose monopolies are interfered with, and underhand attacks by the trouble-makers and intriguers who pervade public life'. Thus, while he had his notorious flaws, which Mr Skrine admitted were numerous, the politicians he dealt with were no better, so that the Dewan could always find a justification for more repression.[64]

In any case, an alternative would be just as problematic. 'In the first place the Maharajah and his mother are so united in their conviction of the justice of their cause and their faith in Sir CP, that nothing short of a direct command from His Excellency [the Viceroy] would move them, and this might result in abdication.' Then there was the fact that any successor to the Dewan would find it exceedingly hard to work, 'with the [Junior] Maharani sitting on his head and the trouble-makers and tale-bearers hard at work at undermining his influence all the time'. The Congress too would settle for none other than one of their own nominees. 'It would be impossible to grant this without committing the State to responsible government, which the rulers do not believe in and are determined not to promise.'[65] But Sir CP and the Junior Maharani themselves were liable, he felt, for this current crisis, even though they were equally the only combination capable of grappling with it firmly—for the time being at any rate.

> If they had been wiser Sir CP and the Maharani would have realised that you cannot have a dictatorship except on the solid basis of a well-organised and intensely loyal party, and of a thoroughly centralised and disciplined administrative machine. They would have felt their way carefully from the start, raised the standard of the public services, and doled out constitutional reforms and economic schemes year by year as required to maintain their popularity. Instead, in their passion for Travancore's glory, they launched out on ambitious innovations such as a bicameral Legislature, a University, State banking, Temple-entry, pretentious schemes for the uplift of the depressed classes, and vast hydroelectric and other public works. Character, technical skill, and experience were alike lacking in the personnel required to bring these schemes to fruition and they served merely to antagonise powerful vested interests, to flatter the Travancoreans and make them want more, and to boost the State out of all proportion to its achievements.[66]

The Resident was speaking plain power politics here, which was something the Senior Maharani had understood during the Regency; that reforms and schemes though necessary must be timed and that no monarchy could work outside the material and social context of its existence. Travancore was part of a larger framework of British India and of colonial rule, and there were limitations on what the royal family could and could not offer and achieve. The system of absolute despotism was also such that its ultimate unfairness awaited exposure, and benevolent government merely bought time to keep the monarchy in the good books of an increasingly demanding, restive population. The only way the royal family, in an age of proliferating democratic consciousness, could remain relevant was by rising above petty politics, being impartial in its attitude, and creating strong institutions that could accommodate the aspirations of their subjects or offer avenues for their frustrations to be vented without toppling the hierarchy. Sethu Lakshmi Bayi had worked in this direction and proved herself, earning, as Louise Ouwerkerk remarked, 'the unstinted love and respect of her people'.[67]

But the Junior Maharani returned to the age of royal patronage rather than institutional rule, and acted like 'a more amiable Catherine de Medici' who was 'fully recognised by the local people'. It was to her, states Ouwerkerk, that 'they went for favours, for jobs or promotions for themselves and their relatives. Inevitably she was surrounded by sycophants and flatterers who warped her judgement.'[68] She knew a great deal and was intelligent, 'but she wants to introduce too many changes at once, which is unrealistic'.[69] Where the royal family were meant to be as discreet as possible, revealing themselves strategically to sustain popularity, while retaining their quaint charm and semi-divine remoteness, the Maharajah's mother was everywhere. By 1940, a statue was erected of her in the capital, ostensibly by public subscription to recognise 'the part she played in the cause of humanity and in the all round progress of the state',[70] not helped by allegations that Christians were coerced to contribute and that surplus funds were diverted to Hindu organisations.[71] Where Sethu Lakshmi Bayi was awarded the Crown of India for her administrative prowess, in 1936 the Maharajah would openly request the Viceroy for a similar bauble for his mother.[72] The application, incidentally, was denied, just as the statue of the Junior Maharani would also disappear some years later, after it was allegedly decapitated.[73]

Similarly, while the Senior Maharani received honorary doctorates for her work, the Junior Maharani and her son, reported the Resident, donated Rs 1 lakh to a university that recriprocated with similar honours.[74] In imitation of the Paramount Power, orders and titles that sounded lavishly bombastic were designed, with little relevance for the masses. The effort ended in embarrassment, for no sooner had the 'Order of the Conch' (with the Junior Maharani as the 'Lady of the Order') been constituted, along with the 'Order of Martanda', than the Government of India strictly told the Maharajah to have them revoked.[75] In 1936, when discussions were on to federate the princely states under a new political structure, Sir CP informed Delhi that 'the price of Travancore's adhesion is the addition of 2 guns to the Ruler's permanent salute'. Negotiations were actually about the Rs 40 lakh, a monumental sum, the state lost every year due to an old Interportal Trading Convention from the reign of Ayilyam Tirunal, but evidently the Maharajah was 'prepared to make some financial sacrifice' and allow this bleeding to continue, if his dynasty were flattered with a more fashionable gun salute.[76] In other words, while the tide was flowing towards greater democratisation and ultimately to India's independence, the royal family were blinded by their own autocracy, revelling in obsolete notions of prestige and glory and in pursuit of impotent emblems of princely greatness.[77] Indeed, even five decades later, the Junior Maharani's son would refer to the 7,600 sq. miles of land that was Travancore as a veritable 'empire'.[78]

By 1944 things had not improved and the then Resident, Mr Todd, noted after a year in office that the state was a 'one man show' because of which 'intrigue and favouritism' flourished and in turn had 'driven out individualism and sapped energy and initiative'.[79] 'Although the Dewan's flair for publicity keeps [the] Maharajah and Maharani in a dignified limelight,' he added, 'I do not think the Ruling family are in close enough contact and sympathy with their people. The Senior Maharani, when Regent, was very popular with the people but the Junior Maharani does not seem to appeal to the common herd. The scandal attached by rumour to the association of the Junior Maharani and the Dewan can, I am sure, be discounted but there is no doubt that the former well appreciates her family's dependence on the protecting strength of their indomitable adviser.'[80]

> For some 10 years now Sir C.P. Ramaswami Iyer has been in Travancore. First as legal adviser to the Junior Maharani struggling to end the galling Regency of her rival, the Senior Maharani, then through the Federation negotiations and up through the many years as Dewan, Sir C.P. Ramaswami Iyer has become the only power in the land ... [He has a] quick brain and arresting personality ... [but was] Intolerant of opposition to his set purpose, contemptible [sic] of his colleagues—or rather subordinates, for he brooks no colleagues, he is yet too proud of his established reputation to associate himself with scandalous misrule or a weak case ... Vain, he is very susceptible to flattery, although he evaluates flattery from an Indian on a different scale from the flattery of a European. From the former he expects and demands it, from the latter he, at heart, prefers and feels complimented by, friendly candour. Likes to be treated as a cosmopolitan, man of the world rather than as an Indian; and although he pays lip service to nationalism and his religion

> he voices, privately, much contempt for his politically minded compatriots and the superstitions of the ultra-devout ... There is a grandiloquent bi-cameral legislature but driven on the tightest of bearing reins, and little individualism is shown by the opposition—or tolerated for long. The Dewan does not believe in democracy in an Indian State.[81]

Referring to the approach of Independence, Mr Todd felt Travancore would entertain, like other well-run political units in India, aspirations for freedom. 'But can,' he asked, 'sovereignty be sustained on imported talent and imported vitality? Many sovereign States import experts for a brief period and for a definite purpose, but what of a State which must import its Prime Minister and the heads of all important departments? Sovereignty,' the Resident concluded, 'is not in the name alone, but in the purity and temper of the metal.'[82] It was something of a prescient pronouncement, for when the time came, indeed the Maharajah would do his best to retain Travancore as an independent kingdom, aided, as always, by Sir CP in this mission which was, from its onset, doomed for disastrous failure. Travancore was forged on the eve of the British Empire in India, and the destiny of its Ivory Throne was also to fade with its patron power.

While the Dewan controlled all aspects of the administration, his efforts were not futile and were successfully reflected in the finances of the state. By 1943 the treasury collected Rs 375 lakh, and by 1944 the revenues were expected to exceed Rs 400 lakh.[83] Since the Second World War was raging, the Government of India were somewhat disappointed that only Rs 23 lakh had been offered that year for the war effort instead of a more generous amount.[84] But while these numbers were a natural progression from the historically well-administered system of the state, the *reputation* of the principality exceeded its due, mainly because, as the Viceroy put it, of 'much propaganda of a competitive and slightly aggressive kind'. He also felt that the government 'is a good deal less solid than that of Mysore, as it depends on the personality of the Dewan who seems to have a finger in every pie'.[85] In Mysore, the Maharajah had developed strong institutions, while in Travancore it was a sturdy Sir CP propping up a good-looking façade of stability. Writing in his diary in 1945, Lord Wavell noted:

> The Maharajah of Travancore is entirely overshadowed by his mother, the Junior Maharani, and by the very forcible Dewan, Sir C.P. Ramaswami Iyer. He is not altogether a fool, but does not have a chance with these two dominant personalities; there is no doubt that Travancore is a one-man show, and the one man is Sir C.P. There is no doubt about his efficiency, his

charm when he chooses to exert it, or his determination to get his own way. How good the state administration really is behind its impressive façade is hard to say.[86]

The practice, evidently, was for the Junior Maharani, the Maharajah and their Dewan to meet every day. 'Thatha would go to Kowdiar Palace in Trivandrum,' his granddaughter would write, 'dressed in a dhoti, long coat, turban, and *angavastram* (long cloth worn over the shoulder, sometimes around the neck), with a load of files. The Maharajah, Maharani, Thatha and officers concerned would all sit on the floor on mats in a big hall and hold discussions.'[87] Sometimes Sir CP's forceful dominance was less dignified; for example, once he walked into Kowdiar Palace and flung a file at the Maharajah, who was playing tennis. 'My Brother,' the Elayarajah would tell, 'was a perfect gentleman and instead of reacting, silently ignored and swallowed this affront. But I could not take it. I just could not digest the sight of my Brother being insulted thus. I paid him [Sir CP] back in the same coin.' The Maharajah's brother, who had something of a temper, picked up the file and flung it right back at the astonished Dewan.[88]

In many ways, in fact, the younger son of the Junior Maharani was proving to have a mind of his own, and strong convictions he would not renounce in the interests of simple obedience or mere courtesy. Writing about him as early as 1938, when he was only fifteen and about to appear at his first big public function as chief guest, the Resident mused that 'Sir CP will presumably write his speech for him, but the boy's got plenty of character and will of his own—much more than the pleasant young Maharajah unfortunately. There may be serious trouble one day in that quarter,' Mr Skrine mischievously added, 'not so much between the two brothers as between the Elayarajah and his imperious mother.'[89] The statement was an interesting one, and indeed by the end of the 1940s the Maharajah's brother would embark on some very unexpected plans, not least of which was to extend a warm hand of friendship to Sethu Lakshmi Bayi's side of the royal family.

18

Rivers of Blood

With the surrender of the Axis forces in the summer of 1945, the Second World War came to an end, culminating with the suicide of its wicked architect, Adolf Hitler. The honour of victory for the Allies in Europe was, however, largely a moral one for the time being, as emerging from the war they found, for the second time in a generation, their economies in monumental ruins, with grave social unrest simmering underneath. The world after 1945 was a new place, its previous character only barely recognisable. Great imperial houses had been toppled and emasculated; communism raised its head in a horrified Western heartland; Europe was divided; and the Cold War was about to commence. Great Britain, the world's most formidable empire, was about to forfeit its proud appellation of 'great', and the sun was beginning to set on the debris of what was once Pax Britannica. It was the dawn of a whole new era, shaped by an epic battle of ideology and politics between the United States and the Soviet Union, at the end of which destined to emerge was the world as we know it today.

The repercussions of these vast changes were naturally felt in India, the jewel in the British Empire's crown, yearning to cut loose and chart its own fate. With finances in a precarious state, and with Gandhi determined to wrest India free, the British Crown had no option but, ultimately, to concede Independence after two centuries of an unequal marriage. It was a time of public rejoicing in British India. The Congress and its arch-rival, the Muslim League, though, fought over the spoils of a hard-won war, doomed to divide India in violence. But what of those great 'Pillars of the Raj', those aristocrats and princes, without whom a proverbial handful of Englishmen could never have prevailed in a tumultuous subcontinent as this? Of those who saved the British in their time of need and financed their armies; whose loyalty during the Great Rebellion of 1857 tendered 'breakwaters in the storm which', as Lord Canning declared with grateful relief, 'would have swept us in one great wave'?[1] The fairy-tale wonder and extravagance of the Raj could never have flourished had it not been for the faithful allegiance of this assortment of India's most unpredictable, colourful gentlemen: the Maharajahs.

It was the British who, by the middle of the nineteenth century, united India, a chaotic patchwork of warring states and decayed empires, into a singular political and economic entity. Yet the destinies of two-fifths of the subcontinent, with all its many millions, remained in the hands of 'native' princes and chiefs (they were never acknowledged as kings). Lord Macaulay dismissed them as 'nominal sovereigns sunk in indolence and debauchery, chewing *bhang*, fondling concubines, and listening to buffoons' while others decried them as vulgar 'sinks of reaction and incompetence and unrestrained autocratic power'.[2] Of the nearly 600 regal houses in India, most were petty potentates presiding over 'postage stamp' principalities. Only forty qualified as 'real' princes, with the stately devices of royalty and incomes higher than at least a million rupees.[3] Their defences and foreign relations surrendered to the Paramount Power, they were in return guaranteed for their fealty a degree of internal autonomy. A hierarchy of jealously guarded and supremely bombastic privileges and titles, not to speak of carefully numbered gun salutes, distinguished and flattered the more important, wealthier princes from their lesser peers. At the apex stood, thus, the Nizam of Hyderabad, one of the richest men in the world who alone was entitled to the style of His *Exalted* Highness. At the bottom languished a 'prince' whose 'princely state' did not extend beyond a few acres of grassland nobody cared about.

As a rule, the Nawabs and Maharajahs of India were a race grown fat lording over the abiding miseries of their impoverished subjects. 'Though their lives are intertwined with the destinies of several millions of the human race,' lambasted one critic, 'few can boast to the qualifications or the character that entitles a man to assume the functions of kingship.'[4] Indeed, the vast majority of India's princes were known not for their emphatic solicitude for the masses as much as for the notoriously glamorous lifestyles they led, all at the expense of their suffering subjects. With an average of eleven titles, 5.8 wives, 12.6 children, 9.2 elephants shot, 2.8 private railway cars, 3.4 Rolls Royces, and 22.9 tigers killed, the Maharajahs had plenty to keep them merry while their people toiled through the business of everyday survival.[5] It was a peculiar sight in India to see splendid palaces towering above a barren setting of destitution and hardship. But the princes were by and large blind to the world around them, more interested in playing up their competitive ostentations, than applying themselves to good government.[6]

Thus, the robust Maharajah of Patiala, for instance, is said to have spent his time collecting concubines with great avidity; at the height of its glory his harem comprised 350 handpicked ladies, earning him the byname His *Exhausted* Highness. In Kapurthala the reigning prince declared he was a reincarnation of Louis IV of France and built himself a miniature Versailles in the Himalayan foothills.[7] The sixth Nizam of Hyderabad collected diamonds and baubles with a connoisseur's keenness, although he was perhaps better known for beginning a family tradition of sending out all his clothes to be laundered in Paris. Even when committing suicide, princes could not be more inventive; one particular prototype methodically drank himself to death in his favourite European hotel; his drink of choice: expensive champagne. Interestingly, their people too found remarkably creative means to attract princely attention for their problems. In an amusing episode, the Nizam ran over a poor old woman when out on a drive. A generous amount was granted to her family as compensation, but very soon observers noted that 'whenever the Nizam went motoring there was much difficulty in clearing the road of the aged poor, who had been deliberately put in the way by their impecunious relatives'.[8]

There were, of course, exceptions that proved this rule of royal depravity. For every dozen or so of degenerate, conceited princes, there was perhaps one good ruler who sought to provide his subjects a standard of life superior to that in British-ruled provinces. Mysore, one of the greatest princely states, was famously progressive and more industrialised than any other part of India. In Baroda, the British did its people a favour by deposing a Maharajah who spent his time commissioning carpets of pearls, and installing in his place a young prince who would earn the love and respect of his subjects by far-sighted policy. In the 1940s, the ruler of Jaipur imported a minister from Mysore and sought to replicate its successes in his desert principality, starting schools, abolishing purdah, and so on. And, of course, in the south there was Travancore, guided by a line of fairly enlightened rulers into the higher echelons of progressive governance, winning appreciation from all quarters.

It was quite natural, then, that when talk commenced of India's independence from British rule, the more prominent princely states despised being classed with the predominantly north Indian 'Rolls Royce' Rajahs, who were little more than exotic feudal lords and anachronisms that survived into modernity. Even some of those who viewed their principalities as personal estates, such as the Nizam of Hyderabad, entertained serious hopes of attaining complete independence owing to their wealth. In the late 1920s, when the Government of India contemplated dominion status for the subcontinent under Lord Irwin and desired to bring the princes within its purview, the latter fought strongly for their rights. The Paramount Power, whose influence arose from individual treaty relations with the Maharajahs, could not transfer such authority to any elected government that might rule in British India, they had argued. Travancore too, at the time under Sethu Lakshmi Bayi, made it clear that the state had every right to sign fresh alliances as an independent unit with any such elected government in greater India.[9] The principality, well administered, wealthy, and with a relatively moderate royal family, felt it *deserved* to be allowed to continue in power.

By 1946, however, the tide was flowing in a quite different direction. As Louise Ouwerkerk noted, 'When Independence drew near, the Princes changed from bulwarks into stumbling blocks.'[10] Repeated and determined attempts to constitute a federation, comprising princely states and British provinces, had failed. Independence for India looked more feasible than ever, and the Maharajahs began to fret about their future. It was at this time that Sir CP, who had in the 1930s advocated Travancore's claim to be treated as independent in any future arrangements contemplated by the Paramount Power, decided to strengthen the position internally so as to weather the storm inevitably lying ahead. He knew, tells Robin Jeffrey, 'that public opinion in the State would oppose independence, and favour Travancore's joining an Indian union led by Gandhi, Nehru, and the Indian National Congress'. And so, 'if the plans for an independent Travancore were to have a chance of success, he would need the support of local politicians'.[11] Unfortunately for the Dewan, however, from the time he arrived in the state in 1931, through the Abstention Movement and later the demand for responsible government in 1938–39, he had been far from a darling to local leaders, most of whom had, at some point or the other, had to languish in jail at his authoritarian instance.

By the end of the war, the Government of India once again allowed elected governments in the provinces (they had resigned in 1939 when India was dragged into war without the consent of its people), and Sir CP realised that, for all their hatred towards him, the leaders of the Travancore State Congress, 'were yearning for a share' themselves in the local administration.[12] These men, after all, were part of the legislature before the movement for responsible government forced them into the political wilderness. In 1944 they had returned, with smaller numbers, and acted as a popular opposition to the government, but they wished now to be more than suspended in a state of perpetual hostility. They had the ambition and skills to function in government, and were individuals of education and standing. The Dewan decided to exploit the natural frustration that arose among many of them, as a result of his own policies ironically, and present himself now in a new, more friendly avatar as a messiah of change prepared to work with, rather than against, them. The gates of the government, he determined, would be thrown open to the political outcasts, in what was meant to be a moment unique in its magnanimity.

Early in 1946, therefore, Sir CP announced a grand scheme evidently based on the 'American Model', to share power in a partnership between the princely regime (with himself as its executive), and its elected representatives. 'He appears to have calculated,' Jeffrey continues, 'that he could devise a constitutional carrot, tempting enough to win [the politicians'] cooperation, yet one that would leave the substance of power with the princely government.'[13] Adult suffrage was offered but there would be no elected minister at the helm of affairs. The prerogative to appoint the executive head, it was clarified, would continue to vest with the Maharajah. Those elected representatives, then, would instead be formed into committees that could oversee different aspects of the administration.[14] The idea was not at all an innovation by Sir CP; as early as the 1920s, Sethu Lakshmi Bayi had involved, precisely for these reasons and with astute objectives, members of the public through boards in the process of government. The Maharajah's administration wound this down, realising belatedly its virtues some fifteen years later, at its own peril; by this time ambitions had exceeded the old wine in new bottles that the royal regime had on offer.

The Travancore State Congress responded to the invitation by first terming it 'definitely retrograde and undemocratic'. But behind the rhetoric they were exhausted, and perhaps driven by the ambition of some of their own leaders, proved willing to negotiate terms with Sir CP.[15] Others, however, were not anxious to play. Trouble arose not so much from the State Congress as from a new element in the state's politics: communists. They were backed mainly by the Ezhava community, in alliance with 'agricultural workers, boatmen, fishermen, and various other lower occupational groups'.[16] The Ezhavas, ever the bane of Sir CP's glory in Travancore, had become even stronger by the 1940s, after successfully battling for temple entry in the last decade. And their emergence was married to industrial successes in the two important districts of Alleppey and Shertallai in north Travancore, which also boasted the first trade union in the state, the Travancore Labour Association. By now it had transformed itself into the Coir Factory Workers' Union, and with 7,400 fee-paying members, this was perhaps the biggest of fifty unions in the state; Shertallai alone had eleven with 15,000 out of 20,000 local workers registered.[17] All of them, it became clear, were prepared to stand up to the Dewan and scotch his latest flirtations with the State Congress.

The workers had initially, in fact, supported the State Congress during its agitation for responsible government in the late 1930s. But the crushing of that movement and the subsequent loss of steam, on Gandhi's instructions, alienated their faith in what they now perceived as a bourgeois party. By 1940 it was happily, then, that a new Travancore branch of the Communist Party of India (CPI) assumed control of the unions and the thousands of workers affiliated to them.[18] It was these very workers and skilled labourers, not the educated middle classes, who now obstructed the compromise contemplated between the State Congress and Sir CP, determined to demand complete and absolute responsible rule in Travancore. As always, when the Dewan's calculations floundered due to an unexpected contingency, he utilised all the forces at his disposal to have his way. As one scholar states:

> The government of Sir C.P. Ramaswami Iyer prepared to face the threat with a combination of the carrot and the stick. First it unleashed a reign of repression aimed especially against organised labour, both industrial and agricultural. Shertallai was made the centre of these repressive measures. The area had a number of big landlords who had become angered at the new activities of the agricultural labourers and provided full support to the government, offering even their residence and other buildings for use as police and army camps ... The All Travancore Trade Union Congress (ATTUC) expressed its protest against these by organising a one-day general strike. In October 1946 C.P. called a tripartite conference at which he offered the ATTUC representatives what is said to have been an attractive economic package as well as representation in [the new] parliament on condition that the unions accept his proposed constitutional reforms and call off their political agitation. The offer was rejected. Within days after this, the two taluks of [Alleppey] and Shertallai were filled with units of the police, the reserve police, and the army, who set up camps at various centres throughout the region.[19]

In response to the Dewan's intimidation, the unions set up 'people's camps' of their own, with volunteers armed with spears and country weapons; the five camps in Shertallai alone had 2,378 workers, ready for a confrontation with the government.[20] On 22 October the unions struck work, days before the new 'American Model' was to come into force. Things took a violent turn when on 24 October a group of what were now considered rebels attacked a police camp in Punnapra. In the skirmish that followed, a number of policemen and many workers were killed. Sir CP immediately declared martial rule and took personal charge of the police and army. 'Rivers of blood', as the Valiya Koil Tampuran put it, were about to flow in Travancore.[21]

On 27 October the army surrounded a camp at Vayalar, where they encountered stiff resistance from the rebels. Machine-gun fire was then ordered and more than 150 people lost their lives. Similar attacks were mounted on other camps, killing another 130 individuals elsewhere that same day. 'It is estimated that about a thousand people lost their lives [altogether] in the Punnapra-Vayalar outbreak,' remarks the historian Sreedhara Menon.[22] As the CPI would later declare, this agitation became 'a bright page' in the 'revolutionary memories of Kerala' and a 'red signature in the history' of the land in 'a struggle of resurrection of self righteous workers against all injustices of a repressive, exploitative state'.[23] Equally significantly, it was the first time since the rebellion of Velu Tampi against an unpopular monarch and his government in the early nineteenth century that the people of Travancore had resorted to arms against the dispensation now ruling them. The distance of the regime, in an ivory tower of its own, shielded loyally by Sir CP, was perhaps most evident in that while the streets flowed with the blood of his subjects in Punnapra–Vayalar, the Maharajah was busy in the capital making merry with the Governor of Madras and other distinguished guests at a grand banquet.[24]

With the army entering the fray, and with many lives lost, the movement quickly disintegrated. But it had won a moral victory. Punnapra–Vayalar was 'a rude shock to public opinion all over the State and stiffened the attitude of the people against the Dewan', who was now more despised than ever.[25] By 31 October the strikes were called off and more than sixty organisations were banned, including the ATTUC and the CPI. 'Many leaders and participants of the revolt were jailed and tortured, many went underground, and the movement seemed to have been crushed for the time being.'[26] But it cost Sir CP the goodwill of the Congress too, not only in Travancore but also outside. During an event he attended in Bombay, 'a thousand Malayalis' came to demonstrate against him with posters bearing the words 'Punnapra-Vayalar' and the man was compelled to use the back door to leave the venue. 'Hatred,' noted Louise Ouwerkerk, 'was swelling to bursting point.'[27] Given the outrage among the public, all hopes for the new 'American Model' fell through unceremoniously. When the offer was first made, workers had declared: 'American Model, *Arabikadalalil*': take your American Model and dump it in the Arabian Sea. While Sir CP didn't quite do that, it became clear there was no way his constitutional reform was going to succeed now. So Travancore returned to the absolute rule of its Dewan for all practical purposes as it ventured into the historic year of 1947.

On 18 February 1947 the great patricians of Britain assembled in Parliament with the elected representatives of their people to hear from their Prime Minister, as historians have termed it, 'a funeral oration for the British Empire'.[28] 'His Majesty's Government,' announced Clement Attlee, 'wishes to make it clear that it is their definite intention of take the necessary steps to effect the transference of power into responsible Indian hands by a date not later than June 1948.'[29] It was a stunning declaration. The fabulous journey of a small mercantile nation from its tiny, frosty island to building the world's greatest and most imposing empire had come to an end. 'The loss of India,' Winston Churchill had years before warned, 'would be final and fatal to us. It could not fail to be part of a process that would reduce us to the scale of a minor power.'[30] He was correct. Britain's days of glory were coming to an end, it's decline hastened by the ravages of war.

The task of relinquishing British rule in India was entrusted to the thoroughly flamboyant and famously charming Lord Mountbatten, a great grandson of Queen Victoria, cousin to the reigning (and final) King Emperor, not to speak of a dozen other European monarchs, and an accomplished naval figure and wartime hero. It was an unorthodox selection for a lofty office that had hosted such glacially cold characters like Lord Curzon. Many considered Mountbatten 'a playboy who used his royal connection to slip out of his dinner jacket into a naval uniform, and temporarily abandon the dance floor of the Café de Paris for the battlefield'.[31] He was wealthy (mainly through marriage to a glamorous heiress) and had the looks of a Hollywood film star, an extraordinary contrast from the sedate and soldier-like Lord Wavell, his predecessor in Delhi. He himself was at first most reluctant to take up the job, trying to persuade the king to find someone else. But that was not to be. In divorcing Britain from its greatest treasure in the East, George VI hoped to project his best face. And Louis Mountbatten was that chosen face.

Having arrived in India, Mountbatten got down to business and parleyed with all the important national leaders. He struck a close friendship with Nehru, and found Gandhi, who inflicted his favourite, but fairly revolting, goat's curds on him, to be 'rather like a little bird'.[32] He even struggled to charm his way to win Jinnah's trust. In what was perhaps inevitable, eventually the bloody partition of India was announced, and the Mountbatten Plan, as it was called, was declared to the world on 3 June 1947. The princely states were told that, at least in theory, the Paramount Power's relationship with them would terminate, and they would be free to choose their own destinies. In effect, this meant picking either India or Pakistan for most Maharajahs. Some, however, like Hyderabad, Kashmir and Travancore decided they would elect to stay independent, unique as they were in their own ways. On 11 June, therefore, Sir CP ambitiously, and as it would turn out, wishfully, announced that on 15 August 1947 when Britain officially resigned the Government of India, 'In law as well as in fact, Travancore will become an independent country.'[33]

As Sreedhara Menon states, in doing this, the Dewan 'was only echoing His Masters' Voice or to put it more correctly, that of Their Royal Highnesses of Travancore, the son and the mother'.[34] A few days later the Maharajah featured on local radio to declare personally that 'Travancore will reassume its independence and sovereignty in full measure.'[35] The news was not received with enthusiasm in any quarter, save a dwindling handful of royalists. The declaration of independence, the Resident informed Delhi, had become a subject of 'sharp controversy' though Sir CP explained that the decision was taken 'when the [Indian National] Congress accepted the partition of India', adding untruthfully that it had the blessings of 'a vast majority' of the people.[36] Travancore was again, then, launched into 'the vortex of a political struggle' as the Congress rejected this quest for freedom, and 'the government resorted to a series of repressive measures to meet the situation'.[37] The Dewan in the meantime hopelessly entertained grand plans of seeking United Nations membership, even defending his stand to London by playing on fears attendant upon the slowly materialising Cold War. 'Travancore,' he announced, influenced by his first-hand hatred of communists, 'cannot be forced to join a Dominion whose leaders have at this critical juncture in world history established diplomatic relations with the Soviet Republic.'[38] The State Congress in the meantime was treated roughly, as a telegram from one of its leaders suggests:

> Terrorist organisation composed of *goondas* formed throughout the State under control of police and other Government agencies to wreck public

> meetings and assault public men ... Life of public men in danger. Members of [these] organisations parade public streets arms with *lathis*, knives and other weapons ... Life and property insecure ... Condition rapidly degenerating into widespread violence ... Travancore subjected to unbridled dictatorship by an irresponsible non-Travancorean Dewan.[39]

While agitation picked up around the state, Sir CP met with representatives of the British Crown to whom he complained that the Paramount Power was pushing the princes around hastily. 'He then went on to say that Travancore had no wish to have anything to do with the communal questions which had split [India]. They had no quarrel with either India or Pakistan but wished to be left alone. He was convinced in his own mind that civil war was more or less inevitable—that it would take place within a short time' and that 'even Mr Gandhi must inevitably come round to this view'.[40] The Dewan was invited to Delhi to confer with the Viceroy, who knew that his scheme for independence was a dangerous one and decided to coax him to get the Maharajah to accede his state to Nehru's India.

But Sir CP 'was going to the meeting determined to reject any such proposal outright. He was, however, concerned about the threats of an economic boycott of Travancore by India.'[41] By this time with his characteristic, though in this instance misguided, proactive zeal, the Dewan had even negotiated an agreement with Jinnah 'for the supply of foodstuffs from Pakistan' and 'it had already been agreed to exchange representatives between Travancore and Pakistan. He would also send representatives to other countries, for example Turkey. Whether His Majesty's Government recognised what he was doing at this stage did not immediately concern him.'[42] Mountbatten found Sir CP, 'who has been bombarding me with telegrams and issuing statements to the press', very emotionally agitated about the whole affair and sought to calm him down first.[43]

> At my meeting with him on the 22nd July he started off by presenting his own case through the medium of a series of files. The first of these contained a number of rather amusing cartoons, to which he took the greatest exception, and in particular one published that very morning showing him being spanked by me at this very meeting! The next contained a number of rude cuttings about himself. I advised him to follow the example of Lord Balfour and not to read the newspapers if he was going to let himself get upset in this way. The next file contained cuttings to prove that Gandhi was a dangerous sex maniac who could not keep his hands off young girls. He considered him to be the most dangerous influence in India, and said that if he insisted on

> backing the unstable Nehru against the realistic Patel he would break up the Congress Party within two years. Sir C.P. said that he was not prepared to ally himself with such an unreliable Dominion.
>
> By the end of an hour, Sir C.P. had worked off his emotional upset. He claimed that the statements which he himself had made were devised for the consumption of the people of Travancore itself, who were the highest educated in India. He declared that Travancore would never accede to the Dominion of India: he had indeed already made preliminary terms with Mr Jinnah, including a trade agreement. I pointed out to Sir C.P. that there could be no objection on the part of the Dominion of India to a trade treaty between Travancore and Pakistan. I went on to say that the States have never controlled their own foreign affairs and defence; and to emphasise the advantages of accession on these two subjects and on communications.[44]

Finally, declared the Viceroy with characteristic modesty, 'after I had worked on him for more than two hours, he came round as far as to say he might consider a treaty with India. I felt that we had made some progress and let him go and sent V.P. Menon to work on him.'[45] But by the next day Vallabhbhai Patel made it clear that Travancore could have no special treaty with India and would have to accede like all the other principalities. Mountbatten also informed Sir CP that money was already being channelled into the State Congress 'in anticipation of starting internal trouble' should the Maharajah not accede by 15 August, 'and that I was confident that there was more to follow'. The Dewan then asked the Viceroy to write the Maharajah a letter with all his proposals. 'As I gather the Maharajah is completely under Sir CP's thumb, I cannot but feel that this advice has at least left the door open for Sir CP to come in at the last possible moment, provided he finds that I have been able to get every other State into line.'[46]

Within ten days of this meeting between the Dewan and the Viceroy, however, the Maharajah cabled 'though not without hesitation' his consent to accede the state with India.[47] A number of events and considerations led to a change of heart after those early, and ill-adviced, public declarations of independence. The Maharajah at some level seemed to have calculated that the Paramount Power would assist princes like him in preserving their sovereignty. But as Sir CP warned him two years before, 'English character in general and Englishmen in particular will always swim with the tide. To rely upon British help and advice would be unwise.'[48] But perhaps what affected the Maharajah more was an incident on 25 July. Sir CP was the chief guest at a music concert, where as usual he reasserted the impending 'new era of sovereign independent status for Travancore'. The music began and ended, and the time of his departure came. That is when the lights suddenly went out and an assailant attacked the Dewan with a billhook. Only the angavastram wrapped around his neck in his usual style, and trained breath control saved Sir CP as he was rushed to his doctors.[49] Rattled, in the palace the hitherto cocooned Maharajah realised he had to change his mind. On 28 July the Dewan wrote to him a serious (and historically fascinating) letter from his hospital bed:

> On my return from Delhi and after reading the narrative I deliberately advocated the cause of accession subject to the conditions and concessions made by the Viceroy, so that you may not hear only one side. The next day I gave you my own point of view. The alternative is either accession i.e. becoming a part of the Dominion or treaty or alliance or being independent. There is no middle course and no face saving formula. This was clear from my talk with the Viceroy. If you accede you get some advantages but are not different from Baroda, Gwalior and Patiala except as to customs and some financial matters. If you do not accede, you will have to fight a hard battle with some assistance from Jinnah in the forthcoming civil war in India (which is certain within six months). I expect the rise of half a dozen principalities in India (as in the 18th century) after the massacre of the Congress leaders (in November and December). Those who can fight out the terrible battle will emerge as rulers but the risk of life and property is 75 to 25. I realised this some months ago and made it clear to Your Highness and you then decided to fight it out. ... The events that have happened must have made a great impression on you. They have not changed my mind but made me fully realise that your lives are in jeopardy and those of persons near and dear to you. It is either death or victory ... If you consider that your people are not ready for a fight and that they are not worth fighting for, the path of compromise is inevitable. Such compromise or concession should, if it is to be effective, be wholehearted. Accession as suggested by the Viceroy with the concessions made by him is the first essential.[50]

The result was that the Junior Maharani and the Maharajah, who had so far hoped to 'fight it out' now sheepishly changed their mind, not least when it became clear that there were those who were capable of making violent attacks on even someone like Sir CP, who inspired such dread and fear. Mountbatten noted with some smug satisfaction then: 'Shortly after [Sir CP's] return, he was assaulted with a billhook and very nearly killed. The [Congress] turned the heat full on and Travancore immediately gave in. The Maharajah telegraphed his acceptance of the Instrument of Accession to me personally, and C.P.'s friends have been trying to get Patel to call off the [agitation of the Congress]. He is trying to do this but is having very considerable difficulty, since C.P. had really driven them beyond endurance. The adherence of Travancore after all C.P.'s declarations of independence has had a profound effect on all the other States and is sure to shake the Nizam.'[51] The vacillating Nizam would, as it happened, require some military persuasion, and there is every possibility that had Sir CP and the Maharajah remained determined in their previous position, 'Nehru would have marched the [Indian] army into Travancore' as well.[52]

By the end of July Sir CP realised that responsible rule would now have to be implemented, preparing therefore to resign from his position. 'It is impossible for me to function here as one of several Ministers or what is inevitable under the [expected] Constitution, as a kind of Secretary to H.H.,' he wrote. 'By temperament and training, I am unfit for compromises, being autocratic and over decisive. I don't fit,' he concluded, finally acknowledging the writing on the wall, 'into the present environment.'[53] In his decline everyone in Travancore abandoned the man, and an exit was his only option. On 19 August 1947, after twelve years of ruling Travancore and undoubtedly taking it to unprecedented levels of prosperity (revenues now stood at Rs 9 crore), Sir CP retired from the Dewan's office as the most hated premier in all its history. Ever so canny and clever, the man who really made the Junior Maharani and the last Maharajah of Travancore, ultimately failed to choose the right side in his final battle with history. He left for his house in Ooty, and for all his material contributions to the state, its people were delighted to see the back of him.

A fortnight after his departure, the politically chastened Maharajah announced a fresh constitution, inaugurating, at long last, responsible rule in Travancore. A proclamation issued called for 'a representative body consisting of persons elected on the basis of adult franchise' in Travancore, to meet no later than 1 January 1948. Only matters pertaining to the royal family, temples, and other such subjects were excluded from its purview, but for the first time the state would have an elected Dewan.[54] P.G.N. Unnithan, a senior government official and relative of the royal family, was appointed to lead the state in the meantime.[55] After State Congress leaders were released from prison and all negotiations were completed, on 24 March 1948 the state's first popularly elected government then came to power. The new minister was Pattom Thanu Pillai, and others in his administration included C. Kesavan and T.M. Varghese, all of whom had the unique distinction of not only being Congressmen, but also of having been imprisoned by the very state they now ruled during the regime of their hated predecessor.[56]

Sir CP, in the meantime, was destined to lead the last two decades of his life in a sort of cushioned obscurity. He now converted into an admirer of the nationalists. 'May I take this opportunity,' he wrote to Patel, 'to convey to you my sincere felicitations,' adding how be could not 'refrain from paying my tribute to the consummate talents of leadership manifested by you and Pandit Jawaharlal Nehru'.[57] Perhaps having realised belatedly the turn of the tide, Sir CP decided to placate the very men he once cordially despised. By 1958, he would even tell a blatant lie by claiming that what he had advocated for Travancore was not 'independence' but 'autonomy'.[58] For all this, Sir CP appears to have left Travancore with a bitter taste in his mouth. Writing to the Maharajah in 1949, he returned titles and honours the latter bestowed on him, because of the ruler's 'acquiescence [in] or approval of the removal of the bust in the Legislative Chamber and Your Highness' silence or inaction in respect of [the declaration of a certain Congress leader] that he knew my assailant and was prepared to produce him'.[59]

What relations, if any, he maintained in the years that followed with the Junior Maharani and the Maharajah are not known. But as Louise Ouwerkerk would remark, 'At no time either at the height of his power or after his fall, did he cast the blame for the disastrous policies where it belonged', i.e., at the doors of Kowdiar Palace.[60] 'He was not a free agent: he supported their policies—even those that were foolish and impracticable, he announced them as his own—he defended them, worked them out, took the blame for what went wrong, braved the storms of hatred and calumny and the threats to his life. He was indeed a "daring pilot in extremity".'[61] Even in his fall, he remained dignified enough not to vent frustration at his former royal masters in Travancore, though his general opinion about Indian princes seems to offer an insight into his regret. 'Generally speaking,' he would dryly observe in 1948, 'all the great Kshatriya rulers—descendants of the Sun and Moon—behave like mendicants and sycophants and have no more spirit than a parcel of frightened rabbits or sheep. They deserve [their] fate and I congratulate Patel on the brilliant results of his [policy to get princely states to accede to India].'[62]

Sir CP became, in retirement, an international speaker and served as the vice chancellor of two universities, since Nehru refused to give him any greater role ('This man's perfidy is too recent to be overlooked,' he reportedly remarked).[63] In 1966, aged eighty-seven, he went to London to collect material for what would have been his riveting memoirs. But he died there suddenly on the 26 September, sitting in an armchair at the Liberal Club.[64] A.G. Noorani says in a description of the man, 'Friend and foe alike spoke of his gifts in the superlative. An erudite lawyer, gifted advocate, and born administrator, this consummate politician was also deeply interested in the arts, especially Carnatic music, and in literature. Clarity of thought and precision in expression were matched by a sense of humour and gift of repartee. Add to these an impressive personality and you get the measure of a forceful personality admired by most, respected by many, feared by some, but distrusted by a significant number.'[65] As one of the conspirators in his assassination attempt would later add: 'We did not mean to kill him; killing was too good for him. We meant to send him away from the state humiliated and disgraced—and we succeeded.'[66] Travancore, an awkward entity created with the devoted assistance of Tamil Brahmins, went down also with one of the greatest Tamil Brahmins who ever lived. And its dynasty's most loyal adherent became also its ultimate gravedigger.

As war rumbled halfway across the world in Europe, and while Sir CP and the Junior Maharani committed themselves to a battle against communists, life in Satelmond Palace in the 1940s had continued with an isolated, dreamlike tranquillity. Great changes were, it was known, rapidly approaching, indeed occurring with each passing day, and the Senior Maharani was horrified by the repression that had been unleashed in the state. But nobody was certain what precisely the future held in store. A keen eye was levelled on their disintegrating surroundings, growing more and more violent, and on the tottering world at large. Sethu Lakshmi Bayi was by now hors de combat, having surrendered to the Junior Maharani after the Sripadam dispute in 1939. The avenues for harassment were rapidly depleting and by the early 1940s there was little left for the authorities to rake up at her expense. Her estate in Peermade was seized by the Maharajah—it would be returned after Independence by the Indian government.[67] Then, in 1941, the Maharajah threatened to terminate her pension if she did not pay him regular courtesy calls. But if he was looking to pick a fight, he was treated instead to the uncomplaining obedience of his injunctions by a disappointed woman. Despite being older than his mother, the Senior Maharani yielded to present herself and pay her respects at Kowdiar Palace as and when its masters pleased.[68]

Having surrendered everything she had, whether it was status in the royal family, official duties in the Sripadam, or even the management of her wider ménage, Sethu Lakshmi Bayi found her mind evolving from a feeling of deep hurt and pain to a sense of considerable liberation. It was also a moral victory for her, since the people of Travancore recognised and empathised with her. 'The general feeling was that the Senior Maharani was not treated the way she deserved to be,' states one prominent individual from the time,[69] and successive Residents also noted that one of the primary causes for the Junior Maharani's unpopularity was her harassment of her widely respected cousin. But Sethu Lakshmi Bayi did not concern herself with a contest with the Junior Maharani any more. That phase of her life had ended (not due to choice to begin with), and she rose above it all with an almost ascetic determination, which also served as the only moral consolation and historical weapon for one in her position. The pomp and glamour of royal life was maintained around her carefully, but she knew it was a shell devoid of all its meaning. So she cared no longer for that old world, dissolving, much like she had during the unhappy 1910s, into a world of books and family. And indeed, this was a more joyous immersion than dwelling on injustices, past or present.

'The day at Satelmond Palace,' the Maharani's nephew would recall, 'began at around 6:30 in the morning. It was always the Valiya Koil Tampuran who was up first because he had to have breakfast before seven o'clock. And while his meal was served, he would listen to Soviet news on the radio! Of all the channels, he preferred the English broadcast from Russia, since it was wartime and he wanted to hear the "other angle" to the story. He had an old, loud radio with a valve and Exide batteries. Every few days it would have to be carried to the garage and recharged. It was so blaring that we could hear it even in our part of the grounds. And when the Russian broadcast began, everyone knew it was time to wake up and get on with the day.' Rama Varma would then stroll around the gardens, and sit down to read a formidable stack of newspapers. 'He spoke Tamil well, but he couldn't read it, and one of his menservants used to read the Tamil papers from the stack, loud, from end to end, for him. It was fascinating to watch this activity every day, and to observe the Valiya Koil Tampuran sit there, his eyes shut, absorbing all the information.'[70]

By this time Sethu Lakshmi Bayi would be dressed, and ready to start her day. 'She no longer had those long hours of prayers, and spent most of her time in her enormous bedroom. There was on one side an exquisite canopied four-poster bed, which she used as her night bed and slept in. But once she got ready in the morning, she would not sit there and instead used her day bed, with bolsters and cushions for support. She could sit and read like this for hours, and if she tired, she would recline and continue.'[71] At some point in the morning the Valiya Koil Tampuran would, as usual, arrive to pay his respects. 'It was so wonderful to watch them,' Princess Rukmini recalls. 'They had such a formal marriage. Grandfather always addressed her as "Your Highness", but she didn't call him anything in particular. He never took a seat in her room till she asked one of her maids to bring in a chair. And while they were together, all these women would wait in the anteroom.'[72] It was a curious situation and whether, by now, husband and wife maintained conjugal relations is not known.

Though the Maharani's lunches remained elaborate affairs, she only hosted banquets on festive occasions, preferring to eat in the privacy of her room ordinarily. Everyone else also had their own personal kitchen arrangements into the 1940s, with their own menus and requirements, all guided, however, by a member of the palace staff who informed 'concerned members of the family of their obligations on special days in the Hindu calendar'.[73] Rama Varma had a simple meal of his own. 'He only ever ate toast, roasted vegetables and something they called *karipatti*, which was made from jaggery of the palmyra tree.'[74] Up on the first floor, Princess Lalitha and Kerala Varma, who had started something of an innovation by sharing a bedroom, ate their meals separately, since their timings varied from those of the parents. Princess Indira, similarly, dined independently in her own apartments, because her husband Kuttan was perpetually unwell right from the time of their wedding, and could not move about too much. The happiest and most delighted beneficiaries of this system and the delicious variety it offered were the children. 'We could join grandfather if we liked,' remembers Princess Parvathi, 'but we had to let him know in advance so that he could instruct his cooks. Or we could eat with our parents who enjoyed very relaxed meals. Grandmother's were the grandest, and we all sat on silk mats and ate, and aunt's were rather quiet and dignified, though I remember her frequently eating with grandfather too.'[75]

After lunch everyone resumed their various activities. The Maharani would go back to read or enjoy an afternoon siesta. If she were in the library, the girls often joined her. 'We would all sit down around her, and she would read to us from English books or from Malayalam novels. My sister Uma could never sit for too long, and she used to run off at the first opportunity she got! Grandmother never said anything, but when she later asked us questions from the book we were reading and debriefed us about the story, Uma would be in a fix. She would try her best to persuade us to tell her the stories, but we wouldn't tell her!'[76] Princess Uma, as it happened, preferred spending the afternoons with her grandfather. 'At around three o'clock he used to drink some coconut water, and then prepare for his walk, when I would join him,' she remembers. 'He had a wonderful collection of jokes and loved a laugh. I used to be a handful in those days, and one of my favourite afternoon activities was to hide his belongings in all sorts of curious places. He had a lovely collection of walking sticks, with engraved silver tops. I used to sneak into his place to cart these out, and then find some forgotten chandelier somewhere and hang them there. He always knew who had done it, but he humoured me.'[77]

The girls also, however, went their own way later in the afternoon. Rukmini was the Maharani's pet and perpetual companion. 'Though she was our grandmother too,' tells Parvathi, 'Uma and I found the Maharani a little awe-inspiring and even unapproachable sometimes. She always had so many people around her, and such an aura. But Rukmini was always with her. While we played outside, she would be inside, right next to grandmother, playing board games with her, or reading a book, or having long conversations on some childish subject or the other.'[78] Indeed, Sethu Lakshmi Bayi evolved an unusual fondness towards her eldest granddaughter, which was to last all her remaining life, singling out Princess Rukmini to receive her emotional as well as financial largesse. 'She was always a very smart, attractive child,' tells Princess Indira, 'and she was mother's first grandchild. So she became attached to her and doted on her, to the extent that my sister used to worry the Maharani would spoil the girl.'[79] 'I think,' tells Sethu Lakshmi Bayi's nephew, 'she looked at Rukmini as heiress to the Attingal lineage. Even in terms of features and complexion, they were similar.'[80] Rukmini herself admits her special treatment.

> I remember once breaking a fabulous marble statue at Kovalam. I ought to have got a real whack but grandmother scolded the servants instead. In fact when father scolded me now and then for some mischief or the other, I would run and tell grandmother, and she would then tell father off for scolding me. Another time I remember sitting in a chair near her and reading, and by accident I dropped the book from my hands. She wouldn't let me pick it up, and summoned one of her maids instead. She didn't do this for the others, or even for herself. But for some reason, she pampered me till my parents were worried it would all go to my head. Whatever I did, grandmother never scolded me. That was one of the things my sisters resented. She would reprimand them for things but I could get off scot-free no matter what![81]

But even Rukmini could not always have her way. Miss Watts, now quite old, was a regular visitor at Satelmond Palace, calling at least once a week. 'She was a tall lady—rather plump, with curly hair and twinkling hazel eyes, behind round, gold-rimmed glasses,' Princess Lakshmi would later say. 'She was a very jolly woman, and we used to look forward to her visits because she would bring the most delicious guava toffee I have ever eaten.'[82] On one particular visit, however, Miss Watts brought with her not only her usual toffee, cake or other presents she always carried for the Maharani, but also a pig! 'She presented the pig to me,' laughs Princess Rukmini, 'and I was so very overjoyed at my new pet. I think Uma and Parvathi had mixed feelings about it, but I was certain grandmother would let me keep it in my room. You can then imagine how crestfallen I was when she said, "Nothing doing, and you had better leave that animal outside." She pampered me, but grandmother had not the remotest inclination to allow a pig to trot about her palace halls!'[83]

While Rukmini, thus, spent her time with Sethu Lakshmi Bayi, Uma would be running around with restless energy. 'She couldn't sit in one place for more than a few minutes,' laughs Princess Parvathi, 'and before you knew it, she was in the next room, trying to climb onto something or wriggling into a giant bison skull, and god knows what! I had no alternative but to run after her, and often when she played a prank, I was punished for it as a reluctant accessory to the crime.'[84] One of the favourites of all the children was troubling, rather unmercifully, the soldiers at the gate. As per custom, every time these guards encountered a member of the royal family, normally on entering or leaving the palace premises, they had to stand up, present arms, blow the trumpet, and play the state anthem. 'Uma would stealthily evade all our servants and pattakkars, with me in tow, and walk up and down the drive ten times, so these poor men couldn't get a moment's rest. And then, just when they sat down, glad to see our backs, she would jump out of a bush somewhere, and the soldiers would be back on their tired feet—trumpets, drums, and all! It was quite entertaining for us girls though we did harass those poor souls a great deal, now that I think of it.'[85]

The little Princess Lakshmi was too young at this time, and spent most of her time with nannies and her mother, sometimes peering into the schoolroom where her sisters had their lessons. Rukmini had a set of her own tutors, while Uma and Parvathi learnt from another group. 'We had a common Sanskrit master, and a dance teacher called Indira Tankachi, but only Rukmini really took to dance.'[86] Later in the afternoon, the Maharani often went out for her drive around the capital. 'That was quite impressive,' tells Uma. 'I remember sitting in her Sunbeam, which was always a unique experience, because only her car had soldiers on the footboards and stately outriders on horses. There would be huge crowds of people on the roads, and though we were only children, it was clear to us that grandmother was somebody of great importance, with all these people bowing and showing so much reverence. When we went out driving with our parents, it was never as impressive.'[87]

Sometimes the girls played *pallankuzhi*, a traditional game using a wooden board and the bright, colourful seeds of the *manjari* tree. At teatime they would gather around the aunts and others, 'although we really hung around only for the *palaharams* (sweets) there were to eat.'[88] Then in the evenings they would go to chitchat with their grandfather at a previously decided time. 'We could always run in and out and see him when we liked, but he still liked to have a fixed, formal time for everything, a rigid exactness from which he would never deviate. He would get up at exactly the same time every morning; breakfast and take his meals at exactly the same times in the day. And he would send messages to mother saying, "I will see my grandchildren from this hour to this hour today, thank you very much", and we had to be presented on the dot to him.'[89] For all these rules, however, he was a lot of fun to be around. As a grandson would later tell, 'With grandmother it was always comfortable. With grandfather it was always interesting. His stories were gripping and he never minced words or hid anything, even from us children. He had extremely strong opinions about everything and everybody. He hated Nehru and thought him an upstart; he took to hating Indira Gandhi after Nehru died; and he agreed wholeheartedly when Sarojini Naidu called Gandhi India's own Mickey Mouse!'[90]

But his favourite activity with his granddaughters was teaching them to shoot. 'He had an impressive collection of guns, and he had stopped going into the jungles by the time we were around. So we used to squat with him on the kitchen parapet, where he waited to shoot palm civets that lived in the trees on the grounds or foxes that wandered into the palace compound. Sometimes we went up to the attic in the evenings and shot from there, and on other occasions he taught us target shooting. At Kovalam he would make us study constellations in the sky, though we much preferred using the telescope to look for ships out at sea. And all throughout he would regale us with stories and anecdotes about his times in the forest, and we had great fun. Grandmother never approved of his teaching us to shoot, but we enjoyed it, and so she never stopped it either.'[91] The Valiya Koil Tampuran was thrilled by the enthusiasm of his grandchildren, and even tried to get them to take an interest in riding, which their father too had started to enjoy. 'Uma and Parvathi did not take to it, but I enjoyed riding very much, and grandfather and I would have endless talks about horses,' recalls Rukmini.[92]

> Grandfather was an amazing individual. He used to write plays in his spare time, which were dramatised and enacted in our family theatre at the back of Satelmond Palace. I remember one play where there happened to be a stabbing scene, with a real dagger, for effect, and the actors were so engrossed in their parts that the stabbing became actual! The poor victim was rushed to hospital, but nothing serious happened to him, luckily. Grandfather was also the editor of a magazine called *Microcosm*. He would also invite others to contribute. His editorials, which would criticise some current politician, author or other persons in the limelight, were masterpieces of caustic humour and wit.[93]

On previously decided dates, the girls were all packed into a car with their parents and taken to Kowdiar Palace for their formal visits, Indira and her husband going separately. 'There were some standard questions they asked us all the time, and we were always taught the correct answers in advance. These were routine things about our studies and things like that, but grandmother always ensured we did not slip up. But the Junior Maharani sometimes asked us very unexpected questions too, and mother would become extremely tense at such moments. She did not mind general queries, but if we were asked about our personal relationships with grandmother, for example, she always got worried.'[94] Uma and Parvathi did not quite find these visits to Kowdiar Palace enjoyable. 'We seldom met them except on these courtesy calls, so we felt like strangers. And there was all this formality around the Maharajah, and we had to bow before him,' recalls the latter. 'I remember spending many of these visits hiding behind mother. You can imagine that if I found grandmother in retirement awe-inspiring, the ruling prince was even more daunting a prospect!'[95] But the Junior Maharani knew that it was Princess Rukmini for whom Sethu Lakshmi Bayi harboured a soft corner, and so she received special attention at Kowdiar Palace too:

> They were very nice to me, especially the Junior Maharani. She would take my hand or carry me inside, and I remember mother disliking this, since she did not know what was happening. The fact that she took me into her personal apartments, made her uneasy. But all the Junior Maharani did was to give me sweets and talk to me. The Maharajah was a delightful man and he had all these tricks up his sleeve to entertain children. But it troubled everyone else, and when we returned I was interrogated about what they did and what they had said, and so on. They were not comfortable that the

> Junior Maharani singled me out, though I myself don't remember anything upsetting. The Maharajah's sister would sometimes join, and she was also very sweet and kind, and very pretty. We did hear murmurings about the dispute, but leaving aside the formality of our meetings, in person they were very nice, charming people.[96]

As the girls grew, they would sometimes gang up and break rules set by adults in the palace. 'We could run all around the large halls and play in the courtyard and the gardens. But the attic on the third floor was off limits,' reveals Princess Lakshmi. 'That was never going to restrain our curiosity in those days, though, and we would smuggle food upstairs and hold midnight feasts with all our cousins. Of course, this was until one night one of the servants woke up. They used to sleep around our beds, and we had to tiptoe carefully out of the room. That night, on not finding us there, they looked for us and discovered our secret, threatening to report the whole thing to our parents. Those were unforgettable days, which none of our own grandchildren today could possibly imagine!'[97] When the family visited Vellayini, the attic there was a magical place, full of objets d'art collected by the Valiya Koil Tampuran or presented to the Maharani by visiting dignitaries, who over the decades had included personalities as diverse as the Nobel laureate Rabindranath Tagore[98] and Edda Mussolini, daughter of the Italian dictator.[99] 'There was a beautiful spiral staircase that went up to the attic from the first-floor hall where mother and aunt's apartments met, and we had an elegant model of the palace compound up there—all the buildings, the trees, the mandapam—made entirely of beautiful carved ivory. It was absolutely exquisite! We once came across a gold-lace turban with an aigrette, full of diamonds and emeralds, topped with a plume. It caused a sensation!'[100]

Visiting Pothencode was even more thrilling. 'Grandmother was not very wise when it came to her own money,' tells Rukmini. 'She managed the finances of the state very well, but she was personally exceedingly generous to anyone and everyone who sought her help. It was that old-fashioned, queenly munificence; she could never say no when someone sought her assistance. Grandfather did not condone this, because he knew some people exploited her. But she was very wilful and determined, and he could never stop her. So instead, she gave him certain sums of money for safekeeping, which by the end grew into a massive fortune—we know because the estate duties on his death were mind-boggling, and this was only a small part of grandmother's fortune! And he used to keep a good portion of this in gold and precious stones at Pothencode. There were cabinets full of jars of gems, arranged by type and colour; pink diamonds in one, blue diamonds in the next, rubies in the third and so on. I remember being so amazed when I saw it all for the first time. He even had furniture with secret drawers and fittings, where he hid some of his treasure, and gold tea sets and plates and things like that. He always complained that grandmother was squandering all her money, but she never, ever listened.'[101]

> He had the finest collection of gems, among which were the famous solitaire studs that Kerala Varma Valiya Koil Tampuran, his uncle, used to wear in his ears—9.8 carat diamonds of unmatched brilliance! Grandfather gave one each to mother and aunt and they were made into pendants. He personally chose his stones to eliminate flaws and hence all the ones he purchased were without blemish. On the other hand, grandmother was not so fond of jewellery and therefore the ones she bought were not so faultless. I am certain people fooled her over the price. She made jewellery for her daughters and grandchildren and had no interest whatsoever in owning any herself. Grandpa was also a very fastidious interior decorator of his homes, not to mention superb architect. He purchased the most exquisite artefacts and furniture for his houses and had them so tastefully arranged. His taste I must say was really excellent. He also loved perfume! He always smelt fantastic! Grandma on the other hand was warm and cosy and so very comfortable to be with. She had this very sweet baby powder fragrance about her, quite different from grandpa's exotic and heady scents![102]

Through all these halcyon years, however, there remained a pall over the royal household that the marriage of Princess Indira was not as carefree and happy as her sister's, and that she continued childless. This was because Kuttan's health did not improve with the passage of years. 'He was a very nice, gentle person,' remembers Princess Rukmini, 'and he used to give us children lots of presents, since he did not have any of his own. He bought me my first camera when I was six. But he was constantly ill, and aunt was very disturbed in the 1940s because of this.'[103] He did enjoy the occasional good spell; during one such time, Kerala Varma and he flew to Madras in the aircraft the Junior Maharani had recently acquired, thrilled at their first journey by flight.[104] But Kuttan never did recover, and it was belatedly that he was diagnosed with liver cancer. By then, however, it was too late. Princess Indira took him to Madras to the hospital of Lt Col Pandalai, the Elayarajah's father-in-law, but nothing could be done. Kuttan died in 1949, leaving Sethu Lakshmi Bayi's quiet, beloved younger daughter a widow at twenty-three.

'At first aunt was devastated. For the four years of their marriage, she was constantly nursing him, and his loss affected her terribly. To this day, she does not like talking about it. But she was close to grandmother, who helped her come to terms with the loss.'[105] Princess Indira slowly recovered, after a psychological convalescence in Trichinopoly, where she was sent with her aunt Kutty Amma, and on her return she would chart a new course among members of the royal family. 'She always had a remarkable intellectual bent of mind,' tells a cousin, 'and so the Maharani encouraged her to study to get her mind off things.'[106] Indira became the first female member of the royal family to go to college, and eventually to obtain a degree in psychology. She attended her intermediate classes at the Women's College in Trivandrum, in a day and age where royalty was hardly seen without its regal marks and distinctions. 'I used to go to class barefoot for some reason,' she would chuckle, 'and I think they were surprised to see me. They were all dressed in silks, with jewellery and make-up, and all that, and though I was the Senior Maharani's daughter, I didn't dress like them. I think they were even disappointed by my lack of fashion sense.'[107] Except for the first few times, Indira also did not arrive at college with an escort or in a state car. 'My aunt Kochu Thankam's husband used to drive into town everyday to drop his children, and I used to go with him. It was a very ordinary affair.'[108]

Independence in 1947 was a sensational development at Satelmond Palace. 'I think it was obvious to grandmother that Travancore would have to accede to India, and she thought trying to fight for independence was foolish in those circumstances.'[109] Sethu Lakshmi Bayi was also, as it happened, a great admirer of Nehru. In 1931, towards the end of the Regency, he had actually visited Trivandrum, but the Maharani did not see him to avoid ruffling the Government of India.[110] On another visit in the early 1950s also she would be unable to meet Pandit-ji who was by now Prime Minister. However, she collected all his books, read his biographies, and even kept neatly cut paper clippings about him. 'I think she understood him on an intellectual level, in the way the Valiya Koil Tampuran never comprehended. He, like Sir CP, did not trust Nehru, and even thought that the departure of the British was the worst thing for India, and would lead to civil war. But the Maharani disagreed.'[111] Either way, the advent of freedom for India was a great event. 'It was a situation none of them had imagined ever possible till the war began,' tells Princess Rukmini, 'and they were all doubtful about the future of Travancore, its people, and about all of us; what would become of us, the younger generation of the family, if our state became irrelevant?'[112]

The children themselves did not then care for what was happening, living in a fairyland of their own. The assassination attempt on Sir CP, the threat of attacks from communists, and the fear the Maharajah himself revealed in the end did not give too much comfort to the Maharani, but as the date set for India's independence approached, everyone waited with bated breath for the new era to begin; or at least the younger ones did. 'All of us stayed up for Nehru's midnight broadcast,' remembers a nephew, 'both the daughters of the Maharani, and all of us cousins. The very fact that we stayed up was saying something, not only because of the irony of a royal party tuning into the announcement of a future republic. We really wanted to be participants at a historic moment and we were very conscious that this was one of those rare times that came once in a lifetime. I still remember the intonation of Nehru's voice and other details of that broadcast! It was a very exciting evening.'[113]

But while Lalitha and Indira, with their young cousins and relations stayed up that night for India's 'tryst with destiny', Sethu Lakshmi Bayi was in bed, fast asleep. A new age was upon them, and she needed her rest before it dawned.

19

The Reluctant Princess

While it took Sir CP and Kowdiar Palace much time to wake up and smell the coffee, there was one rather unexpected individual in the royal house who did, surprisingly, foresee the phenomenal changes that were about to transform everything for them. Princess Lalitha was neither the penetrating intellectual in her family, nor especially politically inclined. But underneath her disarming exuberance and charm she had firmly fixed principles and a keen eye that was sensitive to events transpiring around her. 'We always thought of Lalitha as a woman of the masses,' tells a sister-in-law, 'and I used to think that if she ventured into politics, she would have been a great success.'[1] And not only did the princess comprehend that a great wave of change was about to overwhelm the state and its presiding dynasty, but she also charted measures to prepare for it, and weather the all-altering era that inevitably lay ahead.

'Lalitha,' recalls a cousin, 'had certain strong convictions about society and people. Even as a child she disliked being different from others.' This was quite unusual for a princess who was meant to revel in her uniqueness, surrounded always by influences meant to reinforce that very feeling of being special. 'She hated all those marks of royalty, and those forms of address. She used to love everybody. Even the servants, so accustomed to worshipping her family, were surprised by how interested she was in them and their lives.'[2] In keeping with her own sensibilities, then, Lalitha initiated a number of small but significant changes to ensure she was, to the extent reasonably possible, treated in as ordinary a manner as possible. 'We never called her princess or Highness,' remembers another cousin. 'She was *akka*, or elder sister, to us. She would have it no other way.'[3]

Within the palace too she modified a few things. 'Mother's establishment was always more relaxed, and that formal character, which pervaded everything else at Satelmond, was largely absent,' remarks Parvathi. 'She used to have lots of relatives and other visitors whom she entertained freely and not in the courtly style that she was meant to follow.' At one time she even encouraged servants to stop calling her Tampuratti (princess) and refer to her just as amma (mistress), just like in other households of ordinary families. They were horrified at the idea and though, because of her insistence, they would address her that way, the moment her back was turned, they would go back to 'Her Highness'.[4] Sethu Lakshmi Bayi, interestingly, never stood in her daughter's way, permitting her to lead her life the way she deemed best. 'I think grandfather,' tells Rukmini, 'expected mother to maintain all those royal standards, but mother, as usual, was stubborn about doing otherwise, and since grandmother did not object, nobody stopped her.'[5]

After the end of the war, Princess Lalitha did the unthinkable: she moved out of the palace, in pursuit of her own freedom. 'It sounds very simple now,' tells her cousin, 'but at the time it was an extraordinary thing to do. Most people aspired to live like princes, with servants and luxury and all that wealth, but here was this young woman running away from it; giving up her golden spoon for something much more ordinary.'[6] While Satelmond Palace extended over 28 acres of land, some years before the Maharani privately purchased an adjacent property as well. 'We used to call it *akkarakunnu*—the hill on the other side—and she had it registered in the names of her daughters. There used to be an old, distinctly unattractive building there, which was in Lalitha's share of the property. It was a typical, *agraharam*-style village house, without modern amenities and structures, and definitely a far cry from the palace. Sometimes, less important guests were accommodated there, but it was mostly abandoned all those years.'[7]

Now, however, Lalitha and Kerala Varma took it upon themselves to proceed to the building, have it whitewashed, and spruced up for the exclusive use of their children and themselves. 'She was very determined to leave that starchy palace environment. "I won't have my children grow up like this," she used to say, and she always complained about how wrong the royal lifestyle was. I think it also affected her that she had not, in all these years, seen her mother genuinely happy in the palace.'[8] As her daughter would add, 'She hated the titles, and the servants, and the guards, and the unnecessary flattery and traditional sycophancy that plagued the palace. I remember her saying things like "It was completely crazy" or if we asked her something years later, she would say, "I don't wish to remember all that." It was a sentiment she sternly clung to all her life. In fact it was as if she were always waiting for the opportunity to give it all up.'[9] While the Valiya Koil Tampuran did not approve, 'He knew,' remembers the cousin, 'that she was perfectly capable of defying him when it came to such things, and that she had made up her mind. But it wasn't in a negative sense. In fact he used to walk everyday to the cottage at akkarakunnu to see her and the children, and they too every day drove across to the palace to be with the Maharani.'[10]

Overnight, thus, the girls were plucked from Satelmond Palace to this private house next door, leaving behind all that rigid protocol that enveloped their antiquated lifestyle. But this was merely a preparation for what really lay ahead, for Princess Lalitha had even more ambitious plans. 'Once Independence came,' Rukmini describes, 'mother decided to leave Trivandrum altogether. Moving to akkarakunnu was the first step, but she realised that no matter how "ordinary" she tried to become, in the end she was the princess of Travancore and would always be treated like that in the state's capital.' But if she left the state itself and went somewhere else, she would have more freedom and a better shot at leading the ordinary life she so craved. 'In fact it was her life's greatest ambition to become a housewife!'[11] Sethu Lakshmi Bayi did not like the idea of being separated from her daughter and the girls, but as usual, she did not obstruct Lalitha's plans, perhaps well aware that the world was changing and more than cosmetic changes were the need of the hour. 'I think the Maharani's greatness lay in her breadth of mind. While she herself might not have agreed with many things, she never imposed her views on her children. She let Lalitha make her own choices and live life on her own terms, which in a time of joint families, not to speak of royal families, was a very unique quality.'[12]

And so began Lalitha and Kerala Varma's wanderings. 'In 1948, we spent six months or thereabouts,' the latter would tell, 'in Kotagiri. The Maharani visited us there, and I remember her going as a guest of honour to St Mary's Convent. Then we had a long stint in Coonoor till finally we landed up in Kodaikanal.'[13] For the first two places, Lalitha took with her the children's tutors, an English companion called Miss Netto ('who also acted as our tailor and designed some lovely frocks'),[14] and a nurse, Alice, besides the usual servants on her payroll. In Kodaikanal, however, she discarded the academic staff and decided it was time the children went to a public school. 'It was called Presentation Convent,' Uma recalls fondly, 'and we were absolutely thrilled to be wearing uniforms for the first time in our lives. We had seen cousins and relatives go to school like this, and always felt we were missing out on something. I think most children hate going to school, but we loved it.'[15] Rukmini adds, 'I think mother herself had always wanted to go to school. But because she never had the opportunity, she was keen her children went.'[16]

One of the family's close friends at this time was none other than the Junior Maharani's younger son, the Elayarajah Martanda Varma. 'We first began to socialise on friendly terms,' Kerala Varma would recall, 'sometime towards the end of the war. I used go out riding in Trivandrum, as did the Elayarajah, and often our paths would cross. His wife Radha and he subsequently used to visit us at Kovalam when we stayed there for picnics and hosted little parties. And for some reason, when we went off to hill resorts in the late 1940s, the Elayarajah would follow with his wife and daughter, and we would have a very jolly time, all of us together. He really wanted to do something to patch up the old disputes, and to get to know this side of the family.'[17] Lalitha's cousins, who were in their teens, had also joined them that summer, one of whom recalls an amusing episode involving the Elayarajah:

> The house Lalitha rented in Kodaikanal did not have many bedrooms and so my brothers and I slept in the living room. The windows did not have bars and we left them open at night, because there was a lovely breeze. One morning, at around seven o'clock, the Elayarajah jumped in through the window! We were all shaken out of our sleep, but he hushed us quickly and told us to be quiet. He had come to surprise Lalitha and Kerala Varma, who were, to his greatest joy, adequately surprised and frankly a little taken aback. We all had an early breakfast with him, and he then left. Radha wasn't part of this incident, but we would all meet up practically every day and go to the local clubs or for walks and drives. It was a lovely holiday and I think the children of the 'warring Maharanis' got on very well indeed. The Elayarajah, like Lalitha, had some of that delightful irreverence and independence of thought, and a great appetite for fun.[18]

Indeed, while there was a deficiency of trust between the two palaces, Lalitha personally had no problems and trusted the Elayarajah almost implicitly. It was in Kodaikanal that they received news, for instance, of Kuttan's death in 1949. While she and Kerala Varma left for Trivandrum immediately, they did not tell the children, who were entrusted to the Elayarajah and his wife instead. 'Radha was an exquisitely beautiful woman,' recalls Rukmini, 'and I think we had a good time with them, until we figured out what happened in the palace. Then we were upset, but they took good care of us. I think the Junior Maharani's sisters were also there, and one of them, Bhavani, had a roaring sense of humour and she loved Uma and me and entertained us a great deal when we were upset. The youngest sister, Rajamma was there too, and she had her son with her, whom we called Kunjannan. He was, to us little girls, this strong, teenaged, older boy we were all in awe of at the time.'[19]

While the girls went to school in Kodaikanal, Lalitha took driving lessons, or chit-chatted with Radha, when their husbands set out to explore the hills on horseback. At one time all of them very nearly got into a car accident too. The Elayarajah was driving Lalitha's Buick but miscalculated a U-turn on a cliff. On another occasion, Lalitha was trying to negotiate a hairpin bend and almost went over, with the girls in the back.[20] Save for such situations, however, it was a beautiful time for the young parents and their four children, away from the capital. 'But,' as Rukmini tells, 'it was difficult to make it permanent.' In those days these hill stations practically shut down when the season ended, and everyone made an exodus back to the plains. Schools functioned, because they were boarding schools, and even the hospitals were closed. 'So we had to return to the palace. Mother disliked this, but grandfather insisted we spend at least some months there, so off we would go, lock, stock and barrel, back to Trivandrum and to being little princesses.'[21]

Changes, in the meantime, were afoot in the capital also. Although India had attained independence, the Maharajahs continued to sit uneasily upon their anachronistic thrones, having only surrendered foreign relations, communications and defence to the new Government of India. In internal matters, they remained independent. By 1948, however, plans were formulated to merge the princely states with India, and constitute new political units across the country. This was, essentially, a death blow to the princes, who were about to lose all their authority. Nehru's government was essentially politely asking their entire class to retire from history. In 1948, Mountbatten himself visited Trivandrum ('I remember his imposing motorcade driving up the gates of Satelmond Palace')[22] and commenced preliminary talks, after which the famous V.P. Menon, an uncompromising and redoubtable civil servant, who served as Home Minister Vallabhbhai Patel's right-hand man, arrived the following year to chart out the details.

Menon was a tough taskmaster who did not particularly care for the princes, though his mandate was to diplomatically win them over. He would tell how as a poor boy struggling to make his way through life, 'I went to a shop one day and watched a Maharani buy a hundred expensive saris. Another time I was present when a Maharajah walked into a sporting goods shop and casually ordered 100,000 rupees worth of hunting rifles. And one day on my civil service assignments, I was stopped at 15 different state customs posts on a thirty-mile drive through Kathiawar. I thought it was time this sort of nonsense was stopped.'[23] And as destiny would have it, it was for him to dissolve the old states forever, and obliterate them from the maps, really delivering a funeral oration to the last standing vestiges of the British Raj.

The proposal for Travancore was to merge with Cochin into a united bloc. The Maharajah was offered the position of Rajpramukh, a kind of ceremonial governor, and the ruler of Cochin was to be his deputy or Upa-Rajpramukh. Chithira Tirunal, however, insisted on not having a deputy, which, as Menon noted, 'was certainly unfair to the Maharajah of Cochin', but because the latter was too old in any case, he did not object.[24] As it happened, Cochin's last princely ruler made few impositions on the Government of India. He had 'practically no demands at all. A typical request of his was that free copies should continue to be supplied to him of the *Panjangam* or Almanac, which was published by the Cochin Government annually, and was priced at a few annas! He was prepared to efface himself completely in order that his people might enjoy a larger life.'[25] The Maharajah's privy purse there was fixed at Rs 2,35,000 per annum.[26]

Chithira Tirunal, however, took some more time and effort to persuade. 'The devotion of the present Maharajah,' Menon noted with a hint of annoyance, 'to Sri Padmanabha [his family deity] borders on fanaticism.'[27] He told the Government of India that since he ruled the state on behalf of the deity, this belief would have to be accommodated, or else he would be compelled to abdicate. 'I told him,' Menon later wrote, 'not to take a pessimistic view of the position; that there were few problems which human ingenuity could not solve.'[28] After a liberal annual grant was settled on the temple, the Maharajah came to his own privy purse. Chithira Tirunal had been drawing Rs 27 lakh per annum, which Menon felt was too extravagant. Instead, Rs 18 lakh was offered and accepted, all of which was his personal income.[29] He evidently dedicated a portion to the temple, but others in the royal family, such as the Senior Maharani and her children had neither any claim on this, nor did they request it. The Maharajah was also persuaded to give up the 20,000 acres of Crown lands he controlled, though he retained the Sripadam Estate for some more years. In addition to this, as Rajpramukh he was given an allowance of Rs 3,66,000, so that altogether, Chithira Tirunal's finances remained stout in consolation for relinquishing his ancestral inheritance.[30]

In what was unusual, Menon decided to settle allowances on junior members of the royal family also, which came as a blessing to Sethu Lakshmi Bayi and her daughters, who would otherwise have lost their sources of income. 'The Valiya

Koil Tampuran had some eccentric demands, like being allowed to continue owning guns without licence and the Senior Maharani hoped her Regency pension would be paid for life.'[31] Sethu Lakshmi Bayi's regular allowance was fixed at Rs 50,000, equal to the Junior Maharani's; indeed, it was for the first time in history that the Junior Maharani was at par with the matriarch of the royal house. To placate the Maharajah's mother, additionally, and to win her son's cooperation in the negotiations, her daughter, the First Princess, was given a higher allowance of Rs 22,000 while Princesses Lalitha and Indira received Rs 19,000 each per annum.[32] The Elayarajah had a handsome Rs 1,26,000 while his wife received Rs 3,000. Consorts of female members of the royal house received Rs 4,000, while the junior girls, including the direct nieces of the Maharajah, had Rs 10,000 each.[33] Thus the Junior Maharani's family, exclusive of Chithira Tirunal's luxurious privy purse, received a grant of Rs 2,49,000 every year, and Sethu Lakshmi Bayi and her family had Rs 1,36,000.

What moved Menon to make this exception in Travancore–Cochin by settling on junior members of the royal families also an income was a moving visit to Cochin. Here he encountered the royal family, living very much like commoners for no other reason than that there were too many of them. Cochin, a fifth the size of Travancore, in 1949 had a remarkable 223 princes and 231 princesses, some of whom, due to the want of resources, even took up ordinary vocations like government service and teaching. He would later write:

> I met some of these princes and princesses. As I talked with them I was reminded of an aviary in a certain State, which possessed a rare collection of birds. When the State was integrated the popular ministry, apparently on the principle of *ahimsa* [non-violence] let the birds loose! The poor creatures were soon devoured by other birds and beasts of prey. The princesses, at any rate, had all along led a sheltered existence; most of their husbands, instead of supporting them, had themselves to be maintained by the State. I felt it would be inhuman to expose the princesses to a competitive world without making some sort of a provision for them. The Government of India subsequently decided to continue the allowances to those members of the ruling family who were living on the day the covenant was signed. No responsibility was accepted in respect of any further additions to the ruling family.[34]

It was essentially an act of generosity towards Cochin's princesses. But it came to the rescue of the Senior Maharani and her daughters in Travancore, who had financial independence from Kowdiar Palace now, and for whom too the relentless bars of the gilded cage were finally thrown open. They were to taste, for the first time in decades, something they had long craved: freedom.

On 19 August 1949 Lalitha and Kerala Varma arrived in Bangalore, where they had chosen to spend their next sojourn away from the palace. Many years before, in 1933, Sethu Lakshmi Bayi herself had wanted to visit this 'garden city', with its wide, tree-lined avenues and pretty boulevards and parks, but had not been granted permission to go from Kowdiar Palace.[35] Now it was her sister's son who visited a friend here and returned with an excellent review for Lalitha and her husband. Promptly, then, the couple and their daughters drew up their plans for the city, and arrived here with their retinue. A house was found in Malleswaram, and they began what, little did they realise at the time, was destined to become a permanent stay.

Although perched in the middle of the territories of the Maharajah of Mysore, Bangalore had been under British control until Independence. This arrangement dated back to the late eighteenth century when the East India Company defeated Tipu Sultan and reinstated the Hindu Wodeyar dynasty as rulers of that principality. Troops of the company, who according to treaty were to be stationed permanently in the state, were moved from the malarial environs of Seringapatnam to the village of Bengaluru, with its more salubrious climate that suited the English officers. Over the years, two towns formed here: the old 'City', which remained with the Maharajah, and the new 'Cantonment' under British rule. 'City and Cantonment were separated by a wide belt of undulating green', marked by 'parks, lake, orchards, golf courses, and playing fields, interspersed with a few handsome official residences and public buildings'.[36] Localities called 'towns' such as Benson Town, Fraser Town, and Richmond Town, began to develop, and the city attracted large numbers of foreign as well as Anglo-Indian settlers, while the older areas, under the Maharajah's control, remained predominantly Hindu.

'Bangalore in those days, was really like a resort town but it did not have the disadvantages of places like Kodaikanal,' remembers Rukmini. 'Because of its military presence, the city did not close down when the season ended, and there was no dearth of excellent, even famous, schools here. The crowd in general was also highly polished and unusually cosmopolitan; I would say even more than Bombay. There were very many Europeans, right down to the early 1970s, working as heads of foreign firms in the city. It had a very leisurely pace, but one never got bored in Bangalore. There was always something to do.'[37] Lalitha and Kerala Varma, then, took the decision to settle here for good. In September 1949, a house was purchased at No. 9 (later reassigned as No. 8) Richmond Road from a Persian family, the Kazeroonis, who were relatives of the former Dewan of Mysore, Sir Mirza Ismail. On 3 October, the family moved in with great jubilation into what was finally their own little home in their own little place.[38]

Lalitha got down briskly to the task of decorating and setting up her household. 'It's really quite amazing how she did it. She took to it like a duck to water, as if she had always been living like this.' Suddenly, Lalitha was driving her own car, cooking in her own kitchen, sending her kids off to school—things she had ardently hoped to one day be able to do when she lived in the palace. 'I still remember how thrilled she was when she came back from the market in Malleswaram one day and announced, "Children, I have seen my first brinjal today!" She had never really seen raw vegetables before. Or for that matter a real kitchen. I can't explain how excited she was about setting up her own home in Bangalore, on her own terms, and with none of that "royalty business" she so resented. She always wanted to become an ordinary person, and she was able to do that now, in a perfect jiffy. One day we were there in the palace, with all our kowtowing attendants and guards, and the next in an ordinary house in Bangalore, becoming completely new people.'[39]

The first thing Lalitha did was to enrol the girls into the Baldwin Girls' School that was just across the road from their new bungalow. 'Our titles were dropped and we became ordinary children,' recalls Uma. 'I was Her Highness Bharani Tirunal Uma Bayi Tampuran earlier. Now I became simply Miss Uma Varma, daughter of Mr and Mrs Kerala Varma. In fact we felt it was rather backward to flaunt any royal titles any more, and if anyone asked, we were told to say that our father was an industrialist.'[40] This was not entirely surprising an innovation. From the time of her marriage in 1938, even when she was in the palace, Lalitha had been signing letters as 'LKV'—Lalitha Kerala Varma. No longer did she want to be known as the Second Princess of Travancore, and Bangalore offered her the opportunity to discard an identity she always resented and thought of as alien. 'She often used to declare to us in jest, "The only thing I love about Kerala is Kerala Varma!"'[41] But what Rukmini thought was 'the most amazing thing' was that 'mother did not falter at any of these regular, housewifely things. It is so marvellous how she did this, how a woman brought up in a palace could change like that. We became a very close-knit family of father, mother and children for the first time.'[42] Lalitha's cousins were also astonished by her ability to adapt. 'If the maids had some trouble or were not available, she was perfectly capable of picking up a broom and sweeping the house herself—none of that ladylike helplessness for which princesses were notorious.'[43] During a holiday in Bombay, she would also take all her girls for a commute by public transport with photographs revealing bewildered co-passengers in the background wondering who these clearly upper-class bus travellers were. 'Mother wanted to educate us,' Rukmini giggles, 'but I think we were so pampered that we only looked at it as a joyride.'[44]

The public, even in Bangalore, certainly recognised that this new, exuberant family with four daughters were not ordinary, no matter how hard they tried to fit the bill. 'It was a great sensation at the time that we had come away like this, leaving a whole palace behind. You only needed to disembark at the station and say you wanted to go to Travancore House and they knew exactly where to bring you.'[45] Part of this was because Lalitha had a great deal of help in this enterprise to become an ideal housewife. 'We came away from that artificial lifestyle in Satelmond,' remarks Rukmini, 'but some of it came with us. Our favourite servants were brought to Bangalore, and mother had two assistant cooks in the kitchen, where she was breaking new ground as an excellent chef. There were two live-in maids, a gardener, two drivers, an errand boy and a local maid for outside work. But it was nothing like the scores we had in the palace. There must have been ten at most.'[46] Clearly, Lalitha had a fair amount of assistance even in her new life.

Soon the family evolved a very relaxed, westernised lifestyle, complete with two pet Alsatians, Rex and Regina. The girls would go off to school in the morning, which was at first something of a struggle. 'There was some teasing in the beginning,' remembers Uma, 'that we were princesses and all that, but after some time those girls got over the novelty.'[47] There were barely any Indians, however, at Baldwin's in those days. 'The whole place was run by European nuns and Anglo-Indian ladies, and the city itself was a mini-England. Most of the girls were English or French, and there were one or two Americans. We were among the few Indians in the school. There was only one other Indian girl in my class called Farida,' remembers Rukmini, 'and Uma and Parvathi had Sir Mirza's family in their cohort. Our best friends naturally were also Europeans, with names like Gale and Irene, and I remember a Swedish girl called Brigitte too.'[48] Some relations mumbled that it was too unorthodox to introduce the princesses to this crowd, but Lalitha thought it was excellent exposure.

Kerala Varma, in the meantime, began to lead a gentleman's life, since he had all the time in the world for such indulgences. He would go out riding in the mornings and was a popular member of the Turf Club where he played polo and owned a much coveted, award-winning racehorse at one time. His musical interests were pursued with great diligence, as was a new-found hobby for gardening. 'I have never met,' laughs Rukmini, 'any other man who knows so much about flowers and gardening or who can arrange flowers in such a wonderful style. Father consistently won awards for the best garden at neighbourhood competitions, and there were these haughty old Englishmen who huffed and puffed and always resented losing the prize to this young Indian man!'[49] He also spent a good amount of time at the Bangalore Club, where his friends included some of the leading businessmen in the city. 'They also often went out for receptions the Mysore Maharajah had when he visited the city, or for parties organised by Vittal Mallya and other industrialists.'[50] By the 1960s, Kerala Varma himself would venture into entrepreneurship, and establish a number of small concerns: a cables factory, a mechanical tools enterprise, a ceramic tiles unit and so on. 'I also remember father playing a lot of tennis and golf,' tells Parvathi, 'but it was he who ensured we did our homework everyday, and his steward Hariharan taught us mathematics. Till he started his companies, he was very much a house husband just as mother was a housewife.'[51] Lalitha, all along, was en route to becoming a prominent socialite in the city.

> There were three famous Lalithas in Bangalore in those days: Lalitha Varma, Lalitha Mallya, and Lalitha Ubhayakar. The second was of course Vittal Mallya's wife, and the third came from the Ubhayakar family who were called the 'merchant princes' of Bangalore. But it was mother's parties that were truly legendary. Nothing like the way people do it these days. The house was full of gaiety in those days. The food never ran out, there were special waiters and others brought in if it was a big affair, tables and chairs put out in the garden, and streams of visitors. The fare was always vegetarian but there would be pies and cakes and many delicacies, the recipes for which she picked up after coming to Bangalore. And the regular guests included people who could never, in the old 'royal' days, have socialised with mother so easily. Lots of prominent Muslims, Christian planters who had houses in Bangalore (including from Kerala who were technically mother's 'subjects' at one time!), members of the Mysore and Jaipur royal families, and a lot of that sort of crowd. Mother was the driving force behind it all, and everyone loved her.[52]

But these were her large parties. Smaller parties happened every few days; as Lalitha's nephew put it, 'If someone sneezed on Richmond Road, aunt would declare that it was time for a party.'[53] Characteristically, then, she wasn't especially particular about the guest list and believed in the old saying of the more the merrier. 'I remember,' tells a sister-in-law, 'how one afternoon, before a party she and I went shopping on Commercial Street. And every other person we ran into was a friend of Lalitha's. She invited all of them that evening—and they all showed up! They loved her energy and joie de vivre. They loved spending time with her.'[54] Sometimes the results were a little disturbing, though Lalitha took them in her stride with a laugh. 'So many people, scores of them literally, ate at the Richmond Road house everyday,' recalls a cousin, 'that once some absolute strangers, a weird group of men, came in, sat down in one of the verandahs, and were served hot meals from the kitchen. Lalitha played the perfect hostess and was so gregarious that we presumed she knew them. After they left when we asked her who they were, she came back with: "Haven't the faintest."'[55] Rukmini explains, however, that 'mother had a rule that anyone who came home, no matter what their background or purpose, had to be given a meal. So these men were probably told by someone to sit in the verandah and mother happily served them.'[56]

The children, as they grew older, were welcome to join in the perennial party that was life at No. 9 during those early years. 'Our friends from school loved coming to meet mother, because she enjoyed pampering them, and if it weren't for pieces of antique furniture and all those paintings of our princely ancestors, they could never have guessed we used to be "royal".'[57] It was Kerala Varma of whom everyone seemed to be in awe. 'We used to think he looked like a film star,' laughs a cousin, 'with his suits and the horses and all his other sports. He was a very confident person and Lalitha allowed him to develop a personality of his own.'[58] While the girls were younger, they were brought out only for half an hour to meet the guests, before returning to their rooms. But as they grew, they were allowed to party too. 'Mother loved to give all of us a great time, but father was always concerned, since we were girls, and there were always boys trying to flirt,' laughs Rukmini. 'In fact at one time there was this menace of local boys on bicycles throwing love letters and notes over our walls. Father posted guards all around, so the silly chaps were caught if they were up to any mischief.'[59]

The Bangalore Club became a favourite haunt of the family. 'In earlier days they did not welcome Indians unless they were princes, but by the 1950s this was relaxed and businessmen were also allowed. So, father made many Indian friends there too, and mother also would go and spend time at the club.'[60] Relations visiting from Kerala or even from Madras were amazed by the ambience and culture of the Bangalore Club. 'See,' explains a cousin, 'we grew up in a big city too, but it wasn't anglicised the way Bangalore was. We were even well off but not royal like Lalitha and family. I still remember going to the club with Rukmini for a party in the 1960s. It was magical—an aesthetic experience, with all these handsome men and lovely, uninhibited women. Rukmini was a phenomenal beauty and all the men were eager to dance with her. She was the life of the party. And there was a lot of champagne, though we ourselves behaved like country cousins and didn't touch anything, sitting tight with wide eyes, trying to digest this glamorous world. We always wondered whether we would ever be able to live like this even after we grew up and married.'[61]

As the girls grew into their teens, they began to evolve minds of their own. Rukmini was excellent at school, winning awards, participating in numerous activities, becoming captain of Watson House and so on. Uma inherited much of her mother's rebelliousness. 'I still remember one morning,' chuckles Rukmini, 'father waking up and seeing Uma with her hair cropped short. Tony Curtis, the Hollywood star, was a rage at the time, and all the girls were taken up with him. Uma decided to cut her hair, and standing before a mirror chopped it all off into what was meant to be Curtis's hairstyle. Father was livid. She used to be a prankster, like grandfather, and every now and then her teachers would send notes to father that she had teased a certain girl or played a practical joke on someone.'[62] Parvathi, on the other hand, 'had a frightful temper, though she loved machines and things like that. She also became a very good driver and had this mechanical bent that quite impressed everyone. She also took to playing the veena very well, like father.'[63] Lakshmi was still young, but in due course would prove to be just as determined as her mother and older sisters were.

Sethu Lakshmi Bayi, in the meantime, became very curious herself as to how her grandchildren were faring in their modern avatars and lives in a whole new city. 'I think,' tells Rukmini, 'I was the only one who had some trouble adjusting, and that is why I became very competitive at school. Uma and the others were raised by mother, but I was raised by grandmother in that royal style and it took me a while to adjust to life outside the palace.'[64] To study this first-hand, in March 1950, the Maharani arrived in Bangalore with ten servants. 'The whole place was overrun with servants, but what we did was that five rooms in one wing of the house were set aside for grandmother to use, while all of us used the other wing.'[65] The new lifestyle of her family was an eye-opener for Sethu Lakshmi Bayi, but she quite enjoyed the breath of fresh air that was freedom in this alien city. Some things, however, horrified her. 'Grandmother just couldn't get it into her head,' laughs Parvathi, 'that we crossed the road to go to school. She was so alarmed that her grandchildren were doing something "so dangerous" that for all of her stay, we had to come out of the house, get into a rather imposing car, and we'd be driven across the road to school! Uma hated this and the moment the car halted, she would jump out and run away, salvaging her reputation before any of the other girls saw us arrive this way.'[66]

By May, the Maharani returned to the palace, delighted with Bangalore but unhappy to be away from her family who seemed to be doing so well there that Sethu Lakshmi Bayi felt a little left out. 'Life goes on here as usual, though it is hardly worth calling it life,' she wrote to Lalitha later that year. 'Kutty Amma comes here every morning so I don't even go to the *nalukettu* [old house] these days. I spend most of my time in prayers and so the days go on.'[67] She was soon to return, however, for in 1951 it was announced that Lalitha was pregnant with her fifth child. Promptly, Sethu Lakshmi Bayi arrived at Richmond Road, and in September the newest sister in the line, Ambika, was born. She was the first member of the royal family to arrive not in a palace, but faraway from the old principality, and for whom Travancore and all the old stories from Satelmond, Lalindloch, or Halcyon Castle, were just that: stories.

Growing up, then, Ambika, who never experienced that old lifestyle, had a different view from her older sisters. 'This whole palace thing was very distant from my upbringing,' she would say, 'and with my mother underplaying it so much, there was never any reason to explore that past. Whatever I heard was from my sisters, but given the way I grew up, I still can't imagine them in a scenario like that.'[68] To begin with, the whole family spoke barely any Malayalam any more. 'It was mainly because of our schooling with all these European girls, and we only used Malayalam with our household staff. I can read the language with difficulty but I cannot write it. I remember classmates at school teasing me because we had lots of servants and attendants all over the place, but mother gave us the feeling that we were no different from them. She dinned it into us, and actually even gave me the impression that we were not well off at all.'[69] On visits to Kerala, Ambika found the palace 'regal and all that' but it never made an impression on her. 'As far as I was concerned, Bangalore was home.'[70] She would go on: 'I remember being taken to meet the Maharajah once in Trivandrum and I was told I had to bow to him. I had no intention of doing any such thing. Grandmother was a queen and I had never bowed to her, so I saw no reason to bow to this man. Grandmother's sister, Kochu Thankam, was shocked at my refusal. I never met the Junior Maharani, but I had heard stories about her. I was always close to mum, and I think some of her influence rubbed off on me. She balked at being called a princess, though she respected her mother's work. I vividly remember visiting grandfather at Harippad once with mum, and he received her with fireworks and this enormous shiny banner that screamed, "Welcome Home Princess." She almost cried! He was trying to give her a warm reception, but she felt awful and embarrassed. So this royalty tag is not for me, thank you. It doesn't fit in anywhere, except in obscure stories, which I can never relate to fully.'[71]

Many years later, Ambika's son would study medicine in Trivandrum. 'Now you can imagine that if I didn't understand it myself, Ajit, a generation later, barely knew anything about this royal past. He got a bit of this "prince" business and some of his local Malayali batchmates would talk about it. He then became eager to learn about his heritage and culture, but as an objective interest and not to form any lofty opinions about being "royal". He's a doctor now, living in England, and working like any other professional. And that is how it should be, don't you think?'[72] Lalitha's older girls had lived in and knew the palace and the gilded world around it, but Ambika began with a clean slate of her own. And Lalitha ensured she provided her a lifestyle and upbringing that was as ordinary as possible. Mission Housewife appeared to be successfully under way.

Sethu Lakshmi Bayi, in the meantime, was enjoying her stay in Bangalore that lasted nearly a year on this occasion. 'I think grandmother had a lot of fun after a very, very long time,' remarks Rukmini. In the old days in the palace, going out to the movies, for instance, was a complicated affair. 'One had to decide a week in advance, then inform the manager, who would seek permission from the Valiya Koil Tampuran, who then communicated this to the Maharani. Then the manager would call the cinema and a balcony would be reserved. But the royal family could not be seen at a public venue, so they could enter only once the lights were out. Of course the Maharani never went for these, and it was mainly Lalitha and us cousins.'[73] In Bangalore now, however, it was a less bureaucratic affair. A balcony would still be reserved 'and we would start from home in a few cars,' tells Rukmini. 'We'd all enjoy a historical film, of which there were many in the 1950s, covering Greek or Roman history. Years later I remember watching *Ben-Hur* with her. There were only a few theatres in Bangalore in those days, like the Plaza or the Rex, and one called the Globe. She used to sit with her feet up on the seats in front of her, and really enjoyed the freedom. She could never do these things in Trivandrum, where if she stepped on to the streets people would be bowing and falling at her feet with all that traditional reverence. I think she really understood what mother meant when she said she wanted to be liberated from the weight of heritage. She was personally orthodox but she was able to understand and condone our choice for a different lifestyle.'[74]

But the Maharani's long stay was not merely for reasons of leisure. A second marriage had been proposed for Indira with a suitable boy of the Kilimanoor family. She had dissolved into her intermediate studies after Kuttan's death and though she did not speak very much, she finally consented to marrying again. The groom's name was also Kerala Varma, though he was better known as KK. A qualified lawyer, he was actually two years junior to Indira, but what perhaps the more orthodox might have deemed a major disqualification was the fact that he was something of a patriotic radical. Their son would later tell: 'Father was a nationalist and an ardent admirer of Subhash Chandra Bose and his particular brand of nationalism. In fact, when I was born, he even wanted to name me after Bose, but my mother put her foot down. Ironically, when he was a student in college, he had once taken down a portrait of my grandmother from a wall and replaced it with one of Bose. Little did he realise then that he was destined to one day marry that very Maharani's daughter and right into the royal family he thought had seen its day.'[75]

The wedding in May 1952 was a quiet affair, again breaking tradition with its venue at Lalitha's house in Bangalore. 'None of the seven-day weddings like before,' remarks Rukmini. 'In fact, leaving aside the priests and others in the main hall performing all the religious ceremonies, it was quite westernised. I remember we had this massive, tall white wedding cake that all of us couldn't wait to dig into. Aunt herself was all dressed in white, and with how pretty she naturally was, she looked radiant. But the most hilarious part was when the *homam* was going on. The priest, one Kuttappa Sastrigal, was this tiny little man and he was going around the fire chanting mantras, when suddenly his dhoti fell off! We were all in splits, but he quickly pulled it up and proceeded like nothing had happened.'[76] Later that year, the Maharani purchased a house for Indira on Nungambakkam High Road in Madras. 'I would have continued to live in the palace,' Indira tells, 'but once my sister left there was this idea that I too could lead a life of my own. So my husband and I came away from the palace. At first we toyed with the idea of going to Hyderabad but then settled on Madras.'[77]

While Indira continued her higher studies, KK, who was an alumnus of the Presidency College and had an MA in Hindi (acquired in pursuit of his nationalism), practised as a lawyer in the Madras High Court for some years, before venturing into business. In 1963, he would set up what became an iconic company in the city called India Meters. 'It was *the* big company in Madras till the Birlas started Cimmco some years later.'[78] By 1974, however, India Meters, started with a paid-up capital of Rs 74 lakh, would suffer substantial losses, and KK would relinquish his investment in it. As Rukmini now laughs, 'I think both father and uncle were very unlucky in business, trusting the wrong people. None of that generation, which had only just moved away from the palace, really had a good business mentality, and the tendency was to give money to others.' Nobody thought in terms of profit and loss and there was a great deal of generosity others exploited. And because there was more money where it came from, mistakes were often repeated by the husbands who suddenly had all their doting wives' inheritance at their disposal. 'They made their employees very happy, but in the long run their businesses suffered. Some of the younger children in our family are doing well now, but if we were told to do business, we'd have been resounding flops as well!'[79]

Into the early 1970s, KK would venture into the hotel industry. As one journal from the time put it, Hotel Ganpat was Madras's first 'posh Luxury Hotel in the heart of the city' with an investment of Rs 60 lakh.[80] 'It was,' his son tells, 'one of the most popular hotels and had some very good restaurants, patronised by film stars and politicians and the who's who of Madras. Then when the Taj came up on the same road, father thought, "Had it!" But it remained very popular for many more years. Again, it was some bad business decisions and a tendency to believe in the wrong people that ended father's association with the hotel.'[81] When Lalitha and her family from Bangalore visited Madras, they loved going to Ganpat for buffet lunches. 'Uncle was always happy to indulge us and the food kept coming and coming, and often some of the staff would point out a Tamil movie star or an important dignitary dining near us. Uncle knew everyone there was to know in Madras.'[82] The Valiya Koil Tampuran was the only one who felt his sons-in-law ought to stay out of business if they were not good at it. 'He never gave a penny of his own money,' tells Rukmini, 'and he died a very rich man [with a personal estate valued at some Rs 62 lakh]. It was all grandmother's wealth, which she had carefully saved during the Regency, that funded our ill-fated forays into business!'[83]

Indira's life in Madras, however, was vastly different from Lalitha's. She went out to play tennis with Mary Clubwala at the Ladies' Recreation Club and attended meetings of the Literary Society, but remained, for most part, 'painfully shy'.[84] On some occasions, as the wife of a leading industrialist, she would be invited to appear as the chief guest at the Filmfare Awards, for instance, with personalities like Kamala Das, otherwise leading a private life. 'We didn't understand the royal past very much either,' her son tells, 'because it had all changed by then. Besides, we were known as the children of the owner of Hotel Ganpat or India Meters, not as members of the Travancore royal family. Now in hindsight, of course, I can understand we were different from other children.

Where they walked to school, we used to go in a car. Small things like that. After my MA when I worked as a journalist in Bombay, I got used to living in small, crammy apartments. And one day I came home and sat in our drawing room and thought to myself how many people could fit into that one room alone. It offered perspective but we were not spoilt to begin with. We did not lead excessively affluent lives, and there were other "commoners" who were wealthier than us. Aunt had a much more lavish lifestyle in Bangalore actually. Here with us, mother gave us a Western influence while father, who was a scholar and wrote books and translated Sanskrit works, added an Indian element into everything. All the real glamour was in Bangalore. We were more Malayali in that sense, and there was an aura of rigour with more traditional habits in Madras.'[85] Indira's son would only glean some of his royal heritage first-hand in the 1960s, in fact. Writing about it later, he would say:

> I was ten when I was introduced to a broken legacy. Schooling in [Madras] was a no-nonsense affair, riotous and ordinary. During one of my vacations, I was taken to Attingal ... There we were welcomed into the old family temple with traditional honours, mind-boggling for a schoolboy. For the first time I was confronted with the trappings of royalty. Shirtless and sweating, wearing a brand new gold-bordered dhoti, I was horrified to find the probing gaze of a couple of hundred locals focussed upon me. My mother, aunt, and sister bore the limelight more gracefully. There were pipes blowing, and drums. Our grand procession made its way from the palace buildings to the temple. I was in the forefront, a most uneasy exhibit. My eyes were rooted to the ground. My hands clutched a rebellious dhothi. Each step was torture.[86]

It was in 1953 that Indira gave birth to her daughter, Shobhana, and then in 1955 to her son, Shreekumar.[87] Sethu Lakshmi Bayi's first grandson was not born in Madras, though, but in Bangalore in 1953 when Lalitha gave birth to a boy, after five girls in a line. 'Mother was delighted that she had a son. She loved us girls, but after so many daughters a son was a welcome addition, and we too were very thrilled about having a brother.'[88] 'I am counting the days,' wrote the Maharani from Trivandrum, 'for the Xmas holidays to begin, so I can see all of you again, especially my little grandson!'[89] The advent of Balagopal and then Shreekumar two years later gave Sethu Lakshmi Bayi much joy. It was in 1909 that she had nearly had a son, when the baby died, and now forty-four years later, for the first time there was a male heir in her branch of the royal house, even if by this time it meant little. In due course, when Balan and Shreekumar were a year old respectively, they were dedicated to Sri Padmanabhaswamy, like all male members of the dynasty were. 'You had to present the baby before the shrine and walk away, without looking back. The child now belonged to the deity, not to you.'[90]

Balan's birth, however, revealed some of Lalitha's extravagance and the fact that while she had left the palace, that royal tendency towards excessive generosity, so evident in her mother, had not left her. Her cousin tells how,

> ... normally it was Kochu Thankam who helped with her pregnancies, but due to some reason when it was Balan's time, it was *my* mother [the Maharani's sister-in-law] who went to Bangalore to assist Lalitha. At some point she told her, 'I think this time you are going to have a boy.' Lalitha laughed it off, saying she would quite like a son but she was probably never going to have one. And then when Balan was born, she was so overjoyed that she called my mother and said, '*Ammayi*, tell me whatever you want as a present and you shall have it!' My mother thought for a while and said that there was this pink chandelier in Kovalam that she liked. But that was in Kerala, and Lalitha wanted to give her a present immediately. So she took my mother into her bedroom, opened a safe there, and literally scooped up loose diamonds in her hands. She wrapped it in a handkerchief and insisted my mother take it. My father was furious when mother returned to Madras with literally two handsful of diamonds! 'Did you go there to help with the baby or fish for presents?' he admonished her. But he also knew what Lalitha could be like when she was in a mood to be generous.[91]

Laughing about it now Rukmini remarks, 'Well this is what I mean when I say we are not cut out to do business. I have seen my mother giving away gold necklaces and parts of what used to be an extensive collection, to servants and maids. She always said she didn't wear them in any case, and if they made the staff happy, that was fine.' Similarly, she knew perfectly well that the servants pilfered from the stores. 'But unless it was extremely egregious, she did not stop it. Grandfather used to bemoan and compare this to grandmother, who was also very similar in giving away everything with a great and almost unrealistic sense of munificence. "Mother and daughter will squander everything," he would warn, but as usual, he knew his remonstrations were hardly going to stop them. In that sense they remained in that royal mould, unable to give up that traditional benevolence.'[92] In Madras, Indira and her husband were very generous too, extending their patronage to the Hindu cause. 'We had in the 1960s a guru,' recalls Shreekumar, 'and I remember not only him but literally hundreds of his followers and disciples being hosted by us regularly.'[93]

In the meantime, in 1952, the Elayarajah also settled down in Bangalore with his wife and children. A beautiful mansion was constructed on Cunningham Road and during the initial years Radha and he remained on close terms with Lalitha and Kerala Varma. 'They were always invited to our parties and came most of the time, and we used to go there when they had functions. But after some time, it petered out and they started moving in different circles. But the Elayarajah would still visit now and then, and we would do likewise, and years later his children were friendly with some of ours. But that phase where father and mother, and the Elayarajah and Radha were always together came to an end. But I think they were glad that much of the old suspicion between the two families, at least in Bangalore, had been resolved and they could all meet for the occasional relaxed lunch or tea, and have a good time.'[94]

During one of these years a distinguished visitor called on Lalitha and the girls in the form of the Maharajah himself. 'It was the early 1950s definitely, and I think it was after the Elayarajah moved here. He came with his sister and her children and family, and it was a very pleasant meeting.'[95] In the photographs that survive of this visit, however, the contrast between Lalitha and her little ex-princesses in Bangalore and the Junior Maharani's grandchildren is evident. The latter, in south Indian silk attire, look strikingly different from a harassed-looking Lakshmi in a little frock, or an Uma looking completely nonplussed on her rather large bicycle, or Rukmini, in her early teens, and dressed in a salwar kurta, unheard of in Kerala. The meeting went warmly, however, and Sethu Lakshmi Bayi was pleased to hear that the Maharajah had visited her daughter. 'As usual', though, laughs Rukmini, 'grandfather called for caution. "It is curiosity about how you are all faring that has brought them there," he warned, "so you had better not get carried away into thinking of becoming permanent friends." He was ever the realist and always on his guard, even when the Maharajah had just come to say hello. But of course he had his reasons and there was all that history.'[96]

And indeed there was. Despite varied best efforts to patch up, there was too much odium from the past, and a real reconciliation between the two branches of the royal family of Travancore, even when power and titles had become redundant, remained elusive. Sethu Lakshmi Bayi's daughters had chosen to move on. And soon it would be the turn of the Maharani herself.

THE END

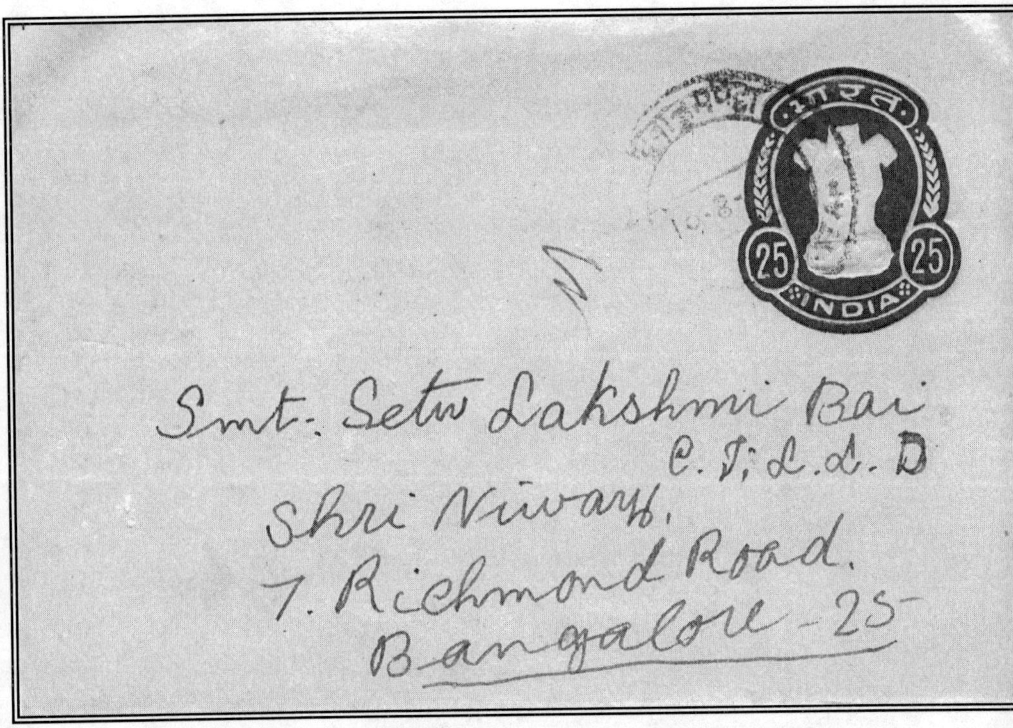

'Smt. Sethu Lakshmi Bayi'

20

Once I Had a Kingdom

'I have had to cut down from twenty-four cooks to twelve cooks!' fumed a thoroughly harassed Valiya Koil Tampuran to his grandchildren when they arrived one summer in the 1950s.[1] Great many changes were stirring Satelmond Palace since the departure of both of Sethu Lakshmi Bayi's daughters to the siren call of life in more exciting cities. And Rama Varma was not pleased by the myriad adjustments he had to manage. The strength of the household staff was heavily pruned; from the 300 servants who once presented themselves for service, the Maharani now employed not more than seventy people.[2] A natural consequence was that a great deal of that quaint formality about her lifestyle ceased to exist. The soldiers at the gates were asked to suspend the custom of treating the world to trumpets and a now meaningless Travancore anthem every time Sethu Lakshmi Bayi went out, and the number of active pattakkars was reduced. Suddenly, now that the establishment had to be maintained out of the Maharani's reduced allowances, there was no necessity for those whose sole job was to bow and strut about regally up and down the palace halls all day. The past was melting away.

Sethu Lakshmi Bayi was also troubled with a great deal of loneliness during these years, but as usual, played it down with her inborn optimism. 'I am getting used to being alone, really. So long as I hear from you fairly often, how you are all getting along, I shall feel all right,' she wrote to a concerned Lalitha on one occasion. On a festive day, when the palace earlier overflowed with streams of visitors and family, its great halls ringing with the laughter of the girls dancing and feasting, she missed them even more. 'Though I shall spend a rather lonely Vishu, the thought of you all will keep me quite happy.'[3] 'Grandmother was very pained to be separated from all of us because family meant everything to her,' tells Rukmini, 'but she knew it had to be done.'[4] As Sethu Lakshmi Bayi herself wrote, 'We have to make sacrifices for the children's sake,' for 'We can have no idea through what all paths life is going to lead them. They must be trained and prepared to face everything.'[5] She still met her family twice a year for fairly prolonged stretches of time. Tells Uma:

> During the winter vacations we would all show up at the palace. It was the busiest season for grandmother, because she would get about finding more servants to take care of our needs, instructing the cooks to prepare our favourite dishes, bringing in teachers to brush up our Malayalam and to make sure we didn't forget our lessons, and things like that. During the summer vacations she would take a house in the hills, and we would drive down from Bangalore, and aunt from Madras, and spend several months all together.[6]

In 1954, the Maharani rented her usual house in Coonoor called 'Stalisfield', while Lalitha took 'Cedara' nearby. Aspect Lodge had been sold by now, although they passed it on walks and remembered fondly their times there. Sethu Lakshmi Bayi arrived before Lalitha did, and seems to have been extremely active in charting out the logistics of the holiday. 'We have brought the Sunbeam and Hindustan,' she wrote to her daughter. 'I am going to suggest that we send the Sunbeam to you. With two cars it will be much safer and ever so much more convenient. You both and the little ones can come in the Sunbeam, and Hariharan can drive the three older girls in the Buick. And you can bring all the maids with you, and most of all you can bring a lot of luggage with you. How else will you manage, I can't imagine!'[7] A few days before the Bangalore party started out, she also sent them suggestions on rest houses on the way. 'I have got all the information you wanted,' she declared triumphantly, her brimming enthusiasm manifest in her writing.[8]

But these vacations never lasted as long as she would have liked, and for the next several months she would wait eagerly for her daughters and the children to return. The year 1955 was a significant one in the family, as the Maharani turned sixty. Lalitha and Indira were determined to organise a celebration. The Valiya Koil Tampuran was away in Bangalore for surgery, though, and Sethu Lakshmi Bayi was not herself very keen. 'Don't you think it would be in very bad taste, if nothing else, to be making elaborate arrangements [for celebrations] now? Your father never liked the idea and now God also seems to be against it ... Console, yourself,' she concluded, 'it is just fate.'[9] But her daughters were not prepared to acquiesce. Rama Varma was persuaded to give his blessings for a big commemoration, and everyone came down to Trivandrum for the birthday. The Maharani, who for decades now had been relatively reclusive, would have liked it to be a private, family affair, but that was not to be. 'I feel really quite nervous,' she wrote, 'about all these strange people coming. Let us hope there won't be any displeasure. I tried to dissuade Indira from going to invite "them" [i.e., the Junior Maharani] ... but she is determined to do her bit! What does father say? The only pleasurable thing about it all is that I shall be able to see you all, even if only for a day or two!'[10]

The arrival of the princesses from Bangalore always brought with it great excitement in Trivandrum. 'I think,' tells the Maharani's nephew, 'these girls, with their unusual clothes, bobbed hair, convent mannerisms, always talking in English, seemed a wonder to the old folk in Trivandrum.'[11] Soon after their arrival they would be invited to join the Junior Maharani at Kowdiar Palace for tea. 'That old business of paying courtesy calls had ended,' remembers Rukmini, 'but we went out of politeness, and they were always very gracious towards us. The Junior Maharani always wanted to know what we were studying, who our friends were and so on. I don't think she liked it much when we came out with a string of Christian names, and I remember her shaking her head and saying we must always remember our Hindu roots!'[12] Sethu Lakshmi Bayi found this rather amusing. 'The other day,' she wrote to Rukmini, 'the Junior Maharani remarked that you were all getting too much of the Christian atmosphere and outlook by going to school and mixing with that crowd. For instance, she said, you were all "touching wood" for something or other, all the time. What the Christians implied by this is, she explained, that in imagination they were touching the wood of Christ's cross to ward off evil and bring good luck! Now what do you think of that!'[13]

But even letters were no permanent antidote to her loneliness, and it slowly became obvious that she craved the company of family members. It was much like her cheerless growing-up years when she yearned for visits from her parents and siblings. At that time she had had no option but to carry on. Now, however, her position had been altered altogether, and there was no 'duty' or dynastic obligation to which she was bound to stay true. 'The palace and all that began to mean very little to her if we were not there to share that life,' remarks Uma, and slowly Sethu Lakshmi Bayi began to consider a life-changing decision.[14] For the time being, however, there were other concerns to keep the Maharani busy. In 1952, the estate in Peermade, which had been given to Indira, was sold, and soon afterwards Lalitha disposed of her estate in Devikulam; both had fallen into disuse and become cumbersome to maintain. By 1955, Lalindloch Palace, of all their family's favourite memories, was also set to be lost. 'There is a note in the *Kerala Kaumudi*,' the Maharani informed, 'to say that the Government has sanctioned the taking over of Vellayini for the AV College.'[15] A new agricultural college was contemplated next to the Vellayini Lake, and Lalindloch with its 100 acres of grounds and the palace buildings, was right in the middle of the proposed location. Political uncertainty meant that nothing was done immediately, as governments fell only to be replaced by other equally unstable minority regimes. 'God alone knows what is going to happen about Vellayini now,' Sethu Lakshmi Bayi wrote again. 'Anyway, I have dismantled the old house almost completely.'[16] By July 1955, however, the keys were entrusted to the government and the Maharani awaited news on their compensation. Though at first she was given to believe that 'they mean to deal fairly'[17] when the final cheque for Rs 9 lakh arrived, she didn't find that especially satisfactory. Unwilling to bicker and haggle, though, she let it be. There would be no more jaunts at the country house, and the sale of Vellayini marked the end of an era.

As the years passed, more and more property had to be relinquished, each severing with it a part of her many memories of bygone times. When V.P. Menon came to negotiate terms with the royal family, certain properties were set aside as the Maharajah's 'private' estate and the rest given over to the people. The latter, however, was selling some of these and the Maharani tried to object stating that the term 'private' did not mean they were the personal possessions of the Maharajah as an individual to alienate, but were in fact properties of the entire royal family.[18] Her objections, while acknowledged, however, were not redressed, and the Maharajah continued with the sales. By 1964, the Valiya Koil Tampuran would lose Halcyon Castle at Kovalam for a pittance of Rs 5.26 lakh when the government decided to acquire it. This upset him extremely, and in a fit of anger, on receiving the government's notice, he is said to have slammed his desk and thrown everything on it on to the floor.[19] A move was also afoot to take over Villa Manimala at Pothencode, but Rama Varma put his foot down when his last and only remaining property was threatened. 'I think,' he is said to have caustically remarked to the minister concerned, 'we are to quietly accept all this because we committed one grave mistake. And that is that for seven years Her Highness served Travancore faithfully as Regent.' An embarrassed minister cancelled the acquisition order, and the Valiya Koil Tampuran was able to retain Pothencode for many more years, till it was sold after his demise in the late 1970s.[20]

But Sethu Laksmi Bayi was fated to make her peace with all her losses, and one after another she gave up her possessions in what used to be Travancore. For a greater storm was about to uproot her permanently. In 1956, the three regions of Travancore, Cochin and Malabar were merged, after certain adjustments of territory with neighbouring Tamil Nadu, into the united state of Kerala. A new ministry would come to power in 1957 under the control of the communists, though it became obvious in the previous year itself that the wind was now blowing in that direction. It is said that the communists had an axe to grind against the royal family not only as a matter of principle but also because of the tragic Punnapra–Vayalar incident that had become an unforgettable highlight in their political evolution. The royal family now had to confront a great deal of retaliation as a consequence. And though the Senior Maharani had had little to do with the ruthless brutality of Sir CP's regime, she was not spared. Bad luck, it appeared, was determined to hound Sethu Lakshmi Bayi.

In April 1956 she reported to her daughters that the servants in the palace had formed a union under one of the cooks and a driver. 'Nobody had thought of rebelling until then,' remembers Rukmini, 'because they were paid well, and like in the old days, their meals, clothes, accommodation and other needs were all taken care of. Moreover they only worked two weeks at a time. Grandfather was quite convinced that this rebellion was due to outside instigation.'[21] Whether or not there was any such provocation, the fact was that while all of Kerala went down the communist road and labour unrest became the order of the day, Satelmond Palace could hardly remain a sunny paradise. Promptly, in a matter of days, the state's labour officer got involved. 'God alone knows how it is all going to end,' a clearly distressed Sethu Lakshmi Bayi wrote. 'There is a tense atmosphere here altogether.'[22] Eventually, the situation was defused when Rama Varma made it clear that labour laws did not apply to domestic servants, also pointing out that if working conditions were *really* as dreadful as they claimed, they were free to leave and that he was confident he could get by with the assistance of others who would be more than happy to work at the palace on existing terms.[23]

By 1957, however, the union raised its head again, having received a boost of confidence from the swearing-in of a communist Chief Minister in Kerala. A hunger strike was called, and on a certain day the Maharani woke up to find barely anyone in the palace. It did not help that in March that year she had suffered a heart attack, and Lalitha and Indira began to worry for her safety. 'It was difficult because the palace was not built like a modern house,' recalls Rukmini. 'It was a large establishment, and when servants refused to operate it, the whole place fell apart. Even many suppliers stopped catering to grandmother, because they were communist sympathisers. It was very worrying.'[24] Everywhere they turned, Sethu Lakshmi Bayi and her husband only saw difficulty. The Junior Maharani also faced similar troubles, but had resources to grapple with them. At Satelmond, so isolated from power and influence for decades, there was no such option. Soon there was open defiance of the Valiya Koil Tampuran and even the Maharani, with slogans being shouted in their hearing. 'You can't imagine it. It was her home, and there was a rebellion in her courtyard.' The climax of all this came was when one morning Sethu Lakshmi Bayi was informed by her sisters that the old Travancore flag had been taken down from the roof. Fluttering atop Satelmond Palace now instead was a communist banner. That was a tremendously poignant moment for her. While Rama Varma was furious and promised to get to the bottom of this, the incident confirmed the Maharani in a decision she had been contemplating for some time now. Turning to her husband she evidently said, 'I think it is time for us to go.'[25]

It was Rukmini who first came up with the proposal that Sethu Lakshmi Bayi should leave the palace and come and stay with her daughter. 'I heard all about the union,' she wrote in a letter in May 1956 when trouble had first occurred. 'Why don't you dismiss all the servants and come and stay with us in Bangalore? You can just bring your most trusted servants, or better still, we will do everything for you instead. You can stay sometimes with us, and sometimes with Auntie in Madras. Or, which will be delightful, you could stay all the while with us! Can't you come? Be sure we will look after you more closely than ever a miser can look after his hard-won gold!'[26] With all these problems confronting her, and with new ones grimacing, not to speak of the grinding deteriorations of age, Sethu Lakshmi Bayi came around to the view that perhaps her granddaughter's suggestion was the wisest course for the future. It was not going to be an easy journey ahead; nobody had ever remotely conceived having one day to leave the palace and lead a different kind of life in a strange new world. But, with that profound courage that had never left her side, the Maharani decided to take a leap and adapt to the future. From Her Highness Sri Padmanabha Sevini Vanchi Dharma Vardhini Raja Rajeshwari Maharani Pooradam Tirunal Sethu Lakshmi Bayi Maharajah C.I., she was about to embark upon the final years of her life as simply Smt. Sethu Lakshmi Bayi.

By October, Lalitha and Kerala Varma arrived in Trivandrum, and a scheme was formulated to extract the Maharani from the palace. She was now practically under house arrest, with maidservants refusing to cooperate. K.G. Menon, the Chief Secretary of Kerala, arranged for police protection.[27] 'Till the car was brought to the front porch that morning,' remembers Sethu Lakshmi Bayi's nephew, 'nobody knew she was leaving.'[28] Plainclothes policemen had earlier been deployed on the grounds to rein in the union should the situation threaten to get violent. Then the Maharani suddenly appeared at the porch, entered the car with Rama Varma, and departed just as quickly. 'Grandfather later told me,' states Rukmini, 'that the servants had planned a demonstration near the gates and they were waiting there. They were quite stunned and taken aback by her abrupt departure.' But what moved him most was not their going into exile like this. 'It was the way grandmother, who never hurt a fly in all her life, was forced to leave.' As they drove out of the gates, Rama Varma asked his wife whether she would like to have a last look at their home. But the Maharani refused. She didn't want to behold her Satelmond, the home she designed with her husband and where she reared her children, the palace from where she had once ruled, like that, besieged by a mob screaming slogans. Towards the end of his life, with tears in his eyes the Valiya Koil Tampuran would tell Rukmini, 'I asked her to have a last glimpse. But she never looked back.'[29]

The Maharani knew, deep in her heart, that she was not destined to return. So her first stop before she reached the railway station was at the gates of the Sri Padmanabhaswamy Temple. She sent her driver to drop some coins into the collection box near the entrance, and turning in her seat, offered final prayers to her family deity. It was in his name that she had ruled the country, and it was in his presence that she now renounced it. It was to him that her dynasty and ancestors had pledged their fidelity and allegiance. And now, it was her fate, as the last of Travancore's queens and one of the ultimate representatives of her lineage, to sever that bond. She had not worshipped in the shrine since 1936 but now, seated in her car, she addressed the deity directly and said, 'Please forgive me. I must leave.'[30] Her Humber then reached Trivandrum Central, a station she had built, and drove on to the railway platform, where as usual, a special carriage was reserved for her. A crowd, restrained by the police, gathered at the sight of these unusual happenings and many recognised their queen, bowing as she emerged from her car. The Maharani acknowledged the obeisance of her people for the last time in her life and boarded the train. As it pulled out of the station and the lush green fields and thatched cottages outside Trivandrum flashed past her window, tears filled Sethu Lakshmi Bayi's eyes. The Valiya Koil Tampuran sat down opposite her, struggling for words to console his royal wife, departing unsung and unthanked from the land she had helped build. But before he could say anything, she wiped her tears. Quietly picking up a book she had been reading, she turned its page and with that famous resilience and forbearance that was the hallmark of her journey through life, began a new chapter.

'Grin and bear it', her mother had taught her. And so she did.

'I am thinking of buying a house in Bangalore,' the Maharani wrote to her sister from Madras. 'It is the house just next door to my daughter's. The owner is planning to sell it. If only I could get it, it would be so convenient.'[31] Sethu Lakshmi Bayi had gone from Trivandrum to Madras, where at the Egmore station waiting to receive her were her brothers and their families. She went to Harrington Road to her brother's house first before moving to Indira's place, where Shobhana and Shreekumar were delighted to welcome their grandmother. But plans to make Madras a permanent home had to be discarded because of the sweltering heat. Bangalore, then, with its more equable climate, was chosen as Sethu Lakshmi Bayi's new place of residence and her home in exile.

On 16 February 1958, the Maharani started out from Madras and at Kolar she was pleasantly surprised to see Lalitha, Kerala Varma and the children waiting to escort her to Richmond Road. She arrived in her majestic Humber but that great change that had suddenly enveloped her was patent for all to see. The soldiers on the footboards were gone, the outriders and escorts were no more, that stately procession around her had dissolved; it was all now a memory of times gone by. When she got out of her car on that strange highway, Sethu Lakshmi Bayi was no longer that great, splendid queen she had once been, but merely a grandmother, a regal lady in white. She was driven to Lalitha's house, where, as during her previous stay, a wing was set aside for the use of her ménage. A fortnight later Lalitha and Kerala Varma, who had planned a holiday in Europe, took their leave, while the Maharani got down to the construction of her bungalow next door. 'Having come to Bangalore,' tells Uma, 'she promptly moved on with her life. She refused to dwell on the past.'[32]

Purchasing the house at 7 Richmond Road was not a straightforward affair, however, since it had been leased to the military, and only after prolonged negotiations was the property released. The owner also sensed Sethu Lakshmi Bayi's keenness to acquire it; therefore selling it for twice the market rate.[33] For greater privacy, she also purchased vacant land from the bungalows around her, setting her home in the midst of vast gardens. Added to Lalitha's property, the whole 4 acres of land offered much scope for landscaping and gardening, and before long the Maharani was mapping the layout of her home with her architects.[34] The existing building was allowed to stand, but in addition to this a new wing was constructed with two very large bedrooms ('halls really'), a drawing room, a library and several verandahs and porticos. The library, however, was only a shadow of its former glory, since a portion of the Maharani's collection was donated to the Agricultural College in Vellayini when the government acquired Lalindloch.[35] Looking at the house from the gate, after it was completed, it seemed like a huge, long building, with a number of outhouses and ancillary premises. 'There were fountains, a lotus pond and lawns all around, with a rose garden, and white benches and several trimmed bougainvillea. One part was kept woody, like a forest.'[36] The bungalow was named 'Shrinivas' and would be the Maharani's home for the remainder of her life.

The move to Bangalore was not easy for Sethu Lakshmi Bayi. She had been reared from the age of five as a queen, and had known no other way of life. But she adapted to the change that had overwhelmed her old world and emerged as a new person from under that thick blanket of conventions that had hitherto cloaked her life. 'She became more relaxed,' Indira would explain, 'after she left the palace. I think she was happier after all that glory and fanfare of palace life had gone, and she herself realised how much better and more peaceful it was this way.'[37] Her grandchildren also noticed that she seemed to become a different person. 'That aloofness we sensed as children,' Parvathi recalls, 'vanished. She became granny to us, plain and simple. She was still extremely dignified right to the end, but that aura of being this iconic Maharani receded into the background. She was more approachable, very relaxed and light-hearted, and every day after we came back from school and completed our homework, we would run off and be with her. That old palace habit, of all of us squatting around her and reading books became a daily affair.'[38]

Some of the younger grandchildren, like Ambika and Balan, also got to know their grandmother better as a person. 'She had a sense of humour and she loved a laugh,' tells Ambika. 'It was amazingly delicate and gentle, but a clever one. It was also unbelievable how much she knew. She always spoke to us about things we were interested in. In fact it is now that I realise that she really didn't speak about herself or what she had gone through in life. It was all what we wanted to talk about.'[39] Of course the person most delighted to be with the Maharani was Rukmini, her pet and favourite. 'It was obvious,' remembers a cousin, 'that the Maharani loved her family, but Rukmini came first in her affections.'[40] Ambika too sensed this. 'Rukmini was always different from the rest of us. She was always at grandmother's, while we lived with mother, and she behaved in a very different way too.'[41]

Rukmini describes her own relationship with Sethu Lakshmi Bayi:

> I never, ever heard grandmother complain about having to leave her home and palace. Once or twice when I pressed her to talk to me about the harassment she faced, she brushed it aside saying, 'Those were just some things in a land far, far away.' But she was really like a psychiatrist as far as I was concerned! I could speak to her about anything and everything under the sun. If I had problems with girls in school, I could come and talk to her. Or if a particular boy wanted to be friends with me, I could ask her what to do. Father would be furious at the very suggestion and say, 'Keep off!' But grandmother would listen, and say things like, 'You may speak to him if you like, but be careful,' and so on. She always gave the best advice and was always willing to listen. After my marriage, I know she did not fully approve of my lifestyle, but she was too kind to say so, though, now and then, when sneaking servitors informed her of my late hours—returning from parties after 2 a.m. and the likes—there was a mild reprimand. Her arrival made me feel much better, because I hadn't quite come to terms with leaving the palace in the way mother and my sisters had. But watching grandmother do it so well was simply amazing. In hindsight the ease with which she cut herself from her past, without even the slightest hint of a fuss about it, is what really sets her apart.[42]

The Maharani's routine didn't change too drastically for the first many years. 'She woke up early in the morning, but didn't rise from bed. She would continue lying down, reciting prayers and only much later would she actually get up. Her morning ablutions took an age, and then a silver service for breakfast with milk, idlies and her favourite chutney. At first she used to have those elaborate palace-style baths with many oils and all that, but after a decade or so, that stopped. She then dressed and settled into her day bed to read, followed by lunch, which also took an age. Then in the evenings she would walk in the gardens, go for a drive with some of us, or we would come and sit around her and chatter, like teenaged girls do!'[43] The number of servants was greatly reduced. From eight personal maids, she now had two women in constant attendance, a Brahmin cook and a Brahmin lady server, and a few other servants and odd-job men. 'But these people found it difficult to adjust in Bangalore and slowly the Brahmins returned to Kerala. And when it became difficult to find replacements in the kitchen, grandmother accepted a Nair lady.'[44]

That, by itself, proved a phenomenal reorientation for Sethu Lakshmi Bayi.

In earlier days Nairs were not permitted anywhere near the royal family during meals. And now she had a Nair cook. During the time of the Temple Entry Proclamation, it was fundamentally caste prejudice that prevented the Maharani from giving the move her blessings. But now she saw the futility of that attitude. So much had changed and she accepted these alterations in her personal lifestyle with an increasingly liberal serenity. 'Grandmother,' tells Ambika, 'was orthodox in her personal habits. But she was willing to change and saw it had to be done. I know my mother was instrumental in this. She used to go see her every evening, and over the years she witnessed this great transformation. By the 1970s, she had Christian maids, and she not only interacted freely with them, but also grew so fond of them that she used to give them presents and money very generously.'[45] By the end of her life it would be a lady called Mary who nursed her ('a real chatterbox, but devoted to grandmother'),[46] and Sethu Lakshmi Bayi surprised herself by increasingly giving up the ritualism and antiquated habits that only a few years ago had seemed immutable. Though there was a certain element of tragedy (often in the minds of outsiders) that a once-majestic, hallowed figure such as her had to accept a series of ceremonial deprivations and make unexpected adjustments at so late a time in her life, the Maharani herself did not resent any of this. 'My happiest days have been in Bangalore,' she would confide in a nephew.[47] 'I know it was painful for her to give it all up in Trivandrum,' remarks Rukmini, 'but all the same, grandmother, despite her gentleness, was a strong woman, and she didn't believe in being miserable when one had the option to adapt and find happiness.'[48] For someone who had gone through many ups and downs in life, happiness, Sethu Lakshmi Bayi had learned the hard way, was to be consciously enjoyed, not demanded as a gift from the world around.

It was in fact the Valiya Koil Tampuran who amused the children with his enduring old-world idiosyncrasies even as his wife altered so much about herself and her ways. 'He continued to lead a gentleman's life and didn't spend all the year in Bangalore,' tells Shreekumar. 'He had a room there, one in Madras with us, and then during winter months he would retire to Pothencode, where he still maintained a large staff of servants and got some of that old palace feel.'[49] When indoors, he dressed in a closed-collar shirt (minus the diamond buttons from the good old days, however), and a mundu, but he never, ever stepped outside except in a three-piece ('or, on his worst days, two-piece') suit. 'He also had some regular beggars in Bangalore. He would go by car to Commercial Street and they looked forward to his visits. It was quite amusing because he always distributed exactly the same amounts of money to exactly the same set of beggars.'[50] Rama Varma might have left the old world behind him, but he had no intention of seeking a divorce from discipline, even where it concerned the distribution of his parsimonious charities.

In daily life too he remained steadfast. If he were in Bangalore, he would call on the Maharani after breakfast and spend an allotted duration with her. He always complained, however, that the Maharani too ought to have a more rigorous schedule. He was himself up at dawn, and even read his books for fixed periods, never going a moment over the hour, even if he had reached a very exciting part in the story. By nine o'clock at night he would be in bed. 'Grandmother on the other hand, would stay up past midnight. Her dinners would go on for hours, and we would all be chit-chatting around her, mother sprawled on a very cosy sofa she had, and the rest of us stretched out in various parts of the room. And then, after we said goodnight, she had her prayers, so it was rarely before one o'clock in the morning that she slept. Naturally she woke up later than grandfather, who would complain that this was all unhealthy. He never said this to her directly. He would come and berate us for keeping her up all night.'[51]

Some of Sethu Lakshmi Bayi and Rama Varma's most loyal old retainers and attendants stayed many years with them in Bangalore. For the Maharani it was her youngest sister Kochu Thankam who ran her household, while the latter's husband served as her secretary. 'It was quite amusing,' laughs Rukmini, 'to hear him run all her financial affairs by grandmother, who had really lost interest in these things. For instance, if she wanted to gift a certain sum of money to somebody for a wedding, she would send him a message. He would then rush to her room and say, "No no, Your Highness, we cannot give them so much. We can give them some but not so much." And she would demand, "Why not? Go to the bank and get some money." The poor man would then be forced to reveal to her that there wasn't that much money in the bank any more to begin with.'[52] But she wouldn't budge. Instead, the Maharani accepted economies in the running of her own household, but couldn't, in her old stately fashion, accept recommendations that she should not help those in need. 'If there was a request even from someone unfamiliar, she would still do her bit for them. She was prepared to make sacrifices personally, but she felt she had a duty to those who still saw her as their queen and expected her patronage and support.'[53] Then, of course, there were the annual presents she sent out to her brothers. 'It was just seven rupees! But every year it would reach before their respective birthdays, and

I remember her youngest brother remarking that it was the most wonderfully exciting thing to wait and wait for it, till the very end of his days.'[54]

The Valiya Koil Tampuran's servants, however, found themselves dealing with a shrewd taskmaster who kept tabs even on the stores. 'They were like these relics of the past that didn't fit in at all in Bangalore, still bowing and doing all that.'[55] But these chaste, old-fashioned people were also sitting targets for the girls' pranks. Rama Varma had four menservants: one Tampan, two Tiruppads, and a Balan Nair. 'They were always with grandfather when he went for a walk, or set out with a camera to take pictures in town, following him at a respectable distance. We called Nair the Shah of Iran because, you won't believe it, he looked exactly like the Shah!' chuckles Rukmini. One of the Tiruppads, on the other hand was christened Marilyn Monroe behind his back 'because of his rather ample bosom'.[56] Tampan was the favourite: 'He used to do this ridiculous dance. If we were glum, he'd burst into the room and start his performance till we were in splits!'[57] On another occasion Kunjukrishna Pillai, the Maharani's driver, a very simple, orthodox man, with great faith in stories about devils and yakshis, was treated to the sight of an apparition in white under a tree in the garden. It gave the man a spectacular fright and only later did he realise it was poor Shobhana dressed up and parked there by Rukmini for the express purpose of scaring the living daylights out of him.[58]

By the time great-grandchildren were born in the family, with more distant a connection to the palace than even their parents, and who never knew Sethu Lakshmi Bayi as a queen, the old attendants in her house offered glimpses of a fast fading but still perfectly magical world. These children grew up in an urban Bangalore, playing cricket or football and going to school with so many other ordinary friends. Kerala as well as the esteem their family and ancestors commanded there was a notion that was as remote as it was alien. Yet there were charming childhood experiences in the Maharani's house. 'I remember how Tampan used to sit and prepare the karipatti that the Valiya Koil Tampuran had with his toast,' remembers one of them. 'It was fascinating to watch. He would have this huge vessel with something similar to molten chocolate in it, stirring it slowly with a giant ladle. We were never eager to have it when it was dry and powdered, but always wanted a taste when it was pasty, and in semi-liquid form. It was so wonderful and fascinating to observe, and occassionally our friends from school would join in and return just as amazed by all these traditional practices. Sometimes we would be teased as "princes" and all that, but really it was more traumatic an experience than something to gloat about by then. If I were truly a prince, where was my palace? Or my Rolls Royce? We were even bullied over this.'[59]

It was in 1958 that the Maharani decided to get Rukmini married. 'It was the one time,' tells her nephew, 'that she imposed her will on someone in the family. Never before, and never after did it happen. But that one time it did.'[60] While Lalitha and Kerala Varma were in Europe, Rukmini had revealed to her that she had plans to become a doctor and wanted to apply for medical school in Madras after her intermediate studies at Mount Carmel College. 'That was the only dispute I had with grandmother,' she now remembers. 'I said I wanted a career, but she disagreed and said very firmly that she wanted to see me settled as soon as possible. Father was very much in favour of my studying medicine, but grandmother would not hear of it. She knew medicine would take years and people told her I would never marry, like her niece who became a doctor and chose to remain a spinster. By the time my parents returned, grandmother had already taken her decision. Very rarely did she exercise her power in the family, but when she did, nobody dared say anything.'[61] And so Rukmini, a former head girl at Baldwin's, put aside all the prizes and certificates she had won at school for science, preserving them to this day in an old trunk, and decided to obey her grandmother.

It was a fateful decision. Had Rukmini studied further, proceeded to live in a hostel like other students, and embarked on a career, so too might have her sisters. As destiny would have it, however, that was not to be. When Uma wanted to pursue art at the Sir J.J. School in Bombay, she too was told she could not, and it was only after marriage that she received some training from the Fine Arts College in Madras, interrupted prematurely, then, by the advent of children. It didn't help that Lalitha, though independent in spirit, deliberately did not want her children to be particularly career-minded. 'She wanted them all around her, living blissful domestic lives in Bangalore. She, like the Maharani, had seen the worst of what power and ambition could do to human beings and she didn't want any of that for her children. She simply wanted them to be ordinary, content people.'[62] The only person to break out of the mould was Lakshmi because of her determination. But that was a decade later. In 1958, Rukmini concludes, 'I was told categorically that I should not entertain hopes of studying, and must accept a proposal.'[63]

The candidate eventually chosen for Rukmini was Devi Prasad of the Poonjar Rajah's house, a distant relation who was introduced to the family when he came to Bangalore for his engineering studies. By the time Lalitha and Kerala Varma returned from their holiday, not only had Sethu Lakshmi Bayi confirmed this proposal but wedding preparations had actually begun. Kerala Varma accepted his mother-in-law's command, but was disappointed. 'She threw it all away,' he would later regret, referring to Rukmini's excellent academic prospects had she pursued them.[64] In January 1959, the wedding was celebrated at the Guruvayur Temple, in a departure from the old custom of conducting such ceremonies in the palace. 'It was like a Page 3 event at the time, with pictures in the papers. And at Guruvayur, in what is unthinkable today, the whole temple complex was closed to the public and we had it to ourselves. When we came out, there were crowds of people waiting to see us, and a lot of excitement.'[65] A decade after Independence, royalty still seemed to command much enthusiasm—or at any rate, curiosity—among the public in Kerala.

In December 1959, Rukmini had her first son and Sethu Lakshmi Bayi's eldest great-grandchild, Venugopal. 'He was born under the star Rohini, which is Krishna's star, and grandmother was so delighted, since Krishna was all she prayed and talked about! So she selected the name and called him Venu.'[66] The 1960s and early 1970s, in fact, were a period of unprecedented joy for the Maharani. Her granddaughters were married during these years, and many new additions were made into the family. All the girls had grown into smart, intelligent women, making the most of their opportunities despite being denied official careers. 'Grandmother was always at the head of all this, advising us, listening to us, and really delighted that we were able to lead lives with greater freedom than she had ever imagined possible in her day. I think she was very happy that in leaving the palace and making that sacrifice, at least she had allowed us a chance to develop our individualities.'[67]

In the 1960s, the Maharani constructed a palatial house for Rukmini within her compound, which locals took to calling 'The Palace on Richmond Road', and soon the place was constantly abuzz with visitors and with the sounds of music and dance. Rukmini had trained under the famous U.S. Krishna Rao and his wife Chandrabhaga Devi, mastering the Bharatanatyam dance form. Soon she would shock conservative opinion by giving a few charity performances, and by the middle of that decade would start her own dance school, attracting many (including foreign) students. But it all had to be wound down when someone from the family discovered that she had also been modelling and video reels were being displayed in cinemas across the state. 'Everyone was shocked,' she now recalls, 'even though I had modelled for an innocent brand of silk saris, and there was nothing scandalous about it.'[68] Either way, most of the family were united in their opinion that she should not get into entertainment, and with that Rukmini's forays into dance came to a premature conclusion. 'But I had grandmother behind me through all this,' she now tells, 'and I used to give her private performances in her bedroom whenever I felt an urge to dance.'[69]

Happily enough, however, dance was replaced by painting, in which Rukmini proved a great success, winning international acclaim. The Governor of Karnataka opened her first big exhibition in 1973 while in 1974 President V.V. Giri inaugurated a show in Delhi. A year later a tour of Europe followed, with successful exhibitions in Germany, arranged by C. Ranganathan (a grandson of Sir CP's, ironically, and who, as 'Rungie', was a tennis partner to Devi Prasad, while his sister Geetha was Rukmini's best friend). By 1976, Rukmini was in London where Lord Mountbatten ('a very naughty old man') opened her show, also singing praises of the Maharani. Into the early 1980s, Rukmini held exhibitions at prestigious venues in Bombay, where the press reported a 'stampede' to view her paintings.[70] Art was not an easy journey either, to be sure. To begin with, Rukmini painted in an unfashionable realist style during an age of avant-garde and abstract expressionism. To add to this, her work became controversial for depicting male as well as female nudes, including in settings borrowed from Hindu mythology. Religious authorities and figures censured her work while haughty art critics thought she could have avoided such 'obsolete' art altogether. But Rukmini had the advantage of painting for her own sake and not for money or to win approval from contemporary artists, and she carried on despite obstacles. Exhibitions, however, had to be declined so as not to provoke the orthodoxy, and her paintings disappeared quietly into more tolerant international collections.

Uma, in the meantime, was also breaking new ground. In 1961, she married a cousin of Devi Prasad's who was a chartered accountant. The couple went to Madras for a year, before returning to Bangalore, where they moved into a house on Promenade Road. 'Father,' tells Uma, 'had bought a plot of land in Frazer Town and constructed bungalows for all of us. And when my husband and I returned from Madras it was all furnished, with a staff ready for service, and grandmother gave me a car as a present. So we really didn't need to do anything ourselves.'[71] While Rukmini went from dance to painting, Uma began with art and then moved onto other interests. In 1963, she gave birth to the Maharani's eldest great-granddaughter, Radhika, who remembers Uma being 'completely absorbed' by art in the 1960s.

'She had a studio on the first floor and one had to hop, skip and jump each time we passed the room, to avoid stepping on a canvas or a tube of paint. It was full of her works, and she began with realism and slowly went through all possible styles, down to abstract and contemporary art.'[72] More importantly,

Uma in the 1960s and '70s had some strong socialist leanings, like Lalitha at one time. She used to have debates and arguments on the topic with Kerala Varma consistently, often storming out of the house after intense, fiery discussions. By 1971 she ventured into the world of fashion by starting Bangalore's first designer boutique. A team was painstakingly put together, with the now famous Prasad Bidapa as her assistant. 'Uma,' he recollects, 'was well known in Bangalore at the time, and it was she who really brought the idea of fashion to the city. She was a catalyst not only in my career but also for the whole fashion scene here.'[73] A number of high-profile shows followed and her star model was a 'fantastic, absolutely stunning' young girl,[74] later to become famous as a politician and future minister in the Government of India, Renuka Choudhry.

Uma also travelled extensively to source textiles and material from across the country, all by herself, on trains, planes and buses, with an unusual degree of freedom and independence. 'In those days she looked quite Anglo-Indian,' tells Rukmini. 'Her bobbed hair was always coloured a deep red, and she was quite fair, and used to dress only in Western clothes—skirts, trousers, and the likes.'[75] Sometimes when she went to Kerala and stayed at Ulloor with relatives, Uma used to board a bus to Trivandrum city in the afternoon. 'Forget most people realising that this distinct-looking lady was "Princess Bharani Tirunal Uma Bayi Tampuran" of Travancore, most didn't even have a clue that she was a Malayali!'[76] Uma quite enjoyed travelling with the masses in this manner, and as part of her bohemian lifestyle, often went to meet with artists and poets across the country, or on trips exploring historical places. To further avoid detection when she went to Trivandrum, she always reserved her room at The Mascot under the name of Mrs Sharma or Mrs Raveendran. 'It was a lot of fun,' she laughs now, 'though I only did it because the name Varma was a giveaway.'[77] Her boutique, however, closed down after a few years owing to want of trained hands to help her run the place. 'I had to do everything on my own, but I know grandparents were very proud of it. Grandfather used to come and sit with me in the afternoons, and he was always encouraging of the kind of work we did.'[78] Very likely, he was also puzzled.

In 1963, Parvathi was married to a member of the Cochin royal family. It was the first time such an alliance had occurred between Kerala's two princely dynasties. 'It was all over the Malayalam papers,' recalls the groom, Ravi Varma, 'and even the dimensions of the plantain leaves on which the feast was served were recorded!'[79] In what was different, however, Parvathi's husband refused to surrender his public sector job in Kerala and come up to Bangalore. Both Rukmini's and Uma's husbands had, in the old palace style, stopped working after their marriages. 'We had 800 rupees every month as our allowance,' tells Rukmini, 'and with other provisions and presents our father or grandmother made, we were very well off.'[80] Both their husbands, then, had large farms on the outskirts of Bangalore, where they spent their time. Ravi, however, wanted to work, and so Parvathi joined him in Cochin, where she finished her studies and obtained an MA in Sanskrit. 'In the beginning they were worried how she would manage after growing up in Bangalore, because Cochin is very orthodox. But we were all so surprised when she proved perfectly capable of waking up at 5:30 in the morning, bathing in a tank and going to temples, and not only living a rigorous life but impressing the old dames in Cochin by how well she did it!'[81]

For the next many years Parvathi remained in Kerala, sometimes even living in places like Mannar, a small town where Ravi's work took him. 'Locals would come sometimes on hearing I was a princess of Travancore. I never knew what to do at such moments because Bangalore had wiped all that out.'[82] But Kerala Varma was concerned about his daughter living in Kerala in conditions he thought must have been difficult. 'Once he came to visit us at Chowara where my husband and I were living in this palace that belonged to the Cochin side,' remembers Parvathi. 'He was so upset on seeing me alone in that massive building, with only one or two servants, that he turned around on the highway on his way back and came and spent another two days with me.' Yet again, on hearing of a robbery in their palace, Kerala Varma despatched at his expense a guard with an Alsatian all the way from Bangalore. On visits to her parents, however, Parvathi's husband came in for special treatment. 'Since I came from Cochin, which was an independent royal family and not from one of the aristocracy within Travancore, the Valiya Koil Tampuran was at first hesitant to sit in my presence. It was quite embarrassing, but we eventually got to know each other better and he became more relaxed.'[83] A few years later, Parvathi and Ravi returned to Bangalore when the latter found a new job, and Sethu Lakshmi Bayi purchased a property for them at Palace Orchards as a present.

The royal husbands, as a rule, treated the Maharani with a solemn reverence. 'When my father married into the family,' tells Devi Prasad and Rukmini's son, 'his mother told him, "There are two gods you must worship. One is the God in the heavens and the other is Her Highness the Maharani." And so he was very much in awe of her.'[84] Ravi also thought very highly of Sethu Lakshmi Bayi due to her reputation in his own family. 'It was generally remarked that the Senior Maharani was not only a great queen but also a genuinely good human being. Everyone only had positive things to say about her.' There was also a family story about how during weddings and celebrations in Cochin, the Maharajah of Travancore used to send gold ornaments and presents. Because of a historic rivalry between the two sides most Maharajahs sent presents of really poor quality. 'We were told that it was only after Maharani Sethu Lakshmi Bayi came to the throne that she stopped this petty mockery and made certain that if gifts were coming from Trivandrum, they were befitting and not merely an attempt to insult Cochin.'[85] For Rukmini, though, Parvathi's marriage was the culmination of destiny. 'You know how Martanda Varma never managed to conquer Cochin. So I used to tell my sister, "Parvathi, where great warriors and Maharajahs failed, you have done it! You have conquered Cochin's heart!"'[86]

Lakshmi, in the meantime, grew from a smart teenager of the Beatles' generation, into a determined young woman who decided she wanted to have a professional life. After her graduation she told her parents she was applying to the Lady Shriram College in Delhi for a postgraduate degree, and that she didn't want to complete her studies after marriage like Parvathi. 'They humoured me at first, thinking there was no harm in applying. But once I got in, mother said she had no intention of sending me all the way to Delhi. Eventually, we reached a compromise, and I was allowed to go to Mysore, only a few hours out of Bangalore.'[87] Lakshmi, then, became the first member of the family to move into a public hostel. 'She never advertised or gave a hint about her background,' remarks a classmate, 'but others used to talk about her as a member of a royal family and how she was born in a palace. She cloaked it all with modesty: no arrogance, no superiority complex, no condescending attitude. Instead, she had an admirable and unique quality in a time when society was still very caste and class conscious. She was warm, elegant, gracious and very "cool"!'[88] Lakshmi also stood up for her principles, even if it included picking a fight with Lalitha. Arguments would ensue each time holidays approached as the daughter would insist on travelling by bus to Bangalore with the other girls, while her mother was dead against it, determined to send a chauffer. Similarly, Lalitha couldn't help but pamper her children once these little tiffs had passed: for Lakshmi's birthday, her mother once showed up in Mysore with a twenty-five-course dinner, much to the delight of her hostel-mates, tired of the dry food they were accustomed to eating there.[89]

It was 1968 when Lakshmi married Raghu, also from the Cochin family, and sometime later the two went to Germany where he finished his engineering studies. 'It was great fun, and I saved up and travelled around Europe. It was the time when the hippies were coming to India, and we were going out and wandering in Europe!'[90] On their return to Bangalore, Lakshmi began her career as a lecturer, and strangely enough Sethu Lakshmi Bayi, who had stood in

Rukmini's way, was hugely delighted. 'I think,' tells Rukmini, 'it was because by Lakshmi's time a great deal had changed. Besides, grandmother used to say that if she hadn't been adopted into the royal family and installed as Maharani, she would have liked to be a teacher. So she was happy with Lakshmi's choice for a career.'[91] By 1972, Ambika, who studied psychology, and would volunteer with the Spastic Society in due course, was married to Jeeth, a surgeon and a captain in the Indian Army, before both of them migrated to England and stayed there until the late 1980s while she obtained higher qualifications.

Balan, in the meantime, emerged as the pampered favourite of his mother, and tended to get into all kinds of mischief as he grew up. 'When he was around twenty, father's secretary came in one morning and showed father the newspaper with a picture of Balan in it. Without telling anyone, he had participated in a motorcycle race all the way from Bangalore to Madras, and come back. It was only when the photograph was printed that we found out! Father was furious, but mother,' laughs Rukmini, 'loved him for it.'[92] By this time he was a popular young man in Bangalore, famous for his long hair and for driving a Buick to college. Legions of girls at bus stops would wait to be offered a lift by 'the Prince of Travancore' and dozens of hearts were broken when in 1973 Balan left for the United States for his MBA at Berkeley. Upon his return two years later, he took over Kerala Varma's business concerns. Sethu Lakshmi Bayi's other grandson, Shreekumar, in the meantime, was more academically and intellectually inclined, and went on to obtain an MPhil before becoming a journalist with *The Indian Express*. Living in Bombay, he 'hung out with the likes of Amjad Khan (who spouted *shayari* to him), Raj Kapoor, Dilip Kumar and Dev Anand (who invited him to join a political party he was starting), while writing for *Cinema Today*'.[93] He returned to Madras in due course to become a professor and an award-winning playwright and novelist. Shobhana too distinguished herself in her studies, becoming a lawyer in the Madras High Court, and a prominent socialite in the city. In the words of one of her legal contemporaries, 'She was so beautiful and intelligent that the whole Madras Bar wanted to marry her!'[94]

With even Sethu Lakshmi Bayi's grandchildren marrying and settling down, her Richmond Road house was inundated with little children. In 1962 Lalitha had, shortly after her thirty-eighth birthday, given birth to her youngest child, a daughter called Devika, twenty-two years Rukmini's junior. 'I remember grandmother once sitting in bed and telling stories,' recalls Rukmini, 'and there must have been a dozen kids all around her. And I thought, here was this woman who once yearned for children of her own and made pilgrimages and religious vows, and now towards the end of her life, she was surrounded by so many! I knew it made her very happy.'[95] The entire family would get together regularly, as Radhika recalls. 'We would all meet every Sunday, and we children had a great time playing games. [Lalitha] would have prepared a sumptuous meal for all of us, and at the end we all had to loudly say, LUHSY (Lalitha, you have surpassed yourself!).'[96] After lunch the children would then run over to the Maharani and the Valiya Koil Tampuran. 'I looked forward to these visits. She used to keep a jar of Nutrine sweets ready for all of us and we would sit beside her, at times on the floor below, or on a large armchair nearby and listen to her stories or read children's comic strips from the *Illustrated Weekly*. Sometimes when we fought, great-grandmother was like a soothing balm. She always enquired about our studies and interests, and since she knew I was interested in art,' continues Radhika, now a painter, 'she said I should cultivate and pursue it.'[97]

Everything about the Maharani fascinated the younger children. 'I remember seeing the inside of her stately black Humber,' remembers Radhika, 'and thought it looked like a drawing room, and not at all like our cars. It had a sofa and armchairs around which I could walk.'[98] The car impressed others in the family too. 'It had no number plate but the old Travancore royal crest, and we all were quite taken up with that, since we had never lived in the palace.'[99] However, as the Maharani's activities became increasingly confined to her home, the Humber was sold in 1967 and old Kunjukrishna Pillai, its driver, pensioned off. Her lunches too amazed the children. 'I would go and peer curiously into her large silver plate and the small silver bowls with curries in them, and finally eye the potatoes in the *pacha sambar*. She would lovingly take out the potato and drop it into my open mouth. At times even when we were two or three kids, there were enough potatoes to give each of us as we sat admiring the bright red, polished, soft, leather slip-on shoes at her bedside.'[100] The Valiya Koil Tampuran, now in his eighties, also became gentler than before. As Radhika tells:

> I used to accompany him on his walks around the garden and watch him play Diabolo or 'devil on two sticks' as he used to call it. A strange game with two sticks and a string tied to them. He would throw a wooden hourglass shaped object up in the air and catch it on the string with the sticks. The whole feat was quite amazing. He also had a collection of magic toys. He used to pull them out and show us various tricks. We would watch the little magic show in amazement. On his walks he would also pluck some jasmine flowers and keep it in his palm. Much later he would put his hands on our nose so we could smell the fragrance.[101]

He also liked playing games of vocabulary. 'He used to give us these brilliant old dictionaries he had, with the history of each word in it, and ask us to choose any. He always knew what every word we threw at him meant, even some very unusual ones starting with Z.'[102] But what really fascinated the children were the prayers. For all their westernised lifestyle, members of Sethu Lakshmi Bayi's family remained fairly religious and had their respective japams in the afternoon. Lalitha worshiped Shiva while Indira had Ganapati. The Valiya Koil Tampuran's japams were impressive. 'He would sit down cross-legged on a little mat on the floor in one corner of the room. There were no idols or pictures of any god, not even a lamp was lit anywhere nearby. His eyes closed, fingers in a mudra, his back straight and upright, he would remain in silence. At times we kids might even enter the room, making noise, but he wouldn't stir. After around forty-five minutes or so, he would open his eyes, bow down and prostrate. Then from a small box he would take out a little vibhuti and put it across his forehead and from another box a little sandalwood paste to apply in the centre of his forehead. He would get up and greet us, never scolding us for the noise.'[103] Rukmini's sons were close to the Valiya Koil Tampuran, with Venu sharing his interest in hunting and sport. 'One memorable story he told us,' remembers his brother, Jay, 'was when Jim Corbett was commissioned to shoot a troublesome maneater, but failed, and great-grandfather took it out. But by the 1970s he regretted having killed all these animals. We used to throw stones at the red-throated garden lizards and he used to tell us to stop, telling how the ecstasy when you got your shot evaporated into agony when you saw the dead eyes. I also remember how he used to come to our rooms, whenever we were unwell, and sit by our bedside and talk to us. That was always special—this grand old man making conversation with us children, and taking everything we said very, very seriously.'[104]

Sethu Lakshmi Bayi, all along, loved hearing news of babies being born in the family. 'In those days,' laughs Devika, 'there were babies being born every year, since my sisters obliged one after the other. And *amooma* [grandmother] rewarded the first person that came to her with the happy news. Of course we would all vie for the honour. I got lucky one time and rushed to her when my nephew was born, and I was given a beautiful brass bell in the shape of Hanuman.' The Maharani wanted the girls in the family to be perfect, cultivated young ladies. 'She used to give Radhika and me tips on how to conduct ourselves as proper young women—a challenge for her, since I was most unladylike and loved nothing more than to slide into my jeans and run around with Venu and Jay!'[105] As it happened, it was Jay who spent a lot of his time with Sethu Lakshmi Bayi in the 1970s. As he recollects:

> I remember sitting with great-grandmother and talking to her for hours on end. We would talk about a lot of small things as well as the books I had read from her collection. I remember she was surprised that I wanted to read her Georgette Heyer books as well as *The Scarlet Pimpernel* by Baroness Orczy and others by Frank G. Slaughter, Rider Haggard, etc., at a very young age. As I was staying in the same house as her for several years, I managed to develop a close relationship with her and she played an important role in my younger days as a guiding light. She also taught us stories from the epics, one chapter a day, and in such detail that it took her hours to finish a chapter. And when we finished, we'd ask to begin the whole thing over again, because she was an expert storyteller. She also told me once that we must aim to be cultured people and that a cultured person is someone who knows something about everything and everything about something. That is why she read such a great deal, and really seemed to know about everything under the sun.[106]

On his visits from Madras, Indira's son also shared a similar relationship with the Maharani. 'From my early teens I used to write and it was a typical summer habit to sit by her side and read out my stories,' recalls Shreekumar. 'I don't know, now that I think of it, whether she enjoyed it or whether she sat there and listened simply because I gave her no alternative! I would inflict a series of macabre murder stories upon her. But she definitely paid attention. I once mentioned a medicine to cure syphilis in a story, not knowing what it was, and she promptly stopped me and asked me to remove it if I didn't know what it meant. I also listened to music with her—Yesudas, Devarajan and so on. She always pointed out the inflections and nuances of the singer's rendition. She was very knowledgeable about classical music. Sometime in the 1970s Yesudas himself came to pay his respects and sang in person for her, and I was fortunate to be present. She really enjoyed that.'[107]

By the 1970s, Sethu Lakshmi Bayi had completed her transformation into an astonishingly liberal person and all the orthodoxy she imbibed early in life had dissolved altogether. 'As I got older,' Balan would later remark, 'what I remember most vividly was her interest in the things we were doing, what we were planning to do with our lives, what the new India was all about.'[108] The Maharani was genuinely interested in the world and the nation of young Indians emerging around her, even if she, as a symbol of another era, didn't entirely fit into it. Proof of her growing openness came some years down the line when Jay and Radhika made marriages that many of their wider family did not approve. 'I wanted to marry a Kannadiga girl,' remembers Jay, 'my childhood sweetheart, and it was great-grandmother who gave her support first.'[109] But while this was still acceptable, since he was a male member of the family, what was much more controversial was Radhika falling in love with a friend of Venu's. She was Sethu Lakshmi Bayi's eldest great-granddaughter, and a representative of the Attingal line. And to have her marry outside the community, many thought, was sacrilegious. But Radhika told Uma and Lalitha about her decision when she was seventeen, and about to leave for Madras for art school. 'I think they hoped that five years down the line, by the time I returned, I would have given up my plans and would fall in line. Grandmother asked me to let her know whether I still felt the same way when I came back. And I did.'[110]

The boy in question was Tosher Hormusjee, the son of a Parsi businessman. Even Uma, who was otherwise remarkably rebellious, was uncertain. But somehow news reached Sethu Lakshmi Bayi of the discussion in the family. So one day, when Tosher came by, the Maharani summoned him for an interview. When he went in, she asked him a number of questions about his career, interests and his parents. 'At the end of the interview a maidservant instructed him to bow down to her. I don't think he had ever bowed to anyone before that.' Tells Radhika. 'Great-grandmother asked me when I went to see her later if I was really interested in this boy, to which I said yes.'[111] Promptly, then, Uma and Lalitha were called in and the Maharani commanded, 'Whatever Radhika wants, you must allow it. It is her decision and her life.'[112] 'It was such a boost of confidence for me. Even Tosher said that at a time when there was so much opposition from all quarters, he couldn't believe that my great-grandmother greeted him and welcomed him to the family. He was very impressed by her. I wondered how someone so elderly, who had lived all her life in an orthodox palace, could be so broad-minded. But I guess she was just that special lady.'[113]

Indeed, it was in this decade that Sethu Lakshmi Bayi truly unhinged herself from the past, taking one step after another towards achieving an almost spiritual peace and detachment. All her worldly possessions were given up by now, and even her jewellery and almost all her money had been divided among family members. In 1971 the Government of India, in terminating the privy purses of the ex-princes, also discontinued the Maharani's pension. Though it would be restored a decade later, she received the unexpected termination ungrudgingly.[114] In the meantime a court case had sprung up with the Maharajah. In 1971, the properties of the royal family were divided, but only the Sripadam was taken into account. Chithira Tirunal claimed the entire set of palaces and buildings in Trivandrum, known as Valiya Kottaram, as his private property. Lalitha and Indira were both incensed that even Satelmond, their childhood home, was the

Maharajah's 'private property' and prolonged litigation commenced, though the Maharani herself was personally against the idea. 'She really didn't want to fight and have anything to do with Trivandrum any more.'[115]

Sethu Lakshmi Bayi's attachment even to Satelmond Palace had now ceased. In 1951, in what felt like a lifetime ago, she had cared about it, and obtained from V.P. Menon an assurance, since the Maharajah was unwilling to give her one, that 'Your Highness' rights and those of your children to stay at Satelmond Palace so long as you desire will be respected and safeguarded.'[116] But as soon as she had left the palace, Kowdiar Palace demanded the surrender of its keys on the grounds that the Maharani no longer used it, and that it was the private property of the Maharajah.[117] Again this assertion was denied as ludicrous and patently unjust. But a few decades down the line her thinking had changed. Sometime in the early 1970s the Maharajah had created, through a generous endowment and with the government's backing, the Sree Chithira Tirunal Institute for Medical Sciences and Technology in Trivandrum.[118] The premises were not very appealing, however, and its head, Dr M.S. Valiathan, had for some time been looking for a place with a greater heritage. It was at this time that he met the Maharani's son-in-law, KK, a friend of his, and was surprised by his suggestion: 'Why don't you take Satelmond?'[119] By this time the place resembled a haunted house and though there was a permanent caretaker, it was rather run-down. Occasionally, the younger boys in the family took city friends there to camp and party, but the family had no particular use of the property. Dr Valiathan, therefore, promptly explored the possibility of acquiring this as the headquarters for his institute. 'One great asset,' he remembers, 'was that the Maharajah and his mother as well as the Senior Maharani and her daughters had a lot of goodwill for us.'[120] An agreement was drafted that pending court proceedings between the two families, a government-allotted compensation would be reserved, and later claimed by the victors. By 1976, the paperwork was drawn up and all Dr Valiathan needed was signatures.

But that is when the Junior Maharani changed her mind and decided against giving the palace over. Her secretary, Vaidyanath Iyer, informed Dr Valiathan that 'the Maharani says there is no need for this transaction, and we cannot ask her any questions'.[121] The Chief Minister of Kerala even suggested another location, but the doctor was determined to have Satelmond, with all its beauty and majestic history. Luckily for him, this was the time when Prime Minister Indira Gandhi proclaimed the Emergency, and fear of the government was on an all-time high. One evening the caretaker at the palace called to inform Lalitha that the police had arrived at Satelmond and forced their way in, with plans to convert the palace into a police camp. Dr Valiathan promptly rang Vaidyanath Iyer and appealed to him that a medical research facility was a nobler alternative to letting the palace become, of all things, a place for trainee policemen to drill around in their undergarments. That very evening the Maharajah agreed to sign the papers. Along with KK, Dr Valiathan then flew to Madras and obtained Indira's signature, leaving immediately afterwards for Bangalore. All that could go wrong on the way did—the plane was delayed and their luggage was misplaced—and it was nearly 11:30 at night when they got out of the airport.

'We thought we would never see the Senior Maharani that night, but when we rang Mrs Kerala Varma she said, "No, no, mother is waiting for you."' And so the two men called at Shrinivas late that night. 'I had seen her last as a boy of ten,' Dr Valiathan, who was related through his father to the Maharani,[122] now tells, 'and she was there again that night, and her daughter, and Kerala Varma, were all around her. She took the agreement and smiled. She said to me, "Valiathan, you must have come to Satelmond several times." I said yes. And she said to me as she signed the papers, "Aah, this is freedom at midnight!" It was a joke based on the book by Dominique Lapierre and Larry Collins, and everybody had a laugh. That was the amazing thing. There was no sorrow or anger or regret at losing the palace. She had lived there and ruled over millions of people from there. But there was no bitterness at losing it. She was so cheerful. She had a complete sense of detachment by then. It was a mark of her greatness.'[123]

What pained Dr Valiathan in due course was that the Supreme Court in 1991 accepted the Maharajah's contention that all these palaces were his private property and that other members of the royal family could only claim what was left of the Sripadam.[124] 'I had a moral dilemma, because I knew the Senior Maharani had lived there and her family were in physical possession; it was from them that I received the keys to the palace, but here I was giving away the money to the Maharajah's side. I feel morally guilty to this day about that moment, but I could not do differently since it was a court order.' Dr Valiathan then made 'a feeble attempt to set up a Satelmond International Symposium for Biomedical Technology in the Maharani's name, but nothing came of it in the long run.' Today, other than a painting with a plaque presented by her family, there is nothing to commemorate the fact that she had reigned over a kingdom from that very palace, just as there is no monument to Sethu Lakshmi Bayi anywhere in Kerala to this day. 'It is a regret,' he concludes, 'that will be with me for the rest of my life.'[125]

But Sethu Lakshmi Bayi herself did not mind all this, nor that Satelmond now housed an institution named after the Maharajah. 'She never blamed him at all, you know,' tells Rukmini. 'She thought of him as a very gentle soul.'[126] On the contrary, she was delighted that her beloved palace was now once again cared for by its new owners and maintained in all its glory, while serving the public cause. Around the same time that she signed the palace away, permanently and decidedly severing her connection to the past, the Government of India also passed the Urban Land Ceiling Act by which no person was permitted to own more than a certain extent of property in Indian cities. Under its clauses, the Maharani's home in Bangalore was too large for single ownership, and she was compelled to cut up and divide even the compound of Shrinivas among her grandchildren. Rukmini inherited the house she lived in, Ambika the wing at the back, Devika the kitchen buildings, while other grandchildren received shares of land. Similarly, property she owned on Miller Road and Spencer Road went to Indira's children. Shortly after this, when some visitors called on her, Sethu Lakshmi Bayi, never one given to emotional demonstrations, showed herself as having accepted all these travails of her life with a smiling forbearance. Looking extremely fragile and shrunken, nearly bedridden by now, in a very tender voice she said: 'Once I had a kingdom. But that is gone. Then I thought Satelmond was mine, but that is gone too. Then I thought this house was mine, but now I can only say this room is mine.'[127]

The Maharani smiled as she said this, but the hearer was moved to tears.

In December 1975, when Rukmini was on a visit to London, she received news that the Valiya Koil Tampuran was gravely ill and admitted to hospital. 'I knew it was serious the moment I heard that grandmother had gone to see him there, because she never, ever went out.'[128] Rama Varma had, for many years now, had a very delicate internal constitution and he used to take great care, therefore, of his food habits. But in the winter of 1975 he suffered a serious attack of indigestion, and one by one his organs began to fail until he lapsed into a coma. 'I still remember him in his hospital bed, unconscious and with all sorts of tubes and wires on him,' recalls Shreekumar.[129] Devi Prasad and Rukmini landed just in time, for on 29 December, the Valiya Koil Tampuran died at the St Philomena's Hospital in Bangalore aged eighty-six. A letter he had written, addressed to 'Her Highness Maharani Sethu Lakshmi Bayi' was delivered to his wife shortly afterwards. Its contents are not known, for the Maharani had it destroyed after she read it, but it was apparently a final expression of fealty and a last message of gratitude from him to the woman he owed everything.[130] In death also, Rama Varma had been meticulously prepared, leaving behind not only this letter but also an exhaustive, detailed will with a codicil running into sixteen pages.[131]

'It was a great loss for all of us, but particularly for grandmother. For a long time after this she did not speak,' recalls Rukmini.[132] Others too noticed the dramatic effect her husband's death had on the Maharani. 'She suddenly aged. I had never thought of her as frail until then, but slowly she began to fade away.'[133] Indeed, Sethu Lakshmi Bayi was terribly affected by the passing of the man who had been her companion from the time she was a girl of ten—from those merry games of hopscotch through to the Regency and beyond. Through thick and thin, she relied on his support, and though they did not always agree—whether during her reign or afterwards on matters of financial prudence—he had been the Maharani's most faithful, even if somewhat unromantic, well-wisher. His death was also a sombre confirmation of the fact that the world she represented and had once presided over with such aplomb was truly gone forever. By the 1960s, most of her brothers had died (as had Miss Watts), and in 1978 Kochu Thankam, her long-standing companion, would retire to Kerala. Some years later the Maharani's other sister Kutty Amma also died. With the Valiya Koil Tampuran's passing away, even his faithful attendants departed to enjoy his bequests to them. One by one, everyone associated with her court disappeared, leaving Sethu Lakshmi Bayi behind, all alone. She was defined by these people and that grand old world they populated together. In 1982, even her youngest brother, seventeen years her junior, passed away suddenly. When informed about this, she asked, 'Before me?'[134]

By now the Maharani had little by way of her individuality except her greatly dignified demeanour. The Valiya Koil Tampuran, until he died, had always reminded the family that this gentle lady was a queen who had ruled and controlled the destinies of millions at one time. But Sethu Lakshmi Bayi herself never spoke about it. She must have been proud of what she had achieved, however, for she carefully preserved all her private papers and documents from the Regency in a black trunk under her bed; the work of her lifetime locked up in a nondescript box and tucked away, just like she hid her sentiments from everybody else. Even her grandchildren—the offspring of a new India—did not quite comprehend the scale of her achievements until after her death when that trunk was opened. But none of this seemed to matter any more, and a kind of loneliness crept into Sethu Lakshmi Bayi's mind. Her body had become frail and uncooperative, and she couldn't get by without the aid of Mary and her nurses. She remained alert and still read a great deal, but slowly began to lose interest in everything. 'She was always particular,' remembers her nephew, 'about her clothes and appearance, but in these final years she lost interest even in all that.'[135] She had given up everything she had; in fact when she died there was only some of her pension money left in her bank. For a woman of such famous generosity, she had little left to give away. And once all those principal personalities from her generation too died or departed, she became the last standing woman. Once they had all surrounded her and looked up to her in awe. Now it was her fate to watch them fade away and to be left behind as the last of her line.

In 1983, news arrived from Trivandrum that the Junior Maharani had died. Sethu Lakshmi Bayi received this information in silence. 'I still remember telling her,' states Rukmini, 'and she had this pensive expression. A look of resignation, really, and she let out a heavy sigh. She didn't say anything about what she felt or thought.'[136] It was the culmination of an epic battle between the two Maharanis, but in the end an anticlimax. The truth was that the world and era they had battled in was no longer relevant; the Ivory Throne that had provoked a generation of quarrels now belonged in a sparsely visited museum. With the passage of time, both women became frail, weak and old, succumbing to that great equaliser, death. There were perhaps regrets, or perhaps there weren't. In 1979, in fact, the Junior Maharani called on Sethu Lakshmi Bayi unexpectedly. The cousins had not seen one another for over twenty-two years. 'When we told her that the Junior Maharani, the Maharajah and others were coming,' recalls Uma, 'she wasn't keen at all. She asked, "But why now, why at this time? I don't want to meet anyone. Can't you say I'm not well?" It wasn't because she disliked them. It was just that she had evolved beyond the history she shared with them.'[137] Or perhaps Sethu Lakshmi Bayi, who had always been conscious of her dignity and walked with her head held high, did not wish to be seen unable to walk at all. At Lalitha's insistence, however, she agreed, and the visitors spent several hours with her. 'Grandmother was very cordial, and received them warmly. The Junior Maharani couldn't climb up the steps into the house, so I remember it was Venu who cradled her up and carried her in.'[138] For all her initial reluctance, photographs of the visit, nonetheless, depict a Sethu Lakshmi Bayi who looked positively radiant and happy at this final encounter with her former nemesis, who ironically looks rather glum.

With even that great 'villain of the piece' from her life and times bowing out, Sethu Lakshmi Bayi moved into a mood of deep contemplation. 'I remember the small rectangular room where she spent her last days, lonely and occasionally visited,' Shreekumar would later write, 'watching the dusk slip in and out of a series of windows.' And once 'towards the end, she confessed she was in danger of "forgetting how to talk". An inherent optimism kept her going. It is frightening to consider such a darkening of life.'[139] But this was perhaps an inevitable conclusion to the story of this Maharani. For the first twenty years after she renounced her royal past in favour of a new life in Bangalore, Sethu Lakshmi Bayi was extremely content. She was essentially the heart and soul of her massive, doting family, surrounded always by people and finally enjoying unsullied happiness of a kind she had never known when she had lived and acted as a queen. Everyone looked forward to being with her, and compensated for what she had given up in Trivandrum with their love and affection.

But such pristine days could not last forever, and by the 1980s things began to change. Lalitha and Indira were now approaching their sixties and even the Maharani's grandchildren were moving towards middle age with their own cares and concerns. The youngest generation, her great-grandchildren, too had grown into adulthood and were part of an urban crowd, 'indistinguishable', as Louise Ouwerkerk put it, 'from the other charming young things that make up the smart set of Bangalore'.[140] 'The last thing we wanted to do at that age,' comments Jay, 'was to stay at home with family.'[141] To them Sethu Lakshmi Bayi was a beloved matriarch and grandmother, but no longer did her tales from the epics enthral them like they once had. 'She lost her regular company,' Jay adds, 'and though we tried to spend time with her occasionally, in hindsight I realise we got carried away with our little lives and could have done better. It was only afterwards that we realised her great sacrifice and how much we owed to her. But, alas, it was too late by then.'[142] Balan too, in retrospect, entertains similar feelings:

> When she left Trivandrum and moved to Bangalore, I was around five years old. To me she was my amooma who lived in the house next door and who we would go visit and spend time with and who would always give us sweets ... It was only later, looking back at her life, that I came to realise how much change she had had thrust upon her. One day, a little girl playing in her own backyard, the next day a princess and a queen, and then back to being an ordinary person. Throughout it all, she conducted herself the very same way, with the same qualities of approachability, integrity, and dignity. Perhaps the biggest lesson that I have learnt is that a person must stay the same whatever life throws at you. I hope that I am living a life now that she would be proud of and upholding the values that made her the person she was ... a great soul living in our midst.[143]

By 1984, Sethu Lakshmi Bayi retreated into a perpetually meditative state. 'If you can visualise a life of constant prayer and meditation, broken only by occasional intrusions of the outside world,' tells Lakshmi, 'you can picture her state of mind as the last years of her life advanced. She had a "peace that passeth understanding". To me, she became the ultimate in spiritual evolution, my Holy Grail!'[144] In December that year the British anthropologist Adrian Mayer, who was perhaps the last outsider to see the Maharani, called on her for an interview. By this time she was clearly moving towards her end. 'She was in bed,' he recalls, 'a small, fragile lady with a sheet drawn over her, her voice a mere whisper.'[145] During their discussion, Sethu Lakshmi Bayi would murmur her answers to Rukmini, who would then elucidate them for the scholar. Yet Mayer knew that this old, dying woman, surrounded by her white sheets and still exuding that dovelike quality, had created history. Writing later he would say, 'To all who know Kerala she was a person of great social and historical importance and I feel it a great privilege to have been able to meet her.'[146]

A few days after Mayer's visit, for New Year's Eve, the Maharani, now missing most teeth and physically diminished in the extreme, asked Mary to dress her better than usual. For it was a family custom for everyone, from the adults down to the children, to get into fancy dress and burst into her room at midnight shouting, 'Happy New Year!' Sethu Lakshmi Bayi would clap in glee and laugh at all the costumes arrayed before her, before proceeding with the usual ritual of handing out toffee to everybody present. For the new year of 1985 also she waited in bed for the party to begin, but midnight came and went and nobody arrived to greet her. It so happened that Lalitha was unwell and didn't want the Maharani to find out. Everyone had, therefore, stayed away from the latter's room. In great disappointment, she went to bed, giving the sweets to her nurses and servants instead. The whole family felt sorry to have let her down, hoping to make it up to her the following year. But they were not destined to have a second chance. In February 1985, Sethu Lakshmi Bayi began to groan in pain and doctors realised that bones in her body had shattered, causing her great agony. Medication did not help and on 22 February she passed away at the Mallige Medical Centre in Bangalore, cremated afterwards like anybody else at the Wilson Garden Electric Crematorium. She knew her time had come, for as she was being carried away to hospital, she called out to Rukmini's son, and said to him in a pained whisper, 'Jay, I am going away.'[147]

Epilogue

Legend has it that the genesis of the House of Travancore was tainted by a terrible curse. When Martanda Varma succeeded to the throne, his consolidation of power in those tumultuous years rested upon the annihilation of the local aristocracy, including two particularly influential adversaries. Their names were Padmanabhan and Raman Tampi, and they were the luckless sons of the penultimate Rajah. The mainstream narrative, spun retrospectively to weave a righteous halo around Martanda Varma, goes to great lengths to tell how these wicked brothers aspired to their father's throne in contravention of matrilineal law. And when their unholy machinations crossed all limits of mercy and reason, the rightful royal heir put them to death according to the gruesome mandates of local justice.

But an obscure Tamil ballad, *Tampimar Kathai*, recounts an alternative version of that bloody episode. This chronicle speaks of a lustful Martanda Varma who coveted the hand of the late ruler's daughter, the exquisite Ummini Tanka. Her brothers gave their consent, but on the condition that her offspring should be guaranteed succession to the throne. As children of a non-Malayali mother, these cousins of Martanda Varma subscribed to patrilineal law, and did not deem their stipulation unreasonable. The Rajah, however, rejected the condition in deference to the dynastic rules of his line. But he was unable to forgive the Tampis' presumption, hereafter plotting to acquire Ummini Tanka by hook or crook.

To coerce the Tampis into submission, he confiscated the vast estates their father had bestowed upon them. In retaliation, the brothers humbled the king on the battlefield with the aid of a mercenary Tamil brigade. In 1729, they besieged

Martanda Varma in his fort at Kalkulam (later sanctified as Padmanabhapuram), claiming an effortless victory. For all the propaganda that depicted Martanda Varma as the very paragon of gallant manliness and brimming heroism to the generations ahead, the king is said to have timidly attempted to slink away in disguise. He was captured, but the Tampis were persuaded to spare his life. It was a clemency that would have fatal consequences for them.

While the Tampis established their rule over the rich district of Nanjanad, a chastened but unforgiving Martanda Varma plotted revenge far away. From direct action, he decided on cunning stratagem. Covertly he bribed the Tamil armies to withdraw from Kerala, agreeing to their commander's condition, in the sacred presence of a temple deity, that he and the Tampis would never cross swords again. But once the charade was played out, and the armies had disappeared into the heat and dust of the Tamil country, the Rajah put into execution his macabre scheme.

In October 1730, Martanda Varma invited the Tampis to his palace in Nagercoil for a casual conference. There he caught Padmanabhan off-guard and killed him. Raman Tampi, sensing treachery, rushed into the chamber, but was overpowered. As a number of men held him down, struggling and thrashing in rage, Martanda Varma, the future hero of modern Travancore, thrust a dagger into his heart. The first victory of the first Maharajah was rooted in cold, crafty murder. But if he had any hopes of marrying Ummini Tanka, they came to naught. For hearing of the treacherous fate of her brothers, the lady cursed the royal house for eternity and slit her throat.

In his career ahead, Martanda Varma was to spill more blood and to commit graver sins, demolishing the old laws of Kerala that stood in the way of his ambition. But the curse of Ummini Tanka unnerved his priests at any rate, for the spirit of this wrathful beauty was conciliated and ceremoniously installed in a temple as a minor deity. And local communities to this day worship the tragic heroine of *Tampimar Kathai* as the Melangode Yakshi.[1]

But if Travancore was afflicted in its inception, its decline two hundred years later too was marred, it is said, by the curse of a woman. In 2011, a council of astrologers was convened in the Sri Padmanabhaswamy Temple in Thiruvananthapuram. Their mission (so to speak) was to consult the stars and determine the cause of a series of troubles that had beset the ex-royal family and the shrine of their deity. The assembled Brahmin astrologers said, according to reports, that things were very bad indeed. Ritual amends were recommended in the form of 100,000 *Tila Homams*, 24,000 *Maha Sudarsana Homams*, 24,000 *Laghu Sudarsana Homams* and a *Sukritha Homam*; fabulous ceremonies to correct lapses accumulated in the conduct of temple rites and traditions over the decades since Independence.[2]

According to eyewitnesses, the astrologers also spoke of a fresh curse that blighted the royal family and demanded urgent ritual settlement. 'There was,' they reportedly declared, 'a queen in this dynasty. She ruled this land and served its deity. But she had to depart with tears in her eyes. Her curse is upon you and continues to unsettle even Padmanabhaswamy.'[3] Many of the believers present, it is said, were confused by this utterance of the astrologers. But to those who knew the history of the royal house, all this pointed to the name of one forgotten woman around whom had fallen a curtain of silence.

The only queen to have left Travancore in tears was Sethu Lakshmi Bayi.

The disappearance of the Senior Maharani and her heirs into the westernised freedoms of Bangalore in the 1950s meant that hereafter the spotlight (largely of exotic curiosity in democratic India) was solely on the successors of the Junior Maharani. And to most in Thiruvananthapuram today, any reference to 'the royal family' conjures up images of only the latter. Sethu Parvathi Bayi and her son, the Maharajah, continued to live in Kowdiar Palace in relative pomp at least until the extravagant Privy Purse paid by the Government of India was abolished in 1971. Though the Maharajah had lost his principality, he was permitted control over the great temple in his capital at the time of the integration of Travancore with India. As 'Ruler of Travancore', under a special covenant, Chithira Tirunal would remain Padmanabhaswamy's mortal representative on earth until his passing in 1991. And till his dying breath this last Maharajah stood famously committed in his religious fervour and passion.

With the death of Chithira Tirunal, his brother, the Elayarajah, succeeded as head of the family and assumed the now-defunct title of Maharajah. Radha Devi and he wound up their life in Bangalore and settled into the Pattom Palace, where they would live till their own deaths. But the Elayarajah's control over the Sri Padmanabhaswamy Temple was contested, and by 2007 legally challenged. It came as a rude shock to him. Following Independence, any significance the Junior Maharani's family retained in Thiruvananthapuram was tied to their control over and religious representation of this shrine. Despite the ascent of numerous communist dispensations to power in Kerala, the family continued to enjoy a minor degree of reverence, and therefore relevance, in the state mainly because of their socio-religious standing vis-à-vis the temple. But once the floodgates of litigation opened, questions began to pile up, and for the first time that traditional estimation was questioned publicly. As the High Court of Kerala noted in its resultant judgment in 2011:

> Public resentment started when the last Ruler's brother ... who after the last Ruler's death took over the control and management of the Temple, arranged to take photographs of the treasures of the Temple and made a claim which was published in the Malayalam Daily *Kerala Koumudi* on 15.9.2007 stating that the treasures of the Padmanabha Swamy Temple are the family properties of the erstwhile Royal Family of Travancore. Several devotees approached Civil Courts in Trivandrum filing Suits for declaration and for injunction against those who are in control and management of the Temple...[4]

The Elayarajah, in response to claims that he had no legal right to the temple or its treasures and that he was in fact mismanaging it, argued that after his brother, he had succeeded as 'Ruler of Travancore'. And under the special covenant, the 'Ruler' alone controlled the temple. He further claimed that the Sri Padmanabhaswamy Temple was a family shrine. The High Court, however, ruled that by the Constitutional Amendment that had abolished the Privy Purse in 1971, the very concept of 'Ruler' had no legal standing anymore, and the Elayarajah's 'succession' to a non-existent title could not be accepted. As for the assertion that the temple was a family estate, the High Court dismissed it as 'absurd'.[5] In order to 'save the Temple and to protect the interest of the devotees and the public at large who have great faith in this Great Temple', it was therefore ordered that the Government of Kerala constitute fresh arrangements for its management. The 'relatives of the late King [had] no right over' it and they were ordered to relinquish control immediately.[6]

The Elayarajah, already eighty-nine at the time, appealed against the decision, and the matter was decided in the royal family's favour in 2020 by the Supreme Court. But while legalities were being argued over, what electrified the public and drew the international press to old, sleepy Thiruvananthapuram was the allure of the mysterious treasures in the temple's vaults that seemed to be the bone of contention. As the High Court remarked in its judgment:

> It is a well-known fact that the Temple has immense treasures, some of which are centuries old and are highly valuable by virtue of its antique value and

> its price in terms of the value of precious metals like gold, silver and stones used in the making. Even though we directed the present management to produce the inventory prepared by the last Ruler ... they refused to produce the same. Some registers produced in the Court were thoroughly incomplete and unreliable. In view of the public claim made by the last Ruler's brother who is presently managing the Temple that the treasures belong to the Royal Family of Travancore, the injunction ... against opening any of the Kallaras (storage place in the Temple) and removal of any valuable item, should continue in force and we order so.[7]

The Supreme Court, on account of fears that temple valuables might be alienated or secreted (one former chief minister of Kerala somewhat ridiculously alleged that the Elayarajah smuggled valuables out in a lunchbox on a daily basis),[8] constituted a special committee to evaluate the *kallaras* and to create inventories of all items. The opening of the vaults, after all, was not unprecedented. In December 1931, according to a news report in *The Hindu* at the time as well as in the account of a contemporary book, one month after the installation of the Maharajah, he had entered the kallaras. Their doors had not been touched in decades and the locks were rusted. Eventually it took over two hours to break into the vault. Floodlights were set up and electric fans blew fresh air into the darkness. By the afternoon the vault was sealed again, but only after several chests of gold, gems, and other valuables had been taken to the palace for 'counting and valuation'.[9]

In 2011, when the process began afresh, however, many more people were involved and the public's imagination exploded as stories leaked out rapidly. As one member of the inspecting panel constituted by the Supreme Court remarked:

> When they removed the granite stone, it was almost perfectly dark, except for a small amount of light coming in through the doorway behind us. As I looked into the darkened vault, what I saw looked like stars glittering in a night sky when there is no moon. Diamonds and gems were sparkling, reflecting what little light there was. Much of the wealth had originally been stored in wooden boxes, but, with time, the boxes had cracked and turned to dust. And so the gems and gold were just sitting in piles on the dusty floor. It was amazing.[10]

Heaps and heaps of gold coins, some belonging to the Roman era and others from the time of the Napoleonic wars, were discovered. The press was abuzz with talk about gem-studded idols of Vishnu, of eighteen-foot-long gold chains, of sacks full of grain made of gold, a crown breathlessly coated in diamonds, and more. With the passage of each day, the value rose till the first four vaults were estimated to possess treasure worth up to $22 billion. What captivated the public even more was the final, deepest vault, which remains sealed to this day. Stories abound about a serpent emblem on its forbidding iron doors and about curses that will afflict anyone who dares to venture within and commit sacrilege; this vault is said to be directly located beneath the shrine of Padmanabhaswamy. The Elayarajah also objected, due to similar reasons, to the opening of this particular kallara, with the astrological consultation of *devaprasnam*, described above, being convened to determine the deity's feelings on the subject.

Evidently, the deity agreed with the Elayarajah.[11]

The courts of law, however, were not wholly convinced. In 2012, the Supreme Court appointed an amicus curiae to study temple affairs and serve, essentially, as its eyes and ears on the ground in Thiruvananthapuram. Gopal Subramanium made many trips to the city to acquaint himself with the history and workings of the shrine and the attendant establishment. A two-volume, 575-page report that emerged in 2014 was scathing in its review of the temple's decades-old administration under the control of the Junior Maharani's family.[12]

In general, the amicus curiae spoke of the appearance of 'large scale breach of moral and fiduciary duties' towards the temple by its incumbent royal managers, adding that it had 'been treated for all effects and purposes as a private fiefdom'. He found a prima facie case of 'breach of trust' and that there was 'a concerted unwillingness to be accountable or to be questioned on any failures in administration'. The amicus curiae added that the Elayarajah, by now deceased, and his family possessed an 'intimidating presence over those who work and serve in the Temple', with 'a fundamental attitude of private ownership', and that more than one member of 'the Palace' had 'manipulated the Temple staff for extraneous reasons'. Convinced that everything was not as it should be, the amicus curiae then spoke to temple employees and guards, some of whom apparently admitted to him that 'if they did their duty fearlessly, they would lose their jobs'. In other words, 'they are clearly suffering from fear and repression' due to 'the overwhelming presence enjoyed by the erstwhile royal family, which has great influence over all temple affairs'.[13]

The devaprasnam, he alleged, was a diversion put up by the royal family to mislead the Supreme Court; in 2007, the Elayarajah had had photographs taken of the articles in the vaults and at that time no devaprasnam was called for before authorising entry into the vaults. But when the Supreme Court gave the same directions, the managers 'raised the bogey of devaprasnam' in order 'to ensure that no proper inventory is maintained of the valuables of the temple'. When the amicus curiae demanded the photographs taken in 2007, the studio responsible confessed to having deleted its soft copies, while hard copies were not produced. Mr Subramanium concluded that 'the stiff resistance on the part of the Temple administration to make available these photographs ... raises suspicions as to the true motive behind this exercise'. It was also reported that the previous inventory, mentioned also by the High Court, had not been made available.[14]

In addition to this, indications were made of alarming financial discrepancies going back decades in the accounts of the temple. 'The temple authorities and the Auditors have failed the minimal standards of financial transparency, and the Amicus does fear that the land and buildings of the temple have been illegally sold and leased.' There was a 'complete lack of inventory' with regard to gold and silver offerings given to the temple for thirty years and he felt that 'financial malfeasance is writ large in the temple'. In much of this, Mr Subramanium held the state as an active supporter of the royal family. It appeared to him that the dominance of the family had 'compelled the State to fall in line' and he found 'it incredible that in a free republican country, the State and its officials actually recognise such exceptional "royal" presence'. The kind of status Kowdiar Palace enjoyed seemed to reveal to the amicus curiae a 'parallelism based on monarchic rule' that could 'predominate the social psyche'. And the royal family, 'riding on the crest of past reputations', enjoyed numerous resultant perks.[15]

Mr Subramanium then recommended that the Supreme Court issue 'an injunction restraining the present trustee [i.e., the current head of the royal house] and his family members from either directly or indirectly interfering with day to day management of the Temple.' It did not help the cause of Kowdiar Palace that two of its own members seemed to side with the amicus curiae. The late Elayarajah's son 'disclosed how [a] coterie of staff members who had royal support defeated any good initiative' in the temple, while the Junior Maharani's only great granddaughter 'wept and wept seeking forgiveness for her family before God'. Her relations, however, objected to the report submitted by Mr Subramanium, with their counsel calling it 'an attempt to defame, dishonour, and discredit the family and to dissociate them from the administration of the age old temple forever'.[16] The Supreme Court, temporarily, asked Kowdiar Palace to withdraw from involvement in the management of the shrine.

For the first time since 1931, the Junior Maharani's family had lost control over what is today recognised as the world's wealthiest temple. And when it was returned in 2020 by the Supreme Court it was with checks and balances, and with participation of the government and other democratic stakeholders.

Kowdiar Palace, with its 100 rooms and imposing façade, still commands respect as a structure of great architectural elegance in Thiruvananthapuram. But its majesty has dulled considerably in recent years; its walls beg for a coat of plaster and paint, its acres and acres of gardens are overrun with weeds, while paintings and objets d'art collected by the Junior Maharani from around the world gather dust. The whole place, creaking and crumbling, stands in wistful, stately dilapidation. Its principal residents today are the two granddaughters of the Junior Maharani; her grandson is now the head of the family following the Elayarajah's death in 2013, and spends much of his time in Mangalore attending to business concerns. Of great grandsons, one lives in the palace with his twin daughters, while another is based in Chennai. The third is a classical musician. The Junior Maharani's great granddaughter is her only heir in the female line. A spirited woman in her sixties now, she caused a minor scandal by marrying a Nair journalist and electing not to have children. Today she lives in a private house of her own, and with her the line of Sethu Parvathi Bayi will terminate.

In the mid-1990s, while the Junior Maharani's daughter, the First Princess, and the Elayarajah were still alive, Kowdiar Palace adopted a relative from the Kolathiri line in Mavelikkara. The event attracted significant attention in the press for its quaint romance, and in an interview the adoptee, a Home Science graduate, assured readers that she remained perfectly normal, though Sanskrit lessons and classical music had been added to her routine. 'We cannot stop temple customs which we are required to perform,' the Junior Maharani's elder granddaughter explained, 'and an heiress is a must for these duties.'[17] As her sister would write with somewhat excessive devotional and dynastic superlatives:

> Since there was no girl for the continuation of Maharani Sethu Parvathi Bayi's branch of the Travancore royal family from which Maharajah Chithira Tirunal hailed, history repeated itself, so that this branch would continue to be blessed with the supreme honour and joy of serving Sree Padmanabha Swamy in the succeeding unnumbered ages. A kshatriya girl

> from ... Mavelikkara was adopted and [due ceremonies were] performed in the presence of [assorted religious dignitaries, family] and guests. Bharani Tirunal Lekha Parvathi Bayi thus became the new member of this branch.[18]

While the case in the Supreme Court has somewhat tempered the optimism with regard to 'unnumbered ages' of prospective temple command, for close to a decade after her adoption, Lekha Parvathi Bayi's name featured every now and then in the press. But suddenly, she disappeared from such association with Kowdiar Palace. Her fate is not entirely clear: some claim that the High Court of Kerala in a judgment related to the temple annulled the adoption, while others point out that she, it was realised later, was too old at the time of adoption, due to which it had to be cancelled. Either way, Lekha Parvathi Bayi, who married and produced a child in 2000, disappeared from the scene just as unexpectedly as she had appeared.

Notwithstanding the antiquated spectacle of royal adoptions in democratic India, the introduction of Lekha Parvathi Bayi was not, in fact, entirely traditional. Adoptions were, in the old days, resorted to when there were no female members in the dynasty or when existing female heirs entertained no prospects of issue.[19] In the 1990s, while Kowdiar Palace was on the brink of extinction after its sole great granddaughter opted out of the business of succession, the branch of the Senior Maharani in Bangalore had a healthy supply of women to fill the ranks of the Attingal line. But possibly because of the traditional animosity between the two houses, or due to the lack of interest that Sethu Lakshmi Bayi's family evinces in Thiruvananthapuram, they were discounted.

To those in the city who still remember the Senior Maharani and are aware that she has descendants, the 'Bangalore royals' appear extremely anglicised. Kowdiar Palace, in that sense, has retained its traditional flavour; every other festive occasion sees members of the Junior Maharani's family feature on Malayalam television, discussing the way things were or matters of culture and royal heritage. In the press most reviews gush homilies, normally about their devotion to Padmanabhaswamy or about their simplicity and asceticism. Much of this curiosity for the royal family revolves around the Junior Maharani's granddaughters and their pronouncements that indicate extreme piety. When asked about a book the younger sister authored, she replied, 'I cannot say I have written the book, I have been allowed to write by Him.' Similarly, 'Adoration of Lord Padmanabha permeates everything the family does. From the time we remember, we grew up with His name.'[20] 'Travancore: Simplicity graces this House', went the title of a fulsome press feature in *The Hindu* in 2003; and a decade later in 2013 another headline in the same paper wasn't particularly refreshing when it said: 'Simplicity hallmark of Travancore royal family.'[21] A typical press review of the family, as for instance in the *Economic Times*, goes:

> As Sree Padmanabha Swamy temple's glittering gems are valued and tagged, it's not just the diamonds that shine but also the royal family of the erstwhile princely state of Travancore. It's an ode to the family's unflinching devotion and integrity that not a penny has gone missing from the billions stored in the cellars of the centuries-old shrine administered by the royals ...What makes the family's story vis-à-vis the temple all the more compelling is that the rulers always knew of the riches, yet never touched them ... Observers talk of the symbolic significance of the practice of royal family members dusting sand off their feet when they emerge from the shrine. 'It was meant to convey that the family members would not take home or misappropriate even a speck of sand belonging to Padmanabha,' they say.[22]

Even the formidable amicus curiae at first appeared to have been in great awe of the family and the deifying halo around it. 'It may also be clarified,' he noted in his preliminary report, 'that the Royal family does not want anything from the Temple's riches for itself. Consistent with tradition, the relationship of the Royal family with the Temple is unique because for them Lord Padmnabha Swamy and the Temple is their "life force". While certain errors,' he added, somewhat uncritically, 'on account of miscommunication or incorrect presentation before the members of the Royal family may have led to certain problems ... it is necessary that the Royal family is associated with the administration of the temple in order to ensure that the Temple is restored at the earliest. In fact, His Highness [sic] Sri Martanda Varma [i.e., the late Elayarajah, then still alive] of the erstwhile State of Travancore visits the Temple daily even at the grand old age of 90 ... The Royal family is also held in high repute especially by the members of the general public and the State Government.'[23]

To Mr Subramanium, in his first stint in Thiruvananthapuram, the Junior Maharani's younger granddaughter, whom he addressed as a Princess, was 'an embodiment of knowledge about the history of the Temple and for whom the Temple is her life's mainstay'. He then expressed admiration of the fact that the Elayarajah could speak Sanskrit, and that another member of the family was a trained classical musician. But after another year in Thiruvananthapuram to investigate temple affairs, the amicus curiae appears to have swiftly distanced his personal respect for the private qualities of the Junior Maharani's heirs from the judicial matter of the family's competence in running the temple. And in this position, his criticism proved devastating to the image Kowdiar Palace had sustained for so many decades in the eyes of the public. A high-profile audit did further damage when it reported to the Supreme Court that as much as 266 kilograms of gold were missing from the temple. And for all those claims that opening the 'serpent' vault would unleash horrendous calamity, since 1990 and under the management of the late Elayarajah, this very kallara had been entered at least seven times.[24]

Naturally, many began to murmur about this discrepancy between the general picture of devotion that envelops the royal family and the increasingly worrying information emerging from court-appointed observers of the reality of the temple's management. The Junior Maharani's family appear to be genuinely pained by these revelations and the attendant beating their reputation has taken. 'This is the saddest moment in their lives and the worst humiliation the family has to endure,' their plea in the Supreme Court read, 'as a result of the unjustified attack on their intense devotion to the Lord and time tested integrity.'[25] In an interview to the *Financial Times*, the Junior Maharani's granddaughter asserted that the family had no desire to appropriate the temple's wealth. 'We have no claim even to one little coin within the temple. We are saying it all belongs to the deity and to him only. We are not fighting to gain control of the riches—not at all. We want our good name vindicated. This is our life. It's not about possessions. We are fighting for our life.'[26]

The future of Sethu Parvathi Bayi's heirless line, ensconced in the decaying Kowdiar Palace, and anxious for authority over the Sri Padmanabhaswamy Temple, that final and only vestige of royal glory, is uncertain.

Tucked away on Bangalore's teeming Richmond Road, Lalitha and Kerala Varma's house today survives as one of the city's last-standing colonial bungalows. Obscured from traffic on the street by a series of erratic constructions, this is a place of nostalgic, somewhat gloomy darkness. Most of the garden, which Kerala Varma tended to in the good old days, has been relinquished to shopping malls, blocks of apartments, and other commercial buildings that tower over the edifice. But like Kowdiar Palace, despite its loss of outwardly grandeur, inside it retains a quaint charm. Its wooden ceilings creak under the weight of ancient chandeliers, dusted occasionally when a man with a tall ladder can be found for hire. Its verandahs, with intricately patterned Italian tiles, open into rooms that have more 'modern' mosaic floors. Furniture is scattered in neglected heaps around the house. Portraits of glorious ancestors hang on the walls, resigned to their fate behind discoloured frames. A handsome grandfather clock stands imperiously in a corner, while books in the study gather dust in cabinets that have not been opened in a decade.

There is to the place, even as it crumbles irreparably, an antique dignity, just as there is something picturesque about the life of its current occupants. Lalitha died in 2008 and Kerala Varma in 2020, aged over 103. For many years their companion was their eldest daughter, Rukmini, now eighty-two. For all her dynamism and glamour in the 1960s and '70s, through the '90s and early 2000s, she lived as a recluse. Rukmini divides her time today between tortuous prayers—in penance for what she calls her accumulated failures and mistakes—and painting. Till recently, every morning her father's attendants would put together two teapoys, mount two stools on them, and hoist a stately armchair to the top so that Rukmini could add a fresh coat of paint to the massive, gigantic mythological canvases she works on.

To those who know in Thiruvananthapuram, Sethu Parvathi Bayi won that historic twentieth-century battle between the two Maharanis of Travancore. After all, her heirs still reside in a grand old palace in Kerala, enjoying public reverence, though recent events have unexpectedly dulled the lustre of their name. On the other hand, Sethu Lakshmi Bayi's heirs haven't left a place to call home in the land their ancestors ruled. Nobody remembers them, and those who know faintly of the Senior Maharani are dying. The veneration devout royalists feel towards the last Maharajah to this day means that the story of Sethu Lakshmi Bayi is never told, and her name is only taken in whispers. To the devout, Chithira Tirunal was god-incarnate because of his love for his family deity. The history with his aunt, however, reveals that even earthly gods have their share of prejudices and are, ultimately, human. Besides, they argue, Sethu Lakshmi Bayi left years ago. And since she chose to renounce her royal heritage, her obscurity is her fate.

While Kowdiar Palace has had to fight battles to protect its reputation (and arguably to hold on to the eroding relevance it still enjoys in Thiruvananthapuram courtesy the temple), the heirs of Sethu Lakshmi Bayi watch with distant curiosity what unfolds in their old family capital. They have had to fight their own battles, though these were somewhat more personal in nature. The greatest tragedy in this side of the dynasty lies in Rukmini's story. The Maharani's favourite, praised for her beauty and talent and lavished upon with presents and fortune, is today a shadow of the woman she was once. And her life began to unravel a little after the demise of her protective, doting grandmother.

In 1988, Rukmini's youngest son, Ranjith, died in Bangalore in an accident. He was only twenty years old, and his mother never recovered from the shock. For years she shunned attention, locking herself up quite literally in a punishing routine of hours and hours of prayers and rituals. She gave away all her expensive goods to family and relations, dressing in tattered old mundus thereafter. As her renunciation of the good life became almost an obsession, she separated from her husband. The woman who was once so pampered that she couldn't cross a road without someone to hold her hand, now left the house only for pilgrimages to temples, travelling in buses full of oblivious strangers. She sold the 'palace on Richmond Road', that mansion her grandmother had presented her; today, Sethu Lakshmi Bayi's final abode hosts an unremarkable apartment building. The Maharani's granddaughter divided all her money and even furniture between Venu and Jay. For some time she lived alone in a gloomy flat with her only remaining property: her dead son's motorbike. Then one day Lalitha rose to the occasion and decided she would not let Rukmini descend from grief into madness. She went to her and brought her to her father's house. And since then Rukmini has resided there, having also made a promise to her dying mother that she would not leave while Kerala Varma lived.

The death of Rukmini's son was the first big tragedy in what was until then a life of great bliss for Lalitha ever since she relinquished the scheming world of palaces and princes. As she remarked after the accident in 1988: 'In all these years I have been very happy. But for the first time now I have known sorrow.'[27]

Adversity came to Indira also in Chennai. Much money was lost in ill-fated business ventures and to incompetent managers. Having moved from her imposing house on Nungambakkam High Road, she died in a much smaller, somewhat depressing place in Neelankarai. There was more than great affluence even then—at least eight or nine members of staff ran Indira's household when I visited in 2011. A fleet of cars was permanently parked outside, awaiting a mistress who never left. Indira seemed to spend most of her time in bed. But the greatest loss she suffered was also personal, when in 2001 Shobhana's only child died, plunging her into a grief from which she too has still not recovered. As she wrote at the time:

Blood of my blood, flesh of my flesh,
Beat of my pulse, song of my heart,
Did I love you too much dear one?
Did jealous fate resent the gift,
Of so much love to a single soul,
And take you, leaving me bereft?[28]

But these two scarring episodes aside, the Senior Maharani's successors state that they are happy, and do not mind their obscurity in the eyes of their former subjects in old Travancore. As Uma explains: 'Every now and then we discuss how we should not have given up all our properties in Kerala, how maybe we should have fought the government for at least some of them, how we should have done some things differently. But would I go back to the palace and to that life? Never!' It is, to the outsider, difficult to believe that there is no sense of regret at having given up the glories of heritage, but Uma is determined in her position. 'You have to remember,' she explains, 'that it is because mother came away from all that, and because grandmother made her great sacrifice that the younger ones in our family today are so successful and leading good lives. If we had continued in the palace, living in some wishful cocoon about being "royalty" while the world around us changed, we would have done a great disservice to these children. They would belong neither in the past nor in the present.'[29]

She has a point. While the first two generations that came out of the palace did not completely succeed in freeing themselves from the easygoing life that was guaranteed by the affluence and wealth that accompanied them, much of that has now dissipated. And confronted with prosperity of a much more regular nature, the generations that followed have moved on in life and got down to work. Today, Venu, Sethu Lakshmi Bayi's eldest great grandchild, is a business executive in Sydney, with his Australian children graduates in medicine and law respectively. Jay divides his time between the United States, Europe and Bangalore in his pursuit of hyperrealism in art, while his daughter worked in Vietnam and now lives in Germany. Balan's daughter worked with the International Water Management Institute in Sri Lanka and is a climate change and water expert, while his son is a Berlin-based lighting designer. Shreekumar's children are employed as an illustrator and audio engineer respectively. One of Uma's sons is an environmentalist while the other spent years on a kibbutz in Israel. Parvathi counts among her children a surgeon, while Lakshmi's daughters are both professionals in the United States. Devika's eldest son works at Amazon in London, with dreams of retiring to Cape Town with his South African wife, while her middle son is setting up a business in India. Her youngest is a professional actor in Canada.

What is interesting is that many of this proliferation of men and women descended from Sethu Lakshmi Bayi, spread across the world now, have never set foot in Kerala. While the press, when referring to 'the royal family of Travancore' alludes entirely to the seven individuals descended from the Junior Maharani, the line that actually has female successors is the thirty-member-strong Senior Maharani's branch. While Kowdiar Palace has no female heirs to carry on the temple traditions they seem desperately anxious to preserve, the scions of what was once Satelmond Palace do not seem particularly interested in effecting a return to those traditions. Whether Balan and Shreekumar, both successors to the Junior Maharani's grandson who currently heads the dynasty, intend to ever take over what their grandmother renounced needs to be seen when the time comes. Indications are, however, that the family has little interest in positions of authority. As Lakshmi dryly remarks, 'What line of succession? What title? The temple should be protected and its customs upheld, but I don't think the deity exists to flatter anyone's vanity or sense of self importance.'[30]

This attitude seems to have permeated the younger ranks of Sethu Lakshmi Bayi's line. In recent years, many of her great grandchildren and their issue have become curious about their history, but still maintain a studied distance. As Shreekumar's younger son states,

> ... my personal stance is that I'm not really interested in royalty. It had its place in history, sure, but I find it's time people stopped associating themselves with legacies like they matter ... There's nothing more distressing than twenty-first-century people proclaiming to be something more special than others on the basis of ... what exactly? The nitty gritty is that it certainly doesn't help when people introduce you saying, 'This is Raja Ravi Varma's grandson.' No, he wasn't my grandfather. And I don't have his paintings etched on my forehead. I like art and respect history. But maybe we should leave behind some of the weight we're carrying. I don't like to be allowed in temples where I feel no connection, while folks who might really feel some satisfaction from their prayers stand at the door. And the whole thing's caste-based, so by now we should have realized that it stinks of every sort of arrogance. I guess I can call myself lucky for certain privileges but it's better to have earned it. And since I haven't earned it and in some sense live off the last trickles of that wealth, I feel ... guilty?[31]

That urge to rebel against the crushing weight of history, which began with Lalitha in the 1940s, has not taken leave of Sethu Lakshmi Bayi's heirs. But there is increasing curiosity in Thiruvananthapuram on account of the fact that the line of the Attingal Ranis today exists in the form of Lalitha's descendants alone. And true to the world of today, these present-day Attingal heiresses are independent women with lives of their own. Of the four girls through whom the line will continue, for whatever purpose, into the future, the eldest, Ambika's daughter, is a scientist. Radhika's daughter, with Zoroastrian blood through her Parsi father, is a national-level women's rugby player. Parvathi's granddaughter worked at an investment consultancy and is now pursuing a career in music. And Lakshmi's only granddaughter goes to college in the United States. None of these girls fit the bill of the traditional Attingal Rani, though there is in their contemporary independence, if one insists on stretching romance and nostalgia, a distant glimpse of those original warrior queens. But the world has changed, and the Attingal Rani has become irrelevant.

Much of the royal heritage in Sethu Lakshmi Bayi's family has been reduced to stray pieces of furniture and to the artworks that adorn their homes. But even as the Maharani's line merges and melts into contemporary India, Rukmini remains as a final living monument to the era that once was, rich with memories, sorrowful with regrets, but a reflective testament to times gone by. The Maharani's house has already been torn down to make way for today's buildings. Soon it will be the turn of Kerala Varma's home as well, for it is prime real estate which he has stated in his will must be sold. What will Rukmini, who has given away everything, do when she loses the roof over her head and the protection put in place by her late father? 'Well, you see,' she says, laughing, 'my grandmother made such a great transformation, moving from a huge palace in Kerala to a house in Bangalore and becoming a nobody. I am already a nobody! And in a few years I will make my own transformation from this house to a little hut somewhere on the outskirts of Bangalore. That is what will happen!'[32]

Even in this exaggeration, there is an element of tragedy.

When Lalitha first arrived in Bangalore in 1949 and found a home for herself, a home away from the gilded world she despised and where generations of her family would now be reared, filling its every nook and cranny with stories and memories, she lit in one room of the bungalow an oil lamp. It was a *kidavilakku*, an eternal flame that she, in gratitude to the heavens for granting her the freedom she craved, promised to keep burning for as long as she drew breath. Till 2008, Lalitha tended to her lamp, and as she lay on her deathbed she entrusted it to Rukmini. The latter has since dutifully followed her mother's instructions and nourished the flame. But one day not so far away in the future, Rukmini knows that the time will come when No 8 Richmond Road will go. And on that day, as she lets the lamp burn out after a lifetime of over seventy years, it will be her charge to release all those succeeding children of Sethu Lakshmi Bayi's bloodline, already spreading around the globe, from their adopted roots in Bangalore as well.

When the time comes, it will be Rukmini's duty to close the final chapter of this story.

Notes

Please note that all italics within quoted text are the author's.

INTRODUCTION: THE STORY OF KERALA

1. Nigel Cliff, *The Last Crusade*, p. 3.
2. See Nigel Cliff, op. cit., for more on Europe's background at this time.
3. Ibid., pp. 82–84.
4. Zamorin is the anglicised version of Samutiri.
5. K.K. Nair, *By Sweat and Sword*, p. 23.
6. Jonathan Gil Harris, *The First Firangis*, pp. 84–89.
7. K.K. Nair, op. cit., p. 134.
8. Not least because da Gama, before taking off, decided to kidnap a number of random, bewildered fishermen from the beach and carry them off with him to Portugal where they were baptised as Christians with great fanfare.
9. Hermann Gundert and T. Madhava Menon, *Kerala Pazhama*, p. v, and Mansel Longworth Dames, *The Book of Duarte Barbosa*, Vol. I, p. 95.
10. The Zamorin had defeated the Kolathiri some years before when a prince of that family eloped with a Calicut princess, incensing the former.
11. K.V. Krishna Ayyar, *The Zamorins of Calicut*, pp. 165, 168.
12. The Zamorin could raise 30,000 men at a day's notice and 100,000 in three days. See K.K. Nair, op. cit., p. 74.
13. Quoted in K.V. Krishna Ayyar, op. cit., p. 207. The Zamorin, it is noteworthy, allowed the residents of the fort, women and children included, safe exit before he tore it down. This was a courtesy the Portuguese never extended to him in their attacks.

14. See, for instance, A.P. Ibrahim Kunju, *Rise of Travancore*, p. 2.
15. Of course, the local Rajahs also learnt to use this strategy against the Europeans. As early as 1513 the Portuguese would complain that they knew 'why the king of Cochin having 30,000 Nairs and the king of Cannanore having 60,000 do not go to destroy Calicut; because they want to keep up this dispute (between Calicut and the Portuguese) till the end of time. They (Cochin and Cannanore) do not wish to make war, but want us to do so.' The Dutch would state the very same when writing to the Rajah of Cochin 200 years later: 'I do not know how much blood has been spent by the Dutch East India Company to aggrandize your family ... The Company is not averse to giving support to Cochin agreeably to our treaty, but they will not at all times send soldiers to fight your Highness's battles.' See K.K. Nair, op. cit., p. 13.
16. Heber Drury, *Letters from Malabar by Jacob Canter Visscher*, p. 64.
17. According to Krishna Ayyar, op. cit., the Zamorin had sometime in the fifteenth century defeated the Quilon (Kupaka) Rajah, invading his territories up to Odanad, and in return was ceded some territory, rights in the Sri Padmanabhaswamy Temple, and paid tribute. The temple rights were later transferred to a Nambutiri family who continued to enjoy these *koyma* privileges even into the 1930s.
18. Quoted in R.S. Whiteway, *The Rise of Portuguese Power in India*, p. 27.
19. K.K. Nair, op. cit., p. 26.
20. Syed Iqbal Hasnain, *Muslims in North India*, p. 110, and Tirithdas Hotchand, *Shah Abdul Latif's Immortal Song*, p. 43.
21. See Nigel Cliff, op. cit.
22. One of the reasons the Syrian Christians did not warm up to the Portuguese was also that the arrival of the latter coincided with a 'sudden strengthening of the Syrians' ties to the west Asian patriarchates' and there was 'an influx of west Asian bishops and attendant monks who arrived in India claiming authority from the Nestorian Catholicos'. The Syrians received them with 'ecstatic adulation' even as the Portuguese considered them 'vile Nestorian heretics'. See Susan Bayly, *Saints, Goddesses, and Kings*, p. 259.
23. Susan Bayly (1984), 'Hindu Kingship and the Origin of Community', *Modern Asian Studies*, Vol. 18, No. 2, p. 194.
24. Susan Bayly, *Saints* ... op. cit., p. 252.
25. See Susan Bayly, 'Hindu Kingship ...' op. cit., for more on this topic.
26. The *Wesleyan-Methodist Magazine* (1812) (Google Books), p. 101
27. Henry E.J. Stanley, *A Description of the Coasts of East Africa and Malabar by Duarte Barbosa*, p. 128.
28. K.K. Nair, op. cit., p. 117.

29. As K.K. Nair states, because war was such a regular affair here, the Nairs developed the institution of the *ankam* where representatives fought instead of entire armies, keeping casualties to the minimum even while settling wars and politics. The system appears to have impressed even the Portuguese, for in 1661 their commander challenged the Dutch to an ankam where a single champion would take on five Dutch nominees. See K.K. Nair, op. cit., p. 104.
30. Krishna Ayyar, op. cit., p. 171. Susan Bayly even speaks of Christian chavers in her work, citing an instance in the sixteenth century when some such Christian warriors vowed to kill the Rajah of Cochin for their lord, the Vadakkumkur Rajah, and even succeeded in their mission.
31. K.K. Nair, op. cit., p. 72.
32. Ibid., p. 58.
33. See Mansel Longworth Dames, op. cit., p. 42. There were some exaggerations, of course, and women could not select partners from below their caste and social standing on pain of death. In Edward Grey's *The Travels of Pietro Della Valle in India*, p. 379, we read: 'The Gentile Nairi have no peculiar Wives; but all Women are common amongst them; and when any man repairs to visit one of them, he leaves his weapon at the door, which sign sufficiently debars all others from entering in to disturb him; nor does this course beget any difficulty or jealousie ... The children neither seek to know nor many times do know who their Father is but their descent by the Mother is alone considered, and according to that all inheritances are transferred. The same rule is observed among Princes and their Wives, the Queens, who are the King's Sisters, being used to marry other neighbouring Kings, and to go into their States to have children, who are to succeed in the Kingdoms of their Uncles, and by this means are of Royal blood both by Father and mother. These Princesses are held in great esteem by the Kings, their Husbands; yet if they are minded to try other Men they are not prohibited, but may and often times do so, making use of whom they fancy for their pleasure, but especially of some Brachman, or other of their Husband's principal Courtiers, who with their privity and consent are wont to converse and practise with them most intrinsecally (sic) in the Palace.'
34. See Wendy and Rex Rogers, *The Psychology of Gender and Sexuality*, p. 207.
35. Mansel Longworth Dames, op. cit., p. 124.
36. J. Talboys Wheeler, *A Short History of India*, pp. 119–20.
37. The Dutch governor Adriaan Moens would in fact tell how the Zamorins, once 'the most powerful and the most wealthy' in Kerala fell because they 'did not maintain their authority sufficiently but allowed pretty well all the courtiers to meddle with the affairs of the kingdom, and even the women had their say in State affairs, especially the mothers of the heir apparent'. See *Selections from the Records of the Madras Government* Vol. 13, p. 132.

38. F. Fawcett, *Nayars of Malabar*, p. 198.
39. John Henry Grose, *A Voyage to the East Indies*, p. 244.
40. Adriaan Moens, the Dutch governor, would note in 1781 that the Zamorins had by this time lost all their spirit. Shortly after the debacle in 1766, Hyder Ali had to withdraw from Kerala due to his wars in the north and a new Zamorin returned to Calicut. However, he proved singularly inefficient and could not hold his own during the second invasion by Hyder some years later. 'The indifference of the Zamorin to the Nabob's last invasion was surprising to me. He heard that the Nabob had taken possession of the neighbouring kingdoms of Cotteate, Coddagamale and other territories thereabout one after the other, and that his turn was to come next, and yet he remained absorbed in trifles instead of thinking of the defence of his kingdom. Not a month before he had to flee, I received letter after letter from him dealing only with the appointment of a Namburi (sic) or priest in the Triporatty (Tripurayar) pagoda by the king of Cochin, in regard to which he had not been consulted. The position in regard to this pagoda is that the appointment of the Nambudri must be made after both the Zamorin and the king of Cochin have been informed. He asked as strongly for my support in this matter as if his head and the existence of his kingdom depended on it. Whilst he was busy with the dispute about this pagoda, the Nabob took one fort of his after the other till, without having made any resistance to speak of, he took to his heels after having first let himself be nicely befooled by the French Governor of Mahe, and left his kingdom a prey to the Nabob.' See *Selections from the Records of the Madras Government*, Vol. 13, p. 133.
41. In a single engagement, for instance, the Zamorin lost 18,000 soldiers once, and according to Krishna Ayyar he could raise well over 100,000 soldiers altogether.
42. Leena More, *English East India Company*, p. 10.
43. B. Sobhanan, *Rama Varma of Travancore*, p. 12. As late as the 1830s Travancore paid a formal tribute to the Nawab of Arcot before he was removed by the British, and the tribute was transferred to the latter.
44. Fra Bartolomeo quoted in Shungoonny Menon, *A History of Travancore*, p. 182. The Dutch were less flattering, though they too respected his ability. Julius Stein van Gollenesse would note how Martanda Varma was 'an able and untiring prince, but very cruel and so conceited and arrogant that he aims at nothing less than the supremacy over the whole of Malabar; and no doubt he would have gained his object had not the Hon'ble [Dutch] Company been in his way.' See *Selections from the Records of the Madras Government*, Vol. 13, p. 53.
45. Sheikh Zainuddin Makhdum would state: 'There are in Malabar chieftains whose territories do not exceed one Parasang ... while others have powers over more extensive territories. Of these some have at their command one hundred soldiers or less, or two hundred to three hundred, thousand, five thousand,

ten thousand, thirty thousand, hundred thousand and more, and so on. Some territories join in league and are governed by two or three persons together. And of them some have greater power and bigger army. Quarrels and skirmishes take place occasionally among them but this does not affect their coalition rule.' See K.K. Nair, op. cit., p. 110.

46. Quoted in Mark de Lannoy, *The Kulasekhara Perumals of Travancore*, p. 28.
47. See the ballad *Tampimar Kathai* and Ibrahim Kunju's work for more on this.
48. P.K.S. Raja, *Mediaeval Kerala*, p. 185.
49. According to the contemporary Dutch governor, Julius Stein van Gollenesse, 'The other states have, without harmony (which is seldom found in the ruling families), little power; but this chief [Martanda Varma] on the contrary has with the help of the English, had all the noblemen of the state, both Pulas and Gurips, put to death or banished the country except the Pula of Bariatto. Since that time he not only rules supreme but by confiscating their goods and lands he has so increased his treasures and revenues that he excels the other rulers in the greatness of his expenditure.' See *Selections from the Records of the Madras Government*, Vol. 13, p. 53.
50. The leader of these mercenaries was one Ponnu Pandya Thevan.
51. Desperate times, however, called for desperate measures. The Thekkumkur Rajah, a Nair prince ruling from Changanassery, tried to keep the Travancore armies at bay by assembling a vanguard of Brahmins. Traditionally, as the premier caste in society, Brahmins were inviolable and enjoyed immunity from military assault. But here again Martanda Varma shoved custom aside by ordering his men to shoot them all down and engage with the unprepared Thekkumkur soldiers cowering behind. In 1750, the Thekkumkur family also went into exile in Calicut. Even the Brahmin Rajah of Purakkad, a small but prosperous principality with its capital at Ambalapuzha, was not spared, despite the fact that he had been a Travancore ally. As the Dutch commander in Cochin lamented, 'Who would have thought that Travancore would not have spared Porca in acknowledgment of his assistance, the more so because he was a Brahmin.'
52. Cochin actually had been involved in earlier wars as well against Travancore, and in 1746 its Rajah was particularly irked when Martanda Varma attacked the Tiruvalla Temple, of which the former was protector. His soldiers began to harvest the paddy from the temple's fields, but the Brahmin trustees formed a guard and beat the soldiers out using sticks and brooms, and warded them off. See Mark de Lannoy, op. cit., p. 123. As for the fall of the Dutch, Martanda Varma defeated them in the famous Battle of Colachel in 1741. The event has since been cast as a great national event, and as the 'first' example of an Indian 'power' defeating a European naval force. But as Ibrahim Kunju remarks, 'as a

military affair, it was nothing spectacular' and Travancore's victory was partly due to good luck. 'On 7th August, a red-hot ball fired from the Travancore side fell into a barrel of gun powder and caused a conflagration in the [rice] stockade [of the Dutch, during the battle at Colachel]. The whole rice supply was consumed in the conflagration. Unable to get supplies from their ships, the Dutch were forced to surrender. The Dutch evacuated the stockade and a large number of muskets and a few pieces of cannon fell into Travancore hands.' See Ibrahim Kunju, *Rise of Travancore*, pp. 41–42.

53. Such was the psychological importance of this victory over an otherwise formidable Tipu Sultan that his personal standard, captured by the Nairs, is still brought out during processions of the Sri Padmanabhaswamy Temple, the most important shrine connected with the Travancore family.
54. V. Nagam Aiya, *Travancore State Manual*, Vol. I, p. 367. In 1880 Martanda Varma's descendant, Maharajah Visakham Tirunal would remark: 'One of my illustrious predecessors, the Maharajah who died in the Malabar year 933, corresponding with the year 1757, the year in which that master-architect, Clive, laid the foundation-stone of the British Indian Empire in the field of Plassey, calling his successors to his bedside, gave them his last words of advice to the effect that "These Englishmen appear to be destined to rise to such power and glory as are hitherto unparalleled. Be it your constant aim and endeavour to secure their friendship and support." These precious and prophetic words ring in my ears as clearly as when they were uttered a century and quarter ago. May those words continue to be the most prized heirloom in my family to the remotest posterity!' See *India's Women: The Magazine of the Church of England Zenana Missionary Society*, Vol. I, p. 29.

CHAPTER 1: A PAINTER PRINCE

1. The uncle was Rajaraja Varma, a painter and pupil of Alagiri Naidu of Tanjore.
2. E.M.J. Venniyur, *Raja Ravi Varma*, p. 5.
3. Ibid.
4. Erwin Neumayer and Christine Schelberger, *Popular Art*, p. 39.
5. C. Rajaraja Varma quoted in Rupika Chawla, *Raja Ravi Varma*, p. 46.
6. S. Ramanatha Aiyar, *A Brief Sketch of Travancore*, pp. 167–168.
7. Venniyur, op. cit., p. 8.
8. Ibid. p. 6.
9. This patron was Krishna Menon, the father in law of Sir Chettur Sankaran Nair, who would go on to become President of the Indian National Congress.

10. Author's interview with Rosscote Krishna Pillai and Advocate Ayyappan Pillai. Kalyani Pillai's father, Nadavarambath Kunjukrishna Menon, was a friend of Punnakkal Easwara Pillai, who already had more than one wife in Trivandrum at the time he married her. One of his descendants was the consort of Prince Asvathi Tirunal.
11. One local story in Trivandrum tells that Easwara Pillai one day returned home early and found the Maharajah sneaking out through the window. He just sighed and took Kalyani Pillai to the palace and handed her over.
12. Read Deepanjana Pal, *The Painter*.
13. Venniyur, op. cit., p. 15.
14. Ibid., p. 21.
15. Ibid., p. 23.
16. This included dressing in a sari, and judging from an 1868 photograph, Kalyani Pillai was probably the first Malayali woman to wear one.
17. Nagam Aiya, *Travancore State Manual*, Vol. III, p. 335.
18. Letter dated 20/01/1909 from the Senior Rani to Kuttan Tampuran (TRF). As early as two years after Ayilyam Tirunal's death, a missionary in Trivandrum would note the following about Kalyani Pillai: 'The late Maharajah's widow has received me four times. She is too busy with her adopted daughter's children, who seem almost always to be ill, to have time for regular study, but is still glad to see me, and to read the Bible whenever I go. Her eyes are beginning to fail her, though she is not an old woman, and yet I think she reads little by herself. She is very thin and delicate looking, and has lost much of her beauty; then of course she wears no jewels now, and that changes a native woman's appearance very much. She seems so friendless and lonely that I feel very sorry for her, and long, O so much, to get her to trust in the best of Friends; but she is so bound by Hindu chains that nothing but God's grace can set her free.' See *India's Women: The Magazine of the Church of England Zenana Missionary Society*, Vol. II, p. 34.
19. P. Ramakrishna Pillai, *Visakhavijaya*, p. 149. Ayilyam Tirunal, in the words of his brother, who of course had his own axe to grind, 'had never subjected himself to strict moral discipline, either extraneous or self imposed' and we are told that 'he used to make indiscriminate advances to women, which are indicated in some old verses' and also in local gossip in Trivandrum.
20. *The Lady* dated 11 January 1912.
21. Henry Bruce, *Letters from Malabar*, p. 79. The missionary Augusta Blandford decades before also lamented how 'This most extraordinary law has led, as could be expected, to much misery and jealousy and family dissension in the long course of its continuance in Travancore; and even to strangers it is painful on state occasions to see the Rajah's sons standing among the attendants behind

their father's throne while the Princes, their cousins, are seated on chairs of state!' See *India's Women: The Magazine of the Church of England Zenana Missionary Society*, Vol. I, p. 25

22. Samuel Mateer, *Native Life in Travancore*, p. 118
23. *The Lady*, op. cit.
24. Letter dated 19/09/1924 from the Resident to the Pol. Sec. GOI (IOR/R/1/1/1530 (2)).
25. Divakara Varma's note on life in Satelmond Palace. Divakara Varma is a great grandson of Raja Ravi Varma and nephew of Maharani Sethu Lakshmi Bayi.
26. Letter dated 19/09/1924 from the Resident to the Pol. Sec. GOI (IOR/R/1/1/1530 (2))
27. *The Lady*, op. cit.
28. Visscher quoted in Binu John Mailaparambil, *Lords of the Sea*, p. 40.
29. The East India Company also paid a pension, called *malikhana*, to the family.
30. It may be of interest to know that the Rani had cancer of the mouth but would not allow outside doctors to diagnose the area. So it was Ravi Varma who sketched the insides of her mouth for the durbar physicians, although these grotesque works now appear to be lost, or so goes the story.
31. Pierre Loti, *India*, p. 56.
32. I am grateful to Lakshmi Raghunandan for allowing me access to her extensive collection of the personal letters of Lakshmi Bayi. The Travancore royal family's interest in the English language appears to have been an early one, and Martanda Varma's successor, popularly called Dharma Rajah, was apparently conversant in the language. Dutch records noted in 1787 that he 'reads the English newspapers of London, Madras, and Calcutta whereby he has acquired much knowledge which would be sought in vain in other Malabar princes'. See *Selections from the Records of the Madras Government,* Vol. 13, p. 38.
33. For her loyalty to her husband she was invested with the Order of the Crown of India in 1881. As Augusta Blandford noted: 'This substantial acknowledgment from the Queen of her admiration of the Rani's virtues will, I feel sure, do good to the cause of morality; and the women of Travancore will long remember to tell their children of the noble Rani who waited in sorrow and widowhood five years for her absent husband, and was publicly honoured by England's Queen Empress.' See *India's Women: The Magazine of the Church of England Zenana Missionary Society*, Vol. II, p. 33
34. Pierre Loti, op. cit., p. 56.
35. Letter dated 20/02/1895 from the Senior Rani to her niece Mahaprabha (Raghunandan, p. 2).
36. Letter dated 06/03/1896 from the Senior Rani to Sir Sheshiah Shastri (Raghunandan, pp. 12–13).

37. Reference is to Kunjaru Rajah who was an ancestor of Dr M.S. Valiathan.
38. There was in fact one more sister between the Ranis and Kochupanki, but she died.
39. This person does not wish to be named.
40. Letter dated 18/12/1899 from the Elayarajah to the Resident (IOR/R/2/892/278). Augusta Blandford also refers to alcoholism in the family and in general among wealthy women when she speaks in 1882 of the death of the brother of Kochupanki and the two Ranis of Travancore 'who had been suffering from some time from abcess (sic) in the liver, brought on by his own intemperance. European brandy is the curse of most of the rich idle men in this country, and I fear the evil is increasing rather than diminishing. They are forbidden by their Sastras to indulge in strong drink of any kind, consequently all they take is in private after dark. They sometimes shut themselves up for days, with the enemy close at hand, and feign sickness so that their drunken state should not be found out. I know one rich family where the old father and all his sons drank deeply; the daughter, a lovely girl of sixteen, a favourite pupil of mine years ago, was married to a man of rank, who drank till he died; then she was given to another hard drinker, who also spent much of his time in gambling, and has, I fear, taught the poor girl to play cards and drink too. Her coarse bloated features are a sad sight to one who remembers her former beauty and girlish light heartedness. I little thought when I saw her in her cloth of gold dress on her wedding day that she would come to this.' She also adds how the Junior Rani had 'been speaking words of warning to her sons' on the matter of drinking. See *India's Women* ... op. cit., Vol. II, pp. 33–34.
41. The unnamed source mentioned above.
42. See Rupika Chawla, op. cit., p. 30.
43. Venniyur, op. cit., p. 29.
44. Rupika Chawla, op. cit., p. 32. His full name was Pururuttathi-Nal Kerala Varma Tampuran (1876–1912), while the younger boy was Revathi-Nal Rama Varma Tampuran (1880–1971). Ravi Varma himself was also Pururuttathi-Nal.
45. Uma (1882–1971), lovingly called Kochomana, remains forgotten in many biographical accounts on Raja Ravi Varma.
46. Author's interview with Rukmini Varma, great-great granddaughter of Raja Ravi Varma and granddaughter of Maharani Sethu Lakshmi Bayi.
47. His full name was Pooram-Nal Kerala Varma Koil Tampuran and he was the author of the *Amarakosa Padartha Prakashika*.
48. His full name was Tiruvonam-Nal Kerala Varma Koil Tampuran of Paliyakkara.
49. Author's interview with Rukmini Varma. Men could be quite touchy about the size of their kudumis and there is a story about the Rajah of Cochin who ruled

from 1895 to 1914, who once met a Nambutiri Brahmin with a kudumi better than his, and promptly had the man chop it off!

50. Lakshmi Raghunandan, *At the Turn of the Tide*, p. 2.
51. See Kulathu Iyer, *Maharani Sethu Lakshmi Bayi Tirumanasu Kondu*.
52. According to Mahaprabha's great-granddaughter Rukmini Varma, this room was 'a dark, cave-like birth room at the back of the nalukettu. I remember experiencing the strangest, most eerie sensations when I looked within. I felt as if icy cold ghostly fingers were running down my spine! It had a haunting aura about it. The woman who had just given birth could not rise from her bed and had to be attended by special servers who had to enter and exit through separate doors to avoid coming into contact with anyone. Only the midwife had free access to the lady. Very many unfortunate health issues cropped up as a consequence, but nobody dared eschew age-old customs!'
53. Lakshmi Raghunandan, op. cit., p. 4.
54. Charles Allen and Sharada Dwivedi, *Lives of the Indian Princes*, p. 31.
55. Letter dated 06/02/1896 from Sir Sheshiah Shastri to the Senior Rani (Raghunandan, pp. 9–10).
56. Letter dated 18/11/1896 from the Senior Rani to Mahaprabha (Raghunandan, p. 8).
57. Lakshmi Raghunandan, op. cit., p. 14.
58. Prince Revathi Tirunal Kerala Varma died soon after the birth of Sethu Lakshmi Bayi, on 5th December 1895.
59. Ulloor S. Parameswara Aiyar, *Progress of Travancore*, p. 101.
60. The Senior Rani quoted in Lakshmi Raghunandan, op. cit., p. 13.
61. Ibid., p. 14.
62. Expression used in letter dated 14/08/1890 from the Resident to the Chief Sec., Madras Govt. quoted in Robin Jeffrey, *The Decline of Nair Dominance*, p. 313.
63. Letter dated 18/12/1899 from the Elayarajah to the Resident (IOR/R/2/892/278).
64. Ibid.
65. Ibid.
66. Letter dated 12/12/1899 from the Resident to the Chief Sec., Madras Govt. (IOR/R/2/900/390).
67. Letter dated 18/12/1899 from the Elayarajah to the Resident (IOR/R/2/892/278).
68. The father of Lakshmi Bayi, Parvathi Bayi, and Kochupanki was Tiruvonam-Nal Ravi Varma Koil Tampuran of Pallom.
69. Letter dated 18/12/1899 from the Elayarajah to the Resident (IOR/R/2/892/278).

70. He intended, therefore, to veto the adoption by citing a legal precedent from a noble family closely allied to the royal house. This was the Vadasseri Ammaveedu, which was one of the exclusive houses from where the princes of Travancore were permitted to take wives. In the early 1880s there had arisen a need for adoption here, and the last surviving male member had organised a suitable arrangement. But some distant nephews of his, connected to the Ammaveedu in the matrilineal line, objected to the idea, and the then Maharajah had, therefore, disallowed the move. This, the Elayarajah pointed out, showed that senior members of the family could not proceed in such matters without the absolute consensus of all affected parties.
71. Letter dated 16/01/1900 from the Resident to the Chief Sec., Madras Govt. (IOR/R/2/892/278).
72. The Prince and Kuttan Tampuran were about the same age and had studied together for the BA exam some years previously.
73. See Dewan's memorandum (Raghunandan, pp. 17–18).
74. Venniyur, op. cit., p. 46.
75. Letter dated 13/01/1900 from the Resident to the Chief Sec., Madras Govt. (IOR/R/2/900/390).
76. Letter dated 12/12/1899 from the Resident to the Chief Sec., Madras Govt. (IOR/R/2/892/278). The Elayarajah had reason to be spiteful. Partly due to the intrigues of the palace bureau, the Maharajah had been on bad terms with the late Prince Revathi Tirunal, and many suspected foul play in his early demise. Since then Chathayam Tirunal also became hostile to Mulam Tirunal, who reciprocated in kind. He would humiliate the Elayarajah on ceremonial occasions by not allowing him to sit next to him, and stopped giving him the customary gifts during festivals and important religious occasions. Chathayam Tirunal was also unhappy because the Maharajah would not defray the expenses of his daughter's wedding from the Civil List, as she was not from an Ammaveedu (i.e., one of the select families from where alone princes could choose spouses) and hence unrecognised by the state.
77. Letter dated 30/04/1900 from the Chief Sec., GOI to the Madras Govt. (IOR/R/2/900/390) The British were eager to ensure legality and the opinion of the Advocate General of Madras, confirmed the Maharajah's stand.
78. Letter dated 17/08/1900 from the Elayarajah to the Resident (IOR/R/2/880/56).
79. Letter dated 05/08/1900 from the Resident to the Elayarajah (IOR/R/2/880/56).
80. Lakshmi Raghunandan, op. cit., p. 26.
81. Letter dated 18/12/1899 from the Elayarajah to the Resident (IOR/R/2/892/278)

CHAPTER 2: THE QUEEN OF THE KUPAKAS

1. Ulloor S. Parameswara Aiyar, *Progress of Travancore*, p. 106. Curzon was rather uncharitable to Indian princes and acted in a generally high-handed manner, deposing or curtailing the powers of some fifteen rulers during his time as Viceroy.
2. Rumour in Trivandrum still has it that he was poisoned, but the Resident's letters show that Asvathi Tirunal, like his brother, was very unhealthy and obese.
3. Letter dated 12/12/1899 from the Resident to the Chief Sec., Madras Govt. (IOR/R/2/892/278).
4. Letter dated 07/06/1901 from the Resident to the Chief Sec., Madras Govt. (IOR/R/2/900/394).
5. Letter dated 07/06/1901 from the Resident to the Chief Sec. Madras Govt. (IOR/R/2/900/394).
6. Valiya Koil Tampuran's diary entry dated 15/06/1901 (Raghunandan, p. 29).
7. In the nineteenth century, Ayilyam Tirunal Gowri Lakshmi Bayi succeeded as Senior Rani in 1808, aged eighteen; Uttrittadhi Tirunal Gowri Parvathi Bayi in 1814, aged thirteen; Pooradam Tirunal Lakshmi Bayi in 1854, at twenty-five; and Bharani Tirunal Lakshmi Bayi in 1857, aged nine.
8. Author's interview with Shreekumar Varma, a grandson of Maharani Sethu Lakshmi Bayi.
9. Author's interview with Rukmini Varma.
10. The consecration occurred on Avittom day in Mithunam month of 482 Malayalam Era.
11. Some believe the adoption was made by his successor Udaya Martanda Varma.
12. P.K.S. Raja, *Mediaeval Kerala*, p. 59.
13. Gouri Lakshmi Bayi, *Sree Padmanabha Swamy Temple*, pp. 147–148.
14. Thus families like the Thottattil Asaris, who were carpenters, and the Ponnara Panickers, who were Nair bodyguards, all travelled south with the Ranis, where their descendants can still be traced.
15. There were powerful women behind the throne elsewhere in India too, but unlike the Attingal Ranis they did not directly or openly exercise power.
16. The original Attingal Ranis gave rise to a number of branches in the royal family. It was the older girl installed at Attingal while the younger was known as the Kunnumel Rani. Her descendants were the Rajahs of Kottarakara and Nedumangad, while those of Quilon and Kayamkulam emerged from the first Attingal Rani.
17. In recent years due to a variety of factors historians have been reluctant to ascribe to the Ranis the kind of power and consequence they actually enjoyed.

T.K. Velu Pillai insists that their territory was only an 'estate' granted by the Travancore Rajah for their upkeep, and that he had all other reins over it. 'The Rani of Attingal,' he would write, 'had no political duties to perform. She had neither territory nor subjects except in the sense that the people paid their respect to her as a member of the ruling family. What she possessed was nothing more than the control over the revenues of the district and an outward state and dignity. Such powers as she exercised were nothing more than delegated powers.' Sreedhara Menon, similarly, concluded that 'The Attingal Ranis did not exercise sovereign powers but in view of their close relations with the Venad [i.e. Travancore] royal family they enjoyed [only] a special status.' These views, sadly, could not be more wrong.

18. Leena More, *English East India Company and the Local Rulers in Kerala*, pp. 12–13.
19. Nagam Aiya, *Travancore State Manual*, Vol I, p. 288. This is the queen of Quilon but Aiya treats her as an Attingal Rani. This is quite possible because all these families were related and there were adoptions among them every now and then. In the 1690s, for instance, when the Peraka Tavazhi branch of the family became extinct due to the want of heirs in that line, the territory was taken over by the Attingal Rani, who then resolved the succession through an adoption from another branch of the Kupaka family.
20. Leena More, op. cit., p. 13.
21. See Krishna Chaitanya's *A History of Malayalam Literature*, p. 42, and Leela Devi's *History of Malayalam Literature*, p. 13.
22. John Wallis, *A Short Treatise by Way of Essay of Attinga* (IOR/G/40/22).
23. Quoted in K.P. Padmanabha Menon, *History of Kerala*, Vol II, p. 27.
24. Louise Ouwerkerk and Dick Kooiman, *No Elephants for the Maharaja*, p. 41.
25. Leena More, op. cit., p. 44.
26. Translation of an Ola given by Her Highness the Queen of Attinga to the Rt Hon. English East India Company on 29/06/1694 (IOR/E/3/50 f223).
27. Translation of a paper given by John Brabourne of the English East India Company to Her Highness the Queen of Attinga (IOR/E/3/50 f224).
28. English Version of a letter from the Queen of Attinga to Sir John Gayer dated 15/04/1695 (IOR/E/3/51 f25).
29. K.P. Padmanabha Menon, op. cit., p. 347.
30. Leena More, op. cit., p. 60.
31. *Selections from the Records of the Madras Government*, Vol. 13, p. 53.
32. Leena More, op. cit., p. 69.
33. Ibid. p. 77.
34. Mark de Lannoy, *The Kulasekhara Perumals of Travancore*, p. 29.

35. Leena More, op. cit., p. 75
36. Reference is to Peraka Tavazhi.
37. Leena More, op. cit., p. 82.
38. Their occasional bullying of the princes seems to have affected the masculine sensibilities of later Rajahs, however, and into the nineteenth century, the traditional influence of the Attingal Ranis was carefully played down in modern renditions of history, diminishing them into glorified dependents of their brothers as best, even as folklore continued to celebrate their triumphant past.
39. Quoted in K.P. Padmanabha Menon, op. cit., Vol II, p. 27
40. Quoted in Leena More, op. cit., p. 29
41. Ibid. p. 30
42. Ibid.
43. John Keay, *The Honourable Company*, p. 254.
44. Author's interview with J. Devika.
45. Leena More, op. cit., p. 117.
46. The Rani, it is said, blamed her nobles for it later, but the Travancore Rajah and the Dutch who called her 'that cunning woman' held her complicit in the plot.
47. Mark de Lannoy, op. cit., p. 33.
48. The Quilon Rajah was part of these treaties, however, proving again his superiority to the Kupaka prince ruling Travancore.
49. John Wallis, op. cit.
50. Mark de Lannoy, op. cit., p. 42.
51. Later historians would claim this Silver Plate Treaty never existed because it could not be found. It did, however, exist till the early nineteenth century and the famous British Resident Col Munro has written about how it was destroyed during a succession dispute in 1810. He also notes how he met many old people at court who had seen and knew the contents of the treaty in detail and in his letter dated 12/06/1813 to the Chief Secretary at Fort St. George he writes: 'I entertain no doubt either of its having been executed or of the terms upon which it was concluded.' See IOR/R/1/1/1532 (1).
52. Mark de Lannoy, op. cit., p. 139. The honour was repeated again on the 9th of June 1782 when the Attingal Rani (mother to the famous Dharma Rajah who succeeded Martanda Varma) died and an 86-gun salute was fired in her honour, that number being her age at the time. See *Selections from the Records of the Madras Government*, Vol. 13, p. 160.
53. Leena More, op. cit., pp. 136–137.
54. Quoted in K.P. Padmanabha Menon, op. cit., Vol. II, p. 29. Nagam Aiya in his *Travancore State Manual*, Vol. 1, p. 356, similarly quotes the English Chief of Anjengo in 1757 who spoke of 'our Priviledges which we obtained from the

Queen of Attinga, in whose Territories the Fort is situated. Her country is now in the absolute power of the King of Travancore, and he holds the Heiress of the Family under restraint in the Palace of Attinga, but being of the same Family himself, does not otherwise treat her ill.'

55. Quoted in Ibrahim Kunju, *Rise of Travancore*, pp. 16–17.
56. Letter dated 28/11/1810 from the Resident to the Chief Sec., Fort St. George (IOR/R/1/1/1532 (1)).
57. Letter dated 21/03/1813 from the Resident to the Chief Sec., Fort St. George (IOR/R/1/1/1532 (1)).
58. T.K. Velu Pillai, *Travancore State Manual*, Vol. II, p. 299.
59. According to Dr R.P. Raja, Kupaka was always another name for Attingal and the Queen of Kupaka was the Attingal Rani. Author's interview with R.P. Raja.
60. Samuel Mateer, *Native Life in Travancore*, p. 128. In the early seventeenth century Pietro Della Valle also noted: 'I will not omit to mention the manner how those who entered saluted the King; for I saw more than one do it, and particularly a Youth who enter'd a good while after the King by one of those little Gates; to whom in particular the King spake much, and of whom he seemed to make great account. In his salutation he advanced his joyned Hands over his Head, then, parting them a little so extended and exalted, he smote them lightly together twice, or thrice, to wit the palm of one hand with the for longest Fingers of the other joyned together; which whole action he repeated twice, or thrice. Such as had weapons lifted them up their joyned Hands above their Heads, with their Swords, Ponyards, Bucklers, or other Arms, in them; and instead of striking with their fingers, as by reason of their Arms they could not, they bowed down their Hands so conjoyned and made the points of their Swords touch the ground.' See Edward Grey, *The Travels of Pietro Della Valle in India*, p. 368.
61. Samuel Mateer, op. cit., p. 129.
62. Statement by Gouri Parvathi Bayi to the author. Gouri Parvathi Bayi is the granddaughter of Sethu Parvathi Bayi.
63. The Palace Manual even details the roles of attendants, including where they should be standing and so on.
64. Charles Allen and Sharada Dwivedi, *Lives of the Indian Princes*, p. 34.
65. Letter dated 28/06/1929 from Louise Ouwerkerk to her mother (MSS EUR F232/60). Some decades before, Augusta Blandford recorded an incident as follows that showed how these 'vexatious rules extend[ed]' to the smallest matters: 'For instance, I was sitting one day with the senior Rani, and in the midst of her reading she was seized with a violent fit of coughing. I said, "Do drink a little water, it will relieve you." She looked up smiling and said, "You forget that I must not take any till I have bathed, because you have been near me," and added "it is very troublesome to follow all these rules." What a

monstrous system! The mere presence of an English lady to be so polluting. I wonder the people do not rise en masse and throw off the hated yoke, but many, alas! hug their fetters, and would not cast them away if they could.' See *India's Women: The Magazine of the Church of England Zenana Missionary Society*, Vol. I, p. 294.

66. Author's interview with Divakara Varma. Dr Lakshman was a Malabar Thiyya.
67. Gouri Parvathi Bayi's statement to the author.
68. Charles Allen and Sharada Dwivedi, op. cit., pp. 199–200.
69. Henry Bruce, *Letters from Malabar*, p. 84.
70. *The Lady* dated 11/01/1912.
71. Kulathu Aiyar, *Her Highness Sethu Lakshmi Bai*, p. 3
72. Shreekumar Varma draft of 'Those Were the Daze' which was published in Anita Nair's *Where the Rain is Born.*
73. Kulathu Aiyar op. cit., p. 3.
74. Author's interview with Rukmini Varma.
75. Ibid.
76. Kulathu Aiyar, op. cit., p. 5.
77. Author's interview with Rukmini Varma and also a profile of the Senior Rani in *The Globe* dated 05/09/1924 and in *The Lady* op. cit.
78. Kuppuswamy Aiyangar, *The Ranis of Travancore*, p. 7.
79. *The Feudatory and Zemindari India*, Vol. 6, No. 3, p. 115.
80. Kulathu Aiyar, op. cit., p. 3.
81. Kulathu Iyer, *Maharani Sethu Lakshmi Bayi Tirumanasu Kondu*, p. 19.
82. *The Lady* op. cit.
83. O.M. Thomas, *Under the Knife*, p. 64. The Maharani's grand piano was donated to the Women's College in Trivandrum, where it still remains.
84. Henry Bruce, op. cit., p. 86.
85. Letter dated 22/02/1929 from the Resident to the Pol. Sec. GOI (IOR/R/1/1/1849).
86. Kuppuswamy Aiyangar, op. cit., pp. 7–8.
87. Ibid.
88. Charles Allen and Sharada Dwivedi, op. cit., p. 113.
89. Ibid.
90. Letter dated 11/08/1904 from the Senior Rani to Mahaprabha (Raghunandan p. 33).
91. The Junior Rani quoted in T.N. Gopinathan Nair, *Avasanate Naduvazhiyude Amma*, p. 17.
92. O.M. Thomas, op. cit., p. 64.

93. P.K. Narayana Pillai, *Kerala Varma*, p. 91.
94. 1875 letter (A) in IOR/R/2/891/256.
95. 1875 letter (B) in IOR/R/2/891/256.
96. 1875 Anonymous letter (A) in IOR/R/2/891/256.
97. Letter dated 07/07/1875 from the Valiya Koil Tampuran to the Resident (IOR/R/2/891/256).
98. P. Ramakrishna Pillai, *Visakhavijaya*, p. 94.
99. Letter dated 26/01/1877 from Kerala Varma to the Maharajah (IOR/R/2/891/260). The full text is as follows: To, His Highness the Maha Rajah of Travancore. Before the Royal feet of His Most Gracious and Extremely Kind hearted Highness the Maha Rajah of Travancore, the Most Benign and Sovereign Protector of this Slave and his family, this most guilty, most deeply penitent and most humble Slave prostrates himself and most respectfully begs to submit this humble supplication.

    With the most sincere repentance and most contrite sorrow, Slave begs to state at Your Highness' feet the great treasonous acts he committed against Your Highness who has been all along treating him with uniform kindness and favor (sic). He is at the same time unable to account for the almost sudden and temporary transition of his mind which enticed him with such a heinous offence and can attribute it to nothing but his ill fate. Your Highness' Slave wrote one or two letters against Your Highness to the First Prince. He wrote that anonymous letter to the Dewan and when questioned about it by Your Highness first with great kindness privately and then officially through the Acting Resident, Slave basely and dishonestly denied any knowledge about it. Slave addressed to Your Highness' Self, his own Sovereign Protector, an anonymous letter like the one to the Dewan. Slave also wrote a Malayalam anonymous letter to Your Highness' address giving an utterly false and scandalous report. Slave wrote to some of the Europeans at Trivandrum going out an ungrounded suspicion which occurred to him without any reason at the time, of Your Highness and the First Prince having been the abettors of the supposed murder of his brother and uncle who died on their return from a tour to Benares. Slave is fully convinced and admits that all the above letters are highly treasonous, and even should Your Highness pass a sentence of life imprisonment with fetters and hard labor (sic), Slave should not think it too heavy a punishment for his offences. Slave most humbly and repentantly admits also that he did the following very wrong things: he was corresponding unnecessarily to some newspapers: He felt somehow an inclination to Christianity: He suspected without any ground somebody having poisoned him: He had got unto that most abominable and forbidden vice of drinking and became a regular drunkard: Wanting stronger narcotics he took to the intemperate use of Bhang and some other stuffs. Having insidiously wronged his Sovereign Protector and Benefactor who has these 20 years been treating him with exceeding kindness and done him every possible good; having proved basely ungrateful to the Royal Family whose salt he and his family are to this day eating; and having treacherously given serious annoyance to Your Highness' Government by his depraved character, Your Highness' humble Slave cannot possibly entertain the faintest hope of obtaining a kind pardon even from so condescending and tender hearted a Sovereign as Your Highness. But feeling the most sincere compunction of conscience and most heartfelt, contrite and (illegible) remorse for all his past misconduct, Your Highness' most humble Slave begs to throw himself at Your Highness' Royal feet and with tears in his eyes most piteously implores Your Highness' kind forgiveness once for the serious offences he has committed. Whatever be Your Highness' Slave's future destiny by the nature of the arrangements Your Highness makes in disposing of him whether to quit his native country and all relations and his days as an exile and a beggar or to rove as a Fakir and perish in the snowy regions of the Himalayas, he will submit to it as his fate; but he will bear Your Highness' Command with his head bowed down and shall never deviate even a hair breadth from it. Your Highness' Slave begs to subscribe, (Signed) Kerala Varmah, State Prisoner.

100. P. Ramakrishna Pillai, op. cit., p. 12.
101. Letter dated 12/05/1885 from the Elayarajah to the Valiya Koil Tampuran (TRF).
102. P.K. Narayana Pillai, op. cit., p. 101.
103. Ibid. p. 49.
104. The Senior Rani quoted in Lakshmi Raghunandan, op. cit., p. 62.

CHAPTER 3: THREE CONSORTS

1. This was the marriage of the late Junior Rani Bharani Tirunal Parvathi Bayi.
2. Undated letter from Kochukunji to Mahaprabha (Raghunandan p. 44).
3. Author's interview with Dr R.P. Raja. The Parappanad family lost eleven male and nine female members during the invasions when they were taken away to Coimbatore by Tipu Sultan's men and forcibly converted to Islam. After the Sultan's defeat they remained outcaste and that branch of the family died out in subsequent years. This family were known as the Kuriyedathu Kovilakam.
4. This was Pooradam Tirunal Lakshmi Bayi, the mother of Maharajah Mulam Tirunal.
5. This was Ayilyam Tirunal Rukmini Bayi, the mother of Maharajah Ayilyam Tirunal and Maharajah Visakham Tirunal. Rukmini Bayi's mother, Gowri Lakshmi Bayi, was also married to a Parappanad Rajah.

6. Undated letter from Kochukunji to Mahaprabha (Raghunandan p. 44).
7. Charles Allen and Sharada Dwivedi, *Lives of the Indian Princes*, p. 180.
8. Author's interview with Rukmini Varma. Rajaraja Varma possibly met Ravi Varma at the wedding itself, following which he was asked to model for the latter.
9. Ibid.
10. Lakshmi Raghunandan, *At the Turn of the Tide*, p. 44.
11. Author's interview with Rukmini Varma.
12. The Valiya Koil Tampuran's diary entry dated 27/02/1906 (Raghunandan, p. 45).
13. The head priest was always the senior Brahmin of the Kakkattu Pohtti family.
14. Author's interviews with Rukmini Varma and Divakara Varma.
15. Among the ten Koil Tampuran families of Travancore, women were always married to Brahmins.
16. Rajaraja Varma married a Nair lady and enjoyed a happy marriage and had several children, including two beautiful daughters, and lived in a large bungalow in Trivandrum. The place is now known as Tampuran Mukku. Rajaraja Varma and Rama Varma had three sisters, Amba, Ambika and Ambalika, and were children of Thrikkettannal Ittiyengala Tampuratti and Kallampally Raman Nambutiri.
17. Rupika Chawla, *Raja Ravi Varma*, p. 123, and author's interview with Rukmini Varma.
18. The marriage had a number of elaborate rituals and ceremonies spread over many days, details of which are available in *The Pallikkettu of H.H. Lalitamba Bayi* by Kulathu Aiyar. See also *Programme of Functions Connected with the Marriage of Her Highness the Senior Ranee* (TRF).
19. Author's interviews with Rukmini Varma and Uma Varma, both granddaughters of Maharani Sethu Lakshmi Bayi and Rama Varma.
20. I am grateful to Shobhana Varma, a granddaughter of Maharani Sethu Lakshmi Bayi and Rama Varma, for showing me many books from Rama Varma's collection.
21. Author's interview with Jay Varma, a great-grandson of Maharani Sethu Lakshmi Bayi and Rama Varma.
22. Author's interview with Rukmini Varma.
23. O.M. Thomas, *Under the Knife*, p. 67.
24. Charles Allen and Sharada Dwivedi, op. cit., p. 185.
25. Lakshmi Raghunandan, op. cit., pp. 56–57.
26. Partha Mitter, *Art and Nationalism in Colonial India*, p. 180.
27. Ibid.

28. See Rupika Chawla, op. cit. for more on this, and Partha Mitter, op. cit., p. 179 for the review of Ravi Varma's work by Tagore.
29. C. Rajaraja Varma quoted in S.A. Pillai, *Raja Ravi Varma and his Art*, p. 13.
30. Lakshmi Raghunandan, op. cit., pp. 54–55.
31. He was the son of one Rohini-Nal Tampuratti of Kilimanoor by her husband, Attupurathu Nambutiri and was born in 1884.
32. Uma Maheswari, *Thrippadidanam*, p. 113, and T.N. Gopinathan Nair, *Sree Chithira Thirunal*, p. 10.
33. Author's interview with Rukmini Varma.
34. Letter dated 14/12/1929 from Louise Ouwerkerk to her mother (MSS EUR F232/60).
35. Kulathu Aiyar, *Her Highness Sethu Lakshmi Bai*, p. 5
36. Author's interview with Dr R.P. Raja.
37. See letter dated 21/02/1935 from the Resident to the Pol Sec., GOI, and letter dated 21/03/1935 from the Under Pol. Sec., GOI (IOR/L/PS/13/1283).
38. Note dated 23/04/1926 on the Exceptional Political Position of the Senior Rani of Travancore in IOR/R/1/1/1532 (1). Also see Note on Kharitas to Senior Ranis of Travancore in IOR/R/2/900/408. I am also grateful to Lakshmi Raghunandan for showing me all the Kharitas Sethu Lakshmi Bayi received during her time as Senior Rani, down till the Viceroyalty of Lord Mountbatten. The text of a typical kharita, as sent by Lord Irwin on 16th April 1926 to Sethu Lakshmi Bayi goes: 'My esteemed friend, His Most Gracious Majesty the King Emperor of India, having appointed me to be Viceroy and Governor-General of India, in succession to the Right Hon'ble The Earl of Reading, I write to inform Your Highness that I assumed charge of my office at Bombay on the 3rd April 1926. Your Highness may rest assured of the friendliness of the sentiments which I entertain for you and of my earnest wishes for your continued prosperity. I desire to express the high consideration which I entertain for Your Highness and to subscribe myself, Your Highness' sincere friend, Irwin (signed) Viceroy and Governor-General of India.'
39. Ibid. The Maharajah was always 'His Highness Sri Padmanabha Dasa Vanchi Palace [personal name] Kulasekhara Kiritapathi Manney Sultan Maharajah Rajah Rama Rajah Bahadur Shamsher Jang' while the Senior Rani was 'Her Highness Sri Padmanabha Sevini Vanchi Dharma Vardhini Raja Rajeshwari Rani [personal name] Sahiba'. The Maharajah had some more titles after his personal name, which were given by the Nawab of Arcot which the Attingal Rani did not share.
40. Instance described in Lakshmi Raghunandan, op. cit., p. 41.
41. Marthanda Varma, *Travancore: The Footprints of Destiny*, p. 85.
42. Ibid. p. 92.

43. T.N. Gopinathan Nair, *Avasanate ...* op. cit., p. 8.
44. Author's interview with Dr R.P. Raja.
45. Letter dated 20/01/1916 from the Senior Rani to Kuttan Tampuran (TRF).
46. John Paton Davies, *China Hand*, p. 83. This was not necessarily unheard of. In the early seventeenth century, Pietro Della Valle would note about the Zamorins and their ostensible orthodoxy as follows: 'These Ceremonies of not being touch'd and the like, of which in publick demonstration they are so rigorous, yet in secret, and when they please, they do not exactly observe; and 'twas told us of this King that he is a great drinker of Wine, though rigorously prohibited by his Religion, and that he hath sometimes eaten and drunk at the same Table with the Portugals very familiarly; and that he is a Man of very affable humour and a great friend to a jovial life, which also his carriage towards us demonstrated.' See *The Travels of Pietro Della Valle in India*, p. 376.
47. Junior Rani's granddaughter at a presentation at the Asian Art Museum in San Francisco; video available at https://www.youtube.com/watch?v=lj6bliCSNbg (accessed 02/01/2015).
48. Simon de Burton, 'Maharajas of the road' in *The Telegraph* dated 08/11/2013 http://www.telegraph.co.uk/luxury/motoring/14583/maharajas-of-the-road.html (accessed 24/11/2014).
49. Henry Bruce, *Letters from Malabar*, p. 84.
50. Kuppuswamy Aiyangar, *The Ranis of Travancore*, p. 7.
51. Gouri Parvathi Bayi's statement to the author.
52. Ibid.
53. Lakshmi Raghunandan, op. cit., p. 64.
54. Letter dated 14/01/1908 from the Senior Rani to Mahaprabha (Raghunandan, p. 62).
55. Letter dated 26/10/1911 from the Senior Rani to Mahaprabha (Raghunandan, p. 68). As it happened, this youngest sister, Kochu Thankam, became her lifelong companion and aide, even in the years after the Senior Rani renounced life in the palace.
56. Letter dated 08/09/1912 from the Senior Rani to Mahaprabha (Raghunandan, p. 75).
57. Author's interview with Indira Varma, the younger daughter of Maharani Sethu Lakshmi Bayi.
58. Author's interview with Rukmini Varma.
59. I am grateful to Lakshmi Raghunandan, Rukmini Varma, and Shobhana Varma for showing me books from the Senior Rani's collection. They are all granddaughters of Sethu Lakshmi Bayi.
60. Kulathu Aiyar, op. cit., p. 7.

61. Ibid. p. 9.
62. Letter dated 13/01/1916 from the Senior Rani to Kuttan Tampuran (TRF).
63. See Lucy Moore, *Maharanis* (Google Books).
64. Letter dated 12/02/1909 from Kochukunji to Mahaprabha (Raghunandan, p. 66).
65. Author's interview with Dr R.P. Raja.
66. Letter dated 18/02/1909 from Kochukunji to Mahaprabha (Raghunandan, p. 66).
67. Gouri Parvathi Bayi's statement to the author.
68. Author's interview with Dr R.P. Raja.
69. Author's interview with Rukmini Varma. One story tells how Mahaprabha one day, upon her return from Trivandrum, heard from a trusted steward of someone having made offensive remarks about her. 'She was undaunted and maintained her regal and imposing status. She did not bat an eyelid, nor did she lose her composure. She assured the steward she would deal with it, and when she entered the room where the members of her family were gathered, she directed one freezing look at the offender, which completely unsettled the latter!'
70. Kulathu Aiyar, op. cit., p. 2.
71. Author's interview with Rukmini Varma.
72. According to Rukmini Varma, Ravi Varma's elder son, Kerala Varma, had a wife from Thrissur, 'a very beautiful lady, who till the end of her days after his departure in 1912 maintained a kidavilakku—an eternal lamp—in the hope of his return one day.' Kerala Varma even had a daughter, who married one of Kochukunji's sons. It is believed that Kerala Varma might have gone to Goa and converted to Christianity and had a second family there. Rukmini Varma remembers meeting a Goan man with a photograph of Kerala Varma, whom he claimed as an ancestor, sometime in the 1970s.
73. Author's interview with Dr R.P. Raja.
74. This descendant of Raja Ravi Varma who spoke to the author does not wish to be named.
75. Letter dated 20/09/1924 from the Resident to the Pol. Sec., GOI (IOR/R/2/884/161).
76. During the author's interview with Advocate Ayyappan Pillai, he too affirmed that the disputes between the two Ranis began on relatively petty grounds, which in Malayalam are called *soundarya pinakkums*. The Senior Rani's daughter Indira Varma also stated that their aunts and relations told of how the rivalry between the cousins began because of such relatively petty issues as beauty and looks. On 23/11/2014 at her speech at the Sethu Lakshmi Bayi Memorial Lecture in Trivandrum, the Junior Rani's granddaughter would remark that even servants of the latter would sing in Malayalam, '*Lakshmi Bayi Maharani; Lakshanam*

Othuru Tirumeni'. Loosely translated, this is an appreciation of the Senior Rani's queenly demeanour and beauty.

77. R.P. Raja, 'Tiruvithamkur Rajakudumbathinte Aradhyapurushan' (Malayalam) in *Ayyaguru Mahasamadhi Varshika Smaranika* (2003) (Thiruvananthapuram: Ayya Mission), pp. 28–29.
78. Author's interview with Dr R.P. Raja.
79. Letter dated 22/02/1929 from the Resident to the Pol. Sec., GOI (IOR/R/1/1/1849).
80. See Chapter 10.
81. Author's interview with Divakara Varma.
82. This person does not wish to be named.
83. Author's interview with Rukmini Varma.
84. Letter dated 15/09/1912 from the Senior Rani to Mahaprabha (Raghunandan, p. 75).
85. Letter dated 22/09/1912 from the Senior Rani to Mahaprabha (Raghunandan, p. 75).
86. Letter dated 08/09/1912 from the Senior Rani to Mahaprabha (Raghunandan, p. 75).
87. Ulloor S. Parameswara Aiyar, *Progress of Travancore*, p. 137.
88. Letter dated 08/11/1912 from the Senior Rani to Mahaprabha (Raghunandan, p. 77).
89. In reality he was named Rama Varma and added the 'Bala' himself at the time of his accession to power. However, to prevent confusion with the other Rama Varmas in this book, I refer to him by his preferred name of Balarama Varma.
90. Dewan P. Rajagopalachari quoted in *Proceedings of the Fourth Meeting of the Sri Mulam Popular Assembly of Travancore,* p. 12 quoted in Annexure A, IOR/R/1/1/3371.
91. These were the Vanchiyur Mahadeva Temple, Veerakeralapuram Sri Krishna Temple, Avanavanchery Ayyappa Temple, Nilamelkunnu Sri Krishna Temple, Avaneesvaram Mahadeva Temple, Mampazhakonam Temple, Elampa Siva Temple, Kattayilkonam Devi Temple, and the Chittankulangara Dharmasastha Temple.
92. Kulathu Aiyar, op. cit., p. 8.
93. Letter dated 09/01/1914 from Rama Varma to Kuttan Tampuran (Raghunandan, pp. 82–83).
94. Lakshmi Raghunandan, op. cit., p. 81.
95. See Valiya Koil Tampuran's letter to the Senior Rani quoted in T.N. Gopinathan Nair, *Avasanate* ... op. cit., p. 41.
96. Kerala Varma's diary entry dated 29/03/1913 (Raghunandan, p. 88).

97. Kerala Varma's diary entry dated 15/05/1913 (Raghunandan, pp. 81–82).
98. Author's interview with Advocate Ayyappan Pillai.
99. Gouri Parvathi Bayi's statement to the author.
100. Author's interview with Dr R.P. Raja.
101. Letter dated 01/12/1912 from the Senior Rani to Mahaprabha (Raghunandan, p. 77).
102. Letter dated 25/02/1915 from the Senior Rani to Mahaprabha (Raghunandan, p. 90).
103. Letter dated 01/12/1912 from the Senior Rani to Mahaprabha (Raghunandan, p. 77).
104. Letter dated 13/02/1914 from Rama Varma to Kuttan Tampuran (Raghunandan, p. 87).
105. Letter dated 29/01/1914 from the Senior Rani to Kuttan Tampuran (Raghunandan, p. 83).
106. Letter dated 29/01/1914 from the Senior Rani to Mahaprabha (Raghunandan, p. 84).
107. Ulloor S. Parameswara Aiyar, *Essays on Travancore*, p. 25
108. Palace letter dated 24th Makaram 1089 Malayalam Era in IOR/R/1/1/3371. The decision was to give 84,000 panams to the Junior Rani, 336,682 panams to the establishment, and 211,300 panams to the Senior Rani, and it was taken by Mulam Tirunal.
109. Kuttan Tampuran's diary entry dated 06/04/1914 (Raghunandan, p. 85).
110. Letter dated 10/02/1914 from the Senior Rani to Mahaprabha (TRF).
111. Mahakavi Kumaran Asan quoted in P.K. Narayana Pillai, *Kerala Varma*, p. 103.
112. Letter dated 05/01/1915 from the Senior Rani to Mahaprabha (Raghunandan, p. 91).

CHAPTER 4: THE SECOND FAVOURITE

1. Letter dated 22/07/1915 from the Senior Rani to Kuttan Tampuran (Raghunandan, p. 97).
2. Appendix to G.O. No. 321 (Political) dated 14/05/1900 (IOR/R/2/892/278).
3. Author's interview with Rukmini Varma.
4. Letter dated 18/12/1899 from the Elayarajah to the Resident (IOR/R/2/892/278).
5. Ulloor S. Parameswara Iyer, *Progress of Travancore*, p. 35.
6. Louise Ouwerkerk and Dick Kooiman, *No Elephants for the Maharaja*, p. 66.
7. She died giving birth to a son named Nagercoil Sri Narayanan Tampi. He grew up, in what was unusual, not in his maternal home, the Nagercoil Ammaveedu,

but at his father's palace, until he was eighteen when he was granted his own establishment at the Tanjore Ammaveedu.

8. Letter dated 03/04/1882 from Mulam Tirunal to the Valiya Koil Tampuran (TRF).
9. Ulloor S. Parameswara Iyer, op. cit., p. 205.
10. Lord Pentland's speech quoted in ibid. p. 142.
11. Ibid. p. 205.
12. P. Ramakrishna Pillai, *Visakhavijaya*, p. 149.
13. M.J. Koshy, *KC Mammen Maappilai*, p. 204.
14. Note dated 25/01/1908 in IOR/R/1/1/1019.
15. Ibid.
16. Note dated 27/02/1907 in IOR/R/1/1/993.
17. Robin Jeffrey, *Decline of Nair Dominance*, p. 102.
18. As Louise Ouwerkerk states, 'So strong was the tradition that the ruler stood above the actual business of administration, that although his consent to the carrying out of a death sentence was necessary, the death warrant was always signed by a special palace official, so that the wrath of the gods would not fall on the Raja'. The special officer was the Fouzdar. See Louise Ouwerkerk and Dick Kooiman, op. cit., p. 64.
19. M.J. Koshy, *Genesis of Political Consciousness in Kerala*, pp. 63–64.
20. Robin Jeffrey, op. cit., p. 146.
21. M.J. Koshy, *Genesis* ... op. cit., p. 64.
22. Letter dated 12/12/1899 from the Resident to Madras Govt (IOR/R/2/892/278).
23. N.P. Unni, *Sanskrit Plays of V Krishnan Tampi*, p. ix.
24. Ulloor S. Parameswara Iyer, op. cit., p. 101. His name was Vadasseri Sri Velayudan Tampi.
25. She was adopted into the Vadasseri Ammaveedu along with her family.
26. T.K. Velu Pillai, *Travancore State Manual*, Vol. II, p. 709. The daughter's name was Bhagavathi Pillai.
27. *The Lady* dated 11/01/1912.
28. The story goes that Visakham Tirunal while on tour met the teenaged Sanku Pillai and was impressed by his personality, and took him on his personal staff. His father was from Chittezhathu house in Minnamthottam, while his mother came from Njarakkattu house in Chavara. I am grateful to my friend Sharat Sunder Rajeev for this information, which he collected from a great-nephew of the man.
29. K. Ramakrishna Pillai quoted in A. Sreedhara Menon, *Triumph and Tragedy in Travancore*, p. 333.

30. M.J. Koshy, *Genesis* ... op. cit., p. xi.
31. Justice T. Sadasiva Aiyar quoted in Robin Jeffrey, op. cit., p. 200.
32. Note dated 27/02/1907 in IOR/R/1/1/993.
33. Robin Jeffrey, op. cit., p. 313. Rumours, interestingly, continue to this day about this in Trivandrum.
34. Ibid., p. 217.
35. Ibid., p. 345.
36. Editor's Note in Ulloor S. Parameswara Iyer, op. cit., p. 139.
37. Robin Jeffrey, op. cit., p. 318.
38. Guptan Nair, *C.V. Raman Pillai*, p. 36.
39. Ibid. p. 33.
40. Robin Jeffrey, op. cit., p. 220.
41. See *The Travancore Deportation* by K. Ramakrishna Pillai. 'Ramakrishna Pillai did not spare even the Maharaja for his insane luxuries and extravagant expenses. The Maharaja spent more than a lakh of rupees for the useless and superstitious Thalikettu ceremony of his daughter in Vadasseri Ammaveedu. "Our sense of justice compels us to state that by such luxurious spendings, the rulers make the people lose their loyalty to the Maharaja." Again: "The palace appropriates a substantial part of the government treasury for itself. The amount is not used for justifiable expenses, but for pomp and luxury, for tours and feasts. A few sycophants and favourites of the Dewan, in addition to their normal salaries amass considerable wealth ... while the people are not benefitted in any way."' See P.C. Joshi and K. Damodaran, *Marx Comes to India*, p. 88
42. A number of people in Trivandrum consider poisoning the cause of these deaths.
43. Author's interview with Divakara Varma.
44. Kerala Varma's diary entry dated 27/04/1905 (Raghunandan, pp. 42–43).
45. Kuttan Tampuran's diary entry dated 17/08/1914 (Raghunandan, p. 86).
46. Ibid.
47. Kuttan Tampuran's diary entry dated 15/07/1914 (Raghunandan, p. 86).
48. Kuttan Tampuran's diary entry dated 21/09/1914 (Raghunandan, p. 86).
49. Lakshmi Raghunandan, op. cit., p. 85.
50. Kuttan Tampuran's diary entry dated 25/02/1914 (Raghunandan, p. 84).
51. Letter dated 20/06/1929 from the Resident to the Pol. Sec., GOI (IOR/R/2/885/175).
52. Letter dated 19/09/1924 from the Resident to the Pol. Sec., GOI (IOR/R/1/1/1530 (2)).
53. Kuttan Tampuran's diary entry dated 03/04/1914 (Raghunandan, p. 85).
54. Letter dated 27/10/1929 from the Resident to the Pol. Sec., GOI (IOR/R/2/885/175).

55. Kuttan Tampuran's diary entry dated 23/03/1914 (Raghunandan, p. 85).
56. Kuttan Tampuran's diary entry dated 26/01/1914 (Raghunandan, p. 87).
57. Senior Rani quoted in Lakshmi Raghunandan, op. cit., p. 86.
58. Kuttan Tampuran's diary entry dated 22/09/1914 (Raghunandan, p. 89).
59. Kuttan Tampuran's diary entry dated 18/10/1914 (Raghunandan, p. 90).
60. Author's interview with Uma Varma.
61. Letter dated 15/09/1912 from the Senior Rani to Kuttan Tampuran (TRF).
62. Kuttan Tampuran's diary entry dated 01/07/1914 (Raghunandan, p. 86).
63. Swaminathan was the husband of Ammu Swaminathan and the father of Mrinalini Sarabhai and Lakshmi Sehgal. Sarabhai's husband, Vikram Sarabhai, incidentally died at Halcyon Castle in Kovalam, once a beach palace belonging to Rama Varma.
64. Letter dated 15/07/1916 from the Senior Rani to Kuttan Tampuran (Raghunandan, p. 98).
65. Author's interview with Dr R.P. Raja.
66. One brother, called Rajan Tampuran, married Mulam Tirunal's daughter and secured a portion of her fortune when she died. He was also the father of a Malayalam actress called Ambika, a cousin of the Travancore Sisters. Another called Kochurajan Tampuran was in government service in various jobs, including superintending the Trivandrum Museum. A third called Kuttan Tampuran was in Jamshedpur, while one Unni Tampuran was a Port Officer in Alleppey.
67. Their names were Thrikketta-Nal Martanda Varma Tampuran (1893–1964) (who features as the baby in Ravi Varma's *There Comes Papa* in Mahaprabha's arms); Makayiram-Nal Kerala Varma Tampuran (1901–1965); Swathi-Nal Rama Varma Tampuran (1906–1941); Pooram-Nal Ravi Varma Tampuran (1907–1962); and Swathi-Nal Rajaraja Varma Tampuran (1911–1983). The Maharani's sisters were Asvathi-Nal Bhageerathi (Kutty Amma) Tampuratti (1902–1984) and Thriketta-Nal Uma (Kochu Thankam) Tampuratti (1909–2004). She also had a sister who died named Ammukutty (d. 1908). The Senior Rani's first brother married a cousin called Manorama from the Edassery Pattaveetil house of Mavelikkara, and whose father was Rama Varma, younger son of Raja Ravi Varma. The second married Meenakshi, a graduate and the daughter of Sir M. Krishnan Nair from his second wife. Meenakshi hailed from Malabar's famous Parakkat family and it was her brother who was married to the Cochin Jew. The brother who married the Zamorin's granddaughter Padma was actually offered the principalship of the Zamorin's College in Calicut after his studies in London, but in the bargain ended up marrying his granddaughter as well. The lady's father was also a member of the Zamorin family and was known as Collector Tampuran. Padma hailed from the Chengalath family of Malabar.

The youngest brother married the daughter of Prabhakaran Tampan, Member of the Madras Legislative Council, and member of the Kuthiravattathu Tampan (Moopil Nair) family who were originally prominent members of the Zamorin's court and one of the biggest zamindars in Malabar. The brother who was unwell and died in the 1940s was married to Kunjikutty Tampuratti, a Kshatriya lady, whom he wed quite late. She met him at a wedding and insisted she would only marry him. They never had children but she remained an important figure within the family until her demise. I am grateful to Divakara Varma and Prabha Menon, nephew and niece respectively of Sethu Lakshmi Bayi, for information on the extended family of the Senior Rani.

68. Author's interview with Rukmini Varma.
69. See File H151/1924 of IOR/L/PS/15/60 for information on the award of the Kaiser-i-Hind to Bhagavathi Pillai, daughter of Maharajah Mulam Tirunal.
70. See Lucy Moore, *Maharanis* (Google Books)
71. Letter dated 10/06/1915 from the Senior Rani to Kuttan Tampuran (Raghunandan, p. 95).
72. Letters dated 06/07/1915 and 15/07/1915 from the Senior Rani to Kuttan Tampuran (Raghunandan, p. 95).
73. A.B. Clarke, *In Kerala*, p. 88.
74. Ibid., p. 91.
75. Ibid., p. 145.
76. Letter dated 15/07/1915 from the Senior Rani to Kuttan Tampuran (Raghunandan, pp. 95–96).
77. Letter dated 23/07/1915 from the Senior Rani to Kuttan Tampuran (Raghunandan, p. 97).
78. Ibid.
79. Letter dated 31/07/1915 from the Maharani Gaekwar to the Senior Rani (TRF).
80. Letter dated 01/07/1916 from the Maharani Gaekwar to the Senior Rani (TRF).
81. The name of this mistress was Madame Grenier and she was ostensibly the Gaekwar's secretary. In 1928 his daughter, Indira Devi, complained to the Secretary of State in London about how she could not travel with her father in the same boat because of the presence of this lady and her mother was 'annoyed' that she had already had lunch with the Madame once before. In a telegram from the Viceroy to the Secretary of State, the former noted that 'the lady is a divorcee of Franco-Spanish extraction, and relationship with Gaekwar is not that of master and secretary. Maharani greatly resents the relationship.' See IOR/L/PO/5/14 (II).

82. Author's interview with Goda Varma, husband of Maharani Sethu Lakshmi Bayi's granddaughter, Shobhana, who is also a nephew of the Junior Rani's husband.
83. Letter dated 31/07/1916 from the Senior Rani to Kuttan Tampuran (Raghunandan, p. 99).
84. Mukundan Tampi was a disciple of Raja Ravi Varma's who is reported to have commented that he 'would brush us all off the face of the earth with his brush!' It is supposed that Tampi could have attained much fame and success had he not been addicted to drink, which destroyed his career. He was also related to Rama Varma through his father, who was a Koil Tampuran of Harippad.
85. Author's interview with Rukmini Varma.
86. Kulathu Iyer, *Maharani Sethu Lakshmi Bayi Tirumanasu Kondu,* p. 32 and author's interview with Rukmini Varma.
87. Lakshmi Raghunandan, op. cit., p. 100.
88. The Senior Rani quoted in ibid.
89. Letter dated 06/02/1920 from the Senior Rani to Kuttan Tampuran (TRF).
90. Author's interview with Prabha Menon.
91. Letter dated 12/04/1920 from the Senior Rani to Kuttan Tampuran (TRF).
92. This is not verified but was told to her granddaughter Uma when she visited the temple by the authorities there.
93. The Valiya Koil Tampuran quoted in Lakshmi Raghunandan, op. cit., p. 102.
94. Ibid. p. 103.
95. Ibid. p. 104.
96. Letter dated 25/04/1920 from the Senior Rani to Kuttan Tampuran (TRF).
97. Letter dated 26/04/1920 from the Senior Rani to Kuttan Tampuran (TRF).
98. S. Guptan Nair, op. cit., p. 38.
99. T.K. Velu Pillai, *Travancore State Manual,* Vol. II, p. 701.
100. The Senior Rani quoted in Lakshmi Raghunandan, op. cit., p. 104.
101. *The Feudatory and Zemindari India,* Vol. IX, No. 4, p. 184.
102. Author's interview with Rukmini Varma.
103. Ibid.
104. Letter dated 22/03/1922 from the Senior Rani to Kuttan Tampuran (Raghunandan, p. 105).
105. Letter dated 07/04/1922 from the Senior Rani to Kuttan Tampuran (Raghunandan, p. 105).
106. Letter dated 10/04/1923 from the Senior Rani to Kuttan Tampuran (TRF).
107. See Uma Maheswari, *Thrippadidanam* (Malayalam).
108. This nephew would go on to become the renowned neurosurgeon Dr R.M. Varma.

109. Letter dated 08/09/1922 from the Senior Rani to Kuttan Tampuran (TRF).
110. The Senior Rani quoted in Lakshmi Raghunandan, op. cit., p. 105.
111. Author's interview with Rukmini Varma.
112. Lakshmi Raghunandan, op. cit., p. 106.
113. The Senior Rani quoted in ibid. p. 106.
114. According to Advocate Ayyappan Pillai, this name suddenly made the name Lalithambika very popular in Travancore among Nairs and others.
115. GCSI: Knight Grand Commander of the Order of the Star of India and GCIE: Knight Grand Commander of the Order of the Indian Empire; these were both British honours conferred on Mulam Tirunal.
116. Gouri Lakshmi Bayi, op. cit., p. 160.
117. Letter dated 05/10/1917 from the Maharajah to the Viceroy (IOR/R/1/1/616).
118. K.P. Padmanabha Menon, *History of Kerala*, Vol. II, pp. 2–3.

CHAPTER 5: HER HIGHNESS THE MAHARAJAH

1. This is the famous slogan of the Tourism Department of Kerala.
2. Quote from '*Report on the Fourth Tour of HE The Hon. Sir Arthur Lawley GCIE, KCMG to Cochin and Travancore*', p. 58 (Sir Arthur was the Governor of Madras, 1906–11).
3. The author's own great grandmother is said to have found a corpse in her town house upon a visit after the floods. The whole place was sealed off, the property sold, with the lady returning to her ancestral home in the country, mentally unable to come to terms with what had happened.
4. Chief Secretary's Press Note dated 02/08/1924 (Bundle No. 217, File No. 509/27 KSA).
5. Report of the Mannar Flood Relief Deputation dated 28/08/1924 (Bundle No. 217, File No. 509/27 KSA).
6. Chief Secretary's Press Note dated 02/08/1924 (Bundle No. 217, File No. 509/27 KSA).
7. Chief Secretary's notification dated 28/08/1924 and Income Tax Commissioner's circular dated 25/08/1924 (Bundle No. 217, File No. 509/27 KSA).
8. Report of the Land Revenue and Income Tax Commissioner (Raghunandan pp. 122–24).
9. See Resolution on Principles to be observed during Minority Administrations in Native States (IOR/R/1/1/615).
10. Vikram Sampath, *Splendours of Royal Mysore*, p. 517.
11. K.P. Padmanabha Menon, *History of Kerala*, Vol. IV, p. 324.

12. K.K. Nair, *By Sweat and Sword*, p. 299. Indeed, this attitude would come up in Bhopal also, where the local female rulers would have a tough time convincing the British of their rights. See *The Career of an Indian Princess* by Sambhu Chandra Mukhopadhyaya.
13. R.P. Raja, *New Light on Swathi Thirunal*, p. 197.
14. M.E. Watts, *Circumstances of the First Regency in Travancore* (Raghunandan, Appendix A, and letter dated 30/04/1926 from the Dewan to the Resident in IOR/R/1/1/1532 (1)).
15. I. Matthew, 'Travancore a Hundred Years ago: The Times of the Ranees and Colonel Munro' published in *The Kerala Society Papers* II, Series 8.
16. James Welsh, *Military Reminiscences*, Vol. II, pp. 144,146.
17. Ibid.
18. See Appendix to Notes quoting Col. Munro in IOR/R/1/1/1532 (1).
19. See Sir T. Sadasiva Aiyar's judgment in Lakshmi Narayani vs. Kanakku Padmanabhan Parameswaran 1906 cited in IOR/R/1/1/1532 (1).
20. Letter dated 19/09/1924 from the Resident to the Pol. Sec., GOI (IOR/R/2/884/161).
21. Ibid.
22. See Lakshmi Raghunandan, op. cit., pp. 112–113.
23. Ibid.
24. See Kulathu Iyer's *Maharani Sethu Lakshmi Bayi Tirumanasu Kondu.*
25. Sethu Lakshmi Bayi had been told an hour before the durbar about the honour.
26. See, for instance, Gazette Extraordinary issued on 23/10/1926.
27. See Chapter 16 for more on this.
28. Robin Jeffrey, *The Decline of Nair Dominance*, p. 77.
29. The Maharajahs who enacted these changes did so only half-heartedly as Robin Jeffrey explains in his seminal *The Decline of Nair Dominance*.
30. There was every hope for victory. In the 1880s converted Christians obtained the right to use temple roads like 'high-caste' Syrian Christians when they complained to the Resident when some Nadar Christians were beaten up for using temple roads. When the Resident was told they were low caste, he thundered: 'I could not admit that Her Majesty the Empress or any person holding the Christian faith should be called "low caste" because of the religion they hold' and the government had quietly but promptly allowed all Christians access to these roads. See Louise Ouwerkerk and Dick Kooiman, No *Elephants for the Maharaja*, p. 56.
31. Perhaps one of the more striking public processions involved one where a Nambutiri was mounted on an elephant with a Pulaya, holding an idol, and paraded around Vaikom to send out a message of solidarity between the highest and the lowest.

32. Quoted in S. Raimon, *Selected Documents on Vaikom Satyagraha*, p. 5.
33. See Robin Jeffrey's 'Temple Entry Movement in Travancore', *Social Scientist*, Vol. 4, No. 8 (1976), p. 15.
34. Gandhi quoted in *The History of Freedom Movement in Kerala*, Vol. II, p. 153.
35. Reference is to Visakham Tirunal.
36. P.K.K. Menon, *The History of Freedom Movement in Kerala*, Vol II, p. 161.
37. Dewan quoted in *The Madras Mail* dated 12/03/1925.
38. Rama Varma, in the words of his grandson Shreekumar, 'hated the Congress, hated Nehru', and disagreed with the nationalist movement. His other grandchildren also attest to this.
39. In complete contrast to her husband, the Maharani's grandchildren remember her as idolising Gandhi and being an ardent admirer of Nehru's, whose every speech, every book and every essay she collected.
40. Quoted in J. Devika, *Her-Self*, p. 85.
41. J. Devika, *En-gendering Individuals*, p. 206.
42. Apparently the idea was indeed Gandhi's.
43. 'So strong,' Louise Ouwerkerk would remark, was the tradition that the ruler stood above the actual business of administration, that although his consent to the carrying out of a death sentence was necessary, the death warrant was always signed by a special palace official, so that the wrath of the gods would not fall on the Raja.' See Louise Ouwerkerk and Dick Kooiman, op. cit., p. 64.
44. T.K. Ravindran, *Vaikkam Satyagraha and Gandhi*, p. 99.
45. P.K.K. Menon, op. cit., Vol. II, p. 382.
46. O.M. Thomas, *Under the Knife*, p. 21.
47. P.K.K. Menon, op. cit., Vol. II, p. 382.
48. Ibid.
49. Ibid.
50. Ibid.
51. See *Young India* for 26/02/1925.
52. Ibid.
53. P.K.K. Menon, op. cit., Vol. II, p. 382.
54. See *Young India* for 19/02/1925.
55. Dewan Raghavaiah quoted in *Young India* dated 26/02/1925.
56. See letter dated 26/01/1925 from the Resident to the Pol. Sec., GOI (IOR/R/1/1/1530 (2)).
57. Lakshmi Raghunandan, op. cit., p. 128.
58. Quoted in T.K. Ravindran, op. cit., p. 196.

59. Gandhi also understood this. In his speech dated 03/04/1925 in Palitana, he said that he had 'seen in Travancore that if the subjects do their duties, the Maharani will manage to do hers. But if the subjects remain recalcitrant, the Maharani cannot do anything, however much she wants.'
60. Letter dated 18/03/1925 from Gandhi to the Police Commissioner of Travancore quoted in S. Raimon, *Selected Documents on Vaikom Satyagraha*, p. 160.
61. See *Young India* for 02/04/1925.
62. P.K.K. Menon, op. cit., Vol. II, p. 354.
63. See *Pioneer Mail and Indian Weekly News* for 25/09/1925.
64. The roads, it should be noted, were always open to non-Hindus. The population figures are from the 1921 *Travancore Census Report*.
65. Nihal Singh's profile of the Maharani in *The Baltimore Sun* dated 23/03/1929.
66. Quoted in T.K. Velu Pillai, *Travancore State Manual*, Vol. II, p. 716.
67. See Lakshmi Raghunandan, op. cit., pp. 131–32.
68. See *Young India* for 02/04/1925.
69. Gouri Lakshmi Bayi, *Thulasi Garland*, p. 382.
70. A. Sreedhara Menon, *Kerala History and its Makers*, p. 209. It is crucial here to understand that merely allowing people into or around temples, which was socially a great gesture, is not greater than giving them economic and educational facilities. The author's own opinion is that Sethu Lakshmi Bayi ought to be remembered for these latter aspects of her reign, instead of because of the former alone. The intentions of the reformers, including Gandhi, in allowing low-caste groups into temples is today questionable, as they seem to have been eager to unite the Hindu community for political purposes, rather than on purely compassionate grounds. Sethu Lakshmi Bayi, in fact, did her best to prevent this seeing minority groups as political aspects in their own right rather than constituents under a Hindu umbrella.
71. See *Young India* dated 26/04/1925.
72. Story related by Goda Varma.
73. Letter dated 20/09/1924 from the Resident to the Pol. Sec., GOI (IOR/R/2/884/161).
74. See *The Pioneer* dated 05/09/1924.
75. Letter dated 19/09/1924 from the Resident to the Pol. Sec., GOI (IOR/R/1/1/1530 (2)).
76. Letter dated 26/01/1925 from the Resident to the Pol. Sec., GOI (IOR/R/1/1/1530 (2)).
77. The *Madras Mail* dated 23/04/1925.

CHAPTER 6: A CHRISTIAN MINISTER

1. The Rani quoted in Shungoonny Menon, *A History of Travancore*, p. 378.
2. Ibid. p. 365.
3. For a while Col. Munro was formally appointed Dewan of Travancore. In what was unprecedented, he was permitted to make proclamations and issue Acts by his hand and under his seal.
4. I. Matthew, 'Travancore a Hundred Years Ago: The Times of the Ranees and Colonel Munro' in *Kerala Society Papers* II, Series 8.
5. Quoted in Appendix to the *Report from the Select Committee on the Affairs of the East India Company 16 August 1832*, p. 289 (available on Google Books at https://books.google.co.in/books?id=lEBmQbMae1gC&printsec=frontcover#v=onepage&q&f=false, accessed 02/10/2015)
6. Ibid. pp. 296.
7. Eventually the Rani did give birth to a son and the grateful colonel presented a silver umbrella to the temple, which is used in ceremonies to this day. Gowri Lakshmi Bayi, of course, was prompt in announcing that she had 'placed this child of mine on the bosom of the Company'.
8. Susan Bayly, *Saints, Goddesses and Kings*, p. 285.
9. Shungoonny Menon, op. cit., p. 383.
10. As the Chief Secretary of Fort St. George wrote to the Resident on 23/08/1814, he was to 'carefully abstain from any open interference in the administration of the country...continuing however at the same time to afford privately, both to the Ranee and the Dewan, but invariably in terms of conciliation and respect, the reasonable assistance of good Council, with a view to the permanent interests of the alliance, and to the progressive improvement of the country.' See Michael H. Fisher, *Indirect Rule in India*, p. 215.
11. Reference is to Swathi Tirunal (1829–1846), who was prevented from doing so by his aunt and brother, but who could not see eye to eye with the Residents.
12. Robin Jeffrey, *The Decline of Nair Dominance*, pp. 56–57.
13. Ibid. pp. 57–58.
14. Letter dated 21/11/1855 from Lord Harris to the Rajah (TRF) Also see Parliamentary Papers Vol. 25 (1859), p. 32 (available on Google Books at https://books.google.co.in/books?id=VvQSAAAAYAAJ&printsec=frontcover#v=onepage&q&f=false, accessed 20/08/2015).
15. Letter dated 30/12/1855 from the Rajah to C.F. Kohlhoff, Conservator of Forests in Travancore (TRF).
16. Robin Jeffrey, op. cit., p. 84.
17. Ibid., p. 66. Visakham Tirunal, for instance, had once lamented that Travancore was India's most priest-ridden country, but as he lay on his deathbed in 1885,

he wouldn't let even his Nair wife come near him, and surrounded himself with these very priests so that he would find his way to heaven unblemished.

18. Quoted in ibid. p. 66.
19. This was an all India phenomenon actually. See M.J. Akbar's *Tinderbox: The Past and Future of Pakistan* (2012) (New York: Harper Perennial).
20. K.R. Ushakumari, *Changanassery Parameswaran Pillai*, p. 28.
21. S. Guptan Nair, *C.V. Raman Pillai*, p. 33. As late as 1934 in a memorial submitted by the Christians to the government it would be 'admitted with regret that even highly cultured men hardly rise above communal considerations in public affairs'. See *Travancore: The Present Problem* (1934).
22. The exception was Nanu Pillai (1877– 80). Until 1872 the Dewans were a train of Raos (i.e., Tanjore Marathi Brahmins) after which some Tamil Brahmins were also thrown in. It was only in 1914 that the next and last Nair Dewan was appointed in the form of Sir M. Krishnan Nair.
23. George Mathew, *Communal Road to a Secular Kerala*, p. 53.
24. With economic competition mounting, 'sons of the soil' is an often-heard expression even in the twenty-first century, as demonstrated, for instance, in the state of Maharashtra by the Maharashtra Navanirman Sena.
25. Robin Jeffrey, op. cit., p. 234.
26. This 'outsider' issue was raised in other states also, such as Mysore, where Sir M. Visvesvaraiah was the first 'native' Dewan.
27. Letter dated 26/01/1925 from the Resident to the Pol. Sec., GOI (IOR/R/1/1/1530 (2)).
28. *The Jenmabhoomi* quoted in Lakshmi Raghunandan, op. cit., p. 163.
29. *The People* dated 30/03/1925.
30. Letter dated 20/02/1925 from the Maharani Regent to the Resident (IOR/R/2/884/147).
31. Chandy was a member of the Executive Council of Mysore and later became Vice Chancellor of Mysore University.
32. Report for the Second Half of March 1925 and letter dated 07/04/1925 from the Resident to the Pol. Sec., GOI (IOR/R/1/1/1531).
33. Report for the Second Half of March 1925 (IOR/R/1/1/1531).
34. Letter dated 07/04/1925 from the Resident to the Pol. Sec., GOI (IOR/R/1/1/1531).
35. Letter dated 13/03/1925 from the Maharani Regent to the Resident (IOR/R/2/884/147). She was not alone in these views. Changanassery Parameswaran Pillai, a prominent Nair, for instance, wrote that 'in the present condition of the State, Watts is an ideal Dewan.' See K.R. Ushakumari, op. cit., p. 40.

36. Quoted in letter dated 07/04/1925 from the Resident to the Pol. Sec., GOI (IOR/R/1/1/1531).
37. Ibid.
38. Letter dated 13/03/1925 from the Maharani Regent to the Resident (IOR/R/2/884/147).
39. Reference is to Sir A.R. Banerjee and J.W. Bhore.
40. In his letter dated 04/05/1925, the Dewan of Cochin informed Mr. Cotton that the opposition was simply 'seeking to assign some plausible reason for not bringing him in' where there was none. See IOR/R/2/884/147.
41. *The Feudatory and Zemindari India*, Vol IV, No 10, p. 432.
42. Information gathered from Linda D'Silva of the Watts family, K.R. Ushakumari, op. cit., p. 41, *The Malabar Advocate* dated 28/03/1925 and the *Madras Mail* for 09/05/1925. Mr Watts's siblings, excluding Miss Watts, included a sister who was a doctor in Lucknow, another sister who was apparently a well-known musician, a brother who was a surgeon in Calcutta, and another brother who retired as a Forest Officer. One of his uncles, Maurice La Bouchardiere, was a professor.
43. Letter dated 16/05/1925 from the Resident to the Pol. Sec., GOI (IOR/R/1/1/1531).
44. See Lakshmi Raghunandan, op. cit., pp. 162–64.
45. T.K. Velu Pillai, *Travancore State Manual*, Vol. II, p. 756.
46. O.M. Thomas, *Under the Knife*, p. 67.
47. See Supplement to the *Western Star* dated 20/11/1928 and Kulathu Iyer's *Maharani Sethu Lakshmi Bayi Tirumanasa Kondu.*
48. Author's interview with J. Devika.
49. Letter dated 02/04/1925 from Mr Watts to the Maharani Regent (Raghunandan pp. 165–66).
50. Letter dated 07/05/1925 from the Maharani Regent to Mr Watts (Raghunandan pp. 167–68)
51. Report for the Second Half of December 1924 (IOR/R/1/1/1583).
52. Lakshmi Raghunandan, op. cit., pp. 170–71.
53. He could not do much with the sword, since his religion prohibited access to the temple and participation in most of its ceremonies. On such occasions the Devaswom Commissioner would carry the sword on his behalf.
54. R.K. Varma's letter to Kuttan Tampuran quoted in Lakshmi Raghunandan, op. cit., p. 173.
55. *The Feudatory and Zemindari India,* Vol IV, No 10, p. 434.
56. Report for the Second Half of June 1925 (IOR/R/1/1/1531).
57. K.K. Nair, *By Sweat and Sword*, pp. 22, 29.

58. Letter dated 23/11/1921 from the Governor of Madras to the Rajah of Cochin (File 61, 'Entertainment of Travancore as Partner in Cochin Harbour Scheme', NAI).
59. Letter dated 04/08/1921 from the Rajah of Cochin to the Governor of Madras (File 61, 'Entertainment of Travancore as Partner in Cochin Harbour Scheme', NAI).
60. Letter dated 14/09/1921 from the Dewan of Cochin to the Sarvadhikaryakkar of Cochin (File 61, 'Entertainment of Travancore as Partner in Cochin Harbour Scheme', NAI). Sir Robert would also remember in his *Cochin Saga*: 'The old State rivalries and prejudices had not entirely died away; personal prestige still counted for much and Travancore was five times as big as Cochin and much richer in natural resources.'
61. To be fair, even the Rajah of Cochin wanted to leave but his Dewan insisted.
62. Lakshmi Raghunandan, op. cit, p. 148.
63. Ibid. p. 369.
64. *The Indian Express* dated 27/06/1936.
65. C Unnikrishnan, '75 Years ago, Cochin Port happened' at http://www.hindu.com/thehindu/mp/2003/05/26/stories/2003052600380100.htm (accessed 20/09/2012).
66. *The Indian Express* dated 01/04/1935.
67. See File No. 214, CE/34 and File No. 286, CE/35 (NAI).
68. A. Sreedhara Menon, *Triumph and Tragedy in Travancore*, p. 318.
69. C. Unnikrishnan, op. cit.
70. Sallyamma Job and Tomy Varghese, 'Dynamics of Foreign Trade in Kerala' in R.K. Mishra & Nandita Sethi eds. *Rethinking India's Growth Strategy*, p. 556 (2008) (New Delhi: Concept Publishing Company).
71. See http://www.cochincustoms.nic.in/revenue.htm (accessed 27/09/2012).
72. The *Pioneer Mail and Indian Weekly News* dated 19/06/1925, and Dewan's address to the Sri Mulam Popular Assembly, 1927.
73. George Mathew, *Status of Panchayati Raj in the States of India*, p. 2 (1995) (New Delhi: Institute of Social Sciences).
74. T.K. Velu Pillai, *Travancore State Manual*, Vol. II, p. 713.
75. P.D. Johnny, *Decentralization of Power at the Panchayat Level in Kerala and the Gandhian Vision of Gram Swaraj* (unpublished thesis submitted to the Mahatma Gandhi University, Kottayam, in 1994), p. 147.
76. These seven panchayats were Bhoothapandy, Nedumangad, Paravoor, Sambavarvadaka, Ayiroor, Ettumanoor, and Perumbavoor.
77. Jessy V. Mathews, 'Origin of Local Self Government in Travancore' in the *Journal of Kerala Studies*, 1989, Vol. 16, and P.D. Johnny, op. cit., p. 147.

78. P.D. Johnny, op. cit., pp. 148–49.
79. P.J. Cherian, William Logan's *Malabar Manual*, Vol. I, p. 244.
80. K. Saradamoni, *Matriliny Transformed*, p. 61.
81. I.K.K. Menon, *The Rajarshi of Cochin*, p. 47.
82. Margaret Child-Villiers, *Fifty One Years of Victorian Life*, p. 170.
83. He admits somewhat rudely that she 'could not boast of anything which may be called beauty and she had nothing which might be considered accomplishment' and that most of his cousins thought he was only trying to please the Rajah. See I.K.K. Menon, op. cit., p. 18.
84. Author's interviews with Roscotte Krishna Pillai and J. Devika.
85. See K. Saradamoni, op. cit., p. 10. This lady was Janaki Amma and her third husband was C. Rajaraja Varma, the brother of Raja Ravi Varma.
86. Quoted in J. Devika, *En-gendering Individuals*, p. 55
87. Ibid., p. 60.
88. Robin Jeffrey, op. cit., p. 136.
89. Ibid. p. 157.
90. K. Saradamoni, op. cit., p. 65.
91. A larger portion of the debate, as Devika studies, focussed on women having to remove the loose upper-cloth they wore, much like a *dupatta*, when they were in the presence of high castes. However, what is forgotten here is that men had to do the same in the presence of higher-caste women as well. It was a salutation based on caste and not on sex.
92. Quoted in J. Devika, op. cit., p. 73.
93. Robin Jeffrey, 'Legacies of Matriliny' in *Pacific Affairs*, Vol. 77, No. 4, p. 650.
94. Robin Jeffrey, 'Matriliny, Marxism and the Birth of the Communist Party in Kerala' in *The Journal of Asian Studies*, Vol. 38, No. 1, p. 80.
95. Robin Jeffrey, *Decline* ... op. cit., pp. 169, 305.
96. See Nair Regulation of 1912.
97. Quoted in 'The Family Organization in the South-West of India' by J. Puthenkulam in Tulsi Patel ed., *The Family in India*, p. 249 (2005) (New Delhi: Sage Publications).
98. J. Devika, op. cit., pp. 78–79.
99. As Augusta Blandford recorded in her 'Mission Work Among High Caste Hindu Women in Trevandrum' in *The Missionary Conference: South India and Ceylon*, p. 174, the 'wise good [Rani] instead of yielding to the entreaties of her friends and taking another consort, lives in strict seclusion' and employed her time 'profitably' by reading the Bible, 'especially the New Testament, which she much admires.'
100. J. Devika and Binitha Thampi, *New Lamps for Old*, p. 77.

101. Robin Jeffrey, *Decline* ... op. cit., p. 227.
102. G. Arunima, *There Comes Papa*, p. 1.
103. Ibid.
104. Dewan's Address to the Sri Mulam Popular Assembly (1929), p. 12 (TRF).
105. Report for the Second Half of October 1925 (IOR/R/1/1/1584).
106. Details of the tirumudikalasam are taken from K.V. Krishna Ayyar's *The Zamorins of Calicut*, p. 32. That Sethu Lakshmi Bayi enjoyed the tirumudikalasam and all other ceremonies connected with the sovereign is seen from the fact that at the time of her retirement she requested the *continuation* of these, as will be seen later.
107. See the *Madras Mail* for 23/11/1925 and V. Narasimhan Thampy, *Travancore Royal Family and Valia Kottaram*, pp. 111–28 for a description of the ruler's birthday processions.
108. Charles Allen & Sharada Dwivedi, *Lives of the Indian Princes*, p. 202. It was not *just* these women who lined the pathway, however. Poets would also wait there for the Maharani, as her granddaughter would remember, and recite verses from their eulogies, presumably in the hope of gaining some favour.
109. See Elizabeth Glover, *Great Queens*, p. 110.

CHAPTER 7: MALICE DOMESTIQUE

1. Report for the First Half of January 1926 (IOR/R/1/1/1584).
2. Ibid.
3. Ibid.
4. Louise Ouwerkerk & Dick Kooiman, *No Elephants for the Maharaja*, p. 74.
5. Ibid., p. 74. Indeed, according to the former Dewan P. Rajagopalachari, she was 'in every respect superior in intellect and ability' to her cousin in Satelmond Palace. See Report for the First Half of January 1925 (IOR/R/1/1/1584).
6. Letter dated 19/09/1924 from the Resident to the Pol. Sec. GOI (IOR/R/1/1/1530 (2)).
7. Louise Ouwerkerk and Dick Kooiman, op. cit., p. 74.
8. T.K. Velu Pillai, *Travancore State Manual*, Vol. I, p. 31.
9. Letter dated 19/09/1924 from the Resident to the Pol. Sec., GOI (IOR/R/1/1/1530 (2)).
10. Ibid.
11. Letter dated 14/12/1929 from Louise Ouwerkerk to her mother (MSS EUR F232/60).
12. Kenneth J. Panton, *Historical Dictionary of the British Monarchy*, p. 217 (2011) (Lanham, Maryland: Scarecrow Press).

13. Lucy Moore, *Maharanis* (Google Books).
14. Secret Note in IOR/L/PO/5/14 (1).
15. Ibid.
16. In a presentation at the Asian Art Museum in February 2012, the Junior Maharani's granddaughter would refer to their 'great' friendship along with lively anecdotes.
17. Report for the First Half of December 1925 (IOR/R/1/1/1584).
18. These were initiated by the head of the Kilimanoor family and her husband's uncle.
19. Recounted by her son Martanda Varma in *Travancore: The Footprints of Destiny*, p. 92.
20. Report for the First Half of February 1926 (IOR/R/1/1/1584). The Government of India assumed the position of guardians to minor princes.
21. Secret Note in IOR/L/PO/5/14 (1).
22. Report for the First Half of February 1926 (IOR/R/1/1/1584).
23. Ibid.
24. Ibid.
25. Report for the First Half of January 1926 (IOR/R/1/1/1584).
26. Ibid.
27. The musician had already gone away on leave as soon as the scandal broke.
28. Report for the First Half of February 1926 (IOR/R/1/1/1584).
29. Ibid.
30. Letter dated 20/03/1926 from the Junior Maharani to the Maharani Regent (Raghunandan, pp. 226–27).
31. Letter dated 01/03/1926 from Dr. Pugh to the Junior Maharani (Raghunandan, pp. 227–28).
32. Letter dated 24/03/1926 from the Maharani Regent to the Junior Maharani (Raghunandan, p. 228).
33. Lakshmi Raghunandan, *At the Turn of the Tide*, p. 229
34. Letter dated 04/04/1926 from the Junior Maharani to the Maharani Regent (Raghunandan, p. 230).
35. Letter (undated) from the Maharani Regent to the Junior Maharani (Raghunandan, p. 231).
36. Letter (undated) from the Maharani Regent to the Resident (Raghunandan, p. 32).
37. Author's interview, for instance, with P. Ramji, whose father Parthasarathy Iyengar was the Municipal Chairman of Alleppey in the early 1940s. He recounted general views of members of the royal house and of this perpetual

comparison between the Maharanis. Other interviewees also spoke of this comparison.

38. Louise Ouwerkerk & Dick Kooiman, op. cit., p. 74.
39. This tikka would become popular in Kerala in its day as the 'Regent *gopi*'.
40. Louise Ouwerkerk & Dick Kooiman, op. cit., p. 9.
41. A favourite image of this was an iconic 1924 photograph of Sethu Lakshmi Bayi and her daughter. Clad in her regular white attire, with a protective arm around the infant Princess Lalitha, she looks out at the viewer with a warm face, wearing the slightest hint of a smile, her expressive eyes revealing sympathy and affection. For years this picture would hang in many households in Travancore, receiving prayers and sincere veneration from thousands every day.
42. Letter dated 09/04/1929 from the Resident to the Pol. Sec., GOI (IOR/R/1/1/1849).
43. See ibid.
44. I.K.K. Menon, *The Rajarshi of Cochin*, p. 268. Also, author's interview with Robin Cotton, nephew of the Resident. The lady in question was Violet Mainwaring, the daughter of Sir Philip Mainwaring. The marriage, as it happened, was doomed right from the start.
45. O.M. Thomas, *Under the Knife*, p. 67.
46. Author's interview with Dr R.P. Raja.
47. T.K. Velu Pillai, op. cit., pp. 717–18.
48. See *The Baltimore Sun* dated 24/03/1929.
49. Maurice Dekobra, *The Perfumed Tigers*, p. 121.
50. Ibid.
51. Quoted in Lakshmi Raghunandan, op. cit., p. 245.
52. Author's interview with Rukmini Varma.
53. See Bundle No. 226, File No. 2050/26 (KSA) In what is interesting, only eight hours before the birth of Princess Indira, the Maharani had passed a proclamation by which tenants of the Kandukrishi Crown Lands and of Sripadam were allowed to pay their dues in cash instead of in paddy, a longstanding demand that Mulam Tirunal had not satisfied in his nearly forty-year reign.
54. The *Madras Mail* dated 27/10/1926 .
55. Another custom the Maharani terminated at this time involved a grandee called the Vanjipuzha Pandarathil. This was a Brahmin aristocrat from Chengannur and in the days of Martanda Varma, he had sheltered the Attingal Rani and her son, the heir. As a distinction it was announced later that the Pandarathil would have the ceremonial position of father to the royal family, and every baby was proclaimed as a child of the Vanjipuzha Pandarathil. Sethu Lakshmi Bayi

ended this and everywhere it was announced instead that Princess Indira was the daughter of Rama Varma.

56. Quoted in Hector Bolitho, *Victoria and Albert*, p. 44 (1938) (London: Cobden Sanderson).
57. Quoted in Lakshmi Raghunandan, op. cit., p. 221.
58. Report for the First Half of December 1924 (IOR/R/1/1/1583).
59. Letter dated 19/09/1924 from the Resident to the Pol. Sec., GOI (IOR/R/1/1/1530 (2)).
60. Ibid.
61. Report for the First Half of November 1924 (IOR/R/1/1/1530 (2)).
62. Report for the Second Half of November 1925 (IOR/R/1/1/1584).
63. Report for the First Half of November 1924 (IOR/R/1/1/1530 (2)).
64. Ibid.
65. Ibid.
66. Report for the First Half of December 1924 (IOR/R/1/1/1583).
67. Report for the Second Half of January 1925 (IOR/R/1/1/1584), and Lakshmi Raghunandan, op. cit., pp. 157–58.
68. Report for the First Half of January 1925 (IOR/R/1/1/1584).
69. Report for the First Half of February 1926 (IOR/R/1/1/1584).
70. See Lakshmi Raghunandan, op. cit., pp. 224–226. It might be conjectured that the raise was given to keep the Dewan quiet after his blackmailing of Rama Varma. This does not appear to be the case as the Maharani did not grant him the amount he wanted, giving him only half the desired raise after prolonged negotiations and consultation with the Government of India. Also, at a later time when the Dewan would blackmail her with the threat of resignation, she would not tolerate it and would ask him to leave.
71. Report for the First Half of April 1926 (IOR/R/1/1/1584).
72. Resident's Note (IOR/R/2/884/157).
73. Letter dated 01/12/1925 from the Resident to the Valiya Koil Tampuran (IOR/R/2/884/157).
74. Letter dated 01/12/1925 from the Resident to the Maharani Regent (IOR/R/2/884/157).
75. Robin Jeffrey, *The Decline of Nair Dominance*, p. 219.
76. The *United India and Indian States* dated 31/07/1925.
77. Letter dated 01/12/1925 from the Maharani Regent to the Resident (IOR/R/2/884/157).
78. Letter dated 01/12/1925 from the Resident to the Maharani Regent (IOR/R/2/884/157).

79. Some of the other papers in Travancore were *Samadarsi, Malabar Advocate, The Standard, The Trivandrum Daily*, the *Sudarsanam, The Citizen*, the *Kerala Deepam*, the *Jenmabhoomi*, the *Desabhimani*, the *Prabhata Taraka*, the *Sree Vazhumcode*, the *Malayali*, the *Kerala Chandrika, Yuvakeralam, Veerakeralam*, the *Kerala Kaumudi, Amritha Bharathi, Swadeshabhimani, The Travancore Times, Keralabhimani*, and more.
80. Lakshmi Raghunandan, op. cit., p. 235.
81. Robin Jeffrey, 'A Sanctified Label' in D.A. Low ed. *Congress and The Raj*, p. 442.
82. P.K.K. Menon, *The History of Freedom Movement in Kerala*, Vol. II, pp. 585, 588.
83. Report for the Second Half of November 1925 (IOR/R/1/1/1584).
84. P.K.K. Menon, op. cit., Vol. II, p. 591.
85. Letter dated 11/10/1929 from Louise Ouwerkerk to her mother (MSS EUR F232/60).
86. Just as in independent India Prime Minister Nehru too would seek to curb 'communal writing'. See Robin Jeffrey (2000), *India's Newspaper Revolution: Capitalism, Politics and the Indian Language Press* (New York: Palgrave Macmillan), p. 184.
87. Robin Jeffrey, 'A Sanctified Label...', p. 442.
88. See *The Press in Kerala*, pp. 3,7, 9.
89. Letter dated 01/12/1925 from the Maharani Regent to the Resident (IOR/R/2/884/157).
90. K.M. George, *Kesari Balakrishna Pillai*, p. 30.
91. Letter dated 01/12/1925 from the Maharani Regent to the Resident (IOR/R/2/884/157).
92. Report for the Second Half of May 1926 (IOR/R/1/1/1584).
93. See *The Regulations & Proclamations of Travancore*, Vol. VI, p. 1167.
94. Letter dated 10/06/1926 from the Maharani Regent to the Resident (Raghunandan, p. 234).
95. Report for the First Half of June 1926 (IOR/R/1/1/1584).
96. Report for the Second Half of November 1925 (IOR/R/1/1/1584).
97. Quoted in Lakshmi Raghunandan, op. cit., p. 183.
98. Report for the First Half of June 1926 (IOR/R/1/1/1584).
99. Report for the Second Half of June 1926 (IOR/R/1/1/1584).
100. Ibid.
101. Ibid.
102. K.R. Ushakumari, *Changanassery Parameswaran Pillai*, p. 43.
103. Report for the Second Half of August 1926 (IOR/R/1/1/1584).
104. P.K.K. Menon, op. cit., Vol. II, pp. 596–605.

105. *Report on Administration of Travancore* for 1929–30, p. 257 (IOR/V/10/2080).
106. K.R. Ushakumari, op. cit., p. 9.
107. Quoted in Lakshmi Raghunandan, op. cit., p. 313.
108. T.K. Velu Pillai, op. cit., Vol. II, p. 696.
109. Robin Jeffrey, *Decline* ..., p. xxiii.
110. Ibid., p. 162.
111. T.K. Velu Pillai, op. cit., Vol. I, p, 9.
112. K.R. Ushakumari, op. cit., p. 43.
113. Robin Jeffrey, *Decline* ..., p. 162.
114. Letter dated 13/09/1938 from the Resident to his mother (MSS EUR F154/23).
115. In fact she was so determined to keep a check on journalism in Travancore, that when some papers moved to small British enclaves along the state's coast where the government could not touch them, she even proposed to purchase these 'for a decent money compensation' from the Government of India. Quoted in Lakshmi Raghunandan, op. cit., p. 315.
116. Letter dated 25/03/1925 from P. Rajagopalachari to Sir Vasudeva Rajah (IOR/R/1/1/1531).
117. See the Memorial from The People of Travancore in IOR/R/1/1/1532 (1).
118. Ibid.
119. Ibid.
120. Ibid.
121. Letter dated 04/09/1926 from the Acting Resident to the Pol. Sec. GOI (IOR/R/1/1/1532 (1)).
122. Report for the Second Half of July 1925 (IOR/R/1/1/1584).
123. With the exception of her granddaughters Rukmini and Lakshmi, nobody this author interviewed in her family had ever known that she had suffered from tuberculosis. In fact they were rather shocked. Even Rukmini and Lakshmi had only heard her refer to it very vaguely, and knew no details.
124. Report for the First Half of December 1926 (IOR/R/1/1/1584).
125. Report for the Second Half of September 1930 (IOR/L/PS/10/1118).
126. Gloria Paris, *A Child of Sanitariums*, pp. 1–2.
127. Report for the Second Half of April 1925 (IOR/R/1/1/1151).
128. See Lakshmi Raghunandan, op. cit., p. 246.
129. It was, interestingly enough, Mr. Watts who came to him as a friend with words of comfort and warmth at that difficult moment. 'It is the fate of all unflinching and unselfish workers,' he sympathetically wrote, 'to be misrepresented and

misunderstood...And I pray that Heaven may give you the strength to pursue without fear or favour the same straight course you have so far taken...What Her Highness and I know so well, others must inevitably come to learn.' See Lakshmi Raghunandan, op. cit., p. 247.

130. Author's interview with Divakara Varma.

131. O.M. Thomas, op. cit., p. 68.

132. Precedents, in fact, gave him enough scope to exercise his talents, insofar as he did so quietly. When Gowri Lakshmi Bayi was in power, for example, her consort's 'valuable counsel was always sought and obeyed in all important affairs of State.' When she died, as Valiya Koil Tampuran he continued to advise his sister in law, Gowri Parvathi Bayi, in matters of government. See Nagam Aiya, *Travancore State Manual*, Vol. I, p. 456.

133. Letters in the Maharani's collection show a number of representations addressed to 'His Highness' Rama Varma, seeking favours. His responses that are available therein all ask the applicants to approach the government and not him.

134. Undated draft for a press note (TRF).

135. Report for the Second Half of November 1926 (IOR/R/1/1/1584).

136. Letter dated 20/06/1929 from the Resident to the Pol. Sec., GOI (IOR/R/2/885/175).

137. Letter dated 28/06/1930 from the Resident to the Pol. Sec., GOI (IOR/L/PS/10/1118).

138. Letter dated 28/06/1930 from the Resident to the Pol. Sec., GOI (IOR/L/PS/10/1118).

139. Report for the First Half of December 1926 (IOR/R/1/1/1584).

140. Letter dated 07/07/1919 from Louise Ouwerkerk to her mother (MSS EUR F232/60). A letter the Valiya Koil Tampuran wrote to his brother in law also shows that while he did have a position of influence with the Maharani, he acted essentially as her secretary, though only at the beginning of her rule. 'During the early years of the Regency,' he would write in 1936, 'I was myself attending to all Her Highness' confidential correspondence, including typing. I did not mind that much in those days except when the volume of work was unusually heavy. But now having enjoyed freedom from clerical and typing work for some time, I find it somewhat hard to have to do them again ... I feel the grinding effects of age are partly responsible for my present listlessness.' See letter dated 14 Vrishchikam 1111 ME from the Valiya Koil Tampuran to Kunjunni, husband of the Maharani's sister Kochu Thankam (TRF).

141. S.B. Patterson's note dated 12/02/1925 (IOR/R/1/1/1530 (2)).

CHAPTER 8: TEA AND TROUBLES

1. There is another version of the story that tells how he cut off his eyelids and cast them into the dust, and that the first tea shrubs grew on that spot. See Laura Martin's *Tea: The Drink that Changed the World* (2007) (Tokyo: Tuttle Publishing).
2. See Sarah Rose's *All the Tea in China: Espionage, Empire, and the Secret Formula for the World's Favourite Drink* (2010) (London: Arrow Books).
3. Heather Lovatt and Peter de Jong, *Above the Heron's Pool*, p. xv.
4. S. Uma Devi, *Plantation Economies of the Third World*, pp. 64–65.
5. Ibid., p. xiv.
6. Paul Erik Baak, *Plantation Production and Political Power*, p. 182.
7. Heather Lovatt and Peter de Jong, op. cit., p. 16.
8. Paul Erik Baak, op. cit., p. 63.
9. Heather Lovatt and Peter de Jong, op. cit., p. 27.
10. Paul Erik Baak, op. cit., p. 86.
11. Letter dated 11/12/1874 from the Resident to the Chief Sec. Govt. of Madras (IOR/R/2/891/253). Ayilyam Tirunal at the time had a personal fortune of five or six lakh rupees, which he intended to leave to his consort and dependants. His brother Visakham Tirunal, however, did venture into plantation in partnership with none other than the Dewan Sir T. Madhava Rao.
12. Paul Erik Baak, op. cit., p. 65.
13. Ibid., p. 167.
14. Ibid., p. 156.
15. *Travancore at the British Empire Exhibition at Wembley*, pp. 26, 42.
16. Ibid., p. 12.
17. Ibid., p. 26.
18. Chief Secretary quoted by the Dewan in Proceedings of the Travancore Legislative Council dated 24/11/1926 (IOR/R/2/884/163).
19. Dewan's response to K.P. Nilakantha Pillai in Proceedings of the Travancore Legislative Council on 24/11/1926 (IOR/R/2/884/163).
20. Letter dated 15/07/1926 from G. Brooke to the Dewan (IOR/R/2/884/163).
21. Dewan's response to K.P. Nilakantha Pillai, op. cit.
22. Chief Secretary's Note dated 13/11/1926 to the EDB (IOR/R/2/884/163).
23. Ibid.
24. Proceedings of the Travancore Legislative Council dated 24/11/1926 (IOR/R/2/884/163).
25. Report for the First Half of December 1926 (IOR/R/1/1/1584).
26. Dewan's response to N. Kochukunju Pillai in Proceedings of the Travancore Legislative Council dated 24/11/1926 (IOR/R/2/884/163).

27. Report for the Second Half of April 1927 (IOR/R/1/1/1644).
28. Dewan's response to K.P. Nilakantha Pillai, op. cit.
29. Letter dated 25/02/1927 from the Resident to the Junior Maharani (IOR/R/2/884/163).
30. *The Feudatory and Zemindari India*, Vol VI, No 7, p. 314.
31. Representation dated 21/03/1927 from the Sri Mulam Popular Assembly to the Dewan (IOR/R/2/883/163).
32. Paul Erik Baak, op. cit., p. 167.
33. Letter dated 09/06/1927 from Brooke Bond to the Dewan (IOR/R/2/884/163).
34. Paul Erik Baak, op. cit., p. 178.
35. K.C. Mammen Mappillai, *Reminiscences*, p. 132.
36. *The Feudatory and Zemindari India*, Vol VI, No 7, p. 313.
37. Dewan's address to the Sri Mulam Popular Assembly dated 21/02/1927.
38. Ibid.
39. Paul Erik Baak, op. cit., p. 179.
40. Ibid., pp. 170–71.
41. Police Report on a meeting dated 02/04/1927 (Bundle No 543, File 1074, KSA).
42. N.E. Kurien and N.E. Elias quoted in Paul Erik Baak, op. cit., p. 157.
43. Robin Jeffrey, *The Decline of Nair Dominance*, p. 28.
44. Ibid.
45. *Report on the Administration of Travancore* for 1926–27, p. 133.
46. See Administrative Reports for those two years.
47. Lakshmi Raghunandan, *At the Turn of the Tide*, pp. 221–22
48. *Travancore at the British Empire Exhibition*, p. 12.
49. M.A. Oommen, 'Rise and Growth of Banking in Kerala' in *Social Scientist*, Vol. 5, No. 3, p. 26, and Dick Kooiman, *Communalism and Indian Princely States*, p. 63.
50. M.A. Oommen, op. cit., pp. 28–29, and Dick Kooiman, ibid. Oommen actually states that only 252 of the companies were actually banks.
51. K.N. Raj and Michael Tharakan, 'Agrarian Reform in Kerala and its Impact on the Rural Economy' in Ajit Kumar Ghose ed. *Agrarian Reform in Contemporary Developing Countries*, p. 31.
52. *Report of the Banking Enquiry Committee*, Vol. I, p. 160.
53. The 1931 Census estimated 428,321 people employed in the primary sector.
54. See *Report on the Administration of Travancore* for 1924–1925, p. 101, and the Dewan's Address to the Sri Mulam Popular Assembly, February 1929.
55. Dewan's Address to the Sri Mulam Popular Assembly, February 1928.
56. *Report of the Banking Enquiry Committee*, Vol. I, p. 54.

57. Dewan's Address to the Sri Mulam Popular Assembly, February 1927, and *Report on the Administration of Travancore* for 1927–1928, p. 30.
58. Letter dated 07/04/1925 from the Resident to the Pol. Sec. GOI (IOR/R/1/1/1531).
59. Lakshmi Raghunandan, op. cit., pp. 312–13.
60. Robin Jeffrey, op. cit., p. 182.
61. Letter dated 07/04/1925 from the Resident to the Pol. Sec., GOI (IOR/R/1/1/1531).
62. Letter dated 18/03/1925 from the Junior Maharani to the Resident (IOR/R/1/1/1531).
63. Letter dated 03/04/1925 from the Junior Maharani to the Resident (IOR/R/1/1/1531).
64. Letter dated 07/04/1925 from the Resident to the Pol. Sec. GOI (IOR/R/1/1/1531).
65. Letter dated 18/03/1925 from the Junior Maharani to the Resident (IOR/R/1/1/1531).
66. Letter dated 27/03/1925 from the Resident to the Junior Maharani (IOR/R/1/1/1531).
67. Memorandum dated 18/04/1925 (IOR/R/1/1/1531).
68. For instance although it was the late Junior Rani Parvathi Bayi who had had sons while the late Senior Rani Lakshmi Bayi had none, it was the latter who remained superior and the former continued merely as Junior Rani.
69. Memorandum dated 18/04/1925 (IOR/R/1/1/1531).
70. Letter dated 24/04/1925 from the Resident to the Pvt. Sec. to Viceroy (IOR/R/1/1/1531).
71. Ibid.
72. Report for the Second Half of April 1925 (IOR/R/1/1/1531).
73. Ibid.
74. Telegram dated 06/05/1925 from the Pvt. Sec. to Viceroy to the Junior Maharani (IOR/R/1/1/1531).
75. Letter dated 19/02/1927 from the Junior Maharani to the Resident (IOR/R/2/884/163).
76. Letter dated 25/02/1927 from the Resident to the Junior Maharani (IOR/R/2/884/163).
77. Letter dated 24/09/1924 from the Resident to the Pol. Sec., GOI (IOR/R/2/884/151).
78. Letter dated 10/12/1924 from the Dewan to the Resident (IOR/R/2/884/151).
79. Letter dated 24/09/1924 from the Resident to the Pol. Sec., GOI (IOR/R/2/884/151).

80. Letter dated 10/12/1924 from the Dewan to the Resident (IOR/R/2/884/151).
81. Letter dated 24/09/1924 from the Resident to the Pol. Sec., GOI (IOR/R/2/884/151), and letter dated 13/01/1925 from the Maharani Regent to the Resident (IOR/R/2/884/151).
82. Letter dated 17/12/1925 from the Resident to the Pol. Sec. GOI (IOR/R/2/884/151).
83. Letter dated 12/04/1925 from the Junior Maharani to the Resident (IOR/R/1/1/1531).
84. Letter dated 04/09/1925 from the Maharani Regent to the Resident (Raghunandan, pp. 206–210).
85. For instance, there was a figure of Rs. 40,000 earmarked for donations and presents to be made by the ruler on state occasions. While the Junior Maharani demanded access to these funds on behalf of her son, Sethu Lakshmi Bayi made it clear that during his minority, it devolved upon her to make these grants as head of the royal family. Similarly, a request for Rs. 25,000 specially to make ornaments for the Maharajah was declined, as the family's personal treasury, the Chellamvagai, had an allocation of its own and any new jewellery required could be crafted there. The biggest dispute, however, arose with the Rs. 1,12,000 earmarked for conducting the two principal annual festivals of the Sri Padmanabhaswamy Temple. The Junior Maharani again claimed this responsibility for herself, while Sethu Lakshmi Bayi, as interim monarch, clarified that she herself would, in keeping with convention, oversee the festivals until the Maharajah came of age.
86. Lakshmi Raghunandan, op. cit., p. 314.
87. Letter dated 14/12/1926 from the Maharani Regent to the Resident (Raghunandan, Appendix C, pp. 40–41).
88. Letter dated 14/12/1926 from the Maharani Regent to the Resident (Raghunandan, Appendix C, p. 40).
89. Letter dated 10/11/1925 from the Maharani Regent to the Resident (Raghunandan, Appendix C, pp. 30–31).
90. Letter dated 24/04/1925 from the Resident to the Pvt. Sec. to Viceroy (IOR/R/1/1/1531).
91. Maharani Regent's note dated 29/01/1102 ME to the Dewan (Raghunandan, Appendix C, pp. 36–40).
92. Letter dated 14/12/1926 from the Maharani Regent to the Resident (Raghunandan, Appendix C, pp. 40–42).
93. Report for the First Half of January 1927 (IOR/R/1/1/1644).
94. Letter dated 14/12/1926 from the Maharani Regent to the Resident (Raghunandan, Appendix C, p. 40).
95. Report for the Second Half of April 1925 (IOR/R/1/1/1531).

96. Report for the First Half of January 1927 (IOR/R/1/1/1644).
97. Report for the Second Half of January 1927 (IOR/R/1/1/1644).
98. Report for the First Half of April 1927 (IOR/R/1/1/1644).
99. Report for the First Half of November 1927 (IOR/R/1/1/1644).
100. Ibid.
101. Report for the First Half of October 1927 (IOR/R/1/1/1644).
102. Dewan's address to the Sri Mulam Popular Assembly dated 27/02/1928.

CHAPTER 9: THE BOUDOIR DEWAN

1. Thus, for instance, while the Rajah of Kayamkulam fled in 1746, for three years the nobles of the state continued to resist the advance of Travancore. Nagam Aiya also refers to rebellions breaking out in the domains of the Thekkumkur and Vadakkumkur Rajahs after they too had gone into exile. See Nagam Aiya, *Travancore State Manual*, Vol. I, p. 352.
2. Martanda Varma was hardly being innovative here. As Abraham Eraly tells in *The Age of Wrath*, when Harihara and Bukka, the founders of the Vijayanagar Empire, who had been taken as prisoners to Delhi and converted to Islam, returned to the south and set up their state following the collapse of the Delhi sultanate, a sage advised them to 'adopt Virupaksha, a Shaivite deity, as [their] patron god, and to rule the kingdom as a surrogate of the god, so as to overcome the persisting public misgivings about the legitimacy' of these brothers reverting as Hindu Rajahs after having lived a decade as Muslims.
3. A member of the present-day Travancore royal family said to me on condition of anonymity: 'It occurs to me that the deity was used by the rulers as a symbol of their own power and might, and assuming the position of Dasa, was, in fact, a height of arrogance, for it gives the ruler absolute power to do anything in the name of the Lord! And very conveniently the deity is literally shutting his eyes to it, as he is depicted in Yoganidra! I think this form of the Lord was very cleverly chosen by the first ruler of this dynasty, to satisfy his ego and the subsequent egos of his heirs.'
4. Closer home, it was the Purakkad Rajahs who ruled their state on behalf of the deity of the Ambalapuzha Temple. They assumed the title of Devanarayana. Louise Ouwerkerk tells that while strategy lay behind the move, which 'placed him and his lands above the control of the erstwhile rebellious nobles, and won over the powerful temple priests to his side. This it undoubtedly was; but its effects were more far-reaching than a political manoeuvre. Sri Padmanabhadasa became the proudest title of the Rajas; they inherited a tradition of total dedication to the service of Travancore. Their lives were simple, their wants modest, their devotion to duty exemplary; and this tradition persisted until the last Maharaja retired into private life in 1950, lamenting that he could not serve

his god and his state to the end.' See Louise Ouwerkerk and Dick Kooiman, *No Elephants for the Maharaja*, p. 35.

5. A.P. Ibrahim Kunju, *Rise of Travancore*, p. 118, and *Selections from the Records of the Madras Government*, Vol. 13, p. 110.
6. Susan Bayly, *Saints, Goddesses, and Kings*, p. 66.
7. The Dutch sources are explicit in this. The accounts of the governor Julius Stein van Gollenesse state how the Travancore Rajah, the ruler of Elayadathu Swarupam, and of Peraka Tavazhi (essentially branches of the Kupaka family) were all Nairs, while the Rajah of Pandalam and the ruler of Cochin were Kshatriyas, while the Devanarayana of Purakkad was a Brahmin. Clearly Gollenesse understood the three categories and he placed the Travancore royal family among the Nairs. See *Selections from the Records of the Madras Government*, Vol. 13, pp. 53–60. The fact that the members of this family used the Kshatriya title of Varma does not point to actually being Kshatriya in caste; the Thekkumkur and Vadakkumkur Rajahs were Varmas but never wore the sacred thread and were considered upper-caste Nairs or Samantas. Females of the family (Rani Umayamma, for instance) had names like Nairs, and as late as 1810 when Rani Gowri Lakshmi Bayi came to power, Col. Munro proclaimed her as 'Attingal Moopil Lakshmi Amma', with even newspapers abroad referring to her as 'Ranah Letchma Amah' and 'Princess Letchma Amah' (See the *Glasgow Herald* dated 01/11/1811, for instance). For Munro's proclamations, see IOR/R/1/1/1532 (1). Interestingly, in his subsequent proclamations in 1813 after the birth of a son to 'the Rani Maharajah' and later when Gowri Parvathi Bayi came to power, the appellation 'Bayi' comes into fashion, suggesting it was these Ranis who adopted what was essentially a Tanjore style name in Travancore. Thus, 'Attingal Moopil Lakshmi Amma, the Valiya Tampuratti Avargal' becomes 'Lakshmi Bayi Maharajah', followed to power by 'Parvathi Bayi Maharajah'.
8. See *Selections from the Records of the Madras Government*, Vol. 13, p. 110.
9. Mark de Lannoy, *The Kulasekhara Perumals of Travancore*, p. 145. In fact in a meeting with Martanda Varma the Cochin Rajah elected to stand because while Martanda Varma was forbidden to sit, he was more powerful and the Cochin Rajah did not wish to offend him by taking a seat even if custom permitted it.
10. *Selections from the Records of the Madras Government*, Vol. 13, p. 100. Also see Susan Bayly, op. cit., p. 67 where she quotes a contemporary record from the Mackenzie Collection in which Martanda Varma himself tells how he built two great temples and 'thus we have done in charity but now I am desirous of wearing the Janava [sacred thread]...round the neck and I am informed by the learned Brahmins that to enable me to do so I should have a Golden Cow made and must worship it, after which I am to entertain many Brahmins and make them glad, then may I wear the sacerdotal thread'. Adrian Mayer, the sociologist,

who interviewed Sethu Lakshmi Bayi shortly before her death shared his interview transcripts with me in which also the Maharani herself remarks that hiranyagarbha was needed so that the ruler could be 'made into the Maharajah'.

11. Abraham Eraly, *The First Spring*, p. 303.
12. See P. Shungoonny Menon's work, for example.
13. P. Shungoonny Menon, *A History of Travancore*, pp. 171, 289.
14. As late as the 1940s a British Resident would record this 'peculiarly unassailable' position of the Maharajah because of Martanda Varma's actions which made the rulers 'sanctified hereditary officials of the temple in the eyes of all good Hindus'. See letter dated 24/04/1944 from the Resident to the Sec. to Viceroy (IOR/L/PS/13/1285).
15. K.K. Nair, *By Sweat and Sword*, p. 90.
16. Ibid. p. 88.
17. Susan Bayly, op. cit., p. 68.
18. Ibid., p. 58.
19. Jonathan Gil Harris, *The First Firangis*, p. 75.
20. *Report of the Travancore Banking Enquiry Committee*, Vol I, p. 22.
21. Robin Jeffrey, *The Decline of Nair Dominance*, p. 4.
22. *Selections from the Records of the Madras Government* Vol. 13, p. 54–55.
23. He was later known as Rajah Kesava Das.
24. Robin Jeffrey, op. cit., p. 13.
25. Nagam Aiya, *Travancore State Manual* Vol. I, pp. 417–18.
26. 'It was the immemorial right of the people to approach the king directly with their demands and grievances,' tells Louise Ouwerkerk, 'and stories of great gatherings of people directly approaching the king abound in Travancore history.' Hiranyagarbha and other ceremonies put a distance, but Velu Tampi still marched right in and had his way, when it was needed.
27. Nagam Aiya, op. cit., Vol. I, p. 420.
28. Ibid., p. 424.
29. Ibid., pp. 430, 432.
30. He declined and is said to have passed on information to the Company.
31. Nagam Aiya, op. cit., Vol I, p. 436.
32. Ibid., p. 445.
33. James Welsh quoted in Robin Jeffrey, op. cit., p. 6.
34. Ibid., p. 16.
35. Michael H. Fisher, *Indirect Rule in India*, p. 215.
36. Ibid., p. 214.
37. Robin Jeffrey, op. cit., p. 7.

38. Michael H. Fisher, op. cit., p. 215.
39. Nagam Aiya, op. cit., Vol. I, p. 492.
40. Robin Jeffrey, op. cit., pp. 148–49.
41. Nagam Aiya, op. cit., p. 493.
42. Robin Jeffrey, op. cit., p. 67.
43. Minute dated 28/01/1871 in IOR/R/2/891/251.
44. See letters and correspondence in IOR/R/2/891/251.
45. Quoted in Robin Jeffrey, op. cit., p. 67.
46. Ibid., p. 69.
47. Ibid., p. 148.
48. Ibid., p. 8.
49. Ibid., pp. 99–100.
50. Ibid., p. 295.
51. Ibid., p. 154.
52. Ibid. pp. 149, 146.
53. Ibid., p. 198.
54. Report for the Second Half of March 1925 (IOR/R/1/1/1531).
55. Letter dated 15/08/1928 from the Maharani Regent to the Resident (Raghunandan, pp. 326–28).
56. Supplementary to Report for the Second Half of February 1938 (MSS EUR F154/46).
57. *The Feudatory and Zemindari India*, Vol IV, No. 11, p. 507.
58. Ibid.
59. O.M. Thomas, *Under the Knife*, p. 18
60. Ibid., p. 20.
61. Ibid., pp. 19–21.
62. Ibid., p. 68.
63. Ibid., p. 69.
64. *The Feudatory and Zemindari India*, Vol IV, No. 10, p. 434.
65. Letter dated 03/01/1926 from the Dewan to the Valiya Koil Tampuran (Raghunandan, p. 223).
66. Letter dated 16/03/1926 from Miss Watts to the Maharani Regent (Raghunandan, pp. 224–26).
67. Ibid. The officers were the Commandant of the Nair Brigade and the Police Commissioner who altogether cost the state more than the Dewan. They were both British officers.
68. Letter dated 22/04/1926 from the Resident to the Pol. Sec., GOI (IOR/R/1/1/1531).

69. Letter dated 16/03/1926 from Miss Watts to the Maharani Regent (Raghunandan pp. 224–26).
70. Note by the Dewan in Lakshmi Raghunandan, op. cit., p. 252.
71. Report for the Second Half of January 1927 (IOR/R/1/1/1644).
72. Ibid. See also Report for the First Half of February 1927 (IOR/R/1/1/1644).
73. Report for the First Half of February 1927 (IOR/R/1/1/1644).
74. Report for the Second Half of January 1927 (IOR/R/1/1/1644).
75. *The Feudatory and Zemindari India*, Vol VI, No. 3, p. 118.
76. Lakshmi Raghunandan, op. cit., p. 316.
77. Report for the Second Half of April 1927 (IOR/R/1/1/1644).
78. Report for the Second Half of June 1927 (IOR/R/1/1/1644).
79. Report for the First Half of June 1927 (IOR/R/1/1/1644).
80. Report for the First Half of May 1927 (IOR/R/1/1/1644).
81. Report for the Second Half of August 1927 (IOR/R/1/1/1644).
82. Report for the Second Half of September 1927 (IOR/R/1/1/1644).
83. *The Feudatory and Zemindari India*, Vol VII, No. 10, p. 481.
84. Lakshmi Raghunandan, op. cit., p. 300–01.
85. Ibid., pp. 301–02.
86. Ibid., p. 302
87. Letter dated 12/02/1928 from the Resident to the Maharani Regent (Raghunanandan, p. 304).
88. Report for the First Half of September 1928 (IOR/R/1/1/1746).
89. Report for the Second Half of March 1928 (IOR/R/1/1/1746).
90. Lakshmi Raghunandan, op. cit., p. 303.
91. Ibid. p. 316.
92. Letter dated 15/08/1928 from the Resident to the Pol. Sec., GOI (IOR/R/1/1/1760).
93. Letter dated 15/08/1928 from the Maharani Regent to the Resident (Raghunandan, pp. 326–28).
94. Letter dated 15/08/1928 from the Resident to the Pol. Sec. GOI (IOR/R/1/1/1760).
95. Ibid.
96. Ibid.
97. Report for the First Half of August 1928 (IOR/R/1/1/1760).
98. Report for the First Half of April 1928 (IOR/R/1/1/1746).
99. Letter dated 15/08/1926 from the Maharani Regent to the Resident (Raghunandan, pp. 326–28).

100. Letter dated 15/08/1928 from the Resident to the Pol. Sec. GOI (IOR/R/1/1/1760).
101. Lakshmi Raghunandan, op. cit., p. 331.
102. Telegram dated 22/08/1928 from the GOI (IOR/R/1/1/1760).
103. Letter dated 21/08/1928 from the Dewan to the Maharani Regent (Raghunandan, p. 332).
104. Report for the First Half of April 1929 (IOR/R/1/1/1819).
105. Lakshmi Raghunandan, op. cit., p. 333.
106. Report for the Second Half of April 1929 (IOR/1/1/1819).
107. Report for the Second Half of June 1929 (IOR/R/1/1/1819).
108. Report for the Second Half of April 1929 (IOR/R/1/1/1819).
109. Letter dated 27/10/1929 from the Resident to the Pol. Sec. GOI (IOR/R/2/885/175).
110. Letter dated 17/08/1928 from the Maharani Regent to the Resident (Raghunandan, pp. 330–31).

CHAPTER 10: BLACK MAGIC

1. Quoted in Nagam Aiya, *Travancore State Manual*, Vol. I, p. 452.
2. His full name was Tampi Martandan Iravi and he was a son of Karthika Tirunal Dharma Rajah who succeeded Martanda Varma.
3. Nagam Aiya, op. cit., p. 457.
4. Ibid.
5. Ibid., p. 458.
6. T.K. Vijayamohan's 'Ummini Tampi' in T.K. Ravindran ed. *Journal of Kerala Studies*, Vol V, Part 1, 1978, p. 268.
7. Ibid.
8. T.K. Vijayamohan's 'The Institution of Devadasis in Travancore' in T.K. Ravidran ed. *Journal of Kerala Studies* Vol V, Part 1, 1978, p. 472.
9. Ibid., p. 476.
10. Ibid., p. 477.
11. Ananda Lal, *The Oxford Companion to Indian Theatre*, p. 32 (2004) (Delhi: Oxford University Press).
12. Rupika Chawla, *Raja Ravi Varma*, p. 318.
13. See Vikram Sampath, *Voice of the Veena* (Google Books).
14. See V. Gangadhar, *M.S. Subbulakshmi* (Google Books).
15. J. Devika, 'The Aesthetic Woman' in *Modern Asian Studies*, Vol 39, No 2, 2005, p. 481.
16. T.J.S. George, *MS: A Life in Music*, p. 91.

17. J. Devika, op. cit., p, 483.
18. R. Nandakumar quoted in ibid., p. 482. And he still got in trouble for this!
19. Krishnaveni Ammal's memorandum in IOR/Q/13/1/11.
20. Ibid.
21. Ibid.
22. T.J.S. George op. cit., p. 83.
23. T.K. Vijayamohan, 'The Institution of Devadasis in Travancore' in T.K. Ravindran ed. *Journal of Kerala Studies*, Vol. V, Part 1, 1978, p. 478.
24. Letter dated 20/06/1929 from the Resident to the Pol. Sec., GOI (IOR/R/2/885/175).
25. Letter dated 15/11/1929 from the Maharani Regent to the Resident (IOR/R/2/885/175).
26. The *Princely India* dated 13/07/1932.
27. *The Feudatory and Zemindari India*, Vol. X, No. 12, p. 619.
28. Ibid.
29. J. Devika, *En-gendering Individuals*, p. 109.
30. Ibid.
31. Saju Chelangad, 'The Forgotten Star' in *The Hindu* dated 24/11/2013 at http://www.thehindu.com/features/cinema/the-forgotten-star/article5383387.ece (accessed 24/11/2014).
32. Ibid.
33. Saju Chelangad, 'Of Monarchs and Movies' in *The Hindu* dated 09/03/2014 at http://www.thehindu.com/features/cinema/of-monarchs-and-movies/article5764301.ece (accessed 24/11/2014).
34. 'Mixed fortunes for the daughters of Travancore' in *The Economist* (blog) dated 28/03/2013 at http://www.economist.com/blogs/banyan/2013/03/women-kerala (accessed 10/08/2014).
35. *The Feudatory and Zemindari India*, Vol. X, No. 12, p. 614.
36. Lakshmi Raghunandan, *At the Turn of the Tide*, p. 133.
37. Narayani Harigovindan, *A History of the Employment of Women in the Government Services of Travancore*, p. 107. The motion was defeated since it was argued that there was no law preventing equal chances in any case.
38. Dewan's Address to the Sri Mulam Popular Assembly (1931).
39. J Devika, *En-gendering ...*, p. 117.
40. Narayani Harigovindan, op. cit., p. 115, and J Devika, *En-gendering ...*, p. 182.
41. Narayani Harigovindan, op. cit., p. 119.
42. *Report on the Administration of Travancore* for 1927–28 p. 177.
43. Letter dated 28/06/1929 from Louise Ouwerkerk to her mother (MSS EUR F232/60).

44. *Report of the Unemployment Enquiry Committee* (1928), p. 17.
45. Ibid., p. 18.
46. Dewan's Address to the Sri Mulam Popular Assembly (1928).
47. J. Devika, *En-gendering* ..., p. 331.
48. Ibid.
49. *Report on the Administration of Travancore* for 1926–27, p. 139.
50. Resolution of the Board dated 27/05/1929 (Bundle No 22, File No 1241/29 KSA).
51. Letter from V. Mary dated 29/05/1929 (Bundle No 22, File No 1241/29 KSA).
52. Letter dated 10/12/1929 from the Board to the Chief Sec. (Bundle No 22, File No 1241/29 KSA).
53. J. Devika, *En-gendering* ..., pp. 183–84.
54. Quoted in Robin Jeffrey, 'Governments and Culture' in *Pacific Affairs*, Vol. 60, No. 3, 1987, p. 466.
55. Dewan's Address to the Sri Mulam Popular Assembly (1930).
56. Report for the First Half of October 1928 (IOR/R/1/1/1746).
57. Report for the First Half of November 1928 (IOR/R/1/1/1746).
58. Letter dated 20/06/1929 from the Resident to the Pol. Sec. GOI (IOR/R/2/885/175).
59. Report for the First Half of January 1928 (IOR/R/1/1/1746).
60. Dewan's Note dated 11/01/1928 (Raghunandan, pp. 292–96).
61. Ibid.
62. Ibid.
63. Ibid.
64. Ibid.
65. Ibid.
66. Letter dated 22/02/1929 from the Resident to the Pol. Sec., GOI (IOR/R/1/1/1849).
67. Nagam Aiya, *Travancore State Manual*, Vol. II, p. 65.
68. Letter dated 22/02/1929 from the Resident to the Pol. Sec. GOI (IOR/R/1/1/1849)
69. Ibid.
70. Ibid.
71. Ibid.
72. Ibid.
73. Ibid.
74. Ibid.
75. Note that 23/02/1929 from the Dewan to the Maharani Regent (Raghunandan, pp. 357–60)

76. Letter dated 22/02/1929 from the Resident to the Pol. Sec., GOI (IOR/R/1/1/1849).
77. Ibid. In his diaries auctioned at Bonham's Harvey could speak of the 'wicked uncles' and 'relentlessly ambitious' mother of the Maharajah, also adding that he was 'superstitious and convinced of the absurdest possibilities' and once described to him a story about how a certain sorcerer turned bullets into water. See description of the diaries at https://www.bonhams.com/auctions/18942/lot/370/ (accessed 20/06/2014).
78. Ibid.
79. Ibid.
80. Letter dated 23/04/1929 from the Resident to the Pol. Sec. GOI (IOR/R/1/1/1849).
81. Ibid.
82. Letter dated 22/02/1929 from the Resident to the Pol. Sec. GOI (IOR/R/1/1/1849).
83. Vijaya Raje Scindia with Manohar Malgonkar, *The Last Maharani of Gwalior*, p. 137.
84. Letter dated 22/02/1929 from the Resident to the Pol. Sec. GOI (IOR/R/1/1/1849).
85. Ibid.
86. Ibid.
87. Ibid.
88. Ibid.
89. Letter dated 13/03/1929 from the Resident to the Pol. Sec. GOI (IOR/R/1/1/1849). It must be mentioned here that the Resident mentions one or two incidents, which, however, I have chosen not to include in this book.
90. Dewan's Note dated 23/02/1929 to the Maharani Regent (Raghunandan, pp. 357–60).
91. Letter dated 25/02/1929 from the Resident to the Dewan (Raghunandan, p. 363–64).
92. Letter dated 07/03/1929 from the Resident to the Pol. Sec. GOI (IOR/R/1/1/1849).
93. Lakshmi Raghunandan, op. cit., p. 366.
94. Letter dated 09/04/1929 from the Resident to the Pol. Sec. GOI (IOR/R/1/1/1849).
95. Ibid.
96. Letter dated 08/03/1929 from the Junior Maharani to the Resident (IOR/R/1/1/1849).

97. Letter dated 26/04/1929 from the Resident to the Pol. Sec. GOI (IOR/R/1/1/1849).
98. Ibid.
99. Letter dated 23/04/1929 from Captain Harvey to the Resident (IOR/R/1/1/1849).
100. Letter dated 09/04/1929 from the Resident to the Pol. Sec. GOI (IOR/R/1/1/1849).
101. Letter dated 06/05/1929 from the Pol. Sec. GOI to the Chief Sec. Madras (IOR/R/1/1/1849).
102. Letter dated 30/05/1929 from the Chief Sec. Madras to the Pol. Sec. GOI (IOR/R/1/1/1849).
103. Letter dated 19/03/1929 from the Pol. Sec. GOI to the Resident (IOR/R/1/1/1849).
104. Mr Cotton's letter dated 05/12/1927 quoted in letter dated 09/04/1929 from the Resident to the Pol. Sec. GOI (IOR/R/1/1/1849).

CHAPTER 11: IN LETTERS OF GOLD

1. Letter dated 09/04/1929 from the Resident to the Pol. Sec. GOI (IOR/R/1/1/1849).
2. Report for the Second Half of April 1929 (IOR/R/1/1/1819).
3. Ibid.
4. I am grateful to Abhed Kiran Kandamath for telling me about this story.
5. Report for the Second Half of June 1929 (IOR/R/1/1/1819).
6. Ibid.
7. Letter dated 29/06/1929 from Mr Watts to the Maharani Regent (Raghunandan, pp. 368–69).
8. Letter dated 05/09/1929 from the Resident to the Maharani Regent (Raghunandan, p. 376).
9. Letter dated 20/06/1929 from the Resident to the Pol. Sec. GOI (IOR/R/2/885/175).
10. See Bundle No 265, File No 404 KSA.
11. See *Reports on the Administration of Travancore* for 1923–24 and 1928–29.
12. Ibid.
13. Supplement to the *Western Star* dated 19/11/1928.
14. Ibid.
15. See *Report on the Administration of Travancore* for 1923–24 and 1929–30 and Dewan's Address to the Sri Mulam Popular Assembly (1931). The 62 lakhs

mentioned includes not only budgetary allocation but also expenses incurred on telephone, electricity, and other schemes then underway.

16. *The Feudatory and Zemindari India,* Vol. X, No. 7, p. 326.
17. T.K. Velu Pillai, *Travancore State Manual,* Vol. IV, p. 158.
18. Ibid.
19. Dewan's Address to the Sri Mulam Popular Assembly (1928).
20. Robin Jeffrey, *The Decline of Nair Dominance,* p. 103.
21. T.K. Velu Pillai, op. cit., Vol. IV, p. 165.
22. Ibid.
23. *The Feudatory and Zemindari India,* Vol. X, No. 12, p. 617.
24. See Bundle No. 403, File No. 453 (KSA) and T.K. Velu Pillai, op. cit., Vol. IV, p. 166.
25. Ibid., pp. 168–72.
26. Dewan's Address to the Sri Mulam Popular Assembly (1930).
27. *The Feudatory and Zemindari India,* Vol. X, No. 12, p. 611.
28. Ibid., p. 618.
29. T.K. Velu Pillai, op. cit., Vol. IV, p. 166.
30. Dewan's Address to the Sri Mulam Popular Assembly (1930).
31. Dewan's Address to the Sri Mulam Popular Assembly (1932).
32. Maurice Dekobra, *The Perfumed Tigers*, p. 118.
33. Louise Ouwerkerk and Dick Kooiman, *No Elephants for the Maharaja*, p. 6.
34. *Report on the Administration of Travancore* for 1926–27, p. 138.
35. *Report on the Administration of Travancore* for 1928–29, p. 175.
36. *The Feudatory and Zemindari India,* Vol. X, No. 12, p. 613.
37. Dewan's Address to the Sri Mulam Popular Assembly (1930).
38. *The Feudatory and Zemindari India*, Vol. X, No. 7, p. 325.
39. M.A. Oommen, 'Rise and Growth of Banking in Kerala' in *Social Scientist,* Vol. 5, No. 3, 1976, pp. 28–29.
40. K. Varkey Joseph, *Migration and Economic Development of Kerala,* p. 86, and T.K. Velu Pillai, *Travancore State Manual,* Vol. III, p. 20.
41. K. Varkey Joseph, op. cit., p. 86.
42. The smallest denomination of currency in Travancore was the copper 'kasu'. Sixteen kasus made one chuckram. The kasus were so small that they could not be counted individually and were scattered over a wooden board with sixteen tiny holes. Four chuckrams made one panam or fanam, and seven panams made one Travancore rupee, while a half chuckram more made a British rupee (which was the colonial state's way of showing their superiority).
43. *The Feudatory and Zemindari India*, Vol. X, No. 12, p. 616.

44. *The Feudatory and Zemindari India*, Vol VI, No. 5, pp. 257–58.
45. Ibid.
46. *Report on the Administration of Travancore* for 1924–25, p. 72.
47. C.M. Ramachandran, *Problems of Higher Education in India*, p. 100.
48. Resident's speech at the investiture durbar of the Maharajah on 09/11/1931 (IOR/R/2/887/186).
49. P.R. Gopinathan Nair, 'Education and Socio-Economic Change in Kerala' in *Social Scientist*, Vol. 4, No. 8, 1976, pp. 33, 37.
50. Ibid. p. 42.
51. Daniel Jivanayakam, *Training Teachers for English Schools in Travancore*, pp. 45, 56, 58–59.
52. Dewan's Address to the Sri Mulam Popular Assembly (1928).
53. Ibid.
54. *The Feudatory and Zemindari India*, Vol. X, No. 12, p. 615.
55. Dewan's Addresses to the Sri Mulam Popular Assembly (1931 and 1932).
56. Supplement to the *Western Star* dated 19/11/1928.
57. *Report on the Administration of Travancore* for 1925–26, p. 95.
58. Ibid., pp. 121–22.
59. Dewan's Address to the Sri Mulam Popular Assembly (1926).
60. *Report on the Administration of Travancore* for 1929–30, p. 34.
61. Dewan's Address to the Sri Mulam Popular Assembly (1930).
62. T.K. Velu Pillai, *Travancore State Manual*, Vol. IV, p. 158.
63. *Report on the Administration of Travancore* for 1927–28, p. 138.
64. Resident's speech at the investiture durbar of the Maharajah on 09/11/1931 (IOR/R/2/887/186).
65. K. Narendranath quoted in Mary E. Clark, *In Search of Human Nature*, p. 400.
66. Viceroy's speech in *The Feudatory and Zemindari India*, Vol. IX, No. 4, p. 193.
67. Rajyashree Kumari Bikaner, *The Maharajas of Bikaner*, p. 85.
68. India House Report on Rukmini Varma's Exhibition in 1976 (TRF).
69. Indira Varma's note to the author on her mother.
70. Letter dated 14/12/1929 from Louise Ouwerkerk to her mother (MSS EUR F32/60).
71. *The Feudatory and Zemindari India*, Vol. X, No. 12, p. 604.
72. Letter dated 07/01/1931 from Ulloor S. Parameswara Iyer to the Palace Special Office (TRF).
73. Letter dated 27/09/1929 from Louise Ouwerkerk to her mother (MSS EUR F232/60) Dick Kooiman in the introduction to *No Elephants for the Maharaja* says Louise only met the Junior Maharani in 1931, but this letter shows they

had their first meeting in 1929. See Louise Ouwerkerk and Dick Kooiman, *No Elephants for the Maharaja*, p. 9.

74. Letter dated 26/08/1929 from the Resident to the Pol. Sec. GOI (IOR/R/2/886/177).
75. See Caroline Keen's *Princely India and the British* for more about these subjects.
76. Report for the Second Half of August 1927 (IOR/R/1/1/1644).
77. Letter dated 14/08/1927 from the Resident to the Maharani Regent (Raghunandan, pp. 258–59).
78. Letter dated 03/08/1927 from the Pvt. Sec. to Viceroy to the Resident (IOR/R/2/886/177).
79. Viceroy's note on his meeting with the Junior Maharani on 03/08/1927 (IOR/R/2/886/177).
80. This was also mentioned in letter dated 25/07/1927 from the Resident to the Pvt. Sec. to Viceroy (IOR/R/2/886/177) indicating that Mr Cotton already knew about this decision.
81. Letter dated 05/12/1927 from the Resident to the Pol. Sec. GOI (IOR/R/2/886/177).
82. Ibid.
83. Letter dated 03/01/1928 from the Pol. Sec. GOI to the Resident (IOR/R/2/886/177).
84. Ibid.
85. Letter dated 16/08/1928 from the Resident to the Pol. Sec. GOI (IOR/R/2/886/177).
86. See letters dated 06/12/1936 and 13/09/1938 from C.P. Skrine to his mother (MSS EUR F153/22 and F154/23).
87. A. Raghu, *CP: A Short Biography*, p. 22.
88. Author's interview with Advocate Vijayaraghavan.
89. A. Raghu, op. cit., p. 27.
90. Report for the First Half of January 1928 (IOR/R/1/1/1746).
91. A Raghu, op. cit., p. 30.
92. Letter dated 11/10/1928 from the Resident to the Pol. Sec., GOI (IOR/L/PS/13/1283). The words recall Sir T. Madhava Rao who also served for long years and was known to hanker not for money as much as for fame.
93. Louise Ouwerkerk and Dick Kooiman, op. cit., p. 121.
94. Letter dated 23/04/1929 from the Resident to the Dep. Pol. Sec. GOI (IOR/R/1/1/1828).
95. Ibid.
96. Pol. Sec. GOI's note dated 08/05/1929 (IOR/R/1/1/1828).
97. Ibid.

98. Ibid.
99. Letter dated 26/08/1929 from the Resident to the Dep. Pol. Sec. GOI (IOR/R/2/885/177).
100. Letter dated 29/08/1929 from D. Sankaran Iyer to the Valiya Koil Tampuran (Raghunandan, pp. 373–75).
101. Letter dated 26/08/1929 from the Resident to the Pol. Sec. GOI (IOR/R/2/885/177).
102. Letter dated 05/09/1929 from the Junior Maharani to the Resident (IOR/R/2/885/177).
103. Letter dated 05/09/1929 from the Resident to the Dep. Pol. Sec. GOI (IOR/R/2/885/177).
104. Letter dated 18/09/1929 from the Junior Maharani to the Resident (IOR/R/1/1/1828).
105. Ibid.
106. Letter dated 20/09/1929 from the Resident to the Junior Maharani (IOR/R/2/885/177).
107. A. Raghu, op.cit., p. 30.
108. Pol. Sec. GOI's note dated 27/09/1929 (IOR/R/1/1/1828)
109. Letter dated 04/10/1929 from the Dep. Pol. Sec. GOI to the Resident (IOR/R/1/1/1828).
110. Ibid.
111. Memorandum to the Viceroy (IOR/R/2/886/178).
112. Ibid.
113. Ibid.
114. Ibid.
115. Ibid.
116. Letter dated 17/01/1930 from the Dep. Pol. Sec. GOI to the Resident (IOR/L/PS/10/1118).
117. Memorial to the Viceroy dated 02/09/1929 (IOR/L/PS/10/1118).
118. See IOR/R/1/1/2037.
119. Memorial to the Viceroy dated 02/09/1929 (IOR/L/PS/10/1118).
120. Letter dated 27/09/1929 from Louise Ouwerkerk to her mother (MSS EUR F232/60). I am also grateful to Rosscote Krishna Pillai for telling me a story about Rama Varma who was 'firm but not unprincipled', telling how, since everyone presumed he was the power behind the throne, his father A.R. Pillai once wrote to him asking if he could have the position of Director of the zoo and public museum in Trivandrum. 'The Valiya Koil Tampuran told him politely that he could not oblige and asked him not to write to him with similar requests again.'

CHAPTER 12: MOTHER AND SON

1. K.M. Panikkar, *Malabar and the Dutch*, p. 22.
2. Susan Bayly, 'Hindu Kingship and Origin of Community', *Modern Asian Studies*, Vol. 18, No. 2, 1984, p. 190.
3. Robin Jeffrey, *The Decline of Nair Dominance*, p. 281.
4. Ibid. pp. 103, 101.
5. Ibid. p. 13.
6. Nagam Aiya, *Travancore State Manual*, Vol. I, p. 361.
7. Nagam Aiya, *Travancore State Manual*, Vol. II, p. 277.
8. Robin Jeffrey, op. cit., p. 4.
9. Susan Bayly, op. cit., p. 189.
10. K.M. Panikkar quoted in Robin Jeffrey, op. cit., p. 4.
11. Susan Bayly, op. cit., p. 209.
12. Robin Jeffrey, op. cit., p. 33.
13. Ibid., p. 129.
14. Ibid.
15. Ibid., p. 126.
16. Ibid., p. 192.
17. Ibid., p. 207.
18. Robin Jeffrey, 'Matriliny, Marxism, and the Birth of the Communist Party in Kerala' in *The Journal of Asian Studies*, Vol. 38, No. 1, 1978, p. 84.
19. Robin Jeffrey, Decline ..., p. 192.
20. Ibid., p. 110.
21. Ibid., pp. 179–80.
22. M.J. Koshy, *K.C. Maammen Mappilai*, p. 84.
23. Robin Jeffrey, *Decline* ..., p. 194.
24. K.V. Joseph, *Migration and Economic Development of Kerala*, p. 151.
25. Robin Jeffrey, *Decline* ..., p. 246.
26. Ibid., p. 247.
27. Ibid., p. x.
28. Samuel Mateer, *Native Life in Travancore*, p. 353.
29. K.V. Joseph, op. cit., p. 131.
30. Report for the Second Half of November 1929 (IOR/R/1/1/1819).
31. Author's interview with J. Devika.
32. Lakshmi Raghunandan, *At the Turn of the Tide*, p. 313.
33. Dick Kooiman, 'Political Rivalry among Religious Communities' in *Economic and Political Weekly*, Vol. 28, No. 7, 1993, p. 288.

34. Ibid., p. 289.
35. Ibid., p. 292.
36. K.R. Ushakumari, *Changanassery Parameswaran Pillai*, Appendix IV, p. 148.
37. Letter dated 28/04/1930 from G. Sankaran Nair to the Pol. Sec. GOI (IOR/R/1/1/1985).
38. Letter dated 28/06/1930 from the Resident to the Pol. Sec. GOI (IOR/R/1/1/1985).
39. Letter dated 22/04/1930 from G. Sankaran Nair to the Pol. Sec. GOI (IOR/R/1/1/1985).
40. Letter dated 12/08/1930 from G. Sankaran Nair to the Dep. Pol. Sec. GOI (IOR/R/1/1/1985).
41. Author's interview with Divakara Varma.
42. Letter dated 12/08/1930 from G. Sankaran Nair to the Dep. Pol. Sec. GOI (IOR/R/1/1/1985).
43. Letter dated 28/06/1930 from the Resident to the Pol. Sec. GOI (IOR/L/PS/10/1118).
44. Mr Nair's complaints were dismissed along with the previous memorial against the Regency sent in 1929. See IOR/R/1/1/2037.
45. Lakshmi Raghunandan, op. cit., p. 373.
46. Letter dated 16/03/1931 from the Resident to the Pol. Sec. GOI (IOR/R/1/1/1985).
47. Letter to the Editor on Travancore Politics in the *Princely India* dated 20/07/1932.
48. Letter dated 16/03/1931 from the Resident to the Pol. Sec. GOI (IOR/R/1/1/1985).
49. Letter dated 01/01/1930 from the Resident to the Pol. Sec. GOI (IOR/R/2/885/177).
50. Ibid.
51. Report for the First Half of January 1930 (IOR/R/1/1/1889).
52. Letter dated 31/08/1929 from the Maharani Regent to the Resident (IOR/R/2/885/177).
53. Letter dated 03/09/1929 from the Resident to the Maharani Regent (IOR/R/2/885/177).
54. Letter dated 04/09/1929 from the Maharani Regent to the Resident (IOR/R/2/885/177, and Raghunandan, p. 382).
55. Report for the Second Half of September 1929 (IOR/R/1/1/1819).
56. Report for the First Half of April 1928 (IOR/R/1/1/1644).
57. Letter dated 27/09/1929 from the Maharani Regent to the Resident (IOR/R/2/885/177). Some of the names suggested were K.S. Srinivasa

Achariya, Rao Bahadur Gopalaswami Iyengar, and Rao Bahadur U. Rama Rao, K.C. Manavedan Raja of the Zamorin's family, and Rao Bahadur P.T. Srinivasa Achari.

58. Letter dated 03/10/1929 from the Resident to the Dep. Pol. Sec. GOI (IOR/R/2/885/177).
59. Letter dated 02/11/1929 from the Maharani Regent to the Resident (IOR/R/2/885/177).
60. Letter dated 01/10/1929 from the Maharani Regent to the Resident (IOR/R/2/885/177, and Raghunandan, p. 383).
61. Letter dated 30/12/1929 from the Maharani Regent to the Resident (IOR/R/2/885/177).
62. Quoted in Letter dated 09/04/1929 from the Resident to the Pol. Sec. GOI (IOR/R/1/1/1849).
63. Letter dated 04/09/1929 from the Resident in Travancore to the Resident in Mysore (IOR/R/2/885/177).
64. Letter dated 17/01/1930 from the Pol. Sec. GOI to the Resident (IOR/R/2/885/177).
65. Letter dated 10/02/1929 from the Resident to the Pol. Sec. GOI (IOR/R/1/1/1905).
66. Letter dated 26/01/1930 from the Resident to the Junior Maharani (IOR/R/2/885/177).
67. Ibid.
68. Report for the First Half of April 1930 (IOR/R/1/1/1889).
69. Letter dated 09/07/1930 from Sir CP to the Pol. Sec. GOI (IOR/R/1/1/1905).
70. Report for the Second Half of April 1930 (IOR/R/1/1/1889).
71. Report for the First Half of June 1930 (IOR/R/1/1/1889).
72. Letter dated 04/10/1929 from Louise Ouwerkerk to her mother (MSS EUR F232/60).
73. Report for the Second Half of August 1930 (IOR/L/PS/10/1118).
74. Report for the First Half of July 1930 (IOR/R/1/1/1889).
75. Ibid.
76. Ibid.
77. It is normally said that he was compelled to abdicate because he corresponded with Germans, but his descendants in a biography have dismissed these stories.
78. I.K.K. Menon, *The Rajarshi of Cochin*, p. 24.
79. Report for the Second Half of July 1928 (IOR/R/1/1/1746).
80. I.K.K. Menon, op. cit., p. 260–61.
81. Report for the First Half of October 1927 (IOR/R/1/1/1644).
82. Report for the First Half of July 1930 (IOR/R/1/1/1889).

83. Ibid.
84. Ibid.
85. Report for the Second Half of July 1930 (IOR/R/1/1/1889).
86. Telegram dated 11/04/1930 from A.S. Menon to the Pvt. Sec. to Viceroy (IOR/R/1/1/1905).
87. Letter dated 22/02/1930 from the Resident to the Pol. Sec. GOI (IOR/R/1/1/1905).
88. Dewan's Address to the Sri Mulam Popular Assembly (1931).
89. See *Report of the Economic Depression Enquiry Committee.*
90. P.J. Thomas, 'India in the World Depression', *The Economic Journal*, Vol. 45, No. 179, 1935, pp. 469–70.
91. Ibid. p. 473.
92. Dewan's Address to the Sri Mulam Popular Assembly (1931).
93. Quoted in *Report of the Economic Depression Enquiry Committee.* p. 10.
94. Quoted in Ferdinand Mount, *The Tears of the Rajas*, p. 306.

CHAPTER 13: LA REVANCHE

1. See S. Gopal's 'Drinking Tea with Treason' in William Roger Louis ed. *Adventures in Britannia* (pp. 145–158).
2. Ibid.
3. S. Gopal, *The Viceroyalty of Lord Irwin*, p. 1.
4. S. Gopal, 'Drinking Tea with Treason', op. cit.
5. Ibid.
6. Piers Brendon, *The Decline and Fall of the British Empire*, pp. 383–84.
7. S. Gopal, 'Drinking Tea with Treason', op. cit.
8. Ibid.
9. Rajmohan Gandhi, *Gandhi*, p. 327.
10. Sankar Ghose, *Jawaharlal Nehru*, p. 68.
11. Ibid.
12. K. Natwar Singh, *The Magnificent Maharajah*, p. 255 (2009) (Delhi: Rupa) (Google Books).
13. Ibid.
14. See Jaswant Singh, *Jinnah: India, Partition, Independence (2009) (Delhi: Rupa Publications) (Google Books).* It is likely Jinnah's dislike originated in a personal grudge. A story goes that his wife, Ruttie Jinnah, once wore a low-cut dress to a banquet at the Governor's house when Willingdon was the Governor of Bombay, and Lady Willingdon, not very subtly, asked an ADC to bring a wrap 'in case' Mrs Jinnah felt cold. Jinnah stood up and said, 'When Mrs Jinnah feels cold, she will say so and ask for a wrap herself.'

15. K. Natwar Singh, op. cit., p. 255.
16. V. Sriram, 'Madras's Pushy First Lady', *The Hindu* dated 23/10/2013 at http://www.thehindu.com/news/cities/chennai/madras-pushy-first-lady/article4023512.ece (accessed 01/10/2014)
17. T.N. Kundra, *Glimpses of Indian National Congress: From Inception to Attainment of Freedom (1885–1947)*, p. 92 (1996) (Delhi: Regency Publications).
18. Rajmohan Gandhi, op. cit., p. 327.
19. Philip Williamson, *National Crisis and National Government*, p. 167.
20. S. Gopal, 'Drinking Tea with Treason', op. cit., and Rajmohan Gandhi, op. cit., p. 328.
21. Arthur Herman, *Gandhi and Churchill*, p. 375.
22. Piers Brendon, op. cit., p. 387. As it happened, by 1935 he was compelled to admit the genuine aspirations of India's people, leading to the Government of India Act of 1935, allowing Indians a role in the administration.
23. Saroja Sundararajan, *Sir C.P. Ramaswami Aiyar*, p. 272.
24. Ibid.
25. T.N. Gopinathan Nair, *Avasanate Naduvazhiyude Amma*, p. 46.
26. Shankunthala Jagannathan, *Sir C.P. Remembered*, p. 83.
27. A. Raghu, *CP: A Short Biography*, p. 30.
28. T.N. Gopinathan Nair, op. cit., p. 46.
29. Marthanda Varma, *Travancore: The Footprints of Destiny*, p. 107.
30. Shankunthala Jagannathan, op. cit., p. 84.
31. Marthanda Varma, op. cit., p. 108.
32. Saroja Sundararajan, op. cit., p. 272, and see IOR/R/2/885/177 Vol. III.
33. Letter dated 23/06/1931 from Pol. Sec. GOI to the Resident (IOR/R/2/886/186).
34. P.K.V. Kaimal, *Revolt of the Oppressed*, p. 127.
35. A. Raghu, op. cit., p. 30.
36. Saroja Sundararajan, op. cit., p. 223.
37. Shakunthala Jagannathan, op. cit., p. 83.
38. Pol. Sec. GOI's note dated 18/06/1931 (IOR/R/1/1/2071).
39. Saroja Sundararajan, op. cit., p. 674.
40. Khushwant Singh in *Why I Supported the Emergency and Other Essays* (Google Books).
41. Ibid.
42. Jarmani Das and Rakesh Bhan Dass, *Maharani: Love Adventures of Indian Maharanis and Princesses*, p. 46 (1972) (New Delhi: S. Chand).
43. Louise Ouwerkerk and Dick Kooiman, *No Elephants for the Maharaja*, p. 76.

44. Mentioned in S. Muthiah's *Madras Miscellany* (Google Books).
45. Piers Brendon, op. cit., p. 387.
46. See Arun Gandhi's *Kasturba: A Life* (Google Books).
47. V. Sriram, op. cit.
48. K. Natwar Singh, op. cit., p. 224.
49. Kirpal Singh and Annie Matthew, *Middle School Social Sciences*, H89 (2009) (New Delhi: Frank Brothers and Co.). Thus Amrita Shergill Marg in Delhi was named Ratendon Road after her son while Brassey Avenue was named after her grandfather. Then there was the Willingdon Hospital, Willingdon Airport, Willingdon Crescent, and Willingdon Island, to name a few.
50. Resident's note dated 05/07/1931 (IOR/R/2/887/186) and telegram dated 06/07/1931 to GOI (IOR/R/1/1/2071).
51. Resident's note dated 05/07/1931 (IOR/R/2/887/186).
52. Ibid.
53. Ibid.
54. Telegram dated 02/07/1931 from GOI to the Resident (IOR/R/1/1/2071 and IOR/R/1/1/2164).
55. Pol. Sec. GOI's note dated 09/07/1931 (IOR/R/1/1/2071).
56. Ibid.
57. Ibid.
58. Telegram dated 06/07/1931 from the Resident to GOI (IOR/R/1/1/2071). The Resident raised concerns for the Maharani in this telegram, stating that he would inform her only after hearing back from Simla. Their go-ahead was received the following day. See Letter dated 08/07/1931 from the Resident to the Pol. Sec. GOI (IOR/R/1/1/2071).
59. Pol. Sec. GOI's Note dated 09/07/1931 (IOR/R/1/1/2071).
60. Telegram dated 02/07/1931 from the GOI to the Resident (IOR/R/1/1/2071 and IOR/R/1/1/2164).
61. Ibid.
62. Dep. Pol. Sec., GOI's Note dated 09/07/1931 (IOR/R/1/1/2071).
63. Letter dated 10/07/1931 from the Pol. Sec., GOI to the Resident (IOR/R/1/1/2071).
64. Ibid. The Junior Maharani's family seem to still suspect the Resident, and her granddaughter, in her statement to the author, said: 'The Resident tried to get the regency extended by implying that my uncle was not up to the mark. Grandmother went directly to the Viceroy and asked him to be the judge of her son's capacity. The Viceroy did this much to the annoyance of the Resident. My uncle took over as the Head of State immediately afterwards. Maybe the Resident construed this as interference.' This view, however, is not accurate since the Resident did not try to extend the Reency because the Maharajah was not

up to the mark, but tried to have the Viceroy stick to the pre-decided date of the termination of the Regency so as to protect the position of Sethu Lakshmi Bayi.

65. Dep. Pol. Sec., GOI's Note dated 09/07/1931 (IOR/R/1/1/2071).
66. Letter dated 10/07/1931 from the Pol. Sec. GOI to the Resident (IOR/R/1/1/2071).
67. Pol. Sec., GOI's note dated 14/07/1931 (IOR/R/1/1/2071).
68. Ibid.
69. Ibid.
70. Ibid.
71. Lord Willingdon quoted in A. Sreedhara Menon, *Triumph and Tragedy in Travancore*, p. 7.
72. Letter dated 13/08/1931 from the Maharani Regent to the Resident (IOR/R/2/887/186).
73. Letter dated 31/07/1931 from the Dep. Pol. Sec., GOI to the Resident (IOR/R/1/1/2071).
74. Ibid.
75. Resident's Note dated 05/07/1931 (IOR/R/2/887/186).
76. Report for the First Half of August 1931 (IOR/R/1/1/2065).
77. Ibid.
78. Report for the First Half of August 1931 (IOR/R/1/1/2065).
79. Letter dated 11/07/1931 from the Maharani Regent to the Resident (IOR/R/2/887/186).
80. Letter dated 18/08/1931 from the Viceroy to the Maharani Regent (IOR/R/1/1/2071).
81. Pol. Sec., GOI's note dated 28/07/1931 (IOR/R/1/1/2071).
82. Ibid.
83. Letter dated 19/08/1931 from the Maharani Regent to the Viceroy (IOR/R/1/1/2071). It should be mentioned here that by a typing error, the date on this letter is written as 9 August 1931. But the stamp of the post office on it shows that it was sent on 19 August 1931.
84. Letter dated 04/10/1931 from the Dewan to the Resident (IOR/R/2/887/186).
85. Ibid.
86. The Travancore Government Gazette Extraordinary dated 23rd Thulam 1107 corresponding to 9th November 1931 (IOR/R/2/887/186).
87. Letter dated 10/11/1931 from the Resident to the Pol. Sec., GOI (IOR/R/1/1/2071).
88. See Chapter 16 ahead.
89. Letter dated 02/07/1931 from the Pol. Sec. GOI to the Resident (IOR/R/1/1/2164).

90. Shungoonny Menon, *A History of Travancore*, p. 401
91. Ibid. p. 475.
92. Letter (undated) from the Maharani Regent to the Resident (Raghunandan, p. 182).
93. Letter dated 16/02/1926 from the Pol. Sec., GOI to the Resident (IOR/R/1/4/40 (2)).
94. Political Department's M.I. Huk's note dated 06/08/1925 (IOR/R/1/4/40 (1)).
95. Political Department's K.S. Fitze's note dated 07/08/1925 (IOR/R/1/4/40 (1)).
96. M.I. Huk's note dated 06/08/1925 (IOR/R/1/4/40 (1)).
97. Letter dated 16/02/1926 from the Pol. Sec., GOI to the Resident (IOR/R/1/4/40 (2)).
98. Letter dated 23/10/1929 from the Dep. Pol. Sec., GOI to the Resident (IOR/R/1/1/1864).
99. Letter dated 04/08/1931 from the Resident to the Pol. Sec., GOI (IOR/R/1/1/2164).
100. Ibid.
101. Ibid.
102. Col. Morrison quoted in ibid.
103. Ibid.
104. Ibid.
105. Ibid.
106. Ibid.
107. Ibid.
108. Telegram dated 09/12/1931 from the Resident to the GOI (IOR/R/1/1/2164).
109. Ibid.
110. Letter dated 05/12/1931 from Sir CP to the Pvt. Sec. to Viceroy (IOR/R/1/1/2164).
111. Letter dated 22/02/1932 from the Resident to the Pol. Sec., GOI (IOR/R/1/1/2164).
112. Ibid.
113. Ibid.
114. Letter dated 03/03/1932 from the Viceroy to the Maharajah (IOR/R/1/1/2164).
115. Letter dated 04/04/1932 from the Maharajah to the Viceroy (IOR/R/1/1/2164).
116. Letter dated 01/04/1932 from the Maharajah to the Dewan (IOR/R/1/1/2164).

117. Letter dated 18/04/1932 from the Senior Maharani to the Resident (IOR/R/1/1/2164).
118. Ibid.
119. Ibid.
120. Ibid.
121. Ibid.
122. Ibid.
123. Letter (undated) from the Senior Maharani to the Dewan (IOR/R/1/1/2164).
124. Sir CP quoted in letter dated 28/04/1932 from the Resident to the Pol. Sec., GOI (IOR/R/1/1/2164).
125. Ibid.
126. Ibid.
127. Ibid.
128. Ibid.
129. Ibid.
130. Ibid.
131. Ibid.
132. Letter dated 18/04/1932 from the Senior Maharani to the Resident (IOR/R/1/1/2164).
133. Ibid.
134. Letter dated 02/05/1932 from the Senior Maharani to the Resident (IOR/R/1/1/2164).
135. Letter dated 28/05/1932 from the Resident to the Pol. Sec., GOI (IOR/R/1/1/2164).
136. Sir CP quoted in ibid.
137. Ibid.
138. Ibid.
139. Sir CP quoted in ibid.
140. Ibid.
141. Ibid.
142. Ibid.
143. Maharajah quoted in ibid.
144. Ibid.
145. Ibid.
146. Ibid.
147. Ibid.
148. Ibid.
149. Letter dated 31/07/1932 from the Resident to the Pol. Sec., GOI (IOR/R/1/1/2164).

150. Ibid.
151. Ibid.
152. Ibid.
153. Letter dated 20/06/1932 from the Senior Maharani to the Resident (IOR/R/1/1/2164).
154. Letter dated 15/08/1932 from the Viceroy to the Maharajah (IOR/R/1/1/2164).
155. Ibid.
156. Letter dated 15/08/1932 from the Maharajah to the Viceroy (IOR/R/1/1/2164).
157. Ibid.
158. Ibid.
159. Ibid.
160. Letter dated 09/10/1932 from the Senior Maharani to the Resident (IOR/R/1/1/2164).
161. Ibid.
162. Letter dated 04/08/1931 from the Resident to the Pol. Sec., GOI (IOR/R/1/1/2164).
163. Gouri Lakshmi Bayi, *Sree Padmanabha Swamy Temple*, p. 140.
164. Letter dated 28/04/1932 from the Resident to the Pol. Sec., GOI (IOR/R/1/1/2164).
165. Report for the First Half of November 1924 (IOR/R/1/1/1530 (2)).
166. Letter dated 01/11/1931 from the Maharani Regent to the Valiya Tampuran of Cochin (Raghunandan pp. 404–05).

CHAPTER 14: A REAL LITTLE GRANDE DAME

1. Quoted in Lakshmi Raghunandan, *At the Turn of the Tide*, p. 407.
2. Letter dated 01/11/1931 from the Maharani Regent to the Valiya Tampuran of Cochin (Raghunandan, pp. 404–05).
3. Indira Varma, 'Halcyon Days at Kovalam', *The Hindu* dated 25/12/2005 at http://www.thehindu.com/thehindu/mag/2005/12/25/stories/2005122500410600.htm (accessed 08/10/2014).
4. Letter dated 25/11/1930 from the Maharani Regent to the Valiya Tampuran of Cochin (Raghunandan, p. 407).
5. Emily Gilchriest Hatch, *Travancore: A Guide Book for the Visitor*, p. 173.
6. Author's interview with Rukmini Varma.
7. Author's interview with Divakara Varma.
8. Author's interview with Uma Varma.

9. Author's interview with Rukmini Varma.
10. Letter dated 08/08/1941 from Princess Lalitha to the Valiya Koil Tampuran (TRF).
11. Author's interview with Rukmini Varma.
12. Ibid.
13. Ibid.
14. Ibid.
15. Divakara Varma's note to the author on life in Satelmond Palace.
16. Author's interview with Lakshmi Raghunandan.
17. Author's interview with Rukmini Varma.
18. Ibid.
19. Divakara Varma's note on life in Satelmond Palace. The cook's name was Kerala Varma Pandarathil and his assistants were called Thengamulaku while other aides who cut vegetables were called Murakkari.
20. Author's interview with Rukmini Varma.
21. Charles Allen & Sharada Dwivedi, *Lives of the Indian Princes*, pp. 203–04.
22. Author's interview with Uma Varma.
23. Charles Allen & Sharada Dwivedi, op. cit., pp. 203–04.
24. Author's interview with Uma Varma.
25. Author's interview with Prabha Menon.
26. They are Dr R.M. Varma, the famous neurosurgeon, and Dr Suseela Varma who was a spinal cord injury specialist.
27. Author's interview with Divakara Varma.
28. Ibid.
29. Ibid.
30. Author's interview with Prabha Menon.
31. Ibid.
32. Ibid.
33. Indira Varma quoted in Shreekumar Varma, 'Benign Presence', *The Hindu* dated 05/02/2006 at http://www.thehindu.com/todays-paper/tp-features/tp-sundaymagazine/benign-presence/article3219363.ece (accessed 03/04/2015).
34. Ibid.
35. Author's interview with Rukmini Varma.
36. Ibid.
37. Charles Allen & Sharada Dwivedi, op. cit., p. 34.
38. Ibid. p. 213.
39. See T. John Samuel, *Many Avatars; One Life* (Google Books).
40. Ibid.

41. Indira Varma's note to the author on her mother.
42. Author's interview with Divakara Varma.
43. Author's interview with Uma Varma.
44. Author's interview with Rukmini Varma.
45. Author's interview with Rukmini Varma.
46. Author's interview with Uma Varma.
47. Pooyam Tirunal Gouri Parvathi Bayi's remarks at the Maharani Sethu Lakshmi Bayi Memorial Lecture in Trivandrum on 23/11/2014. She remarked that as children to get them to bathe and use oils and other such things they didn't particularly enjoy, the servants used to tell them that if they wanted to look as good as Sethu Lakshmi Bayi, they must do all this.
48. Author's interview with Rukmini Varma.
49. Author's interview with Uma Varma.
50. Author's interview with Indira Varma.
51. A 1932 letter from Princess Lalitha to the Senior Maharani (TRF).
52. (Undated) Letter from Princess Lalitha to the Maharani Regent (TRF).
53. (Undated) Letter from Princess Lalitha to the Maharani Regent (TRF).
54. Author's interview with Uma Varma.
55. Author's interview with Rukmini Varma.
56. Ibid.
57. Letter dated 21/07/1937 from Princess Lalitha to the Valiya Koil Tampuran (TRF).
58. Ibid.
59. Ibid.
60. Letter dated 08/08/1941 from Princess Lalitha to the Valiya Koil Tampuran (TRF).
61. Author's interview with Rukmini Varma.
62. Ibid.
63. Ibid.
64. Ibid.
65. A typical card found in the TRF collection.
66. Indira Varma's note to the author on her mother.
67. Indira Varma, 'Halcyon Days at Kovalam' op. cit.
68. *The Indian Express* dated 23/03/1948.
69. Indira Varma, 'Halcyon Days at Kovalam' op. cit.
70. Princess Lalitha quoted in Lakshmi Raghunandan, op. cit., p. 413.
71. Lakshmi Raghunandan's essay to the author on Rama Varma.
72. Indira Varma, 'Halcyon Days at Kovalam' op. cit.

73. Ibid.
74. Lakshmi Raghunandan's essay to the author on Rama Varma.
75. Indira Varma, 'Halcyon Days at Kovalam' op. cit.
76. Ibid.
77. Ibid.
78. Author's interview with Rukmini Varma.
79. Lakshmi Raghunandan's essay to the author on Rama Varma.
80. Author's interview with Rukmini Varma.
81. Author's interview with Devika Radhakrishnan. Devika Radhakrishnan is a granddaughter of Maharani Sethu Lakshmi Bayi and Rama Varma, the Valiya Koil Tampuran.
82. Radhika Varma Hormusjee's note to the author. Radhika Varma Hormusjee is a great-granddaughter of Maharani Sethu Lakshmi Bayi and Rama Varma, the Valiya Koil Tampuran.
83. Letter dated 08/08/1941 from Princess Lalitha to the Valiya Koil Tampuran (TRF).
84. Author's interview with Dr R.M. Varma.
85. Author's interview with Indira Varma.
86. Lakshmi Raghunandan, op. cit., p. 412.
87. Divakara Varma's note to the author on life in the palace.
88. Nihal Singh, 'Her Highness of Travancore', *The Baltimore Sun* dated 24/03/1929.
89. Letter dated 06/12/1936 from CP Skrine to his mother (MSS EUR F154/22).
90. John Stewart, *Envoy of the Raj*, p. 176.
91. Ibid.
92. Letter dated 06/12/1936 from CP Skrine to his mother (MSS EUR F154/22).
93. Letter dated 19/05/1933 from the Chief Secretary to the Senior Maharani's Private Secretary (Bundle No. 266, File No. 738 KSA).
94. Letter dated 03/03/1933 from the Senior Maharani to the Resident (IOR/R/2/887/198).
95. Letter dated 18/02/1933 from the Sarvadhikaryakkar to the Dewan (IOR/R/2/887/198).
96. Letter dated 03/03/1933 from the Senior Maharani to the Resident (IOR/R/2/887/198).
97. Ibid.
98. Ibid.
99. Ibid.
100. See IOR/R/2/884/146 for an inventory and valuation of the Chellamvakai.

101. This person does not wish to be named.
102. Letter dated 03/03/1933 from the Senior Maharani to the Resident (IOR/R/2/887/198).
103. Ibid.
104. Letter dated 18/02/1933 from the Sarvadhikaryakkar to the Sripadam Karyakkar (IOR/R/2/887/198).
105. Letter dated 31/05/1932 from the Sarvadhikaryakkar to the Sripadam Karyakkar (IOR/R/2/887/198).
106. Letter dated 03/03/1933 from the Senior Maharani to the Resident (IOR/R/2/887/198).
107. Letter dated 09/11/1107 M.E. from the Sripadam Karyakkar to the Sarvadhikaryakkar (IOR/R/2/887/198).
108. Letter dated 31/01/1108 M.E. from the Sripadam Karyakkar to the Sarvadhikaryakkar (IOR/R/2/887/198).
109. Letter dated 31/01/1108 M.E. from the Sarvadhikaryakkar to the Sripadam Karyakkar (IOR/R/2/887/198).
110. Letter dated 10/03/1108 M.E. from the Sripadam Karyakkar to the Sarvadhikaryakkar (IOR/R/2/887/198).
111. Letter dated 03/03/1933 from the Senior Maharani to the Resident (IOR/R/2/887/198).
112. Letter dated 18/04/1933 from the Resident to the Senior Maharani (IOR/R/2/887/198).
113. Resident's note dated 15/06/1933 (IOR/R/2/887/198).
114. Ibid.
115. Ibid.
116. Ibid.
117. Ibid.
118. He is mentioned as 'Rajabhakta' in the *Report on the Administration of Travancore for 1936–37*, p. 10.
119. Author's interview with Indira Varma.
120. Author's interview with Divakara Varma.
121. See letter dated 21/02/1935 from the Resident to the Pol Sec., GOI, and letter dated 21/03/1935 from the Under Pol. Sec., GOI (IOR/L/PS/13/1283).
122. Letter dated 30/09/1938 from C.P. Skrine to his mother (MSS EUR F154/23).
123. Letter dated 16/07/1937 from C.P. Skrine to his mother (MSS EUR F154/22).
124. John Paton Davies, *China Hand,* p. 83.
125. Report for the First Half of September 1932 (IOR/R/1/1/2224).
126. Ibid.

127. Helen Cameron Gordon, *Hindu Life and Customs*, p. 177.
128. Report for the Second Half of March 1934 (IOR/R/1/1/2510).
129. Report for the Second Half of November 1932 (IOR/R/1/1/2224).
130. Helen Cameron Gordon, op. cit., p. 177.
131. Author's interview with Dr R.P. Raja, and Gita Aravamudan, *Disappearing Daughters*, p. 160 (2007) (New Delhi: Penguin).
132. Report for the Second Half of August 1932 (IOR/R/1/1/2224).
133. *The Princely India* dated 07/08/1932.
134. Report for the Second Half of August 1932 (IOR/R/1/1/2224).
135. A. Sreedhara Menon, *Triumh and Tragedy in Travancore*, p. 276.
136. Louise Ouwerkerk and Dick Kooiman, op. cit., p. 213.
137. Ibid.
138. Extract from letter dated 21/02/1945 from the Viceroy to the Secretary of State (IOR/L/PS/13/1285).
139. *Speeches of Sachivottama Sir CP Ramaswami Aiyar*, p. 23

CHAPTER 15: A PALACE COUP

1. Letter dated 24/03/1818 from the Resident to the Chief. Sec. Madras (IOR/R/1/1/1532 (2)).
2. Ibid.
3. Ibid.
4. Ibid. Chathayam Tirunal is referred to in these documents as the Amah Rajah while her daughters are Burnee Ternal (Bharani Tirunal) and Ootarum Ternal (Uthram Tirunal). The pretender prince, Visakham Tirunal Kerala Varma, is called Kerul Warmah.
5. Ibid.
6. Ibid.
7. Ibid.
8. Ibid.
9. Letter dated 28/11/1810 from the Resident to the Chief Sec. Madras (IOR/R/1/1/1532 (1)).
10. Letter dated 24/03/1818 from the Resident to the Chief. Sec. Madras (IOR/R/1/1/1532 (2)).
11. Ibid.
12. Ibid.
13. Ibid.
14. Ibid.
15. Ibid.

16. Ibid.
17. Ibid.
18. Ibid.
19. Ibid.
20. Ibid.
21. Report for the First Half of October 1932 (IOR/R/1/1/2224).
22. T.K. Velu Pillai, *Travancore State Manual*, Vol. II, p. 734.
23. *Princely India* dated 27/07/1932.
24. Report for the Second Half of August 1932 (IOR/R/1/1/2224), and the *Princely India* dared 13/07/1932.
25. Report for the First Half of October 1932 (IOR/R/1/1/2224).
26. Ibid.
27. Louise Ouwerkerk & Dick Kooiman, *No Elephants for the Maharaja*, p. 121.
28. Report for the First Half of October 1932 (IOR/R/1/1/2224).
29. Louise Ouwerkerk and Dick Kooiman, op. cit., p. 121.
30. John Bright-Holmes, *Like It Was: The Diaries of Malcolm Muggeridge*, p. 124. Muggeridge added: 'I have always had illusions about him...the sort of charm engendered by promiscuity and living beyond your income, the sort of bonhomie etc. etc. When I actually met him, I found him rather dingy and commonplace. There was certainly no sparkle. We spoke about politics. He seemed uneasy. I have a feeling [and here Muggeridge was wrong] that his innings is drawing to a close. Of course, it's been a pretty good one.'
31. Louise Ouwerkerk & Dick Kooiman, op. cit., p. 121.
32. Report for the First Half of October 1932 (IOR/R/1/1/2224).
33. Letter dated 02/01/1935 from the Resident to the Pol. Sec. GOI (IOR/R/1/1/2734).
34. Ibid.
35. Ibid.
36. Ibid.
37. Ibid.
38. Ibid.
39. Letter dated 02/11/1935 from the Resident to the Pol. Sec. GOI (IOR/R/2/888/207).
40. Ibid.
41. Letter dated 14/11/1935 from the Pol. Sec. GOI to the Resident (IOR/R/2/888/207).
42. Letter dated 20/11/1935 from the Resident to the Pol. Sec. GOI (IOR/R/2/888/207).

43. Letter dated 02/11/1935 from the Resident to the Pol. Sec. GOI (IOR/R/2/888/207).
44. A. Sreedhara Menon, *Triumph and Tragedy in Travancore*, p. 11.
45. Letter dated 31/08/1936 from the Maharajah to the Resident (IOR/R/2/888/207).
46. Letter dated 01/09/1936 from the Maharajah to the Resident (IOR/R/2/888/207).
47. A. Raghu, *CP: A Short Biography*, p. 31.
48. The Resident was first of the opinion that there was a 'remarkable unanimity of opinion here that [CP] would refuse such an offer if made [i.e. the Dewanship] as it would not, it is judged, pay him, but that he will have his own nominee appointed instead.' The Political Secretary, however, felt it was 'most unlikely' CP would decline such an offer. See IOR/R/1/1/2859.
49. A. Raghu, op. cit., p. 34.
50. Quoted in Thomas J. Nossiter, *Communism in Kerala*, p. 99.
51. Letter dated 02/01/1935 from the Resident to the Pol. Sec. GOI (IOR/R/1/1/2734).
52. Letter dated 02/11/1935 from the Resident to the Pol. Sec., GOI (IOR/R/2/888/207).
53. Letter dated 02/04/1928 from the Resident to the Pol. Sec. GOI (IOR/L/PS/10/1118). This conversation was had when Mr Dodwell, the Maharajah's teacher, was saying his goodbye, and it was reported that the Junior Maharani was upset that her sixteen-year-old son had said this openly. Louise Ouwerkerk also noticed this, later saying how 'asked his opinion out of the blue, [the Maharajah] evaded an answer until he had "thought it over".' See Louise Ouwerkerk and Dick Kooiman, op. cit., p. 74.
54. Mahadev Desai, *The Epic of Travancore*, p. 98.
55. Shreekumar Varma, 'Benign Presence', *The Hindu* dated 05/02/2006 at http://www.thehindu.com/todays-paper/tp-features/tp-sundaymagazine/benign-presence/article3219363.ece (accessed 03/04/2015).
56. B.R. Ambedkar, *What Congress and Gandhi have done to The Untouchables*, p. 317.
57. Ibid.
58. T.K. Velu Pillai, *Travancore State Manual*, Vol. II, p. 768.
59. A. Sreedhara Menon, *Kerala History and its Makers*, p. 210.
60. G. Mahadevan, 'Temple Entry Proclamation the Greatest Act of Moral Freedom', *The Hindu* dated 12/11/2011 at http://www.thehindu.com/todays-paper/tp-national/tp-kerala/temple-entry-proclamation-the-greatest-act-of-moral-freedom-uthradom-tirunal/article2620727.ece (accessed 07/10/2014).

61. See letters in IOR/R/2/889/226.
62. T.K. Velu Pillai, *Travancore State Manual*, Vol. II, p. 753.
63. Mahadev Desai, op. cit., p. 42.
64. Dick Kooiman, *Communalism and Indian Princely States*, pp. 131–32.
65. *The Indian Express* dated 08/04/1939.
66. Dick Kooiman, 'Political Rivalry among Religious Communities' in *Economic and Political Weekly*, Vol. 28, No. 7, 1993, p. 293.
67. A. Sreedhara Menon, *Triumph and Tragedy in Travancore*, p. 276.
68. Dick Kooiman, 'Political Rivalry ...', op. cit., p. 288.
69. Marthanda Varma, *Travancore: The Footprints of Destiny*, p. 118
70. A. Sreedhara Menon, *Triumph* ..., op. cit., p. 118.
71. *Notes on the Present Position of Christians in Travancore* by the Travancore Peace Bloc (1946).
72. Ibid.
73. Ibid.
74. See Memorandum of Grievances submitted to Sir C.P. Ramaswami Iyer KCIE, Dewan of Travancore by a Deputation of the All Travancore Joint Political Congress (1936) and Full Notes of Proceedings of the meeting between the All Travancore Joint Political Congress and the Dewan on 28/10/1936 (IOR/R/2/889/220).
75. S. Ramnath Aiyar, *A History of Travancore*, pp. 126, 128.
76. Letter dated 02/01/1935 from the Resident to the Pol. Sec. GOI (IOR/R/2/888/210).
77. Ibid.
78. Letter dated 26/09/1935 from the Resident to the Pol. Sec. GOI (IOR/R/2/888/207).
79. Ibid.
80. Louise Ouwerkerk and Dick Kooiman, op. cit., p. 70.
81. James Chirayankandath, 'Communities at Polls', *Modern Asian Studies*, Vol. 27, No. 3, 1993, p. 657.
82. Robin Jeffrey, 'Temple Entry Movement in Travancore', *Social Scientist*, Vol. 4, No. 8, 1976, p. 18.
83. T.K. Velu Pillai, *Travancore State Manual*, Vol. II, pp. 740–41.
84. Ibid. p. 743.
85. James Chirayankandath, op. cit., p. 657.
86. A. Sreedhara Menon, *Triumph* ..., op. cit., p. 137, and *Notes on the Present Position of Christians in Travancore* op. cit.
87. *Travancore: The Present Political Problem* by the All Travancore Joint Political Congress, p. 1.

88. Dick Kooiman, 'Communalism and Indian Princely States', *Economic and Political Weekly,* Vol. 30, No. 34, 1995, p. 2129.
89. James Chirayankandath, op. cit., p. 659.
90. Louise Ouwerkerk & Dick Kooiman, op. cit., p. 68.
91. James Chirayankandath op. cit., p. 646.
92. Ibid. p. 660.
93. Ibid.
94. Louise Ouwerkerk and Dick Kooiman, op. cit., p. 87.
95. T.K. Velu Pillai, *Travancore State Manual,* Vol. II, p. 747.
96. George Mathew, *Communal Road to a Secular Kerala,* p. 94.
97. James Chirayankandath, op. cit., p. 660.
98. Ibid.
99. Ibid., p. 662.
100. Dick Kooiman, 'Communalism and Indian Princely States' op. cit., p. 2129.
101. Ibid.
102. Letter dated 06/11/1936 from the Resident to the Pol. Sec. GOI (IOR/R/2/889/220).
103. A. Sreedhara Menon, *Triumph* ..., op. cit., p. 151. The movement included Muslims, Ezhavas, Latin Catholics, Syrian Catholics, Jacobites, Marthomites, Protestants, and organisations represented included the SNDP Yogam, the Wajanathul Muhamadiyya Association, All Travancore Muslim Service League, Travancore State Catholic Congress, and so on.
104. George Mathew, op. cit., pp. 94–95.
105. James Chirayankandath, op. cit., p. 661.
106. Robin Jeffrey, 'Temple Entry Movement in Travancore' op. cit., p. 18.
107. Ibid.
108. Ibid.
109. Robin Jeffrey, *Decline* ..., op. cit., p. 210.
110. Robin Jeffrey, 'Temple Entry Movement in Travancore', op. cit., p. 20.
111. Ibid.
112. Louise Ouwerkerk and Dick Kooiman, op. cit., p. 142.
113. Mahadev Desai, op. cit., pp. 128–29.
114. Marthanda Varma, op. cit., p. 131.
115. Louise Ouwerkerk and Dick Kooiman, op. cit., p. 92.
116. Robin Jeffrey, 'Temple Entry Movement in Travancore' op. cit., p. 20. Sir CP sometimes went out of his way to preserve Hindu principles. In 1944, for instance, when capital punishment was abolished in the state, the Resident wrote that the basic reason was that for centuries Brahmins and women were not liable

to it and now the government was being criticised for favouring Brahmins. CP decided to do away with capital punishment as a whole instead of adding Brahmins to the list. See Letter dated 24/11/1944 from the Resident to the Sec. to Viceroy (IOR/L/PS/13/1285).

117. George Mathew, op. cit., p. 95.
118. Memorandum of Grievances..., op. cit.
119. Resident's note dated 07/08/1936 (IOR/R/2/889/223).
120. Ibid.
121. Mahadev Desai, op. cit., p. 162.
122. Notes on the Present Position of Christians..., op. cit.
123. Robin Jeffrey, 'Temple Entry Movement in Travancore', op. cit., p. 22.
124. George Mathew, op. cit., p. 111.
125. B.R. Ambedkar, op. cit., p. 318.
126. Mahadev Desai, op. cit., p. 129.
127. James Chirayankandath, op. cit., p. 663.
128. Louise Ouwerkerk and Dick Kooiman, op. cit., p. 222.
129. Dick Kooiman, 'Communalism and Indian Princely States', op. cit., p. 2129.
130. A. Sreedhara Menon, *Triumph...*, op. cit., p. 193.
131. Ibid. p. 118.
132. Louise Ouwerkerk and Dick Kooiman, op. cit., p. 129.
133. Mahadev Desai, op. cit., p. 151.
134. T.K. Velu Pillai, *Travancore State Manual*, Vol. II, p. 767.
135. Ibid.
136. Mahadev Desai, op. cit., p. 151.
137. Author's interview with Dr R.M. Varma, who remembers this visit by Gandhi to Satelmond Palace.
138. Mahadev Desai, op. cit., p. 151.
139. Ibid. p. 235.
140. Author's interview with Divakara Varma.
141. Letter dated 24/04/1937 from C.P. Skrine to his mother (MSS EUR F154/22).
142. Louise Ouwerkerk and Dick Kooiman, op. cit., p. 95.
143. B.R. Ambedkar, op. cit., p. 318.
144. Author's interview with Divakara Varma.
145. Author's interview with Lakshmi Raghunandan.
146. Louise Ouwerkerk and Dick Kooiman, op. cit., p. 93.
147. Report for the First Half of February 1927 (IOR/R/1/1/1644).
148. Report for the Second Half of September 1930 (IOR/L/PS/10/1118).
149. Author's interview with Dr R.P. Raja.

150. Supplementary to the Report for the Second Half of February 1938 (MSS EUR F154/46).
151. Author's interview with Divakara Varma.
152. Author's interview with Rukmini Varma.
153. Ibid.
154. Letter dated 27/07/1939 from the Senior Maharani to the Resident (IOR/R/1/1/3371).
155. Letter dated 23/09/1938 from C.P. Skrine to his mother (MSS EUR F154/23).
156. See Bundle No. 25, File No. 1194 KSA. In a letter dated 23/07/1932 the Dewan informed the Sarvadhikaryakkar of the Maharajah that as per precedent, the last Regent had 'her name continued to be shown above that of the Elayarajah.' To this on 10/08/1932 the Sarvadhikaryakkar responded: 'I am commanded by His Highness the Maharajah to inform you ... that Her Highness' place in the Almanac will be shown after that of His Highness the Elayarajah.'
157. B.R. Ambedkar, op. cit., p. 319.

CHAPTER 16: THE ULTIMATE ECLIPSE

1. 'The hopes of Lakshmi Bayi, the sister of the Maharajah of Travancore have again been disappointed,' wrote the Resident in his Report for the First Half of April 1936. 'Such an occurrence happening a second time will be a severe blow to the mother of His Highness as it gravely endangers the change of the succession to the gadi being retained in her line.' Evidently the 'calamity' occurred after Kochukunji had Dr Mary and her staff withdraw, and placed the pregnant princess under the care of an ayurvedic practitioner (IOR/L/PS/13/1283).
2. Report for the First Half of January 1938 (IOR/R/1/1/3047).
3. Letter dated 24/04/1944 from the Resident to the Pvt. Sec. to Viceroy (IOR/L/PS/13/1285).
4. Report for the First Half of January 1938 (IOR/L/PS/13/1283).
5. Letter dated 23/09/1938 from CP Skrine to his mother (MSS EUR F154/23).
6. Author's interview with Indira Varma.
7. Author's interview with Kerala Varma, the son in law of Maharani Sethu Lakshmi Bayi.
8. Author's interview with Rukmini Varma.
9. Charles Allen and Sharada Dwivedi, op. cit., p. 180.
10. Author's interview with Rukmini Varma.
11. Ibid.
12. Author's interview with Divakara Varma.
13. Author's interview with Kerala Varma; he was the son of Vasudevan Nambutiri

of Puliyadu Illam of Thittappally and of Ambika Cherukutty Tampuratti of Kilimanoor.

14. Author's interview with Rukmini Varma.
15. Lakshmi Raghunandan, *At the Turn of the Tide*, p. 414.
16. Ibid.
17. Author's interview with Rukmini Varma.
18. Author's interview with Kerala Varma.
19. Author's interview with Divakara Varma.
20. Letter dated 19/07/1929 from Louise Ouwerkerk to her mother (MSS EUR F232/60).
21. Author's interview with Divakara Varma.
22. Author's interview with Indira Varma.
23. Ibid.
24. Letter dated 12/03/1938 from 'Molly Gardner' to 'Verra Rattler' (TRF).
25. Letter dated 23/09/1928 from C.P. Skrine to his mother (MSS EUR F154/23). The actual ceremonies were more detailed and are explained in Kulathu Iyer's *The Pallikettu...* op. cit. Also see *Thirumadampu of His Highness Martanda Varma* by K.P. Subramonia Iyer, who notes on pp. 5–6 how these materials from Princess Lalitha's wedding were used for the 'thread ceremony' of the Maharajah's brother, a decision which was 'a supreme act of self-sacrifice on the part of His Highness the Maharajah, for generally no pandal as such is used for a similar occasion a second time'.
26. Letter dated 23/09/1928 from C.P. Skrine to his mother (MSS EUR F154/23).
27. Ibid.
28. Letter dated 27/07/1939 from the Senior Maharani to the Resident (IOR/R/1/1/3371).
29. Letter dated 13/06/1935 from the Sripadam Karyakkar to the Sarvadhikaryakkar (IOR/R/1/1/3371).
30. Letter dated 23/03/1935 from the Sarvadhikaryakkar to the Sripadam Karyakkar (IOR/R/1/1/3371).
31. Letter dated 26/10/1935 from the Sarvadhikaryakkar to the Sripadam Karyakkar (IOR/R/1/1/3371).
32. Ibid.
33. Letter dated 02/08/1933 from the Chief Secretary to the Sripadam Karyakkar (IOR/R/1/1/3371).
34. Letter dated 07/11/1934 from the Chief Secretary to the Sripadam Karyakkar (IOR/R/1/1/3371).
35. Letter dated 24/01/1934 from the Chief Secretary to the Sripadam Karyakkar (IOR/R/1/1/3371).

36. Letter dated 17/02/1934 from the Sripadam Karyakkar to the Chief Secretary (IOR/R/1/1/3371).
37. Proceedings of the Third Meeting of the Sri Mulam Popular Assembly, p. 28 (IOR/R/1/1/3371).
38. Proceedings of the Fourth Meeting of the Sri Mulam Popular Assembly, p. 12 (IOR/R/1/1/3371).
39. Ibid.
40. Letter dated 06/09/1910 from the Chief Secretary to the Senior Dewan Peishkar (IOR/R/1/1/3371).
41. *Travancore Land Revenue Manual* (1915), Vol. III, pp. 1,15, 67 (IOR/R/1/1/3371).
42. *Travancore Land Revenue Manual* (1936), Vol. III, p. 17 (IOR/R/1/1/3371).
43. Letter dated 13/02/1939 from the Sarvadhikaryakkar to the Sripadam Karyakkar (IOR/R/1/1/3371).
44. Letter dated 31/03/1939 from the Sripadam Karyakkar to the Sarvadhikaryakkar (IOR/R/1/1/3371).
45. Letter dated 05/05/1939 from the Sarvadhikaryakkar to the Sripadam Karyakkar (IOR/R/1/1/3371).
46. Letter dated 13/10/1114 ME from the Sripadam Karyakkar to the Sarvadhikaryakkar (IOR/R/1/1/3371).
47. Ibid.
48. Ibid.
49. Letter dated 21/07/1939 from the Sarvadhikaryakkar to the Sripadam Karyakkar (IOR/R/1/1/3371).
50. Letter dated 27/07/1939 from the Senior Maharani to the Resident (IOR/R/1/1/3371).
51. Ibid.
52. Letter dated 19/12/1938 from the Sarvadhikaryakkar to the Sripadam Karyakkar (IOR/R/1/1/3371).
53. Letter dated 05/08/1938 from the Sarvadhikaryakkar to the Nithiachilavu Karyakkar (IOR/R/1/1/3371).
54. Letter dated 27/07/1939 from the Senior Maharani to the Resident (IOR/R/1/1/3371).
55. Ibid.
56. Ibid.
57. See the voluminous exchange of letters on these topics in IOR/R/1/1/3371 Annexure G.
58. Letter dated 27/07/1939 from the Senior Maharani to the Resident (IOR/R/1/1/3371).

59. Ibid.
60. Letter dated 14/08/1939 from the Resident to the Senior Maharani (IOR/R/1/1/3372).
61. Letter dated 30/08/1939 from the Senior Maharani to the Resident (IOR/R/1/1/3372).
62. Letter dated 25/09/1939 from the Senior Maharani to the Resident (IOR/R/1/1/3372).
63. Ibid.
64. Letter dated 26/09/1939 from the Sarvadhikaryakkar to T.S. Sankaranarayana Iyer (IOR/R/1/1/3372).
65. Letter dated 27/09/1939 from the Senior Maharani to the Resident (IOR/R/1/1/3372).
66. Letter dated 28/09/1939 from the Resident to the Senior Maharani (IOR/R/1/1/3372).
67. Letter dated 22/10/1939 from the Senior Maharani to the Viceroy (IOR/R/1/1/3372).
68. Letter dated 30/09/1939 from the Senior Maharani to the Resident (IOR/R/1/1/3372).
69. Letter dated 09/10/1939 from the Senior Maharani to the Resident (IOR/R/1/1/3372).
70. Legal Opinion of Sir Tej Bahadur Sapru dated 25/09/1939 (IOR/R/1/1/3372).
71. Letter dated 27/08/1939 from the Senior Maharani to the Resident (IOR/R/1/1/3371).
72. See the whole correspondence on this matter in IOR/R/1/1/3371 Annexure B
73. Letter dated 13/10/1114 ME from the Sripadam Karyakkar to the Sarvadhikaryakkar (IOR/R/1/1/3371). Also see Annexure C of the same file.
74. Letter dated 27/07/1939 from the Senior Maharani to the Resident (IOR/R/1/1/3371).
75. Letter dated 14/10/1939 from the Senior Maharani to the Resident (IOR/R/1/1/3372).
76. Letter dated 22/10/1939 from the Senior Maharani to the Viceroy (IOR/R/1/1/3372).
77. Ibid.
78. Ibid.
79. Letter dated 19/10/1939 from the Senior Maharani to the Resident (IOR/R/1/1/3372).
80. Ibid.
81. Ibid.
82. Telegram dated 20/10/1939 from the Senior Maharani to the Viceroy (IOR/R/1/1/3371).

83. Letter dated 29/11/1939 from the Resident to the Pol. Sec., G.O.I. (IOR/R/1/1/3372).
84. Ibid.
85. Author's interview with Dr R.P. Raja.
86. Legal Opinion of Kuttikrishna Menon dated 29/11/1939 (IOR/R/1/1/3372).
87. Ibid.
88. Telegram dated 19/12/1939 from the Senior Maharani to the Viceroy (IOR/R/1/1/3372).
89. Letter dated 09/12/1939 from the Pol. Sec., GOI to the Dewan (IOR/R/1/1/3372).
90. Letter dated 26/12/1939 from the Viceroy to the Senior Maharani (IOR/R/1/1/3372).
91. Hugo s'Jacob, *The Rajas of Cochin*, p. 84.
92. Letter dated 28/11/1810 from the Resident to the Chief Sec. Madras (IOR/R/1/1/1532 (2)).
93. Letter dated 12/06/1813 from the Resident to the Chief Sec. Madras (IOR/R/1/1/1532 (2)).
94. S.C. Mukhopadhyaya, *The Career of an Indian Princess*, pp. 6–7.
95. Caroline Keen, *Princely India and the British*, pp. 112–14.
96. Ibid.
97. Saradamoni, *Matriliny Transformed*, p. 68.
98. Ibid. p. 18.
99. Ibid.
100. Minutes of Evidence taken before the Select Committee of the House of Lords Appointed to Enquire into the Present State of Affairs of the East India Company (1830), Part I, p. 394, available on Google Books at https://books.google.co.in/books?id=e5hRAAAAYAAJ&printsec=frontcover&dq=Minutes+of+Evidence+taken+before+the+Select+Committee+of+the+House+of+Lords+appointed+to+enquire+into+the+Present+State+of+Affairs+of+the+East+India+Company+%281830&hl=en&sa=X&ved=0CBwQ6AEwAGoVChMI7pvFm5HdxwIVzKCUCh2_pAig#v=onepage&q&f=false (accessed 02/10/2015).
101. Saradamoni, op. cit., p. 68.
102. Caroline Keen, op. cit., p. 117.
103. Ibid., pp. 110, 112.
104. Ibid.
105. Ibid., pp. 25, 27.
106. Ibid., pp. 30–31.
107. Letter dated 12/06/1813 from the Resident to the Chief Sec. Madras (IOR/R/1/1/1532 (1)).

108. Ibid.
109. Ibid.
110. Letter dated 13/08/1813 from the Resident to the Chief Sec. Madras (IOR/R/1/1/1532 (1).
111. Letter dated 03/09/1813 from the Governor General, Fort William to the Governor General, Fort St George (IOR/R/1/1/1532 (2)).
112. Letter dated 04/10/1814 from the Chief Sec. Madras to the Resident (IOR/R/1/1/1532 (2)).
113. It was thus that the Maharajah was not allowed to become Karnavan aged 16 in 1928, for instance, and also why the late Elayarajah's objections to the adoption in 1900 were dismissed.
114. Note dated 10/02/1927 by H.R. Lynch Blosse of the Political Department, GOI (IOR/R/1/1/1532 (1)).
115. Ibid.
116. Quoted in ibid.
117. Quoted in Appendix to Notes by J.P. Thompson of the Political Department, GOI (IOR/R/1/1/1532 (1)).
118. Note dated 10/02/1927 by HR Lynch Blosse of the Political Department, GOI (IPR/R/1/1/1532 (1)).
119. Letter dated 28/09/1926 from the Acting Resident to the Pol. Sec. GOI (IOR/R/1/1/1532 (1)).
120. Ibid.
121. Letter dated 24/11/1927 from the Viceroy to the Secretary of State (IOR/R/1/1/1532 (1)).
122. Letter dated 25/06/1928 from the Pol. Sec. GOI to the Resident (IOR/R/1/1/1532 (1)).
123. Telegram dated 23/01/1940 from the Resident to GOI (IOR/R/1/1/3372).

CHAPTER 17: THE VILLAIN OF THE PIECE

1. Letter dated 20/09/1938 from Princess Lalitha to the Senior Maharani (TRF).
2. Author's interview with Parvathi Varma.
3. Author's interview with Rukmini Varma.
4. Author's interview with Dr R.M. Varma.
5. Lakshmi Raghunandan, *At the Turn of the Tide*, p. 417.
6. Letter dated 25/09/1939 from the Senior Maharani to the Resident (IOR/R/1/1/3372).
7. Author's interview with Indira Varma.
8. Author's interview with Divakara Varma.

9. Letter dated 22/11/1939 from the Maharajah to the Senior Maharani (IOR/R/1/1/3372).
10. Letter dated 20/12/1939 from the Senior Maharani to the Resident (IOR/R/1/1/3372).
11. Letter dated 27/12/1939 from the Senior Maharani to the Viceroy (IOR/R/1/1/3372).
12. Report for the Second Half of February 1940 (IOR/R/1/1/3499).
13. Lakshmi Raghunandan, op. cit., p. 418.
14. Author's interview with Rukmini Varma.
15. Lakshmi Raghunandan, op. cit., p. 418.
16. This person does not wish to be named.
17. Bharani Tirunal Uma Bayi Tampuran (b. 29 December 1941); Rohini Tirunal Parvathi Bayi Tampuran (13 February 1943); and Makham Tirunal Lakshmi Bayi Tampuran (b. 12 April 1946). They are named in the final Travancore almanacs and government directories, and the rest of Princess Lalitha's children were born after Independence and the integration of the princely states.
18. Their names are Pooyam Tirunal Gouri Parvathi Bayi Tampuran (b. 7 September 1942) and Aswathi Tirunal Gouri Lakshmi Bayi Tampuran (b. 4 July 1945).
19. Letter dated 24/11/1944 from the Resident to the Sec. to Viceroy (IOR/L/PS/13/1285).
20. He was the son of the Valiya Koil Tampuran's sister Ambalika and the very candidate Princess Lalitha had refused to marry in 1938.
21. *The Indian Express* dated 15/05/1945.
22. Report for the Second Half of August 1945 (IOR/L/PS/13/1298). Radha Devi was actually a *sister* of Mrs Pandalai. She and Col. Pandalai adopted her youngest sibling, who was many years her junior. Col. Pandalai had a famous temper. The story goes that once in the army a British officer behaved badly towards him, to which when he came on another occasion for an examination, the Colonel put him on a stretcher and had him branded! He then produced evidence during a court martial that branding was a legitimate method of treating mental imbalance. His wife originally came from Kayamkulam but grew up near Kovalam. Col. Pandalai was one of five brothers who were all sons of a Tampuran from the Mavelikkara family. The first and third were judges, the fourth an engineer, and the youngest looked after family affairs. Col. Pandalai was the second. I am grateful to Divakara Varma for these family stories and details.
23. Letter dated 24/04/1944 from the Resident to the Sec. to Viceroy (IOR/L/PS/13/1285).
24. In 1932 Ila Devi, the Princess of Cooch Behar and daughter of the Junior Maharani's friend Indira Devi was considered but the proposal fell through

when it was realised the bride would never be a Maharani (see letter dated 29/11/1932 from the Resident to the Under Secretary to GOI in IOR/L/PS/13/1283). Then in 1936 the Junior Maharani interviewed a girl from the family of the Paliyath Achan (see Report for the Second Half of March 1936 in IOR/L/PS/1283). Finally in 1944 also a proposal was under consideration but the death of his nephew, apparently, put the Maharajah off any plans to marry (see letter dated 24/04/1944 from the Resident to the Sec. to Viceroy in IOR/L/PS/13/1285). In what was a bizarre case, one Govinda Kaimal also tried to lobby to have the Maharajah marry one of his daughters and tried to influence the Maharajah's grandfather to enable this, even submitting a proposal to the Junior Maharani (IOR/R/1/1/3218).

25. Letter dated 24/04/1944 from the Resident to the Sec. to Viceroy (IOR/L/PS/13/1285).
26. Nilkan Perumal, *The Truth about Travancore*, p. 74.
27. John Paton Davies, *China Hand*, p. 83.
28. Gouri Lakshmi Bayi, *Sree Padmanabhaswamy Temple*, p. 162.
29. Letter dated 29/06/1938 from C.P. Skrine to his mother (MSS EUR F154/23).
30. Ibid.
31. Ibid.
32. Letter dated 05/04/1938 from the Resident to the Pol. Sec. GOI (IOR/R/1/3080).
33. Letter dated 29/06/1938 from C.P. Skrine to his mother (MSS EUR F154/23).
34. Letter dated 13/09/1938 from C.P. Skrine to his mother (MSS EUR F154/23).
35. A. Sreedhara Menon, *A Survey of Kerala History*, p. 293.
36. Letter dated 13/09/1938 from C.P. Skrine to his mother (MSS EUR F154/23).
37. Louise Ouwerkerk and Dick Kooiman, *No Elephants for the Maharaja*, p. 135.
38. Memorial dated 08/01/1939 from All Subjects of Travancore (IOR/L/PS/13/1283).
39. Statement of Dr N.S. Pillai of Attingal (IOR/R/1/1/3218).
40. T.M. Mathew, *Dr G Ramachandran: A Historical Biography*, p. 209 (2010) (Thesis submitted to the Mahatma Gandhi University's Faculty of Social Sciences).
41. Ibid.
42. Ibid., p. 217.
43. Letter dated 10/08/1939 from Mahatma Gandhi to the Dewan (IOR/R/1/1/3316).
44. Letter dated 15/08/1939 from the Dewan to Mahatma Gandhi (IOR/R/1/1/3316).
45. Louise Ouwerkerk and Dick Kooiman, op. cit., p. 153.

46. Letter dated 13/09/1938 from C.P. Skrine to his mother (MSS EUR F154/23).
47. *The English Writings of Rabindranath Tagore* Vol. II, p. 832.
48. Letter dated 13/09/1938 from C.P. Skrine to his mother (MSS EUR F154/23).
49. Letter dated 23/09/1938 from C.P. Skrine to his mother (MSS EUR F154/23).
50. Letter dated 30/09/1938 from C.P. Skrine to his mother (MSS EUR F154/23).
51. Letter dated 23/09/1938 from C.P. Skrine to his mother (MSS EUR F154/23).
52. Letter dated 13/09/1938 from C.P. Skrine to his mother (MSS EUR F154/23).
53. Ibid.
54. Louise Ouwerkerk and Dick Kooiman, op. cit., pp. 176, 200.
55. Ibid. p. 204.
56. Mahadev Desai, *The Epic of Travancore*, p. 94.
57. Letter dated 12/08/1930 from G. Sankaran Nair to the Dep. Pol. Sec. GOI (IOR/R/1/1/1985) and Report for the First Half of December 1929 (IOR/R/1/1/1819).
58. Note dated 04/09/1936 from the Political Secretary (IOR/R/1/1/2859).
59. Letter dated 11/10/1938 from the Resident to the Pol. Sec. GOI. (IOR/L/PS/13/1283).
60. Author's interview with P. Ramji, son of 1940s Alleppey Municipal Chairman, Parthasarathy Iyengar.
61. Letter dated 11/10/1938 from the Resident to the Pol. Sec. GOI (IOR/L/PS/13/1283).
62. Ibid.
63. Ibid.
64. Ibid.
65. Ibid.
66. Ibid.
67. Louise Ouwerkerk and Dick Kooiman, op. cit., p. 72.
68. Ibid., p. 74.
69. Ibid., p. 9.
70. Report for the First Half of November 1940 (IOR/R/1/1/3500)
71. *Notes on the Present Position of Christians in Travancore* by the Travancore Peace Bloc (1946).
72. Letter dated 15/03/1936 from the Maharajah to the Viceroy (File No. 7, 195-H/36 in the National Archives, Delhi).
73. The author could not independently verify this.
74. Report for the First Half of December 1942 (IOR/R/1/1/3786).
75. See Gazette Extraordinary dated 12/11/1936 and Tony McClenagham, *Indian Princely Medals*, p. 252.

76. Letter dated 06/12/1936 from A.C. Lothian, Representative of the Government of India, to the Pol. Sec. GOI (IOR/L/PS/13/750).
77. See also Dick Kooiman, 'The Guns of Travancore or How much Poweder may a Maharaja blaze away?' in *Indian Economic Social History Review* Vol. 43, No. 3, 2006, pp. 301–22. Travancore originally had a 17-gun salute till 1867 in which year it was raised to 19. It had a local 21-gun salute but this was not recognised by the Government of India, much to the consternation of successive Maharajahs. What Chithira Tirunal wanted was a recognised dynastic permanent gun salute of 21.
78. Marthanda Varma, *Travancore: The Footprints of Destiny*, p. 101.
79. Letter dated 24/04/1944 from the Resident to the Pol. Sec. GOI (IOR/L/PS/13/1285).
80. Ibid.
81. Ibid.
82. Ibid.
83. Report for the Second Half of July 1943 (IOR/1/1/3927).
84. Letter dated 11/09/1944 from the Resident to the Sec. to Viceroy (IOR/L/PS/13/1285).
85. Letter dated 21/02/1945 from the Viceroy to the Secretary of State (IOR/L/PS/13/1285).
86. Penderal Moon, *Wavell: The Viceroy's Journal*, p. 112.
87. Shakunthala Jagannathan, *Sir C.P. Remembered*, p. 86.
88. Marthanda Varma, op. cit., p. 135.
89. Letter dated 28/02/1938 from C.P. Skrine to his mother (MSS EUR F154/23).

CHAPTER 18: RIVERS OF BLOOD

1. Rajendra Prasad, *Asif Jahs of Hyderabad*, pp. 90–91.
2. Ibid. p, 86.
3. Kanhayalal Gauba, *His Highness*, pp. 32–33.
4. Ibid. p. 142.
5. *Life Magazine* dated 21/04/1947.
6. I have, since the publication of this book in 2015, nuanced this general negative picture of the Maharajahs as a class in my 2022 work, *False Allies*.
7. Dominique Lapierre and Larry Collins, *Freedom at Midnight*, pp. 173–74.
8. Michael O'Dwyer quoted in Clark Worswick, *Princely India: Photographs by Raja Deen Dayal 1884–1910* (New York: Alfred A. Knopf), p. 42.
9. Memorandum to the Butler Committee (1928). See also A. Sreedhara Menon, *Triumph and Tragedy in Travancore*, p. 225. At the time the princes had

also tried to argue that Paramountcy depended on the treaties, which the Butler Committee rejected, stating that Paramountcy was to be Paramount, even if it went beyond the purview of the treaties. However, the claim of the Maharajahs that their subordinate status could not be transferred to anyone else from the British Crown was accepted. See Ambedkar's 'Paramountcy and the Claim of the Indian States to be Independent' at http://www.ambedkar.org/ambcd/51.%20Paramountry%20and%20the%20Claims%20of%20the%20Indian%20States.htm (accessed 15/09/2014).

10. Louise Ouwerkerk and Dick Kooiman, *No Elephants for the Maharaja*, p. 4.
11. Robin Jeffrey, 'India's Working Class Revolt', *Indian Economic Social History Review* Vol. 18, No. 2, 1981, p. 107.
12. Ibid.
13. Ibid.
14. Ibid.
15. Ibid., p. 108.
16. Sekhar Bandopadhyay, *From Plassey to Partition*, p. 435.
17. Robin Jeffrey, 'India's Working Class Revolt,' op. cit., pp. 105–06.
18. Ibid.
19. Joseph Tharamangalam, *Agrarian Class Conflict*, p. 74.
20. Ibid. p. 75.
21. Author's interview with Rukmini Varma.
22. A. Sreedhara Menon, *A Survey of Kerala History*, pp. 293–94.
23. See http://www.cpimkerala.org/eng/struggles-72.php?n=1 (accessed 14/10/2014).
24. Louise Ouwerkerk and Dick Kooiman, op. cit., p. 246.
25. A. Sreedhara Menon, *A Survey ...*, pp. 292–94.
26. Joseph Tharamangalam, op. cit., p. 75.
27. Louise Ouwerkerk and Dick Kooiman, op. cit., p. 248.
28. Dominique Lapierre and Larry Collins, op. cit., p. 63.
29. Ibid. p. 65.
30. Ibid. p. 68.
31. Ibid. p. 41.
32. Ibid. p. 110.
33. Sir CP's statement (IOR/L/PS/13/1842).
34. A. Sreedhara Menon, *Triumph...*, p. 261.
35. Ibid. p. 378.
36. Report for the First Half of June 1947 (IOR/L/PS/13/1299).
37. A. Sreedhara Menon, *A Survey...*, p. 294.
38. Statement dated 06/07/1947 (IOR/L/PS/13/1842).

39. Thanu Pillai's telegram dated 10/07/1947 in B. Krishna, *India's Bismarck*, p. 102.
40. Note dated 21/07/1947 by the Deputy High Commissioner (IOR/L/PS/13/1842).
41. Ibid.
42. Ibid.
43. Viceroy's report dated 25/07/1947 (IOR/L/PO/6/123).
44. Ibid.
45. Ibid.
46. Ibid.
47. A.G. Noorani, 'C.P. and Independent Travancore', *Frontline*, Vol. 20, No. 13 dated 04/07/2003 at http://www.frontline.in/static/html/fl2013/stories/20030704000807800.htm (accessed 15/10/2014)
48. A. Sreedhara Menon, *Triumph*..., pp. 233–34.
49. A.G. Noorani, op. cit.
50. A. Sreedhara Menon, *Triumph*..., pp. 388–89. Also see A.G. Noorani, op. cit.
51. Viceroy's report dated 01/08/1947 (IOR/L/PO/6/123).
52. A.G. Noorani, op. cit.
53. Ibid.
54. Quoted in letter dated 10/09/1947 from Sir Terence Shone to Sir P.J. Patrick (IOR/L/PS/13/1842).
55. P.G.N. Unnithan was the son of a Harippad Tampuran from the Valiya Koil Tampuran's family, and his sister was married to Rama Varma, the son of Raja Ravi Varma. Their daughter, Manorama, in turn was married to Sethu Lakshmi Bayi's older brother, R. Martanda Varma, whom she called annan.
56. A. Sreedhara Menon, *A Survey*..., p. 294.
57. B. Krishna, op. cit., p. 103.
58. A.G. Noorani, op. cit.
59. Ibid.
60. Louise Ouwerkerk and Dick Kooiman, op. cit., p. 77.
61. Ibid.
62. B. Krishna, op. cit., p. 103.
63. Louise Ouwerkerk and Dick Kooiman, op. cit., p. 280.
64. A.G. Noorani, op. cit.
65. Ibid.
66. Louise Ouwerkerk and Dick Kooiman, op. cit., p. 271.
67. Lakshmi Raghunandan, *At the Turn of the Tide*, pp. 418–23.
68. See letters dated 20/08/1941 from the Sarvadhikaryakkar to the Senior Maharani's Karyakkar, and his reply dated 08/09/1941 (Raghunandan, pp. 424–25).

69. Author's interview with Advocate Ayyappan Pillai.
70. Author's interview with Divakara Varma.
71. Author's interview with Rukmini Varma.
72. Ibid.
73. Author's interview with Divakara Varma.
74. Author's interview with Parvathi Varma.
75. Ibid.
76. Ibid.
77. Author's interview with Uma Varma.
78. Author's interview with Parvathi Varma.
79. Author's interview with Indira Varma.
80. Author's interview with Divakara Varma.
81. Author's interview with Rukmini Varma.
82. Author's interview with Lakshmi Raghunandan.
83. Author's interview with Rukmini Varma.
84. Author's interview with Parvathi Varma.
85. Ibid.
86. Ibid.
87. Author's interview with Uma Varma.
88. Author's interview with Rukmini Varma.
89. Ibid.
90. Author's interview with Shreekumar Varma.
91. Author's interview with Rukmini Varma.
92. Ibid.
93. Ibid.
94. Ibid.
95. Author's interview with Parvathi Varma.
96. Author's interview with Rukmini Varma.
97. Author's interview with Lakshmi Raghunandan.
98. He presented the Maharani during his visit in 1922 a copy of his *Thought Relics*.
99. Edda Mussolini visited in December 1928. See report for the Second Half of December 1928 (IOR/R/1/1/1746).
100. Author's interview with Rukmini Varma.
101. Ibid.
102. Ibid.
103. Ibid.
104. Author's interview with Divakara Varma.
105. Author's interview with Rukmini Varma.

106. Author's interview with Divakara Varma.
107. Author's interview with Indira Varma.
108. Ibid.
109. Author's interview with Rukmini Varma.
110. Report for the Second Half of May 1931 (IOR/R/1/1/2064) and author's interview with Kerala Varma.
111. Author's interview with Divakara Varma.
112. Author's interview with Rukmini Varma.
113. Author's interview with Divakara Varma.

CHAPTER 19: THE RELUCTANT PRINCESS

1. Author's interview with Malathi Varma, who is married to Dr R.M. Varma, the nephew of Maharani Sethu Lakshmi Bayi.
2. Author's interview with Dr R.M. Varma.
3. Author's interview with Divakara Varma.
4. Author's interview with Parvathi Varma.
5. Author's interview with Rukmini Varma.
6. Author's interview with Divakara Varma.
7. Ibid. It was later rented to a Swami who led a very reclusive life, according to Divakara Varma. 'All that we know is that he kept some cows and every evening would take his Plymouth car and get grass feed for them and return. The front gate was always chained and padlocked. Sometime in the 1950s the property was sold to one Commander S.P.N. Nair, who evicted the Swami, and I think it is a housing colony today.'
8. Ibid.
9. Author's interview with Ambika Varma.
10. Author's interview with Divakara Varma.
11. Author's interview with Rukmini Varma.
12. Author's interview with Divakara Varma.
13. Author's interview with Kerala Varma.
14. Author's interview with Uma Varma.
15. Ibid.
16. Author's interview with Rukmini Varma.
17. Author's interview with Kerala Varma.
18. Author's interview with Divakara Varma.
19. Author's interview with Rukmini Varma. The sisters are Bhavani Tampuratti and Rajamma Tampuratti and Kunjannan is Dr R.P. Raja.
20. Author's interview with Kerala Varma.

21. Ibid.
22. Author's interview with Divakara Varma.
23. Michael Edwardes, *The Last Year of British India*, p. 203
24. V.P. Menon, *The Story of the Integration of Indian States*, p. 281.
25. Ibid. p. 282.
26. Ibid. p. 288.
27. Ibid. p. 282.
28. Ibid. p. 278.
29. Ibid. p. 286.
30. Ibid.
31. Author's interview with Divakara Varma.
32. Lakshmi Raghunandan, *At the Turn of the Tide*, p. 436. Till then the Senior Maharani's daughters were receiving just over 8,000 rupees per annum, while the Maharajah gave his sister nearly three times that figure. It was the Indian government that corrected this anomaly in the interest of fairness.
33. See Kerala Gazette (1963) for these figures. These allowances would be continued even after Indira Gandhi terminated privy purses to Maharajahs in 1971. As of 2009, the Elayarajah (who died in 2013) received Rs. 491,400; while Princess Indira's allowance was Rs. 85,800 (Princess Lalitha and the Junior Maharani's daughter, and the Maharanis themselves, had died). The junior princesses, granddaughters of the two Maharanis, had Rs. 39,000 each, while the Junior Maharani's only grandson had Rs. 78,000. The only living consort in 2009 was Kerala Varma who had Rs. 15,600.
34. V.P. Menon, op. cit. p. 288.
35. Eric Stracey, *Growing up in Anglo-India*, p. 14 (1999) (Madras: East West).
36. Author's interview with Rukmini Varma.
37. The house was purchased from an Iranian gentleman called Mr Kazerooni and his wife, who was a niece of the Dewan. She was also a descendant of the legendary Ali Asker, the famous merchant and horseman at the Mysore Maharajah's court.
38. Author's interview with Rukmini Varma.
39. Author's interview with Uma Varma.
40. Author's interview with Ambika Varma. Ambika Varma is a granddaughter of Maharani Sethu Lakshmi Bayi.
41. Author's interview with Rukmini Varma.
42. Author's interview with Prabha Menon.
43. Author's interview with Rukmini Varma.
44. Ibid.
45. Ibid.
46. Author's interview with Uma Varma.

47. Author's interview with Rukmini Varma.
48. Ibid.
49. Ibid.
50. Author's interview with Parvathi Varma.
51. Author's interview with Rukmini Varma.
52. Author's interview with Shreekumar Varma.
53. Author's interview with Malathi Varma.
54. Author's interview with Prabha Varma.
55. Author's interview with Rukmini Varma.
56. Ibid.
57. Author's interview with Prabha Varma.
58. Author's interview with Rukmini Varma.
59. Ibid.
60. Author's interview with Prabha Varma.
61. Author's interview with Rukmini Varma.
62. Ibid.
63. Ibid.
64. Ibid.
65. Author's interview with Parvathi Varma.
66. Lakshmi Raghunandan, op. cit., p. 437.
67. Author's interview with Ambika Varma.
68. Ibid.
69. Ibid.
70. Ibid.
71. Ibid.
72. Author's interview with Divakara Varma.
73. Ibid.
74. Author's interview with Shreekumar Varma.
75. Author's interview with Rukmini Varma.
76. Author's interview with Indira Varma.
77. Author's interview with Shreekumar Varma.
78. Author's interview with Rukmini Varma.
79. *The Southern Economist*, Vol. 9, p. 148 (Google Books).
80. Author's interview with Shreekumar Varma.
81. Author's interview with Jay Varma.
82. Author's interview with Rukmini Varma.
83. Author's interview with Shreekumar Varma.
84. Ibid.

85. Shreekumar Varma draft of 'Those Were the Daze', which was published in Anita Nair's *Where the Rain is Born.*
86. Swathi Tirunal Shobhana Bayi Tampuran and Punartham Tirunal Shreekumar Varma Tampuran.
87. Author's interview with Rukmini Varma.
88. Lakshmi Raghunandan, op. cit., p. 439.
89. Author's interview with Uma Varma.
90. Author's interview with Prabha Varma.
91. Author's interview with Rukmini Varma.
92. Author's interview with Shreekumar Varma.
93. Author's interview with Rukmini Varma.
94. Ibid.
95. Ibid.

CHAPTER 20: ONCE I HAD A KINGDOM

1. Author's interview with Rukmini Varma.
2. Fifty people served inside the palace while the remainder were outside staff.
3. Lakshmi Raghunandan, *At the Turn of the Tide*, p. 444.
4. Author's interview with Rukmini Varma.
5. Lakshmi Raghunandan, op. cit., p. 438.
6. Author's interview with Uma Varma.
7. Lakshmi Raghunandan, op. cit. p. 440.
8. Ibid.
9. Ibid., p. 443.
10. Ibid., p. 443–44.
11. Author's interview with Divakara Varma.
12. Author's interview with Rukmini Varma.
13. Lakshmi Raghunandan, op. cit., p. 439.
14. Author's interview with Uma Varma.
15. Lakshmi Raghunandan, op. cit., p. 442.
16. Ibid.
17. Ibid.
18. Letter dated 21/02/1958 from the Maharani's Secretary to the Maharajah's Secretary (TRF).
19. Author's interview with Rukmini Varma.
20. Author's interview with Advocate Ayyappan Pillai. The whole place is now in ruins and seems to have been vandalised, though occasionally Malayalam films are shot there.

21. Author's interview with Rukmini Varma.
22. Lakshmi Raghunandan, op. cit., p. 445.
23. Author's interview with Rukmini Varma.
24. Ibid.
25. Ibid.
26. Lakshmi Raghunandan, op. cit., p. 445.
27. Menon's son would later marry the Maharani's niece Prabha Menon.
28. Author's interview with Divakara Varma.
29. Author's interview with Rukmini Varma.
30. Ibid.
31. Lakshmi Raghunandan, op. cit., p. 449. The owner was one Subba Rao.
32. Author's interview with Uma Varma.
33. In fact some years later her neighbour would be assessed for wealth tax at a rate higher than normal because the value of his property, instead of Rs. 1.5 per square foot was assessed at Rs. 3 per square foot, which the Maharani had paid.
34. The architects later formed the famous firm, Chandavarkar & Thacker.
35. Author's interview with Rukmini Varma.
36. Radhika Varma Hormusjee's note to the author.
37. Author's interview with Indira Varma.
38. Author's interview with Uma Varma.
39. Author's interview with Ambika Varma.
40. Author's interview with Prabha Varma.
41. Author's interview with Ambika Varma.
42. Author's interview with Rukmini Varma.
43. Ibid.
44. Ibid.
45. Author's interview with Ambika Varma.
46. Author's interview with Lakshmi Raghunandan.
47. Author's interview with Dr RM Varma.
48. Author's interview with Rukmini Varma.
49. Author's interview with Shreekumar Varma.
50. Ibid.
51. Author's interview with Rukmini Varma.
52. Ibid.
53. Ibid.
54. Ibid.
55. Ibid.

56. Ibid.
57. Author's interview with Jay Varma.
58. Author's interview with Rukmini Varma.
59. Author's interview with Jay Varma.
60. Author's interview with Divakara Varma.
61. Author's interview with Rukmini Varma.
62. Author's interview with Prabha Varma.
63. Author's interview with Rukmini Varma.
64. Author's interview with Kerala Varma.
65. Author's interview with Rukmini Varma.
66. Ibid.
67. Ibid.
68. Ibid.
69. Ibid.
70. Information collected from press cuttings and other papers from the collection of Rukmini Varma.
71. Author's interview with Uma Varma.
72. Ibid.
73. Author's interview with Prasad Bidapa.
74. Author's interview with Uma Varma and Prasad Bidapa. Mrs Chowdhury herself did not reply to confirm this when contacted.
75. Author's interview with Rukmini Varma.
76. Ibid.
77. Author's interview with Uma Varma.
78. Ibid.
79. Author's interview with Ravi Varma.
80. Author's interview with Rukmini Varma.
81. Author's interview with Ravi Varma.
82. Author's interview with Parvathi Varma.
83. Author's interview with Ravi Varma.
84. Author's interview with Jay Varma.
85. Author's interview with Ravi Varma.
86. Author's interview with Rukmini Varma.
87. Author's interview with Lakshmi Raghunandan.
88. Author's interview with Vanitha Dayananda, a classmate of Lakshmi Raghunandan's from the 1960s.
89. Ibid.

90. Author's interview with Lakshmi Raghunandan.
91. Author's interview with Rukmini Varma.
92. Ibid.
93. Divya Kumar, 'Writing it Right', *The Hindu* dated 09/04/2010 at http://www.thehindu.com/features/metroplus/writing-it-right/article392830.ece (accessed 24/11/2014).
94. Author's interview with Advocate Vijayaraghavan.
95. Author's interview with Rukmini Varma
96. Radhika Varma Hormusjee's note to the author.
97. Ibid.
98. Ibid.
99. Author's interview with Jay Varma.
100. Radhika Varma Hormusjee's note to the author.
101. Ibid.
102. Author's interview with Jay Varma.
103. Radhika Varma Hormusjee's note to the author.
104. Author's interview with Jay Varma.
105. Author's interview with Devika Radhakrishnan.
106. Author's interview with Jay Varma.
107. Author's interview with Shreekumar Varma.
108. Balagopal Varma's speech at the Maharani Sethu Lakshmi Bayi Memorial Lecture on 23/11/2014 (Audio file supplied by Jay Varma).
109. Author's interview with Jay Varma.
110. Radhika Varma Hormusjee's note to the author.
111. Ibid.
112. Author's interview with Uma Varma.
113. Radhika Varma Hormusjee's note to the author.
114. Lalitha, however, felt it was an injustice to her mother who had served the people and filed a court case that the Maharani won a few years before her death.
115. Author's interview with Rukmini Varma
116. Letter dated 01/05/1951 from V.P. Menon to the Senior Maharani (TRF).
117. See letter dated 25/01/1958 from the Maharajah's Karyakkar to the Senior Maharani's Private Secretary, and the latter's response dated 21/02/1958 (TRF).
118. Altogether the Maharajah's family donated some Rs. 58 lakhs.
119. Author's interview with Dr. M.S. Valiathan.
120. Ibid.
121. Ibid.

122. Dr Valiathan's great-grandfather was Kunjaru Rajah, an uncle to Raja Ravi Varma's wife who was grandmother to Sethu Lakshmi Bayi.
123. Author's interview with Dr M.S. Valiathan.
124. See Revathinnal Balagopala Varma vs His Highness Shri Padmanabhadasa Balarama Varma (Since Deceased) And Others (judgement) dated 28//11/1991 for the Supreme Court ruling, and also *Princely States and Reform in Hindu Law* by Arun Mohan for details about the case in the High Court of Kerala.
125. Author's interview with Dr M.S. Valiathan. The amount agreed was Rs. 20 lakh, which by 1991 went up to Rs. 55 lakh, adding interest.
126. Author's interview with Rukmini Varma.
127. Ibid.
128. Ibid.
129. Author's interview with Shreekumar Varma.
130. Author's interview with Rukmini Varma.
131. Author's interview with Jay Varma.
132. Author's interview with Rukmini Varma.
133. Author's interview with Shreekumar Varma.
134. Author's interview with Prabha Menon.
135. Author's interview with Divakara Varma.
136. Author's interview with Rukmini Varma.
137. Author's interview with Uma Varma.
138. Ibid.
139. Shreekumar Varma's draft of 'Those were the Daze', which was published in Anita Nair's *Where the Rain is Born*.
140. Louise Ouwerkerk & Dick Kooiman, *No Elephants for the Maharaja*, p. 279.
141. Author's interview with Jay Varma.
142. Ibid.
143. Balagopal Varma's speech at the Maharani Sethu Lakshmi Bayi Memorial Lecture on 23/11/2014, op. cit.
144. Author's interview with Lakshmi Raghunandan.
145. Author's interview with Adrian Mayer.
146. Letter from Adrian Mayer to Rukmini Varma (TRF).
147. Author's interview with Jay Varma.

EPILOGUE

1. Ibrahim Kunju, *Rise of Travancore*, pp. 22–24.
2. 'Vault B should not be opened: Astrologers', *The Hindu* dated 13/08/2011

at http://www.thehindu.com/news/national/kerala/vault-b-should-not-be-opened-astrologers/article2348090.ece (accessed 28/06/2015).

3. These persons do not wish to be named.
4. Uthradom Thirunal Marthanda Varma vs The Union of India on 31 January 2011 available at http://indiankanoon.org/doc/1198234/ (accessed 28/06/2015).
5. Ibid.
6. Ibid.
7. Ibid.
8. 'Kerala Temple: Achuthanandan takes royal family to court', *NDTV* dated 24/08/2011 at http://www.ndtv.com/thiruvananthapuram-news/kerala-temple-achuthanandan-takes-royal-family-to-court-465224 (accessed 28/06/2015).
9. A. Srivathsan, 'When the vault was opened in 1931', *The Hindu* dated 06/06/2013 at http://www.thehindu.com/news/national/kerala/when-the-vault-was-opened-in-1931/article2201786.ece (accessed 28/06/2015).
10. Jake Halpern, 'The Secret of the Temple', *The New Yorker* dated 30/04/2012 at http://www.newyorker.com/magazine/2012/04/30/the-secret-of-the-temple (accessed 28/06/2015).
11. 'Vault B should not be opened: Astrologers', *The Hindu*, op. cit.
12. See 'Report by Gopal Subramanium, amicus curiae appointed by the Supreme Court in the Sri Padmanabhaswamy Temple case' in *The Hindu* at http://www.thehindu.com/news/resources/report-by-gopal-subramaniam-amicus-curiae-appointed-by-the-supreme-court-in-the-sree-padmanabhaswamy-temple-case/article5939933.ece (accessed 28/06/2015).
13. Ibid.
14. Ibid.
15. Ibid.
16. Prabhati Nayak Mishra, 'Royal family of Travancore puts forward their story in Padmanabhaswamy temple controversy', *DNA* dated 03/11/2014 at http://www.dnaindia.com/india/report-royal-family-of-travancore-puts-forward-their-story-in-padmanabhaswamy-temple-controversy-2031552 (accessed 28/06/2015).
17. 'Princess Bharani', *Hinduism Today*, February 1996 at http://www.hinduismtoday.com/modules/smartsection/item.php?itemid=3569 (accessed 28/06/2015).
18. Gouri Lakshmi Bayi, *Sree Padmanabhaswamy Temple*, p. 189.
19. See the Rules of Procedure for Adoption dated 1747 in Ibrahim Kunju, op. cit., p. 149.

20. Kausalya Santhanam, 'Writer with a royal lineage', *The Hindu* dated 16/08/2011 at http://www.thehindu.com/features/friday-review/history-and-culture/writer-with-a-royal-lineage/article2455596.ece (accessed 28/06/2015).
21. See http://www.thehindu.com/thehindu/mag/2003/03/30/stories/2003033000700700.htm and http://www.thehindu.com/news/cities/Thiruvananthapuram/simplicity-hallmark-of-travancore-royal-family/article4712319.ece (accessed 28/06/2015).
22. Ananthakrishnan G, 'Sree Padmanabha Swamy temple: Lord Vishnu's royal servants guard his riches', *The Economic Times* dated 05/07/2011 at http://articles.economictimes.indiatimes.com/2011-07-05/news/29738859_1_royal-family-sree-padmanabha-swamy-temple-erstwhile-princely-state (accessed 28/06/2015).
23. 'Sree Padmanabha Swamy Temple case: Amicus curiae's report to the Supreme Court', *The Hindu* dated 08/11/2012 at http://www.thehindu.com/news/resources/sree-padmanabha-swamy-temple-case-amicus-curiaes-report-to-the-supreme-court/article4077408.ece (accessed 26/08/2015).
24. '266 kg gold missing from Kerala's Sree Padmanabhaswamy Temple: Audit Report', *NDTV* dated 14/02/2015 at http://www.ndtv.com/cities/266-kg-gold-missing-from-keralas-sree-padmanabhaswamy-temple-audit-report-739461 and Krishnadas Rajagopal, 'Padmanabhaswamy temple vault was opened seven times: Vinod Rai', *The Hindu* dated 13/08/2014 at http://www.thehindu.com/news/national/kerala/padmanabhaswamy-temple-vault-was-opened-seven-times-vinod-rai/article6309994.ece (accessed 28/06/2015).
25. Prabhati Nayak Mishra, op. cit.
26. Amy Kazmin, 'The battle for custodianship of the Sree Padmanabhaswamy Temple', *Financial Times* dated 19/09/2014 at http://www.ft.com/intl/cms/s/0/170f515a-382e-11e4-a687-00144feabdc0.html#axzz3eN5jrJgi (accessed 28/06/2015).
27. Author's interview with Jay Varma.
28. Indira Varma in Gayatri Rao ed. *Curtains: Stories by 9 Women* (Google Books).
29. Author's interview with Uma Varma.
30. Author's interview with Lakshmi Raghunandan.
31. Author's interview with Karthik Varma.
32. Author's interview with Rukmini Varma.

Index

Bibliography

Note: In addition to the titles listed here, which are mainly secondary sources, in the notes for this book can be found other volumes that I have referred to, articles from journals such as the *Social Scientist*, the *Modern Review*, and so on, as also the catalogue numbers and details of papers and primary archival material from the India Office Archives in London (marked IOR or MSS), the Kerala State Archives (marked KSA), the private papers of the Travancore royal family (marked TRF), and material sourced from the National Archives of India in New Delhi (marked NAI). Letters and reports published in *At the Turn of the Tide* by Lakshmi Raghunandan have been marked with the relevant page numbers (for instance: Raghunandan, p. 25) after mentioning the date and other details.

Due to the exhaustive numbers of files and material involved, it has not been possible to list them here. Similarly, material obtained from newspapers and journals, including rare ones such as the *Feudatory and Zemindari India*, have been individually named in the notes with relevant dates and information. A few books viewed online through Google Books have been marked accordingly.

Aiya, V. Nagam (1999), *Travancore State Manual*, Vols. I, II and III (Thiruvananthapuram: Kerala Gazetteers Department)

Aiyar, R. Kulathu (1916), *Her Highness Sethu Lakshmi Bai, Senior Ranee of Travancore: A Short Life Sketch* (Madras: Methodist Publishing House)

Aiyar, S. Ramanatha (1903), *A Brief Sketch of Travancore, The Model State of India: The Country, Its People and Its Progress* (Trivandrum: Western Star Press)

Aiyar, S. Ramanath (1938), *A History of Travancore* (Madras: Srinivasa Varadachari & Co.)

Aiyar, Ulloor S. Parameswara (2003), *Essays on Travancore* (Trivandrum: Government Press)

Aiyar, Ulloor S. Parameswara (1998), *Progress of Travancore under H.H. Sree Moolam Tirunal* (Thiruvananthapuram: Govt. of Kerala)

Aiyangar, Kuppuswamy (1906), *The Ranis of Travancore* (Bombay: MC Rutnagar & Co.)

Allen, Charles and Dwivedi, Sharada (1984), *Lives of the Indian Princes* (London: Century Publishing)

Ambedkar, B.R. (1945), *What Congress and Gandhi have done to the Untouchables* (Bombay: Thacker & Co. Ltd.)

Arunima, G. (2003), *There Comes Papa: Colonialism and the Transformation of Matriliny in Kerala, Malabar c. 1850-1940* (New Delhi: Orient Longman)

Ayyar, K.V. Krishna (1938), *The Zamorins of Calicut: From the Earliest Times down to AD 1806* (Calicut: Norman Printing Bureau)

Baak, Paul Erik (1997), *Plantation Production and Political Power: Plantation Development in South-West India in a Long-Term Historical Perspective, 1743-1963* (Delhi: Oxford University Press)

Bandyopadhyay, Sekhar (2006), *From Plassey to Partition: A History of Modern India* (Hyderabad: Orient Longman)

Bayi, Gouri Lakshmi (1995), *Sree Padmanabha Swamy Temple* (Bombay: Bharatiya Vidya Bhavan)

Bayi, Gouri Lakshmi (1998), *Thulasi Garland* (Mumbai: Bharatiya Vidya Bhavan)

Bayly, Susan (2003), *Saints, Goddesses and Kings: Muslims and Christians in South Indian Society 1700-1900* (Cambridge: Cambridge University Press)

Bikaner, Rajyashree Kumari (2012), *The Maharajas of Bikanar* (New Delhi: Amaryllis)

Brendon, Piers (2008), *The Decline and Fall of the British Empire: 1781-1997* (London: Vintage)

Bright-Holmes, John (ed.) (1982), *Like it Was: The Diaries of Malcolm Muggeridge* (New York: William Morrow)

Bristow, Robert (1967), *Cochin Saga: A History of Foreign Government and Business Adventures in Kerala, South India, by Arabs, Romans, Venetians, Dutch, and British together with the Personal Narrative of the Last Adventurer and an Epilogue* (Cochin: Paico)

Bruce, Henry (1909), *Letters from Malabar and On the Way* (London: G. Routledge & Sons)

Chaitanya, Krishna (1971), *A History of Malayalam Literature* (New Delhi: Orient Longman)

Chawla, Rupika (2010), *Raja Ravi Varma: Painter of Colonial India* (Ahmedabad: Mapin Publishing)

Cherian, P.J. (ed.) (2000), *William Logan's Malabar Manual Vol. I* (Thiruvananthapuram: Kerala Gazetteers Department)

Child-Villiers, Margaret (1922), *Fifty-One Years of Victorian Life* (New York: E.P. Dutton and Company)

Clark, Mary E. (2002), *In Search of Human Nature* (London: Routledge)

Clarke, A.B. (1916), *In Kerala: A Recort of the Tour in South India with Their Highnesses the Maharaja and Maharani Gaekwar* (Bombay: Bennett, Coleman & Co. Ltd)

Cliff, Nigel (2012), *The Last Crusade: The Epic Voyages of Vasco Da Gama* (New York: Harper Perennial)

Commons, House of (1859), *Parliamentary Papers: Accounts and Papers: East India: Annexations of Territory; Afghanistan; King of Delhi; Oude; Travancore* (London: House of Commons)

Dames, Mansel Longworth (2002), *The Book of Duarte Barbosa Vol. I* (New Delhi: Asian Educational Services)

Davies, John Paton (Jr) (2012), *China Hand: An Autobiography* (Philadelphia: University of Pennsylvania Press)

Dekobra, Maurice (1930), *The Perfumed Tigers: Adventures in the Land of the Maharajahs* (translated by Neil Wainwright) (London: Brewer and Warren Inc.)

Desai, Mahadev (1937), *The Epic of Travancore* (Ahmedabad: Navajivan Karyalaya)

De Lannoy, Mark (1997), *The Kulasekhara Perumals of Travancore: History and State Formation in Travancore 1671 to 1758* (Leiden: CNWS)

Devi, R. Leela (1977), *History of Malayalam Literature* (Trivandrum: Educational Supplies Depot)

Devi, S. Uma (1989), *Plantation Economies of the Third World* (Delhi: Himalaya)

Devika, J. (2005), *Her-self: Early Writings on Gender by Malayalee Women 1898-1938* (Kolkata: Stree)

Devika, J. (2007), *En-gendering Individuals: The Language of Re-forming in Twentieth Century Keralam* (Hyderabad: Orient Longman)

Devika, J. and Thampi, Binitha, *New Lamps for the Old* (Unpublished Proofs)

Directors, The Honourable Court of (1833), *Appendix to the Report from the Select Committee of the House of Commons on the Affairs of the East India Company* (London: The Honourable Court of Directors)

Drury, Heber (1862), *Letters from Malabar by Jacob Canter Visscher* (Madras: The Adelphi Press)

Edwardes, Michael (1963), *The Last Years of British India* (London: Cassell)

Eraly, Abraham (2011), *The First Spring: The Golden Age of India* (New Delhi: Viking)

Fawcett, F. (2004), *Nayars of Malabar* (New Delhi: Asian Educational Services)

Fisher, Michael H. (1998), *Indirect Rule in India: Residents and the Residency System* (Delhi: Oxford University Press)

Fuller, C.J. (1976), *Changing Cultures: The Nayars Today* (Cambridge: Cambridge University Press)

Gandhi, Rajmohan (2008), *Gandhi: The Man, His People, and the Empire* (Berkeley: University of California Press)

Gauba, Kanhayalal (1931), *His Highness: Or the Pathology of Princes* (Lahore: Times Publishing Company)

George, K.M. (1989), *Kesari Balakrishna Pillai* (Madras: Sahitya Akademi)

George, T.J.S. (2004), *MS: A Life in Music* (New Delhi: HarperCollins)

Ghose, Ajithkumar ed. (1983), *Agrarian Reforms in Contemporary Developing Countries* (London: Croom Helm)

Ghose, Sankar (1993), *Jawaharlal Nehru: A Biography* (Bombay: Allied Publishers)

Glover, Elizabeth (1928), *Great Queens: Famous Women Rulers of the East* (London: Hutchinson & Co.)

Gopal, Sarvepalli (1957), *The Vicerouyalty of Lord Irwin: 1926-1931* (Oxford: Clarendon Press)

Gordon, Helen Cameron (2000), *Hindu Life and Customs* (New Delhi: Mittal Publications)

Grey, Edward (ed.) (2010), *The Travels of Pietro Della Valle in India* (Cambridge: Cambridge University Press)

Grose, John Henry (1766), *A Voyage to the East Indies: Began in 1750 with Observations continued till 1764 Volume I* (London: S. Hooper)

Gundert, Hermann and Menon, T. Madhava (2003), *Kerala Pazhama: Antiquity of Kerala* (Thiruvananthapuram: International School of Dravidian Linguistics)

Harigovindan, Narayani (1998), *A History of the Employment of Women in the Government Services of Travancore* (Dissertation submitted to the Department of History, University of Kerala)

Harris, Jonathan Gil (2015), *The First Firangis: Remarkable Stories of Heroes, Healers, Charlatans, Courtesans & other Foreigners who Became Indian* (New Delhi: Aleph Book Company)

Hasnain, Syed Iqbal (2009), *Muslims in North India: Frozen in the Past* (New Delhi: Har Anand Publications)

Hatch, Emily Gilchriest (1939), *Travancore: A Guide Book for the Visitor* 2nd Edition (Calcutta: Oxford University Press)

Herman, Arthur (2009), *Gandhi & Churchill: The Epic Rivalry that Destroyed an Empire and Forged our Age* (New York: Bantam Dell)

Hotchand, Tirithdas (1963), *Shah Abdul Latif's Immortal Song: The Song of Kinjhar Lake* (Hyderabad: Pardeep Publications)

India's Women: The Magazine of the Church of England Zenana Missionary Society Vol. I (1881) and Vol. II (1882) (London: James Nisbet & Co.)

Iyer, A. Padmanabha (1940), *Souvenir of the Sashtiabdapurthi of Sachivothama Sir C.P. Ramaswami Aiyar* (Trivandrum: ARV Press)

Iyer, K.P. Subramonia (1941), *Thirumadampu of His Highness Marthanda Varma Elaya Raja of Travancore* (Trivandrum: Government Press)

Iyer, R. Kulathu (1929), *Maharani Sethu Lakshmi Bayi Tirumanasukondu* (Malayalam) (Trivandrum: VV Press)

Iyer, R. Kulathu (1939), *The Pallikkettu of H.H. Lalitamba Bayi: The Second Princess of Travancore: A Short Account* (Trivandrum: Chandra Press)

Jagannathan, Shakunthala (1999), *Sir CP Remembered: To Thatha with Love* (Mumbai: Vakils, Feffer & Simons Ltd.)

Jeffrey, Robin (2014), *The Decline of Nair Dominance: Society and Politics in Travancore 1857-1908* (New Delhi Manohar)

Jivanayakam, Daniel (1931), *Training Teachers for English Schools in Travancore* (New York: Columbia University)

Joseph, K. Varkey (1988), *Migration and Economic Development of Kerala* (Delhi: Mittal Publications)

Joshi, P.C. and Damodaran, K. (1975*), Marx Comes to India: Earliest Indian Biographies of Karl Marx* (Delhi: Manohar)

Kaimal, P.K.V. (1994), *Revolt of the Oppressed: Punnapra–Vayalar, 1946* (New Delhi: Konark)

Keay, John (1994), *The Honourable Company: A History of the English East India Company* (New York: Macmillan)

Keen, Caroline (2012), *Princely India and the British: Political Development and the Operation of Empire* (New York: IB Tauris & Co. Ltd.)

Kerala, Government of (1977), *The Press in Kerala* (Trivandrum: Department of Public Relations)

Kooiman, Dick (2002), *Communalism and Indian Princely States: Travancore, Baroda, and Hyderabad in the 1930s* (Delhi: Manohar)

Koshy, MJ (1972), *Genesis of Political Consciousness in Kerala* (Trivandrum: Kerala Historical Society)

Koshy, MJ (1976), *K.C. Mammen Mappillai: The Man and his Vision* (Trivandrum: Kerala Historical Society)

Krishna, B. (2007), *India's Bismarck: Sardar Vallabhbhai Patel* (Mumbai: Indus Source Books)

Kunju, A.P. Ibrahim (1976), *Rise of Travancore: A Study of the Life and Times of Martanda Varma* (Trivandrum: Kerala Historical Society)

Lapierre, Dominique and Collins, Larry (1975), *Freedom at Midnight* (New York: Simon and Schuster)

Loti, Pierre (1996), *India* (New Delhi: Asian Educational Services)

Louis, William Roger (ed.) (1995), *Adventures with Britannia: Personalities, Politics and Culture in Britain* (Austin: University of Texas)

Lovatt, Heather and de Jong, Peter (1993), *Above the Heron's Pool: A Short History of the Peermade /Vandiperiyar District of Travancore* (London: Putney)

Low, D.A. (ed.) (1977), *Congress and the Raj: Facets of the Indian Struggle* (London: Heinneman)

Madras, Government of (1909), *The Fourth Tour of H.E. The Hon. Sir Arthur Lawley G.C.I.E., K.C.M.G. to Cochin and Travancore* (Madras: Government Press)

Maheswari, S. Uma (2011), *Thrippadidaanam: Sree Uthradam Thirunal Marthanda Varmayude Rajasmaranakal* (Malayalam) Kozhikode: Mathrubhumi Books)

Mailaparambil, Binu John (2011), *Lords of the Sea: The Ali Rajas of Cannanore and the Political Economy of Malabar (1663-1723)* (Leiden: Brill Academic Publishers)

Mappillai, K.C. Mammen (1980), *Reminiscences* (Kottayam: Malayala Manorama)

Mateer, Samuel (1883), *Native Life in Travancore* (London: WH Allen & Co.)

Mateer, Samuel (1871), *The Land of Charity: A Discriptive Account of Travancore and its People* (London: John Snow and Co.)

Mathew, George (1989), *Communal Road to A Secular Kerala* (New Delhi: Concept Publishing)

Mathew, George (1995), *Status of Panchayati Raj in the States of India* (New Delhi: Institute of Social Sciences)

Matthew, I. (1931), *Travancore a Hundred Years Ago: The Times of the Ranees and Colonel Munro: Reprint of an Article Appearing in The Kerala Society Papers* (Trivandrum: City Press)

McClenaghan, Tony (1996), *Indian Princely Medals: A Record of the Orders, Decorations and Medals of the Indian Princely States* (New Delhi: Lancer)

Menon, A. Sreedhara (2008), *Kerala History and its Makers* (Kottayam: DC Books)

Menon, A. Sreedhara (2001), *Triumph and Tragedy in Travancore: Annals of Sir CP's Sixteen Years* (Kottayam: Current Books)

Menon, A. Sreedhara (2007), *A Survey of Kerala History* (Kottayam: DC Books)

Menon, I.K.K. ed. (1994), *The Rajarshi of Cochin: Autobiography and Biography of Maharaja Sir Sri Rama Varma* (Trivandrum: Kerala State Archives)

Menon, K.P. Padmanabha (1986), *History of Kerala: Written in the Form of Notes on Visscher's Letters from Malabar Vols. I-IV* (New Delhi: Asian Educational Services)

Menon, P. Shungoonny (1878), *A History of Travancore From the Earliest Times* (Madras:Higginbotham & Co.)

Menon, P.K.K. (2001), *The History of Freedom Movement in Kerala Vol. II (1885-1938)* (Trivandrum: Govt. of Kerala)

Menon, V.P. (1985), *The Story of the Integration of the Indian States* (Hyderabad: Orient Longman)

Mitter, Partha (1995), *Art and Nationalism in Colonial India*, 1850-1922 (Cambridge: Cambridge University Press)

Mohan, Arun (1990), *Princely States and the Reform in Hindu Law* (Bombay: N.M. Tripathi)

More, Leena (2003), *English East India Company and the Local Rulers in Kerala* (Tellicherry: IRISH)

Moon, Penderel (1973), *Wavell: The Viceroy's Journal* (London: Oxford University Press)

Mount, Ferdinand (2015), *The Tears of the Rajas: Mutiny, Money and Marriage in India, 1805-1905* (London: Simon & Schuster)

Mukhopadhyaya, S.C. (1869), *The Career of an Indian Princess: The Late Begum Secunder of Bhopal* (Calcutta: Anglo-Sanskrit Press)

Nair, Anita (ed.) (2002), *Where the Rain is Born: Writings About Kerala* (New Delhi: Penguin)

Nair, S. Guptan (1992), *C.V. Raman Pillai* (New Delhi: Sahitya Akademi)

Nair, KK (2012), *By Sweat and Sword: Trade, Diplomacy and War in Kerala through the Ages* (New Delhi: Manohar)

Nair, T.N. Gopinathan (1992), *Avasanate Naduvazhiyude Amma: Sri Sethu Parvathi Bayi Thirumanassinte Jeevitakatha* (Malayalam) (Trivandrum: St Joseph's Press)

Nair, T.N. Gopinathan (1996), *Sree Chithira Thirunal: Avasanathe Naduvazhi* (Malayalam) (Thiruvananthapuram: Department of Cultural Publications, Government of Kerala)

Neumayer, Erwin & Schelberger, Christine (2003), *Popular Indian Art: Raja Ravi Varma and the Printed Gods of India* (Oxford: Oxford University Press)

Nossiter, Thomas J. (1982), *Communism in Kerala: A Study in Political Adaptation* (London: Royal Institute of International Affairs)

Notes on the Present Position of Christians in Travancore by the Travancore Peace Bloc (1946) (Madras: Good Pastor Press)

Ouwerkerk, Louise & Kooiman, Dick (1994), *No Elephants for the Maharaja: Social and Political Change in the Princely State of Travancore* (New Delhi: Manohar Publications)

Pal, Deepanjana (2009), *The Painter: A Life of Ravi Varma* (New Delhi: Random House India)

Panikkar, K.M. (1931), *Malabar and the Dutch* (Bombay: Taraporevala)

Perumal, Nilkan (1939), *The Truth About Travancore* (Madras: R.J. Ram & Co.)

Pillai, Poovattoor Ramakrishna (1990), *Visakhavijaya: A Study* (Thiruvananthapuram:

Anitha Publications)

Pillai, P.K. Narayana (1988), *Kerala Varma* (Delhi: Sahitya Akademi)

Pillai, K. Ramakrishna (1911), *The Travancore Deportation: A Brief Account of the Deportation of Mr K Ramakrishna Pillai BA* (Kottakkal: Ramgopal & Co.)

Pillai, S.A. (1928), *Ravi Varma and his Art* (Quilon: S.A. Pillai)

Pillai, T.K. Velu (1996), *Travancore State Manual Vols. I-IV* (Trivandrum: Government of Kerala)

Prasad, Rajendra (2010), *Asif Jahs of Hyderabad: Their Rise and Decline* (Hyderabad: Prachee Publications)

Raghu, A (1998), *CP: A Short Biography of CP Ramaswami Aiyar* (Delhi: Prestige Books)

Raghunandan, Lakshmi (1995), *At the Turn of the Tide: The Life and Times of Maharani Setu Lakshmi Bayi, the Last Queen of Travancore* (Bangalore: Maharani Setu Lakshmi Bayi Memorial Charitable Trust)

Raimon, S. (ed.) (2006), *Selected Documents on Vaikom Satyagraha* (Trivandrum: Kerala State Archives Department)

Raja, P.K.S. (1966), *Mediaeval Kerala* (Calicut: Navakerala Co-op. Publishing House)

Raja, R.P. (2006), *New Light on Swathi Thirunal* (Thiruvananthapuram: INDIS)

Ramachandran, C.M. (1987), *Problems of Higher Education in India: A Case Study* (Delhi: Mittal Publications)

Ravindran, T.K. (1975), *Vaikkam Satyagraha and Gandhi* (Trivandrum: Sri Narayana Institute of Social and Cultural Development)

Report on the Administration of Travancore for 1923-24 (1925) (Trivandrum: Government Press)

Report on the Administration of Travancore for 1924-25 (1926) (Trivandrum: Government Press)

Report on the Administration of Travancore for 1925-26 (1927) (Trivandrum: Government Press)

Report on the Administration of Travancore for 1926-27 (1928) (Trivandrum: Government Press)

Report on the Administration of Travancore for 1927-28 (1929) (Trivandrum: Government Press)

Report on the Administration of Travancore for 1928-29 (1930) (Trivandrum: Government Press)

Report on the Administration of Travancore for 1929-30 (1931) (Trivandrum: Government Press)

Report on the Administration of Travancore for 1930-31 (1932) (Trivandrum: Government Press)

Report on the Administration of Travancore for 1931-32 (1933) (Trivandrum: Government Press)

Report on the Administration of Travancore for 1936-37 (1938) (Trivandrum: Government Press)

Report of the Banking Enquiry Committee of Travancore Vol. I (1930) (Trivandrum: Government of Travancore)

Report of the Travancore University Committee 1923-24 (1925) (Trivandrum: Government Press)

Report of the Travancore Economic Depression Enquiry Committee (1931) (Trivandrum: Government Press)

Report of the Travancore Unemployment Enquiry Committee (1928) (Trivandrum: Government Press)

Rogers, Wendy and Rogers, Rex (2001), *The Psychology of Gender and Sexuality: An Introduction* (New York: Open University Press)

Sampath, Vikram (2008), *Splendours of Royal Mysore: The Untold Story of the Wodeyars* (New Delhi: Rupa)

Saradamoni, K. (1999), *Matriliny Transformed: Family, Law and Ideology in Twentieth Century Travancore* (New Delhi: Sage Publications)

Scindia, Vijaya Raje with Malgonkar, Manohar (1987), *The Last Maharani of Gwalior: An Autobiography* (New York: State University of New York)

Sekhar, G.P. (ed.) (1938), *Speeches & Messages of His Highness Sir Bala Rama Varma, Maharaja of Travancore* (Trivandrum: Radh-Ind)

Selections from the Records of the Madras Government Volume 13 (1911) (Madras: Government Press)

S'Jacob, Hugo (2000), *The Rajas of Cochin, 1663-1720: Kings, Chiefs and the Dutch East India Company* (New Delhi: Munshiram Manoharlal Publishers)

Sobhanan, B. (1977), *Rama Varma of Travancore: His Role in the Consolidation of British Power in South India* (Cochin: Sandhya Publications)

Speeches of Sachivottama Sir C.P. Ramaswami Aiyar (1937) (Trivandrum: Government Press)

Sreedhar, K.P. (ed.) (1939), *Travancore Re-Born* (Kottayam: Good Shepherd Press)

Stanley, Henry E.J. (1865), *A Description of the Coasts of East Africa and Malabar in the Beginning of the Sixteenth Century by Duarte Barbosa* (London: The Hakluyt Society)

Stewart, John (1989), *Envoy of the Raj: The Career of Sir Clarmont Skrine, Indian Political Service* (Maidenhead: Porpoise)

Sundararajan, Saroja (2002), *Sir CP Ramaswami Aiyar: A Biography* (New Delhi: Allied Publishers)

Thampy, V. Narasimhan (1976), *Travancore Royal Family and Valia Kottaram*

(Trivandrum: Narasimhan Thampy and Government of Kerala)

Tharamangalam, Joseph (1981), *Agrarian Class Conflict: The Political Mobilization of Agricultural Labourers in Kuttanad, South India* (Vancouver and London: University of British Columbia Press)

The All Travancore Joint Political Congress (1934), *Travancore: The Present Political Problem* (Calicut: Empire Press)

The English Writings of Rabindranath Tagore, Vol. II (2006) (New Delhi: Sahitya Akademi)

The Regulations & Proclamations of Travancore Vol. VI 1100-1105 M.E. (1930) (Trivandrum: Sridhara Press)

Thomas, OM (1970), *Under the Knife: Candid Studies of Some Kerala Notables* (Allahabad: New Book Syndicate)

Travancore at the British Empire Exhibition, Wembley (1924) (London: Haycock, Cadle & Graham)

Unni, N.P. (ed.) (1977), *Sanskrit Plays of V. Krishnan Tampy* (Trivandrum: B Vallippilla Kochamma)

Unni, N.P. (1980), *A History of Mushika Vamsa* (Trivandrum: Kerala Historical Society)

Ushakumari, K.R. (2009), *Changanassery Parameswaran Pillai and the Socio Political Evolution of Modern Travancore* (Thiruvananthapuram: Author)

Varma, Uthradom Tirunal Marthanda (2010), *Travancore: The Footsteps of Destiny: My Life and Times under the Grace of Lord Padmanabha: As told to Uma Maheswari* (New Delhi: Konark)

Venniyur, EMJ (1981), *Raja Ravi Varma* (Trivandrum: Govt. of Kerala)

Welsh, James (1830), *Military Reminiscences: Extracted from A Journal of Nearly Forty Years' Active service in the East Indies* Vol. II (London: Smith, Elder and Co.)

Wheeler, J Talboys (1880), *A Short History of India and of the Frontier States of Afghanistan, Nipal, and Burma* (London: Macmillan and Co.)

Whiteway, R.S. (1989), *The Rise of Portuguese Power in India: 1497-1550* (New Delhi: Asian Educational Services)

Williamson, Philip (2003), *National Crisis and National Government: British Politics, the Economy, and Empire, 1926-1932* (Cambridge: Cambridge University Press)

Author's Note and Acknowledgements

In the six years I have spent putting together this book, I have received help, guidance and assistance from a number of people.

I owe my thanks, firstly, to my parents for their generous financial support in the early years of the project, when I did not have an income of my own, and for asking no questions as to what I was doing. I hope the result will not entirely horrify them as they finally discover what it is that I was working on these past several years.

I must also specially thank my sister Indrani for pulling me into reading and writing years ago at a time when I was happy to find less inspiring distractions!

In 2009, I began a long correspondence with Lakshmi Raghunandan, granddaughter to Sethu Lakshmi Bayi and author of *At The Turn of the Tide* (1995), a phenomenal volume that compiles all of the Maharani's important correspondence and papers. This book is one of the foundations for my own work, and I am grateful to Lakshmi also for giving me access to the other material, some from the mid-nineteenth century, which she has with her. Lakshmi and her husband Raghu tolerated me for long hours at their home in Bangalore since our first meeting in 2011, sometimes permitting my intrusions even beyond midnight.

That same year, Lakshmi introduced me to Rukmini Varma, her reclusive sister and Sethu Lakshmi Bayi's favourite grandchild, who has been a most bountiful source of stories as well as all varieties of details about the Maharani. Since then, Rukmini, besides interviews that I formally had with her, has entertained hundreds of hours of calls, almost always made late at night, to clarify doubts and to answer questions that came up every now and then. I am particularly thankful to her for taking such an interest in my writing, since she does not normally receive visitors or have interactions these days outside family circles.

Rukmini's son Jay has also, since 2013, been a great source of memories about the life Sethu Lakshmi Bayi led after she left the palace for Bangalore.

Similarly, Uma Varma, witty and irreverent, opened her doors to me, particularly with regard to her memories of the Valiya Koil Tampuran, and received many phone calls from me over the years from London. She too took more than a passing interest in this book and proactively followed up with me whenever there was something new that she thought would add to my research.

Her daughter, Radhika Varma Hormusjee, gave me a beautiful essay of her memories of her great grandparents and of the life the family led in Bangalore, and went out of her way to help photograph the paintings I wanted to include in this book.

Parvathi and Ravi Varma, Ambika Varma, Balagopal and Vidya Varma, and Devika Radhakrishnan offered valuable inputs that have enriched this book, as did the late Dr R.M. Varma and his wife Malathi. Kerala Varma, the Maharani's son-in-law, who will soon turn a hundred years old, was also a store of information and spoke to me on several occasions despite ill health, for which I am grateful. I thank also Mr Prasad Bidapa and Dr Vanitha Dayananda for their contributions.

Divakara Varma, the Maharani's nephew, corresponded with me over email and gave me answers to many questions, and in 2014 we met for an exhaustive discussion in Nagercoil before he returned to Canada. To him and for his phenomenal recollection of detail I express my gratitude.

Ambassador C. Ranganathan spoke to me over the phone about his own experience of knowing members of Sethu Lakshmi Bayi's family and about his grandfather, Sir C.P. Ramaswami Iyer. Urmila Devi, whose uncle was the last ruler of princely Mysore, also supplied me some material and told me of her recollections of the Maharani's family after they had moved to Bangalore.

My friend and the distinguished author Vikram Sampath receives a special mention here for all his determined encouragement and help in Bangalore on each of my visits. Whenever I grew frustrated while writing or neglected my manuscript, it was Vikram who, through cutting emails, reminded me that it was too early for me to claim a writer's block, and I would need to churn out more than one book to join that club!

I am grateful to Indira Varma, Sethu Lakshmi Bayi's daughter, in Chennai for seeing me in December 2011 despite poor health and even though she was in mourning at the time following K.K. Varma's death earlier that year. I am thankful to Shreekumar Varma and his wife Geeta for their interviews with me, as also to Shobhana Varma, who gave me a note about her grandmother's principal accomplishments as ruler. Her husband Goda Varma, who is a nephew of Maharajah Chithira Tirunal on the side of his father, the Kochu Koil Tampuran, also gave me some comments that were of value.

In Chennai, I also met Prabha Menon, the Maharani's niece, who regaled me with old stories, which were very valuable since they offered an entirely different perspective that was at once close but not as intimate as was the case with direct members of Sethu Lakshmi Bayi's family.

I am grateful to Advocate Vijayaraghavan and his uncle Mr P. Ramji who belong to an old family of Tamil Brahmins in Alleppey, and who passed to me stories that were current in 1940s Travancore about its royal family and Dewan.

In Thiruvananthapuram, my thanks are due first to my friend Sharat Sunder Rajeev, who since 2008 has aided me in a number of ways with my research and guided me towards the right people, acting also every now and then as my Malayalam translator. Advocate Ayyappan Pillai, a nonagenarian who lived through the Regency years and vividly remembers the rule of Sir CP, and is one of the city's most respected figures, gave me honest perspectives on a number of matters. 'Rosscote' Krishna Pillai told me some interesting facts over the phone. I am also grateful to Abhed Kiran Kandamath for snippets of information he would send me occasionally, and to Soheb Vahab, who painstakingly unearthed material from dusty shelves in libraries scattered across the city.

J. Devika, whose incisive scholarship and brilliant mind never cease to amaze me, not only gave me an interview but also sent me unpublished proofs of her book, as well as pointed me to other valuable sources of information, without which I could not have got my head around a number of themes covered in this volume. Both in London and in Thiruvananthapuram we followed up on my research, and her guidance has been of singular value.

Mr Sadasivan Nair helped facilitate my access to the Kerala State Archives and aided me in navigating what initially seemed like a daunting, endless network of permissions from assorted officials.

Mr Sasidhara Varma's carefully constructed family tree of the Mavelikkara Kolathiri line offered the material through which I was able to chart more easily the family tree that features in this book.

Dr M.S. Valiathan, the medical luminary who acquired Satelmond Palace for the Sri Chithira Tirunal Institute in the 1970s and observed Sethu Lakshmi Bayi during a poignant moment in her life, was frank in recalling that episode and his memories of the events leading up to it.

Linda D'Silva, a great-niece of M.E. Watts, the Dewan, contributed a number of details, and Robin and the late Nicolette Cotton, relations of C.W.E. Cotton, the Resident, hosted me for lunch at their charming house and provided me all the papers they had with them. Prof Adrian Mayer of the School of Oriental and African Studies, who was the last outsider to see the Maharani a few months before her death, also spoke to me at length about that episode at his house in London.

Arighna Gupta, my able research assistant in Delhi, combed the National Archives there diligently for an entire summer and helped me locate all the material I needed. In Pune, my friend Shivang Joshi took a proactive interest in the book and designed what I think is an excellent cover, for which I thank him.

Narayani Harigovindan of the French embassy in Delhi fished out for me her very well-researched postgraduate thesis on women in the Travancore state services, after the subject of my book came up quite out of the blue at a meeting.

I must also thank in particular Dr Shashi Tharoor, my employer in 2011–12, who was most encouraging about my writing. Lord Bilimoria in London, with whom I worked in 2012–13, went out of his way to enable me to focus on my manuscript despite the pressures of work by offering me a certain part of each month off, for which I am very grateful.

Jonathan Raymond Guillemot, on whom I inflicted broad overviews of the book and its story, offered inputs at critical moments, without which my writing would have evolved in a direction that, in retrospect, I think would have been heavily unsuitable.

Prof. Robin Jeffrey, without whose classic *The Decline of Nair Dominance* (1976) serious students of Kerala history would be poorer in their store of knowledge, read through parts of my manuscript and offered his comments. His book is the other source of information that is foundational to my own research, and for this and for producing one of the best books ever written on Kerala and its people, I express my thanks to him.

I was introduced to Prof. Jeffrey by our mutual friends, the delightful Khyrunnisa and Prof. Vijayakumar in Thiruvananthapuram, whose hospitality and friendship has been one of the enduring rewards I have received in the process of writing this book.

While working on this book I have referred extensively to the collections of the India Office Archives at the British Library in London, which form the primary source of material as will be seen in the endnotes appended to this book. What I subsequently discovered at the National Archives in Delhi had already been found in London, though I was able to unearth some records of interest at the Kerala State Archives. Besides the extensive collections of the British Library, I also referred to the library of King's College London, where I was a student; of the London School of Economics; of the School of Oriental and African Studies; of the University of Oxford; and the University of California, Berkeley, among others.

At U.C. Berkeley, Lisa Hong's assistance is appreciated, while Karen Robson of the library of the University of Southampton sent me some material from the archives of Lord Mountbatten, for which I remain grateful. Wendy Wilson of *The Lady* in London kindly sent me an image I had located in their archives, and Agata Rutkowska of the Royal Collection provided me valuable assistance in tracing other similar pictures.

My only regret has been that in writing this book the family of the Junior Maharani of Travancore chose for most part not to participate in my research. Her son, the last Elayarajah, whom I met on two different occasions, had his office acknowledge receipt of my formal interview request, but repeated reminders were ignored. He passed away in late 2013.

The Elayarajah's daughter, Parvathi Devi, agreed to see me in April 2014 but at the last minute rang to cancel the appointment. The Junior Maharani's only great-granddaughter, my friend, the refreshingly original Lakshmi Nalapat, took me out for several lunches and dinners, but also decided not to speak on record. Her brother, Rama Varma, too politely declined. The Junior Maharani's nephew, the historian and scholar Dr R.P. Raja, however, spoke to me on record, and for being the first person to make an exception and to see me, I thank him. In 2015, the Junior Maharani's eldest grandchild, Gouri Parvathi Bayi, also agreed to send me a written statement containing her memories and some anecdotes. Despite its briefness, I have referred to and quoted from it in this book and am grateful to her for offering me this in lieu of an interview.

This Gouri Parvathi Bayi did despite knowing that the primary records I had accessed for my book were frequently far from complimentary to the Junior Maharani. I also requested her to allow me to go through any papers her family might have at Kowdiar Palace, but this was declined. As she noted at the end of her statement to me:

> None of this is probably what you want but this is the way my grandmother was and no old British papers can tell me and scores of other people who knew her, anything different. Is it not possible that some of the Britishers were prejudiced/resentful? As for the regency, I will not share with you any of the records that are less than complimentary or tell you anything negative

> about [Sethu Lakshmi Bayi's] branch of the family. At the end of the day that is what they are—another offshoot of our own family. Blackening your own is not what we were taught to do.

Implicit in this, I suspect, is a charge that my intention is to 'blacken' the family (or the Junior Maharani's side of it) through this book. My belief, however, from the start has been that history, especially so many decades after its protagonists have passed away, must be an objective affair, and the strength of written records—official letters, confidential reports, fortnightly assessments of the Residents, and so on—cannot be discarded in order to preserve a popular image of historical figures. These British observers, it must be acknowledged, had their prejudices. But insofar as witnessing the internal dynamics of the ruling dynasty went, theirs is the view closest to unbiased objectivity. As A. Sreedhara Menon, the distinguished historian, noted in his final masterpiece, *Triumph and Tragedy in Travancore* (2001), the confidential records of British authorities 'help us view the events of the period in their true perspective'.

In the eyes of history there cannot and should not be any sacred cows. However, I recognise and understand the position taken by Gouri Parvathi Bayi and her family.

Finally, thanks are due to my publishers at HarperCollins India for their enthusiasm and support for this book. V.K. Karthika, my brilliant editor, has been singular in her guidance. It has also been a pleasure working with her excellent team, especially with Shantanu Ray Chaudhuri, Amrita Talwar and Bonita Shimray. Together they have given me more attention and support than first-time authors can ordinarily demand, making the whole process of publishing this book more relaxed and cheerful than I would have at first anticipated.

About the Author

Manu S. Pillai is a historian and writer whose other books include *Rebel Sultans* (2018), *The Courtesan, the Mahatma & the Italian Brahmin* (2019) and *False Allies* (2021). Formerly Chief of Staff to Dr Shashi Tharoor, MP, he has worked at the House of Lords in Britain and with the BBC on its 'Incarnations' history series. A winner of the Sahitya Akademi Yuva Puraskar, he has been a columnist at *Mint Lounge*, while his other writings have appeared in *The Hindu*, *Open* magazine, *The Times of India*, *Hindustan Times*, *The New Statesman* and other publications.

Manu holds a PhD from King's College London. *The Ivory Throne* is his first book.

30 Years *of*

HarperCollins *Publishers* India

At HarperCollins, we believe in telling the best stories and finding the widest possible readership for our books in every format possible. We started publishing 30 years ago; a great deal has changed since then, but what has remained constant is the passion with which our authors write their books, the love with which readers receive them, and the sheer joy and excitement that we as publishers feel in being a part of the publishing process.

Over the years, we've had the pleasure of publishing some of the finest writing from the subcontinent and around the world, and some of the biggest bestsellers in India's publishing history. Our books and authors have won a phenomenal range of awards, and we ourselves have been named Publisher of the Year the greatest number of times. But nothing has meant more to us than the fact that millions of people have read the books we published, and somewhere, a book of ours might have made a difference.

As we step into our fourth decade, we go back to that one word – a word which has been a driving force for us all these years.

Read.